THE ROUGH GUIDE TO

Iceland

KT-463-991

There are more than two hundred Rough Guide titles
covering destinations from Alaska to Zimbabwe
and subjects from Acoustic Guitar to Travel Health

Forthcoming travel guides include
Devon & Cornwall • Ibiza • Malta
Tenerife • Vancouver

Forthcoming reference guides include
Cuban Music • Latin: 100 Essential CDs • Personal Computers
Pregnancy & Birth • Trumpet & Trombone

Rough Guides Online
www.roughguides.com

ROUGH GUIDE CREDITS

...tor: Geoff Howard
...s editor: Mark Ellingham
...torial: Martin Dunford, Jonathan Buckley, Jo
Mead, Kate Berens, Amanda Tomlin, Ann-Marie Shaw,
Paul Gray, Helena Smith, Judith Bamber, Orla Duane,
Olivia Eccleshall, Ruth Blackmore, Claire Saunders,
Gavin Thomas, Alexander Mark Rogers, Polly Thomas,
Joe Staines, Lisa Nellis, Andrew Tomičić, Richard Lim,
Duncan Clark, Peter Buckley, Sam Thorne, Lucy
Ratcliffe, Clifton Wilkinson, David Glen (UK); Andrew
Rosenberg, Mary Beth Maioli, Stephen Timblin, Yuki
Takagaki (US)
Production: Susanne Hillen, Andy Hilliard, Link Hall,
Helen Ostick, Julia Bovis, Michelle Draycott,

Katie Pringle, Robert Evers, Mike Hancock, Robert
McKinlay, Zoë Nobes
Cartography: Melissa Baker, Maxine Repath, Ed Wright,
Katie Lloyd-Jones
Picture research: Louise Boulton, Sharon Martins
Online: Kelly Cross, Anja Mutić-Blessing, Jennifer Gold,
Audra Epstein (US)
Finance: John Fisher, Gary Singh, Edward Downey,
Mark Hall, Tim Bill
Marketing & Publicity: Richard Trillo, Niki Smith,
David Wearn, Chloë Roberts, Birgit Hartmann (UK);
Simon Carloss, David Wechsler, Kathleen Rushforth (US)
Administration: Tania Hummel, Demelza Dallow,
Julie Sanderson

ACKNOWLEDGEMENTS

David would like to thank: Njóla and Álfrún, the snow
angels; big thanks also to Meimei and Loftur, and
Gerry and Robin.

James would like to thank, in Iceland: the ambassador
par excellence, Kristbjörn Egilsson, for his unending
patience and expert knowledge on the use of all things
Icelandic; Ólafur Guðbrandsson for the use of his
comfortable flat in Reykjavík and his Icelandic
classes; wonderful Knútur at the tourist office in
Akureyri, for his patience and last minute help; and
Petrína Bachman, formerly of the Icelandic Embassy
in London, for her superb sense of humour.
In Britain: Juliet Schaffer who couldn't believe it
was happening all over again; Alan Davey for his

superb knowledge of the sagas; GO, for taking a
risk; Michelle Boon at Icelandair for her cocktail
dress; Steinunn Pálsdóttir at Arctic Experience; and
above all Lance Price, who had no hesitation in
dropping everything to hike in Hornstrandir.

The editor would like to thank: Kate Davis for extra
Basics research; Susannah Wight, for conscientious
proofreading; Maxine Repath and The Map Studio,
Romsey, Hants, for meticulous cartography; Sharon
Martins for cappuccinos and picking the pictures;
Louise Boulton, for the steamy front-cover picture;
Rob Evers for patient typesetting; and Kate Berens,
Claire Saunders, Gavin Thomas and Olivia Eccleshall
for tea, coffee and snakes.

PUBLISHING INFORMATION

This first edition published March 2001 by
Rough Guides Ltd, 62–70 Shorts Gardens,
London WC2H 9AH.
Distributed by the Penguin Group:
Penguin Books Ltd, 27 Wrights Lane, London W8 5TZ
Penguin Putnam, Inc. 375 Hudson Street, NY 10014,
USA
Penguin Books Australia Ltd, 487 Maroondah Highway,
PO Box 257, Ringwood, Victoria 3134, Australia
Penguin Books Canada Ltd, 10 Alcorn Avenue, Toronto,
Ontario, Canada M4V 1E4
Penguin Books (NZ) Ltd, 182–190 Wairau Road,
Auckland 10, New Zealand
Typeset in Linotron Univers and Century Old Style to an
original design by Andrew Oliver.
Printed in Spain by Graphy Cems.
Illustrations in Part One and Part Three by Edward Briant.

Illustrations on p.1 & p.285 by Robert Evers.
© David Leffman and James Proctor 2001
No part of this book may be reproduced in any form
without permission from the publisher except for the
quotation of brief passages in reviews.
336pp – Includes index
A catalogue record for this book is available from the
British Library
ISBN 1-85828-597-6

The publishers and authors have done their best to
ensure the accuracy and currency of all the information
in *The Rough Guide to Iceland*; however, they can
accept no responsibility for any loss, injury, or
inconvenience sustained by any traveller as a result of
information or advice contained in the guide.

THE ROUGH GUIDE TO

Iceland

written and researched by

David Leffman and James Proctor

ROUGH
GUIDES

THE ROUGH GUIDES

TRAVEL GUIDES • PHRASEBOOKS • MUSIC AND REFERENCE GUIDES

 We set out to do something different when the first Rough Guide was published in 1982. Mark Ellingham, just out of university, was travelling in Greece. He brought along the popular guides of the day, but found they were all lacking in some way. They were either strong on ruins and museums but went on for pages without mentioning a beach or taverna. Or they were so conscious of the need to save money that they lost sight of Greece's cultural and historical significance. Also, none of the books told him anything about Greece's contemporary life – its politics, its culture, its people, and how they lived.

So with no job in prospect, Mark decided to write his own guidebook, one which aimed to provide practical information that was second to none, detailing the best beaches and the hottest clubs and restaurants, while also giving hard-hitting accounts of every sight, both famous and obscure, and providing up-to-the-minute information on contemporary culture. It was a guide that encouraged independent travellers to find the best of Greece, and was a great success, getting shortlisted for the Thomas Cook travel guide award, and encouraging Mark, along with three friends, to expand the series.

The Rough Guide list grew rapidly and the letters flooded in, indicating a much broader readership than had been anticipated, but one which uniformly appreciated the Rough Guide mix of practical detail and humour, irreverence and enthusiasm. Things haven't changed. The same four friends who began the series are still the caretakers of the Rough Guide mission today: to provide the most reliable, up-to-date and entertaining information to independent-minded travellers of all ages, on all budgets.

We now publish more than 150 titles and have offices in London and New York. The travel guides are written and researched by a dedicated team of more than 100 authors, based in Britain, Europe, the USA and Australia. We have also created a unique series of phrasebooks to accompany the travel series, along with an acclaimed series of music guides, and a best-selling pocket guide to the Internet and World Wide Web. We also publish comprehensive travel information on our Web site:

www.roughguides.com

HELP US UPDATE

We've gone to a lot of effort to ensure that the first edition of *The Rough Guide to Iceland* is accurate and up-to-date. However, things change – places get "discovered", opening hours are notoriously fickle, restaurants and rooms raise prices or lower standards. If you feel we've got it wrong or left something out, we'd like to know, and if you can remember the address, the price, the time, the phone number, so much the better.

We'll credit all contributions, and send a copy of the next edition (or any other Rough Guide if you prefer) for the best letters. Please mark letters: "Rough Guide Iceland Update" and send to:
Rough Guides, 62–70 Shorts Gardens, London WC2H 9AH, or Rough Guides, 4th Floor, 345 Hudson St, New York, NY 10014.
Or send email to: mail@roughguides.co.uk
Online updates about this book can be found on Rough Guides' Web site at www.roughguides.com

THE AUTHORS

David Leffman first visited Iceland in 1981, and has been back and forth ever since in-between travelling around east Africa and Southeast Asia, working as a photographer, and co-authoring Rough Guides to *Australia*, *China*, and *Indonesia*. When not doing anything else, he can be found scuba diving near his home in Queensland.

James Proctor first fell in love with Iceland whilst working as the BBC's Scandinavia correspondent during the early 1990s, after which he returned to Reykjavík to study Icelandic at the University of Iceland, although his pitiful use of declensions still bemuses most Icelanders. When not in Iceland, James resides with his partner in the south of France: however, after a summer of searing heat, there are few places more appealing than the cool climes of Iceland. James is also the co-author of the *Rough Guide to Sweden*.

CONTENTS

Introduction ix

● CHAPTER 4: THE WEST FJORDS 163–189

● CHAPTER 5: NORTHWEST ICELAND 190–219

● CHAPTER 6: MÝVATN AND THE NORTHEAST 220–245

● CHAPTER 7: THE EASTFJORDS AND THE SOUTHEAST 246–275

● CHAPTER 8: THE INTERIOR 276–283

PART THREE CONTEXTS 285

LIST OF MAPS

MAP SYMBOLS

--- --- ---	Chapter division boundary	◉	Accommodation	⚑	Golf course
═══	Major road	▣	Restaurant/pub	🏊	Swimming pool
═══	Minor road	⊔⊔⊔⊔	Rift	ⓘ	Tourist office
= = =	Unpaved road/track	/|\\	Hill	⊠	Post office
- - - -	Footpath	᷄᷄	Mountains	■	Building
◆	Point of interest	▲	Peak	↥	Church (regional maps)
★	Bus stop	⇃	Waterfall	➕	Church (town maps)
✈	Airport	⩔	Spring	⊞	Cemetery
✗	Airstrip	/|\\	Volcano	▧	Park
🅟	Petrol station	⊛	Crater	▨	National park
🅿	Parking	☗	Fort	▩	Forest
═══	Waterway	∴	Ruins	↝	Glacier
⛫	Hut	♥	Museum	∴	Beach
⚠	Campsite	ⵢ	Lighthouse	ᶾᶾ	Lava flow

INTRODUCTION

Resting on the edge of the Arctic Circle and sitting atop one of the world's most volcanically active hotspots, **Iceland** is nowadays thought of for its striking mix of magisterial glaciers, bubbling hot springs and rugged fjords, where activities such as hiking under the Midnight Sun are complemented by healthy doses of history and literature. It's unfortunate, then, that one of the country's earliest visitors, the Viking Flóki Vilgerðarson, saw fit to choose a name for it that emphasized just one of these qualities, though perhaps he can be forgiven in part: having sailed here with hopes of starting a new life in this then uninhabited island, a long hard winter in around 870 AD killed off all his cattle. Hoping to spy out a more promising site for his farm he climbed a high mountain in the northwest of the country, only to be faced with a fjord full of drift ice. Bitterly disappointed, he named the place *Ísland* (literally "ice land") and promptly sailed home for the positively balmy climes of Norway.

A few years later, however, Iceland was successfully settled and, despite the subsequent enthusiastic felling of trees for fuel and timber, visitors to the country today will see it in pretty much the same state as it was over a thousand years ago, with the **coastal fringe**, for example, dotted with sheep farms, a few score fishing villages and tiny hamlets – often no more than a collection of homesteads nestling around a wooden church. An Icelandic town, let alone a city, is still a rarity and until the twentieth century the entire nation numbered no more than 60,000. The country remains the most sparsely populated in Europe, with a population of just 272,000 – over half of whom live down in the southwestern corner around the surprisingly cosmopolitan capital, **Reykjavík**. **Akureyri**, up on the north coast, is the only other decent-sized population centre outside the Greater Reykjavík area.

But if the coast is thinly populated, Iceland's **Interior** remains totally uninhabited and unmarked by humanity: a starkly beautiful wilderness of ice fields, infertile lava and ash deserts, windswept upland plateaux and the frigid vastness of Vatnajökull, Europe's largest glacier. Even in downtown Reykjavík, crisp, snow-capped peaks and fjords hover in the background, evidence of the forces that created the country. And Iceland's location on the Mid-Atlantic ridge also gives it one of the most volcanically active landscapes on Earth, peppered with everything from naturally occurring hot springs, scaldingly hot bubbling mud pools and noisy steam vents to a string of unpredictably violent volcanoes, which have regularly devastated huge parts of the country. It's something that Icelanders have learned to live with: in June 1998, when Reykjavík was rocked by a major earthquake, the ballet dancers at the National Opera performed right through it without missing a step.

Historically, the **Icelanders** have a mix of Nordic and Celtic blood, a heritage often held responsible for their characteristically laconic approach to life – taps in hotels often drip, buses don't depart to the stroke of the driver's watch, and everybody, including the President and the Prime Minister, is known by their first name. The battle for survival against the elements over the centuries has also made them a highly self-reliant nation, whose dependence on the sea and fishing for their economy is virtually total – hence their refusal to allow foreign trawlers to fish off Iceland during the diplomatically tense 1970s, sparking off three "Cod Wars", principally with Britain. However, their isolated location in the North

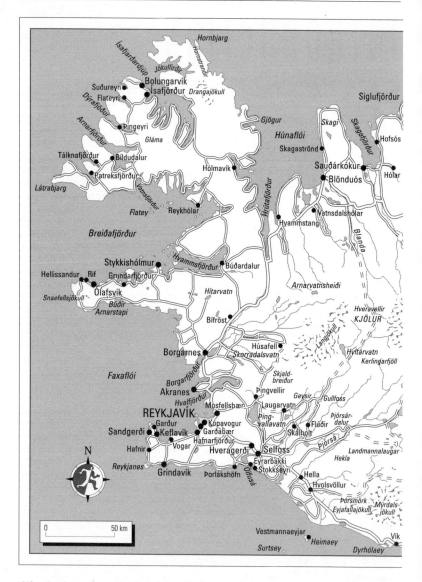

Atlantic also means that their island is frequently forgotten about – Icelanders will tell you that they've given up counting how many times they've been left off maps of Europe – something that deeply offends their strong sense of national pride. For all their self-confidence though, they can seem an initially reserved people – until Friday and Saturday nights roll around, when the *bjór* starts to flow, and turns even the most monosyllabic fisherman into a lucid talkshow host, right

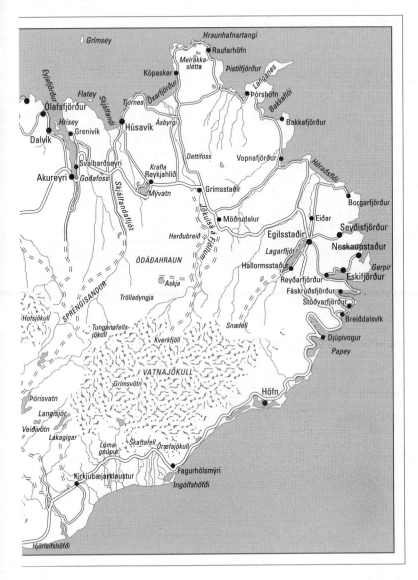

down to reciting from memory entire chunks of medieval sagas about the early settlers.

Where to go

It's difficult to imagine the emptiness of a country that is as large as England or the US State of Kentucky yet has a population of barely a quarter of a million (in comparison with England's 48 million). Route 1, the **Ringroad**, runs out from **Reykjavík** to encircle the island, with all long-distance buses and domestic planes beginning their journeys from the city. It may be small, but what Reykjavík lacks in size it more than makes up for in stylish bars, restaurants and shops, and the nightlife is every bit as wild as it's cracked up to be – during the light summer nights, the city doesn't sleep. The world's most northerly capital also boasts cinemas, an opera, a symphony orchestra and a dance company, as well as the usual string of museums and galleries. Reykjavík makes a good base for visiting the original geyser at **Geysir**, which gave its name to all other such hot springs around the world, and the spectacular waterfalls at **Gullfoss**. The **Reykjanes Peninsula**, home to the country's only international airport at Keflavík and therefore the first sight most travellers get of Iceland, is renowned for its teeming birdlife and its whales, which are frequently spotted off the peninsula's western tip.

Outside the relatively densely populated **southwestern** corner, the wilder side of Iceland begins – open spaces of vivid green edged by unspoilt coastlines of red and black sands all set against a backdrop of brooding hills and mountains. The main draw of the **West Coast** is the towns of **Borgarnes** and **Reykholt** and the surrounding countryside, where there's barely a feature that's unassociated with the **sagas**, such as **Keldur**, a farm where dramatic scenes from *Njal's Saga* were played out.

Away from the Ringroad, the **Snæfellsnes Peninsula** with its dramatic views of the glacier at its tip is one of country's most accessible hiking destinations. Arguably Iceland's most dramatic scenery is found in the far northwest of the country, the **West Fjords**, where tiny fishing villages nestle at the foot of table-top mountains or are tucked away in the neck of narrow fjords which offer protection from the ferocious Arctic storms which batter this exposed part of the country. **Ísafjörður** is the only settlement of any size in the region and makes a good base from which to strike out on foot into the wilderness of the **Hornstrandir Peninsula**. Beautifully located at the head of **Eyjafjörður** on the north coast, **Akureyri** is rightfully known as the capital of the north and functions as Iceland's second city. With a string of bars and restaurants it can make a refreshing change from the small villages elsewhere on the north coast. From here it's easy to make trips to reach the island of **Grímsey**, the only part of Icelandic territory actually within the **Arctic Circle**, and nearby **Siglufjörður**, for an insight into the twentieth-century herring boom that once made this tiny village the country's economic powerhouse.

The country's biggest tourist attraction outside the capital is **Lake Mývatn**, an hour to the east of Akureyri. The lake is a favourite nesting place for many species of ducks and other waterfowl and is surrounded by an electrifying proliferation of volcanic activity, including long-dormant cinder cones and the still-steaming lava fields at **Krafla**, which last burst forth in the 1980s. North of Mývatn, the small town of **Húsavík** is one of the best places in the country to organize summer whale-watching cruises, while just inland to the east, the wilds of **Jökulsárgljúfur National Park** offer superlative hiking along deep river gorges to the spectacular **Dettifoss**, Europe's most powerful waterfall. Across on the east coast, the **Eastfjords** centre on **Egilsstaðir** and the port of **Seyðisfjörður**, where Iceland's only international ferry docks, and offer further walking opportunities – both coastal and around the fjords, and inland to the volcanic spire of **Snæfell** – in a part of the country which regularly receives the driest and warmest weather. The small town of **Höfn** in the southeast corner is a good base from which to visit Europe's biggest glacier, the mighty **Vatnajökull**, either on a skidoo trip or on foot through **Skaftafell National Park**. Further to the west the nearby glacial lagoon, **Jökulsárlón**, offers the surreal chance to cruise alongside floating icebergs which were once part of the glacier itself. Iceland's most rewarding long distance hiking route is also found in this corner of the country – the **Þórsmörk trail** is one of the world's most exhilarating walking paths.

The **south coast** is marked by vast stretches of black, volcanic coastal sands punctuated by tiny villages that unfortunately are prone to some of the country's foulest weather – the town of **Vík** is Iceland's wettest but boasts teeming seabird colonies. Just off the south coast, and easily reached by ferry from Þorlakshöfn, the **Vestmannaeyjar (Westman Islands)** sport the world's largest puffin colonies and were propelled into the world headlines during the 1960s and 1970s by a series of volcanic eruptions that created a new island, **Surtsey**, and also threatened to bury the town of **Heimaey** under lava and ash.

Iceland's barren **Interior** is best tackled as part of a guided tour – it's much easier to let experienced drivers of all-terrain buses pick their way across lavafields and cross unbridged rivers than to try it yourself. Parts of the Interior's fringes are also feasibly explored on foot, however, and even by bus it's perfectly possible to break your journey anywhere and camp – you'll be sharing the stunning scenery with only the ghosts of the early settlers who perished in its bleak, grey-sanded lava deserts.

When to go

Though milder than you might think, Icelandic **weather** is notoriously unpredictable. In **summer** there's a fair chance of bright and sunny days and temperatures can reach 17°C but these are interspersed with wet and misty spells when the temperature can plummet to a chilly 10°C. Generally speaking if it's wet and windy in the southwest it'll be sunny and warm in the northeast, which receives more than its fair share of sunshine in the summer months, much to the dismay of city slickers at the other end of the country. Most budget accommodation is

CLIMATE IN ICELAND		
Average daily temp (°C)		**Rainfall (mm)**
Max	**Min**	
REYKJAVÍK		
Jan	2	-2	89
Feb	3	-2	64
March	4	-1	62
April	6	1	56
May	10	4	42
June	12	7	42
July	14	9	50
Aug	14	8	56
Sept	11	6	67
Oct	7	3	94
Nov	4	0	78
Dec	2	-2	79

only open from late May to early September, and it's at these times, too, that buses run their fullest schedules. Many bus routes through the Interior don't start until late June or early July when the snow finally melts. Although Iceland lies south of the Arctic Circle and therefore doesn't experience a true **Midnight Sun**, nights are light from mid-May to early August across the country. In the north the sun never fully sets during June. Between September and January the *Aurora Borealis* or **Northern Lights** can often be seen. They appear as an eerie, oscillating curtain of green, blue or pale orange light in the night sky.

Winter temperatures fluctuate at 7–8°C either side of freezing point and heavy snowfall and avalanches block many of the roads. There's little chance of accommodation other than in the large hotels in Reykjavík and the other main towns, and hiking and camping are out of the question. However, a stay in the capital at this time means a lack of crowds and at Christmas its streets are bathed in the glow of candles burning behind every window. Bear in mind though that daylight in midwinter is limited to a few hours – in Reykjavík, sunrise isn't until almost 11am in December; the sun is already sinking slowly back towards the horizon after 1pm; and by 3.30pm, it'll be dark again. Further north in Ísafjörður, reckon on around one and a half hours' less daylight than in Reykjavík.

GETTING THERE FROM BRITAIN AND IRELAND

Until recently, Iceland was one of the most expensive countries in Europe to reach from Britain, due in large part to Icelandair, Iceland's national airline, holding a monopoly on the route. Furthermore, the lengthy ferry journey from Scotland, via the Shetland and Faroe Islands to Iceland's east coast port, Seyðisfjörður, is very expensive. However, in 2000, the low-cost airline GO began summer-only flights into Iceland's international airport, Keflavík, and prices have since tumbled as Icelandair brought its fares broadly in line with those offered by its new rival.

FLIGHTS

Between May and September, **GO** fly four times weekly from London Stansted to Keflavík (3hr) for £120–290 return fare. The frequencies may change from season to season, so check with the airline for the latest information.

Icelandair operate from both London Heathrow and Glasgow to Keflavík. From April to September, the Heathrow flights (3hr) operate twice daily (once on Sat); from October to March, the frequency is reduced to one daily on Monday, Wednesday and Saturday, but remains at two daily for the rest of the week. From Glasgow (2.5hr), they fly once daily, except on Saturdays from October to March, when there's no service. Summer (April–Sept) return fares range from £280 to £400 from both destinations; out of season, they generally fall to £200–350, but it's worth checking with Icelandair directly, or visiting its

Web site, for any **special offers** – deals can see prices fall to just £179.

One of the best ways to find **discounted flights** to Iceland is to look on the Internet (see box on p.4); good site to check out include *www.cheapflights.co.uk*, *www.deckchair.co* and *www.lastminute.co.uk*. Other classified sections of the Sunday newspapers. If you live in London, *Time Out* magazine and the *Evening Standard* occasionally throw up good offers. It's always worth calling one of the **discount flight agents** (see box on p.4), who sell slightly reduced Icelandair flights as part of package deals, such as STA Travel and Usit CAMPUS for youth and student reductions, although such discounts with Icelandair only amount to £30 or so.

FERRIES

Although it's possible to travel by sea to Iceland, the journey is only recommended to those with a cast-iron stomach, since the frequent gales, storms and unsettling swell of the North Atlantic can well and truly quash romantic images of riding the waves to your destination. To make things a little easier though, from 2002 a new ferry will replace the *Norröna*, which currently plies the route, and will be altogether more luxurious than the current ship, featuring a swimming pool, Jacuzzi, saunas, and even a fitness centre.

The Faroese shipping company **Smyril Line** operate a once-weekly car and passenger **ferry** between mid-May and early September from Lerwick, on Shetland, to Seyðisfjörður, in eastern Iceland, departing on Wednesday at 2am and arriving on Thursday at 9am. However, the return leg of this journey requires a three-day stopover in the Faroe Islands while the ferry nips down to Denmark, before collecting you again from the Faroese capital, Tórshavn, before heading off for Lerwick. To reach Lerwick from the rest of the UK, you can take the **P&O Scottish Ferries** service from Aberdeen to Lerwick, departing on Monday at 6pm and arriving at 8am on Tuesday. Travelling by this route, though, can be a real endurance test depending on where you're coming from: from

---

FERRY COMPANIES

Smyril Line ☎298/345 900.
P&O Scottish Ferries ☎01224/572615.

AIRLINES, AGENTS AND TOUR OPERATORS IN BRITAIN

AIRLINES

GO ☎0870/607 6543, www.go-fly.com.

Icelandair ☎020/7874 1000, www.icelandair.co.uk.

AGENTS AND TOUR OPERATORS

Arctic Experience, 29 Nork Way, Banstead, Surrey SM7 1PB (☎01737/218810, www.arctic-experience.co.uk). Well-established wildlife holiday specialist, with groups led by naturalists to Iceland, Greenland, Spitzbergen, Alaska and Lapland.

Bridge the World, 47 Chalk Farm Rd, London NW1 8AN (☎020/7911 0900, www.bridgetheworld.com). Good deals aimed at the backpacker market

Explore Worldwide, 1 Frederick St, Aldershot, Hants, GU11 1LQ (☎01252/760 000, www.explore.co.uk; brochure requests 01252/760 100). Small-group tours, treks and expeditions and safaris on all continents, with few supplements for single travellers; the emphasis is on small local hotels.

Flynow.com, 125 Gloucester Rd, London, SW7 4SF (☎020/7835 2000, www.flynow.com); 597 Cheetham Hill Rd, Manchester M8 5EJ (☎0161/721 4000). Large range of discounted tickets.

The London Flight Centre, 131 Earls Court Rd, London SW5 9RH (☎020/7244 6411, www.topdecktravel.co.uk); 47 Notting Hill Gate, London W11 3JS (☎020/7727 4290); Shop 33, The Broadway Centre, Hammersmith tube, London W6 9YE (☎020/8748 6777). Long-established agent dealing in discount flights.

North South Travel, Moulsham Mill Centre, Parkway, Chelmsford, Essex CM2 7PX (☎/fax:01245/608 291, www.northsouthtravel.co.uk). Friendly, competitive travel agency, offering discounted fares worldwide – profits are used to support projects in the developing world, especially the promotion of sustainable tourism.

Regent Holidays, 31 High Street, Shanklin, Isle of Wight PO37 6JW (☎01983/86 4212). Good package operator.

STA Travel, (☎020/7361 6145 or ☎0161/830 4713, www.statravel.co.uk); 86 Old Brompton Rd, London SW7 3LH; 117 Euston Rd, London NW1 2SX; 38 Store St, London WC1E 7BZ; 11 Goodge St, London W1P; 38 North St, Brighton (☎01273/728 282); 25 Queens Rd, Bristol BS8 1QE (☎0117/929 4399); 38 Sidney St, Cambridge CB2 3HX (☎01223/366 966); 75 Deansgate, Manchester M3 2BW (☎0161/834 0668); 88 Vicar Lane, Leeds LS1 7JH (☎0113/244 9212); 78 Bold Street, Liverpool L1 4HR (☎0151/707 1123); 9 St Mary's Place, Newcastle-upon-Tyne NE1 7PG (☎0191/233 2111); 36 George St, Oxford OX1 2OJ (☎01865/792 800); 27 Forrest Road, Edinburgh (☎0131/226 7747); 184 Byres Rd, Glasgow G1 1JH (☎0141/338 6000); 30 Upper Kirkgate, Aberdeen (☎0122/465 8222). Specialists in low-cost flights and tours for students and under-26s, though other customers welcome.

Trailfinders, 1 Threadneedle Street, London EC2R 8JX (☎020/7628 7628, www.trailfinders.co.uk); 215 Kensington High St, London W6 6BD (☎020/7937 5400); 58 Deansgate, Manchester M3 2FF (☎0161/839 6969); 254–284 Sauchiehall St, Glasgow G2 3EH (☎0141/353 2224); 22–24 The Priory Queensway, Birmingham B4 6BS (☎0121/236 1234); 48 Corn St, Bristol BS1 1HQ (☎0117/929 9000). One of the best-informed and most efficient agents for independent travellers.

Usit Campus, national call centre ☎0870/240 1010, www.usitcampus.co.uk; 52 Grosvenor Gardens, London SW1W 0AG (☎020/7730 340); 541 Bristol Rd, Selly Oak, Birmingham B29 6AU (☎0121/414 1848); 61 Ditchling Rd, Brighton BN1 4SD (☎01273/570 226); 37–39 Queen's Rd, Clifton, Bristol BS8 1QE (☎0117/929 2494); 5 Emmanuel St, Cambridge CB1 1NE (☎01223/324 283); 53 Forest Rd, Edinburgh EH1 2QP (☎0131/225 6111, telesales 668 3303); 122 George St, Glasgow G1 1RF (☎0141/553 1818); 166 Deansgate, Manchester M3 3FE (☎0161/833 2046, telesales 273 1721); 105–106 St Aldates, Oxford OX1 1DO (☎01865/242 067). Student/youth travel specialists.

London, for example, the entire journey takes three and a half days.

High season is defined as falling between mid-June and the end of August. During this time, one-way **through fares** from Aberdeen to Seyðisfjörður, available directly from P&O Scottish Ferries (see box on p.3), are £188 for a single couchette (£145 in low season) and £277

(£210) for a two-berth cabin; return tickets cost double these prices, and taking a **car** on this route costs an extra £155 (£123). If you want to just buy a Smyril Line ticket from Lerwick to Iceland, costs are 1320 Danish krónur in high season for a single couchette (920 in low season) and 1900 Danish krónur for a two-berth cabin (1310). Once again, returns cost double and tickets are available through P&O Scottish Ferries.

PACKAGE TOURS

An all-inclusive **package tour** can sometimes turn out to be the cheapest way of doing things, and may be a much easier way of reaching remote areas of Iceland, particularly in winter. The specialist operators listed in the box opposite provide deals ranging from a visit to Reykjavík and the Golden Circle attractions of Geysir and Gullfoss to all-singing, all-dancing adventure holidays involving snowmobiling across Vatnajökull and whale watching in Húsavík.

City breaks invariably work out less costly than arranging the same trip independently: prices include return travel, transfer from Keflavík to your hotel, hotel accommodation and often a city sightseeing tour of Reykjavík. Out of season, prices can be as low as £200 per person for a weekend– contact Icelandair, the main operator for city breaks, for the latest details on dates and prices.

GETTING THERE FROM IRELAND

Since there are neither direct air nor ferry links between Ireland and Iceland, all routes from Belfast and Dublin to Reykjavík lead first to London or Glasgow. By **plane**, it's most straightforward to buy a return ticket to London Heathrow or London Stansted (see box for operators) and then connect on to an Icelandair or GO flight to Iceland (see p.3). If you wish to connect onto the Smyril Line **ferry** (see p.3), you'll first have to make your way to Aberdeen for the ferry to Shetland, though of course this just extends an already lengthy trip.

When it comes to **packages**, you're best off contacting one of the British-based companies listed in the box on p.4.

(see p.3)... (see p.3)... box on p.4.

AIRLINES, AGENTS AND TOUR OPERATORS IN IRELAND

AIRLINES

Aer Lingus, Northern Ireland reservations (☎0645/737 747); Dublin reservations (☎01/705 3333). Branches at: 41 Upper O'Connell St, Dublin; 13 St Stephen's Green, Dublin 2; 12 Upper St George's St, Dun Laoghaire; 2 Academy St, Cork (☎021/327 155); and 136 O'Connell St, Limerick (☎061/474 239).

British Midland, Northern Ireland reservations (☎0345/554 554); Dublin reservations (☎01/283 8833).

KLM UK, Reservations in Northern Ireland (☎0990/074074); in the Republic (☎0345/445588).

AGENTS AND TOUR OPERATORS

Liffey Travel, 12 Upper O'Connell St, Dublin 1 (☎01/878 8322).
Trailfinders, 4–5 Dawson St, Dublin 2 (☎01/677 7888, www.trailfinders.com).
USIT Now, Fountain Centre, College St, Belfast BT1 6ET (☎028/9032 4073); 10–11 Market Parade, Patrick St, Cork (☎021/270 900); 33 Ferryquay St, Derry (☎01504/371 888); 19 Aston Quay, Dublin 2 (☎01/602 1777 or 677 8117, Europe and UK ☎01/602 1600 or 679 8833, long-haul ☎01/602 1700); Victoria Place, Eyre Square, Galway (☎091/565 177); Central Buildings,O'Connell St, Limerick (☎061/415 064); 36–37 Georges St, Waterford (☎051/872 601).

GETTING THERE FROM NORTH AMERICA

From North America, Iceland is only served by Icelandair, Iceland's national carrier, who fly out of a handful of airports in the US but just the one in Canada. All flights go to Keflavík international airport, near Reykjavík, the main point of entry for Iceland.

Fares depend on what time of year you fly: they're most expensive during **high season** (roughly June–Aug and around Christmas and New Year) and are cheapest during **low season** (Nov–March, excluding Christmas and New Year); the remaining months are classified as **shoulder season**, with **fares** somewhere in between. **From the US** Icelandair flights go daily direct to Reykjavík from

DISCOUNT TRAVEL COMPANIES AND TRAVEL CLUBS

Airtech, Suite 204, 588 Broadway, New York NY 10012 (☎1-800/575-TECH or ☎212/219-7000, *www.airtech.com*). Standby seat broker; also deals in consolidator fares and courier flights.

Airtreks.com, High Adventure Travel, 442 Post St, 4th Floor, San Francisco CA 94102 (☎1-800/350 0612 or ☎415/912 5600, *www.airtreks.com*). Round-the-world tickets; Web site features interactive database that lets you build and price your own RTW itinerary.

Council Travel, 205 E 42nd St, New York NY 10017 (1-800/226-8624 or ☎212/822-2700, *www.counciltravel.com*); plus branches in many other US cities. Student/budget travel agency.

Educational Travel Center, 438 N Frances St, Madison WI 53703 (☎1-800/747-5551 or 608/256-5551, *www.edtravel.com*). Student/youth and consolidator fares.

STA Travel, 10 Downing St, New York NY 10014 (☎1-800/777-0112 or ☎212/627-3111, *www.sta-travel.com*); plus branches in Los Angeles, San Francisco, Miami, Chicago, Seattle, Philadelphia, Washington DC and Boston. Worldwide discount travel firm specializing in student/youth fares, student IDs, travel insurance, car rental etc.

Student Flights, Suite A104, 5010 E Shea Blvd, Scottsdale AZ 85254 (☎1-800/255-8000 or ☎602/951-1177, *www.ise.com*). Student/youth fares, student IDs and rail passes.

TFI Tours International, 34 W 32nd St, New York NY 10001 (1-800/745-8000 or 212/736-1140). Consolidator.

Travac Tours, 989 6th Ave, New York NY 10018 (☎1-800/872-8800 or ☎212/563-3303, *www.thetravelsite.com*). Consolidator and charter broker. You can have a list of fares faxed to you by calling toll-free on ☎888/872-8327.

Travel Avenue, Suite 1404, 10 S Riverside Plaza, Chicago IL 60606 (☎1-800/333-3335 or ☎312/876-6866, *www.travelavenue.com*). Discount travel agent.

Travel CUTS, 187 College St, Toronto ON M5T 1P7 (☎1-800/667-2887 or ☎416/979-2406, *www.travelcuts.com*); plus other branches throughout Canada. Student travel organization specializing in student fares, IDs and other travel services.

Travelers Advantage, 311 W Superior St, Chicago IL 60610 (☎1-800/255-0200, *www.travelersadvantage.com*). Travel club; annual membership fee.

UniTravel, Suite 120, 11737 Administration Drive, St Louis MO 63146 (☎1-800/325-2222 or ☎314/569-2501; *www.unitravel.com*). Consolidator.

Worldtek Travel, 111 Water St, New Haven CT 06511 (☎1-800/243-1723 or ☎203/772-0470, *www.worldtek.com*). Discount travel agency.

Worldwide Discount Travel Club, 11601 Biscane Blvd, Miami Beach FL 33181 (☎305/895-2082). Travel club with discounts on package holidays only. Annual membership fee.

AIRLINES IN NORTH AMERICA

Air Canada Canada ☎1-888/247-2262,
US ☎1-800/776-3000, *www.aircanada.ca.*

Icelandair ☎1-800/223-5500,
www.icelandair.com.

New York (US$545 high season, US$298 low season; 5hr), Baltimore (US$545/298; 5hr), Boston (US$545/298; 5hr); six times weekly from Minneapolis (US$725/348; 6hr); and twice weekly from Orlando (US$725/348; 6hr). **From Canada**, they operate three weekly services from Halifax (Nova Scotia) only (CAN$1400/725; 4hr). Air Canada offers daily flights to Halifax from Montreal (CAN$180; 1hr 20min), Toronto (CAN$255; 2hr) and Vancouver (CAN$482; 5hr 40min).

You can normally cut costs by going through a **specialist flight agent** – either a **consolidator**, who buys up blocks of tickets from the airlines and sells them at a discount, or a **discount agent** (see box opposite), who in addition to dealing with dis-

counted flights may also offer special student and youth fares and a range of other travel-related services such as travel insurance, car rental, tours and the like. Bear in mind, though, that penalties for changing your plans on discounted tickets can be stiff. Remember too that these companies make their money by dealing in bulk – don't expect them to answer lots of questions. If you travel a lot, **discount travel clubs** are another option – the annual membership fee may be worth it for benefits such as cut-price air tickets and car rental.

Don't automatically assume that tickets purchased through a travel specialist will be cheapest – once you get a quote, check with the airlines and you may turn up an even better deal. Be

TOUR OPERATORS IN NORTH AMERICA

Adventure Center (☎1-800/227-8747, *www.adventurecenter.com*). Ten-day Land of Fire and Ice tour throughout Iceland, starting at US$2825, land only.

Adventures Abroad (☎1-800/665-3398, *www.adventures-abroad.com*). Canadian-based company with a variety of packages, specializing in small group tours. A fourteen-day Iceland tour starts around CAN$2928, land only.

Borton Overseas (☎1-800/843-0602, *www.bortonoverseas.com*). Adventure-vacation specialists, offering a variety of Iceland tours with biking, hiking and rafting activities, plus farm and cabin stays. The three-night Viking Challenge features hiking, horse riding and mountain biking from US$2067 and includes airfare from the East Coast.

Brekke Tours (☎1-800/437-5302, *www.brekketours.com*). Sightseeing and cultural tours of Iceland, such as the three-day "Iceland Hot Stop" starting at US$225, land only. Call for a brochure.

Icelandair Holidays (☎1-800/779-2899). Iceland tour specialists, offering a variety of tours from basic airfare plus hotel packages to fully escorted tours.

International Gay and Lesbian Travel Association (☎1-800/448-8550, *www.iglta.org*).

Trade group with lists of gay-owned or gay-friendly travel agents, accommodation and other travel services.

Loma Travel (☎1-888/665-9899, *www.loma-travel.com*). Canadian tour operator offering cheap flights, tours and cruises.

Passage Tours (☎1-800-548-5960, *www.passagetours.com*). Tours, ski packages and cheap weekend breaks starting at US$498, airfare included.

Scanam World Tours (☎1-800/545-2204, *www.scanamtours.com*). Group and individual tours and cruises, plus cheap weekend breaks. Four-day tours of Iceland start at US$390, land only.

Scanditours (☎1-800/432-4176, *www.scanditours.com*). Canadian based, with wide range of travel options including individual tours of Iceland. Offices in Toronto and Vancouver.

Scantours (☎1-800/223-7226, *www.scantours.com*). Numerous tours of Iceland; their eight-day Grand Tour of Iceland starts from $1325, land only.

Vantage Deluxe World Travel (☎1-800/322-6677, *www.vantagetravel.com*). De luxe group tours and cruises Scandinavian cruises that stop in Iceland.

advised also that the pool of travel companies is swimming with sharks – exercise caution and never deal with a company that demands cash up front or refuses to accept payment by credit card.

Students might be able to find cheaper flights through the major student travel agencies, such as Council Travel, STA Travel or, for Canadian students, Travel CUTS (see box on p.6 for addresses and phone numbers).

Another source of cheap air fares is the **Internet**; there are a number of Web sites where you can look up fares and even book tickets, such as Airtreks, at *www.airtreks.com*, specialize in RTW tickets (see below) and have a helpful interactive Web site. Also try Travelocity at *www.travelocity.com*, FLIFO Cyber Travel Agent at *www.flifo.com*, or make a bid for a fare at *www.priceline.com*.

ROUND-THE-WORLD TICKETS

If you are travelling to Iceland as part of a longer trip, consider buying a **Round-the-World** (RTW) ticket, although as Icelandair has a monopoly on flights to and from Iceland, fares that allow stopovers for anything over three days are not discounted. Since Iceland is not one of the more obvious destinations for round-the-world travellers, you would probably have to have a custom-designed RTW ticket (rather than an "off-the-shelf" RTW ticket) assembled for you by a travel agent, which can be quite expensive. For example, a New York–San Jose de Costa Rica–Caracas–Paris–Glasgow–Rejkavík–Boston–New York will set you back $1695.

PACKAGES AND ORGANIZED TOURS

There are a number of companies operating **organized tours** of Iceland, ranging from de luxe cruises to cycling holidays. Group tours can be very expensive, and occasionally don't include the airfare, so check what you are getting. Reservations can often be made through your local travel agent; most of the tour operators listed on p.7 also have informative Web site that allow you to book online.

GETTING THERE FROM AUSTRALIA AND NEW ZEALAND

There are no direct flights to Iceland from Australia or New Zealand, and by far the cheapest way of getting there from down under is to find a discounted airfare to London and arrange a flight to Reykjavík from there (see p.3). As London is a major destination for most international airlines flying out of Australia and New Zealand, the high level of competition ensures a wide choice of routes worldwide, with flights via Southeast Asia being the cheapest option. Prices quoted below are for travel to London; see p.3 for the add-on fare for London-Reykjavík flights.

Regular return fares from Australia and New Zealand are seasonally adjusted: **low season** is from mid-January to the end of February and October to November; while **high season** last from mid-May to August and then from December until January. The remainder of the year is classed as **shoulder season**. Tickets purchased direct from the airlines are expensive, and travel agents generally offer much better deals – they also have the latest information on limited special offers and stopovers, and it's their fares which are quoted below. The best **discounts** are offered by companies such as Flight Centres, STA and Trailfinders (see p.10); such outfits can also help with visas, travel insurance and tours. You might also want to have a look on the **Internet**; *www.travel.com.au* offers discounted fares online, as does *www.sydneytravel.com*.

AIRLINES IN AUSTRALIA AND NEW ZEALAND

Air New Zealand Australia ☎13/2476; New Zealand toll-free ☎0800/737 000, or ☎09/357 3000; *www.airnz.com*.
Daily flights to London Heathrow from Sydney, Brisbane, Melbourne and Auckland, with a transfer in LA.

British Airways Australia ☎02/8904 8800; New Zealand ☎09/356 8690; *www.british-airways.com*.
Daily flights to London Heathrow from Sydney, either direct or with a transfer in LA; twice weekly via Perth, with either a transfer or overnight stop in Harare or Johannesburg; and daily from Auckland, with a transfer in LA.

Canadian Airlines Australia ☎1300/655 767; New Zealand ☎09/309 0735; *www.cdnair.ca*.
Several flights weekly to London Heathrow from Sydney, Melbourne and Auckland, with a transfer in Vancouver or Toronto.

Cathay Pacific Australia ☎13/1747 or ☎02/9931 5500; New Zealand ☎09/379 0861; *www.cathaypacific.com*.
Several flights weekly to London Heathrow from Brisbane, Sydney, Melbourne, Perth, Cairns and Auckland, all with a transfer in Hong Kong.

Garuda Australia ☎1300/365 330; New Zealand ☎09/366 1855 or ☎1800/128 510.
Several flights weekly from Melbourne, Sydney, Perth, Darwin and Brisbane in Australia and Auckland in New Zealand to London Gatwick, with either a transfer or an overnight stop in Denpasar or Jakarta.

Icelandair The Australian agent is Nordic Travel, and Bentours can also issue tickets for London–Reykjavík fares; see the Specialist Operators box on p.11 for both; there is no New Zealand agent.

Japan Airlines Australia ☎02/9272 1111; New Zealand ☎09/379 9906; *www.japanair.com*.
Daily flights to London Heathrow from Brisbane and Sydney, plus several flights a week from Cairns and Auckland, all with either a transfer or overnight stop in Tokyo or Osaka. Code-share with Air New Zealand.

Korean Air Australia ☎02/9262 6000; New Zealand ☎09/307 3687; *www.koreanair.com*.
Several flights weekly to London Heathrow from Sydney and Auckland, plus once a week from Christchurch with either a transfer or overnight stop in Seoul.

Malaysian Airlines Australia ☎13/2627; New Zealand ☎09/373 2741 or ☎0800/777 747; *www.malaysiaair.com*.
Several flights weekly to London Heathrow from Sydney, Melbourne, Perth and Auckland, with either a transfer or overnight stop in Kuala Lumpur.

Qantas Australia ☎13/1313; New Zealand ☎09/357 8900 or ☎0800/808 767; *www.qantas.com.au*.
Daily flights to London Heathrow from major cities in Australia, either direct (with a short refuelling stop) or with a transfer in Singapore or Bangkok, plus twice weekly via Perth with either a transfer or overnight stopover in Harare or Johannesburg; daily flights from major cities in New Zealand to London Heathrow via Sydney, and with a transfer in Singapore, Bangkok or LA.

Royal Brunei Airlines Australia ☎07/3221 7757 (no NZ office); *www.bruneiair.com*.
Three flights weekly to London Heathrow from Brisbane, and two weekly from Darwin and Perth, all via Abu Dhabi and with a transfer or overnight stop in Brunei.

Singapore Airlines Australia ☎13 1011; New Zealand ☎09/303 2129 or ☎0800/808 909; *www.singaporeair.com*.
Daily flights to London Heathrow from Brisbane, Sydney, Melbourne, Perth and Auckland, either direct or with a transfer in Singapore.

Sri Lankan Airlines Australia ☎02/9244 2234; New Zealand ☎09/308 3353.
Three flights a week to London Heathrow from Sydney, with a transfer or overnight stop in Colombo.

Thai Airways Australia ☎1300/651 960; New Zealand ☎09/377 3886; *www.thaiair.com*.
Several flights a week to London Heathrow from Brisbane, Sydney, Melbourne, Perth and Auckland, with either a transfer or overnight stop in Bangkok.

United Airlines Australia ☎13/1777; New Zealand ☎09/379 3800; *www.ual.com*.
Daily flights to London Heathrow from Sydney, Melbourne and Auckland, with a transfer in LA.

Virgin Atlantic Airways Australia ☎02/9244 2747; New Zealand ☎09/308 3377; *www.virgin-atlantic.com*.
Daily flights to London Heathrow from Sydney, Melbourne and Adelaide, with a transfer or overnight stop in Kuala Lumpur. Code-share with Malaysia Airlines.

There are also a few companies offering all-inclusive **tours to Iceland** from Australia, though not New Zealand – see the Specialist Operators box opposite.

FLIGHTS FROM AUSTRALIA

Depending on the route and transfer time, **flight times** between Australia and Britain are 22–28 hours via Asia, and 25–30 hours via North America. All **airfares** to London from Australian east-coast gateways such as Brisbane, Sydney, and Melbourne are equally priced, with the domestic carrier Ansett or Qantas providing a shuttle service to the point of international departure. If you're going via Asia, note that scheduled flights from Perth or Darwin are going to cost A$100–200 less than if departing from eastern gateways, though you'll also spend A$400 more if going via the USA from these places.

The cheapest deals are **via Asia** and may involve a night's free overnight stop in the carrier's home city, with accommodation, meals and transfers included in the ticket price – often a welcome

break on long-haul flights. The best low-season bargains are with Sri Lankan Airlines, at around A$1300 return; in high season, the cheapest fares are usually offered by Garuda, Japan Airlines and Royal Brunei, all costing between A$1350 and A$2400. Virgin Atlantic have teamed up with Malaysian Airlines to offer no-frills London flights via Kuala Lumpur for around A$1600 in low season and around A$2600 in high season. Mid-price carriers flying to London include Korean Airlines, Malaysia Airlines, Thai Airways, Singapore Airlines, Cathay Pacific, Qantas, British Airways and Air New Zealand: prices range from A$1899 to A$2600. More expensive, but faster and entailing only a short refuelling stop or a quick change of planes, are Thai Airways, Singapore Airlines, Cathay Pacific, Qantas, British Airways and Air New Zealand, coming in at A$1900–2800.

Flights to London are pricier **via North America**, and all require a change of planes en route (via LA with United Airlines and Air New Zealand, and via Toronto or Vancouver with Canadian Airlines); expect to pay A$2100–3000.

SPECIALIST TOUR OPERATORS IN AUSTRALIA

The following offer tours and advice on travel to Iceland from Australia; there are no specialist operators for Iceland in New Zealand.

Bentours, Level 11, 2 Bridge Street, Sydney NSW 2000 (☎02/9241 1353, fax 9251 1574, *www.bentours.com.au*). Handles Icelandair ticket sales; also offers 3- to 5-day sightseeing packages from Reykjavík.

IT Adventure (Exodus), Level 4, 46–48 York Street, Sydney NSW 2000 (☎02/9279 0491, fax 9279 0492, *www.exodus.co.uk*). Puts together 14-day bus and trekking expeditions to Iceland from the UK, taking in Vatnajökull, Snæfell,

Þingvellir and Skaftafell, with accommodation in hostels or camping.

Nordic Travel, 600 Military Road, Mosman, NSW 2088 (☎02/9968 1783). The regional Icelandair agent and representative for most major Icelandic tour agents, this long-established operator can book you onto pre-existing tours within Iceland or tailor special-interest packages – from driving, hiking or cycling around the highlights to snowbmobiling across Vatnajökull.

FLIGHTS FROM NEW ZEALAND

Fewer carriers fly from New Zealand than from Australia; however, **routes** are just as varied. Japan Airlines, Malaysia Airlines, Thai Airways and Korean Air all fly from Auckland, with a transfer or overnight stop in the carrier's home city, for between NZ$2000 and NZ$2400; Qantas and British Airways, who go **via Sydney**, **Bangkok** or **Singapore**, are more expensive at NZ$2300–$3000, but will get you there about six hours faster.

The most direct route (though still requiring a change of planes) is **via the Pacific and North America**. Air New Zealand and United Airlines fly via LA for between NZ$2200 and NZ$3000. British Airways, going via LA, and Canadian Airlines, via Vancouver, offer flights for about NZ$2499 to NZ$3000. **Via South America**, a normal return fare with Aerolineas Argentinas via Buenos Aires is quite expensive, with a year-round flat rate of NZ$3600; an RTW ticket is a

better bet (see below). Another option is to fly to an Australian gateway city and then on to London (see p.10 & p.3); you'll get a greater choice of airlines and routes this way.

ROUND-THE-WORLD TICKETS

If you're planning to visit Iceland as part of a longer trip, then you'll find that a **Round-the-World** (RTW) airfare offers greater flexibility and is better value than a straightforward return flight. However, as with standard returns from Australia and New Zealand, you'll have to add the airfare to Reykjavík from London or New York to the following prices.

As a guideline – prices are very volatile - a RTW ticket from Sydney or Auckland to Singapore or Bangkok, then on to London, New York, Los Angeles, Auckland and back to Sydney starts at around A$2399/NZ$2899; a ticket from Sydney to Auckland, Santiago, Rio, London, Paris, Bangkok, Singapore and back to Sydney starts at A$2499/NZ$2999.

VISAS AND RED TAPE

Citizens from the European Economic Area (comprising the EU, Switzerland and Liechtenstein), US, Canada, Australia and New Zealand need only a passport valid for at least three months after the planned date of arrival to enter Iceland for up to three months.

European Economic Area nationals, however, may stay longer than three months on condition that they secure work for a further period of three months minimum. Once in employment, there is no time limit on the length of stay in Iceland but **residence and work permits** are required, normally valid for five years, and available from the **Icelandic Statistical Bureau** (Hagstofa Íslands, Pjóðskrá, Skuggasund 3, Reykjavík; ☎560 9850). Non-EU nationals can only apply for residence permits before leaving home, and must be able to prove they can support themselves without working. For further information, contact the relevant embassy in your country of origin or the Icelandic **Ministry of Foreign Affairs** at *www.mfa.is*.

As regards **customs regulations**, all visitors to Iceland, irrespective of country of origin, can bring in the following: either one litre of spirits and one litre of wine, or one litre of spirits and six litres of beer, or one litre of wine and six litres of beer or two litres of wine. In addition to this, 200 cigarettes, or 250g of other tobacco products, are also permitted.

ICELANDIC EMBASSIES ABROAD

Australia and New Zealand: contact the Icelandic Embassy in China: Landmark Tower 1, 802, 8 North Dongsanhuan Road, Chaoyang District, 100004 Beijing (☎86/106590 7795).

Canada: Consulate General, 940 Younette Drive, West Vancouver, B.C. V7T 1S9 (☎604-922-0854); plus consulates in Edmonton, Winnipeg, St John's, Ottowa, Halifax, Toronto, Montreal and Regina.

Republic of Ireland: contact the Icelandic Embassy in the UK.

UK: 2A Hans St, London, SW1X 0JE (☎020/7259 3999)

US: 1156 15th Street NW Suite 1200 Washington DC 20005-1704 (☎202/265 6653); Consulate General, 800 3rd Ave, 36th Floor, New York, NY (☎212-593-2700); plus consulates in Phoenix, Tallahassee, Anchorage, San Francisco, Miami, Chicago, Atlanta, Louisville, New Orleans, Boston, Detroit, Minneapolis, Kansas City, New York, Harrisburg, Dallas, Houston, Norfolk and Seattle.

INSURANCE

A typical travel insurance policy usually provides cover for the loss of baggage, tickets and – up to a certain limit – cash or cheques, as well as cancellation or curtailment of your journey. Most of them exclude so-called dangerous sports unless an extra premium is paid: in Iceland this can mean whitewater rafting and trekking. Read the small print and benefits tables of prospective policies carefully; coverage can vary wildly for roughly similar premiums.

Many policies can be chopped and changed to exclude coverage you don't need – for example, sickness and accident benefits can often be excluded or included at will. If you do take medical coverage, ascertain whether benefits will be paid as treatment proceeds or only after return home, and whether there is a 24-hour medical emergency number. When securing baggage cover, make sure that the per-article limit – typically under £500 equivalent – will cover your most valuable possession. If you need to make a claim, you should keep receipts for medicines and medical treatment, and in the event you have anything stolen, you must obtain an official statement from the police. Bank and credit cards often have certain levels of medical or other insurance included and you may automatically get travel insurance if you use a major credit card to pay for your trip.

Travel agents and **tour operators** are likely to offer some sort of insurance when you book a package holiday, though according to UK law they can't make you buy their own (other than a £1 premium for "schedule airline failure"). If you have a good all-risks home insurance policy it *may* cover your possessions against loss or theft even when overseas. Many private medical schemes such as BUPA or PPP also offer coverage plans for abroad, including baggage loss, cancellation or curtailment and cash replacement as well as sickness or accident.

ROUGH GUIDES TRAVEL INSURANCE

Rough Guides now offers its own **travel insurance**, customized for our readers by a leading UK broker and backed by a Lloyd's underwriter. It's available for anyone, of any nationality, travelling anywhere in the world.

There are two main Rough Guide insurance plans: **Essential**, for basic, no-frills cover, starting at £11.75 (European) and £23.03 (worldwide) for two weeks; and **Premier** – with more generous and extensive benefits – starting at £12.50 (European) and £28.79 (worldwide). Alternatively, you can take out annual **multi-trip insurance**, which covers you for any number of trips throughout the year (with a maximum of 60 days for any one trip), starting at £47.26 (European) and £83.99 (worldwide). Unlike many policies, the Rough Guides schemes are calculated by the day, so if you're travelling for 27 days rather than a month, that's all you pay for. If you intend to be away for the whole year, the **Adventurer** policy will cover you for 365 days from £90 (Europe), £160 (worldwide excluding USA and Canada), and £200 (worldwide including USA and Canada). Each plan can be supplemented with a "Hazardous Activities Premium" if you plan to indulge in sports considered dangerous, such as skiing, scuba-diving or trekking. Rough Guides also does good deals for older travellers, and will insure you up to any age, at prices comparable to SAGA's.

For a **policy quote**, call the Rough Guides Insurance Line on UK freefone ☎0800 015 0906, or, if you're calling from outside Britain, on ☎44/1243 621 046. Alternatively, get an online quote at *www.roughguides.com/insurance.*

Americans and **Canadians** should also check that they're not already covered. Canadian provincial health plans usually provide partial cover for medical mishaps overseas. Holders of official student/teacher/youth cards are entitled to meagre accident coverage and hospital in-patient benefits. Students will often find that their student health coverage extends during the vacations and for one term beyond the date of last enrollment. Homeowners' or renters' insurance often covers theft or loss of documents, money and valuables while overseas, though conditions and maximum amounts vary from company to company.

TRAVELLERS WITH DISABILITIES

Iceland is a fairly well prepared for disabled travellers. Several hotels in Reykjavík and Akureyri have rooms specially designed for disabled guests, larger department stores are generally accessible to wheelchair users, while transport – including coastal ferries, airlines, and a few public tour buses – can make provisions for wheelchair users if notified in advance.

The best idea is to contact the service operators, either directly or through your travel agent; tourist information offices in Reykjavík (see p.46) also have copies of the *Icelandic Hotels and Guesthouses* brochure, which includes a list of hotels accessible to disabled visitors, and the *Accessible Reykjavík* booklet produced by **Sjálfsbjörg**, Reykjavík's Disabled Association and available for free from the main tourist office in Reykjavík.

For advice before you go, there are two US-oriented **Web sites** for disabled travellers, both of which have comprehensive links to other similar sites. Access Able Travel (*www.access-able.com*) has a bulletin board for passing on tips and accounts of accessible attractions, accommodation, guides and resources around the globe. Disability Travel (*www.disabilitytravel.com*) deals in arranging all aspects of travel for the mobility impaired and will at least be able to offer advice on Iceland. Though they are not geared specifically to visitors, ÖBÍ, the Organisation of Handicapped in Iceland (English-language homepage at *www.obi.is/ensk/*) also have a Web site with links

to various organizations for disabled people in Iceland, who again will have information on available services.

There are also **organized tours and holidays** specifically for people with disabilities – the contacts in the box opposite will be able to put you in touch with specialists for trips to Iceland. It's important to know where you may expect help and where you must be self-reliant, especially regarding transport and accommodation. It's also vital to be honest with travel agencies, insurance companies, and travel companions, plus you should think about your limitations, making sure others know about them too. If you don't use a wheelchair all the time but your mobility is limited, remember that you are likely to need to cover greater distances while travelling – sometimes over rougher terrain and in different temperatures to those you are familiar with. If you use a **wheelchair**, have it serviced before you go and carry a repair kit.

People with pre-existing medical conditions are sometimes excluded from **travel-insurance policies**, so check the small print carefully. A **medical certificate** of your fitness to travel, provided by your doctor, is pretty well essential, as some insurance companies or transport operators may insist on it. Make sure that you have extra supplies of drugs, and a prescription including the generic names in case of an emergency. If there's an association representing people with your disability, contact them early in the planning process for advice.

CONTACTS FOR TRAVELLERS WITH DISABILITIES

Australia and New Zealand
DPA (Disabled Persons' Assembly), Level 4, Wellington Trace Centre, 173–175 Victoria Street, PO Box 27-524 Wellington (☎04/801 9100).

Wheelchair Travel, 29 Ranelagh Drive, Mt Eliza VIC 3930 (☎1800/674 468 or ☎03/9787 8861, *www.travelability.com*).

Ireland
Disability Action Group, 2 Annadale Avenue, Belfast BT7 3JH (☎028/9049 1011).

Irish Wheelchair Association, Blackheath Drive, Clontarf, Dublin (☎01/833 8241, fax 833 3873, *iwa@iol.ie*).

UK
Access Travel, 6 The Hillock, Astley, Lancs M29 7GW (☎01942/888 844, fax 891 8811). The sole licensed UK tour operator dealing specifically with travellers with disabilities.

Holiday Care Service, 2nd Floor, Imperial Building, Victoria Road, Horley, Surrey RH6 7PZ (☎01293/774 535, fax 784 647, Minicom 776 943, *holiday.care@virgin.net*).

RADAR (Royal Association for Disability and Rehabilitation), 12 City Forum, 250 City Road, London EC1V 8AF (☎020/7250 3222, Minicom 7250 4119). A good source of advice on holidays and travel abroad.

Tripscope, The Courtyard, Evelyn Road, London W4 5JL (☎020/8994 9294, fax 8994 3618, Minicom 0845/758 5641, *tripscope@cableinet.co.uk*). Information service offering free advice on UK and international travel for those with limited mobility.

US and Canada
Access First Travel, 239 Commercial St, Malden, MA 02148 (☎1-800/557-2047). Current information for disabled travellers.

Directions Unlimited, 123 Green Lane, Bedford Hills, NY 10507 (☎1-800/533-5343). Tour operator specializing in custom tours for people with disabilities.

Jewish Rehabilitation Hospital, 3205 Place Alton Goldbloom, Chomedy Laval, PQ H7V 1R2 (☎450/688-9550, ext 226). Guidebooks and travel information.

Mobility International USA, PO Box 10767, Eugene, OR 97440 (☎541/343-1284 voice & TDD, *www.miusa.com*). Information and referral services, access guides, tours and exchange programmes. Their Web site has useful travel tips and listings of disabled-friendly accommodation and sights, plus information on foreign exchange programmes for the disabled. Annual membership $25 (includes quarterly newsletter).

Society for the Advancement of Travel for the Handicapped (SATH), 347 Fifth Ave, Suite 610 New York, NY 10016 (☎212/447-7284, *www.sath.org*). Non-profit-making travel industry referral service that passes queries on to its members as appropriate; allow plenty of time for a response.

Travel Information Service (☎215/456-9600). Telephone only information and referral service for disabled travellers.

Twin Peaks Press Box 129, Vancouver, WA 98666 (☎360/694-2462 or ☎1-800/637-2256, *www.pacifier.com/twinpeak*). Publisher of the Directory of Travel Agencies for the Disabled ($19.95), listing more than 370 agencies worldwide; Travel for the Disabled ($19.95); the Directory of Accessible Van Rentals ($9.95) and Wheelchair Vagabond ($14.95), loaded with personal tips.

Wheels Up! PO Box 5197 Plant City, FL 33564-5197 (☎1-888/389-4335). Provides discounted airfare, tour and cruise prices for disabled travellers; also publishes a free monthly newsletter and has a comprehensive Web site.

COSTS, MONEY AND BANKS

Due to its small consumer base and dependency on imports, Iceland is an expensive country to visit, even compared to the rest of Europe and Scandinavia. There are ways to minimize costs, whether you're planning to stay in hotels and rent a car, or simply travel between campsites on public buses, but expect to pay substantially more than you're used to for all food, transport and accommodation.

Iceland's **currency** is the **króna** (krónur in the plural), abbreviated to either Isk, Ikr or kr, which divides into 100 **aurar**. Notes come in 5000kr, 2000kr, 1000kr and 500kr denominations, and there are 100kr, 50kr, 10kr, 5kr, and 1kr coins, decorated with sea creatures. You might also encounter 50 or 10 aurar coins, though due to inflation these are seldom seen today. At the time of writing the **exchange rate** was approximately 117kr to £1; 81kr to US$1; 55kr to CAN$1; 45kr to AU$1; and 34kr to NZ$1.

BASIC COSTS

The best way to minimize costs in Iceland is to be as self-sufficient as possible, and bring in full **camping equipment** – or at least a sleeping bag for the cheapest unfurnished hostel-style beds (see p.28) – and make use of the various **bus passes** on offer (see p.22). A **Hostelling International Card** (p.28) will also get you a few hundred krónur a night off official Youth Hostel rates. Bear in mind too that **seasons** affect costs: places to stay and car-rental agencies drop their prices between October and May, though at that time inexpensive summer-only accommodation will be shut, campsites will probably be under snow, and bus services are infrequent or suspended.

Taking all this into account, budget travellers can keep **daily costs** down by camping out every night – mixing campsites with free camping in the wilds – using a bus pass and cooking for themselves, keeping average daily costs for accommodation, travel and food down to around 3000kr (though cyclists can cut this in half) a day. Throw in a few nights in hostel-style accommodation and the occasional pizza and you're looking at 4000kr. Mid-range travel still means using a bus pass to get around, but, favouring hostels and eating out cheaply most of the time, this will set you back about 6000kr a day. Staying only in guesthouses or hotels and eating in restaurants for every meal means that you're looking at daily expenses of anything upwards of 12,000kr.

If you need to **car rental** at any stage, then you can add at least another 5500kr a day, plus fuel – see p.22 for more about this. None of the above takes into account additional costs for entertainment such as tours, entry fees, drinking (an expensive pastime in Iceland – see p.30), or alternative transport such as flights and ferries, for which we've given prices in the guide.

If you do incur any serious expenses – or even just buy a souvenir woollen sweater – take advantage of the fact that visitors can get a partial Value-Added Tax, or **VAT refund** on purchases exceeding 4000kr, provided departure from Iceland is within 30 days of the purchase. The VAT itself totals 24.5 percent of the cost price, though the refund is only 15 percent. You fill out a form at the time of purchase and hand it over with all reciepts at the currency-exchange booth upstairs by the duty-free shop at Keflavík airport (see p.43), where you'll receive your refund in cash; you can ask for this in any currency. If you leave by ferry from Seyðisfjörður (see p.3), get your form stamped at customs and then apply for a refund within three months through Icelandic Tax-free Shopping, PO Box 1200, 235 Keflavík, Iceland.

BANKS AND EXCHANGE

Branches of Iceland's three **banks** – Íslandsbanki, Landsbanki Ísland and Búnaðarbanki – are found

---

CHANGE GROUP OFFICES IN ICELAND

Austurstraeti 20, IS-101 Reykjavík.
Tues–Sun: May–Sept 9am–11pm &
Sept–May 11.30am–7.30pm.

Bankastræti 2, IS-101 Reykjavík.
Mon–Sat: May–Sept 8.30am–8pm &

Sept–May 9:00am–5pm.
Falcon House, Hafnarstræti 3, IS-101 Reykjavík.
Daily: May–Sept 9am–6pm.
Nonni Travel, Brekkugata 5, Akureyri. Daily: May
15–Sept 1 8am–8pm.

---

right around the country, including in many single-street villages, and most sport an **ATM**, often located in a weather-proof lobby that can be accessed outside opening hours. Normal **banking hours** are Monday to Friday 9.15am to 4pm, though a few branches in Reykjavík have longer hours.

All banks handle **foreign exchange**, with the Íslandsbanki charging no commission and the others a nominal fee per transaction. Outside banking hours, you could also try major hotels or **The Change Group**, which has three branches in Reykjavík and one in Akureyri (see the box above) – rates, however, are poor and commissions high in both cases. Banks and the Change Group (which is the Icelandic representative for Western Union) can also arrange **international money transfers**, though you should expect a service charge in the region of 1750kr and for the transfer to take at least a few days.

TRAVELLERS' CHEQUES AND CARDS

Travellers' cheques, available in advance through banks and travel agents, are the safest way to carry your funds around, as they can be cashed in all Icelandic banks and many hotels, and can be replaced if lost or stolen – keep a list of the serial numbers separate from the cheques. Take US dollar or UK sterling denomination cheques, as it's not possible to cash Australian or New Zealand dollar travellers' cheques in Iceland. Some stores and accommodation in Reykjavík also accept US dollar or British notes, though elsewhere you'll have to exchange foreign currency into krónur first.

Credit cards are widely used in Iceland for just about everything. MasterCard and Visa are the major brands, valid not just for shopping but also for **cash advances** over the counter at all banks and a few of the larger post offices. Íslandsbanki also advance cash on Diners' Club, while the American Express agent is Úrval-Útsýn Travel Agency, at Lágmúli 4, Reykjavík. You should also check whether your credit card or home **ATM card** has Cirrus/Maestro/Electron connections, which will allow it to to draw funds directly from your home account through Icelandic ATMs. The fee for this depends on your bank, but can work out as the cheapest way of all to access your money.

HEALTH

Iceland is by and large a healthy country to be in – a small industrial output means that pollution levels are very low. Health care is also excellent and available in most communities, and while language is unlikely to be a problem, tourist offices can also recommend doctors and hospitals – all of whom will anyway be English speaking. No vaccinations are required for visitors to Iceland.

If you're spending much time out of doors, be aware that the **weather** and **distance** might cause difficulties if you need medical attention in a hurry, and it's wise to carry a **first-aid kit**. Two important items to include are a roll of elasticated **sticking plaster** (band aids) and **crepe bandages** – both vital for supporting and splinting sprained muscles or broken bones.

Most problems you'll encounter, however, are minor. Though you might not think the northern sun would be much trouble, it's still strong enough to cause sunburn and eyestrain – especially when reflected off ice or snow – so use **sunscreen** and **sun glasses**. Some sort of hand cream or **moisturiser** and **lip balm** are a good idea too, as the cold dry air, wind and dust can painfully crack exposed skin. **Eye drops** will also relieve irritation caused by dust. **Flies** are not the problem in Iceland that they can be in Scandanavia; Mývatn (see p.227) is the only place you'll encounter them in plague proportions, though very few bite.

About the most serious thing to worry about is **hypothermia**, wherein your core body temperature drops to a point that can be fatal. In Iceland, it's obviously most likely to occur if you get exhausted, wet and cold whilst out hiking or cycling; symptoms include a weak pulse, disorientation, numbness, slurred speech and exhaustion. If you suspect someone is suffering from hypothermia, seek shelter from the wind, rain, and snow, get the patient as dry as possible, and prevent further heat loss – aside from clothing, a foil "space blanket" available from camping stores will help. Sugary drinks can also help (alcohol definitely doesn't), but serious cases need immediate hospi-

tal treatment. The best advice is to do your best to avoid hypothermia in the first place: while hiking, ensure you eat enough carbohydrates, drink plenty of water and wear sufficient warm and weather-proof clothing, including, if necessary, a **hat** – most body heat is lost through the head – and gloves. During the colder parts of the year, **motorists** should always carry a blanket and warm gear too, in case they get stranded by snow.

PHARMACIES AND MEDICAL TREATMENT

There's at least one pharmacy, or **apotek**, in every town in Iceland, as well stocked as any chemist you'll find at home. Most open during normal business hours, though some in Reykjavík and Akureyri stay open longer. **Doctors** are similarly distributed, though if you need **hospital treatment**, you'll need to get yourself to a major regional centre – Reykjavík also has several **health centres** with general practitioners on hand through the day.

INFORMATION AND MAPS

For information before you go, the Icelandic Tourist Board maintains several promotion offices abroad, as do Icelandair and their agents, where you'll be able to pick up brochures of the highlights, plus information on tours, transport and accommodation. There's also heaps of information available about Iceland on the Internet – see the box on p.20 for useful Web sites.

Once you're in the country, Reykjavík's **tourist information centre** (see p.46) has

ICELANDIC TOURIST BOARD OFFICES ABROAD

Australia and New Zealand
There are no Icelandic tourist or airline offices in either Australia or New Zealand; instead, contact Bentours or Nordic Tours (see the "Specialist Operators" box on p.11).

Canada
There are no Icelandic tourist or airline offices in Canada; contact the US office instead.

Ireland
There are no Icelandic tourist or airline offices in Ireland; contact the UK office instead.

UK
Icelandair, 172 Tottenham Court Road, 3rd Floor, London W1P 9LG (☎020/7338 4499, *www.goiceland.co.uk*).

US
Iceland Tourist Board, 655 3rd Ave, 18th Floor, New York, NY 10017-5689 (☎212-885-9700); or PO Box 4649, Grand Central Station, New York, NY 10163-4649.

information and brochures for the whole country, with independent tourist information offices in almost every other town, often housed in the bus station. Wherever you are, your accommodation is another good source of local details; for instance, families may have lived on particular farms for generations, and have very thorough knowledge of the region.

MAPS

A range of excellent **maps** of the country, costing between 800 and 1100kr, is available for all types of use – if you can't find what you want overseas, you'll be able to pick it up in Reykjavík and Akureyri, or sometimes from local tourist offices and fuel stations. In addition to the maps detailed below, Iceland's hiking clubs

---

MAP OUTLETS

AUSTRALIA AND NEW ZEALAND

Map Land, 372 Little Bourke Street, Melbourne (☎03/9670 4383).

The Map Shop, 16a Peel Street, Adelaide (☎08/8231 2033).

Perth Map Centre, 884 Hay Street, Perth (09/9322 5733).

Speciality Maps, 58 Albert Street, Auckland (☎09/307 2217).

Travel Bookshop, Shop 3, 175 Liverpool Street, Sydney (☎02/9261 8200).

Worldwide Maps and Guides, 187 George Street, Brisbane (☎07/3221 4330).

CANADA

International Travel Maps and Books, 552 Seymour St, Vancouver V6B 3J5 (☎604/687 3320, www.itmb.com).

Open Air Books and Maps, 25 Toronto St, M5R 2C1 (☎416/363-0719).

Ulysses Travel Bookshop, 4176 St-Denis, Montréal H2W 2M5 (☎514/843 9447, www.ulyssesguides.com).

IRELAND

Easons Bookshop, 40 O'Connell St, Dublin 1 (☎01/873 381, www.eason.ie).

Fred Hanna's Bookshop, 27–29 Nassau St, Dublin 2 (☎01/677 1255).

Hodges Figgis Bookshop, 56–58 Dawson St, Dublin 2 (☎01/677 4754, www.hodgesfiggis.com).

Waterstone's, Queens Bldg, 8 Royal Ave, Belfast BT1 1DA (☎028/9024 7355); 7 Dawson St, Dublin 2 (☎01/679 1415); 69 Patrick St, Cork (☎021/276 522).

UK

Blackwell's Map and Travel Shop, 53 Broad St, Oxford OX1 3BQ (☎01865/792 792, www.blackwell.bookshop.co.uk).

Daunt Books, 83 Marylebone High St, London W1M 3DE (☎020/7224 2295, fax 7224 6893); 193 Haverstock Hill, London NW3 4QL (☎020/7794 4006).

Heffers Map and Travel, 20 Trinity Street, Cambridge CB2 1TJ (☎01223/586 586, www.heffers.co.uk).

James Thin Melven's Bookshop, 29 Union St, Inverness IV1 1QA (☎01463/233 500, www.jthin.co.uk).

John Smith and Sons, 26 Colquhoun Ave, Glasgow G52 4PJ (☎0141/221 7472, fax 248 4412, www.johnsmith.co.uk).

The Map Shop, 30a Belvoir St, Leicester, LE1 6QH (☎0116/2471400).

National Map Centre, 22–24 Caxton St, London SW1H 0QU (☎020/7222 2466, www.mapsnmc.co.uk).

Newcastle Map Centre, 55 Grey St, Newcastle upon Tyne NE1 6EF (☎0191/261 5622, www.newtraveller.com).

Stanfords, 12–14 Long Acre, London WC2E 9LP (☎020/7836 1321, www.stanfords.co.uk); 29 Corn Street, Bristol BS1 1HT (☎0117/929 9966; www.stanfords.co.uk).*

The Travel Bookshop, 13–15 Blenheim Crescent, London W11 2EE (☎020/7229 5260, www.thetravelbookshop.co.uk).

Waterstone's, 91 Deansgate, Manchester M3 2BW (☎0161/837 3000, fax 835 1534, www.waterstonesbooks.co.uk).

*Stanfords in London is the UK's largest map sellers, and operates a mail order service available on the number given above and on email from sales@stanfords.co.uk.

The UK-wide general booksellers Waterstone's and Dillons usually have comprehensive map departments, as do the less widely found Blackwell's, dotted around the country.

continues overleaf

MAP OUTLETS continued

US

ADC Map and Travel Center, 1636 I St NW, Washington DC 20006 (☎202/628-2608).

Book Passage, 51 Tamal Vista Blvd, Corte Madera, CA 94925 (☎415/927-0960, *www.bookpassage.com*).

The Complete Traveller Bookstore, 199 Madison Ave, New York, NY 10016 (☎212/685-9007, *www.complete.traveller.com*); 3207 Fillmore St, San Francisco, CA 94123 (☎415/923-1511).

Elliott Bay Book Company, 101 S Main St, Seattle, WA 98104 (☎206/624-6600, *www.elliottbaybook.com*).

Forsyth Travel Library, 226 Westchester Ave, White Plains, NY 10604 (☎1-800/367-7984, *www.forsyth.com*).

Map Link Inc., 30 S La Patera Lane, Unit 5, Santa Barbara, CA 93117 (☎805/692-6777, *www.maplink.com*).

Phileas Fogg's Books & Maps, #87 Stanford Shopping Center, Palo Alto, CA 94304 (☎1-800/533-FOGG, *www.foggs.com*).

Rand McNally, 444 N Michigan Ave, Chicago, IL 60611 (☎312/321-1751); 150 E 52nd St, New York, NY 10022 (☎212/758-7488); 595 Market St, San Francisco, CA 94105 (☎415/777-3131).*

Travel Books & Language Center, 4437 Wisconsin Ave, Washington, DC 20016 (☎1-800/220-2665).

Traveler's Choice Bookstore, 2 Wooster St, New York, NY 10013 (☎212/941-1535, *tvlchoice@aol.com*).

*Note: Rand McNally now has more than 20 stores across the US; call ☎1-800/333-0136, ext 2111, or go to www.randmcnally.com *for the address of your nearest store, or for direct mail maps.*

(see p.35) and National Parks (available from park offices on-site) put out a few maps of varying quality for popular nature reserves and national parks.

For **general orientation**, try the widely available *Íslandskort* series published by Mál og Menning bookshop in Reykjavík, which provides a single 1:600,000 sheet of the entire country, along with four separate 1:300,000 maps covering each quarter. Landforms, roads and road types are well defined, and there's a clear distinction made between farms and small settlements – so you can accurately gauge where the next shops are.

The back of each sheet also has a thumbnail sketch of the region's main sights. Geologists should also check out Mál og Menning's *Náttúrufarskort* series, which includes a general **geological** map of Iceland, plus a 1:5000 sheet of Surtsey, the world's newest island.

Lastly, there's Landmælingar Íslands, the Icelandic National Land Survey. Their most popular products are the 1:500,000 **road map**, also available as a booklet; and a series that splits the country into nine sections, covered by five 1:250,000 sheets (there are maps on both sides). In both cases their contour detail is far superior to

ICELAND ON THE INTERNET

Eye On Iceland
www.eyeoniceland.com
Well-planned magazine-style site for travellers to Iceland, with an independent slant. Good coverage of recent news, plus events and issues.

Icelandic Tourist Board
www.icetourist.is
Comprehensive regional run-down of the country, listing the main sights and recommended services.

Iceland Worldwide
www.iww.is
Some excellent photos but lightweight text on travelling around Iceland, plus a monthly

newsletter on practically any topic – such as politics, sport, or travel – to do with the country and a Yellow Pages-style service directory.

Reykjavík City
www.reykjavik.is
Net-zine for Reykjavík, with all upcoming attractions, parties, bands and events.

Travelenet
http://travelnet.is
Tourist brochure with snippets of history, plus practical information on transport, accommodation and tours.

Íslandskort's, and the 1:250,000 set are suitable for most **hiking** demands. Popular hiking areas such as Hekla, Vestmannaeyjar, Skaftafell,and

Mývatn are covered separately in Landmælingar's 1:50,000 series, some of which have 1:25,000 details on the reverse of the sheet.

GETTING AROUND

Iceland's small scale makes getting around fairly straightforward – at least during the warmer months. From Reykjavík, it's possible to fly or catch a bus to all major centres, and in summer there are even scheduled buses through the Interior. In winter, however, reduced bus services and difficult road conditions might make flying the only practical way to travel. It's also easy enough to hire cars or four-wheel-drives, though those on a budget will find cycling a more practical alternative.

On the ground, whether you're planning to take buses around the country, hire a car or cycle about, you'll probably spend a good deal of time on **Route 1**, or *Hringbraut*, the **Ringroad**, which largely follows the coast in a 1500-kilometre circuit of the country via Reykjavík, Akureyri and Egilsstaðir. With the exception of a long gravel run in the northeast between Mývatn and Egilsstaðir, most of the Ringroad is surfaced, and in winter snowploughs do their best to keep the route accessible to conventional vehicles, though you'll still need to take care and use snow tyres.

Elsewhere, while stretches around towns might be surfaced, the majority of Icelandic roads are gravel. Some of these are perfectly decent if bumpy to travel over, while many others – such as **roads through the Interior** – are only navigable in high-clearance four-wheel-drives. Note that interior roads are only open between June and August: exactly when each opens and closes each year – or whether some open at all – depends on

the weather, and the going can be difficult even then.

You can check on the **current road conditions** anywhere in Iceland by logging on to *www. vegag.is*, a continually updated Web site in English and Icelandic that shows maps of the country with roads colour-coded according to their state.

FLIGHTS

Flying in Iceland is good value: the single airfare from Reykjavík to Egilsstaðir, for instance, is around 7000kr – little more than half the price of a one-way bus fare for the same journey – and takes just one hour instead of two days. As an added bonus, you'll get a different take on Iceland's unique landscape from above – flying over Vatnajökull's vast expanse of ice is about the only way to get a grasp of its scale.

The main **domestic carrier** is Flugfélag Íslands, who fly all year from Reykjavík to Vestmannaeyjar, Ísafjörður, Akureyri, Egilsstaðir and Höfn (Hornafjörður) almost daily. From Akureyri, they have less regular connections between April and October to Grímsey, Ísafjörður, Egilsstaðir, Vopnafjörður and Þórshöfn.

Other airlines out of Reykjavík and Akureyri concentrate on connections to remoter settlements across Iceland's northwest and northeast. Íslandsflug is the largest of these operators, and also offers combined air-and-land **tours** of a day's or more duration from Reykjavík to various popular spots: Húsavík for whale watching; Mývatn for the lake and nearby hot pots; and Vestmannaeyjar for puffins and more volcanoes.

Booking flights presents no particular problems, and we've given contact details for airline offices and agents throughout the guide. Note, however, that **bad weather** can cause cancellations at short notice and that it's best to book ahead for summer weekends and holidays. Some sample **fares** from Reykjavík are: Vestmannaeyjar 4500kr single/9000kr return; Akureyri 6000/12,000kr; and Egilsstaðir 7000/14,000kr.

Air passes can be bought in Iceland from Icelandair or Air Iceland offices. The Flugfélag Íslands pass comprises coupons (4 for 20,700kr, 5 for 23,600kr, 6 for 27,100kr; valid for one year on all routes), whereby each is redeemed for a flight; the first can be booked well in advance, the others up to 24 hours before departure. The same conditions apply to the Fly As You Please Pass, which offers twelve days unlimited travel on Flugfélag Íslands routes (32,900kr).

Luggage allowance is 20kg, and you need to **check in** thirty minutes before departure.

BUSES

Buses are pretty much the most convenient way to get around a large chunk of Iceland, and Iceland's umbrella long-distance-bus organisation, **BSÍ** (*www.bsi.is*), based at the bus station in Reykjavík, puts out a free, comprehensive **timetable** of scheduled departures and tours run by various companies. Between May and October, scheduled services cover the entire Ringroad and many other routes, with regular tours tackling interior destinations once the roads open around June – about the only way you'll get to see these remote places unless you've considerable off-road driving experience and the right vehicle.

On the down side, bus travel is expensive, especially for the relatively small distances involved: one-way **fares** from Reykjavík are 5400kr to Akureyri; 6300kr to Höfn; and around 11,000kr to Egilsstaðir. In purely point-to-point terms you may find it costs less to fly (see above), and if you can get a group of three people or so together, car rental (see below) works out even cheaper. Between October and May, the range of buses is also greatly reduced: interior roads close, local services dry up, and even along the Ringroad buses only run as far east as Höfn and Akureyri.

BUS PASSES

Bus passes available from BSÍ and other outlets in Akureyri, Seyðisfjörður, and Egilsstaðir, will save you money on extended bus travel, and also get you **discounts** at many campsites, and five percent off ferry tickets and selected bus tours when booked through BSÍ in Reykjavík. Pass holders can also make use of the **Open Voucher System**, wherein you prepay for sleeping-bag accommodation at hostels, guesthouses or campsites along the way – though you'll barely save any money this way. Passes are not valid on city bus services.

The **Full Circle Pass** costs 19,200kr and lets you orbit the country using scheduled services along the Ringroad, with no time limit. However, you're not allowed to double back on your route, and have to pay extra if you detour off the Ringroad – through the Golden Circle, Interior, or Westfjords for instance – but overall you save around 3000kr on simply paying fares as you go. A **Full Circle-Westfjords Pass** (28,500kr) is essentially the same as the Full Circle, with a Westfjords extension that also allows free passage on the Stykkishólmur–Brjánslækur ferry.

Alternatively, the **Omnibus Pass**, valid from between 7 days (21,000kr in summer, 12,500kr in winter when there are no buses on the Höfn–Akureyri stretch) and 28 days (43,500kr, summer only), allows you to change direction, and covers the entire Full Circle-Westfjords route as well as the Golden Circle. Omnibus Pass holders also get 50 percent off bike rental through BSÍ in Reykjavík.

BUS TOURS AND BUSES THROUGH THE INTERIOR

BSÍ and its operatives also run **tours**, from half-day trips around Þingvellir to overnight traverses of the **Interior**. Passes are not valid on these routes, but you can get off along the way and pick up a later bus – tell them your plans in advance so a space can be reserved for you. Make sure too that you know when the next bus is due – some parts of the country are only covered once or twice a week.

DRIVING

Driving around Iceland allows greater flexibility than taking the bus, but unless you have an off-road vehicle you're going to be more or less restricted to the Ringroad and its more accessible offshoots – and you'll still have to rely on bus tours elswhere. **Car-rental** rates can be reasonable value for a group, and it's also possible to bring in your own vehicle to the country for a limited time. Depending on whether you're in Reykjavík or out in the wilds, **fuel** costs between 84–100kr per litre for petrol (*bensín*). UK, US, Canadian, Australian and New Zealand **driving licenses** are all valid for short-term visits.

CAR RENTAL

Car-rental agencies, offering everything from small economical runarounds to gas-guzzling four-

CAR RENTAL AGENCIES

AUSTRALIA AND NEW ZEALAND
Avis, Australia ☎1800/225 533; New Zealand ☎09/526 2800, *www.avis.com*.

Budget, Australia ☎1300/362 848; New Zealand ☎0800/ 652 227 or ☎09/375 2270, *www.budget.com*.

Hertz, Australia ☎1800/550 067; New Zealand ☎09/309 0989 or 0800 655 955, *www.hertz.com*.

US AND CANADA
Auto Europe ☎1-800/223-5555, *www.autoeurope.com*.

Avis ☎1-800/331-1084, *www.avis.com*.

Budget ☎1-800/527-0700, *www.budget.com*.

Europcar ☎1-877-940-6900, *www.europcar.com*.

Hertz US ☎1-800/654-3001; Canada ☎1-800/263-0600, *www.hertz.com*.

Kemwel Holiday Autos ☎1-800/422-7737, *www.kemwel.com*.

UK AND IRELAND
Avis ☎0870/606 0100; Northern Ireland ☎0990/900 500; Eire ☎01/874 5844, *www.avis.com*.

Budget ☎0800/181 181; Eire ☎0800/973 159, *www.budgetrentacar.com*.

Europcar ☎0345/222 525; Eire ☎01/676 7476, *www.europcar.com*.

Hertz ☎0870/844 8844; Northern Ireland ☎0990/996 699, Eire ☎01/676 7476, *www.hertz.com*.

Holiday Autos ☎0870/400 0011; Northern Ireland ☎0990/300 400; Eire ☎01/872 9366, *www.kemwel.com*.

wheel-drives, are found right around Iceland. In smaller places the selection will be limited, and rental counters are usually located at the local airport or bus terminal. Avis, Hertz and Europcar are the most widespread of the international companies, with plenty of indigenous operators such as ALP, who give slightly better rates – contact details are given throughout the guide.

Rental-rate options boil down to two types: a **daily rate**, which covers the first 100km, after which you pay upwards of 28kr per additional kilometre; or an **all-inclusive rate**, which fixes a flat daily fee – obviously of benefit if you're planning a relatively short-term, long-range excursion. Check that advertised prices include **tax and insurance**, known as CDW (Collision Damage Waiver) – they often don't – and note that if you're planning on a **one-way rental** (hiring the car in Reykjavík and leaving it in Akureyri, for instance) you'll have to pay an additional relocation fee. It's always worth bargaining, especially if you're planning a lengthy rental period or are in Iceland outside the tourist season; some companies even wait until you return the car before working out which rental option will give you the best rate for the time and distance covered.

Including CDW, **prices** for a small sedan start around 3600kr per day, plus additional kilometre fees, rising to 6000–9000kr per day for unlimited kilometres. Even after factoring in petrol costs, the lower end of this scale works out favourably compared to bus travel for two or more people.

For a four-wheel-drive, however, you're looking at 12,000kr per day at the very least, plus heavy fuel consumption.

BRINGING YOUR OWN VEHICLE

The vehicle ferry from Scandanavia and Scotland to Seyðisfjörður in the Eastfjords (see p.3) makes **bringing your own vehicle** into Iceland fairly straightforward. Assuming you have been living outside Iceland for the previous twelve months, you're allowed to import the vehicle and 200 litres of fuel duty free for a period of one month starting from date of entry. You'll also need to produce proof that the vehicle is fully insured for Iceland and to bring along its registration certificate and your driving licence, before a duty-free import permit is granted. Permits can often be extended for up to three months after arrival, but overstay your permit and you'll be liable to full import duties on the vehicle.

For further information, contact the Directorate of Customs, Tryggvagötu 19, 150 Reykjavík.

DRIVING REGULATIONS AND ROAD CONDITIONS

Icelanders have a cavalier attitude to **driving** in conditions that most other people would baulk at – they have to, or would probably never get behind the wheel – and take dirt tracks and frozen twisting mountain roads very much in their stride, barely slowing for any hazards. Native drivers also tend to gravitate towards the road's centre and don't slow down much or move over for oncoming traffic, which can be very disconcerting at first. Aside from the weather and potential road conditions, however, low-volume traffic makes for few problems.

Cars are left-hand drives and you drive on the right as in the US, though the opposite to the UK, Australia and New Zealand. The **speed limit** is 50km an hour in built-up areas, 90km an hour on surfaced roads, and 80km an hour on gravel. **Seat belts** are compulsory for all passengers, and **headlights** must be on at least half-beam all the time.

Two **roadsigns** you'll soon become familiar with out in the country – even if you stick to the Ringroad – are "*Einbreið brú*", indicating a single-lane bridge sometimes also marked by flashing yellow beacons; and "*Malbik endar*", marking the end of a surfaced road. Along the southeast coast, the northeast and some interior roads, **sandstorms** can be a serious hazard and have been known to overturn vehicles and strip the paint off cars; stretches of the Ringroad where these might occur are marked with orange warning signs.

Otherwise, the most common hazard is having other vehicles spray you with windscreen-cracking **gravel** as they pass; slow down and pull over to minimize this, especially on unsurfaced roads. When there's snow – though you'd be unlucky to come across much around the Ringroad during the summer – you'll find that the road's edges are marked by evenly spaced yellow poles; stay within their boundaries. The trick to **driving on snow or ice** is to avoid skidding by applying the brakes slowly and as little as possible, and to remember that momentum is key: even if you're barely crawling along, while you're still moving forward you should keep the wheels spinning and resist the temptation to change gear, as you'll lose your impetus by doing so. In winter, everyone fits studded **snow tyres** to their cars to increase traction, so make sure any vehicle you rent has them too. Pack a good blanket or sleeping bag in case you get stuck by snow in your car, and always carry food and water.

FOUR-WHEEL-DRIVING AND ROUGH ROADS

Iceland's **interior routes,** plus some shorter **gravel tracks** off the Ringroad to Þórsmörk and elsewhere, can be really rough, with stretches of sand, boulders, ice or rivers to negotiate, and should only be tackled in a high-clearance **four-wheel-drive vehicle** with an experienced driver. Four-wheel-drive-only roads are designated with an "F" on road maps (for instance, the Kjölur route is F35), and it is illegal to take conventional motor vehicles on them.

Even on remoter roads, however, you'll probably see some traffic as recreational four-wheel-driving is very popular in Iceland – witness the numbers of "super jeeps", with jacked up heavy-duty chassis and giant wheels. In April 2000, a convoy of these monsters even managed to cross eastwards over Vatnajökull, successfully dragging each other over the ice, crevasses and half-frozen rivers along the way.

Precautions include not tackling any four-wheel-drive roads alone; being properly equipped with all rescue gear and tools (and know in advance how to use them); and always carrying more than enough fuel, food and water. It's also wise to tell someone reliable where you're going and when you'll be back, so that a rescue can be mounted if you don't show – but don't forget to contact them when you do get back safely. You'll also need **advance information** on road and weather conditions; check out *www.vegag.is* and try local tourist offices, or the Reykjavík BSÍ bus terminal (see p.46).

Rough roads have their own hazards. To minimize them, stay on any marked tracks; you'll also prevent further damage and erosion to Iceland's fragile environment this way. Vehicles easily bog down in deep snow, mud or soft sand, so maintaining forward momentum is vital for getting through all these. If you stop moving forward, your spinning wheels will quickly dig the vehicle in, so take your foot off the accelerator immediately. Hopefully you'll be able to reverse out in low range, otherwise you'll have to start digging.

Rivers are potentially very dangerous, and you need to be in tune with their daily ebb and flow caused by snow or glacial melt through the day – they should be at their lowest in the morning. Some are bridged but many are not; **fords** are marked with a "V" on maps. You need to assess the depth and speed of the river first to find the best crossing point, and select a gear accordingly; changing gear in mid-stream will let water into the clutch. Slacken off the fan belt, block the engine's air intake, and waterproof electrics before crossing. If you stall in mid-stream, turn off the ignition *immediately*, disconnect the battery, winch out, and don't restart until you've ensured that water hasn't entered the engine through the air-filter – which will destroy the engine.

CYCLING

Bad roads, steep gradients and unpredictable weather don't make Iceland an obvious choice for a **cycling** holiday, but nonetheless there are plenty of people who come here each summer just to pedal around. And if you're properly equipped, it's a great way to see the country close-up – you'll also save plenty of money over other forms of transport.

You'll need solid, 18- or 24-speed **mountain bikes** with chunky tyres. You can **rent** these from various hostels in Iceland, or at the BSÍ bus terminal in Reykjavík (where pass holders – see p.22 – get up to a fifty percent discount), for around 1500kr a day. If you're **bringing your own bike** to Iceland by plane, or getting it from one end of the country to the other by air, you'll need to have the handlebars and pedals turned in, the front wheel removed and strapped to the back, and the tyres deflated.

There are bike shops in Reykjavík, Akureyri and a couple of the larger towns, but otherwise you'll have to provide all **spares** and carry out **repairs** yourself, or find a garage to help. Remember that there are plenty of areas, even on the Ringroad, where assistance may be several days' walk away, and that dust, sand, mud and water will place abnormal strains on your bike. You'll definitely suffer a few **punctures**, so bring a repair kit, spare tyre and tubes, along with the relevant tools, spare brake pads, spokes, chain links and cables.

Weather has the most capacity for ruining your enjoyment if you're not prepared for it. In summer, expect a few days of rain, a few of sunshine, a storm or two, and plenty of wind. Around the coast you shouldn't need excessively warm **clothing** – a sweater and waterproof in addition to your normal gear should be fine – but make sure it's all quick-drying. If travelling through the Interior, weatherproof jackets, leggings, gloves and headware, plus ample warm clothing, are essential. Thick-soled neoprene surf **boots** will save cutting your feet on rocks during river crossings.

It's not unfeasible to cover around 90km a day on paved stretches of the Ringroad, but elsewhere the same distance might take three days and conditions may be so bad that you walk more than you ride. Give yourself four weeks to circuit

the Ringroad at an easy pace – this would average around 50km a day. Make sure you've worked out how far it is to the next store before passing up the chance to buy **food**, and and don't get caught out by supermarkets' short weekend hours (see p.31). Note that **off-road cycling** is prohibited in order to protect the landscape, so stick to the tracks.

If it all gets too much, you can put your bike on a bus for a few hundred krónur. If there's space, bikes go in the luggage compartment: otherwise it will be tied to the roof or back. Either way, protect your bike by wrapping and padding it if possible.

For help in planning your trip, contact the **Icelandic Mountain Bike Club** (Íslenski Fjallahjólaklubbúsins, or ÍFHK), who organize club weekends and also have heaps of advice for cyclists. You can download most of this and contact them through their Web site at *www.mmedia.is/~ifhk*, which has English text.

HITCHING

Hitching around Iceland is possible, at least if you have plenty of time. Expect less traffic the further you go from Reykjavík, and even on the Ringroad there are long stretches where you may go for hours without seeing a vehicle. Leave the Ringroad and you might even have to wait days for a lift, though in either case it's likely that the first car past will stop for you.

Having said this, holidaying Icelanders will probably already have their cars packed to capacity, so make sure you have as little gear as possible – without, of course, leaving behind everything you'll need to survive given the climate and long spaces between shops (see p.31). And though Iceland may be a safer place to hitch than elsewhere in Europe, Australia, or the US, doing it still carries inherent risks, and the best **advice** is not to do it.

If you must hitch, never do so alone and remember that you don't have to get in just because someone stops. Given the wide gaps between settlements it will probably be obvious where you are heading for, but always ask the driver where they are going rather than saying where it is you want to go.

The best places to line up lifts are either at campsites, hostels, or the fuel stations which sit on the outskirts of every settlement; it's possible, too, that staff in remoter places might know of someone heading your way.

TOURS

Everywhere you go in Iceland you'll find **tours** on offer, ranging from whale-watching cruises, hikes, pony treks and snowmobile trips across southern glaciers, to bus safaris covering historic sites, interior deserts, hot springs and volcanoes or even joy flights over lakes and islands. Some of these things you can do independently, but in other cases you'll find that tours are the only practical way to reach somewhere.

They can last anything from a couple of hours to several days, with the widest range offered between June and September, though some, such as whale watching, are seasonal. **Booking in advance** is always a good idea, especially in the peak tourist months of July and August, when you may have to wait a couple of days before being able to get on the more popular excursions. Details of tours and operators are given throughout the guide. In winter – which as far as tourism is concerned lasts from September to May – many operators close completely, and those that remain open concentrate on four-wheel-driving and glacier exploration along the fringes of the southern icecaps, as the Interior itself is definitely off-limits by then. While bigger agents in Reykjavík offer trips almost daily in winter, don't expect to be able to just turn up at a small town and get onto a tour – most will require a few days' advance warning in order to arrange everything.

ACCOMMODATION

Icelanders love exploring their country and travel all over it for work and play, and – in summer – almost every settlement has somewhere to stay in the shape of a hotel, guesthouse, hostel or campsite. In addition, farms and some rural schools provide accommodation where you might not expect it. Almost all formal lodgings are found around the settled coastal band; if you're heading into the wilds at any stage, you'll need to camp or make use of huts.

Before setting out, pick up the *Accommodation in Iceland* **brochure** from tourist information outlets, which lists most places to stay – though not all – and official campsites, along with their facilities. Hotels tend to stay open year-round, but many other places **shut down** from September to May, or need advance notice of your arrival outside the tourist season. Where places do stay open, **winter rates** are around 25 percent cheaper than summer ones.

In addition to a range of rooms, several types of places to stay offer **budget** accommodation.

ACCOMMODATION PRICE CODES

Throughout this guide, prices given for **youth hostels** and **sleeping-bag accommodation** are per person unless otherwise specified. **Hotel** and **guesthouse** accommodation is graded on a scale from ① to ⑧; all are high-season rates and indicate the cost of the cheapest double room. The price bands to which these codes refer are as follows:

① Up to 4000kr	③ 6000–8000kr	⑤ 10,000–12,000kr	⑦ 15,000–20,000kr
② 4000–6000kr	④ 8000–10,000kr	⑥ 12,000–15,000kr	⑧ Over 20,000kr

ICELANDIC ACCOMMODATION ORGANIZATIONS

Contact details for specific places to stay are given throughout the guide, many of which are run by the following organisations:

Edda, Hlíðarfótur IS-101, Reykjavík (☎505 0910, fax 505 0915, *www.edda.is*).

Fosshótel, Skipholt 50, Reykjavík (☎562 4000, fax 562 4001, *www.fosshotel.is*). Association of eleven mid-range hotels located at strategic points around the country, including Reykjavík and Akureyri.

Icelandair (contact and bookings through *www.icehotels.is*). Six upmarket hotels in southern Iceland, including the very stylish *Hótel Fluðir* at Fluðir.

Icelandic Farm Holidays, Hafnarstræti 1, 101 Reykjavík (☎562 3640, fax 562 3644, *www.farmholidays.is*). Agent for 100-odd farms offering accommodation around Iceland.

Icelandic Youth Hostel Association, Sundlaugavegur 34, 105 Reykjavík (☎553 8110, fax 588 9201, *www.hostel.is*).

Key Hotels, Borgatúni 32, Reykjavík (☎511 6030, fax 511 6031, *keyhole@centrum.is*). Five top-notch hotels in Reykjavík, Þingvellir, Hveragerði and Akureyri.

Where **made-up beds** are offered, you basically pay for a bed, not the room, so might end up sharing with strangers but for less than the price of a single room. **Sleeping-bag accommodation** is much the same thing and even cheaper, except only a bare bed or mattress is provided, hostel style, and you supply all the bedding – so even if you don't intend to camp, it's worth bringing a sleeping bag.

HOTELS AND GUESTHOUSES

Icelandic **hotels** are for the most part uninspiring places, typically elderly and gloomy or bland, modern, business-oriented blocks, though rooms are comfortable and well furnished as a rule. Bigger establishments might have their own pool, gym, sauna or even casino, and there will always be a restaurant, with breakfast included in the cost of a room. Hotels don't usually have any budget options, though you do occasionally find made-up beds or even sleeping-bag accommodation on offer in country areas. Room **rates** vary depending on the location and facilities, but you're looking at upwards of 9000–12,000kr for a double with en-suite bath, 6000–9000kr without, and about two-thirds of these prices for a single room with and without bath.

Guesthouses (*gistiheimilið*) tend to have a lot more character than hotels, as they're often just converted, family-run homes. Rooms range from the barely furnished to the very comfortable, though facilities are usually shared, and you'll often find some budget accommodation available too. Breakfast is sometimes included, or offered for an extra 750kr or so; some places can provide

all meals with advance notice. As for **prices**, doubles cost 5000kr or more; made-up beds are around 2500kr per person and sleeping-bag accommodation will be about 1700kr.

FARMS

You'll find plenty of **farms** in Iceland, some with histories going back to saga times, that offer accommodation of some kind, ranging from a room in the farmhouse to hostel-style dormitories or fully furnished, self-contained cabins. Many also encourage guests to take part in the daily routine, or offer horse riding, fishing, guided tours, or even four-wheel-drive safaris.

For the most part, farm **prices** are the same as for guesthouses; cabins usually sleep four or more and can work out a good deal for a group at around 8000kr. Come prepared to cook for yourself, though meals are usually available if booked in advance.

SUMMER HOTELS AND EDDA

In Iceland, many country schools open up during the summer holidays as **summer hotels**, fifteen of which come under the Icelandair-owned **Edda** banner (see box above for details). They're aimed at the budget end of things, and usually have a few rooms, large dormitory space, and even mattresses on the floor. Facilities are shared, though most have a thermally heated pool in the grounds and there's always a restaurant.

Costs at summer hotels are slightly less than guesthouses: count on paying around 5000kr for a double, 4000kr for a single, 2000kr for a made-up bed, and 1700kr or less for sleeping-bags.

HOSTELS

The Icelandic Youth Hostel Association (see box below for details) runs 29 **hostels** around Iceland, ranging from big affairs in Reykjavík to old farm-houses sleeping four out in the country. All are owner-operated, have good self-catering kitchens and either offer bookings for local tours or organize them themselves. Some can also provide meals with advance notice and have laundry facilities. Quite a few are open all year too, though you'd be hard-pushed to reach remoter ones until winter was well and truly over – turn up out of season, however, and you'll often receive a warm welcome.

Whatever the time of year, you should **book in advance**; in summer, hostels are often full, and at other times, even if officially open, owners may simply lock up the house and head off somewhere for a few days if they're not expecting guests. Dormitory accommodation is the norm, either in made-up beds (2000kr) or sleeping bags (1500kr), with around a 25 percent **discount** for holders of a Hostelling International card – these have to be bought before you leave home (see box below).

CAMPING

Camping is a good way to minimize expenditure in Iceland, whether you make use of the country's 150 or so campsites or set up for free in the nearest field. It is, however, a **summer-only** option: in winter, campsites and fields alike will probably be buried beneath a metre of snow.

Most **campsites** are no-frills affairs, with level ground, a toilet and cold running water only – in which case, head to the nearest swimming pool for its shower facilities. Those in popular tourist areas may have powerpoints, a laundry and hot showers, for which you'll have to pay extra; on-site shops are unusual, however, so stock up in advance. Campsites in the Interior are very barely furnished, usually with just a pit toilet. **Prices** come in at around 500kr per tent, though sometimes you'll pay the same amount per person instead.

If you're doing extensive hiking or cycling there will be times that you'll have to **camp in the wild**. The main challenge here is to find a flat, rock-free space to pitch a tent over. Where feasible, always seek **permission** for this at the nearest farmhouse before setting up; farmers don't usually mind – and often direct you to a good site – but may need to keep you away from pregnant stock or the like. Note too, that in a few reserves camping is only permitted at designated areas. When camping wild, you can bury anything biodegradeable but should carry other rubbish out with you.

YOUTH HOSTEL ASSOCIATIONS

ICELAND
Bandalag Íslenskra Farfugla, Sundlaugavegi 34, IS-105 Reykjavík (☎553 8110, fax 588 9201, www.hostel.is).

AUSTRALIA AND NEW ZEALAND
Australia Australian Youth Hostels Association, Level 3, 10 Mallet St, Camperdown, NSW 2050 (☎02/9565 1325).

New Zealand Youth Hostels Association of New Zealand, PO Box 436, Christchurch 1 (☎03/379 9970).

UK AND IRELAND
Eire An Oige, 61 Mountjoy St, Dublin 7 (☎01/830 4555, www.irelandyha.org).

England and Wales Youth Hostel Association (YHA), Trevelyan House, 8 St Stephen's Hill, St Albans, Herts AL1 2DY (☎0870/870 8808,

www.yha.org.uk). London membership desk and booking office: 14 Southampton St, London WC2 7HY (☎020/7836 8541).

Northern Ireland Youth Hostel Association of Northern Ireland, 22 Donegall Rd, Belfast BT12 5JN (☎028/9031 5435, www.hini.org.uk).

Scotland Scottish Youth Hostel Association, 7 Glebe Crescent, Stirling, FK8 2JA (☎0870/1553 255, fax 01786/891 350, www.syha.org.uk).

US AND CANADA
Canada Hostelling International/Canadian Hostelling Association, Room 400, 205 Catherine St, Ottawa, ON K2P 1C3 (☎1-800/663-5777 or ☎613/237-7884).

US Hostelling International-American Youth Hostels (HI-AYH), 733 15th St NW, Suite 840, PO Box 37613, Washington, DC 20005 (☎202/783-6161, www.hiayh.org).

CAMPING EQUIPMENT

Aside from bringing in your own equipment, you can **buy** good camping gear at high prices from outdoor supply shops in Reykjavík, or **rent** it from the BSÍ bus terminal.

Your **tent** is going to be severely tested, so needs to be in a good state of repair and built to withstand strong winds and heavy rain – a good-quality dome or tunnel design, with a space between the flysheet and the tent entrance where you can cook and store your backpack and boots out of the weather, is ideal. Whatever the conditions are when you set up, always use guy ropes and a flysheet as the weather can change rapidly.

Also invest in a decent **sleeping bag** – even in summer, you might have to cope with sub-zero conditions – and a **sleeping mat** for insulation as well as comfort. A waterproof sheet to put underneath your tent is also a good idea. Unless you find supplies of driftwood you'll need a **fuel stove** too, as Iceland's few trees are all protected. Butane gas canisters are sold in Reykjavík and many fuel stations around the country, but you're probably better off with a pressure stove capable of taking a variety of more widely available fuels such as unleaded petrol (*blýlaust*), kerosene (*steinolía*), or white spirit/shellite (*hreinsað bensín*).

At popular hiking areas and throughout interior Iceland you'll encounter **mountain huts**, which are maintained by Iceland's hiking organisations (see p.35). The name can be misleading: these can be lavish, multistorey affairs with kitchen areas and dormitories overseen by wardens, though more usually they're very basic wooden bunkhouses that offer no more than a dry retreat from the weather. You'll always have to supply bedding and food and should **book well in advance** through the relevant organisation, particularly at popular sites such as Þórsmörk (see p.116). If you haven't booked you may get in if there's room, but otherwise you'll have to pitch a tent.

Emergency huts, painted bright orange to show up against snow, are sometimes not so remote – you'll see them at a few places around the Ringroad where drivers might get stranded by sudden heavy snowfalls. Stocked with food and fuel, and run by the SVFÍ (Iceland's national life-saving association), these huts are strictly for emergency use only; if you have to use one, fill out the guestbook stating what you used and where you were heading, so that stocks can be maintained and rescue crews will know to track you down if you don't arrive at your destination.

FOOD AND DRINK

Although Iceland's food is unlikely to be the highlight of your trip, things have improved from the early 1980s when beer was illegal

and canned soup supplemented dreary daily doses of plain-cooked lamb or fish. The country's low industrial output and high environmental conciousness – the use of hormones in livestock feed is forbidden, for instance – means that its meat, fish and seafood are some of the healthiest in Europe, with hothouses now providing a fair range of vegetables and even some fruit.

While in Reykjavík and Akureyri the variety of food is pretty well what you'd find at home, menus elsewhere are far less exciting – with sheep outnumbering the people by four to one, there's a lot of **lamb** to get through. You'll often find some variety to the standbys grills or stews, however, even if **salads** have yet to really catch on; otherwise fast food or cooking for yourself will have to see you through.

TRADITIONAL FOODS

Iceland's cold climate and long winters meant that the settlers' original diet was low in vegetables and high in cereals, fish and meat, with **preserved foods** playing a big role. Some of the following traditional foods are still eaten on a daily basis, others crop up mainly at special occasions such as the mid-winter Þorramatur feasts, though restaurants may serve them year round.

Something found everywhere is **harðfiskur**, wind-dried haddock or cod, which you'll see airing on huge racks outside fishing villages; it's commonly eaten as a snack by tearing off a piece and chewing away, though some people like to spread butter on it first. Most Icelandic **seafood** is excellent, though **hákarl** (Greenland shark), is a more doubtful delicacy, as it can only be consumed after being buried for up to six months in sand to break down the high levels of ammonia and neurotoxins contained in its flesh. Different parts of the rotted shark yield either white or dark meat, and the advice for beginners is to start on the milder-tasting dark (*gler hákarl*), which is translucent – rather like smoked glass. Either way, the flavour is likely to make your eyes water, even if connoisseurs compare the taste and texture favourably to a strong cheese. Don't feel bad if you can't stomach the stuff, because neither can many Icelanders.

As for meat, there's ordinary **hangikjöt**, which is hung, smoked lamb, popular in sandwiches and as part of a traditional Christmas spread; **svið**, boiled and singed sheeps' heads; haggis-like varieties of **slátur** ("slaughter"), of which blood pudding (*blóðmör*) is a favourite; and a whole range of scraps pressed into cakes and pickled in whey, collectively known as **súrmatur** – leftover *svið* is often prepared like this, as is *súrsaðir hrútspungar*, or pickled rams' testicles.

Game dishes include the grouse-like ptarmigan (*rjúpa*), which takes the place of turkey at Icelandic Christmas dinners; an occasional reindeer (*hreindýr*) in the east of the country; and puffin (*lundi*) in the south, which is usually smoked before being cooked. In a few places you'll also come across whale or seal meat, as both are still hunted in limited numbers. Rather more appealing to non-Icelandic palates, **salmon** (*lax*), **trout** (*silingur*), and **char** (*bleikja*) are all superb and relatively inexpensive. In addition to smoked salmon, try the similar-looking *gravad*, whereby the fish is marinated with herbs until it's soft and quite delicious.

About the only endemic **vegetable** is a type of lichen that's dried into almost tasteless, resilient black curls and snacked on raw or cooked with milk. Home-produced **cheese** and dairy products are very good, and it's worth trying yogurt-like **skyr**, sold all over the country plain or flavoured with fruit. **Pancakes** known as *flatbrauð* or *laufabrauð* are traditionally eaten at Christmas, and a few places – notably near Mývatn in northeastern Iceland – bake a delicious rye bread called *hverabrauð* in underground ovens (see p.232).

DRINKS

It's been said with some justification that Iceland runs on **coffee**, with just about everyone in the country firmly hooked, a definite café culture in the cities, and decent quality brews offered even at fuel-station cafés. In some rural supermarkets, hot thermoses of free coffee are laid on for customers to help themselves, and wherever you pay for a cup, the price usually includes a refill or two. **Tea** is also pretty popular, though not consumed with such enthusiasm. **Bottled water** and familiar brands of **soft drinks** are available everywhere.

When it comes to **alcohol**, you'll find that it's only sold in bars, clubs, restaurants and the few state-owned liquor stores. Most Icelanders drink very hard when they put their minds to it, most often at parties or on camping trips – the August bank holiday weekend is notorious. It's surprising, then, to find that full-strength **beer** was actually illegal until March 1989, when the 75-year-old prohibition laws were revoked. In Reykjavík, March 1 is still celebrated as *Bjórdagurinn* or **Beer Day**, with predictably riotous celebrations organized at bars throughout the capital. Beer comes as relatively inexpensive, low-alcohol pilsner, and more expensive, stronger lagers.

All **wine** and most **spirits**, naturally enough, are imported, though hard-liquor enthusiasts should try **brennevín**, a local spirit distilled from potatoes and flavoured with caraway seeds or angelica. It's powerful stuff, affectionately known as *svarti dauði* or "black death", and certainly warms you up in winter – you'll also welcome its traditional use to clean the palate after eating fermented shark.

RESTAURANTS, CAFÉS AND BARS

Just about every settlement in Iceland, from villages upwards, has a **restaurant** of some sort. In Reykjavík, and to a lesser extent Akureyri and some of the larger towns, there's a variety of formal establishments offering everything from traditional Icelandic fare to Mexican, Thai, Chinese, and Italian- and French-inspired dishes, and even a couple of **vegetarian** places. This is the most expensive way to dine – expect to pay upwards of 1500kr per person – though keep your eyes peeled for lunch-time **specials** offered at Asian restaurants, or inexpensive fixed-price meals of soup, bread, and stew elsewhere. All-you-can-eat **smorgasbords** or buffets also crop up, especially around Christmas, when restaurants seem to compete with each other over the calorie contents of their spreads of cold meats and **cakes** – the latter something of a national institution.

In the country, pickings are far slimmer, however. Some **hotel restaurants** have fine food, though it's more often filling than particularly memorable; prices can be as high as in any restaurant, but are generally lower. Otherwise, the only place offering cooked food might be nearest **fuel station café**, which typically whip up fast fodder such as burgers, grills, sandwiches and pizzas for a few hundred krónur. Indeed, at times it seems that pizza is Iceland's national dish, and there's even a widespread chain called **Pizza 67**.

Found all over the country, **bars**, besides being somewhere to have a drink, also usually sell meals and are frequently decorated along particular themes – decked out 1950s-style, for example, or hung with fishing memorabilia. **Coffee houses** are less widespread, confined mostly to the cities and a couple of towns, and while some offer light meals most concentrate on serving coffee with cakes and breads.

SELF-CATERING

Self-caterers will save a lot over eating out, though ingredients still cost more than they do at home. There are few specialist food shops besides **fishmongers** and **bakeries**, but at least one **supermarket** – often run by co-operative organisations – in all villages, towns and cities. Don't expect to find them attached to campsites, however, and when travelling about, buy supplies when you can, don't get caught short by weekend shop hours, and know where the next supermarket is. There are no shops in the Interior.

Larger supermarkets can be well stocked with plenty of fresh fruit and vegetables – especially in "hothouse towns" such as Hveragerði in southern Iceland – plus fish and meat. Rural stores, however, may have little more than a few imported apples and oranges and a shelf or two of canned and dried food. Iceland grows its own capsicums, mushrooms, tomatoes and cucumbers, plus plenty of berries and a few bananas, but most other things are imported and therefore fairly expensive.

POST, PHONES, THE INTERNET AND THE MEDIA

Iceland may be remote but its communications are modern and reliable, making it easy to keep in touch with home.

Post offices are located in all major communities and are open from 8.30am until 4.30pm Monday to Friday. **Domestic mail** will generally get to the nearest post office within two working days, though a recipient living out on a farm might not collect it so quickly. For **international post** count on three to five days for mail to reach the UK or US, and a week to ten days to Australia and New Zealand. Anything up to 20g **costs** 35kr within Iceland, 50kr to Europe, and 75kr to anywhere else; up to 50g costs 45/95/135kr.

International **parcels** aren't outrageously expensive – a 500g packet is 435kr to Europe and 900kr to elsewhere – but not particularly fast; ask at any post office about Express Mail if you're in a hurry, though you'll pay far more than for the normal service.

Post restante facilities are available at all post offices; have mail sent to the relevant office marked "to be collected" in English and turn up with your passport. If you can't find an expected letter, check that it hasn't been filed, Icelandic-style, under your Christian name; it might help to have your surname underlined on the letter.

PHONES

Síminn (the name used for Iceland Telecom) offices are usually inside the local post office, where you'll be able to place local and international calls. You'll also often find a row of **payphones** outside – if not, head to the nearest fuel station. You can make **international calls** on payphones too, and they accept either coins or **phonecards** of various values, which you can buy in post offices. Calling from a hotel will be very expensive, and beware of **hotel payphones**, which will start gobbling your money

even if the call goes unanswered. You pay **reduced rates** on domestic calls at weekends and Mon–Fri 7pm–8am; on calls to Europe daily at 7pm–8am; and to everywhere else daily at 11pm–8am.

All **phone numbers** in Iceland are seven digits long, with no regional codes. If you need to use the **phone book** (which you should be able to find chained to the phone box), remember that listings are arranged in order of Christian name – Gunnar Jakobsson, for instance, would be listed under "G", not "J".

If you're bringing in a **mobile phone**, Iceland uses both GSM and NMT networks – ask your provider about whether your phone is compatible. GSM has a restricted range but works around most towns and villages, while NMT covers almost everywhere except a few bits of the Interior.

OPERATOR SERVICES AND INTERNATIONAL CALLS

Operator services in Iceland
Emergencies (fire, ambulance or police) ☎112
International directory enquiries ☎114
International operator ☎115
National directory enquiries ☎118

Phoning Iceland from abroad
To call Iceland from overseas, dial your international access code (see below), then ☎354. then the phone number.
Australia ☎0011
Canada ☎011
New Zealand ☎00
UK ☎00
US ☎011

Phoning overseas from Iceland
To call overseas from Iceland, dial ☎00, then your country code (see below), then the area code minus initial zero, then the phone number.
Australia ☎61
Canada ☎1
New Zealand ☎64
UK ☎44
US ☎1

Country Direct
Country Direct connects you directly to an operator in the country that you dial to:

CANADA
AT&T Canada ☎800 9011
Teleglobe ☎800 9010

IRELAND
☎800 9353

NEW ZEALAND
☎800 9031

UK
British Telecom ☎800 9044, or ☎800 9440, or ☎800 9441
Cable & Wireless ☎800 9088

US
AT&T ☎800 9001
Global One ☎800 9111
MCII ☎800 9002
Sprint ☎800 9003

THE INTERNET

Iceland is one of the highest per-capita users of the Internet, with most homes and businesses connected. For visitors, there are several **Internet cafés** in Reykjavík costing around 500kr an hour; elsewhere, **public libraries** often have free access, though you might have to queue for a couple of hours until a terminal becomes available. If all else fails, accommodation, and even tourist information offices or tour agents, might also allow you to use their facilities if asked nicely, though they're certainly not obliged to.

If you don't have one already, it's worth signing up for a **free email account** with a company such as Yahoo (*www.yahoo.com*) or Hotmail (*www.hotmail.com*), which will allow you to send and receive email messages from anywhere in the world that has Internet access – a good alternative to phones or poste restante. To sign up, log on to the relevant Web site, and follow the instructions; any email sent to you will then stack up in the inbox waiting to be read.

THE MEDIA

Iceland's main **daily paper** is the right-wing *Morgunblaðið*, available all over the country and giving thorough coverage of national and international news. The only real competition is the leftish *Dagur*, though many Icelanders don't consider it such a good read. If your Icelandic isn't up to it, you can also get the **daily news in English** off *Morgunblaðið*'s Web site (*www.mbl.is*), or get a roundup of the main stories through the *Icelandic Review*, an English-language newsheet giving good outlines about main national stories – it's available in Reykjavík's newsagents or online at *www.icenews.is*. Ryekjavík's bookshops – and libraries around the country – also have copies of **British and US newspapers**, though supply is erratic and sometimes a week or more out of date. **International magazines** such as *Time* and *National Geographic* are also available from the same sources.

There are also several **radio stations** with a menu of commercial pop, classical music and talk-back shows. Between late May and early September, the news is also broadcast in English on Radio 1, daily at 8.55am. while the three **television channels** show a familiar mix of soaps, dramas, films and documentaries. All these media are predominantly Icelandic-language only, though films are screened in their original language with subtitles.

OPENING HOURS, HOLIDAYS AND FESTIVALS

open daily from 10am until late afternoon; in smaller communities, however, weekend hours are shorter, and some places don't open at all on Sundays.

Out in the country, **fuel stations** provide some essential services for travellers, and larger ones tend to open daily from around 9am to 11pm. Office hours everywhere are Monday to Friday 9am to 5pm; **tourist offices** often extend these through the weekends, at least in popular spots.

HOLIDAYS AND FESTIVALS

Though Iceland's calendar is predominantly Christian, many official holidays and festivals have a secular theme, and at least one dates from pagan times. Some are already familiar: **Christmas** and **Easter Monday** are both holidays in Iceland and are celebrated as elsewhere in the Western world, as is **New Year**.

Shops are generally open Monday to Friday 9am–6pm and Saturday 10am to mid-afternoon, though you might find that many close for the weekend through the summer. In cities and larger towns, supermarkets are

Harking back to the Viking era, however, **Thorrablot** is a mid-winter celebration originally honouring the weather god Þorri, and became something to look forward to during the bleakest time of the year. Held throughout February, people throw parties centred around the consumption of traditional foods such as *svith* and *hákarl* (see p.30), with some restaurants also laying on special menus.

Sjomannadagur, or Seamen's Day (June 4), unsurprisingly, is one of the biggest holidays of the year, with communities organising mock sea-rescue demonstrations, swimming races and tug-of-war events. This is followed by another break for **Independence Day** (June 17), the day that the Icelandic state separated from Denmark in 1944. Þingvellir (see p.85), the seat of the original parliament east of Reykjavík which hosted the original 1944 event is a good place to head for, though everywhere throws some sort of celebration.

Verslunnarmannahelgi, the Labor Day Weekend, takes place around the country on the first weekend in August. Traditionally, everybody heads into the countryside, sets up camp, and spends the rest of the holiday drinking and partying themselves into oblivion; hit any campsite in the country at this time and you'll be sharing it with thousands of drunken teenagers. On Heimaey in the Westman Islands, **Þjóðhátíð** is held on the same day and celebrated in the same way, though it nominally commemorates Iceland's achieving partial political autonomy in 1874.

One event to look out for, though it's not a single festival as such, is the annual stock round-up, or **rettir**, which takes place in rural areas throughout September. This is when horses and sheep are herded on horseback down from the higher summer pastures to be penned and sorted; some farms offering accommodation allow guests to watch or even participate.

SPORTS AND OUTDOOR ACTIVITIES

Iceland has its own wrestling style, called glíma – a former Olympic sport where opponents try to throw each other by grabbing one another's belts – and there's a serious football (soccer) following; the Reykjavík Football Club was founded in 1899, and an Icelandic consortium owns the English-league club Stoke City. Otherwise, there's not a great obsession with sport as such, with most people here getting outside not to play games but to work or enjoy the Great Outdoors.

The lava plains, black-sand deserts, glacier-capped plateaus, alpine meadows, convoluted fjords and capricious volcanoes that make Iceland such an extraordinary place scenery-wise also offer tremendous potential for outdoor activities, whether you've come for wildlife or to hike, ride, ski, snowmobile or four-wheel-drive your way across the horizon. Further information on these activities is always at hand in local tourist offices, while you can find out more about the few national parks and reserves from the Department of Forestry or various Icelandic hiking organisations (see opposite). Many activities can be done on an organized tour, sometimes with necessary gear supplied or available for rent. Before you set out

to do anything too adventurous, however, check your insurance cover (see p.13).

SWIMMING AND HOT POTS

More of a social activity than anything else, **swimming** is extremely popular with everyone year-round, and it seems mandatory for businessmen to have a dip on their way to work. Just about every town and village has a swimming **pool**, usually heated by the nearest hot spring to around 27°C, almost always with attached outdoor spa baths or **hot pots**. These are a great Icelandic institution and are an incredible experience in winter, when you can sit up to your neck in scalding water while the snow falls thickly around you. Out in the wilds, hot pots are replaced by natural hot springs – a great way to relax trail-weary muscles. Note that at all official swimming pools you are required to shower with soap before getting in the water.

FISHING

As Iceland is surrounded by the richest fishing grounds in the North Atlantic, **sea fishing** has always been seen as more of a career than a sport, though there are limited opportunities out of Keflavík in the southwest.

The country's rivers and lakes, however, are also well stocked with **salmon** and **trout**, pulling in hordes of fly fishers during the **fishing season** (April 1 to September 20 for trout, June 20 to mid-September for salmon). Both fish are plentiful in all the country's bigger waterways, though the finest salmon are said to come from the Laxá (which means Salmon River), in northeast Iceland, and the Rangá in the south. During the winter, people cut holes in the ice and fish for **arctic char**; the best spots for this are east of Reykjavík at Þingvallavatn, and Mývatn, in the northeast (see pp.91 & 227).

You always need a **permit** to fish, which are generally available from local tourist offices and some accommodation, especially on farms. Permits for char or trout are fairly inexpensive and easy to obtain on the spot, but those for salmon are always pricey and often need to be reserved months in advance, as there is a limit per river. For further information, contact the **National Angling Association**, Bolholt 6, IS-105 Reykjavík (☎553 1510, fax 568 4363, *www.arctic.is/angling*); or Icelandic Farm Holidays (see "Accommodation", p.27), who publish a free English-language booklet about trout and salmon fishing in Iceland.

HIKING

Hiking gets you closer to the scenery than anything else in Iceland, and exploring the countryside on foot is how many locals and visitors alike spend much of their time off. In reserves and the couple of national parks you'll find a few **marked trails**, and where they exist you should always stick to them in order to minimize erosion. Elsewhere you'll need to be competent at using a map and compass to navigate safely over the lava, sand, rivers and ice you'll find along the way. If you're unsure of your abilities, there are two **hiking clubs** to get in touch with: **Ferðafélag Íslands** (The Touring Club of Iceland, Mörkin 6, IS-108 Reykjavík; ☎568 2533, fax 568 2535, *www.fi.is*); and **Útivist** (Hallaveigarstigur 1, IS-101 Reykjavík; ☎561 4330, fax 561 4606, *www.utivist.is*). Both run guided treks of a couple of days duration to a week or longer, and maintain various mountain huts in reserves and the Interior where you can book a bunk (see p.29). Local tourist information offices can also put you in touch with guides.

Whether you're planning to spend a weekend making short hikes from camp in a national park,

or two weeks hiking across the Interior, come properly equipped for the likely conditions. **Weather** changes very fast in Iceland, and while there are plenty of sunny summer days, these will be spaced by rain, storms and the real possibility of snow on high ground or in the Interior, and you can get caught out easily even on brief excursions. Always carry warm, weatherproof **clothing**, food, and **water** (there are plenty of places in Iceland where porous soil makes finding surface water unlikely), as well as a torch, lighter, penknife, **first aid kit**, a foil **insulation blanket** and a whistle or mirror for attracting attention. The country is also carpeted in sharp rocks and rough ground, so good quality, tough **hiking boots** are essential – though a pair of **neoprene surf boots** with thick soles are useful to ford rivers.

On lava, watch out for **volcanic fissures**, which are cracks in the ground ranging from a few inches to several metres across and which are usually very deep. These are dangerous enough when you can see them, but blanketed by snow they'll be invisible – take care not to catch your foot or fall into one. Another hazard is **river crossings**, which you'll have to make on various trails all over the country. Rivers levels are at their lowest first thing in the morning, and rise through the day as the sun melts the glacial ice and snow that feeds into them. When looking for a crossing point, the river will be **shallowest** at its widest point; before crossing, make sure that your backpack straps are loose so that if necessary you can ditch it in a hurry. Face into the current as you cross and be prepared to give up if the water gets above your thighs. Never attempt a crossing alone, and remember that some rivers have no safe fords at all if you're on foot – you'll have to hitch across in a vehicle.

WHEN AND WHERE TO HIKE

For the country as a whole, the **best months** for hiking are from June through to August, when the weather is relatively warm, wildflowers are in bloom, and the wildlife is out and about – though even then the Interior and higher ground elsewhere can get snowbound at short notice. Outside the prime time, weather is very problematic and you probably won't even be able to reach the area you want to explore, let alone hike around it.

One of the beauties of Iceland is that you can walk just about anywhere, assuming you can cope with local conditions, though there are, of course, some highlights. Close to Reykjavík, the **Reykjanes Peninsula** (see p.96) offers extended treks across imposingly desolate lava rubble; while trails at **Þingvellir** (see p.85) include historic sites and an introduction to rift valley geology. Further east, **Þórsmörk** (see p.116) is one of the most popular hiking spots in the country, a wooded, elevated valley surrounded by glaciers and mountain peaks with a well-trooden network of paths.

Along the west coast, the **Snæfellsnes Peninsula** (see p.149) is notoriously damp but peaks with the ice-bound summit of Snæfell, the dormant volcano used as a fictional gateway into the centre of the Earth by writer Jules Verne. Further north there's **Hornstrandir** (see p.171), the wildest and most isolated extremity of the Westfjords, a region of twisted coastlines, sheer cliffs and rugged hillwalks. Those after an easier time should head to **Mývatn** (see p.227), the shallow northeastern lake where you can make simple day-hikes to extinct craters, billowing mud-pits, and still steaming lava flows; longer but also relatively easy are the well-marked riverside trails around nearby **Jökulsárgljúfur National Park** (see p.238), which features some awesome canyon scenery. Over in the east, the best of the hikes take in the highland moors and glaciated fringes of the massive Vatnajökull ice cap: at **Snæfell** (see p.253), a peak inland from Egilsstaðir; **Lónsöræfi reserve** (see p.266) near Höfn; and **Skaftafell National Park** (see p.269), another riotously popular camping spot on Vatnajökull's southern edge.

HORSE RIDING

Horses came to Iceland with the first settlers, and, due to a tenth-century ban on their further import to stop equine diseases arriving in the country, have remained true to their original stocky Scandanavian breed. Always used for **riding**, horses also had a religious place in Viking times – a famous example was the stallion Freyfaxi in *Hrafnkel's Saga* (see p.252) – and were often dedicated or sacrificed to the pagan gods; with the advent of Christianity, eating horse meat was banned, being seen as a sign of paganism. Nowadays, horses are used for the autumn livestock round-up, and for recreational purposes.

Icelandic horses are sturdy, even-tempered creatures, and in addition to the usual walk, trot, and canter, can move smoothly across rough ground using the gliding **tölt** gait. The biggest breeding centres are in the country's relatively mild south, but horses are available for **hire** from farms all over Iceland, available with **guides** as needed for anything from an hour in the saddle to two-week-long treks across the Interior. Places to hire horses are given throughout the guide, but if you need to sort something out in advance, contact **Íshestar** (Bæjarhraun 2, 220 Hafnarfjörður; ☎565 3044, fax 565 2113, *www.ishestar.is*), who run treks of all lengths and experience levels right across the country.

SNOW AND ACTION SPORTS

Snow sports – which in Iceland are not just practised in winter – have, surprisingly, only recently begun to catch on. Partly this is because the bulk of Iceland's population lives in the mild southwestern corner of the country, but also because snow was seen as just something you had to put up with; **cross-country skiing**, for instance, is such a fact of life in the northeastern winters that locals refer to it simply as "walking", and were baffled when foreign tour operators first brought in groups to do it for fun.

The possibilities for cross-country skiing are pretty limitless in winter, though you'll have to bring in your own gear. **Downhill skiing and snowboarding** are the most popular snow sports, with two major centres – winter slopes at Bláfjöll (see p.71), only 20km from Reykjavík; and summer skiing at Kerlingarfjöll, close to Hofsjökull glacier in the central interior – accommodation at the latter needs to be booked well in advance, and **rental gear** is available at both.

For something very different, plenty of tour operators offer glacier trips on **snowmobiles**, which are like jet-skis for snow – the only way for the inexperienced to get a taste of Iceland's massive ice fields, though things can get pretty bumpy and most people find a single two-hour excursion is quite enough. Elsewhere, others are just beginning to investigate the possibilities of **rafting** on the larger rivers.

GAY AND LESBIAN TRAVELLERS

Iceland is a very small and closely knit society whose population is barely bigger than that of any average-sized European or American town. In fact, it's generally said that two Icelanders meeting for the first time can usually find people they know in common after just a couple of minutes of conversation – not exactly ideal conditions for a thriving gay scene to develop and indeed for years many gay people upped and left for the other Nordic capitals, most notably Copenhagen, where attitudes were more liberal and it was easier to be anonymous.

However, two things have begun to change all that. First was the establishment of the Icelandic gay and lesbian association in 1978, **Samtökin 78** (Laugavegur 3, ☎552 7878), to promote awareness of homosexuality and gay rights at a political level. This professionally run organisation also offers a support network, not only in Reykjavík, but also out in the tiny towns and villages in the countryside, where attitudes towards homosexuality are not nearly as enlightened. Despite this, there are still many men and women in far-flung villages stuck in the closet because they fear the reaction of people around them should they come out.

The countryside also lacks the effects of the second factor that has changed the lives of so many gay men and women living in the capital – the advent of the bar. The legalization of beer in 1989 meant that **bars** began springing up throughout Reykjavík, bringing people out onto the streets in larger numbers than had ever been the case before. This change in the law made it possible for gay men and women to socialize in pubs in a way that they could only have dreamt of before. Over the past decade, a bar culture has slowly but surely developed in Reykjavík and the city is now confident enough to boast three gay bars (see p.69), though there isn't a single gay bar or any gay scene to speak of in the provinces.

Samtökin's efforts have certainly paid off at the political level – after much lobbying, Iceland's politicians not only agreed to allow gay marriage in 1996 (in effect the right to register legally a partnership between two same-sex partners thus granting legal parity with straight couples), but also to allow gay men and lesbians to adopt children, making Iceland the first country in the world to pass such progressive legislation.

POLICE, CRIME AND SEXUAL HARASSMENT

Iceland is a peaceful country, and it's unlikely that you'll ever even see the police. Most

public places are well lit and secure, people are friendly and helpful, if somewhat reserved, and street crime and hassles are extremely rare.

It's foolish, however, to imagine that problems don't exist, though they mainly revolve around **petty crime** and are largely confined to Reykjavík. Many criminals are drug addicts or alcoholics after easy money; keep tabs on your cash and passport (and don't leave anything visible in your car when you park it) and you should have little reason to visit the **police**. If you do seek them out, you'll find them unarmed, concerned and usually able to speak English – remember to get an insurance report from them in the event you have anything stolen.

As for **offences** you might commit, **drink-driving** is taken extremely seriously here, so don't do it: catch a taxi rather than risk being caught. Being drunk in public in Reykjavík might also get you into trouble, but in a country campsite you probably won't be the only one, and (within reason) nobody is going to care. **Drugs**, however, are treated as harshly here as in much of the rest of Europe.

SEXUAL HARASSMENT

In general, Iceland is an egalitarian society, and, though **women** still sometimes get paid less than men for comparable work, they enjoy a higher economic and social status than in most other European countries. Kvennréþindahreyfingin, the **Women's Rights Movement**, was founded in the early twentieth century and drove through women's right to vote and receive an equal education and, when needed, still assists with the latter.

Sexual harassment is less of a problem here than elsewhere in Europe. You can move almost everywhere in comparative comfort and safety, and although in Reykjavík clubs you might receive occasional unwelcome attentions – or simply be taken aback by the blatant atmosphere – there's very rarely any kind of violent intent. Needless to say, hitching alone, or wandering around central Reykjavík late at night, is unwise. If you do have any problems, the fact that almost everyone understands English makes it easy to get across an unambiguous response.

DIRECTORY

ADDRESSES Addresses in Iceland are always written with the number after the street name.

BOOKS There are bookshops with English-language publications in Reykjavík and Akureyri, but prices are extortionate – about 1900kr for a paperback novel.

ELECTRICITY is 240v, 50Hz AC. Plugs are round pin with either two or three prongs; appliances fitted with overseas plugs need an adaptor.

LAUNDRY Outside of Reykjavík, which has two public laundromats (see p.72), you'll only find laundry facilities at accommodation or better-equipped campgrounds.

NAMES Icelanders have a given name, plus the name of (usually) their father with an attached "-son" for boys and "-dóttir" for girls. So, Jón's son Gunnar is called Gunnar Jónsson, and his daughter Njóla is called Njóla Jónsdóttir. Because of this lack of family names, telephone directories are arranged by given names – using the above example, you'd find Gunnar Jónsson under "G", and Njóla Jónsdóttir under "N" in the phone book. In an effort to preserve national identity, all foreigners taking Icelandic citizenship must also take an Icelandic name.

PHOTOGRAPHY Print and slide film and processing are readily available in Reykjavík, Akureyri, and most supermarkets elsewhere, but like everything else, are very expensive – bring all you'll need.

SOUVENIRS Icelandic woollen sweaters are a practical momento of your trip, and cost around 8000kr. Their characteristic patterns derived around a century ago from Greenland's traditional costumes. As almost all are made in cottage industries, consistent patterns, colours, sizes, shapes and fittings are nonexistent – shop around until you find the right one. Woollen hats and mittens are also good buys; as are proverbially warm eiderdown duvets, stuffed with locally collected duck feathers (very expensive, however); and better-value smoked salmon.

PART TWO

THE
GUIDE

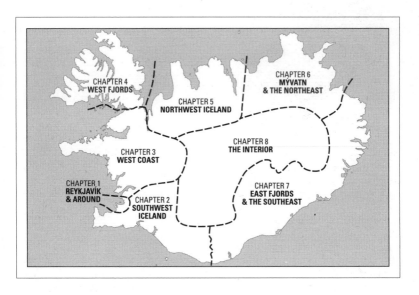

CHAPTER ONE

REYKJAVÍK

T he world's most northerly capital, **Reykjavík** has a sense of space and calm that comes as a breath of fresh air to travellers accustomed to the bustle of the traffic-clogged streets of Europe's other major cities, and often literally so. Although unrepresentative of the majority of the country for its relative urbanization, a visit here is a good place to obtain as true a picture as possible of this highly individual, often apparently contradictory society, secluded on the very edge of the Arctic. While it's true, for example, that Friday- and Saturday-night Reykjavík has earned the place a reputation for hedonistic revelry, with locals carousing for as long as the summer nights allow – despite the legendarily high price of alchohol here – the pace of life is in fact sedate. The tiny centre, for example, is more of a place for ambling around, taking in suburban streets and corner-side cafés set against mountain and ocean scenery, rather than being somewhere to hurtle around between department stores and designer-clothes shops. Similarly, given the city's capital status, Reykjavík lacks the grand and imposing buildings found in the other Nordic capitals, possessing instead apparently ramshackle clusters of houses, either clad in garishly painted corrugated iron or drearily daubed in grey-brown pebbledash as protection against the ferocious North Atlantic storms. This rather unkempt feel, though, is as much part of the city's charm as the blustery winds that greet you as you exit the airport, or the views across the sea to glaciers and the sheer mountains that form the backdrop to the streets. Even in the heart of this capital, nature is always in evidence – there can be few other cities in the world, for example, where greylag geese regularly overfly the busy centre, sending bemused visitors, more accustomed to diminutive pigeons, scurrying for cover.

Today, amid the essentially residential city centre, with its collection of homes painted in reds, yellows, blues and greens, it is the **Hallgrímskirkja**, a gargantuan church made of white concrete towering over the surrounding houses, which is the most enduring image of Reykjavík. Below this, the elegant shops and stylish bars and restaurants that line the main commercial thoroughfare of **Laugavegur**, busy with shoppers seemingly undaunted by the inflated prices of goods – import taxes and cuts by middlemen are to blame – are a consumer's heaven, even if window-shopping is all you can afford.

With time to spare, it's worth venturing outside the city limits into **Greater Reykjavík**, for a taste of the Icelandic provinces – suburban style. Although predominantly an area of dormitory overspill for the capital, the town of **Hafnarfjörður**, is large enough to be independent of Reykjavík and has a couple of museums and a busy harbour, though it's for the summer **Viking Festival** that the town is perhaps best known. Alternatively, the flat and treeless island of **Viðey**, barely ten minutes offshore of Reykjavík, is the place to come for magnificent views of the city and of the surrounding mountains – there are also some enjoyable walking trails here, which lead around the island in an hour or so.

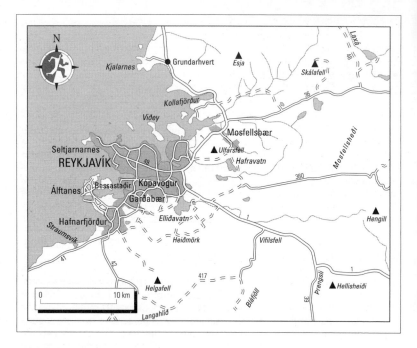

The city also makes a good base for excursions around Reykjavík, including to three of Iceland's most popular attractions: the site of the old **Alþing** at Þingvellir (see p.85), the waterspouts and waterfalls of **Geysir** and **Gullfoss** (see pp.94 & 95), and **Skálholt** (see p.93) church – all within simple reach by public transport – or, more expensively, on day-long guided tours from the city. Also worthwhile is the **Reykjanes peninsula** (see p.96), a bleak lavafield that's as good an introduction as any to the stark scenery you'll find further into Iceland, and home to the mineral-rich waters of the **Blue Lagoon** (see p.101) – the most visited attraction in the country.

Some history

As recounted in the ancient Íslendingabók and Landnámábók sagas, Reykjavík's **origins** date back to the country's first settler, **Ingólfur Arnarson**, who arrived in 874 AD, brought here by his high seat pillars – emblems of tribal chieftainship, tossed overboard from his boat – and settling, in pagan tradition, wherever they washed up. He named the place "smoky bay" (*reykja* meaning "of smoke", *vík* meaning "bay") mistakenly thinking that the distant plumes of steam issuing from boiling spring water were smoke caused by fire. It was a poor place to settle, however, as the soil was too infertile to support successful farming, and Reykjavík remained barely inhabited until an early seventeenth-century **sea-fishing** boom brought Danish traders here, after which a small shanty town to house their Icelandic labour force sprang into existence. Later, in the middle of the eighteenth century, **Skúli Magnússon**, the official in charge of Reykjavík's administrative affairs (*landfógeti*), a man today regarded as the city's founder, used Reykjavík as a base to establish Icelandic-controlled industries, opening several mills and tanneries, and importing foreign craftspeople to pass on their skills. A municipal charter was granted in 1786, when the population totalled a mere 167 – setting the course for Reykjavík's acceptance as Iceland's capital. At the turn of the eighteenth century, the city replaced Skálholt as the national seat of religion and gained the Lutheran Cathedral, Dómkirkjan; eighty years later, with the opening of the new Alþing building, it became the base of the national parliament.

Since independence in 1944, **expansion** has been almost continuous. As a fishing harbour, a port for the produce of the fertile farms of the southwest and a centre for a variety of small industries, Reykjavík provides employment for over half the country's population. Over the past decade, there's been a substantial boom, too, in tourism, with travel agents on every corner and large expanses of land being consumed by building sites throwing up hotels to service the bringers of the new wealth. The city has also pioneered the use of **geothermal energy** to provide low-cost heating – which is why you have to wait for the cold water instead of the hot when taking a shower, and why tap water always has a whiff of sulphur.

Arrival and information

All **international flights** (except those from Greenland and the Faroe Islands, which arrive at Reykjavíkurflugvöllur city airport; see below) arrive at **Keflavík airport** (information on ☎425 0680), 52km west of Reykjavík at the tip of the Reykjanes peninsula. There are two currency-**exchange offices** here, both offering the same rates – one on either side of passport control – plus there's an **ATM** accepting most major credit cards, in the arrivals hall after customs. Brace yourself as you leave the tiny terminal building for howling wind and accompanying horizontal rain. A **taxi** from the airport into Reykjavík will set you back around a whopping 6000kr, so it's far better to take one of the **Flybus coaches** (☎562 1011), which leave from immediately outside the terminal; you'll see departure times, which coincide with arrivals, displayed on monitors once you're through customs. Tickets for this, which can be bought from the Flybus desk in the arrivals hall or on the coach, cost 700kr one way and are also payable by credit card and in major foreign currencies, including UK sterling and US dollars. The journey lasts around 45 minutes and terminates at the *Loftleiðir* hotel (see p.51), 2km from the city centre; from there a shuttle bus (same ticket) takes you to all other major hotels in the city, as well as the campsite (see p.49); alternatively, taxis from here cost around 700kr, while bus #7 (150kr) goes directly into the

---

THE REYKJAVÍK CARD

Available for one, two or three days, the **Reykjavík Card** gives you unlimited transport on the city's buses, access to the main museums, including the National Art Gallery (see p.58), the Ásmundur Sveinsson Sculpture Museum (see p.61) and the Árni Magnússon Manuscript Institute (see p.57), plus admission to seven swimming pools in the capital. Available at the tourist office in Bankastræti (see p.46), the City Hall information desk (see p.56), most hotels and guesthouses, the BSÍ bus terminal (see p.46) as well as at all the city's swimming pools. Costs are 900kr for a 24-hour ticket, 1200kr for 48 hours, and 1500kr for 72 hours

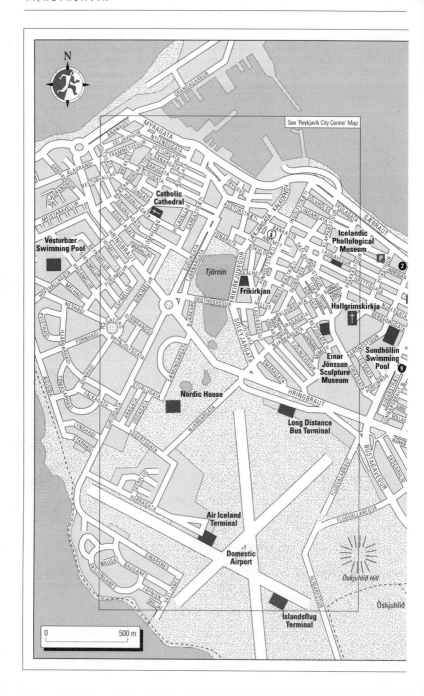

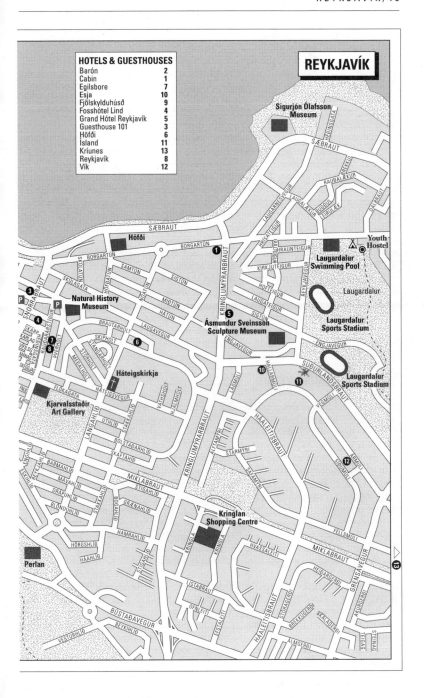

HOTELS & GUESTHOUSES

Barón	2
Cabin	1
Egilsbore	7
Esja	10
Fjölskylduhúsð	9
Fosshótel Lind	4
Grand Hótel Reykjavík	5
Guesthouse 101	3
Höfði	6
Ísland	11
Kríunes	13
Reykjavík	8
Vík	12

REYKJAVÍK

centre – failing that, it's around a thirty-minute walk; the hotel can provide you with a map, but bear in mind that bad weather can make this impractical, particularly if laden with heavy luggage.

Domestic flights, plus those from the Faroes and Greenland, arrive at the **Reykjavíkurflugvöllur city airport**, originally built by the British when they occupied Iceland during World War II and adjacent to *Hótel Loftleiðir*. Remember though that the airport has two terminals, separated by the runway – flights with Íslandsflug use the building behind the hotel, whereas Flugfélag Íslands, who operate the majority of domestic flights, use the terminal on the other side of the runway. There is no direct access from one to the other, so if you need to get between the two, either take a taxi or be prepared to walk for 45 minutes.

Long-distance buses finish their journeys at the **BSÍ bus terminal**, at Vatnsmýrarvegur 10, halfway between the two Reykjavíkurflugvöllur air terminals, about 1km from the centre of town. Inside is a small **tourist information office** (Mon–Fri 9am–5pm; ☎552 2300, *info@bsi.is*), a fairly decent **café** (daily 7am–11.30pm) and a wall of **left-luggage** lockers (Mon–Fri 7.30am–9.30pm, Sat 7.30am–2.30pm, June–Aug also Sun 5–7pm; ☎552 6292; 150kr per day, 400kr per week). All **bus timetables** are published on the net at *www.bsi.is*.

The city's **main tourist information office**, at Bankastræti 2, lies at the foot of the main shopping street, Laugavegur (May–Sept daily 8.30am–7pm; Oct–April Mon–Sat 9am–5pm; ☎562 3045, *tourinfo@tourinfo.is*), where you can get untold amounts of brochures and **maps**, including the excellent free *Map of Reykjavík*, is by far the best source of up-to-date information on both Reykjavík and the rest of the country. If you're travelling independently, you can check your intinerary here with the staff before setting off for the remoter regions.

City transport

Reykjavík is easy to get around. The heart of the city is the low-lying quarter between the harbour and the lake, busy with shoppers by day and with young revellers by night. Most of the sights are within walking distance of here.

Yellow **city buses**, operated by SVR (Strætisvagnar Reykjavíkur; ☎551 2700), depart from the two **main terminals**: Lækjartorg (ticket office Mon–Fri 9am–6pm), at the junction of Lækjargata and Austurstræti; and Hlemmur, at the eastern end of Laugavegur. **Day services** run from 7am to midnight Monday to Saturday, and from 10am to midnight on Sundays: frequencies are roughly every twenty minutes throughout the day and every thirty minutes in the evenings and at weekends; **night buses** run on Friday and Saturday nights only from midnight to roughly 4am. There's a flat, single-trip **fare** of 150kr that must be paid for with exact change; when boarding, simply throw the money into the box by the driver. **Tickets** are only issued if you're changing buses, in which case ask for a "*skiftimiði*", valid for 45 minutes, as you pay. A strip of eight tickets, an "*eitt kort*", can be bought onboard from drivers, from the terminals' **ticket offices** (Lækjartorg Mon–Fri 9am–6pm; Hlemmur Mon–Fri 8am–6pm, Sat & Sun noon–6pm) or, curiously, from any of the city's swimming pools, for 1000kr. Both ticket offices have free **route maps** and **timetables**, plus the **Græna Kortið pass** (3900kr), which gives one month's unlimited bus travel within the Greater Reykjavík area, which covers the surrounding satellite towns, including Hafnarfjörður.

Two **useful routes** are #5, which runs from Lækjartor̃
Reykjavíkurflugvöllur Flugfélag Íslands domestic air term̃
goes to the *Hótel Loftleiðir* for the Íslandsflug domestic terminal ̃
via Hringbraut. If you want to see the city cheaply, bus #5 is excelleñ
running to the airport, it also operates in the opposite direction from L̃
east via the central Hverfisgata, Hlemmur and the swimming pool and cã
in Laugardalur, before swinging west to the Kringlan shopping centre; chang
here for route #6 to take you back into town.

Taxis, driving and cycling

Travelling by **taxi** across the city centre is not as expensive as you might think –
roughly 600–700kr should be enough to take you where you want to go from any
one point to another. The main ranks are centrally located on Lækjargata,
between the junctions with Bankastræti and Amtmannsstígur, as well as opposite
Hallgrímskirkja church on Eiríksgata and Hlemmur. It's also possible to call one
of the main operators for a taxi: Hreyfill (☎588 5522) are best, or try Borgarbíll
(☎552 2440), BSR (☎561 0000) or Bæjarleiðir (☎553 3500). Remember that
Icelandic taxi drivers aren't usually tipped.

Parking in Reykjavík is a relatively straightforward business and certainly not
the nightmare you might expect in a capital city. Most residential streets,
although often full with residents' cars, are unmetered, whereas in the city centre
parking meters are in use. Multistorey **car parks** are dotted around the city centre, most conveniently at Skólavörðustígur. Once again they're all marked on the
tourist office's Reykjavík map. Although the city's **traffic** is generally free-flowing,
even at rush hours, it can be busy on Friday and Saturday nights, when it's wise
to avoid Laugavegur, which mutates into a long snaking line of slow-moving cars.

Bike rental is centrally available from Borgarhjól, at Hverfisgata 50 (☎551
5653), or at the youth hostel or the campsite in Laugardalur (see p.49); all places
charge around 1200kr per day. For cycling around the city, see p.64.

Accommodation

Reykjavík's **accommodation** has been unable to keep up with the escalating
tourist influx, encouraged by the increased frequency of flights between Iceland
and European cities (notably Copenhagen and London), which means that finding

---

kjotorg fer vostrents

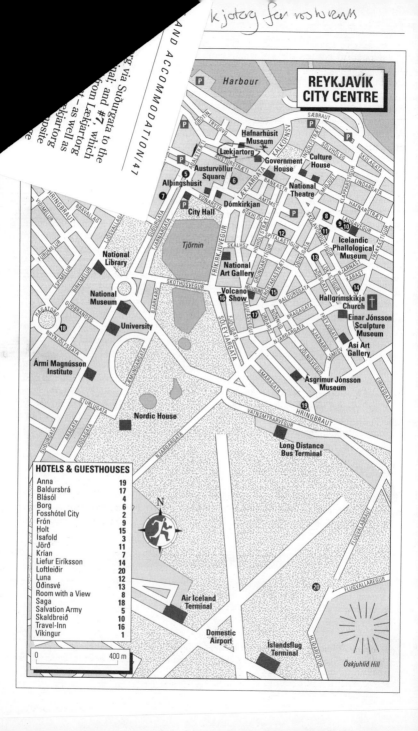

g via Suðurgata to the
cial; and #7, which
from Lækjartorg
t – as well as
kjartorg
ækjartorg
opsite

REYKJAVÍK CITY CENTRE

Harbour

Hafnarhúsit
Museum

Lækjartorg

Austurvöllur
Square

Alþingshúsit

Government
House

Culture
House

National
Theatre

Dómkirkjan

City Hall

Tjörnin

National Library

National
Art Gallery

National Museum

Volcano Show

University

Icelandic
Phallological
Museum

Hallgrímskikja
Church

Einar Jónsson
Sculpture
Museum

Ási Art
Gallery

Ásgrímur Jónsson
Museum

Árni Magnússon
Institute

Nordic House

Long Distance
Bus Terminal

Air Iceland
Terminal

Domestic
Airport

Íslandsflug
Terminal

Öskjuhlíð Hill

HOTELS & GUESTHOUSES

Anna	19
Baldursbrá	17
Blásól	4
Borg	6
Fosshótel City	2
Frón	9
Holt	15
Ísafold	3
Jörð	11
Krían	7
Liefur Eiríksson	14
Loftleiðir	20
Luna	12
Óðinsvé	13
Room with a View	8
Saga	18
Salvation Army	5
Skaldbreið	10
Travel-Inn	16
Víkingur	1

N

0   400 m

somewhere to stay in Reykjavík in the height of summer is not easy. At other times of year the city's limited number of beds can also be stretched, so it's always a good idea to book in advance. If you can't find anywhere to stay in the city centre, there are alternatives in the suburb of **Hafnafjörður**.

The city campsite and the youth hostel

The cheapest place to stay in Reykjavík is the busy city **campsite** (mid-May to mid-Sept; ☎568 6944; 350kr per person, plus 350kr per tent), at Sundlaugavegur 34. Cooking, laundry and shower facilities are available on site. Next door, also at Sundlaugavegur 34, is the excellent **youth hostel** (☎553 8110, fax 588 9201; 1450kr per person), next to Reykjavík's largest swimming pool. As with other forms of accommodation in the capital, the hostel quickly fills in summer and advance booking is recommended; **reservations** are held until 6pm unless otherwise requested. The small **dorms** sleep between two and eight people each. There's also a laundry and kitchen here (the closest supermarket is a two-minute walk from the hostel on Laugalækur), while buying **breakfast** here will set you back 600kr. **Bus #5** runs here from the central Lækjartorg and Hlemmur terminals every twenty minutes; the **Flybus** to and from the airport (see p.43) also stops here. Allow forty minutes to walk into town.

Guesthouses, bed and breakfasts and apartments

Generally cheaper than hotels, but still by no means a bargain at 4000–7000kr for a double, **guesthouses** usually provide kitchens – though **breakfast** is often included in the price – but rooms are always on the simple side, with little to distinguish between them. Other than those we recommend, a central location is as good a reason as any to choose one over another, though bear in mind that many are fully booked weeks in advance throughout July and August. Some homeowners rent out one or two rooms for **bed and breakfast** in summer, often giving an excellent insight into Icelandic family life: rates are slightly lower than at guesthouses. Recommended owners include Anna Sigurðardóttir, at Tryggvagata 14 (☎561 4590, fax 562 8409; 4500kr), centrally located close to the harbour; Hólmfríður Guðmundsdóttir, on the fourth floor at Skólavörðustígur 16 (☎562 5482, fax 562 5482; 5000kr), right in the heart of the city; Eiríkur Rauði, Eiríksgata 6 (☎552 1940, fax 552 1951; 6000kr), behind Hallgrímskirkja church; Sigrún Ólafsdóttir, Skeggjagata 1 (☎562 2240, fax 562 2240; 6000kr), off the busy Snorrabraut, a ten-minute walk from the centre; and Monika Blöndal, Aflagrandi 20 (☎552 3644; 4500kr), in the west of the city, a 25-minute walk from the centre. If these B&Bs or the guesthouses below are full, look out for signs in windows advertising rooms or ask at the tourist office for their lengthy official list.

Anna, Smáragata 16 (☎562 1618, fax 562 1656). Run by the animated and friendly Anna, who lived in the States for 25 years and so speaks excellent English. Excellent value and very handy for the long-distance bus station, and definitely one of Reykjavík's better guesthouses. ③.

Baldursbrá, Laufásvegur 41 (☎552 6646, fax 562 6647). Friendly, modern guesthouse with a fantastic location, right in the city centre and overlooking Tjörnin, though with rather narrow beds and unfortunate floral curtains. Sleeping-bag accommodation 1600kr; ③.

Blásól, Sólvallagata 35 (☎562 6335, fax 562 9410). A good choice in the western part of town, run by an architect and his family. The interior is a fine example of modern IKEA-style Scandinavian design. The rear garden is available to guests. ③.

Egilsborg, Þverholt 20 (☎561 2600, fax 561 2636). Bright, modern place in a peaceful street close to the Hlemmur bus terminal, though none of the rooms is en suite. Sleeping-bag accommodation 1800kr; ②.

Fjölskylduhúsið, Flókagata 5 (☎551 9828, fax 551 2448). Just nine comfortable rooms in this homely guesthouse in a quiet street, just 15 minutes' walk from the centre. ③.

Flókagata 1, Flókagata 1 (☎552 1155, fax 562 0355). Just up the road from *Fjölskylduhúsið*, in a pebble-dashed modern block. The rooms are uninspiring and stuffed with furniture and cheesy fittings, but they are close to the centre and reasonably good value. Sleeping-bag accommodation 1900kr; ③.

Guesthouse 101, Laugavegur 101 (☎562 6101, fax 562 6105). Expensive and totally soulless place at the eastern end of the main shopping street with cheap furniture and cell-like rooms. Worth a look if everything else is full. ④.

Ísafold, Bárugata 11 (☎561 2294, fax 562 9965). An excellent choice in a quiet suburban street in the western part of town. Tastefully appointed rooms, all with shared bath – decorated with wall paintings and stylish furniture. ③.

Jörð, Skólavörðustígur 13a (☎562 1739, fax 562 1735). Central location in an old but basic house, just off the main shopping street. Plain, dull rooms, but they are a steal for the centre of town, though breakfast costs an extra 500kr. ②.

Krían, Suðurgata 22 (☎511 5600, fax 511 5611). Bright, airy and comfortable – and above all spacious – rooms in this good central guesthouse overlooking Tjörnin. Well worth the slightly higher prices. ③.

Kríunes, Lake Elliðaárvatn (☎567 2245, fax 567 2226). A fifteen-minute drive southwest of the city, this is a truly fantastic lakeside choice, a former farmhouse surrounded by high trees and with views of the lake, kitted out with South American-style fittings and furnishings, including brightly coloured rugs. Self-catering facilities available. ③.

Luna, Spítalastígur 1 (☎511 2800). Good, gay-friendly, newly renovated guesthouse in the heart of the city, offering six tastefully decorated but expensive en-suite apartments. Studio apartments 9600kr.

Room with a View, Laugavegur 18 (☎552 7262). Recommended gay-friendly and operated sixth-floor flats on the main shopping street, excellently appointed and with incredible panoramic views from the shared balcony. Kitchen, shower and steambath available. From 4500kr per night.

Salvation Army Guesthouse, Kirkjustræti 2 (☎561 3203, fax 561 3315). The cheapest guesthouse in Reykjavík, often fully booked, despite the narrow rooms with clanking pipes, paper-thin walls and lack of private bath. Although there can be some slightly eccentric local characters in residence, it's a good sensible choice if you're on a tight budget and it's dead central. Breakfast is an extra 600kr. Sleeping-bag accommodation from 1400kr; ①.

Travel-Inn, Sóleyjargata 31 (☎561 3553, fax 562 8370). One of Reykjavík's top three guesthouses in a tastefully renovated old house with good-sized, comfortable rooms overlooking the southern end of Tjörnin and handy for the long-distance bus station on Vatnsmýrarvegur. The rooms with shared bath are good value. ③.

Víkingur, Ránargata 12 (☎562 1290, fax 562 1293). Another good location in the western part of town in a quiet suburban street. Ten simple but modern rooms put this guesthouse towards the top of the list, and it's tremendous value. ③.

Hotels

Without exception, **hotels** in the city are heavy on the pocket. Standards are uniformly high and a buffet **breakfast** is always included in the price, but the average rate for a double with bath is 11,000kr, and even a single without bath will be upwards of 5000kr. If, however, you fancy splashing out for a night or two of luxury, the following are the city's best-value options.

Barón, Barónsstígur 2-4 (☎562 3204, fax 562 3779). En-suite doubles, plus apartments – all with wooden floors, microwaves and showers – most of which have sea views. Apartments can vary greatly in size, so look before you choose. One-bedroom apartment 11,500kr mid–May to mid–Sept, less out of season. ④.

Borg, Pósthússtræti 11 (☎551 1440, fax 551 1420). The city's very first hotel, opened in the 1930s and ever since the unofficial home of visiting heads of state. Reeking with atmosphere, the fifty rooms are all individually decorated in Art Deco style with period furniture. The service can be somewhat unctuous, however. ⑦.

Cabin, Borgartún 32 (☎511 6030, fax 511 6031). Modern hotel with fantastic views from the front rooms of the sea and Mount Esja. Bright colours are the key here – lots of reds, yellows and blues make the décor quite lurid. Unusually, several rooms look onto the central corridor rather than the great outdoors – handy if you find it hard to sleep in the bright midnight sun; these rooms are half the price of normal doubles. Doubles with shower ④.

Esja, Suðurlandsbraut 2 (☎505 0950, fax 505 0955). Big, impersonal and popular with stopover passengers travelling to and from America, but a 25-minute walk from the centre. The stylish rooms have Scandinavian-style wooden décor – those at the front have views over the sea to Mount Esja. Doubles with shower ⑥.

Fosshótel City, Ránargata 4a (☎511 1155, fax 552 9040). A homely place close to the centre, and one of the cheaper hotels, with uninspiring but adequate rooms. ④.

Fosshótel Lind, Rauðarárstígur 18 (☎562 3350, fax 562 3351). Bright, modern and functional hotel about twenty minutes' walk from the centre. Rooms are plain but good value. Doubles with shower ⑤.

Frón, Klapparstígur 35a (☎511 4666, fax 511 4665). Right in the city centre, this good hotel offering nine stylish, modern studio studios and six two-room apartments, each with bath, kitchenette and TV. Studios 8800kr, two-bedroom apartments 9800kr.

Grand Hótel Reykjavík, Sigtún 38 (☎568 9000, fax 568 0675). Although a 25-minute walk from the centre, this is still a good choice for its stylish rooms of marble floors, chrome fittings and wood panels. Also has a romantic restaurant with an open fire in the centre of the dining area. Doubles with shower ⑦.

Höfði, Skipholt 27 (☎552 6477, fax 562 3986). Odd location in the middle of a business area for this former student hostel, around a 25-minute walk from the town. Few creature comforts in the cramped rooms here, but it is cheap, and the doubles come with either bath or shower. ③–④.

Holt, Bergstaðastræti 37 (☎552 5700, fax 562 3025). Part of the French Relais & Châteaux group of hotels, over three hundred paintings by Icelandic artists adorn the rooms and public areas of this luxury, centrally located hotel. Rooms are of the persian carpet, dark-wood panelling, red-leather armchair and chocolate-on-the-pillow variety. Breakfast costs extra. ⑦.

Ísland, Ármúli 9 (☎595 7000, fax 595 7001). Radisson SAS hotel, about 2.5km from the city centre. Stylish light and airy Scandinavian-design rooms with lots of wood panels and glass and chrome, popular with businessmen and rich tourists. ⑦.

Leifur Eiríksson, Skólavörðustígur 45 (☎562 0800, fax 562 0804). Perfect location overlooking the Hallgrímskirkja church, right in the heart of the city. Small and friendly neatly furnished place – the top-floor rooms, built into the sloping roof, are particularly worthwhile for their excellent views. Good value and recommended. Doubles with shower ⑤.

Loftleiðir, Reykjavík city airport (☎505 0900, fax 505 0905). Icelandair-owned hotel popular with stopover travellers. The quiet, carpeted rooms are a little on the small side but perfectly adequate, though, is dull and business oriented. The only hotel in Reykjavík with an indoor swimming pool; separate-sex saunas also available. A longish walk into the city centre, however – reckon on about half an hour. Doubles with shower ⑥.

Óðinsvé, Pórsgata 1 (☎511 6200, fax 511 6201). Great place that's stylish, relaxed and within an easy trot of virtually everything. Rooms here have wooden floors, Scandinavian-style minimalist furniture and a homely atmosphere. Doubles with shower ⑥.

Reykjavík, Rauðarárstígur 37 (☎562 6250, fax 562 6350). Functional and uninspiring hotel, roughly twenty minutes' walk from the centre. Rooms are plain and simple but clean and presentable, though you might find some disturbingly pink furniture in them. Doubles with shower ⑥.

Saga, Hagatorg (☎525 9900, fax 525 9909). Swanky, large Radisson SAS hotel, usually packed with conference delegates dashing up to admire the view from the top-floor restaurant. The rooms, although cosmopolitan in feel and design, with bureaux and comfortable armchairs, are nothing special. Doubles with shower ⑦.

Skjaldbreið, Laugavegur 16 (☎511 6060, fax 511 6070). Plain rooms with floral and net curtains and dull grey carpets, but this is the only hotel on Reykjavík's main shopping street, and is therefore unbeatable for its location. Doubles with bath ⑥.

Vík, Síðumúli 19 (☎588 5588, fax 588 5582). The simple but pleasant rooms in this hotel are popular with German tour groups. It's oddly located in a business district, 30 minutes' walk from the centre but is perfect for good-value, upmarket self-catering, since half the rooms have a kitchen. Doubles with shower ③.

The City

Although small for a metropolis, compared with Iceland's other built-up areas, Reykjavík is a throbbing urban development. If you're planning to visit some of the country's more remote and isolated regions, you should make the most of the atmosphere generated by this bustling port, with its buzzing nightlife and high-brow museums. The collections in the centrally located **National Museum** and **Árni Magnússon Manuscript**, for example, offer a fine introduction to Iceland's stirring past, while outdoors, in the streets and parks you'll find the outstanding work of sculptors **Ásmundur Sveinsson** and **Einar Jónsson**, as well as in two permanent exhibitions – indeed, contemporary art has a high profile in a whole host of art shops and galleries. And yet even with all of this around you, you can never forget that you're bang in the middle of the North Atlantic, with your nearest neighbours being Greenland and the North Pole – a remoteness that is at the core of Reykjavík's appeal.

The city centre is split roughly into two halves by the brilliant waters of the large, naturally occurring pond, **Tjörnin**. To the north and west of this lie, respectively, the busy fishing **harbour**, full of modern hi-tech trawlers and Iceland's now decomissioned whaling fleet, and **Vesturbær**, the city's oldest district, dating back in parts to the Settlement, now largely given over to administration, eating, drinking and entertainment. It's also one of the city's most likeable and picturesque quarters, comprising a spread of well-to-do residential streets, at odds with the concrete apartment blocks on the eastern outskirts of the city. Another gaggle of bars and restaurants are located on **Austurstræti** and **Hafnarstræti** – the location of the Icelandic **parliament** and the main post office, studded with multicoloured rooves and facades, reaching up the hill that begins at Tjörnin's western edge. East of the pond, things become altogether more commercial, as the gently sloping main drag, **Laugavegur,** the city's main shopping street, packed with glitzy designer boutiques and the location for most of the city's bars, restaurants, shops and cinemas, leads towards the **bus terminal**, Hlemmur, which marks the city's edge.

Central Reykjavík

You'd be hard pushed to find a capital city as diminutive as Reykjavík, and a leisurely walk of just an hour or two will take you around almost the entirety of the centre. Such smallness accounts for the city's lack of contrasting and well-defined areas: for simple convenience, we've divided the central portion into two sections separated by the lake, **Tjörnin**, and the road, **Lækjargata**, which runs from the lake to Reykjavík's main square, named **Lækjartorg**. Even the few things of note further out from the centre can be reached in a few minutes on public transport.

Lækjartorg and around

The best place to get your first taste of Reykjavík is the area around **Lækjartorg** and the adjoining pedestrianized **Austurstræti** on its southern side – a general meeting place for Reykjavík's urbanites, where people stroll, strut and sit on benches munching cakes, ice creams and burgers bought from the nearby snack stands and *McDonalds*. It was once overlooked from its western end by the headquarters of the main daily newspaper, *Morgunblaðið*, the implication being that journalists needed only to look through their windows to discover what was happening in the city, which was usually very little – but today the area can be one of the most boisterous in the city. On Friday and Saturday evenings, particularly in summer, hundreds of drunken revellers fill the square when the clubs empty out at 5 or 6am, jostling for prime position – although the noise from the throng can be deafening, the atmosphere is good hearted and not at all intimidating. By day, the area resumes its busy commercial air as people dash in and out of the post office or pop in to one of the city's two main bookshops, Eymundsson. Beyond its junction with Þósthússtræti, Austurstræti gives itself over solely to pleasure, as this is where some of the city's best **bars and restaurants** can be found (see p.65). This is also the location for the **state alcohol store** (see Listings, p.72) a futuristic glass-and-steel structure at no. 10a, where those who want to drink at home have to come and part with vast amounts of cash (see Basics, p.30, for more on this).

Austurvöllur and the Alþingshúsið

Þósthússtræti, running south from Austurstræti, leads into another small square, **Austurvöllur**, a favourite place for city slickers from nearby offices to catch a few rays during their lunch breaks, stretched out on the grassy lawns edged with flowers. Yet the square's modest proportions and nondescript apartment blocks – where Blur's Damon Albarn is rumoured to have a flat – belie its historical importance. This was the site of Ingólfur Arnarson's farm; it's thought he grew his hay on the land where the square now stands, and as such it marks the original centre of Reykjavík. Similarly, the square's central, elevated **statue** of the nineteenth-century independence campaigner Jón Sigurðsson, entitled *The Pride of Iceland, its Sword and Shield,* faces two of the most important buildings in the country – the Alþing and the Dómkirkjan – though you'd never realise their status from their appearance.

The **Alþingshúsið** (House of Parliament) is ordinary in the extreme, a slight building made of grey basalt with the date of its completion, 1881, etched into its dark frontage – yet this unremarkable structure played a pivotal role in bringing about Icelandic independence. In 1798, the parliament moved to Reykjavík from Þingvellir (see p.85), where it had been operating virtually without interruption since 930 AD. Within just two years, however, it was dissolved as Danish power reached its peak, but with great pride and after much struggle, the Alþing regained its powers from Copenhagen as a consultative body in 1843, and a constitution was granted in 1874, making Iceland self-governing in domestic affairs. The Act of Union, passed in this building in 1918, made Iceland a sovereign state under the Danish Crown although the act was open for reconsideration at any time after 1940, but by then Denmark was occupied by the Nazis and the Alþing had assumed the duties normally carried out by the monarch, declaring its intention to dissolve the Act of Union at the end of the war. Today, the modest interior, illuminated by chandeliers, more resembles a town council chamber than the seat of a national parliament.

The adjacent **Dómkirkjan** (Mon–Fri 10am–4pm; free), Reykjavík's Lutheran cathedral, is a neoclassical stone structure shrouded against the weather in corrugated iron, built in 1785 after Christian VIII of Denmark scrapped the Catholic bishoprics of Hólar in the north, and Skálholt in the south, in favour of a Lutheran diocese in what was fast growing into Iceland's main centre of population. The church may be plain on the outside, but venture inside and you'll discover a beautiful interior: perfectly designed arched windows punctuate the unadorned white-painted walls at regular intervals, giving an impression of complete architectural harmony. The Cathedral is now deemed too small for great gatherings and services of state, and the roomier Hallgrímskirkja (see p.59) is preferred for state funerals and other such well-attended functions.

Aðalstræti and Hafnarstræti

From the western corner of Austurvöllur, Kirkjustræti runs the short distance to Reykjavík's oldest street, **Aðalstræti**, which follows the route taken in the late ninth century by Ingólfur Arnarson from his farm down to the sea. Immediately in front of you is the city's oldest building, a squat timber structure which dates back to 1752, formerly a weaving shed and a bishop's residence, now the **Gröf** restaurant (see p.67), where lived Skúli Magnússon (see p.75), High Sherrif of Iceland, who encouraged the development of craft industries here. On the opposite side of the street, a few steps north towards the sea, is Ingólfur Arnarson's **freshwater well**, now glassed over for posterity, which was discovered by sheer fluke when the city council carried out roadworks here in 1992.

Nearby, at the junction of Aðalstræti and **Hafnarstræti**, is another of Reykjavík's beautifully restored timber buildings (covered in corrugated iron for protection), **Fálkahúsið**, one of three buildings in the city where the King of Denmark once kept his much-prized Icelandic falcons before having them dispatched by ship to the Court in Copenhagen. There was outrage recently when the building was converted into a bistro-bar, the *Café Victor* (see p.66), inevitably subjecting the ancient timbers to the wear and tear of hundreds of stomping feet. Despite this, its turret-like side walls and sheer size still impress, especially when you consider the huge amount of timber that was imported for the job, as Iceland had no trees of its own. Cast an eye to the roof and you'll spot two carved wooden falcons still keeping guard over the building, either side of a garish modern representation of a Viking longboat.

Many of the buildings on the south side of Hafnarstræti were formerly owned by Danish merchants during the Trade Monopoly of 1602–1855 (for more on this, see p.291), and indeed, this street, as its name suggests (*hafnar* means "harbour"), once bordered the sea and gave access to the harbour, the city's economic lifeline and means of contact with the outside world. Today, though, the street is several blocks from the ocean after landfill extended the city foreshore. Instead, it is home to some excellent **bars and restaurants**, which together with adjacent, Austurstræti, makes up a rectangular block of eateries and drink-ing-holes, well worthy of exploration (see Eating and drinking, p.65).

Tryggvagata and the harbour

Tryggvagata, a quiet street, one block north of the bustle of Hafnarstræti, is remarkable for two things other than the number of consonants in its name: the imposing blue-and-white **mural** close to its junction with Þósthússtræti, portray-ing fishermen doing battle with the sea, which livens up the otherwise frightfully dull public **customs house**; and the **Hafnarhúsið**, or Reykjavík Art Museum (daily 11am–6pm, Thurs until 7pm; 400kr, Mon free), at Tryggvagata 17. This large, austere building was constructed in the 1930s as warehouse storage and office space for the Port of Reykjavík but has now been converted into a museum displaying work by twentieth-century Icelandic painters such as Jón Stefánsson, Helgi Þorgils – look out for his surreal portrayal of angelic-looking Icelandic boys riding unclothed on the backs of geese – and Ólöf Nordal. A permanent exhibi-tion of the multicoloured cartoon-like work of Icelandic artist Erró is also planned. Although there's plenty of exhibition space here, the layout is less than obvious since the confusing array of corridors, which once linked the former warehouse's storage areas, twists and turns around the museum's supporting concrete and steel pillars, leaving the visitor quite lost at times (there are no guides available). There's also a café, where it's worth taking time out to enjoy the view of the harbour and Mount Esja through the floor-to-ceiling windows.

From the museum, a two minute walk down **Grófin** leads to **Geirsgata**, the busy main road that runs along the southern side of the **harbour**, which has been built around reclaimed land – the beach where vessels once landed their foreign goods is now inland from here. Street names around here, such as Ægisgata (Ocean Street) and Öldugata (Wave Street), reflect the importance of the sea to the city, and a stroll along the dockside demonstrates Iceland's depen-dence on the Atlantic, with fishing trawlers being checked over and prepared for their next battle against the waves, plastic crates of ice-packed cod awaiting transportation to village stores around the country. Above all, you'll see the five black **whaling vessels**, each with a red "H" painted to its funnel (*hvalur* is Icelandic for "whale"). Roped together, they've stood idle since Iceland aban-doned whaling in 1989 and although the Icelandic parliament gave the go ahead for resumption in 1999 (see p.135) it remains to be seen to what extent they will allow the industry to continue.

Tjörnin and around

From the harbour, Þósthússtræti leads south over Austurstræti and Hafnarstræti to Vonarstræti and **Tjörnin**, invariably translated into English as "the pond" or "the lake". *Tjörn* and its genitive form of *tjarnar* are actually old Viking words, still used in northern English dialects as *"tarn"* to denote a mountain lake. This size-able body of water, roughly a couple of square kilometres in size, is populated by a variety of ducks and other birds – including the notorious **arctic tern**, known for its dive-bombing attacks on passers-by, and found at the pond's quieter south-ern end – whose precise numbers are charted on notice boards stationed at sev-eral points along the bank. A walking path leads all around the lake and can make a pleasant hour's stroll, though be careful not to slip on the large amounts of bird droppings at the lake edge.

Occupying prime position on the northern edge of Tjörnin is **Reykjavík City Hall** (Mon–Fri 8am–7pm, Sat & Sun noon–6pm; free). Opened in 1992, it's a showpiece of Nordic design, a modernistic rectangular structure of steel, glass and chrome that actually sits on the lake itself. Inside, in addition to the city's administration offices, is a small café and a fabulous self-standing **topographical model** of Iceland to be found in one of the small exhibition areas. It gives an excellent idea of the unforgiving geography of Iceland – marvel at the sheer size of the Vatnajökull glacier in the southeast (as big as the English county of Yorkshire) and the table mountains of the West Fjords and gain instant respect for the people who live amid such landscapes.

One of the best **views of Reykjavík** can be had from **Suðurgata**, a street running parallel to the western shore of Tjörnin and reached the city hall by walking west along Vonarstræti. Not only is the street lined with tidy little dwellings, but from it you can see across the lake to the suburban houses of the city centre, whose corrugated iron rooves, ranging in colour from a pallid two-tone green to bright blues and reds, have been carefully maintained by their owners – the familiar picture postcard view of Reykjavík.

National Museum

At the junction of Suðurgata and the busy Hringbraut, the closest thing Iceland has to a motorway, is the entrance to the **National Museum**, unfortunately closed for renovation until at least December 2002. Small, but quite comprehensive, the museum aims to give an easily digested summary of the country's past,

MAGNÚSSON'S MANUSCRIPTS

Despite so many of Iceland's sagas and histories being written down by medieval monks for purposes of posterity, there existed no suitable means of protecting them from the country's damp climate, and within a few centuries the unique artefacts were rotting away. Enter **Árni Magnússon** (1663–1730), humanist, antiquarian and professor at the University of Copenhagen, who attempted to ensure the preservation of as many of the manuscripts as possible by sending them to Denmark for safekeeping. Although he completed his task in 1720, eight years later many of them went up in flames in the Great Fire of Copenhagen, and Árni died a heartbroken man fifteen months later, never having accepted his failure to rescue the manuscripts, despite braving the flames himself. As he noted at the time of the blaze, "these are the books which are to be had nowhere in the world"; the original **Íslendingabók**, for example, the most important historical record of the settlement of Iceland, written on calfskin, was destroyed, though luckily it had been copied by a priest in Iceland before it left the country.

The manuscripts were to remain apart from their country of origin until long after Icelandic indepedence in 1944. In 1961, legislation was passed in Denmark decreeing that manuscripts composed or translated by Icelanders should be returned, but it took a further ruling by the Danish Supreme Court, in March 1971, to get things moving, as the Danes were reluctant to see these works of art leave their country. Finally, however, in April that year, a Danish naval frigate carried the first texts, **Konungsbók Eddukvæða** and **Flateyjarbók**, across the Atlantic into Reykjavík, to be met by crowds bearing signs reading "*handritin heim*" ("the manuscripts are home") and waving Icelandic flags. Even so, the transfer of the manuscripts wasn't completed until 1997.

including excavation finds from pagan places or worship and Viking graves, such as items from Bergþórshvoll (see p.111), where Njál, of Njál's Saga, lived. There will also be a collection of religious artefacts, chiefly from the eleventh to thirteenth century, plus a weighty stock of craftworks of the sixteenth to nineteenth centuries. However, the prime exhibit looks set to remain a carved wooden door, which dates to around 1200 and depicts an ancient warrior on horseback slugging it out with an unruly dragon.

The Árni Magnússon Manuscript Institute Not open Sat & Sun

A little further along Suðurgata you pass the bigger of the country's two universities – the other one is a tiny affair in Akureyri – an ugly, pebbledashed monstrosity that overlooks the city airport, before coming to the wonderful **Árni Magnússon Manuscript Institute** (June–Aug daily 1–5pm; Sept–May Tues–Fri 2–4pm on request for small groups; 400kr), housed in the university's Árnagarður building and one of the best places to gain an understanding of both Iceland's literary past and the nation's obsession with books and stories. Named after the learned seventeenth- to eighteenth-century Icelandic scholar (see box), the institute houses some of the most important, often ornately decorated historical accounts, including the *Íslendingabók* (*Book of Icelanders*) and *Landnámabók* (*Book of Settlement*), which both recount the settlement of the country, as well as some of the fact-based fiction – *Njál's Saga*, the *Saga of Eirík the Red* and *Snorri's Saga* – all of which helped establish the high-flying cultural reputation Iceland once enjoyed. Unfortunately, very few of the original manuscripts are now on public display since they're considered too valuable and delicate to be exposed to the light. Instead, they're kept locked away in vaults accessible only to the museum staff, who, only under special circumstances, are allowed to access them – and then only when wearing gloves to protect the vellum. Instead, a small visitors' room allows guests to see some of the less precious originals, as well as plenty of copies of the masterpieces themselves, all housed in a couple of locked glass cabinets. Although the museum is a little disappointing in this respect, it's invaluable in providing background information on the literary tradition in medieval Iceland and on **Árni Magnússon** himself. English-speaking **guides** are on hand for this purpose and will regale you with stories that clearly fill them with pride – to Icelanders, these medieval manuscripts are as much a part of their history as historic buildings and royal palaces are to other nations.

Nordic House

Opposite the university is the **Nordic House**, designed by Finnish architect Alvar Aalto in 1961 and buzzed over by aircraft landing at the nearby domestic airport. Devoted to Nordic culture, with an extensive **library** of books written in all the Nordic languages (daily midday–5pm; free) holding books on virtually any aspect of Nordic life you choose to mention from Faroese knitting to Greenlandic seal hunting. There are also temporary **exhibitions** (often photographic) in the hall (Tues–Fri midday–5pm; free) and frequent evening events, from classical **concerts** to **talks** covering topics from history to politics to music (sometimes in English). Check what's on from the posters inside or from the free tourist magazines at the Tourist Office (see p.46). For speakers of non-Nordic languages, the best part of Nordic House is its **café** (Mon–Sat 8am–5pm, Sun midday–5pm), which serves up a cheap fish lunch (around 700kr) as well as delicious homemade cakes with coffee.

East of Tjörnin: Fríkirkjuvegur, Lækjargata and Government House

A few minutes' walk north from the Nordic House, on **Fríkirkjuvegur**, which runs along the eastern side of Tjörnin, is the **Fríkirkjan**, the Free Lutheran Church, a simple wooden structure painted bright white, whose best feature is its tall tower, useful as a landmark to guide you to the neighbouring **Íshúsið** (Ice House) at Fríkirkjuvegur 7. Once a storage place for the massive chunks of ice, hewn in winter from the frozen lake and used to prevent fish stocks rotting, the building has been completely redesigned and enlarged and now houses the **National Art Gallery** (Tues–Sun 11am–5pm; 400kr, free on Wed). Icelandic art may lack worldwide recognition, but all the significant names are to be found here, including Erró, Jón Stefánsson, Ásgrímur Jónsson, Guðmundur Þorsteinsson and Einar Hákonarson – though disappointingly, lack of space means that the paintings can only be shown in strictly rationed portions from the museum's enormous stock of around 5000 works of art. You can, however, get an idea of the paintings not on display by glancing through the postcards for sale at reception. Drop in, but expect to leave with your artistic appetite no more than whetted; also, note that on entry you have to leave your coat and bag in the lockers provided.

A walk from here back towards Lækjartorg leads on to **Lækjargata** (effectively a continuation of Fríkirkjuvegur), which once marked the eastern boundary of the town; Tjörnin once emptied into the sea through the small brook (*lækur* is Icelandic for "brook") here, which now runs under the road. The cluster of old timber buildings up on the small hill parallel to the street is known as **Bernhöftstorfan** and, following extensive renovation, they now house a couple of chi-chi fish restaurants and the tourist office (see p.46), with its official entrance round the corner in Bankastræti. They're flanked by two of Iceland's most important buildings: the old Reykjavík Grammar School, built in 1844, which once had to be accessed by a bridge over the brook, and housed the Alþing before the completion of the current Alþingshúsið in nearby Austurvöllur square (see p.53); and a small unobtrusive white building at the bottom of Bankastræti, which is, in fact, **Government House** (Stjórnarráðið), another of Iceland's very parochial-looking public offices. One of the oldest surviving buildings in the city, built in 1761–71 as a prison, it now houses the offices of the Prime Minister. Up on **Arnahóll**, the grassy mound behind the building, a statue of Ingólfur Arnarson, Reykjavík's first settler, surveys his domain; with his back turned on the National Theatre, and the government ministries to his right, he looks out to the ocean that brought him here over eleven centuries ago.

Laugavegur and around

From Lækjartorg, turn right into the short Bankastræti and on, up the small hill, into **Laugavegur** (Hot Spring Route), the route once taken by local washerwomen to the springs in Laugardalur. This is Iceland's major commercial artery, holding the main shops and a fair sprinkling of cafés, bars and restaurants. Not surprisingly therefore, on Friday and Saturday evenings in summer it's bumper to bumper with cars, their horns blaring, and with well-oiled revellers hanging out of the windows. However, before you give yourself over to extensive retail therapy, there are a couple of more cerebral attractions worthy of your time and attention in this part of town: the grand former National Library, now the Culture House (daily 11am–5pm; 300kr), at Hverfisgata 15, one block north of and parallel to Laugavegur, has the country's best exhibition on **Viking history**. *Vikings and the New World*, a permanent display on the top floor, tells how Iceland was discovered by Vikings from Norway who then, under the leadership of Eirík the Red, went on to settle Greenland before finally discovering America around the year 1000 AD. Maps, charts and pictures bring the quest for new land in the west to life, and this shouldn't be missed by anyone even vaguely interested in Icelandic history. Downstairs, an entire room is given over to the independence leader **Jón Sigurðsson**, though you probably have to be a national to appreciate fully some of the finer details of his bitter struggle with the Danes, and labelling of exhibits here is in Icelandic only anyway. Another small exhibition shows how Iceland has been perceived by the outside world, and, if the collection of oddly shaped ancient maps on display here is anything to go by, knowledge was pretty scarce.

Back on Laugavegur and a couple of blocks further east, a museum that causes the staff at the tourist office down to road to blush with embarrassment, is the **Icelandic Phallological Museum** at no. 24 (2–5pm: May–Aug Tues–Sat; Sept–April Tues & Sat; 300kr), the most offbeat of all the country's museums. Inside is a collection of the penises of virtually every mammal found either in Iceland or its offshore waters, with over eighty of them on display, from the sizeable member that once belonged to a young male blue whale, now hollowed out, salted, dried and placed on a wooden plaque to that of a rogue polar bear founded drifting on pack ice off the West Fjords, shot by Icelandic fishermen and then castrated. A human specimen has escaped the collection to date, although there's a certificate on the wall signed by a farmer in his eighties who's agreed to donate his apparently ample wedding tackle to the museum on his death.

Hallgrímskirkja

If, after the Phallological Museum, you're in need of spiritual comfort, help is close at hand, since from the lower end of Laugavegur, the tongue-twisting Skólavörðustígur streaks steeply upwards to the largest church in the country, the magnificient **Hallgrímskirkja** (daily: May–Sept 9am–6pm; Oct–April 10am–4pm; tower 10am–5pm). This is a modern concrete structure, whose neatly composed space-shuttle-like form dominates the Reykjavík skyline. Work began on the church, named after the renowned seventeenth century religious poet, Hallgrímur Pétursson, immediately after World War II and still continues, the slow progress due to the task being carried out by a family firm – comprising one man and his son. Each year brings fresh rumours that the thing is about to be completed, the latest addition being the stained-glass window above the door. Opinions on the church's architectural style – the work of architect Guðjón Samúelsson – not least the 73-metre phallic steeple – have split the city over the years, although nowadays locals have grown to accept rather than love it. Most people rave about the organ inside, the only decoration in an otherwise completely bare Gothic-style shell; measuring a whopping 15m in height and possessing over 5000 pipes, it really has to be heard to be believed. The cost of installing it called for a major fundraising effort, with people across the country sponsoring a pipe – if you fancy putting money towards one yourself, for which you'll receive a certificate, have a word with the staff. The tower has a **viewing**

platform (200kr), accessed by a lift from just within the main door, but it's not particularly worth it – you can see much the same for nothing from the *Perlan* restaurant at Öskjuhlíð (see p.63). Incidentally, don't expect the clock at the top of the tower to tell the correct time – the wind up there is so strong that it frequently blows the hands off course. In fact, it's rare for any two public clocks in Reykjavík to tell the same time because of the differing wind conditions throughout the city.

With his back to the church and his view firmly planted on Vínland, the imposing, if somewhat green **statue** of Leifur Eiríksson, *Discoverer of America*, was donated by the US in 1930 to mark the Icelandic parliament's thousandth birthday. It's a favourite spot for photographs and makes as good place as any to survey your surroundings – this is one of the highest parts of Reykjavík and on a clear day there are great **views** out over the surrounding streets of houses adorned with multicoloured corrugated-iron facades.

Einar Jónsson Sculpture Museum

The heroic form of the Leifur Eiríksson statue is found in several others around the city, many of them the work of **Einar Jónsson** (1874–1954), who is remembered more officially by the pebbledash building to the right of the church, which looks like three large adjoining cubes – the **Einar Jónsson Sculpture Museum** (June to mid-Sept Tues–Sun 2–5pm; mid-Sept to May Sat & Sun 2–5pm; 300kr), which is entered from Freyjugata, the street behind the museum. Einar was Iceland's foremost modern sculptor, and this building was given to him as a studio and living space by the Icelandic government in 1923. He worked here in an increasingly reclusive manner until his death in 1954, when the building was given over to displaying more than a hundred of his works – many based on religious and political themes – to the public. A specially constructed group of rooms, connected by slim corridors and little staircases, takes the visitor through a chronological survey of Einar's career – and it's pretty deep stuff. Jónsson claimed that his self-imposed isolation and total devotion to his work enabled him to achieve mystical states of creativity, and looking at the pieces exhibited here, many of them heavy with religious allegory and all dripping with spiritual energy, it's a claim that doesn't seem far-fetched; look out for *The Guardian*, a ghost keeping watch over a graveyard to make sure the dead receive a decent burial. If the museum is closed, you can peek into the garden at the rear of the museum, where several examples of Jónsson's work are displayed alfresco, or admire his most visible work, the statue of independence leader, Jón Sigurðsson, found in front of the Alþingshúsið in Austurvöllur square (see p.53).

ÁSÍ Art Gallery and the Ásgrímur Jónsson Museum

Another, equally admired, modern Icelandic sculptor, **Ásmundur Sveinsson**, once lived further down the same street as the museum, a short walk away at Freyjugata 41, in a striking if somewhat now past-its-prime functionalist building, designed in 1933 by the sculptor and the architect **Sigurður Guðmundsson**. At the time, the combination of the building's uncompromising squat, building-block style, together with Ásmundur's array of in-your-face sculptures in the garden, caused many heads to turn, but these sculptures have since gone to the Ásmundur Sveinsson Sculpture Museum (see opposite), and the building now seems an integral part of the cityscape, serving as **The ÁSÍ (Icelandic Labour Unions) Art Gallery** (Tues–Sun 2–6pm). This trade-union art collection includes a worthy permanent stock of Icelandic masters, backed-up by regular exhibitions of more contemporary fare on the second floor. It's a rather dry place to while away a wet afternoon.

The area between here and Tjörnin is one of the more affluent parts of the city, with houses flourishing a wooden turret or two. From the ASÍ museum, trace your steps back to Hallgrímskirkja before heading down Njarðargata, and after about five minutes you'll come to one of the best preserved and less ostentatious abodes, now the **Ásgrímur Jónsson Museum** (June–Aug Tues–Sun 1.30–4pm; 300kr) at Bergstaðastræti 74, the former home of an artist who became a seminal figure in twentieth-century Icelandic painting. Born on a farm in southern Iceland, Ásgrímur (1876–1958) grew up beside the Hekla volcano until leaving for Copenhagen, then the capital of Iceland, in 1897, to study at the Academy of Fine Arts. Six years later, having developed a style and subject matter that drew heavily from Icelandic landscapes and folklore, he returned to his home country and staged an influential exhibition of his work, reflecting the growing nationalistic mood in the country. The ground floor of this small house is kept as the artist left it when he died in 1958, including his piano which he loved to play; upstairs, you'll find a selection of thirty or forty of his canvases, mostly touching though occasionally violent. Especially pleasing are his paintings from around Húsafell where he depicts knotty birch trees struggling for life on the red volcanic soil set against lush green meadows and the whites of the ice caps.

Kjarvalsstaðir Art Gallery

From the Ásgrímur Jónsson Museum it's a fifteen-minute walk east to the main highway, Hringbraut, beyond its junction with Snorrabraut and then north into Rauðarárstígur, to reach another of Reykjavík's excellent modern-art museums. Despite being surrounded by birch trees and grassy expanses, however, at first sight the **Kjarvalsstaðir Art Gallery** (daily 10am–6pm; 400kr, free Mon), devoted to the work of Iceland's most celebrated artist, **Jóhannes Kjarval** (1885–1972), is an ugly 1960s-style concrete structure, but inside it's a surprisingly bright and airy place. After working during his youth on a fishing trawler, Jóhannes moved abroad to study art, spending time in London, Copenhagen, France and Italy, but it was only after his return to Iceland in 1940 that he travelled widely in his own country, drawing on the raw beauty he saw around him for his quasi-abstract depictions of Icelandic landscapes which made him one of the country's most popular twentieth-century painters. Painting in oils, much of his work is a surreal fusion of colour: his bizarre yet pleasing *Krítik* from 1946–7, a melee of icy blues, whites and greys measuring a whopping 4m in length and 2m in height, is the centrepiece of the exhibition, portraying a naked man bending over to expose his testicles whilst catching a fish, watched over, rather oddly, by a number of Norse warriors. The museum is divided into two halls – the east one shows Kjarval's work, whilst the west hall is dedicated to visiting temporary exhibitions. Whilst it may take a while for his style to grow on you, it's certainly worth dropping by – note, though, that the entrance to the museum, which is actually located in a small area of parkland, is on Flókagata, off Rauðarárstígur.

The Ásmundur Sveinsson Sculpture Museum

If sculpture is more your thing, particularly if you've already seen the man's house (see opposite), you'll want to check out the domed **Ásmundur Sveinsson Sculpture Museum** (daily: May–Sept 10am–5pm; Oct–April 1–4pm; 400kr) at

Sigtún, a twenty-minute walk from the the Kjarvalsstaðir Art Gallery that involves a series of right and left turns that zigzag you northeast through a series of suburban streets. Don't be put off by the list of streets, as it's actually a very straightforward walk: from the museum turn right along Flókagata, left into Stakkahlíð, right into Háteigsvegur, left into Bólstaðarhlíð, right into Háaleitisbraut, left into Kringlumýrarbraut, and finally right into Suðurlandsbraut, from where you'll see the peculiar white igloo shape beyond the trees on your left hand side.

Ásmundur Sveinsson (1893–1982) was one of the pioneers of Icelandic sculpture, and his powerful, often provocative, work was inspired by his country's nature and literature. During the 1920s he studied in both Stockholm at the State Academy and in Paris, returning to Iceland to develop his unique sculptural cubism, a style infused with Icelandic myth and legend, which you can view here at his former home that he designed and built with his own hands in 1942–50. Look, also, at his soft-edged, gently curved monuments to the ordinary working people of the country in the grounds of the museum, many of which once stood outside his house in Freyjugata (see p.60). In case you're wondering why the museum assumes such an uncommon shape for Reykjavík, it's because when Ásmundur planned it, he was experimenting with Mediterranean and North African themes, drawing particular inspiration from the domed houses common to Arabic countries. Inside, a couple of stark white rooms contain more examples of the sculptor's work, including several busts from his period of Greek influence, but the original of his most famous sculpture, *Sæmundur on the Seal*, showing one of the first Icelanders to receive a university education, the priest and historian Sæmundur Sigfússon (1056–1133), astride a seal, psalter in hand, is not on display here but, appropriately, stands outside the main university building on Suðurgata.

Botanical garden and zoo
Barely ten minutes on foot from the Ásmundur Sveinsson sculpture museum, reached by walking east along Engjavegur, the **botanical garden**, part of the Laugardalur sports and recreation area, contains an extensive collection of native Icelandic flora, as well as thousands of imported plants and trees. This place is particularly popular with Icelandic families who come here not only to enjoy the surroundings but also to show kids the adjoining **zoo** (May–Sept daily 10am–6pm; 400kr), where seals, foxes, mink, reindeer and fish caught in Iceland's rivers and lakes are all on hand to keep them busy. Once the attraction of the animals starts to wane, there's a small duck pond, complete with replica Viking longboat, along with other activities based loosely on a Viking theme: a fort, an outlaw hideout and even a go-cart track in the surrounding family park. **Buses** #2, 5, 10, 11, 12 and 15 all run here from the city centre.

Árbæjarsafn Open-Air Museum
From the botanical garden, it's a short bus ride on #10 (originating at the Hlemmur bus terminal) to the **Árbæjarsafn Open-Air Museum** (June–Aug Tues–Fri 9am–5pm, Sat & Sun 10am–6pm; Sept–May Mon, Wed & Fri 1–2pm; 400kr), a collection of turf-roofed and corrugated-iron buildings on the site of an ancient farm that was first mentioned in the Sagas around the mid-1400s. The buildings and their contents record the change that occurred as Iceland's economy switched from farming to fishing – the industrial revolution being heralded by the arrival of the fishing trawler – and Reykjavík's rapid expansion. The pretty turf

church here, dating from 1842, was carefully moved to its present location from Skagafjörður (see p.198) on the north coast in 1960. Next to it, the farmhouse is dominated by an Ásmundur Sveinsson sculpture, the *Woman Churning Milk*, illustrating an all-but-lost traditional way of life.

Höfði and the Museum of Natural History

From Árbær folk museum, a five-minute walk north along Höfðabakki to its junction with Vesturlandsvegur will bring you to the #9 **bus**, which runs from here back into Reykjavík passing **Höfði** on the way, a stocky white wooden structure built in the early 1900s in Jugend style, which occupies a grassy square beside the shore, between the roads Sæbraut and Borgartún. This was the venue of the **Reagan–Gorbachev snap summit** of 1986, called at the suggestion of the former Soviet President, Mikhail Gorbachev to discuss peace and disarmament between the two superpowers. Although agreement was reached in Reykjavík on reducing the number of medium-range and intercontinental missiles in Europe and Asia, the thornier question of America's strategic defence initiative of shooting down missiles in space remained a sticking point. However, the Summit achieved one major goal – it brought the world's attention on Iceland, which, in the mid-1980s, was still relatively unknown as a destination for travellers, in effect marking the beginning of the tourist boom that Iceland is enjoying today.

Whether Gorbachev and Reagan were troubled by the resident Höfði **ghost** isn't known, but it's said to be that of a young girl, who poisoned herself after being found guilty of incest with her brother. Between 1938 and 1951 the house was occupied by diplomats, including one who was so troubled by the supernatural presence that one dispatch after another was sent to the Foreign Office in London begging for a transfer until he finally got his way. In recent years, lights have switched themselves on and off, paintings have fallen off walls and door handles have worked themselves loose. Today – apart from international summitry – the house enjoys a principal function as a centre for the city's municipal functions.

From Höfði, it's a ten-minute walk west along Borgartún and left into Snorrabraut to the **Museum of Natural History** (Tues, Thurs, Sat & Sun: June–Aug 1–5pm; Sept–May 1.30–4pm) at Hverfisgata 116, although much of the museum is of remote interest if you're not eager for rocks and lava samples, it's worth looking out for the stuffed specimen of the extinct Great Auk.

Öskjuhlíð

If you've arrived in Reykjavík from Keflavík airport, it's hard to miss the space-age-looking grey container tanks which sit at the top of the wooded hill, **Öskjuhlíð**, immediately east of the domestic airport. Each contains 4000 litres of water at 80°C for use in the capital's homes, offices and swimming pools; it's also from here that water is pumped, via a network of specially constructed pipes, underneath Reykjavík's pavements to keep them ice- and snow-free during winter. The whole thing is topped by a revolving restaurant, the *Perlan*, a truly spectacular place for dinner – if your wallet can take the strain. The restaurant is, however, one of Reykjavík's best-known landmarks and is the best place for a 360-degree **panoramic view** of the entire city; simply take the lift to the fourth floor and step outside for free. On a clear day you can see all the way to the Snæfellsjökull glacier at the tip of the Snæfellsnes peninsula, as well as the entirety of Reykjavík.

THE SELTJARNARNES–HEIÐMÖRK PATHWAY

When the wind isn't blowing too strongly, the flat surrounds of Reykjavík lend themselves to **cycling** and an excellent, well-marked **pathway** has been laid from the western suburb of Seltjarnarnes via the domestic airport, Öskjuhlíð (see p.63) and the Elliðaárdalur valley, named after the Elliðaá, one of Iceland's best salmon-fishing rivers, to Heiðmörk, a city park immediately east of the it – this route is clearly marked on the excellent *Map of Reykjavík* available from the tourist office (see p.46); for bike rental, see p.47. The salmon season itself runs from April to September and **fishing permits** must be ordered several months in advance of your arrival in Iceland via the tourist office in Reykjavík – reckon on a hefty 6000kr to 10,000kr per day depending on location. Trout fishing is much cheaper – generally 500kr to 6000kr per day – and permits can be obtained at short notice.

East of Öskjuhlíð, the path itself follows the river as it flows into Elliðaárvatn, the largest lake within Greater Reykjavík. Formed thousands of years ago when an outflow of lava dammed the glacial valley here, the lake is 174m above sea level and therefore surrounded by Arctic flora; a walking trail leads around Elliðaárvatn and takes around three hours to complete. Elliðaárdalur, is one of Reykjavík's main **horse-riding** areas – riding tours are booked through the tourist office in Reykjavík with trips varying in length from under an hour to a full day. Bordering the eastern shores of the lake, Heiðmörk, the largest and most popular recreational area in the city, is set between mountains, craters and lavafields and offers 2800 square hectare of forested expanses ideal for mountain biking or hiking – extensive planting began in 1949 to try to avert severe soil erosion from overgrazing and the harsh climate. Walking and cycle paths criss-cross the wooded expanses, dotted with picnic sites, making the area a favourite spot during summer weekends for Reykjavík's inhabitants.

Before leaving the *Perlan*, make sure you see the artificial indoor **geyser simulator** that erupts every few minutes from the basement, shooting a powerful jet of water all the way to the fourth floor it's a good taste of what's to come if you're heading out to the real thing at Geysir (see p.94).

Öskjuhlíð itself was also an important landmark in the days when the only mode of long-distance transport was the horse, as it stood out for miles across the barren surrounding plains – and more recently served as a military base for the British army during World War II. Today though, it's a popular recreation area for Reykjavíkers who, unused to being surrounded by expanses of woodland, flock here by foot and with mountain bikes to explore the **paths** that crisscross its slopes. Although it can be pretty crowded here on a sunny day, you'll easily be able to find a shady glade to call your own.

In fact, Öskjuhlíð has only been wooded since 1950, when an extensive forestation programme began after soil erosion had left the area barren and desolate. Today the western and southern areas of the hill are covered with birch, spruce, poplar and pine – parts of which are now an unofficial nude gay sunbathing area (see p.69). At the southern end of the hill at Nauthólsvík, on Nauthólsvegur road close to the Reykjavík Sailing Club, is an artifical beach of bright yellow sand where it's possible to swim in a sea-water pool, thanks to the addition of hundreds of gallons of geothermally heated sea water into the open-air **pool** (free; no facilities) next to the beach. As with the rest of Reykjavík, the hot water is piped here from the tanks atop the hill.

Eating and drinking

Eating in Reykjavík is expensive, although there are ways to reduce costs a little. Naturally, self-catering is the least costly of all, and the best **supermarkets** in the city centre include: 10–11, close to the Austurvöllur square at Austurstræti 17, which, true to its name, is open from 10am until 11pm; the larger Bónus, at Laugavegur 59; and the best-stocked and largest supermarket in the country, Nýkaup, in the Kringlan shopping centre, at the junction of Miklabraut and Kringlumýrarbraut and reached either on foot in about forty minutes or by taking bus #6 from the city centre. If you're looking to buy booze simply to take away, the **ÁTVR alcohol shops** are at Austurstræti 10a (Mon–Thurs 11am–6pm, Fri 11am–7pm, Sat 11am–2pm); and on the lower level of the Kringlan shopping centre (Mon–Thurs 11am–6pm, Fri 11am–7pm, Sat 11am–2pm). Supermarkets are also the best source of **breakfast** if your accommodation isn't providing any, since cafés generally don't open until around 10am – closing time is variable. Otherwise, expect to pay through the nose for it at one of the city's hotels, reckoning on at least 700kr a head for an extensive buffet selection of cold fish, smoked meats, toast, jam, cereals and coffee. For coffee and snacks during the day, use any of the numerous **cafés** dotted around, many of which mutate into **bars** from 6pm onwards, though this will leave a serious hole in your pocket – expect to pay around 1000kr per head for a cup of coffee, a sandwich and a cake. For a half-litre of beer be prepared to pay around 500kr.

For full meals, many **restaurants** offer lunch specials from 11.30am to 2.30pm. These may be either set dishes or help-yourself buffets costing around 1100kr – look out for "*tilboðsréttir*" or "tourist menu" either posted up in the window or on a display board outside. These generally include a starter such as soup, a meat or fish dish, followed by coffee. If your budget stretches to it (upwards of 3000kr a head), however, you can dine in style in small, atmospheric and high-quality restaurants, though you'll often need to make a reservation for Friday or Saturday evenings in summer, and dress fairly smartly. Most open for dinner around 6.30pm or 7pm and stay open until midnight or 1am on weekday evenings and Sundays, extending their hours until around 3am on Friday and Saturday evenings. There are some decent restaurants around the city serving **international** cuisines, such as Mexican or Mediterranean, though they're no cheaper than the Icelandic ones and are usually of a poorer standard, though a few do surprise. If you're longing for a curry, you'll only be disappointed – Indian food is bland in the extreme, aimed at the Icelandic palate, which has yet to come to grips with lots of spices. There are also a number of similarly priced **fast-food** outlets serving burgers and pizzas, but none is particularly cheap: the *McDonald's* in Reykjavík, for example, is one of the most expensive of its kind in the world.

Cafés

Brennslan, Pósthússtræti, ☎561 3600. Good-value brasserie overlooking Austurvöllur square, with excellent sandwiches from 450kr, tortillas from 650kr, chicken and chips 900kr, or grilled salmon with marinated vegetables in a balsamic and ginger sauce for 890kr. It's a good place for an evening drink, with over 100 different beers to choose between.

Café Ozio, Lækjargata 6a. Friendly restaurant and good bar, especially popular in the evenings with twenty- to thirty-somethings. Soup is 690kr, Greek salad 790kr, cheeseburgers 790kr and lasagne 890kr. It also has really good-value grilled lamb – just 1690kr, with herb sauce and salad. Cocktails cost 850kr and a glass of house red is 550kr, a bottle costs 1950kr. A popular drinking establishment by evening.

Café Paris, corner of Þósthússtræti and Austurstræti. French-style café, with outdoor seating in summer overlooking the Alþingi. Fine central choice for a cup of coffee or a light snack.

Café Victor, Hafnarstræti 1–3. Bistro bar and café in one of the capital's oldest buildings, which once served as the Danish king's falcon house (see p.54). Soup is 350kr, beer from 450kr or full meals from 1100kr. Try the divine oven-baked monkfish with green olive, feta cheese, garlic, tomato and herb sauce for 1150kr. Great ambience by evening, when the café turns into a bar.

Grái Kötturinn, Hverfisgata 16a. Smoky, friendly basement café, good for meeting young Reykjavíkers who come here for the excellent coffee. Open from 8am for breakfast.

Kaffi List, Laugavegur 20A. Immediately recognisable by its huge pink neon sign over the door. Locals love this smart café with a Spanish touch serving tapas and open sandwiches. Count on 1200kr for lunch. Also a lively spot for an evening drink or two.

Kaffi Reykjavík, Vesturgata 2 (☎562 5530). An excellent and popular choice for lunch (soup and a fish dish for 790kr) or dinner. Try the delicious peppered catfish for 1680kr or, more adventurously, the fried guillemot in blue cheese sauce at 1640kr. A bottle of house red is 2300kr; a sound choice for a beer, at 550kr.

Kaffibarinn, Bergstaðastræti. Trades on the rumour that Damon Alburn of Blur has shares in the place – however unlikely. A single ugly building covered in red corrugated iron with green window frames and brown wooden blinds though worth it for the curiosity value. A trendy place for a beer or two.

Kaffivagninn, Grandargarður 10. A little shack down by the harbour, popular with local fishermen who come here for an early morning breakfast – indeed, this is the only place serving breakfast so early, opening at 6am. The menu changes daily but generally offers fish, stew and soup dishes of the day, and while the food may be plain and unadorned, the working atmosphere is great. Open until 7pm.

Mokka, Skólavörðustígur 3a. The oldest café in Reykjavík with a changing display of black-and-white photographs adorning the walls. The place makes a point of not playing music and was the first café in the country to serve espressos and cappuccinos to its curious clientele. Coffee costs 220kr, sandwiches from 310kr. Recommended.

Sólon Íslandus, Bankastræti 7a. Reykjavík's best café, enjoying a perfect position on the main shopping street for people watching. Marble tables and gilt mirrors make for a truly relaxing afternoon over a cafetiere and a piece of chocolate cake.

Restaurants

Á Næstu Grösum, Laugavegur 20b, close to the junction with Klapparstígur. Tasty vegetarian food, with most of the ingredients coming from geothermally heated greenhouses in southern Iceland. The hours are rather short, however – Mon–Fri 11.20am–2pm & 6–10pm, Sun 6–10pm.

Amigos, Tryggvagata 8, ☎511 1333. A decent and relatively inexpensive Mexican place – if you don't mind the fake cacti everywhere – at the corner of Nordurstígur and Myrargata. Nachos for 855kr or enchiladas for 1320kr.

Apótek, corner of Austurstræti and Þósthússtræti. A stylishly modern café, bar and grill restaurant with white-panelled chairs, wooden flooring and top-notch food. Lunch here, consisting of a set fish dish, is particularly good value at around 1100kr.

Einar Ben, Veltusund 1, ☎511 5090. Elegant dining with chandeliers, heavy red drapes, soft lighting – and prices to match. Whale steak with black pepper, dates and rosemary sauce is 1950kr.

Eldsmiðjan, Bragagata 38a. The best pizzas in Reykjavík, from 800kr, made in a real pizza oven that burns Icelandic birchwood. In a backstreet near the Hallgrímskirkja church but definitely worth looking out.

Grænn Kostur, Skólavördustígur 8. Fantastic spicy vegetarian eat-in meals and takeaway, using fresh ingredients and offering a wide variety of dishes. It is annoyingly hard to find, however – turn off Skólavördustígur when you see the sign for the multistorey car park, and it's on your right hand side in the small parade of shops.

Gröf, Aðalstræti 10, ☎551 6323. An atmospheric place located in the oldest building in Reykjavík, with small wooden tables and a very low ceiling, serving expensive seafood and lamb. Open for dinner only from 6pm.

Hornið, Hafnarstræti 4, ☎511 3233. A very popular place with young Reykjavíkers, who flock here for the excellent pizzas (from 850kr) and pasta (from 1320kr). The fish here is also good: dishes are often Italian-inspired, such as the cod with tomatoes and olives (1580kr). Wine here can be inordinately expensive – check carefully before ordering.

Humarhúsið, Amtmannsstígur 1, ☎561 3303. *The* place to eat lobster in Reykjavík, although it is hideously expensive: lobstertails with spinach and saffron orange sauce will set you back a mighty 3360kr. The tasteful décor resembles a homely dining room and even comes complete with a mantelpiece clock.

Ítalia, Laugavegur 11, ☎552 4630. Expensive and average Italian restaurant serving pizzas from 1250kr and pasta from 1350kr.

Jómfrúin, Lækjargata 4. Good choice for lunch, and popular with visiting Scandinavians for its open Danish sandwiches. Rye bread with fried plaice, smoked salmon with caviar, shrimps, asparagus and lemon is fantastic value at 720k.

Naust, Vesturgata 6–8, ☎551 7759. Over eighty excellent fish dishes. served up in a high-seas atmosphere, the dark interior strewn with fishing nets. Dinner only from 6pm.

Pizza 67, Tryggvagata 26. The Reykjavík branch of the pizza chain you'll become well acquainted with on your travels around Iceland. A lunchtime pizza costs around 790kr, though prices rise in the evening,when they start at 900kr. Don't try the meat and fish dishes here – frankly they're too expensive for the rather bland and dingy surroundings.

Skólabrú, Skólabrú 1, ☎562 4455. An old wooden building from 1906, covered in corrugated iron, houses this renowned fish restaurant. Inside the grandfather clock and lace curtains give a homely feel to the restaurant whose fish is especially succulent – try the pan-fried monkfish in fresh pineapple and mango sauce for 1890kr.

Svarta Pannan, corner of Tryggvagata and Þósthússtræti. Slightly dingy-looking but a reliable – and cheap – fast-food outlet with fish and chips for 750kr, burger and chips for 650kr. Alternatively, soup and a turn at the salad bar is 500kr.

Tres Locos, Laugavegur 11, corner with Smidjustígur. Good Mexican food in the centre of town. Chicken enchilladas cost 1300kr, chimichanga is 1400kr.

Vegamót, Vegamótastígur 4, ☎511 3040. A favourite hangout for Reykjavík's trendy young things, who come here for the excellent lunches – chicken burritos are 950kr or lamb brochettes go for 990kr. A popular place for dinner, too, but reckon on 1500kr for a main fish or meat dish.

Við Tjörnina, Templarsund 3, ☎551 8666. One of the best fish restaurants in Reykjavík divided into quaint, cluttered rooms – the interior design reminiscent of an Icelandic grandmother's front room. Daring and delicious cuisine: everything from pan-fried fish cheeks on a bed of cajun-spiced vegetables to charcoal grilled redfish with bananas. If you fancy meat, there's raw smoked guillemot or lightly pan-fried heart of lamb.

Þrir Frakkar, Baldursgata 14, ☎552 3939. Backstreet French-style bistro using purely Icelandic ingredients for its traditional dishes: whale peppersteak 1990kr or pan-fried sole with gorgonzola sauce 1680kr. The traditional *plokkfiskur* (fish and potato mash) is excellent, as is the salted cod with tangy caper and red onion sauce.

Nightlife and entertainment

Thanks to some cunning publicity from the Icelandic Tourist Board, **nightlife** in Reykjavík is now deservedly known across Europe and the States for its partying. Although the scene is actually no bigger than that of any small-sized town in most other countries, what sets it apart is the northerly setting and location for all this revelry – in summer, it's very disorientating to have entered a nightclub in the wee small hours with the sun just about to set, only to emerge a couple of hours

---

WRECKED IN REYKJAVÍK

A rite of passage for all Icelandic teenagers, the **runtur** (literally "round tour") is a drunken pub crawl that generally takes place between at least half a dozen bars and pubs, whatever the weather. Intent on searching out the place with the hottest action, groups of revellers, already well oiled after downing several generous vodkas before setting out, maraud the city centre, particularly on Friday nights. If you come across them, expect to be engaged in conversation or to see some rather unrestrained behaviour – but then nightlife in Iceland isn't known for its subtleties.

---

later (and several thousand krónur poorer) into the blinding and unflattering daylight of the Icelandic morning. Very few people are out much before 10pm, after which time crowds fill the streets and queues develop outside the most popular joints. The light nights mean that summer partying often rarely winds up before 5am or 6am, and it's certainly not uncommon to see hordes of drunken youngsters staggering around Lækjartorg at 4am shivering in the cold air dressed, fashion-consciously, only in their latest T-shirts and jeans – and often in much less.

You'll need plenty of cash for even a few **drinks** (a beer in a club costs upward of 500kr) – and don't be tempted to leave your drink on the bar whilst you go dancing, as the chances are it'll have been drunk by the time you return. Admission fees to **clubs** are not too steep, generally around 300–400kr. As you'd expect, things are liveliest on Friday and Saturday nights, when most places swing until 5 or 6am; closing time the rest of the week is around.

Bars, pubs and clubs

The best spots to start socializing are **bars** and **pubs**, as well as some of the cafés listed on p.65 that turn into bars after 6pm. Remember that, whatever your tradition at home, you won't be expected to buy a round of drinks if you're in company, since that would be virtually ruinous, and that it's quite permissible to nurse one drink through the entire evening. Some of the bars listed below are attached to restaurants but you can always drink without eating.

Don't expect to get into a **club** in style-conscious Reykjavík if you turn up in full hiking gear – the **dress code** is generally smart and Icelandic men often don a tie to go out clubbing. For foreigners things are more relaxed, but you'll feel more comfortable if you're smart-casual. At some places, jeans and sneakers aren't allowed. However you're kitted out, don't be surprised if you're approached and chatted-up as soon as you've set foot through the door.

22, Laugavegur 22. Bar on the main street, with a small dancefloor on the second floor. Once very popular, it's now rather quiet and so is a good place if you want to chat over a beer.

Astro, Austurstræti 22. A smart club full of wannabe yuppies gyrating to the latest sounds on the upstairs glass dancefloor. No jeans or white trainers allowed.

Dubliner, Hafnarstræti 4. Traditional Irish bar with wooden tables and floor. A popular place for an evening pint of Guinness or a beer (500kr). There's also a decent selection of whiskies at 350kr per shot.

Gaukur á Stöng, Tryggvagata 22. The closest thing to a traditional British watering hole, billing itself as Iceland's oldest pub – true enough since it's been plying liquor to the masses since 1985.

Hótel Ísland, Ármúli 9. The disco, *Broadway*, inside is prone to Vegas-style singing and dancing spectaculars, though occasionally with more interesting fare and popular with people of all ages, from teenagers to pensioners.

Kaffi Thomsen, Hafnarstræti 17. More bar than café, with bright neon lights and a dance-floor – though don't expect anyone to be in here much before 11pm.

Nellys, Þingholtsstræti 2–4. American-style bar with a mixed gay and straight crowd, especially at weekends, open till 1am daily and serving Iceland's cheapest beer at 290kr a glass – so understandably popular.

Rex, Austurstræti 9. One of the most chic brasseries in town, with interior design by the UK's Sir Terence Conran, featuring wall mirrors, ornate steel roof supports and an illuminated glass bar. In short, a must.

Samtökin, Laugavegur 3. The best place for gay men and women to meet up – if the other places listed are quiet, the chances are there'll always be someone here.

Sirkus, Klapparstígur 31. Reykjavík's first French wine bar, in an unprepossessing building off Laugavegur. French wine is available by the glass, as is pastis and calvados. Busy at weekends with a Bohemian clientele who don't mind queuing to get in.

Spotlight, Hverfisgata 8–10. Reykjavík's busiest nightclub, with a sizeable dancefloor. Popular also with the capital's gay population on Friday and Saturday nights. *The* place to be seen, and something of a pickup joint, with lots of dark corners hiding roaming hands.

Þjódleikhúskjallarinn, Hverfisgata. Despite its unpronounceable name, the basement café underneath the National Theatre transforms itself into a popular club playing 1970–80s music on Fri and Sat nights (midnight to 3am).

Gay Reykjavík

Although a **gay scene** does exist in Reykjavík, it is very small and at times crashingly provincial in style and scale. There are just three exclusively gay **bars** in the capital – the best choice is the **Samtökin** bar, café and gay library all rolled into one at Laugavegur 3 (☎552 7878, *www.gayiceland.com*), which welcomes lesbians and gay men. To enter, walk through the arch and use the same door as the Norræna travel agency, then take the lift to the fourth floor. A popular and recommended place to meet other gay people is the new – and therefore trendy – *Mannsbar* at Vegamótastígur 4 – this place looks set to become the main meeting place for gay men and women in Reykjavík. The only other option is the smoky, male-only *MSC* leather bar in Ingólfsstræti – ring the bell through the black metal gate opposite the *Sólon Íslandus* café to gain entrance here. Other than the predominantly straight clubs and bars (see opposite), which attract a small but dedicated gay following on Friday and Saturday nights, other places to meet gay men include the sauna at the Vesturbær **swimming pool** (see p.71), and Öskjuhlíð (see p.64), the unofficial nude male-only **sunbathing area** on the western slopes of this wooded hill opposite the *Hótel Loftleiðir*. From the front of the hotel, head for the wide walking and cycling path that runs through the trees around the hill, leaving the path after two to three minutes to cut down towards the edge of the trees.

Gay Pride has no fixed schedule but is always held over a weekend sometime in the summer, generally July or August. It's a small-scale affair, with a procession through the city centre, an evening of dancing and merrymaking and other cultural activities. For further information contact Samtökin (see above).

Live music, theatre and cinema

There's been a strong **rock** music network in Reykjavík for over two decades, represented originally by Björk and the Sugarcubes, and more recently by groups such as Gus Gus, though decent venues have always been thin on the ground, with most gigs taking place in one of the city's restaurants. Besides the local talent, a lot of British and American acts use Icelandair as a cheap way to cross the Atlantic and they often do a show here on the way. Find out what's on by checking with the tourist information office (see p.46) or by looking through their free handout *What's on in Reykjavík*. The following establishments (pubs and hotel) often have live music at weekends, offering anything from jazz to rock: *Dubliner*, at Hafnarstræti 4; *Gaukur á Stöng*, at Tryggvagata 22; *Gröf*, at Aðalstræti 10; and the *Hótel Borg*, at Þósthússtræti 11.

Remarkably, for such a small city, Reykjavík boasts several **theatre** groups, an opera, a symphony orchestra and a dance company. Unfortunately, major theatre productions and classical concerts, by the **Icelandic Symphony Orchestra**, are a rarity in summer, but throughout the rest of the year there are full programmes of both. Events are chiefly held at the *Þjódleikhúsið* (☎551 1200), the National Theatre on Hverfisgata, or the *Háskólabíó* cinema complex (☎562 2255), home to the Symphony Orchestra, off Suðurgata. The **Icelandic Opera** (☎511 4200) is at Ingólfsstræti, and the **City Theatre** (☎568 8000) at Listabraut.

The **cinema** is a better bet if you have time on your hands and little money in your pocket: new international releases are screened with subtitles. Admission is generally 700kr; see any of the newspapers (see Basics, p.33) for full **listings** or call the following cinemas direct: Bíóborgin, Snorrabraut 37 (☎551 1384 or ☎52 5211); Regnboginn, Hverfisgata 54 (☎551 9000); Háskólabíó, on Hagatorg, off Suðurgata (☎530 1919); and Stjörnubíó, Laugavegur 94 (☎551 6500). Háskólabíó is the biggest and best but they're all of a high standard. More unusual is the worthwhile **Volcano Show** at Hellusund 6a (☎551 3230), a three-hour set of films in two showings of recent Icelandic eruptions from daringly close quarters (part one 650kr, part two 850kr). Part one screenings (1hr) begin at 3pm and 8pm year round, with additional shows in summer, with part two (2hr) following at 4.15pm and 9.15pm. Commentary is in English.

Activities

The **swimming pool** is to the Icelanders what the pub is to the British or the coffee shop is to Americans. This is the place to come when in Reykjavík to meet people, catch up on the local gossip and to relax in divine geothermally heated waters. The locals loll around in the pools for hours, as there is no time limit on how long you can stay in the pool. Entrance fees are around 200kr.

Although Reykjavík is surrounded by superb **hiking** terrain, much of it is difficult to reach without your own transport. However, two excellent areas, both accessible by bus, lie within east striking distance of the capital. **Hengill**, south of Reykjavík on the Ringroad towards Selfoss, offers the best hiking opportunities around Reykjavík, whereas **Mount Esja**, between Reykjavík and Akranes, offers steep climbs and superb views from its slopes of the Greater Reykjavík region.

Lastly, there are several opportunites for **skiing** at **Bláfjöll**, **Skálafell** and **Hamragil**, all of which are suitable for varying levels of expertise, from beginner upwards.

Swimming
The abundance of natural hot water around the capital means there's a good choice of **swimming pools**, which are always at a comfortably warm 29°C, often with hot pots at 39–43°C. **Opening hours** during April to September are gener-

ally from 6.30am until around 10pm Monday to Friday, and from 8am or so until 6 or 7pm Saturday and Sunday, while outside these months they may open an hour later and close an hour earlier than this. Remember you must shower without a swimming costume before entering the pools and thoroughly wash the areas of your body marked on the signs by the showers – because pool water in Iceland doesn't contain large amounts of chlorine to kill germs as is common in most other countries. The best three city-centre pools are: Laugardalur, on Sundlaugavegur and adjacent to the youth hostel (see p.49), Iceland's largest outdoor swimming complex, complete with fifty-metre pool, four hot pots, a jacuzzi, steam room, waterslide and masseuse; Sundhöllin, on Barónsstígur and close to Hallgrímskirkja, with an indoor 25-metre pool, two outdoor hot pots, plus single-sex nude sunbathing on outdoor terraces; and Vesturbær, on Hofsvallagata, with an outdoor 25-metre pool plus three hot pots, a sauna, steam bath and solarium. Swimming costumes can be hired for a small charge at all three.

Hiking

Set in an area of lush vegetation, hot springs (harnessed by the Reykjavík District Heating Company to provide central heating for the capital) and volcanic activity, **Hengill** has around 125km of well-marked hiking trails, all detailed on free **maps** available at the tourist information centre in Reykjavík (see p.46). Hengill mountain, which dominates the area, is in fact a volcanic ridge that has erupted several times in the past, and the surrounding area is made up of numerous lavafields, craters, hot springs and bubbling mud pools – it's therefore vital to follow marked paths that have been carefully laid out. To get here, take the 9am long-distance **bus** to Selfoss and ask the driver to let you off at the bottom of the Hveradala hill at Kolvidarhóll, from where you can start hiking, choosing a route that fits your time available and physical ability. To return to the capital, head back for the Ringroad and catch the 4pm bus coming back from Selfoss.

Proudly standing guard over Reykjavík, **Mount Esja** is a familiar sight to anyone who's spent even a few hours in the capital. At 909m, the mountain appears to change colour – from light purple to deep blue, from light grey to golden – depending on the prevailing weather conditions and the light that reflects on the basalt rock and palagonite minerals which make up the mountain, although locals say it depends on her mood. Several hiking trails wind their way around the mountain – once again, a detailed **itinerary** is available from the tourist office – but it's best to start out at Mógilsá where the Icelandic state forestry station has it base. From here an easy path leads up the mountain towards the rocky higher stretches.

Skiing

Although **skiing** is possible in the Reykjavík area, there's so little daylight during the winter period that the amount of time you can actually spend skiing in the day is severely limited. For winter **bus** times to all of the ski areas below, call ☎552 2300.

Thirty minutes by car or bus outside the capital there are three winter downhill skiing areas. The best of the bunch is **Bláfjöll** or Blue Mountains, 20km away with five ski areas of varying difficulty. For cross-country skiing there are tracks of 3–10km, with night skiing available on a five-kilometre route. Get here by taking the Ringroad east until you see a sign for Bláfjöll – turn right onto Route 417 and follow the signs to the mountains.

Skálafell lies to the northeast of Reykjavík and, once again, has beginner, intermediate and advanced hills though it isn't as extensive as Bláfjöll. Incidentally, if you're a fan of chairlifts, you'll find Iceland's longest here at 1500m. Excellent cross-country skiing is also available. From the capital take the Ringroad north until you see a sign for Þingvellir, turn right onto Route 36 and continue until you see a sign for Skálafell, finally turn left into the ski area.

Heading east on the Ringroad for around twenty minutes until just beyond the turn for Route 39 – don't take this road but continue one minute beyond it and turn into the ski area marked on the left – brings you to the **Hamragil** skiing area with its seven ski lifts. Pistes of varying degrees of difficulty are available here, as are some decent cross-country routes.

Listings

Airlines Air Atlanta, Álafossvegur (☎515 7700); Flugfélag Íslands, Reykjavík city airport (☎570 3030); Icelandair (switchboard ☎505 0300, departure and arrival information ☎505 0500, international ticket sales ☎505 0100); Íslandsflug, Reykjavík city airport (☎570 8090).

American Express, Lágmúli 4 (☎568 2050).

ÁTVR alcohol store Austurstræti 10a (Mon–Thurs 11am–6pm, Fri 11am–7pm, Sat 11am–2pm).

Banks and exchange Búnadarbanki Íslands, Austurstræti 5; Íslandsbanki, Bankastræti 5; Landsbanki Íslands, Austurstræti 11; The Change Group, Tourist Information Office Bankastræti 2.

Bookshops Bóksala Stúdenta, Hringbraut; and Eymundsson, Austurstræti 18; Mál og Menning, Laugavegur 18, both sell English-language books and videos on Iceland, Icelandic–English dictionaries and foreign newspapers.

Car rental AB Bílaleiga, Smíðjuvegur 24c (☎557 1831); ALP, Skemmuvegur 20, Kópavogur (☎567 0722); Bílahöllin, Bíldshöfði 5 (☎587 1390); Bílaleigan Geysir, Dugguvogur 10 (☎568 8888); Hasso-Ísland, Hringbraut 62 (☎555 3340); Hertz, Flugvallabraut (☎505 0600).

Dentist For the duty dentist call ☎575 0505. English spoken.

Embassies and consulates Canada, Suðurlandsbraut 10 (☎568 0820); Denmark, Hverfisgata 29 (☎562 1230); Finland, Túngata 30 (☎510 0100); Norway, Fjólugata 17 (☎520 0700); Sweden, Lágmúli 7 (☎520 1230); UK, Laufásvegur 31 (☎550 5100); USA, Laufásvegur 21 (☎562 9100).

Emergencies Fire, ambulance and police ☎112.

Ferries Norræna travel agency, Laugavegur 3 (☎562 6392), for the Smyril Line ferry from Seydisfjörður to the Faroe Islands, the Shetland Islands, Norway and Denmark; Eimskip, Þósthússtræti 2 (☎525 7000); Viðey island, from Sundahöfn (☎568 6199).

Laundry Þvottahúsið Emla, Barónsstígur 3 (☎552 7499).

Lost property Police headquarters, Hverfisgata 113–115 (☎569 9020).

News in English Channel One, FM 92.4 & 93.5 (June–Aug daily 7.30am), or call ☎515 3690; Klassík FM, FM 100.7, carries BBC World Service news Mon–Fri at 9am, midday and 3pm.

Pharmacies Háaleitisapótek, Háaleitisbraut 68 (24hr; ☎581 2101); Lyfjaapótek, Lágmúli 5, near the youth hostel at Laugardalur (9am–midnight; ☎533 2300).

Police Tryggvagata 19 (☎569 9025).

Post office Þósthússtræti 3–5 (☎580 1000; Mon–Fri 10am–4.30pm).

Travel agents BSÍ, Vatnsmyrarvegur 10 (☎562 3320) for bus excursions; Norræna, Laugavegur 3 (☎562 6392), for the Smyril Line ferry from Seydisfjörður; Útivist, Hallveigarstígur (☎561 4330), for excursions and plane tickets.

Out from the city: Greater Reykjavík

Home to three out of every five Icelanders, **Greater Reykjavík** is composed of the neighbouring municipalities of **Seltjarnarnes**, northwest of the city centre, **Mosfellsbær** to the northeast, and, in the southwest **Hafnafjörður, Garðabær** and **Kópavogur**, the last three of which are passed through by the road into the city centre from from Keflavík airport.

Comprising row upon row of neat, tidy suburban dwellings of dormitory over-spill for Reykjavík, all but Hafnafjörður hold little of interest to the visitor. During the past twenty or thirty years several of these places, in particular Kópavogur and Garðabær, have grown enormously, sending shivers down the spines of city planners and politicians in Reykjavík who admit to fighting a losing battle to stem the flow of people from the villages and towns in the rest of the country, and new tax breaks and other incentives are constantly being dreamed up to prevent population overload – and ever-rising prices – in Reykjavík. Whether these measures succeed in the long term remains to be seen.

Hafnafjörður

Stealing the limelight from its neighbours thanks to its dramatic setting amid an extensive lavafield, **Hafnafjörður**, with a population of around 19,000 and just 10km from the capital, is as big as the centre of Reykjavík, although it's not as likeable. The town's prosperity stems from its superbly sheltered harbour (Hafnafjörður meaning "the harbour fjord") – 7000 years ago the volcano, Búrfell (see p.106), around 5km east of the centre, erupted, spewing lava out along the northern side of the fjord which is now home to Hafnafjörður, creating a protective wall. At the beginning of the fifteenth century the village became a strategic centre for trade with England, which was then just starting up, and the harbour was often full of English fishing boats profiting from the then rich fishing grounds immediately offshore. Just seventy-five years later, a dispute broke out between the English and newly arrived German fishermen who challenged, and won, the right to operate out of the burgeoning town. Their victory, however, was shortlived, since Hafnafjörður fell under the trade monopoly of the Danes in 1602, which lasted until 1787, when the place fell into obscurity. Today, apart from being the venue for the **International Viking Festival** (see box on p.74), the place is known for its inhabitants, called **hafnies**, being the unfortunate subjects of many an Icelandic joke – it's said, for example, that local children take ladders when they start at high school, which their parents also use to go shopping with if they hear that prices have gone up. Needless to say, Icelandic humour can be an acquired taste.

The **harbour** is the best place to start your wanderings. Home port for many of Iceland's ocean-going trawlers, it's interesting enough just watching the bustle as fishermen land their catches, wash down their vessels and mend their nets. Here, the arts centre **Hafnarborg** (Wed–Mon midday–6pm; 300kr, free on Mon), is at Strandgata 34. In a fit of generosity the building was donated to the town by a local chemist and his wife in 1983 and today exhibits work by local Icelandic artists as well as doubling as a concert venue – it's worth a quick look, but you're more likely to satisfy your artisitic appetite in Reykjavík.

A stone's throw from here, one block to the north of the harbour, at Vesturgata 8, is the maritime museum, **Sjóminjasafn Íslands** (June–Sept daily 1–5pm; Oct–May Sat & Sun 1–5pm; 300kr) housed in an old wooden warehouse dating from the late

1800s. Inside is a passable if somewhat dull portrayal of Hafnafjörður's seafaring past, although it's the displays on Leifur Eiríksson and his discovery of Vínland that make the museum worthwhile. Next door, at Vesturgata 6, stands Sívertsens-Húsið, the town's oldest building, dated to 1803 and once the residence of local trader, boat builder and man about town Bjarni Sívertsen, today home to a **folk museum** (June–Aug daily 1–5pm; Sept–May Sat & Sun 1–5pm; 300kr). The interior is stuffed with how-we-used-to-live paraphernalia and can easily be skipped in favour of a stroll south along Fjarðargata to the roundabout and the junction with Strandgata for some excellent **views** of the harbour front.

From the harbour front itself it's a ten minute walk to a **viewpoint** at Hamarinn cliffs – to get there, retrace your steps past the harbour front along Strandgata to the junction with Lækjargata, head east along this road and take the footpath up the hill to the wall of lava you'll see, formed from an eruption in the nearby Búrfell volcano; this leads to the viewpoint. The protected wooded natural area up here offers good views out over the harbour and the surrounding countryside and is a pleasant place to have a picnic when the weather's good. Incidentally, the ugly red- and white-striped towers you can see from here, which totally dominate the surrounding flat landscape of lavafields, belong to the vast Swiss-owned aluminium smelter at Straumsvík, which imports its raw materials from Australia and uses local geothermal power to produce the metal.

Practicalities

From Lækjartorg and Hlemmur in the Reykjavík city centre, **bus** #140 runs to Hafnafjörður every twenty minutes Monday to Friday and every thirty minutes at weekends, stopping near the harbour at the **tourist office**, (mid-May to mid-Sept Mon–Fri 8.30am–5.30pm, Sat 9am–3pm, Sun noon–5pm; rest of the year Mon–Fri 1–4pm; ☎565 0661), at Vesturgata 8. When it comes to accommodation there are two **youth hostels** – the larger one, *Hraunbyrgi* (☎565 0900, fax ☎555 1211; 1700kr), is located in Vídistaðatún park on Flókagata, where there's also a **campsite**, (June–Aug; 350kr per person, plus 350kr per tent) with hot and cold running water. Closer to the centre at Strandgata 21, the *Arahús* hostel has a handful of rooms (1700kr) but also offers sleeping-bag accommodation. Hafnarfjörður also has a centrally located **guesthouse**: a small, nameless establishment at Lækjarkinn 2 (☎565 5132; ②) has a handful of rooms, with shared facilities including a kitchen.

THE INTERNATIONAL VIKING FESTIVAL

Undisputedly the best time to be in Hafnafjörður is late June when the **International Viking Festival** (*www.hafnarfjordur.is/vikings*) is held, an orgy of Viking feasts when whole animals are roasted on skewers over open fires, markets are stocked with everything from mead to horned helmets. Events such as wrestling, battles and storytelling also mark the event, which draws thousands of curious visitors keen to learn more about this potent part of Iceland's history. Although the festival can be a little staged and cheesy, it's certainly worth making the effort to see – the spectacle dominates news bulletins for days around the time of the festival. It's held on the open land of **Vídistadatún**, next to the campsite; from the tourist office it's an easy ten-minute walk west on Vesturgata and then north on Flókagata.

Unusually for provincial Iceland, **eating** throws up a wealth of opportunities, but by far the best option is the Viking-theme restaurant, *Fjörukráin*, at Strandgata 50, occupying a cavernous, dimly lit wooden structure dating from 1841. This is the place in Iceland to sample traditional Viking fare: rotten shark and singed sheep's heads are just some of the delicacies on offer. Although it's bit on the tacky side, it's well worth a visit. More conventionally, there's a *Pizza 67* at Reykjavíkurvegur 60, or the respectable *Gafl-Inn* at Dalshraun 13, which serves up sandwiches, fish and meat dishes at reasonable prices – reckon on 1100kr for fish. If you're craving something non-Icelandic, head for *Singapore*, beyond Pizza 67 at Reykjavíkurvegur 68, which has half-decent southeast Asian food; note, however, that these last three are all a good twenty-minute walk from the centre. For excellent fish there's *Tilveran*, in the centre of town at Linnetsstígur 1 – the cod here is particularly good – or the nearby *A Hansen* which also has delicious seafood as well as lamb and meat dishes. For a good **café**, head for *Café Kænan* at Óseyrarbraut 2, which is popular with the fishermen from the nearby harbour – or if the smoking here is too much, there's the smoke-free coffeehouse, *Nönnukot*, at Mjósund 2, where they do some excellent home-made cakes.

Viðey and Lundey

In the Kollafjörður inlet, a nature reserve immediately north of the Laugardalur area of Reykjavík, lies **Viðey** (Wood Island – though it's no longer forested), an island not with a rich historical backdrop. Actually the top of a now extinct volcano and measuring barely 1.7 square kilometres, the land here was first claimed by Reykjavík's original settler, **Ingólfur Arnarson** as part of his estate. Archeological studies have shown that Viðey was inhabited during the tenth century and that a church was located here sometime in the twelfth century, but it was for the Augustinian monastery, consecrated here in 1225, that Viðey is better known. However, the island's monks fled when, in 1539, representatives of the Danish king proclaimed Viðey property of the Lutheran royal crown. Barely eleven years later, in 1550, Iceland's last Catholic bishop, **Jón Arason**, regained possession of the island through an armed campaign, restored the monastery and built a fort here to defend the island from his Lutheran enemies. Little did that help, however, and in the same year, Arason was beheaded and the Reformation, taking place across mainland Europe, began in Iceland.

Two centuries of peace ensued and in 1751 Viðey was given to the royal treasurer and sheriff, **Skúli Magnússon**, with the Rococo-style Viðeyjarstofa, Iceland's first stone building, being built as his residence four years later. In 1817, the island passed into the ownership of the President of High Court, **Magnús Stephensen**, who brought Iceland's only printing press to Viðey, furthering the tiny place's claim as the country's main centre of culture – a reputation that spread from the establishment of the island's Augustinian monastery. Following several more changes of ownership, the City of Reykjavík finally bought the island in 1983.

A short walk up the path from the jetty where the ferry (see below) deposits you is **Viðeyjarstofa**, Skúli Magnússon's residence, the oldest building in the country and now functioning as an expensive but excellent restaurant. Maintained in its original stone form, it was designed in simple Rococco style by the architect who worked on the Amalienborg royal palace in Copenhagen, and the outer walls are made of basalt and sandstone whilst the interior is of Danish brick and timber. Standing next to the restaurant is a **church**, consecrated in 1774, the second oldest in Iceland, and worth a glance inside for its original interior furnishings. Walk east of here to the site of the old fort, Virkid, of which nothing now remains, to see the Skúli Magnússon **monument** (he died here in 1794) and **Danadys** (Danes' Grave), the final resting place for a number of Danish citizens who lived on the island over the centuries.

Other than these few attractions there's little to do on Viðey than enjoy the spectacular views of the mainland and take a stroll on one of the many **paths** that lead around the island. From Viðeyjarstofa, a road heads beyond the island's schoolhouse to the easternmost point, from where a path takes over, following the south coast back towards the ferry jetty, skirting a protected area (closed May & June), home to thousands of nesting birds. Alternatively, from the easternmost point, a track leads back along the north coast past the restaurant and out to the northwestern part of the island, **Vesturey**, a peninsula connected to Heimaey by the small isthmus, Eiði.

North of Viðey is **Lundey**, a tiny steep-sided islet renowned for its staggeringly large population of puffins – it's name means "Puffin Island" – and although it's only possible to see the island as part of an boat cruise (see below) and it's not possible to go ashore, it's still a truly remarkable experience, home to the only **puffin colony** near the capital. From the boat you'll have a great view of the cliffs and grassy slopes which make up the island's sides and the burrows where the puffins live. The smell of guano here is also very strong.

Both islands are easily accessible from Sundahöfn harbour, northeast of Laugardalur and reached by buses #4 from Lækjartorg (see p.46) and #9 from Hlemmur (see p.52) in the city centre. From the harbour, the **ferry to Viðey** (June–Sept Mon–Fri 1pm & 2pm, Sat & Sun every 60min 1–5pm; plus extra sailings Thurs, Fri, Sat & Sun at 7pm, 7.30pm & 8pm) takes just seven minutes. **Boat cruises to Lundey** depart weather permitting (mid-June to mid-August Mon, Wed & Fri 4.45pm; 3000kr) and last 90 minutes to two hours. The boats circle the island several times to give you a good chance to see the puffins up close, clinging to the cliff tops and diving into the sea in search of food. On the return journey they put in at Viðey for about forty minutes before continuing back to Sundahöfn. Bookings are necessary and should be made at the tourist office on Bankastræti (see p.46).

travel details

Buses

The bus details given below are relevant for May to September; for winter times, visit *www.bsi.is*.

Reykjavík to: Akranes (3 daily; 50min); Akureyri (daily; 6hr); Blönduós (daily; 4hr); Blue Lagoon (3 daily; 40min); Borgarnes (3 daily; 1hr10min); Búðardalur (4 weekly; 4hr); Brú (daily; 2hr); Gullfoss/Geysir (daily; 2hr30min); Höfn (daily; 7hr); Hólmavík (3 weekly; 6hr); Ísafjörður (3 weekly; 10hr); Ólafsvík (daily; 3hr); Sauðárkrókur (3 weekly; 5hr); Siglufjörður (3 weekly; 7hr); Skaftafell (daily; 6hr); Stykkishólmur (daily; 2hr30min); Þingvellir (daily; 50min); Þorlákshöfn (daily; 1hr).

Flights

Reykjavík to: Akureyri (7 daily; 50min); Bíldudalur (daily; 40min); Egilsstaðir (3 daily; 1hr); Höfn (2 daily; 1hr); Ísafjörður (3 daily; 40min); Sauðárkrókur (2 daily; 45min); Vestmannæjar (3 daily; 30min).

Ferries

Reykjavík to: Viðey (June–Sept Mon–Fri 2 daily, Sat & Sun 5 daily; 10min).

CHAPTER TWO

SOUTHWESTERN ICELAND

S pread either side of Reykjavík, southwestern Iceland comprises the lava-
ridden Reykjanes Peninsula, and the lakes, rifts, riverlands, glaciers,
islands and volcanoes lying east between the capital and the country's
southernmost reaches around the town of Vík. Despite barely extending
200km from end to end, nowhere else are Iceland's key elements of history and
the land so visibly intertwined, and it's a region that's as important to Icelanders
as it is to tour-group intineraries. Here you'll see where Iceland's original parliament was founded over a thousand years ago, sites that saw the violence of saga-
age dramas played out, together with the area where the country's earliest
churches became seats of power and learning. Culture aside, if you're expecting
the scenery this close to Reykjavík to be tame, think again: the southwest contains some of Iceland's most iconic and frequently explosive landscapes, memorable whether viewed as a simple backdrop to a day's drive around the sights or
treated as an excuse in their own right to spend a week trekking cross-country.

The southwest splits into four well-defined areas. Due east of Reykjavík, the
land drops steadily to the **Hvítá** river system, around which you'll find a clutch of
essential historical and geological features – the ancient parliament at Þingvellir
and Geysir's hot water spout are best known – strung out around an easy route
known as the **Golden Circle**. Just about every visitor to Iceland tackles this, but
far fewer delve southwest of Reykjavík into the Reykjanes Peninsula's less obviously appealing rubble and lava flats, though thermal springs and some fine coastline encourage a detour beyond the country's only international airport at
Keflavík. Further away to Reykjavík's southeast, beyond the Hvítá system you

ACCOMMODATION PRICE CODES

Throughout this guide, prices given for **youth hostels, sleeping-bag accommodation** and **campsites** are per person unless otherwise specified. **Hotel** and
guesthouse accommodation is graded on a scale from ① to ⑧; all are high-season
rates and indicate the cost of the cheapest double room. The price bands to which
these codes refer are as follows:

① Up to 4000kr	③ 6000–8000kr	⑤ 10,000–12,000kr	⑦ 15,000–20,000kr
② 4000–6000kr	④ 8000–10,000kr	⑥ 12,000–15,000kr	⑧ Over 20,000kr

(See p.26 for a full explanation.)

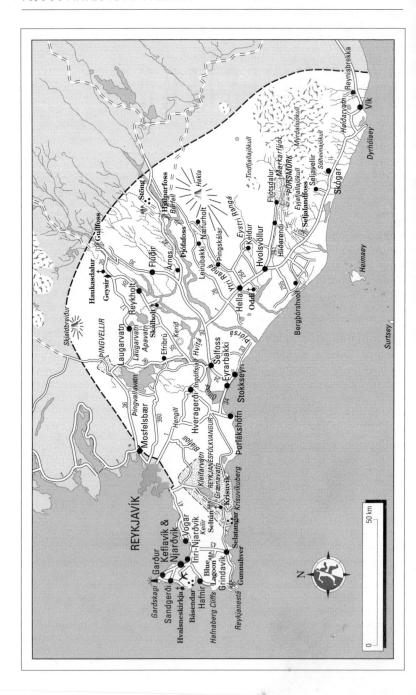

cross the much larger **Þórsá** – Iceland's longest river at 230km – and enter Iceland's **central south**. Dominating the inland scenery is the blasted landscape surrounding **Hekla**, one of the country's most violent volcanoes, while south of here towards the sea, views open up into the pleasant rolling farmland and boggy river plains of **Njál's Saga country**, dotted with ancient farms and landscapes from this most famous of tales. Head east again and you'll soon run up against the heights of the **Mýrdalsjökull** ice cap; mountainous outrunners descend right down to the coast from here, while highland valleys – especially those at **Þórsmörk** – provide some superlative hiking. These slopes end at the pleasant coastal village of **Vík**, which sits on the edge of extensive sand deserts stretching off into southeast Iceland. Offshore, a short ferry ride or flight from the mainland brings you to **Heimaey**, the small, intimate core of the **Westman islands**, alive with seabirds and further recent proof of Iceland's unstable vulcanology.

As a firmly settled, much-visited part of the country, the southwest enjoys good access and almost everything in the region can be reached within a couple of hours from Reykjavík. For general navigation, Mal og Menning's 1:300,000 *Suðvesturland* and the 1:25,000 Landmælinger Íslands' **maps** both cover the area in decent detail, with much better contour information on the latter. Surfaced **highways** cut right through the region, with the country's densest network of **minor roads** heading out from these – though you'll still need to take the **weather** into account when tackling them – it's relatively mild, though this is also the wettest, windiest part of the country, prone to fog along the coast and potentially heavy snowfalls through the year on higher ground. **Public transport** is comprehensive, with regular buses through the year along the highway and out to most of the key sights. The exceptions are remoter tracks to Hekla and Þórsmörk, which open late in the year and require four-wheel-drive vehicles at all times. **Guided-tour** options are legion, and range from bulk-carrier buses through to private jeeps; many run in all seasons.

THE GOLDEN CIRCLE

The name **"Golden Circle"** might be a tourist-industry tag, but it's also apt, as this two-hundred-odd-kilometre circuit east from Reykjavík covers many of Iceland's best-known features and touches on the root of much of its history. Passing through the farming towns of **Hveragerði** and **Selfoss**, which make decent bases for hiking and delving into local history, the route takes in **Þingvellir**, whose dramatic rift valley and associated lake mark the area where the Icelandic state sprang into being in Viking times. East from here on the banks of the Hvítá is the religious centre of **Skálholt**, while following the river northeast takes you to **Gullfoss'** powerful twin cataracts and nearby **Geysir**, the original hot blowhole that has lent its name to similar vents worldwide. Visitors – local and foreign – flock to the main sights, mostly on hurried day-trips or weekend camping excursions; if this sounds discouraging, stay a little longer or explore a little wider and you'll soon escape the crowds.

One way to cover the highlights, particularly if you're pushed for time, is to take a **Golden Circle tour**, leaving daily from the *Hotel Loftleiðir* in Reykjavík (see p.51). These cost 5100kr, last up to seven hours, and are best booked a day in advance (most accommodation and tourist information centres in Reykjavík can do this). With English-speaking guides providing commentary, the tour crams in hothouses at Hveragerði, the church at Skálholt, assorted craters, Gullfoss, Geysir and, unless there's been serious snow, Þingvellir. It's an ambitious schedule for a single day and necessarily superficial, though many people also find that a disproportionate amount of time is given to stopovers at the numerous gift shops and cafés which line the route. Tours do, however, provide a convenient introduction to sights that you can return to later on to explore in depth.

Making your own way around, either head northeast from Reykjavík along Route 36 straight to Þingvellir, or take Route 1 southeast to Hveragerði and Selfoss, from where separate roads run up to Þingvellir and the Geysir–Gullfoss area. **Public buses** from Reykjavík run via Hveragerði and Selfoss to Gullfoss year-round, though Þingvellir is only covered by summer services. **Accommodation** of all kinds is plentiful, but hostels tend to get block-booked by groups at weekends and holidays.

Hveragerði and around

Heading southeast from Reykjavík on Route 1, the road crosses the top end of various flat, lichen-covered lava flows, with **Bláfjöll** and then **Skálafell** rising off to the south, and higher **Hengill** to the north. Gravel tracks head up towards the latter, which fixes the end of the volcanic ridge hemming in the western side of **Þingvallavatn** lake (see p.91), and with a full day it's possible to make a return hike to the rough summit at 800m.

Back on the highway, the road twists down off the ranges to the coastal plains 45km from the capital and the glowing hothouses of **HVERAGERÐI**, a cluster of low buildings on the Vármá (Warm River), nestled beneath steaming fell slopes. Sitting on the edge of a geothermal area, which extends north under the mountains and right up to Þingvellir, a wool mill and hydroelectric dam were built here on the river in the early twentieth century, but the town only really took off in the 1920s when, for the first time in Iceland, the subterranean heat was harnessed to grow vegetables. Today, this has spawned a horticultural school, a clinic specializing in hot-mud cures for arthritis, and scores of hothouses, from small backyard setups to giant commercial affairs, artificially lit to aid the propagation of fruit, vegetables, and exotic plants. That said, there's not a huge amount to see in Hveragerði itself, though some fine **hiking** hereabouts might encourage a stopover.

A small, dishevelled, quiet mesh of streets, the **town** is laid out either side of the main drag **Breiðamörk**, which runs north off the highway through the compact centre, and up towards where hiking trails begin at **Gufudalur**, a valley at the base of the hills. The most obvious thing to do is head for a **hothouse**, and a couple of minutes' walk east off Breiðamörk down Austurmörk brings you to Eden, the darling of Golden Circle bus tours. A gift shop, garden centre and café rolled into one, coffee, ornamental figs, bougainvillea, palms, cactus, heliconias and much trumpeted bananas (which are not exported in bulk, as often reported), bask in a tropical warmth, stolidly defying the outdoor temperatures. Another 100m up Breiðamörk, Blómaborg is a smaller affair, aimed more at Reykjavík residents seeking colourful house plants.

West from here on parallel Hveramörk and overlooked by Hveragerði's rather ordinary modern church, thermal outflows have been turned into a **hot springs park** (300kr; irregular hours), complete with bubbling pools and miniature geyser. It's often open only for groups, so to see the real thing follow the Gufudalur road for about 1km to **Grýla**, a small, erratically active hot spout named after a child-devouring troll.

Practicalities

Hveragerði's shops and services are close together, on or near Breiðamörk, about 300m from the highway. Daily **buses** along Route 1, as well as from Þorlákshöfn, the port for the Westman Islands' ferry (p.123), and the Reykjanes Peninsula (see p.96) pull in on Breiðamörk across from the **post office**, a couple of well-stocked **supermarkets**, and a **bank** with an ATM. **Tourist information**, in the shape of sound advice, regional tour bookings, and **maps** can be had at Ferðaþjónusta Suðurlands (☎483 4280, fax 483 4287, *www.simnet.is/travel*; Mon–Fri 9am–6pm, Sat & Sun 9am–2pm), a travel agent just down the road at Breiðamörk 10.

For somewhere to stay, Hveragerði's **campsite** (400kr per person), east of the centre at the top end of Reykjamörk, has basic facilities and is minimally maintained, and it's better to opt for one of the town's hostel. Close to the bus stop, both the *Hótel Ljósbrá*, Breiðamörk 25 (☎483 4588; ②), and the nearby co-owned *Youth Hostel Ból*, Hveramörk 14 (☎483 4198, fax 483 4088; 1250–1500kr), are well run, clean, and between them offer everything from sleeping-bag space through to double rooms with private bath, though note that both are closed from mid-September to April. A few minutes' walk west, *Gistiheimilið Frumskógar*, Frumskógar 3 (☎ & fax 483 4148; sleeping-bag accommodation 1500kr, ①), offers slightly shabby self-catering doubles and singles (2000kr). Otherwise, there's Hveragerði's business-cum-conference venue, *Hótel Örk*, off Breiðamörk as you head towards the highway (☎483 4700, fax 483 4775; ⑥); rooms are furnished in upmarket motel style, and there's a pool, casino and nightclub. Pick of the local **farmstays** are *Eldhestar* at Vellir, about 2km southeast of Hveragerði (☎483 4884, fax 486 5577, *www.eldhestar.is*; sleeping-bag accommodation 1500kr), which does great guided horse-treks through southern Iceland, lasting anywhere from one hour to two weeks; and *Núpa III*, 3km south of town (☎483 4388; sleeping-bag accommodation 1000kr, 4–6 person cabins from 4000kr; closed mid-Sept to April).

You can get morning coffee and cakes at the **bakery** next to the tourist office. For **restaurant** fare, both the *Hótel Örk* (expensive) and the *Hótel Ljósbrá* (moderate) offer a range of dishes including Icelandic lamb staples, and there's a *Pizza 67* halfway along Breiðamörk. If you're **self-catering** you can take advantage of Hveragerði's glut of vegetables (tasting none the worse for their hothouse origins), and hunt out rectangular loaves of dense, dark, *hverabrauð* – rye bread baked in underground ovens (for more of which, see p.232) – at the bakery or supermarkets on Breiðamörk.

Hiking around Hveragerði

The hills above Hveragerði are covered in **trails** and patterned by plenty of hot springs, hillsides stained by volcanic salts, heathland plants, and, in fine weather, inspiring views coastwards. A range of day-return tracks allow a good sniff around, though with more time it's quite feasible to push right on up to Þingvallavatn lake (see p.91), 18km north. For more about possible routes, ask at the travel agent, the youth hostel, or at the *Hótel Ljósbrá* (see "Practicalities", above).

The easiest option is to head up to **Gufudalur**, the appropriately named Steam Valley; take the road north from Hveragerði beyond Grýla and cross the Vármá, then bear east up the valley for 2km to where pools clog up the scenery with vapour.

For something more ambitious, stay on the road and follow it until you cross a shallow stream at the base of **Dalafell** (347m), about an hour's walk north from town. Bear right just across the stream and follow the bank up **Grændalur**, a particularly pretty valley in summer, with several hot springs to investigate along the way. At the head of the valley you've a couple of options; if you're not after anything too serious, cross west over the ridge, climb the track up Dalafell, then follow it back down to town via Djúpagil or across to Klambragil (see below) – a fifteen-kilometre, five-hour circuit. For a harder alternative (20km), continue north at the top of Grændalur past another thermal area and on to a series of three probable **crater lakes** running below the northeast side of flat-topped **Kyllisfell**. The last lake sits in a long, narrow depression, past which the track descends to another pool, **Djáknapollur**, about 9km from the start of the trail below Grændalur and more or less the halfway point if you're following the paths up to Þingvallavatn. If you're not, however, turn southwest at this point and climb again to a steep, narrow ridge which crests around 500m; from here you could scramble up several scree-covered peaks for the views (or simply the challenge), or just follow the trail southwest along the ridge and over a couple of lower rises to **Klambragil**, another great spot, with a handful of hot springs outflowing into a stream where the water's just about cool enough to enjoy a soak. Following the stream down, you reach the head of **Djúpagil**, the valley descending the west flank of Dalafell, and so return to the trailhead on the Hveragerði road.

Selfoss and around

Some 15km east of Hveragerði, Route 1 passes the junction of roads north towards Þingvellir and the Geysir–Gullfoss area (see p.92), before crossing a suspension bridge over the fast-flowing Ölfusá and running into the unassuming town of **SELFOSS**. Caught between the looming bulk of **Ingólfsfjall** to the north and flat grasslands running to the horizon in all other directions, it's been the centre of Iceland's **dairy industry** for the last seventy years or so and is easily the southwest's largest settlement, with a population of 4000. Although there's little to Selfoss besides its history, good facilities and a crossroads position on the southwest's main roads also combine to make the town a convenient base for a few days, taking in some easy **walks** in the area, climbing Ingólfsfjall, or visiting the nearby coastal fishing villages of **Stokkseyri** and **Eyrarbakki**.

The original English-engineered **suspension bridge** itself, built in 1891, is the reason Selfoss ever came into existence. Before then, roads through the region ran to a point further south, on the Ölfusá estuary, where traffic was ferried across. Rough waters made these ferry crossings hazardous however, and when the bridge was opened it became an immediate success, a focus for the new stores and homes that gradually coalesced into the country's first inland town, drawing trade away from the older coastal settlements. The bridge also gave Selfoss the distinction of being the cause of the country's first **strike**, sparked not over wages but the fact that its builders were supplied with only salmon to eat. The current bridge – which is just about the only two-lane span in the whole of southern

Aerial view of Reykjavík

Höði, Reykjavík

Ásmundir Sveinsson Sculpture Museum

Tjörnin, Reykjavík

Reykjavík

Hallgrímskirkja, Reykjavík   Strokkur, Geysir

Black volcanic sand and sea stack, Dyrhólaey

Midnight sunset

Thermal area, Mývatn

Puffin

Þingvellir

Church and farm on the Öxará, Þingvellir

View from Heimaklettur, Heimaey

Skógarfoss

Iceland – actually dates from 1945, built after the original collapsed when two milk trucks crossed it simultaneously a year earlier. Equally distinctive is Selfoss's modern riverside **church**, just south of the bridge on the same side as the town, whose standard black-tiles-and-whitewash exterior compliments a beautifully elongated bell tower and steeply peaked roof. Inside, exposed wooden rafters and murals based on mostly decorative medieval designs are handsome touches.

For a look at the countryside around Selfoss, cross back over the bridge and head north towards Þingvellir and Gullfoss up Route 350, which squeezes between Öfulsá and Ingólfsfjall's eastern side. A kilometre along this road is a right turning down to the riverside **Laugarbakkar farm**, open for visitors to catch **milking sessions** (daily 8am & 5pm). The view outside takes in the sharp-lined confluence of the clear, glacier-fed Hvítá river system and the darker Sog river, which drains Þingvallavatn lake to the north, to form the Öfulsá – which, in it's turn, flows the final 10km to the sea. Across the river from here, a low cover of birch scrub known as **Þrastaskógur**, the Thrush Forest (probably due to ubiquitous redwings), covers a six-thousand-year-old lava field extending right down to Selfoss; there are riverside **walking tracks** along both sides of the river back to town.

Back on Route 350, and 5km north of Selfoss where Route 350 splits up towards Þingvellir, is Alviðra farm. From there a track ascends straight up to the summit (two strenuous hours) of the flat-topped mountain of **Ingólfsfjall** (551m), a sand-wich of lava and assorted detritus formed by sub-glacial volcanic activity. The mountain is named after Iceland's first official settler, **Ingólfur**, who wintered here in the early 870s before moving on to settle at Reykjavík (for more on which, see Contexts, p.288). Today, the only settlement here comprises a scattering of summer houses, some of which are planted – somewhat alarmingly – on Ingólfsfjall's unstable, boulder-strewn lower slopes.

Practicalities

Coming over the bridge from Hveragerði, the first thing you encounter is a round-about: from here, Eyravegur heads south (right) towards the coast; while Route 1 bears east (left) into Selfoss as Austurvegur to form the kilometre-long high street. At the eastern edge of town, the Esso **fuel station** houses Selfoss' **bus ter-minal**, staging post for services from as far afield as Reykjavík, Vík, Gullfoss and Geysir, the Reykjanes Peninsula, Eyrarbakki, and southeast Iceland. There's also a **tourist office** here (daily 8am–8pm; ☎482 1266), which hands out brochures and advice, as well as a café, along with a **payphone** – there's another outside the post office on Austurvegur. On the same street you'll also find a huge **super-market**, a **library** (Mon–Fri 1–8pm) with English-language weeklies, and sever-al **banks** with ATMs. **Tours** to southwestern sights between the Reykjanes Peninsula and Þorsmörk are operated by Iceland Direct, based at the *Hjarðarból* farmstay (see below; contact through *icedir@eyjar.is*). For **car rental**, Bílaleiga (☎482 3893), based at *Menam* (see below), offers decent rates.

Turn south off Austurvegur at the Esso station and it's 400m to Selfoss's excel-lent **campsite** down on Engjavegur (350kr per tent, plus 350kr per person), which offers plenty of space, powerful showers and well-equipped kitchen facili-ties. Adjacent to this is the *Gesthús Selfossi* (☎482 3585, fax 482 2973, *gesthus@ka.is*), which offers **beds** in cabins sleeping four (6100–7600kr), as well as summer-only sleeping-bag accommodation at the adjacent school (1700kr). All other accommodation is across town: on the roundabout, *Hótel Selfoss* (☎482 2500, fax 482 2524, *hotel@ka.is*; ⑤) is a big, smart affair; they also run the more homely *Hótel Þoristún* (same tel; ②) around the corner. Just off the roundabout, at the start of the coast road, *Menam* (☎482 4099) has sleeping-bag accommodation and made-up beds (1500–2500kr) in small, warm **rooms** above a restaurant. The closest **farmstay** is at *Hjarðarból*, halfway back along the highway towards Hveragerði (☎483 4178, fax 483 4878, *info@iceland-direct.com*; closed mid-Sept to May; ②), where the price includes meals – buses along Route 1 can drop you off.

Selfoss boasts some unexpectedly good **places to eat**. *Kaffi-krús*, opposite the library on Austurvegur, is open from 10am until midnight for coffee and excellent cakes in candlelit ambience, but *Menam* (see above) restaurant's authentic Thai cuisine is a real gem – treat yourself to chicken and green beans in coconut milk for little more than the price of a pizza. For faster food, *Hrói Höttur*, next to the post office on Austurvegur, is a fine pizzeria, while the Esso station café offers sandwiches, burgers, and the like.

Stokkseyri

South of Selfoss, Route 34 runs straight to the coast across the **Flói**, a ten-kilometre stretch of land so flat that halfway across you can see both your starting point and destination. Within sight of the sea you reach an intersection; turn eastwards and it's a couple of kilometres to **STOKKSEYRI**, a village of a few houses, a fish factory, a supermarket and a fuel station congregating around a church behind a protective storm wall. Over the wall is a windswept, vestigial and unattended **harbour** – though even in its heyday in the 1900s it must have been tough to launch a boat here – and, oddly, a little yellow sand beach nestled amongst black, weed-strewn rocks. It's not obvious today, but Stokkseyri was once a busy fishing port whose most famous resident was **Thurídur Einarsdottír**, an early nineteenth-century woman who worked on commercial fishing boats for most of her life and was a fleet foreman for 25 years. The idea of women going to sea wasn't too unusual at the time, but Thurídur is also renowned for sucessfully defending, in court, her then-illegal preference for wearing men's clothing. A couple of old turf-and-stone buildings lurk nearby – one is right beside the church.

The road continues a few kilometres east past a small lake stained red by tannin-rich mud, to a flat-sided **lighthouse**, in front of which is **Rjómabuið Baugsstöðum**, a corrugated-iron buttery from 1905. It's open as a museum in summer, but at other times peer through the window and you'll see a wooden churn and associated paraphernalia, all in working order and powered by a small waterwheel beside the building.

There's no accommodation in Stokkseyri, but at least one **bus** each morning departs for here from Selfoss, continuing on to Eyrarbakki, Þorlákshöfn and Reykjavík before reversing its route in the afternoon. The only **place to eat** is at the fuel station; otherwise, you can buy food from the supermarket.

Eyrarbakki

Four kilometres west from Stokkseyri and just past the intersection, **EYRAR-BAKKI** is a larger version of its neighbour, and from the time of Settlement until the early twentieth century sat on what was counted as the best **harbour** in southern Iceland. But, as at Stokkseyri, it's difficult to understand why Eyrarbakki's fishermen ever relied on a haven as poor as this: there's no shelter from the elements and boats were traditionally launched by dragging and pushing them through the surf into deeper water where they could be rowed out. Nonetheless, fishing and a proximity to the Öfulsá estuary ferry ensured Eyrarbakki's success as a trading centre until the Selfoss bridge was completed; thereafter, decline was compounded when the town's harbour was rendered redundant by a more effective, man-made effort west across the Öfulsá at Þorlákshöfn (see p.123), and the town's fish factory finally closed in the 1990s.

Despite this downturn of fortune, Eyrarbakki is an attractive place with a core that includes plenty of old houses and shops dating back to its glory days. Some have been bought up and restored by city folk as weekend retreats, while others, like the timber-sided **church**, are still in use. Just past the church, the oldest building, Husíð, is another wooden structure, a Norwegian kit-home dating back to 1765 which, along with adjacent buildings, now serves as the **Söfnin museum** (June–Aug daily 10am–6pm, April, May, Sept & Oct Sat & Sun 1–5pm; 400kr). Aside from a random assortment of Eyrarbakki's historical flotsam, a couple of rooms have been refurbished in period style, and there's a partial reconstruction of the once pivotal town store, whose last proprietor – Guðlaugur Pálsson – served customers from 1917 until 1989. Better yet, your ticket includes entry into the **Maritime Museum** (same hours) across the lawn behind, whose centrepiece is a wooden fishing boat of the kind used until the 1930s. It must have taken some courage to go to sea in these broad, open, low-sided vessels, let alone fish from one; sails were used, though boats were classified not by the shape of the sails or overall length, but by the number of oars used to row them – and hence the size of the crew. A few photos and weather-beaten oilskins complete the display. Outside, climb the storm wall for a look seawards at what fishermen were up against as they set off or returned – a difficult entry over a rocky shore.

As at Stokkseyri, there's nowhere to stay and the only **place to eat** is in the service station at the entrance to town. **Buses** are the same as for Stokkseyri, with Reykjavík-bound services first stopping 17km along at Þorlákshöfn, via a causeway over the Öfulsá's improbably broad estuary. If you've your own transport, this latter route takes in heathland, coastal flats, vegetated lava flows and a series of brackish marshland pools, all ideal for **bird-watching** – swans, geese, snipe and godwit are all common.

Þingvellir and Þingvallavatn

The region north of Selfoss is scarred by one of the world's great geological boundaries, a **rift valley** marking where the North American and Eurasian continental plates are physically tearing apart. It was in this monumental landmark that Iceland's clan chieftains, or *goðar*, first gathered in the tenth century to formalize their laws and forge a national identity for themselves (see box, p.86). Although this rift stretches right across Iceland, nowhere else is it so expansively evident – a four-kilometre-wide, forty-metre-deep slash in the landscape, sided in basalt columns and extending for 16km from Iceland's largest lake, **Þingvallavatn**, to the low, rounded cone of the **Skjaldbreiður** volcano in the northeast.

Þingvellir itself – the site where the chieftains met at the southwestern end of the rift – has been protected since 1930 as a national park. **Access** to the area from either Selfoss or Reykjavík is along Route 36, which runs for 40km up to

THE ALÞING AT ÞINGVELLIR

With laws shall our land be built up, but with lawlessness laid waste.

Njál's Saga

By the beginning of the tenth century, Iceland's 36 regional chieftains were already meeting at local **assemblies** to sort out disputes, but as it became obvious that the country had developed from a casual stopover for passing pirates into an established, longer-term base, they recognized the need for some form of overall government. With this in mind, Norwegian law was adapted and the first **Alþing**, or General Assembly, was held in the rift valley north of **Þingvallavatn** in 930 AD, at a place which became known as **Þingvellir**, the **Assembly Plains**. Though the Alþing's power declined through the ages, Þingvellir remained the seat of Iceland's government for the next eight centuries.

The Alþing was held for two weeks every summer, and attendance for chieftains was mandatory. In fact, almost everyone who could attend did so, setting up their tented camps – **buðs** – and coming to watch the courts in action or settle disputes, pick up on gossip, trade, compete at sports, and generally socialize. The whole event was co-ordinated by the **lawspeaker**, while the laws themselves were legislated by the **Law Council**, and dispensed at four regional courts, along with a fifth **supreme court**. Strangely, however, none of these authorities had the power to enforce their verdicts, beyond bringing pressure to bear through public opinion. The adoption of **Christianity** as Iceland's official religion in 1000 AD was one of the Alþing's major successes, but if litigants refused to accept a court's decision, they had to seek satisfaction privately. **Njál's Saga** contains a vivid account of one such event, when a battle between two feuding clans and their allies broke out at the Alþing itself around 1011 AD (see p.108).

This lack of real authority undermined the Alþing's effectiveness, creating a power vacuum in Iceland that ultimately saw Norway and then Denmark assume control of the country. By the late thirteenth century the Alþing was losing its importance, with the lawspeaker's position abolished and the courts stripped of all legislative power. They had rather more ability to act on their judgements though, and from the mid-sixteenth century **public executions** – unknown before – were carried out at Þingvellir. Eventually, while still meeting for a few days every year, the Alþing became a minor affair, and the last assembly was held at Þingvellir in 1798, replaced after 1800 by a national court and parliament at Reykjavík.

A century later, however, and Þingvellir had become the focus of the **nationalist movement**, with large crowds attending various independence debates here – the Danish king even attended Iceland's millennial celebrations at Þingvellir in 1874. It remained a symbol of national identity through the twentieth century, peaking when half the country turned up at Þingvellir to hear the **declaration of independence** from Denmark and the formation of the **Icelandic Republic** on June 17, 1944. Surprisingly few, however, attended ceremonies here in July 2000 to mark a thousand years of Icelandic Chrisitianity, though maybe this was due more to the advent of television and a Millennium hangover than disinterest in Þingvellir's associations.

Þingvellir from Selfoss along Þingvallavatn's eastern shore, and then crosses north of the lake and continues the same distance westwards to Reykjavík – note that the Rekjavík stretch is often shut by winter snowfalls. Coming from Geysir–Gullfoss, it's a straightforward fifty-kilometre trip west via Laugarvatn (see p.93). A decent gravel road also runs south around Þingvallavatn between

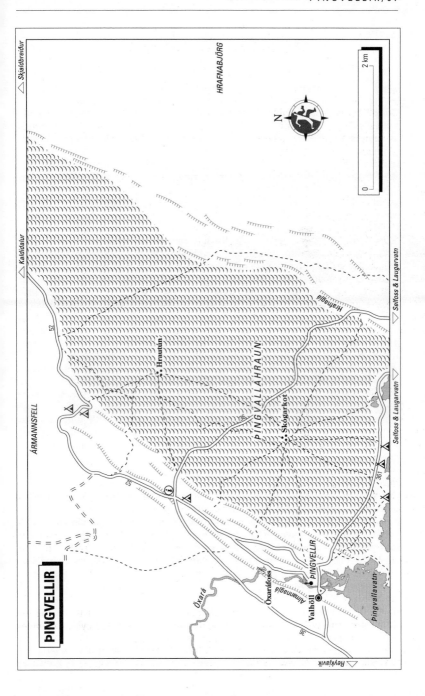

the Reykjavík and Selfoss routes, enabling you to see a slightly less touristed part of the region. **Accommodation** throughout largely boils down to camping, though there's a hotel at Þingvellir and several farmstays scattered around elsewhere.

Þingvellir National Park and around

Þingvellir National Park encompasses the flat moors at the southern end of the rift valley, with boundaries reaching 6km north from Þingvallavatn to the foothills of **Ármannsfell** – said to be the abode of the region's mythical guardian, Ármann Dalmannsson – and around the same distance east towards the solitary massif of **Hrafnabjörg**. The main focus is, of course, Þingvellir itself, a surprisingly small area at the southwestern corner of the park where the narrow **Öxará** – the Axe River – flows down to the lake shore past a **church** and other historic monuments, all hemmed in on the west by the 2km-long **Almannagjá**, the region's most impressive rift wall.

Golden Circle **tours** aside (see p.79), you can reach Þingvellir on summer **buses** from Reykjavík and Selfoss, though from Geysir you'll have to hitch once you reach Laugarvatn; you'll also need your own transport to check out Þingvallavatn's southwestern end. Note that Þingvellir marks the southern terminus of the Kaldidalur route through the Interior (see p.144). Wherever you're coming from, aim for the **information centre** (☎482 2660, fax 3635; daily May–Sept), on Route 36 around 2km north of the church, which sorts out fishing and all **camping permits** (450kr), has a useful three-dimensional model of the region, and doubles as a **café**. A surfaced road runs south from the centre, past the **main campsite**, Almannagjá, and the church, to the lakeside *Hótel Valhöll* (☎482 2622, fax 482 3622; ⑤), the park's only formal **accommodation**. The 1930s building is a bit gloomy but rooms are well furnished and the hotel's upmarket **restaurant** is excellent – and the setting, at the base of Almannagjá's walls, is very imposing. There are three other exposed **basic campsites** east of here, along a quiet, one-kilometre strip of lake shore between Vatnskot and Öfugsnáði bays – of most use to anglers – and a couple more for hikers 3km north of the information centre, beyond the park border at the base of Ármannsfell. **Park rules** protect all plants, animals and natural formations, and prohibit open fires, off-road driving and camping outside designated sites.

Þingvellir

It's hard to overstate the historical importance of **Þingvellir**, though there are very few specific monuments to see, and to capture the spirit of the place you need to familiarize yourself with the buildings and natural formations around which events were played. The best spot for an overview is from a popular **lookout point** on top of Almannagjá, looking down over Þingvellir, the church, hotel and lake; there's a signposted turn-off from the Reykjavík road, or simply follow the path up from the church area. Here you're on the edge of the **North American continental plate**: the Alþing site is directly below, with the church and red-roofed hotel separated by the Öxará which flows south to the lake. Looking northeast up the rift towards the information centre, a flagpole rises in front of where vertical basalt columns topped in rope lava cleave away from the rift wall, while in the distance, Ármannsfell and Hrafnabjörg frame the valley, fist-like and solid. Permanence is an illusion, however – the rift is widening by 1.5cm further each year as the continental plates drift apart. As they move, the valley

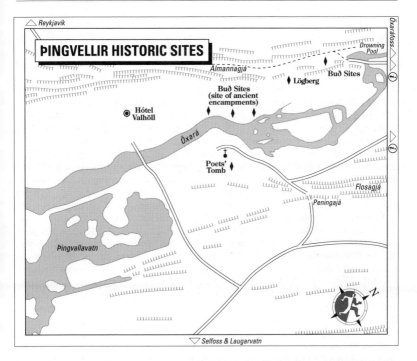

floor sinks, on average, a couple of millimetres anually, though in 1789 it fell half a metre in just ten days after an earthquake. Away in the distance, Skjaldbreiður's apparently low summit is easily overlooked, though at 1060m it's actually one of the highest peaks in view.

A hundred-metre track descends northeast into Almannagjá and down to the flagpole, which marks the presumed site of **Lögberg**, the rock where important speeches were made and the lawspeaker recited Iceland's laws to the masses below. Its exact location is obscure, the victim of subsidence and plain forgetfulness, but this is the place used during twentieth-century assemblies. Continuing along Almannagjá, a plaque and traces of walls outline the remains of an eighteenth-century **buð**, one of the temporary roofed camps raised by participants during assemblies. They seemed to shrink through the ages; the sagas suggest that clans raised *buðs* large enough to accommodate most of their members, though storekeepers and traders presumably kept smaller establishments. This one is small and relatively recent; of the thirty or so *buð* sites located in the area, two are thought to predate the thirteenth century.

Beyond here, the Öxará cascades over Almannagjá as the twenty-metre-high **Öxarárfoss** flows down along the gorge for 150m then breaks through the wall in a brief tumble down onto plains, and so past the church and into the lake. Rift walls near Öxarárfoss are clearly layered, marking falls of ash from at least twenty separate volcanic eruptions, though river rocks themselves are barely worn, suggesting that the Öxará's path is fairly new and supporting oral accounts of the river's diversion into the rift around 1000 AD to provide water for the sizeable chunk of Iceland's population who descended at each Alþing. After Danish laws were enforced in the sixteenth century, **pools** near the second falls were used to drown women convicted of witchcraft or sexual offences (men were beheaded for the same crimes), though the idea of a death penalty was repugnant to Icelanders and few such executions were carried out. During the Christian millennial celebrations in July 2000, a wreath was laid here in atonement for those who were executed before capital punishment was abolished in the late eighteenth century.

Moving down into the valley, cross over the Öxará and follow the road back towards the church. East of here is the splintered wall forming **Flosagjá**, a deep fissure whose southern end has been flooded by underground springs creating **Peningagjá**, an exceedingly clear, deep wishing pool; coins glint silver and electric blue at the bottom. A little further on is the **church**, the site of which was apparently in use – possibly as a giant *buð* – before the Norwegian king Ólafur Haraldsson supplied timber for the first church building in 1018. The current white and blue structure, from 1859, is misleadingly small and unpretentious, as by the eighteenth century Þingvellir church was wealthy, owning a huge swathe of farmland stretching right up the valley. A raised area behind is reserved for the tombs of outstanding Icelanders; at present the only two incumbents are the patriotic poets **Einar Benediktsson** and **Jónas Hallgrímsson**, the latter who also inspired the nineteenth-century independence movement and drew great inspiration from Þingvellir. Former farm buildings next door are now a school and home to the church warden, who doubles as the national park manager, and the marshlands in front were once possibly an island where **duels** at the Alþing were fought, before the practice was banned in the thirteenth century.

Around Þingvellir

Once you've soaked up some history, Þingvellir's surrounds deserve a day or two of exploration. Higher ground aside, the entire valley is covered in the overgrown nine-thousand-year-old lavafield **Þingvallahraun**, product of the up-valley Skjaldbreiður (Shield-broad). Though now extinct, this was the first **shield volcano** to ever be classified, a type that spews out high-volume fluid lava in a steady rather than violent eruption, leaving wide, flattened cones. The valley is beautiful in summer and early autumn, carpeted in patchy pine plantations, dwarf birch forest and heathland plants, with the national park covered in a web of marked **walking and riding trails** – note that some of these cross minor rifts and gorges, which might be dangerously concealed if there has been any snow. To venture further, or climb any of the mountains, you'll need at least basic orienteering skills and the Landmælingar Islands *Þingvellir* 1:25,000 **map**. **Horses** are available through Islenskir Ferðahestar (☎566 7600, fax 566 7629, *trvhorse@centrum.is*), who offer year-round day-trips for 6900kr, and late-night excursions in summer to see Þingvellir under the long dusk light (5000kr).

Of the **marked trails**, the easiest lead east of Þingvellir's church or north from Þingvallavatn's shore, converging 2km on at **Skógarkot**, a sheep farm abandoned in the 1930s – paths from Þingvellir are best, as they cross a couple of interesting rifts and avoid most of the boggy ground you'll find on the other routes. The long-beaked birds zigzagging away in panic at your approach, or flying high to drop earthwards with a strange drumming noise, are **snipe**, or *hrossagaukur* in Icelandic (horse-cuckoo). Skógarkot's ruined but strongly built **stone buildings** occupy a grassy hillock roughly halfway across the valley, not a high position but still elevated enough for you to take in a panorama of distant peaks and rift walls,

and feel dwarfed by the scale of the Þingvallah...
either continue north to another farm site at **Hr...**
the main campsite (another 4km in all); or walk a ...
the valley to where Route 36 climbs the eastern rif...
continental plate – at **Hrafnagjá**, Raven's Rift.

Of the **mountains**, Ármannsfell (765m) is the eas...
a full-day, eight-kilometre return hike to the summi...
southern slopes; there's snow up here until the middle...
not really climbable, but you could hike out here from t...
the base, and return in a very full day – it's about an ei... ...ound-
trip, only really negotiable by taking the road, or marked   ...okógarkot, to
Hrafnagjá before striking northeast cross-country. For Skja...oreiður, you're looking at a two- to three-day hike to the rim of the three-hundred-metre-wide crater,
and need advice on the route from the information centre or one of Iceland's walking clubs (see p.35) before setting out.

Þingvallavatn and around

Þingvallavatn was formed nine thousand years ago when fresh lava blocked off
the outflow of springs rising in a basin to the south of Þingvellir, backfilling it with
water to form a fourteen-kilometre-long lake, Iceland's largest. Although no great
scenic wonder, Þingvallavatn and its sole outflow, the **Sog** river, are surrounded
by alternately rugged hills and undulating moorland, good for both hiking and
bird-watching, while the lake is dotted with three tiny volcanic islands and, on
rare windless days, forms a perfect blue mirror to the sky. Three surprisingly non-
intrusive **hydroelectric stations** at the head of the Sog provide power for the
region, while healthy stocks of char and a dwindling trout population keep the fly
population down and anglers happy – **winter fishing** is especially popular, when
holes have to be cut through the ice. In summer, you can get fishing **permits**
through the information centre or *Hótel Valhöll*; at other times, you'll need to
make enquiries in Reykjavík or Selfoss before heading up here.

You can circuit Þingvallavatn in your own transport along gravel roads which
run around the south side of the lake between both prongs of Route 36.
Otherwise, two-hour-long summer **boat trips**, which troll around the islands after
fish, depart at 11am, 2pm and 5pm every Saturday and Sunday; book in advance
with Þingvallavatnssiglingar, at Skálabrekka farm (☎ & fax 482 3610), which is
just off Route 36 about 5km south of the Þingvellir information centre towards
from Reykjavík.

Around Þingvallavatn

From Þingvellir information centre, the road around Þingvallavatn starts by following Route 36 towards Reykjavík for 11km, before turning southeast onto an
unmarked but substantial gravel road. This runs quickly down to the water on
Þingvallavtn's west shore, and then twists as it passes summer houses below the
line of **Jórukleif**, a spiky-toothed range running along the western lakeshore
from Hengil. After a few kilometres you leave the lake behind and continue
beneath rocky, shattered hills – not really all that tall, but appearing so as they
loom over the road – to where the view opens up at a long valley where
Nesjavallavirkjun, the **Nesjavellir Thermal Power Station** (guided tours
June–Aug Mon–Sat 9am–noon & 1–6pm; free) steams away at the base of steep,

any such projects in Iceland, miles of silver piping, lights, and
e station a strangely organic quality, not out of place in the land-
actical terms, Nesjavallavirkjun supplies Reykjavík with hot water
perheated sources 2km underground, while roadside overflows attract
owl in cold weather. Near Nesjavallavirkjun's entrance, low wooden buildings at *Hótel Nesbúð* (☎482 3415, fax 482 3414; sleeping-bag accommodation
1100kr, ①) provide **accommodation**, hot tubs, and a good **restaurant**; there are
also a range of marked **walking tracks** into the hills from here lasting between
an hour and – if you want to hike all the way to Hveragerði – a day or more.

Back on the road and heading east from the power station, you reach the lake
again at **Hagavík**, a tiny bay fringed in black shingle, then leave it once more and
pass the signed access track to **Olfusvatnsvík** (a 2.5km walk), a marshy bay with
camping potential at the start of signed, seventeen-kilometre **hiking trail** south
to Hveragerði (see p.81). Cross another stretch of moorland and you'll find yourself above **Úlfljótsvatn**, Þingvallavatn's southernmost bay, where a huge cross on
the hillside hovers over a tiny lakeside church. Just beyond here is a bridge
across the Sog to **Írafossstöð hydro station**, lowest of the three – the other two
are invisible from the road – and then you rejoin Route 36 at the few houses comprising **Syðribrú**: turn south to follow the Sog to Selfoss, or north to head back
towards Þingvellir. Not far along in the latter direction is *Efribrú* **farmstay** (☎482
2615 fax 482 2614; sleeping-bag accommodation 1500kr, ②; bookings needed
Oct–May), which offers breakfast for a little extra (or you can self-cater); there
are also **horses** available for hire. A curved basalt gorge by the roadside after
here is the Sog's original exit from Þingvallavatn, now used to regulate outflow
through the power stations. Construction of the uppermost hydro station here in
1937 uncovered a Settlement-era **burial mound** enclosing two skeletons, various
weapons, and a boat, now in the National Museum in Reykjavík.

Geysir and Gullfoss

One way or another, the tangle of roads and tracks northeast of Selfoss follow the
green, marshy swards of the Hvítá basin before joining up some 60km later up
Route 35 at Iceland's two most famous sights: the erupting hot pools at **Geysir**,
and **Gullfoss'** thundering falls, 7km beyond. The three **routes** described below –
via **Laugarvatn**, **Skálhot** or **Flúðir** – can be worked into a variety of circuits, with
Golden Circle tours and public buses giving year-round access from Selfoss and
Reykjavík along the Skálholt route. Coming from Þingvellir, buses only run to
Laugarvatn between July and September, and at other times you'll have to take a
bus to Selfoss first, or hitch to Laugarvatn, to join up with a scheduled service.

Routes: via Laugarvatn, Skálholt and Reykholt

Heading north out of Selfoss, the road to Geysir and beyond initially follows Route
36 towards Þingvellir, but once past Ingólfsfjall and the Sog branches northeast
along Route 35 into a typical Icelandic "forest" of knee-high dwarf birch and willows. Brightly coloured summer houses with high-pitched roofs abound, like a
disorganised, streetless satellite suburb of Selfoss spreading across the under-
growth. Around 5km along Route 35, a signpost and layby east of the road mark
Kerið crater, probably created three thousand years ago by a sudden gas explo-

sion through the ground, leaving a neat, conical hill whose crater is 70m deep and the same distance across. The bottom is flooded and used for farming fish, and there's an easy, fifteen-minute path around the red, gravelly rim, with a view northwest to the similar **Seyðishólar crater**. All Golden Circle tours stop at Kerið for ten minutes or so.

About 25km from Selfoss, Route 37 branches north off Route 35 to meet the Þingvellir–Geysir road at the small town of **LAUGARVATN**. Home to Iceland's National School for Sports – the huge, 1930s-style institution looming above the lake shore – the town is little more than a half-dozen streets sitting on extensive **thermal springs** welling up from the base of rugged hills behind, and looks east over **Laugarvatn** itself, a flat, still lake surrounded by equally flat countryside. Despite its small size and fairly downbeat appearance, however, the town is a popular summer retreat for Icelanders, who come to take advantage of the **waterfront sauna**, to hire sailboards or simply go swimming in the lake, and to follow hiking trails into the bald hills behind – including one that heads north for 14km to Skjaldbeiður (see p.85). If you're tempted to stay, there's a **campsite** (350kr) and the *YHA Dalsel* (✆ & fax 486 1215; sleeping-bag accommodation 1500kr, & made-up bed 2000kr), opposite each other Laugarvatn's north exit, while the *Lindin* **restaurant-bar**, down by the lake, will keep you fed and watered. Beyond Laugarvatn, the road continues northeast along the base of flat-topped fells before rejoining Route 35 just short of Geysir, and year-round **buses** head back to Selfoss and Reykjavík, or on to Geysir and Gullfoss, between twice a week and once a day – though transport west to Þingvellir runs only in July and August.

Skálholt and Reykholt

Stay on the main road after the Kerið crater and you're soon crossing a region of small lakes and streams north of the Hvítá known as **Biskupstungur**, the Bishop's Tongue – a route followed year-round by both Golden Circle tours and **buses**, though these run only a few times a week between September and June.

The name Biskupstungur probably originated after the foundation of the church at **SKÁLHOLT**, which lies off the main road around 40km from Selfoss. It's easy to overdose on churches in Iceland, but Skálholt's definitely warrants a stop: seat of a bishopric since 1056 AD, the huge wooden **cathedral** later established here grew wealthy on land revenues. A **school** was also established – Iceland's first – and by the early thirteenth century there were two hundred people living here, making it the largest settlement in Iceland. Surviving numerous reconstructions and the Reformation, Skálholt became, along with Hólar in northern Iceland, a major seat of learning, and lasted until the region was hit by a catastrophic earthquake in the late eighteenth century. The bishop subsequently shifted to Reykjavík, and Skálholt was largely abandoned, though a chapel was maintained until the church and school were restored and reconsecrated in 1963.

Today, the church is elegantly underplayed, plainly decked out and unusual only for its size. Inside, a mitre over the door identifies Skálholt as a bishopric; there's a nicely proportioned wooden ceiling, abstract stained-glass windows, and a tapestry-like **mosaic** of Christ behind the altar. Reconstruction work in the 1950s also uncovered a thirteenth-century stone **sarcophagus** belonging to Bishop Páll Jónsson, a charismatic churchman who added a tower and sumptuous decorations to the original building: a wooden crook carved with a dragon's head was found with his remains, and the sarcophagus itself is on view here in the summer. Out in front, a twinned rock **sculpture** represents Christianity and

Paganism, while a rough-cut stone monument, 100m away, commemorates Iceland's last Catholic bishop, Jón Arason. Arason was actually bishop at Hólar in the north, but rode south in 1550 and captured Skálholt in an attempt to prevent the Danish king from forcing Lutherism on the country; after a brief struggle he was taken and beheaded by the king's men.

You can **stay** year-round at Skálholt's school (☎486 8870, fax 8994; sleeping-bag accommodation 1200kr, made-up bed 2200kr), or return to the main road from where it's a further 7km to the steaming hillside vents that pin **REYKHOLT** down as another of the southwest's greenhouse villages. The roadside fuel station incorporates a store, **café**, **bus stop**, and **bank**, and is also where to arrange **camping**, with a pool and further **summer accommodation** one kilometre from the road at Reykholt's school-based youth hostel (☎486 8830, fax 8709; sleeping-bag accommodation 1200kr, ①). From here, it's an uneventful 20km to the Geysir–Gullfoss area.

Routes to Geysir and Gullfoss: via Flúðir

You need your own transport, but an alternative route to the Geysir–Gullfoss area follows Route 1 east of Selfoss for 15km, then turns northeast along Route 30 across a peaty, vegetated lavafield known as **Skeið**. It's prime **horse-riding** country, and those interested should call in to the Land and Hestar stables at *Húsatófir* (☎ & fax 486 5560), a farm offering guesthouse accommodation as well as anything from an hour in the saddle for 1300kr to week-long guided treks of varying difficulty. You need to bring your own riding clothes and boots.

Forty-five kilometres from Selfoss, **FLÚÐIR** is not quite a township, more a clutch of services: a **post office**, **bank** with ATM, a **fuel station-cum-roadhouse**, and a stylish **place to stay**, the *Hotel Flúðir* (☎486 6630, fax 6530; ④), whose corrugated iron, granite and wood décor complement excellent views northwest over ridges and icy heights above Laugarvatn. From here it's a sometimes slippery 20km on a mix of bitumen and gravel to where the road twists sharply over the Hvítá river as it channels through a tight pinch of rock-studded conglomerate; the water is eerily quiet, despite visibly strong currents. Five kilometres on is the **Geysir–Gullfoss junction**, where there's **camping**, **beds**, **meals** and **horse riding** available at *Brattholt* farm (☎486 8991, fax 8691; tents 400kr, dorms 1000kr, ①; closed Oct–Feb), whose owner donated Gullfoss to the Icelandic Nature Conservation Council (see p.96).

Geysir

Visible from miles away as a pall of steam rising above the plains, **GEYSIR**'s hot springs turn out to be a grassy slope below **Bjarnfell mountain**, studded with circular pools atop grey, mineral-streaked mounds. The area has been active for thousands of years, but the springs' positions have periodically shifted as geological seams crack open or close down, and the current vents are believed to have appeared following a thirteenth-century earthquake. Just what makes geysers erupt is subject to speculation: some theorists favour gaseous subterranean burps; others believe that cooler surface water forms a "lid", trapping superheated fluid below until enough pressure builds up to burst through as an eruption. What nobody doubts is just how hot the springs are: pool **temperatures** reach 125° C, and even surface water is only just off boiling point – under no circumstances should you wander off marked paths (some vents are covered by a paper-thin crust), step anywhere without looking first, or put any part of your body in the springs or their outlets.

The deep, clear blue **Geysir pool** itself – the Gusher – is, of course, what everyone comes to see, and in its heyday was certainly impressive, regularly spitting its load seventy metres skywards. Sadly, it has actually been inactive since the 1960s, though it used to be triggered for important visitors by dumping forty kilos of soap powder into it, which somehow sparked an eruption. Today, you'll have to be content with the antics of nearby **Strokkur**, the Churn, which fires off a thirty-metre-high spout every few minutes. A split second before it explodes, Strokkur's pool surface forms a distinct dome, through which the rising waters tear through (it's worth try to catch this on film). Lesser spouts in the vicinity include **Blesi**'s inactive twin pools, one clear and colourless, the other opaque blue; the unpredictably tempered **Fata**; and **Litli Geysir**, which does little but slosh around from time to time.

Aside from Geysir, you can also climb well-worn tracks to the summit of **Bjarnarfell** (727m) in a couple of hours for views down on Geysir's surrounds, though it's a miserable proposition in bad weather. Another option is to follow the signposted, 3km-long gravel vehicle track up **Haukadalur** – Hawk Valley – from Geysir to a **forestry reserve** and church. In saga times Haukadalur was an important holding, another famous educational centre that was eventually incorporated into Skálholt's lands. Extensive felling and ensuing erosion put paid to the estate, which was in a sorry condition when turned into a reserve in the 1930s. Since then, the hillsides here have been planted thickly with green pine trees, and thousands of new saplings spread down the valley, coloured in spring by wildflowers. Have a quick look at the nineteenth-century **church** too, whose brass door-ring is said to have belonged to the friendly giant **Bergþór**, who asked to be buried here.

Practicalities

The Geysir thermal area, along with a **roadhouse** and various services, is right by the roadside, 60km from Selfoss and a bit less than that from Þingvellir. All Golden Circle tours and **public buses** stop here for at least an hour, long enough to catch an eruption and get fed, but not to ascend Bjarnfell or get out to Haukadalur. Moving on, there are daily buses all through the year on to Gullfoss, and back to Selfoss and Reykjavík, though you might have to wait a day or two for specific services south via either Laugarvatn or Reykholt.

There's good-value **accommodation** either at *Hótel Geysir* (☎486 8915, fax 486 8715; studio flats with bathroom and kitchen 6500kr, ②), or at the hostel-style *Geysir Guesthouse/Haukadalur III* (☎486 8733; sleeping-bag accommodation 1400kr, made-up bed 1800kr), which tends to get booked out in advance. For food, the roadhouse's **café** is overpriced and mediocre; you'll get a better deal at the hotel **restaurant**, even if you're only after a bowl of soup and coffee. Note that there's no store at Geysir, and you'll need to bring supplies if you're self-catering.

Gullfoss

About 6km up the road from Geysir on the Hvítá river, **Gullfoss** – Golden Falls – can hardly fail to impress, whether in full flood during the spring thaw or frozen and almost still in the depths of winter. Although most people bypass it unknowingly on the bus, the approach road over moorland follows the top of a two-kilometre-long **canyon** sided in organ-pipe basalt columns, into which Gullfoss drops in a pair of broad cataracts: the first steps out ten metres in full view, then the river bends a sharp ninety degrees and falls a further twenty metres into the gorge's spray-filled shadow. **Paths** along the edge are danger-ous when icy, but at other times they allow you to get thoroughly soaked while viewing spray rainbows above the drop.

The falls are now protected as a nature reserve, formed after **Sigríður Tómasdóttir**, daughter of the owner of the estate that incorporated Gullfoss, fought first her father and then the government to stop a hydroelectric dam being built here in the 1920s. Permission to build the dam was granted, but, fanned by Sigríður, public feeling ran so strongly against the project that con-struction never started. The land was later sold to Einar Guðmundsson of near-by *Brattholt* farm (see p.94), who donated it to the Icelandic Nature Conservation Council in 1976.

Gullfoss marks the end of the Golden Circle and conventional vehicle travel in this direction and, unless you're properly equipped to tackle the **Kjölur route** across the Interior (p.280), all roads and daily buses to Selfoss and Reykjavík head back southwest from here.

THE REYKJANES PENINSULA

The **Reykjanes Peninsula**, Iceland's southwestern extremity, provides most vis-itors with their first look at the country, as they exit **Keflavík's** international air-port and take the highway east towards Reykjavík across ubiquitous lavafields. Unfortunately, there's probably nowhere else in the region that's quite so unremittingly bleak and unvegetated – lichen and moss battle it out on the rocks for their share of the landscape – and, lured by grander prospects elsewhere, most people leave Reykjanes behind without a second thought. But if you've a couple of days to fill in, the peninsula is conveniently close to the capital and has a fair amount to offer: Keflavík itself is a departure point for summer **whale-watching trips**; there's wild, rocky scenery and associated **birdlife** right around the coast; ruins and hiking trails inland; winter **skiing**; and – not to be missed – **Blue Lagoon**, one of Iceland's best spas.

With the exception of the Reykjavík–Keflavík highway (Route 41), and the road south off this to Blue Lagoon, **roads** through the region are mostly gravel, and can be rough going at times. **Buses** from Reykjavík and Selfoss cover the region fairly extensively in summer, though you may need to make use of local services or **tours** from Keflavík to reach minor sights; winter transportation is very limit-ed, however. As regards **hiking**, many of the Reykjanes Peninsula's trails are marked by well-made stone **cairns**, nicknamed "priests" (because they point the way but never go there themselves), but you may feel more secure with relevant **maps** as well – Landmælingar Íslands' *Suðurland* 1:250,000 suffices for general navigation. If you're **camping**, be prepared to carry plenty of water (there are very few sources anywhere on the peninsula), and note that there's almost no soft ground to pitch a tent over. Reykjanes' **weather** is very windy and wet – though after rain the contrast between black rocks and green moss is striking – with respectable snowfalls in winter.

The Reykjavík–Keflavík highway

Heading west from the capital, the straight, fast forty-kilometre-long **Reykjavík–Keflavík highway** is the busiest road in Iceland. After the satellite suburb of Hafnarfjörður (p.73) drops away, you're confronted with the peninsula's bald vistas: ranges frame the horizon, with the flat, petrified lava flow of **Þránsskjaldarhraun** in between, blistered with solidified burst gas bubbles and resembling the top of a badly baked cake. As a reference point, look for **Keilir**'s isolated volcanic cone off to the south before you reach the intersection where Route 43 points south to **Blue Lagoon** and **Grindavík**, 33km from Reykjavík; stay on the highway and it's another couple of kilometres before a possible detour coastwards to **INRI-NJARÐVÍK**, a quiet village built around a nineteenth-century church. **Accommodation** here is provided by a barely furnished *Youth Hostel Strönd* at Njarðvíkurbraut 52 (☎421 6211; sleeping-bag accommodation 1400kr, made-up bed 1500kr; airport connections can be arranged), near the church; there are good views over the sea to Snæfellsnes and an easy ten-kilometre **coastal trail** east to the otherwise forgettable hamlet of **Vogar**.

Past the Inri-Njarðvík junction, the highway splits to run either a final few kilometres out to the airport and Reykjanesbær, or down towards **Hafnir** and the southwest peninsula (see p.99).

Reykjanesbær: Keflavík and Njarðvík

Stretching for 5km along the seafront, **KEFLAVÍK**, and its satellite **NJARÐVÍK** – collectively known as **Reykjanesbær** – between them form what is easily the Reykjanes Peninsula's biggest centre. Keflavík was a trading port as far back as the sixteenth century, but it was World War II that established the town's current status, when US defence forces stationed here took advantage of the peninsula's flat geography and built an **airport** west of town. At the war's end, US attempts to make this refuelling and supply base permanent proved unpopular with Icelanders and were abandoned, but following Iceland's joining of **NATO** in 1949 – an event that sparked a riot in Reykjavík – the US pressured Iceland into agreeing to the idea. The base opened in 1951, and Keflavík and Njardvík flourished alongside as service centres, busy through the Cold War era but in its aftermath, like the base itself, slightly at a loss. Many of Reykjanesbær's residents still work at the base, however – and remain ambivalent about the US-NATO presence and its implications for Iceland.

Aside from the odd fighter jet screeching overhead, the effects of all this on Reykjanesbær are implied rather than seen, and the town remains ordinary and functional – not really a stopover of choice unless you want to catch an early flight from the **international airport** (see p.43), just 5km west, or hook up with a **whale-watching tour**. These leave from the harbour mid-April to mid-September, with June through to August as the most likely time to spot minke whales, porpoise and dolphin; if you're exceptionally lucky, blue whales or orca may show, though you may, of course, see nothing at all. Operators include the Whale Watching Centre (☎421 2600, fax 421 2517); H. I. Tourist Service (☎421 7777, fax 421 3361; includes trip to Nature Centre at Sandgerði); or *Hvalbakur* (☎897 3332). Tours last around three hours, cost 2800kr, and you'll need warm clothing.

Practicalities

Reykjanesbær's services are strung out along a couple of kilometres of the main street, Hafnargata, which stretches north from Njardvík to a **roundabout** at the top end of Keflavík, with nothing clearly marking a boundary between the two. The SBK **bus station** is just past this roundabout, with services shuttling to and from here several times daily, year-round, between the airport, Reykjavík, Blue Lagoon, Garður and Sandgerði, with summer services and **tours** to all over the peninsula. All accommodation can arrange an airport bus pickup, or you can call a **taxi** (☎421 4141).

Down at the Njardvík end of town, the **post office** is on the east (sea) side, roughly opposite the turning to the large Samkaup **supermarket** and Reykjanesbær **campsite** (☎ & fax 421 1460; 350kr per person plus 300kr per tent), where they have phones, showers, toilets, plus a small dining room. Moving up into Keflavík, the crossroads with Vatnsnesvegur is where you'll find **banks** and ATMs, and also a **library**, with the usual supply of foreign-language newspapers and magazines. West is the airport road, while east down Vatnsnesvegur is more **accommodation**: almost on the crossroads, at Hafnargötu 57, *Flug Hótel* (☎421 5222, fax 421 5223; ⑦) is a modern transit hotel, as is *Hótel Keflavík* (☎420 7000, fax 420 7002; ⑥), a few doors along at Vatnsvesvegi 12–14, who also run a lower-key guesthouse opposite (same tel; ④).

Continuing up Hafnargata, you'll find several **restaurants**, the best of which is the long-established *Rain* – they've got pizzas, fish dishes and salads (the grilled-chicken salad is very tasty) – and it's also a comfortable place for a drink. From here it's another 500m or so to the roundabout and bus terminal, with Keflavík **harbour** sandwiched between the two.

Around Keflavík

The countryside northwest of Keflavík makes for a good few days' informal coastal camping. **GARÐUR** is the first place to aim for, a tiny, scattered community just 7km from town. A grassed-over ridge marks the remains of an old wall, apparently the original eleventh-century estate boundary; the discovery of nine **Viking graves** found south of here in the 1850s supports the theory. Later associations can be found at the nineteenth-century **Útskálakirkja**, a church built on the site of an earlier place of worship dedicated to Iceland's only saint, **Þorlákur Þórhallsson**, bishop at Skálholt in 1178–93 (see p.93), though not beatified until 1984. Right at Reykjanes' northwestern tip of **Garðskagi**, two **lighthouses** stand next to each other; the older, red-striped affair is right on the seafront and was once used to monitor bird migrations. Its base is a sheltered spot to look seawards – with a pair of binoculars you can spot seals, turnstones, gannets and assorted wading birds.

Heading south of here for another 6km brings you to **SANDGERÐI**, a small fishing village with a busy harbour and another lighthouse, this one bright yellow. Just before the harbour, **Fraeðasetrið Nature Centre** (daily 1–5pm; ☎ & fax 423 7551; 300kr) is a research centre investigating newly discovered invertebrate marine creatures found off Reykjanes, but there's also a display of larger stuffed animals and, for enthusiasts, extensive files on local botany and geology to sort through. Pick of the exhibits is a huge walrus in the lobby; these are unknown from this area, though they appear on the town coat of arms. In summer, the centre also organizes fifteen-minute whale talks and can arrange transport and guides for bird-watching in the area – call ahead for details. *Vitinn* **restaurant**, at the harbour entrance, has good seafood and lamb dishes, and is also a contact for **whale watching** aboard the *Elding* (contact the *Vitinn* on ☎423 7755, fax 423 7780, or phone *Elding* direct on ☎692 4210, fax 554 7420).

A final 7km south past another church, **Hvalsneskirkja**, and a grouping of abandoned, century-old stone sheep-pens, brings you to the end of the road at Bali (Washtub) farm and the orange Stafnes lighthouse; **views** from here take in heavy surf and distant airport buildings. There's a half-day walking **trail** south along the coast from Stafnes to Hafnir (see below), which after about 1km passes the site of **Básendar**, the Reykjanes Peninsula's largest trading town until it was totally destroyed by an overnight storm in January 1799 – killing just one person. Very little remains besides nondescript rubble.

Southwest Reykjanes: from Hafnir to Grindavík

The road to southwestern Reykjanes splits off the Reykjavík–Keflavík highway a little before Keflavík and just after Inri-Njardvík (see p.97), running for 35km past prime bird-watching sites, a scattering of historic and geological sites around **Reykjanestá**, and winding up at the settlement of **Grindavík**, staging post for the warm waters of **Blue Lagoon**.

The first stop is 10km along at **HAFNIR**, another speck of a settlement based around a harbour and old wooden church, by which is a large, rusting **anchor**, a memento from the 1870 wreck of the schooner *Jamestown*. Hafnir's harbour is pretty inactive nowadays, but the adjacent former fish-processing factory has been painted lilac and green and converted into the **Sæfiskasafnið** (May–Sept daily 2–5pm, Sept–April daily 2–3.30pm; 300kr), an aquarium and halibut farm with display tanks full of local fish and crustaceans.

There's a bit more of interest south of Hafnir, where the road crosses a positively lunar landscape strewn with virtually unvegetated lava rubble – probably through a combination of salt spray and sandy soil, which sees rainwater drain straight into the earth. For a closer look, **cairns** around 5km from Hafnir mark the start of the marked, relatively easy fifteen-kilometre **Prestsastígur walking trail** southeast to Grindavik, and also a shorter trail west from a roadside parking bay 2km further on to the coast at **Hafnaberg cliffs**. This latter route takes about 45 tiring minutes over sandy slopes – beware of aggressive, ground-nesting **greater skuas** – past two large volcanic "blisters", and finally ending on top of forty-metre-high cliffs. From spring through to autumn, these are home to tens of thousands of nesting **kittiwakes** and **fulmars**, along with a dusting of **shags** and **black guillemots**, all of which you'll hear (and probably smell) well before you crawl up to look over for a peek – loose soil and strong winds make standing up near the edge extremely dangerous.

Reykjanestá

Ten kilometres south of Hafnir, **Reykjanestá** is the Reykjanes Peninsula's southwestern extremity, the seascapes here embellished by **Reykjanesviti**, one of the area's more interesting lighthouses. To reach it, turn off the main road at the steaming salt-making plant – the only building along the way, but unmistakable anyway – and keep going until you're under the lighthouse around 2km later. Standing some way from the sea atop of a knoll, it replaced Iceland's first lighthouse, which for seventeen years stood on high cliffs overlooking the stormy surf until an earthquake knocked it down in 1896.

From the knoll you should be able to make out **Eldey**, a tall platform of rock rising straight out of the sea 15km to the southwest. This is Europe's biggest **gannet colony**, and has the sad distinction of being where the last known pair of **great auks** (and their single egg) were chased down and killed on June 3, 1844. These flightless sea birds – which confusingly were once referred to as "penguins" – looked like giant razorbills and were common right across the north Atlantic until being hunted into extinction for their meat and oil; for the whole sorry tale, read Erroll Fuller's *The Great Auk* (see "Contexts", p.302). From the mainland at least, it's hard to believe that a flightless bird ever roosted on Eldey's sheer cliffs, but the back of the island has more accessible niches.

Back on land, the foot of the knoll is unusually green, with **arctic terns** nesting amongst the tussocks of grass in early summer – a sign in Icelandic asks you not to collect their eggs. A bumpy circuit back to the main road takes you to another patch of greenery at **Gunnuhver thermal springs**, a small area of bubbling, muddy pools into which an eighteenth-century witch was dragged by a magic rope after she'd killed off her landlord. As always at hot springs, stay on the paths and take care.

Grindavík and the Blue Lagoon

GRINDAVÍK is a sizeable town for this part of the country, a well-serviced fishing port of two thousand souls 14km east of Reykjanestá, where coastal roads and Route 43 north to the Reykjavík–Keflavík highway meet. Like Keflavík, Grindavík has a long history as a trading centre and was important enough to be raided by **pirates** looking for slaves and plunder in 1627; unlike Keflavík, however, the harbour here is still busy and is now given over to a sizeable fishing fleet, whose catches are processed at the large factory here.

For visitors, Grindavík's biggest appeal is its position at the intersection of many of the Reykjanes Peninsula's **walking trails**, which start right at the town's boundaries. Just off Route 43, there's a three-kilometre track heading north to the obvious pinnacle of **Þorbjarnfell** (231m), from where it's possible to link up with further hiking routes east to **Reykjanesfólkvangur** (see p.102); both are well marked. Another good walk follows the coast east from town for 3km to the apex of **Festarfjall** (202m), the remains of a volcano core and splashed with purple, potash-rich rocks. If you'd rather go **horse riding** on these trails, contact Vík Horses (☎426 8303) to arrange time in the saddle.

Grindavík is centred around a kilometre-long main street running off the highway to the harbour. **Buses** from Reykjavík via the Blue Lagoon (daily throughout the year), and Keflavík, Hveragerði, and Selfoss (daily in summer) pull in at a **shopping complex** with **supermarket** and **bank**. For **eating**, there's a pizzeria across the road from here, or you can head straight on to the *Vörr* grill and café-bar at the harbour entrance. Turn left at the shopping centre for the **campsite**, or, if you want a roof over your head, there's a **guesthouse** at the harbour (☎897 6388, 426 8688; dorm bed 1000kr, sleeping-bag accommodation 1400kr, made-up bed 2000kr), opposite the fish factory – though note that this is fairly basic and is really more of a boarding house for local workers, and booking is essential.

The Blue Lagoon

If there's one place visitors make a beeline for in Reykjanes, it's Bláa lónið, the **Blue Lagoon** (April, May & Sept daily 10am–9pm; June–Aug daily 9am–10pm; Oct–March daily 11am–8pm; half-day 800kr, full-day 1000kr). This is a large, milky-blue **thermal spa** just 5km north of Grindavík and an easy forty minutes along surfaced roads from Reykjavík. Popular with Icelanders, the lagoon is an essential trip, especially if you've not yet had an outdoor hot-pot experience – hit this when it's snowing or just on a cold day and soak your body in exhaustingly warm water while your hair, dampened by foggy vapour, freezes solid.

Only 2m deep and surrounded by lava walls, Blue Lagoon is actually artificial, carefully sculpted to turn outflow from the **Svartsengi thermal power station** into a health resort – actually much more attractive than it sounds, as the pool's recent relocation means that you're no longer bathing within sight of the station's glowing lights and organic loops of silver piping. As for the water, Svartsengi taps into steam vents fed by sea water seeping down into subterranean hot pots, and by the time it emerges at Blue Lagoon it has cooled to a comfortable 38°C. There are decoratively positioned caves and arches to swim through, a **sauna**, and silvery-grey **silt** with claims to cure skin ailments – Icelanders scoop handfuls off the bottom and smear it all over their bodies, and the shop also sells beauty products made from this stuff. Whatever the effects on your skin, hair takes a real battering from the lagoon's enriched mineral content; locals rub conditioner in as protection before bathing.

There are several daily **buses** here year-round from Grindavík and Reykjavík, and a rather limited summer service from Keflavík between June and September. The last bus back to Reykjavík departs the spa area at 8pm; for Grindavík it's 6.40pm; and Keflavík, 4.50pm. The **café** at the spa has sandwiches, ice cream and drinks, and there's also a reasonable **restaurant** and **accommodation** down a side road by the power station at the friendly, single-storey *Hotel Blue Lagoon* (☎426 8650, fax 8651; ⑥), who also offer guests free transfers from the airport.

Reykjanes: south coast and Interior

The Reykjanes Peninsula's rough, rubbly **south coast and Interior** comprises a rift system and associated formations running due east of Grindavík. Much of the lower-lying area here is covered in characteristically dire lavafields, rising to equally denuded ridges and peaks which nonetheless make for fine walking. Transport through the area is a bit limited but in good weather it's worth the effort to reach coastal ruins at **Selatangar**, and **Reykjanesfólkvangur's** hot mud pools, lake and hiking tracks. In winter, roads to these places are often impassable, however, and the main point of interest becomes Iceland's biggest **downhill skiing area**, in the mountains at **Bláfjöll**.

During summer, you can get into the area on **buses** running between Selfoss and Reykjavík via Grindavík, but at other times you'll need to hike in or take your own transport. Roads here aren't great, but – aside from access to Móhalsadalur or Bláfjöll (the latter accessed off Route 1 southeast of Reykjaík) – you shouldn't need a four-wheel-drive.

Selatangar

The road east from Grindavík winds over the back of Festarfjall's volcanic core and then twists down again to run parallel to the coast along the base of a rugged, boulder-strewn range. About 12km along, an unsigned track heads 3km south to end at a parking area above a small shingle and sand beach. Have a good look at the distinctive **lava flow** immediately west – you can see how the front hardened into a wall as it hit the water and then piled up with the weight of the lava behind it – before following a **walking track** east, defined by rocks and driftwood. This brings you, in about ten minutes, to the remains of **Selatangar**, a seasonal fishing settlement last used in the 1880s and comprising lava-block dwellings perched above the sea, ranging from buildings the size and shape of a hollow cairn through to large, walled-in caves. There's far more here than you realize at first, but poke around and you'll soon find a score or more sites, some almost completely intact, others just foundations – look for carefully made walls, and neatly framed window and door lintels. No roofs have survived; these may well have been constructed from driftwood (plenty washes up here) or weatherproofed cloth. With near constant wind howling in from the south, rapidly bringing in and dispersing fog with little warning, Selatangar can be quite spooky – some say that there's even a resident ghost – and it doesn't take much imagination to conjure up what life was like here when the place was last occupied.

Reykjanesfólkvangur and Bláfjöll

Reykjanesfólkvangur, a three-hundred-square-kilometre nature reserve, follows the mountainous ranges northeast of Selatangar to their final fling at **Bláfjöll**'s icy heights. It's reached from the main road east from Grindavík, past the Selatangar turning, along an unsigned fourteen-kilometre track that leads through the middle of the reserve along **Móhálsadalur**, an unexpectedly pretty valley with plenty of **camping** potential. Note, however, that access is only possible in summer, and even then you might need at least a vehicle with high clearance. Towards the far end of the valley, there's a gap in the western range where you can follow marked trails 4km west to all-encompassing **views** atop the conical **Keilir volcano**, whose loose scree slopes can be climbed – with care – to its summit (378m).

If you skip Móhálsadalur, you can still see part of the reserve by following the road east from Grindavík, which soon joins Route 42 – which runs between Selfoss and Reykjavík – at **Krísuvík**. Though the site has been farmed since Settlement, today Krísuvík is basically just a wooden **chapel** the size of a large dog kennel on the slopes of a flat, grassy valley. It's another good place to **camp**, and a **hiking** track southeast from the church ends 5km on at the **Krísuvíkurberg** headland, the only spot on Reykjanes Peninsula's coastline with enough soil to support a **puffin colony** – for more on these birds, see the box on p.122.

From Krísuvík, a bumpy 50km eastwards along Route 42 take you to Hveragerði (see p.80), passing the turning south to Þorlákshöfn (see p.123) and ferries to Heimaey (see p.124). North of Krísuvík, however, it's just 2km to **Grænavatn**, a pale-green crater lake, with the **Seltún hot springs** another kilometre further on. This was the site of a moderately impressive geyser until it exploded in October 1999, showering several hundred tons of rock onto the car park and covering the whole area with grey clay. Boardwalks climb up to where hot springs continue to bubble out of the hills above, but the site of the geyser is now just a large, steaming pond.

Beyond Seltún, the road skirts the western shore of **Kleifarvatn**, a five-kilometre-long lake filling the upper reaches of the Krísuvík valley. No camping is allowed along the roadside, partly because the hills here are visibly unstable, though you could **hike** around the eastern side and find a site there.

Bláfjöll

From the top of Kleifarvatn, Route 42 crosses a final ridge of hills and then descends to moorlands for the final 10km run back to the Reykjavík–Keflavík highway at Hafnarfjörður. Halfway along, the unsurfaced Route 417 heads 20km east to the top end of Reykjanesfólkvangur at **Bláfjöll**, the Blue Mountains (700m). The range provides good hiking in summer and, between November and May, is a popular **skiing area**. You can also get here by taking Route 1 east from Reykjavík for 12km and then following the signs south – note that whichever route you follow, during the skiing season you'll probably need a four-wheel-drive vehicle to reach the resort area at **Bláfjallskali**. Most of the eleven slopes here are graded intermediate or beginner level, though there are at least two advanced runs and some off-piste potential, plus extensive cross-country skiing areas, all floodlit to compensate for those short winter days. There's also a **restaurant** and an equipment rental agent on site, but no accommodation.

THE CENTRAL SOUTH

A mesh of glacial-fed riverlands cover the lowland areas of Iceland's **central south**, the hundred-kilometre broad region lying between the lengthy **Þjórsá**, the Bull River, and the clutch of bulky **glaciers** to its west that weigh down Iceland's southernmost tip above the village of **Vík**. It's mixed country: the inland cowers beneath the **Hekla** volcano, whose destructive antics have put paid to regional farming at least twice in recorded history – as ruins in the **Þjórsárdalur** valley illustrate – while the hummocked, grassy plains around the highway are fertile enough to support Iceland's highest concentration of horse farms, and were the setting for many key events of the medieval epic, **Njál's Saga** (see box p.108). Down south, glacial runoffs are responsible for both a handful of picturesque **waterfalls** and a black-sand coastline, while the highland valley of **Þórsmörk** offers some excellent hiking around the edges of the **Mýrdalsjökull** ice cap.

Route 1 runs diagonally through the region to Vík, plied by year-round buses, and off it a variety of roads and seasonal transport run out to the sights. In summer, pretty well everywhere can be reached on **public transport** or **tours** from within the region and, with the exception of tracks to Þórsmörk or remoter inland routes, it's possible to tackle many of the region's roads in a conventional vehicle. In winter, you'll need to check road conditions before leaving the highway in any vehicle.

Þjórsárdalur and Hekla

Entering the region from the east, the highway crosses the Þjórsá over a single-lane suspension bridge around 30km out of Selfoss, with two options for following it northeast upstream. Routes 30 and 32 between them run up the river's western side to hot springs and medieval ruins at **Þjórsárdalur** – all but the final section on sealed roads – while east of the river, a partially surfaced Route 26 gives access to Hekla and seasonal four-wheel-drive tracks north to Sprengisandur and east around the back of Mýrdalsjökull. In summer, buses from Reykjavík and local operators cover much of the region (see the fol-

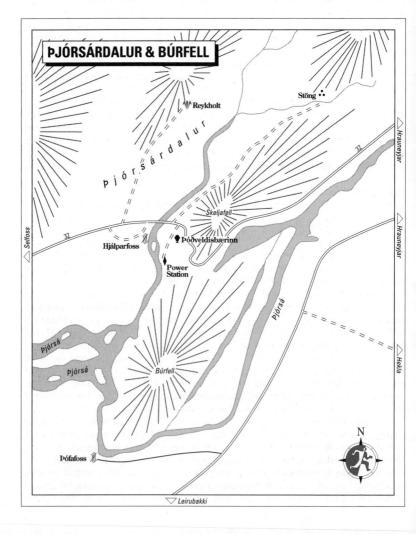

lowing accounts for details); otherwise, access beyond the highway is up to you.

Arnes, Þjórsárdalur and around

The road from Selfoss to Þjórsárdalur is uncomplicated, heading for Flúðir (see p.94) before branching northeast as Route 32 via **ARNES**, little more than a fuel station, store, **guesthouse** (☎486 6048, fax 486 6091; ②) and **campsite**. Once past here, you are within sight of the Þjórsá, with excellent views from a roadside ridge at **Hagafell** straight across the river to Hekla; the table mountain **Búrfell**, and the lower **Skeljafell** to the north, also roughly mark the area to which you're headed.

Thirty kilometres from where you joined Route 32, **Þjórsárdalur** – the Bull River valley – is misleadingly named, as the valley actually sits north of the river, with Búrfell fixing Þjórsárdalur's southeastern corner, and the fifteen-kilometre ridge forming the eastern wall topped by Skeljafell. Aside from a spring-fed trickle, the last thing to flow down here wasn't water but lava from Hekla, eight thousand years ago: subsequent thick falls of ash have regularly wiped out vegetation, making Þjórsárdalur an awesomely sterile place, flanked by brightly coloured cliffs and floored in yellow-grey grit and rocks. As Route 32 crosses the valley's broad mouth, two tracks run northeast off it, giving **access** up Þjórsárdalur, though neither can be completed in conventional vehicles – boggy patches invite detours on to soft gravel, essentially leaving you with the choice of either stopping or deciding which obstruction you'd like to be towed out of.

Hjálparfoss and Stöng

Before tearing off up the valley itself, check out **Hjálparfoss**, a parallel pair of short, foaming falls 100m south of the main road. They drop into a round pool, surrounded by thin basalt columns that both spray in all directions and lie piled up like woodstacks; it would be a fine spot to swim if there wasn't a second, rougher cataract draining the pool towards the power station below Búrfell. Grassy banks do make Hjálparfoss a good place to picnic, however, and there are **harlequin ducks** around in early summer.

A quieter place for a dip – if you can reach it – are the **hot springs** lying 7km up Þjórsárdalur's western side near the abandoned farm of **Reykholt**. There's an easily missed sign for the farm from the main road and, depending on your skills and the weather, conventional vehicles can often get over halfway, leaving a bit of a hike to the springs.

On a completely different tack, follow the signposted Route 327 from the main road another 7km up the valley's eastern side to the remains of **Stöng**; it's a rough and then muddy drive, but even without four-wheel-drive you should be able to get within sight of the red-roofed shelter-shed protecting the site. Set on a small stream below the dark slopes of Stangarfjall, Stöng was the home of a chieftain named **Gaukur Trándilsson** until Hekla erupted in 1104, the first time since Settlement, smothering all of Þjórsárdalur under ash and pumice – there were echoes of this following the mountain's February 2000 hiccup, which carpeted the area ankle-deep in black soot. Stöng was excavated in 1939 and illustrates a typical **Viking homestead**: a longhouse formed the main hall, with a second, smaller hall and two attached outhouses serving as women's quarters, washroom and pens, all built from stone and timber and sided in turf. Neatly built stone foundations, central fireplace and post supports all give a good outline of the original buildings, but it's the stark setting – distant orange and green-streaked valley walls, and patches of pasture clinging on along the stream – which really impress.

For a more complete picture of how Stöng once appeared, return to the main road and take the surfaced turning south marked "Búrfellsstöð", roughly opposite the Stöng junction and immediately below Búrfell. This descends shortly to the power station, but before this follow signs left to **Þóðveldisbærinn** (June to early Sept daily 10am–noon and 1–6pm; 200kr), a complete reconstruction of Stöng. Built in 1974 and based on archeological evidence provided by Stöng and other period sites, this brings the original windowless buildings to life, authentically decked out with everything from hand-cut timber roofing and floors to the fireplace and woollen furnishings.

Búrfell and beyond

Past Þjórsádalur, Route 32 winds up the saddle between Búrfell and Skeljafell and then heads off to the Interior along the banks of the Þórsá. At the top of the saddle there's a four-wheel-drive only track right up to the **transmitter tower** on **Búrfell**'s flattened summit (699m); you can walk it in an hour and, if the weather's unusually good, you won't get a better view of Hekla – just 12km over the river to the southeast – than from here.

Continuing along the Þórsá, you pass a network of dams and spillways, part of an extensive **hydroelectric project** – most impressive of all is a channel, cut 20m deep and parallel with the river, to regulate the flow. It's best viewed from a bridge 10km further along the road, from where you can look back towards Búrfell along the channel's artificially straight walls, or north to where the river explodes out from below another power station into the tight confines of a gorge. Once over the bridge, it's a couple of kilometres to Route 26 and trails around Hekla (see below), or north towards Hrauneyjar farm, first stop on the Sprengisandur route (see p.280).

Hekla and around

Ten kilometres over the Þórsá on Route 1, a lone fuel station and signpost for **Galtalækur** mark the road northeast to Hekla, and as you scoot across the plain, the mountain grows steadily to fill the view and you soon find yourself surrounded by vegetated lava flows. Without your own transport, the best **access to the area** is on BSÍ's Fjallabak buses, which reach most of the places detailed below between July and September on their daily Reykjavík–Skaftafell runs (see p.78, Travel Details).

Those planning to have a closer look at the mountain should pull in 30km along right on Hekla's western edge at *Leirubakki* farm, which can supply fuel, meals by arrangement, outside hot tubs, **horses**, and excellent year-round **accommodation** in a huge, chalet-like, self-catering guesthouse (☎ & fax 487 6591; camping 500kr; dorm bed 1000kr; sleeping-bag accommodation 1500kr, made-up bed 2500kr). Only 3km from the volcano's foothills, the farm also has the latest information on the weather and on routes up the mountain, both of which you'll need constant updating on.

Believed to be the literal entrance to hell in medieval times – a fact that left the mountain unclimbed until daring students Eggert Olafsson and Bjarni Palsson scrambled up in 1750 – **Hekla** is Iceland's second-most-active volcano, with at least eighteen eruptions known to have occurred in the last thousand years. Oriented northeast, the mountain forms a forty-kilometre-long, snow-covered oval ridge cresting at around 1500m; it should be visible for miles around, but a heavy smudge of cloud usually obscures the peak and gives Hekla – Hooded – its name.

Though several thousand years old, Hekla's **earliest recorded eruption** was the one that buried Stöng in 1104 (see p.104), and it has been active, on and off, ever since. Typically, the mountain fires up with very little warning, initially violently spraying out huge clouds of fluorine-rich **tephra** ash, which blankets the landscape, poisons groundwater, and kills fish and livestock. Stöng was by no means the only farm to have been abandoned following such an event – the same eruption is believed to have wiped out twenty similar homesteads – and there are only two working farms around the volcano today. **Lava** follows the ash, welling up at various points along a fissure that splits Hekla's crest lengthways for 5km; during the notorious 1768 eruption – before which the mountain had been dormant for seventy years – flows covered over 65 square kilometres. Eruptions often subside relatively quickly, most of the action occuring within the first few days and followed by months of grumbling – the anguished voices of tormented souls, according to legend.

Hekla has erupted every ten years since 1970, the **most recent eruption** occurring on the evening of February 26, 2000. It wasn't much by the mountain's standards – a plume of ash and steam reaching upwards for 15km and a few days' worth of lava spilling east – but it was notable in that most of Reykjavík descended on the area to watch, only to be trapped on Hekla's slopes by a sudden snowfall. Since then, the mountain's exact height – formerly 1491m – has been unknown, along with the condition of **hiking tracks** to the summit: trails from the north and northeast were buried by ash, and you'll need to make enquiries before setting out.

Þófafoss and Tröllkonuhlaup

Following the main road past *Leirubakki* farm (see above), you immediately find yourself in a wilderness between the Þórsá river and Hekla's western slopes, the ground covered in tiny pieces of lightweight yellow **pumice** that are collected hereabouts for export. After about 5km there's a road towards the mountain itself and **Næfurholt farm**, one of the area's few functioning survivors – though it actually had to be moved after one eruption – then a roadside ridge blocks in Hekla's foothills while the Búrfell mesa springs up ahead of you, looking from this position like the perfect setting for an impregnable fortress. Wheel ruts and guide posts heading off-road towards Búrfell at this point can be followed for 4km to **Þófafoss**, where the river bends right under Búrfell's southern tip in a wide, low waterfall, a friendly splash of blue in a monochrome landscape.

Route 26 continues northeast, passing another waterfall called **Tröllkonuhlaup**, the Troll Woman's Leap, named after one of these unpleasant creatures crossed the river in a single bound while chasing a farmer. Bearing east off this road from here is Route 225, an immediately four-wheel-drive-only track signposted "Hekla" with home-made signs; you need to head this way for the most likely places to start an assault on the peak. Route 26 itself follows the river for 15km up to the junction with Route 32 and the roads to Búrfell and Þjórsárdalur (p.105), or those going northeast via Hrauneyjar farm towards Sprengisandur (p.280).

Njál's Saga country

Heading southeast across the Þórsá on Route 1, the first thing you'll notice are disproportionate numbers of four-wheel-drives towing boxes, and a wide, rolling expanse of pasture, positively reeking of horse – this is one of Iceland's premier horse-breeding areas. The countryside between here and the distant slopes of **Eyjafjallajökull** to the east comprises the plains of the two-pronged **Rangá river** system, the setting for much of the action of **Njál's Saga** (see box below), though parts of this tale were played out right across southern Iceland. With the highway towns of **Hella** or **Hvolsvöllur** as a base, getting out to a handful of the saga sites is straightforward enough, even if you do find more in the way of associations rather than concrete remains when you arrive. You will, however, either need your own transport or to organize **tours** from Hvolsvöllur to visit these – see below for contact details.

NJÁL'S SAGA

There was a man called Mörð Fiddle . . .

Njál's Saga

So begins, rather innocuously, **Njál's Saga**, Iceland's great tale of Viking-age clan warfare and reconciliation. The longest saga of them all, Njál's Saga was written in the thirteenth century, three hundred years after the events it portrays, and owes more to oral tradition than historical sources – though later records and archeology tend to confirm the story's factual basis (dates below are mostly estimates, however).

Told in an immediately accessible, open manner that reveals the protagonists' characters through their actions, the tale centres on the life of **Njál Þorgeirsson** and his family, who are casually ensnared in a minor issue that tragically escalates into a frightful, fifty-year blood feud. Bound by their own personalities, fate, and sense of honour, nobody is able to stop the bloodshed, which ends only after the original characters – and many of their descendants – have been killed. But there's far more to Njál's Saga than its violence, and the tale paints a vivid picture of Iceland at what was, in some ways, an idyllic time: the power of the Alþing at Þingvellir was at its peak, Christianity was overpowering paganism, and the country's independent settlers lived by their own efforts on farming and freebooting.

The tale splits into three uneven parts, beginning in the late tenth century at a point where the fate of several participants is already intertwined. Gifted with foresight and generally respected by all, Njál himself is often a background figure, mediating and advising rather than confronting or fighting, but his sons play a far more active role, especially the proud and ferocious **Skarp-héðinn**. Njál's best friend is the heroic **Gunnar Hámundarson** of **Hlíðarendi**, whose superb martial skills and physical prowess never get in the way of his generosity or sense of justice. Balancing this nobility is the malevolent **Mörð Valgarðsson**, a second cousin of Gunnar's who grows up hating him for his intrinsic goodness and spends the saga's first third plotting his downfall.

Around 970 Gunnar goes against Njál's advice and marries "Thief-eyed" **Hallgerð**, a thorny character who, amongst other things, provokes a violent feud with Njál's household. Njál manages to remain firm friends with Gunnar, but his sons are drawn into the fray by the murder of their foster-father **Þórð**, and the cycle of payback killings begins, quickly spiralling out beyond the two immediate fami-

Hella and around

HELLA, a one-street service centre where the highway crosses the narrow flow of the Ytri-Rangá – also known as the Hólsá, and the western branch of the river Rang – grew through the twentieth century to serve **Rangárvallahreppur**, the fertile farming district beyond Hekla's southwestern extremities. The town is really just somewhere to pause before heading on: aside from historic sites nearby, Hella is close to the volcano, clearly visible 50km to the northeast, and is the start of the inland route behind Mýrdalsjökull – see p.118.

Buses set down east of the river at the shopping centre, where you'll find a fuel station, **supermarket** and **bank** with ATM. **Accommodation** and **camping** is available through the *Gistihúsið Mosfell*, next door to the shopping centre (✆487 5828, fax 487 5004; camping 500kr, cabins 5000kr, ②), and at the *Aegissiða IV*, west of the river behind the Shell petrol station (✆487 5104, fax 487 5171; camp-

---

lies. Mörð sees his chance, and manipulates various disreputable characters into picking fights with Gunnar, who emerges undefeated yet increasingly worn down from each confrontation. At last, Gunnar is ambushed by **Þorgeir Otkelsson**, whose father he killed earlier as a result of Mörð's scheming; he kills Þorgeir too, but is outlawed for it and banished from Iceland at the Alþing in 990. Torn between his respect for the law and love of his country, Gunnar finds himself unable to leave, and is hunted down to Hlíðarendi by a posse led by Mörð and the upstanding chieftain **Gizur the White**. When Gunnar's bowstring snaps during the siege, Hallgerð spitefully refuses to give him two locks of her hair to restring the weapon; "To each their own way of earning fame," says Gunnar, and is cut down.

After an interlude describing Iceland's **conversion to Christianity** in 1000, the violence sparked by Hallgerð thirty years earlier resurfaces when Njál's sons kill her distant relative, the arrogant **þráin Sigfússon**, for his part in Þorð's death. Attempting to placate Þráin's family, Njál adopts his son **Höskuld**, and for a while all seems well. But over the next decade resentment eats away at Njál's sons, and, encouraged by Mörð – who, now that Gunnar is dead, has shifted his vindictive attentions to Njál – they kill Höskuld while he's sowing his fields one sunny morning. Höskuld's influential father-in-law **Flósi of Svínafell** agrees initially to a cash settlement for the murder, but Njál inadvertently offends him at the Alþing in 1011: confrontation is inevitable and the eighty-year-old Njál, bowing to fate, retreats with his sons to his homestead **Bergþórshvoll**. Flósi and his men attack and torch the building, killing all but Njal's son-in-law **Kári**, who, having promised Skarp-héðinn to avenge them all, escapes through the burning roof and runs into the night, his clothes ablaze.

Though a hunted man, public opinion against the burning of Njál runs so high that Kári is able to remain free, and at the following year's Alþing he confronts Flósi and his allies – now known as the **Burners**. Mörð stirs up trouble again and a pitched battle breaks out; in the aftermath, all but Kári accept the Alþing's conditions for peace, which banishes Flósi and the Burners from Iceland until tempers have cooled. For his part, Kári swears vengeance, and swiftly tracks down and kills a group of Burners before fleeing the country himself. For the next few years Kári wanders around northern Europe, picking off a couple more of his enemies, getting caught up in Ireland's battle of Clontarf in 1014, and seeking absolution from the Pope. Eventually returning to Iceland, Kári's ship is wrecked at Ingólfshöfði off the southeast coast; walking inland through a blizzard he seeks sanctuary at Svínafell and becomes reconciled with Flósi, bringing Njál's Saga to an end.

ing 450kr, sleeping-bag accommodation 1500kr, cabins 5500kr). *Laufafel* **restaurant** at the fuel station is good for grills and staples; and you can organize **bike rental** through *Gistihúsið Mosfell* (day/week rental 1100/6000kr), and **horses** through the Árbakki horse-farm (☎487 5041).

Þingskallar and Keldur

Just east of Hella, Route 264 heads north off the main highway back towards Hekla. Seven kilometres along at an airstrip, Route 268 and the Ytri-Rangá branch up to the road on which *Leirubakki* farm sits, on Hekla's western slopes at Næfurholt (see p.106) – a forty-kilometre journey in all, mostly on gravel tracks. About halfway there, **Þingskallar farm** was a medieval assembly site, and traces of around thirty *buðs*, temporary encampments similar to those at Þingvellir (see p.88), have been found in the fields here.

Stay on Route 264 past the airstrip, and 20km east of Hella is the pretty farm of **Keldur** (June–Sept daily 10am–noon & 1–6pm), named after the "cold springs" that seep out from under a grassed-over lava flow to form a sizeable stream winding off across the plains. Keldur is mentioned in Njál's Saga (see box on p.108) as the home of **Ingjald Höskuldsson**, uncle of Njál's illegitimate son. Initially siding with Flósi, as Njál's kinsman Ingjald refused to take part in the burning, he was speared in the leg by Flósi and defected to Kári's side. Although there's a modern farm at Keldur, an older string of a half-dozen **turf-covered halls** almost date back to saga times – part of the central one here was built in the thirteenth century and is Iceland's only extant example of a stave-built hall from this period. There's also a fifty-metre, block-lined **tunnel** running over to an ensemble of stalls, stable and a barn; estimates date this to the eleventh century. Take a moment to register Keldur's location, right on the steep front of one of Hekla's flows: the few **stone walls** defining the fields below were built to limit ash drifts and erosion following periodic eruptions.

While you're in the area, ask at Keldur for directions to **Gunnarsstein**, a boulder where Gunnar and his allies were ambushed by a group led by local horseman **Starkað of Þríhyrningur**, whose red stallion had lost a fight to Gunnar's previously untried black one. The battle that followed contains some of Njál's Saga's most savage imagery; when it was over, Gunnar and his brothers had killed fourteen of their attackers, but at the cost of Gunnar's own son **Hjört** (whose name means "heart"). The tale describes Hjört's burial here afterwards, and in the mid-nineteenth century a mound at the site was indeed found to contain a skeleton and a **bracelet** engraved with two hearts (now in the National Museum in Reykjavík; see p.56).

Oddi

Not mentioned in Njál's Saga, though of a similar vintage, **ODDI**'s couple of houses and prominent, red-roofed **church**, all set on the only hill for miles around, are 5km southwest down the highway from Hella and then the same distance directly south along Route 266. Though you'd hardly credit it today, Oddi was once famous, when the French-educated **Sæmundur Sigfússon** became priest here in 1078 and established an **ecclesiastical school**, whose alumni later included thirteenth-century law speaker, historian and diplomat Snorri Sturluson, and St Þorlákur Þórhallsson. Sæmundur himself is the subject of several legends, including one in which the devil – disguised as a seal – offered to carry him back to Iceland from France so that Sæmundur could apply for the post at Oddi. When they were within sight of the shore, the resourceful Sæmundur brained the devil with a psalter, swam to safety, and got the job. Less to his credit, he's also held responsible for causing Hekla's 1104 eruption by tossing a keepsake from a jilted lover – who turned out to be a witch – into the volcano. Built in 1924, the current church is pretty plain, though it has thirteenth-century relics squirrelled away, and a nice modern organ.

Hvolsvöllur

Eleven kilometres southwest down the highway from Hella you reach the broad, open mouth of the **Markarfljót valley**, along which the intricately tangled shallow river flows westwards out from the Mýrdalsjökull and Eyjafjallajökull caps. Right on the edge is **HVOLSVÖLLUR**, a few short streets off the highway labouring under an unattractive electricity station and transmitter tower. Despite this, it's a good place to get to grips with Njál's Saga country; you're close to the settings for some of the most important scenes in the tale, and Hvolsvöllur itself – or rather the farm, **Völlur**, 5km north – was the homestead of Mörð Fiddle, with whom Njál's Saga opens. Mörð's daughter **Unn** was both Gunnar's cousin, and mother to the tale's arch-villain, Mörð Valgardsson. On a purely practical note, the town is also the last place to stock up on provisions before heading eastwards to **hiking** grounds at Flótsdalur or Þórsmörk.

Hvollsvöllur's only attraction is 150m along Route 261 off the highway, the **Saga Centre** (☎487 8781, fax 487 8782, *www.islandia.is/~njala*). The bulk of this is an entertaining museum, with models of Viking houses and ships; maps, dioramas and paintings showing the location of local sites and the extent of Viking travels across the northern hemisphere; and replica clothes and artefacts. The centre also puts together **guided tours** of the region, along with **saga feasts** in a reconstructed medieval-style hall – a couple of fun hours' worth of food and storytelling, with the staff dressed up in period costume (phone ahead for times and costs). For less conventional ways of getting around, you can organize local **off-road exploring** with Ómar Halldórsson (☎487 8781).

Practicalities

The Hlíðarendi **fuel station**, on a sharp bend on the eastern edge of town where Route 261 leaves the highway for the Saga Centre, and the upper Markarfljót valley, is also the **bus stop**, serviced by year-round buses travelling along the highway between Reykjávik and Höfn, and summer services to and from Þórsmörk (p.117) and the Fjallabaksleið. Hvolsvöllur's array of services – **bank, post office** and **supermarket** – are spread along the main highway, while you can find **accommodation** opposite the Saga Centre at the slightly faded *Hótel Hvolsvöllur* (☎487 8187, fax 487 8391, *hotelhvol@simnet.is*; ③–⑤); 200m further on again are brighter prospects at the popular *Asgarður* guesthouse's cabins or dormitories (☎487 8367, fax 8387, *asgard@simnet.is*; sleeping-bag accommodation 1900kr, ②–③) – they also have outdoor hot tubs. Hvolsvöllur's **campground** is off the highway behind the fuel station – take the road opposite the bank. **Places to eat** are limited to the hotel's restaurant, the fuel station's café, or a small pizza place just up from the Saga Centre.

Bergþórshvoll

South of Hvollsvöllur, follow Route 255 coastwards for 20km off the highway and across the flat, waterlogged countryside to **Bergþórshvoll**, where Njál's homestead sat a thousand years ago. Today, a modern house occupies the low crest 1km from the sea, and there's no visible trace of the original hall, which was besieged by Flósi and his hundred-strong Burners in the autumn of 1011. The two sides (Njál's party consisting of about thirty of his family and servants) met face to face in the open, but, urged by the old man, the defenders retreated into the house, and Flósi – certain that Njál's sons would kill him if they escaped – dishonourably ordered the building to be set alight. After women, children, and servants were allowed to leave, Njál, his wife, and sons burned to death; only "lucky" Kári managed to break out. In support of the story, charred remains found here during twentieth century excavations have been carbon-dated to the saga period.

The Markarfljót valley: Hlíðarendi and Fljótsdalur

It's a beautiful thirty-kilometre run east along Route 261 from Hvollsvöllur up **Fljótshlíð**, the flat-bottomed, heavily farmed border of the **Markarfljót valley**, with the saga site of **Hlíðarendi** and beautiful valley setting at **Fljótsdalur** to draw you out this way. Ahead loom Eyjafjallajökull's black sided, ice-capped heights, while on a clear day the view south extends all the way to the sea; in summer, streams and ponds draining the wetlands in between are alive with **birds** – especially black-tailed godwits, with their vivid orange and black plumage.

Hlíðarendi
The road follows the base of a long line of green hills heading up the valley, whose slopes contrast strongly with the starker-toned mountains opposite. About 15km from Hvollsvöllur there's **accommodation** at *Smaratún* farm (☎487 8471; cabins 5500kr, sleeping-bag accommodation 1350kr, camping 450kr), and a few kilometres further, a side road climbs steeply up to where a small church and handful of buildings command a splendid view of the area. This is **Hlíðarendi**, home to Njál's great friend Gunnar, the most exemplary of all saga characters; unfortunately, however, his fine character always tended to inspire envy rather than admiration. When Gunnar found that his wife **Hallgerð** had encouraged a slave to steal food from the prosperous farmer **Otkel**, he fatefully slapped her – hence Hallgerð's refusal to help him later on (see box on p.108) – and offered Otkel repayment. Otkel's malicious friend Skamkel, however, advised him against accepting, starting the long sequence of blood-letting which led to Gunnar being declared an outlaw. But on his way to the coast to leave Iceland forever, Gunnar's horse stumbled and he looked back to Hlíðarendi across fields of golden corn and newly cut hay, and knew he could never leave his homeland – a rare moment in saga literature when landscape, rather than personality, drives events – and so, returning to Hlíðarendi, met his end.

Though there are a couple of turf outhouses behind Hlíðrendi's church, nothing besides the scenery remains from the saga period – though, as Gunnar felt, this can be ample reward (at least on a sunny day). Look on the plains below for **Stóra-Dímon**, an isolated rocky platform called **Rauðuskriður** in the saga, where Njál's sons Skarp-héðinn and Helgí ambushed Þráin Sigfússon, who had participated in the murder of their foster-father. Þráin spotted them but Skarp-héðinn slid over the frozen river and killed Þráin before he had time to put on his armour, setting in motion events which were to lead directly to the burning of Njál. You can get to Stóra-Dímon from the Flótsdalur road (see below).

Fljótsdalur

East of Hlíðarendi, the hills grow steeper as the valley narrows, with a frill of small, ribbon-like waterfalls dropping down to the roadside. A track pointing south past Stóra-Dimón to Route 1 marks the start of the gravel, and then you're running alongside the Markarfljót's river-system's continually shifting maze of flat, intertwined streams up **Fljótsdalur**, a valley caught between the steep, glaciated slopes of **Tindafjall** to the north and Eyjafjöll to the south. Ten kilometres from Hlíðarendi and 27km from Hvolsvöllur, the road crosses a ford and becomes a four-wheel-drive track; there's a popular **youth hostel** here in a renovated turf house, open from mid-April to mid-October (☎487 8498 or 487 8497; sleeping-bag accommodation 1500kr, self-catering only) – you definitely need to book in advance.

Fljótsdalur forms the southern boundary of the wild Fjallabak Nature Reserve, an area covering the old traffic routes which ran, quite literally, *fjallabak*, "behind the mountains". With the right vehicle you can reach Landmannalaugur's wilderness of crisp peaks and hot springs, and the deep canyon of Eldgjá from here, or hike north up Tindafjall to its ice cap, **Tindfjallajökull** (1462m), via a series of mountain huts – the hostel gives advice on the routes.

Eyjafjallajökull: Skógar and Þórsmörk

Southeast across the Markarfljót's sprawl, the highway finds itself pinched between the coast and **Eyjafjöll**, the mountainous platform for the **Eyjafjallajökull glacier**. Though dwarfed by its big sister Mýrdalsjökull immediately to the east, Eyjafjallajökull's 1666m apex is southwestern Iceland's highest point, and the mountain has stamped its personality on the area: an active **volcano** smoulders away below the ice, which enjoyed major eruptions in the seventeenth and nineteenth centuries and whose sub-glacial melting in 1967 sent a rock-and-gravel-laden flash flood – a *jökulhlaup* – west down the Markarfljót. Less disruptively, the glacier-fed streams running over Eyjafjöll's abrupt southern edges have created a string of roadside **waterfalls** around the town of **Skógar**, one end of a popular hiking trail that runs between the two glaciers to the beautiful highland valley of **Þórsmörk** on Eyjafjallajökull's northern side – also accessible in summer along a four-wheel-drive track.

Seljalandsfoss and Seljavellir

Right at Eyjafjöll's western tip, Route 249 heads north off the highway and around the back of the mountain to Þórsmörk, becoming the four-wheel-drive-only F249 in the process (see p.116). Although conventional vehicles can't manage the whole 30km, there's no trouble reaching **Seljalandsfoss**, a narrow but powerful waterfall that drops straight off the fellside into a shallow pool only a few hundred metres from the highway. Paths run behind the curtain – you'll get soaked but the noise of the falls is impressively magnified – and over to a couple of smaller falls. There's also a **campsite** with a turf-covered shower block at *Hamragarðar* (350kr), a farm. If you're heading on to Þórsmörk, the last **place to stay** is 7km up the road from the highway at *Stóramörk* (☎487 8903, fax 487 8901), a farm with limited year-round sleeping-bag accommodation and bed space (1250–3000kr). Another place to feature in Njál's Saga, Stóramörk was the property of Ketil

Sigfússon, a decent man who had the awkward task of being both Njál's son-in-law and brother to Þráin. Having constantly struggled to dampen down conflict, Ketil later supported Flósi, but was nonetheless spared by Kári after being disarmed by him in a fight.

Back on the highway past the Seljaland-Þórsmörk junction, layered, rough cliffs rise back from the roadside, with plenty more waterfalls cascading over the edges. Twenty kilometres along, the hills suddenly recede, allowing views inland right up to the glacier, and a gravel road heads 3km north up the valley to further **camping** at *Seljavellir* (☎487 8810; 350kr), another farm – call in advance and they'll collect you from the highway. This is an excellent spot, with an outdoor pool and hot tub to relax in, and some wild hiking along the glowering valley and, via **hot springs** and yet more **waterfalls** just below the snowline, up onto Eyjafjallajökull itself.

Skógar, Skógarfoss and the Þórsmörk trail

A further 7km past the Seljavellir road, **SKÓGAR** is an insubstantial collection of buildings set back off the highway at the end of a track beside Skógarfoss, easily the biggest of the local **waterfalls** and worth a look even if you've otherwise already had enough of these things. Other reasons to stop are the entertaining folk museum, or the rewarding two-day **hiking trail to Þórsmörk** up over inter-glacial passes.

Skógar was settled by the twelfth century, and you'll find a detailed record of the region's farming and fishing communities east of the *Edda* hotel at Skógar's **folk museum** (daily 9am–6pm; 300kr). Impromptu guided tours or folk-singing sessions organized by local character and curator Þórður Tómasson are one of the museum's highlights, but even if he doesn't appear the exhibits themselves are interesting enough. Various types of traditional stone and turf farm buildings have been relocated to an adjacent field, while inside the main building, the centrepiece is a ten-metre-long, heavy wooden **fishing boat** from 1855, tough enough to survive being dragged regularly over miles of sand and gravel to be launched. Along with associated fishing gear aranged around the walls, look for the wooden moulds used to cast fish-shaped hook weights – a design considered to be lucky. Contemporary agricultural and domestic items flesh out the rest of the display, though there are a few older items too, most notably a **jade cloak pin** of Viking vintage, an edition of Iceland's first printed **bible**, dated to 1544, and a fourteenth-century fragment from the Book of David written in Icelandic on vellum. Ask to be shown (it's easy to overlook otherwise) the brass **ring** found hundreds of years ago, said to have once adorned a chest of gold hidden behind Skógarfoss by the Viking settler **Þrasi** – legend has it he argued with his children and didn't want them to inherit his wealth.

The **Skógarfoss** falls themselves, at 62m high, are justifiably famous, looking good from a distance and nothing short of huge, powerful and dramatic close up as they drop straight off the plateau – stand on the flat gravel river bed in front of the rainbow-tinged plunge pool, and the rest of the world vanishes into the white mists and noise. A steep but otherwise easy **track** climbs to the top, putting you eye-to-eye with fulmars as they sit on nests or wheel through the spray, beyond which a muddy trail heads upstream to a much smaller but violent cataract and brilliant views coastwards and up across mossy moorland towards the distant glacier cap. If you're properly prepared, you can follow the river in this direction right up to join the Þórsmörk hiking route – see below.

There's a **bank** in Skógar but no other services, and all **places to stay** are open summer only. In Skógar proper, the grey, boxlike school doubles as an *Edda* hotel (☎487 8870, fax 8858; sleeping-bag accommodation 1200kr, dorm 1500kr, singles/doubles 4000/5000kr), while towards the falls is the similar *Grunnskóli*, which has sleeping-bag accommodation (1300kr) and a nearby **café**. Continue on and just short of the falls is a **campsite** (400kr) with toilets and showers. You can also stay at *Drangshlíð* (☎487 8868, fax 487 8869; sleeping-bag accommodation 1000kr, ②; laundry available), a **farmstay** 3km west of Skógar and reached directly off the highway, where, turf-roofed, the outhouses built onto the mouth of a cave here were once used to pen livestock.

The Þórsmörk trail

The twenty-kilometre **Þórsmörk trail** from Skógar, over the Fimmvörðuháls pass between Eyjafallajökull and Mýrdalsjökull, and down the other side to Þórsmörk, is, for its scenery (at least in good weather) and relatively easy grade, a thoroughly enjoyable walk. The first 9km to the pass makes a good day-return hike from Skógar, while most people heading on to Þórsmörk spread the trip over two days, overnighting at one of the two mountain huts en route. It's also perfectly feasible to do the whole Skogar–Þórsmörk stretch in one day if you're reasonably fit and start early enough. The trail is passable only in summer, and even then you should come prepared for possible rain and snow, poor visibility and cold; the track is pretty well defined but it's highly advisable to take a compass and Landmælingar Íslands' 1:100,000 *Þórsmörk-Landmannalaugur* **map**. The Icelandic hiking clubs Útivist and Ferðafélag Íslands also offer **organized hikes** along the route just about every weekend from mid-June to late August; see p.35, in Basics, for their contact details, and note that you'll need to book with them in order to use their huts.

There are two **routes** to set out on, taking either the steep track up to Skógarfoss, or following the four-wheel-drive track between the falls and Skógar's *Edda* hotel. The two trails converge further on, then run up to a small bridge over the Skógá, the only safe point to cross this river. Wherever you begin, a steady four hours should see you below the wide mouth of the Fimmvörðuháls pass at the rather basic **first hut** (500kr), from where it's another twenty minutes to the roomy, well-appointed *Fimmvörðuskáli*, a **second hut** (1000kr) owned by Útivist at the highest point on the route (1043m) – note that this lies several hundred metres west of the main track, and will be booked solid over summer weekends.

If you have the necessary gear and experience on ice, both glaciers are within easy reach from here; if not, your options are to return to Skógar or continue past a lake and on through the pass over snowfields – in clear weather, there are excellent views of the mountains further north during this section. A short, steep stretch beyond (with a chain to help you along) descends to easier slopes and down to Goðaland and *Básar*, the **third hut** (see p.117), at Þórsmörk's eastern end, then it's another few kilometres west along the valley to the rest of Þórsmörk's cabins and campsites – allow six hours in total from Fimmvörðuskáli. There's a daily afternoon **bus** from Þórsmörk back to Reykjavík via Hvolsvöllur; for more about this and further hiking from Þórsmörk itself, see below.

Þórsmörk

Hidden from the rest of the world by encircling glaciers and mountain wilderness, **Þórsmörk** – Thor's Wood – is a series of highland valleys north of Eyjafallajökull, watered by a host of multistreamed glacial rivers that flow west off the heights and down into the Markarfljót. Green-sloped, covered in stunted willow and birch woodland and wildflowers, with icy peaks rising above, this is one of Iceland's most beautiful spots, a forestry reserve since 1921 and, through the summer months, a magnet for everyone from hard-core hikers coming to tackle the numerous trails, to equally energetic partygoers here to unwind in a bucolic setting. For those on a saga quest, Þórsmörk also features indirectly in the latter part of Njál's Saga as the homeland of the boastful comic character Björn, who, despite his innate cowardice, proves a useful ally to Kári in his vengeance against the Burners.

Aside from hiking **trails from Skógar or Landmannalaugur** (see pp.115 & 283), there's only one **road to Þórsmörk**, the thirty-kilometre Route F249 off the highway from Seljalandsfoss (see p.113). Owing to several difficult river crossings and just plain rough conditions, this is a high-clearance, four-wheel-drive-only

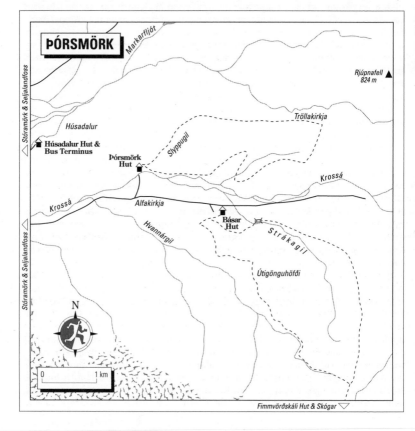

route, and can be quite an adventure in itself. After Stóramork, the road follows the south side of the Markarfljót, and passes a lake at the foot of a short **glacier** descending from the north side of Eyjafjallajökull, before crossing a handful of rivers and reaching the Þórsmörk area. From June 1 until September 15 there's a daily **bus** from Reykjavík's BSÍ terminal via Hvolsvöllur; the Útivist and Ferðafélag Íslands walking clubs (see p.35 for details) also organize **guided hikes** here every weekend in summer, with less frequent excursions year-round – including over New Year.

Accommodation is at designated campsites or using your own sleeping bags in mountain huts (in season, make sure you book in advance). All huts have communal kitchens, with showers a couple of hundred kronur extra, though you'll need to provide **food** – the closest places to buy **supplies** are Hvolsvöllur and Vík. Ideally you'll enjoy sunny weather, but come armed for wet, cold conditions, and carry both Útivist's 1:25,000 **map** of hiking trails, along with Landmælingar Íslands' 1:100,000 *Þórsmörk-Landmannalaugur* sheet, if you plan to do any serious exploration – only a few of the trails are described below. For a totally different take on the area, you could also try **whitewater rafting** on the upper Markarfljót and Emstruá rivers, arranged in advance with *Tindfjöll* (☎487 5557, fax 487 5587, *www.tindfjoll.is*).

In Þórsmörk

Þórsmörk is laid out west–east along the seven-kilometre-long **Krossá river valley** and its offshoots, with the area north of the river generally referred to as Þórsmörk proper, and the area south of the river as **Goðaland**. Walking trails are everywhere, and the **road** runs right to the eastern end of the Þórsmörk area along the south side of the river past the three huts and campsites.

Unless you've hiked up from Skógar (p.114), you'll arrive at the western end of things along the F249; buses wind up off the main road at the small valley of **Húsadalur**, on the north side of the river, where there's a **campsite** (550kr) and a bus-company run **hut** (☎852 5506; 1250kr). A better base, however, lies about 1.5km east of here on foot (or 4km by road from the Húsadalur junction), at Ferðfélag Íslands' popular **Þórsmörk hut** (1350kr) and **campground** in the pleasant valley of **Langidalur**; this sits at the intersection of many of Þórsmörk's hiking trails. An easy couple of kilometres on foot south from here via the bridge over the Krossá below Valahnúkur peak (465m), **Álfakirkja**, the Elves' Church, is an impressive bowl of cliffs facing the mouth of **Hvannárgil**, a 2km-long series of canyons flanking a small river. For a satisfying full-day's hiking north of the river through Þórsmörk's highland meadows – around 14km return from Langidalur – aim for **Rjúpnafell** (824m); a favourite route there runs up through **Slyppugil** gorges and then follows valley slopes up to the peak, returning on a lower path which follows the Krossá back to camp.

To explore south of the river at Goðaland, base yourself a further 2km east of the Þórsmörk hut at Útivist's **Básar hut** (1200kr), where **camping** is also allowed (550kr) at the start of the trail over Fimmvörðuháls to Skógar (see p.115). With Eyjafjallajökull looming above, the landscape here is more extreme than across the river, and the hiking is generally harder, though the two-kilometre trail east to the well-vegetated, rough-edged gorge of **Strákagil** is easy enough. Continue through the gorge and you'll eventually emerge on a grassy hillside below **Heiðarhorn**, a steep spur of rock around 5km from Básar which, with a little effort, can be partially scaled for sweeping views north. From here, it's a further 8km to the

Fimmvörðuháls hut on the Skógar trail (see p.115), or you could bear northwest just 2km on from Heiðarhorn and return to Básar along the ten-kilometre trail skirting the steep-sided peak of **Útigönguhöfði** (805m) – there's a chain to help climb up it if you're really keen.

From Mýrdalsjökull to Vík

The country's fourth-largest ice cap, **Mýrdalsjökull** blocks off and protects southwestern Iceland from the scouring effects of the glacial deserts – **sandurs** – further east, though it's also responsible for creating the extensive strips of black, basaltic sand fringing the 30km of coastline between Skógar and **Vík**. Like neighbouring Eyjafjallajökull, Mýrdalsjökull harbours a powerful volcano, 1300-metre **Katla**, which last erupted in 1918 and is worryingly overdue for another blast – they occur once every seventy years on average. Katla's *jökulhlaups* (volcanically induced flash floods; see p.298 for more about these) have extended the coastline and devastated the area's farms a dozen or more times since Settlement, and the possibility of an imminent eruption is being taken very seriously by locals – though in summer, BSÍ (see p.46) runs **day tours** onto the ice cap from Reykjavík, including a short spin on a snowmobile.

Moving down the coast, the mountains supporting Mýrdalsjökull – and occasional outlying glaciers, such as Sólheimajökull – intrude further and further towards the sea, finally reaching it around Iceland's southernmost tip, **Dyrhólaey**, where they form impressively sculpted cliffs, home to innumerable seabirds. Inland, there's highland scenery around **Heiðarvatn** lake, while back down on the coast past Dyrhólaey, the sleepy village of **Vík** itself marks the beginning of the long cross-desert run into southeastern Iceland. **Route 1** and **buses** link Skógar with Vík, and with everything else within 10km of the highway.

Sólheimajökull, Dyrhólaey and Heiðarvatn

Not far east of Skógar, the highway crosses the shallow, foul-smelling Jökulsá Fulilækur, a glacial river whose sulphurous scent points to origins beneath the ice surrounding Katla. Look upstream from the roadside and you'll see the apparently insignificant, narrow ice tongue of **Sólheimajökull**, one of Mýrdalsjökull's outrunners; a **track** heads up the broad river valley for 5km to the front of the glacier, but you'll need a four-wheel-drive vehicle or at least high clearance for the abundant boggy patches along the way. Close up, Sólheimajökull is steep-faced and heavily streaked in crevasses, and is worth a look if you haven't seen this sort of thing before – though camping here is ill-advised given the current volcanic unrest under Mýrdalsjökull.

Around 12km down the highway from Jökulsa Fulilækur, an unsurfaced, bumpy Route 218 slides 5km coastwards past a handful of farms and then over a causeway to where the country reaches its southernmost extremes at **Dyrhólaey**. As Dyrhólaey's cliffs and – unusally for Iceland – extensive **sand dunes** have been declared a **nature reserve** protecting large seabird colonies, access is only allowed outside the summer nesting season. But even at other times, you won't be able to miss Dyrhólaey's **birdlife**, with every cliffside crevice occupied from April until the winter sets in, white streaks of guano a sign of tenancy. Stumpy, ubiquitous fulmars – gull-like but actually related to albatrosses –

chatter nervously at you from their half-burrow roosts, or soar in on narrow wings for a closer look; out at sea, rafts of eider duck bob in the waves, while razorbills, guillemots and puffins, bills full of fish, dodge scavenging brown skuas on their way homewards.

Once over the causeway, continue straight ahead and you'll find yourself on a rocky shelf above the sea with the swell hammering into the low cliffs at your feet; turn right, however, and the road rises steeply to end at a dumpy, orange **lighthouse** on the hill above. Cross over a wall and out onto a tall, sheer-sided projecting headland to where a **stone cairn** marks the end of the mainland, a suddenly final, incontestable point from where the Atlantic stretches into the horizon. You can't see it from here, but you're actually standing on a sizeable **arch**, which, according to tradition, was big enough for sailboats to pass under. Below to the west, black beaches stretch up towards Skógar; to the east, the weather-sculpted rocks off Vík stand out clearly, though the town itself is hidden behind round-backed **Reynisfjall**, a ridge that divides the southwest's fertile farmland from the bleak expanses of sand on the far side. It also blocks the weather: it's not unusual for it to be snowing one side, and bright and sunny on the other.

Back on the highway towards Vík, the road climbs up over a saddle between the mountainous inland and Reynisfjall itself. At the top of the saddle, a 3km-long sideroad branches northwards off Route 1 to **Heiðarvatn**, a flat, blue oval lake half-circled by heath-covered fells, somewhere to do nothing much for a couple of days. The road ends where the two adjacent farms Stóra-Heiði and Litla-Heiði (☎487 1266 or 487 1265) provide **camping and fishing permits** – the lake is stocked with trout – while there's also a fine twenty-five-kilometre **hiking trail** around to the northeast fells via **Þakgilshellir** – a cave embellished with sixteenth-century graffiti, mostly just names – and then down to the youth hostel at Reynisbrekka, beyond Vík (p.120).

Vík and around

VÍK – more fully known as **Vík-í-Mýrdal** – is a pleasant coastal village nestling on the toe of Reynisfjall's steep eastern slopes, a last haven before taking on the deadening horizons of the **Mýrdalssandur** beyond, the desert laid down by Katla's overflows. Vík got going as a trading station in the late nineteenth century and today serves a few farms and the tourist traffic, with a **wool factory** that's making a name for itself with some innovative designs.

Vík's **older quarter** is south of the highway along the hundred-metre-long main street of Víkurbraut – though the only sight as such is Brydebúð, Vík's original nineteenth-century store, now vacant. A footpath takes you further, following Reynisfjall's margin down to the sea, signposted **Reynisdrangar**, or Troll Rocks. Curiously enough, this leads to about the only place along the shore that you can't see these three tall, offshore spires from; local legend holds them to be petrified trolls, caught by the sun as they were trying to drag a boat ashore. A small colony of **kittiwakes** nests on cliffs above the black-sand beach here, identified from other gulls by their onomatopoeic piping call and black wing-tips. In summer, the open heath east past the roadhouse also becomes a nesting ground for millions of **arctic terns** – don't approach as you'll be mercilessly dive-bombed by every bird you disturb. If the weather is fine, the **trail** up Reynisfjall from the highway also makes for a good hour's climb, ending by the weather station on a muddy hill top, with puffin burrows at your feet and views east of Vatnajökull's mighty ice cap floating above the desert haze.

Practicalities

Vík's hundred-odd houses are laid either side of a two-hundred-metre stretch of the highway: south along Vikurbraut you'll find the **supermarket** and *Hótel Lundi*; while a **post office** and **bank**, and the rest of Vík's accommodation, are strung along the highway. As you head east, one of the last buildings is a fuel station-cum-roadhouse that doubles as the **bus stop** for the year-round services to and from Reykjavík and Höfn.

Top of Vík's **places to stay** is the characterful *Hótel Lundi*, at Vikurbraut 26 (☎487 1212, fax 487 1404; sleeping-bag accommodation 1200kr, ①); the inn-like main house has the better rooms, while cheaper board is in an older, tin-sided building with self-catering facilities. Alternatives are *Gistihús Arsalir*, a big, homely guesthouse on the hillside as you descend to Vík (☎487 1400; sleeping-bag accommodation 1250kr, ②); the lower-budget *Gistihús Katrinar*, on the highway near the bank (☎487 1186; 3500kr); and *Hótel Vík*, a low-key, modern hotel with a pool, off the highway past the post office (☎487 1480; sleeping-bag accommodation 1250kr, 7350kr). There's also a **campsite**, down past the *Hótel Vík* on a good, flat lawn, with shower and toilet facilities. Alternatively, there's summer accommodation in the hills fringing the Mýrdalssandur at the *Reynisbrekka* **youth hostel** (June to mid-Sept; ☎487 1106, fax 1303; ③) 6km east of town along the highway, then 4km north on a gravel road – they might be able to pick you up if you call in advance.

For **places to eat**, *Gistihús Arsalir* has a **café** and both hotels have **restaurants**, while the roadhouse stays open until 9pm serving burgers, sandwiches and coffee. The hotels also set up **tours** ranging from bird-watching hikes to snowmobiling on Mýrdalsjökull; while the tour group Ævintýraferðir (☎487 1334, fax 487 1303) explore Dyrhólaey and the adjacent coastline by boat and amphibious vehicle. **Leaving**, the highway east of Vík is highlighted by two alarming orange **warning signs**, alerting you to the possibility of a Katla eruption and the dangers of sandstorms in Mýrdalssandur. If you're crossing under your own steam, take any sandstorm warnings seriously and note that it's over 70km to the next town, Kirkjubæjarklaustur (see p.273).

VESTMANNAEYJAR

Vestmannaeyjar – the **Westman Islands** – are an archipelago of fifteen or so scattered, mostly minuscule volcanic islands around 10km off the coast south of Hvolsvöllur. The only inhabited one in the group, **Heimaey**, is an easy trip from the mainland, and there are two immediate draws: **Eldfell volcano**, still steaming from its 1973 eruption, an event that doubled the width of the island and almost swallowed **Heimaey town**; and the legendary birdlife, especially the large **puffin** population (see box on p.122). Heimaey is small enough to explore thoroughly in a short time, and you might get to know some of the people too, who form a self-contained community that sees itself as quite distinct from the mainland; don't be surprised if you hear residents talking about "going over to Iceland", as if it were another country. Heimaey aside, the other Westmans are difficult to land on and so only infrequently visited by bird or egg collectors, but you may be lucky and score a trip around **Surtsey**, the group's southernmost outpost and newest island, which sprang from beneath the waves during the 1960s.

Geological babies at only 12,000 years old overall, the Westman Islands were inhabited some time before the mainland was officially colonized in the ninth century by Ingólfur Arnarson and his foster-brother Hjörleifur Hróðmarsson. The brothers had brought British slaves with them who, coming from the lands at the

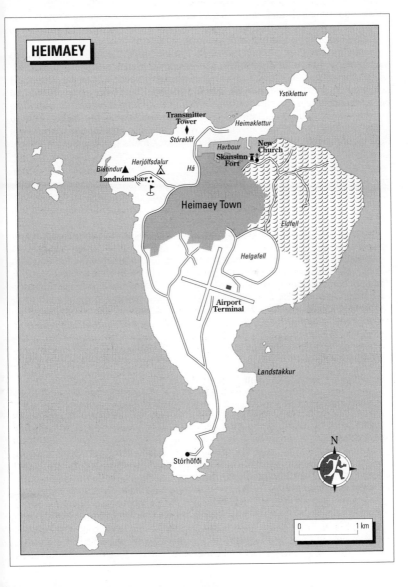

west of the Viking world, were known as **Westmen**; Hjörleifur's revolted, killing him and fleeing to these islands – hence the name – where they were tracked down and slaughtered by a vengeful Ingólfur. Over the succeeding centuries Heimaey became permanently settled by fisher-farmers, but was generally outside the mainstream of Icelandic history until **Algerian pirates** raided on July 16, 1627, killing or enslaving half the population of five hundred. It took some time to get over this disaster, but by the twentieth century mechanization and the country's economic shift from farming to fishing saw Heimaey becoming a prosperous little haven, well positioned for taking advantage of what are still the North Atlantic's richest cod and haddock grounds.

Fresh problems lay ahead, however. The submarine eruption that formed Surtsey turned out to be the prelude to events a decade later on January 23, 1973, when a two-kilometre-long volcanic fissure suddenly opened up eastern Heimaey below the long-extinct cone of **Helgafell**. Within 24 hours the entire island had been evacuated and the new volcano Eldfell was gushing lava in violent spasms; houses were buried beneath the flow, set afire by lava bombs, or simply collapsed under the weight of accompanying ash. Worse still, the lava threatened to block the harbour mouth until halted by the then untried method of pumping sea water

---

PUFFINS

Puffins – *lundi* in Icelandic – belong to the auk family, which includes razorbills and guillemots (murres) and are basically the northern hemisphere's equivalent of penguins. Puffins are, without a doubt, the most charismatic of the auks, plump little birds with an upright build and pied plumage, all set off by bright orange feet and a ridiculous, sail-shaped bill striped yellow and red. This comical livery is compounded by an aeronautic ineptitude: their method of landing seems to consist simply of putting out their feet and stopping flying – bad enough to watch on water, but painful to see them bounce and skid on land. Puffins also seem to get victimized by just about every other seabird species: when feeding young, they fly back from fishing with their catch carried crosswise in the beak like a moustache, a clear signal for gulls, skuas and even razorbills to chase them, hoping they'll drop their chick's meal.

Each April, around six million puffins arrive to **breed** in Iceland from unknown wintering grounds, a sizeable chunk of which home in on Heimaey, excavating nesting burrows in huge, dense colonies on the island's grassy cliffs – surrounding seas are also rich in **herring fry**, on which puffins raise their young. Watching a colony involves a bit of sensory overload at first, and it takes a while before you can sort through the confusion and concentrate on details: pairs excavating and cleaning up burrows with foot and bill, preening each other, or just sunning themselves on the grass; the adults' desperate flights back from their fishing grounds. Fledgeling puffins, or **pufflings** – who lack the adults' colourful bill – leave the nest at night during August, when they often become confused by the town's bright lights and fly, dazzled, into buildings; local cats get fat on this easy prey, but residents round up birds and release them.

Westman Islanders also eat puffins, collecting eggs and netting up to a quarter of a million birds annually as food – all hunters are licensed, and great care is taken to catch only non-breeding birds. The **meat** is dark and rich, and often tangy from being smoked; if you want a taste, several of Heimaey's restaurants offer it during the summer, or you may be able to buy birds more cheaply in the town's supermarkets.

onto the front of the flow. When the eruption ceased in June, Heimaey was two square kilometres bigger, had a new mountain, and, amazingly, a better harbour – the entrance is narrower now, but more effectively shielded from prevailing easterly winds. Only one person was killed during the eruption, but 1700 islanders never returned – around 5000 people live here today – and the disruption to the fishing industry contributed to Iceland's runaway inflation during the late 1970s.

You can get over to Heimaey at any time of year, though you'll find few birds or visitor facilities in winter. If you can choose, pick a sunny couple of days between May and September, which will give you time for walks, intimate contact with puffins and thirty other breeding **bird species**, plus the chance to see whales and seals. If you want to party as well, join in the August Þjódhátíð, a **festival** to commemorate Iceland's first steps towards full independence in 1874, which boils down to three days of hard drinking with thousands of other revellers. As to the Westmans' **weather**, temperatures are amongst the mildest in Iceland, but things can get extremely blustery – the country's highest windspeed, 220km an hour, was recorded here.

Heimaey is well connected to the mainland by flights and ferries. From Reykjavík airport, Flugfélag Íslands operate at least two daily **flights**, with more in summer, and the journey takes about half an hour (3500kr).

The *Herjólfur* car and passenger **ferry** leaves from **Þorlákshöfn**, a small town 20km south of Hveragerði, comprising a port and a sprawl of relief housing for islanders evacuated from Heimaey in 1973. Buses from Reykjavík's bus terminal (700kr) connect with all ferries; Þorlákshöfn's **ferry terminal** is left off the main road as you enter town, where **tickets** for the crossing (1500kr each way) are sold up to an hour in advance. The ferry leaves Þorlákshöfn daily at noon, with extra weekend and summer services (details on ☎483 3413.) An onboard cinema and café make the *Herjólfur* as comfortable as possible, though the crossing (2hr 45min) can be notoriously rough.

There's no reason to linger in Þorlákshöfn, but should you get stuck here overnight, there's a fuel station with burger bar and an adjacent supermarket about 500m from the port entrance; seek **lodgings** at the *Heimagisting* guesthouse at Reykjabraut 19 (☎483 3630; 4650kr) or at the **campsite**, about 1.5km away in the town's residential area.

Heimaey and Surtsey

By far the largest of the Westman Islands, **Heimaey** – the Home Island – is only around 6km in length and, except along the east and north coasts, is pretty flat and grassy. At its broad top end you'll find **Heimaey town** and the harbour faced by a narrow peninsula of sheer-sided cliffs; east of here, buildings are hemmed in by Eldfell, the fractionally higher slopes of Helgafell, and the rough, grey-brown solidified lavafield, Kirkjubæjarhraun. Moving south down Heimaey, you pass the cross-shaped airstrip, beyond which the island tapers to a narrow isthmus, over which the rounded hummock of **Stórahöfði** rises as an end point.

Many of the small islands around Heimaey sport shelter huts, but as their sheer cliffs emphasize, actually landing on them is beyond the scope of casual day-tripping. In fact, of the Westman's other islands, **Surtsey** – 20km to the southwest – is the only one that you might get a close look at, and even that's unlikely.

Heimaey town

Inevitably clustered around it's harbour and pretty quiet outside the peak tourist season, Heimaey's small centre is split by the south-running main street **Heiðarvegur**, with most services and attractions in the streets east of here between the harbour and Hásteinsvegur. Don't miss the **aquarium and natural history museum**, on Heiðarvegur (May–Aug daily 11am–5pm; Sept–April Sat & Sun 3–5pm; 300kr), a mix of stuffed animals and far more entertaining tanks of live marine fauna. Up the road on the corner with Vestmannabraut, Heimaey's **cinema** hosts the summertime **Volcanic Film Show** in English (at least once daily mid-May to Sept; 600kr), an hour-long account of the eruption and snippets about life in the islands – when they run, the evening show is best as there's a question-and-answer session afterwards. A few minutes away down Hásteinsvegur, there's

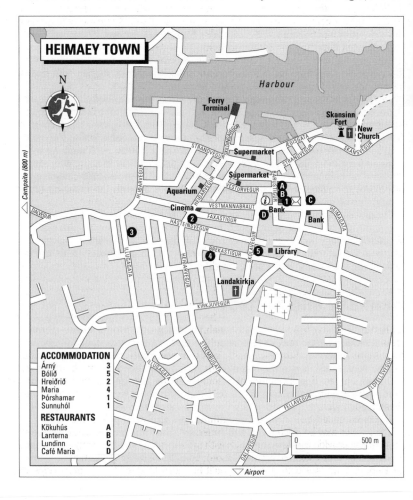

HEIMAEY TOWN

N

Harbour

Ferry Terminal

Skansinn Fort

New Church

△ Campsite (800 m)

STRANDVEGUR

Supermarket

HLÍÐARVEGUR

Aquarium

HEIÐARVEGUR

VESTURVEGUR

Supermarket

BÁRUSTÍGUR

ÆGISGATA

STRANDVEGUR

SKANSVEGUR

DALVEGUR

Cinema

VESTMANNABRAUT

i

A
B
1

C

D Bank

Bank

HEIMAGATA

FAXASTIGUR

HÁSTEINSVEGUR

2

3

ILLUGAGATA

BREKASTÍGUR

SKÓLAVEGUR

4

5 ■ Library

HEIÐARVEGUR

Landakirkja

KIRKJUVEGUR

HEIÐAFELLSBRAUT

STRÉMBUGATA

ILLUGAGATA

FELLAVEGUR

ELDFELLSVEGUR

DALAVEGUR

ACCOMMODATION

Árný	3
Bólið	5
Hreiðrið	2
Maria	4
Þórshamar	1
Sunnuhól	1

RESTAURANTS

Kökuhús	A
Lanterna	B
Lundinn	C
Café Maria	D

0   500 m

▽ *Airport*

also a **Folklore Museum** at the library (June to mid-Sept Mon–Fri 2–5pm; 300kr), whose extensive collection dates from the Algerian invasion onwards, padded out with cases of stamps and coins.

Down at the **harbour**, you'll find a tightly packed fleet of fishing boats and several warehouses, processing their catches and whose yards are piled with kilometres of black and green commercial fishing nets being examined and repaired. Around 500m east along Strandvegur, the road crosses the edge of the 1973 flow and passes a neat square of lava-block walls forming **Skansinn fort**, built after the 1627 pirate episode to house Iceland's first and only army. This wasn't the sole occasion that pirates took advantage of the Westmans' isolation: a sixteenth-century rover named Gentleman John once stole Heimaey's church bell. Next door to Skansinn, a new **church** built from Norwegian-supplied timber was consecrated in mid-2000 to celebrate a thousand years of Christianity in Iceland. The building faces the presumed site of the country's first purpose-built church (rather than a converted pagan shrine), raised by Gissur the White a few years before he championed the new faith at the Alþing in 1000 AD.

Back near the harbour off Strandvegur, you can follow first Kirkjuvegur and then Heimagata below the two-storey-high, steeply sloping **lava flow** that swallowed up the eastern end of town. There used to be several half-crushed houses emerging from the embankment along here, but these have been cleared and now there's just one very weatherbeaten shed in the rubble off Heimagata. Elsewhere, however, collections of little stones painted with windows and doors mark where somebody's home was buried.

For a final idea of just what Heimaey's population went through in 1973, head south to black roofed **Landakirkja** on Kirkjuvegur, the island's main church. Enter the **cemetery** opposite through its arched, wrought-iron gates and on the left you'll find the grave of Theódóra Jónsdóttir, whose two-metre-high memorial is topped by a statuette of an angel, missing a hand. Ash buried this to the angel's thighs; it took Heimaey's residents over a year after the eruption to dig their town out of the black drifts.

Practicalities

Arriving, the airport is a couple of kilometres south of Heimaey – a bus or taxi will be waiting – while the harbour is right in the town. The island's **tourist office** is at Vestmannabraut 38 (Mon–Fri 9am–5pm, plus Sat & Sun 1–5pm in summer; ☎481 1572), where they hand out maps, recommend tours, and book accommodation. Both **banks** – one at the corner of Kirkjuvegur and Vestmannabraut, the other on Bárústigur and with an ATM – handle foreign exchange. For **payphones** either try the **post office** on Vestmannabraut, the town's fuel stations, or the cinema – which also has the town's only public toilet. For general supplies, there are two **supermarkets**: Vöruval, which looks like a domed tent, on Vesturvegur (daily 8am–7pm), and a newer, slightly better-stocked KÁ two streets over on Strandvegur. If you've forgotten some vital bit of outdoor equipment, try the camping-supplies chainstore, 66°N, just west of *Hótel Þórshamar* on Vestmannabraut.

There's a good range of **accommodation** in town, all best booked in advance – in winter, places may be closed, and in summer, full. The guesthouses are all self-catering but can provide breakfast or meals with sufficient warning. The only non-central option is the **campsite** (300kr per person), spectacularly located 1km west of town at Herjólfsdalur (see below), where you'll be lulled to sleep by the mutterings of thousands of fulmars roosting above you; it also has showers and toilets on site. If you're here for the August festivities, come a few days early to find a pitch.

The most central **guesthouse** is *Hreiðrið*, at the corner of Faxastígur and Heiðarvegur (☎481 1045, fax 1414; sleeping-bag accommodation 1400kr, made-up bed 4000kr), a friendly place with half a dozen beds, able to organize everything you'd want to do on Heimaey; guests get a discount for the Volcanic Film Show (see p.124). They also run a summer-only bunkhouse called *Bólið*, further out at Skólavegur 15 (☎481 1045, fax 1414; 1400kr). Other options include made-up bed or sleeping-bag accommodation in the long-established guesthouse *Árný*, a few minutes' walk east of the centre at Illugata 7 (☎ & fax 481 2082; sleeping-bag accommodation 1400kr, made-up bed 3800kr); and the new, purpose-built guesthouse *Maria*, nearby at Brekastígur 37 (☎481 2744, fax 481 2745; ②). Heimaey's only **hotel** is the comparatively plush *Þórshamar*, on Vestmannabraut 28 (☎481 2900, fax 481 1696); the main block has modern twins (④) with TV and bathroom; and there are also cheaper self-catering units opposite (①) and budget accommodation behind at their guesthouse *Sunnuhól*, with made-up beds (2100kr) or sleeping-bag accommodation (1400kr).

Heimaey has plenty of **places to eat**. For coffee and cake, try the bakery, opposite the tourist information on Vestmannabraut, or *Kökuhús* on Bárustígur. Burgers and the like are dished up at the fuel stations, though you'll find better in this line – as well as puffin and grills – at *Lundinn Restaurant Bar and Pub* on the corner of Kirkjuvegur and Heimagata. *Café Maria*, on Vetmannabraut and Skólavegur, is a cosy upmarket café-restaurant, serving relatively expensive though big portions – try their excellent grilled monkfish, lamb or savoury crepes. For a different atmosphere, the mid-range *Lanterna*'s incongruous Greek taverna style surroundings are highly recommended, as is the menu, which covers everything from local puffin, cod and mussels, to grills and salads.

The rest of the island

Heimaey's compact spread of lava and volcanoes – including a still-steaming Eldfell – some stiff cliff hikes around the north peninsula or easier trails down south, and abundant bird life, need a day or two to do them justice, but try and allow extra time to return to favourite spots. It's possible to **walk** everywhere along tracks and roads, though in summer either PH Tours (☎481 2922, fax 481 2007) or Gísli Magnússon, Brekastígur 11 (☎481 1909, fax 481 1927) run informative two-hour daily **bus tours** of the town, lava, volcanoes, and south of the island – including multilingual commentary – with pickups from Heimaey's tourist office and campsite. Also in summer, Viking (☎852 7652, fax 481 1086) leave the harbour daily at 10.30am and 3.30pm for a ninety-minute **boat trip** around Heimaey (1900kr); while Íslandsflug (☎481 3050 or 570 8090) lay on sightseeing **charter flights**.

The lava flow and Heimaklettur cliffs

Steps from Heimagata take you up on top of the 1973 **lava flow**, though it's hard to imagine this huge mass of sharp-sided, weirdly shaped rubble moving at all, let alone flowing. Engraved headstones up here commemorate houses entombed 16m below your feet, and paths lead off in all directions. Heading northeast, you cross the road and end up at a lookout opposite yellow **Heimaklettur cliffs**, a good first spot to spy on seabirds and, currently, **Keiko**, the killer-whale film star of *Free Willy*. Keiko was caught off Iceland but spent most of his 25-odd years in

American aquariums until public pressure following the film saw a massive operation launched to return him to the wild. Penned in the bay below Heimaklettur until he learns to fend for himself, he's recently been taken on "walks" in the open sea, where his keepers hope to introduce him to a pod of wild orca. If he's still in residence, you won't see him make any dramatic leaps for freedom, but may glimpse his oddly floppy dorsal fin break the surface. Chaotic nesting scenes fill the cliffs above, the ledges packed with various types of **guillemots** – if you're wondering how they manage to nest successfully on such incredibly narrow ledges, the secret is in the almost conical shape of their eggs, designed to roll in a circle around their tips, rather than in a straight line over the edge. Red marker poles lead around the coast from here across ankle-twisting debris, with quick asides down to shingle **beaches** or deeper into the flow; half an hour will see you rejoin the road a short distance from Eldfell's north face.

Eldfell and Helgafell

Close to town and not too steep, you won't need much time or energy to climb both Eldfell and Helgafell on any one of a dozen or more tracks. **Eldfell** is easiest, with any one of a number of tracks up the volcano's east or north slopes bringing you to the 205-metre-high rim in about five minutes. One of the first things islanders did on returning in 1973 was to start **turfing** Eldfell's slopes to cover up and stabilize the ash; aerial seed drops during the 1990s also helped, and today about half the cone is well grassed – enough to make it hard to believe that what you're climbing on is so young. Eldfell's top is capped in red-grey scree and lava bombs, with views from the narrow rim of the other Westman islands and the mainland's crisp ice caps. The soil is still steaming up here – in fact, a metre down it's well over 500°C – and there are further hot patches inside the steep-walled **crater**, which the sure-footed can slip and slide down into from the top, and then exit through a gash in the north wall and onto the road.

Immediately southwest of Eldfell, **Helgafell** looks similar but is both taller (226m), and much older at 5000 years of age. The north and southwest faces present the swiftest routes to the summit, which was used as a lookout post during Heimaey's pirate period; today the **crater** is almost filled in, a shallow, sterile depression.

The north peninsula

Heimaey's **north peninsula** is undoubtedly the wildest part of the whole island, a four-kilometre string of sheer-sided cliffs and hills that includes the island's apex. Be aware that some of the tracks described below are potentially very dangerous, and to tackle them you need to be confident on narrow trails with hundred-metre drops either side.

Start a kilometre west of town by the campsite and golf course at **Herjólfsdalur**, a dramatically scaled bowl formed from a long-dead, partially collapsed volcano. Setting for the August festival, there are also the remains of **Landnámsbær** to examine, Iceland's oldest known settlement. While only traces of foundations remain, the type of buildings they recall is typically Norse, marking a longhouse, kitchen area, pigsty and outhouses; carbon-dating places parts of Landnámsbær in the seventh century, though Icelandic historical records say that the farm was founded two hundred years later. Either way, it was abandoned around 1100, perhaps due to overgrazing on the island. The easy hike up the slopes behind looks much steeper than it actually proves to be, and **views** from the top are stupendous, with the peninsula rising precipitously from a wild seascape and Landnámsbær's outline picked out by the early morning sun. The peak to the west is **Blátindur** (273m), its base circled by a slippery path; east is a tricky, if not almost impossible, goat-track along the peninsula to **Há**, though taking this is not recommended – for an easier ascent, return to the western side of the harbour to where there's a rope dangling down the rocks for practising **sprengur**, the traditional cliff-climbing method on Heimaey, used by young men collecting puffins and bird eggs; free beginners' sessions are held here in July (ask at the tourist information for when to turn up). Walk up the grassy hillside behind and you're on Há, from where you can peer down into Herjólfsdalur, or walk north along the rim to opposite the transmitter tower atop of **Stórakliff**. Climbing this latter peak is exhausting work; the track again begins down below on the western side of the harbour, ascending first on steps, then scree, then ropes, and finally, a chain – presumably, transmitter maintainance crews are airlifted in.

The peninsula's northeastern heights are far harder propositions, though you can reach the start on the north side of the harbour easily enough. First is **Heimaklettur**, requiring a rough scramble to reach the Westman Islands' highest point of 283m. Beyond is **Ystiklettur**, regularly visited by puffin collectors but best not attempted without local knowledge and help – if the tourist office can't help, make enquiries at *Hreiðrið* guesthouse (see p.126).

Coastal trails

Due to the airstrip running over the eastern cliffs, it's not possible to circuit Heimaey completely, though that still leaves you with a decent 12km of **coastal trails** to follow. In summer you'll definitely see heaps of **birds**: wheatear, snipe and golden plovers love the island's grassy slopes; ringed plovers, redshanks and purple sandpipers pick over the shoreline for edibles; while skuas, eiders, gannets and auks patrol the seas. And if you've come to Heimaey hoping to see **puffins**, you'll be able to get within touching distance of several million of them.

A clear 6km trail heads down the **west coast** from the golf course, a pleasant couple of hours following the crumbly cliff tops south to Stórhöfði. Initially there's plenty of bald basalt overlaid by later lava flows, which clearly poured over the edge and into the sea, then the path rises almost imperceptibly over spongy grass until, halfway along, you suddenly realize that you're fairly high up above the water. After crossing several fencelines, you run down to sea level again past frames for preparing that Icelandic delicacy, *harðfiskur*, dried fish; you'll get an idea of how windy things get here by the huge bags of rocks weighting the frames down. The little **beach** beyond is good for ducks and waders, then it's a steep, short climb up **Stórhöfði** itself, site of a radio tower and sizeable **puffin colony**, and also an excellent place to scan the seas for **whales** and **gannets**, the latter nesting on the sheer-sided islets to the southwest. On Stórhöfði's south side, a boulder anchors ropes for egg collecting on the rocks below.

From Stórhöfði, carry on up Heimaey's **east coast** to a steeper, rockier and weedier beach, often with some serious surf – this side of the island catches the prevailing winds – and occasional **seals** dodging in and out of the swell. Tidal pools and a couple of interesting **caves** might slow you down for a while – if you can get to them – otherwise climb the messy scree behind up onto a ridge and follow this north until it reaches a fenceline. A stile here gives access to the high, stumpy **Landstakkur peninsula**, complete with another huge **puffin** colony and scenic views. Continuing up the coast, you stay high above the sea with a dramatic drop into the deep blue on one side, and a gentle, grassy backslope on the other. Another stiff stretch uphill and you're at a **beacon** above the airstrip, from where you'll have to cut west across country over to the road and so back up to town.

Surtsey

Surtsey has an interesting history and proves that Heimaey is by no means the only island in the group to bear **volcanic** scars. In the late nineteenth century, **Hellisey** unexpectedly popped out of the waves about 5km off Heimaey's southern tip, the first in a series of underwater eruptions that continued at odd intervals for the next few decades. Then, on November 14, 1963, a colossal explosion, accompanied by towering plumes of steam and ash, heralded Surtsey's birth: within a week, there was a volcano rising 70m out of the sea; April 1964 saw lava appear for the first time; and when the eruption finished three years later, what was suddenly the Westmans' second-largest island covered almost three square kilometres. Erosion has since shrunk it by half, but Surtsey remains of great interest to scientists, who are using it as a model to study how islands are colonised by plants and animals. Unexpectedly, they found that larger plants were the first to become established; previous theories had suggested grasses were first needed to hold the soil together.

As it's a special reserve, **landing on Surtsey** is prohibited unless you're part of a scientific team, and your only chance of a trip over is with Viking (☎852 7652, fax 481 1086), who make four- to six-hour circuits from Heimaey – you'll get a good look but they don't land – once or twice each summer, if they get enough people interested and the weather's good enough.

travel details

Buses

Blue Lagoon to: Grindavík (3 daily; 10min); Hafnarfjörður (3 daily; 30min) Keflavík (June–Aug 2 daily; 15min); Reykjavík (3 daily; 50min).

Eyrarbakki to: Hveragerði (daily; 1hr); Reykjavík (2 daily; 1hr 40min); Selfoss (3 daily; 25min); Stokkseyri (6 daily; 10min); Þorlakshöfn (4 daily; 15min).

Geysir to: Gullfoss (3 daily; 10min); Hveragerði (3 daily; 1hr 50min); Laugarvatn (2 daily; 1hr 20min); Reykholt (daily; 5min); Reykjavík (3 daily; 2hr 30min); Selfoss (3 daily; 1hr 30min).

Grindavík to: Blue Lagoon (3 daily; 10min); Hafnarfjörður (3 daily; 35min); Reykjavík (3 daily; 55min).

Hella to: Höfn (3 weekly; 5hr 15min); Hveragerði (daily; 55min); Hvolsvöllur (daily; 20min); Kirkjubæjarklaustur (3 weekly; 2hr 45min); Reykjavík (daily; 1hr 40min); Selfoss (daily; 35min); Skógar (7 weekly; 1hr 5min); Vík (7 weekly; 1hr 35min).

Hveragerði to: Eyrarbakki (1 daily; 1hr); Geysir (daily; 1hr 35min); Gullfoss (daily; 1hr 45min); Hella (daily; 55min); Höfn (3 weekly; 6hr 20min); Hvolsvöllur (daily; 1hr 25min); Kirkjubæjarklaustur (3 weekly; 3hr 50min); Laugarvatn (2 daily; 1hr 20min); Reykholt (2 daily; 1hr 35min); Reykjavík (daily; 40min); Selfoss (daily; 30min); Skógar (7 weekly; 2hr 10min); Vík (7 weekly; 2hr 40min).

Hvolsvöllur to: Hella (daily; 20min); Höfn (3 weekly; 4hr 55min); Hveragerði (daily; 1hr 25min); Kirkjubæjarklaustur (3 daily; 2hr 25min); Reykjavík (daily; 1hr 50min); Selfoss (daily; 1hr); Skógar (7 weekly; 45min); Vík (7 weekly; 1hr 15min).

Keflavík to: Blue Lagoon (Jun–Aug 2 daily; 15min); Garður (2 daily; 10min); Hafnarfjörður (5 daily; 45min); Reykjavík (5 daily; 1hr); Sandgerði (daily; 10min).

Laugarvatn to: Geysir (2 daily; 30min); Gullfoss (2 daily; 45min); Hveragerði (2 daily; 1hr 20min); Reykjavík (2 daily; 2hr); Selfoss (2 daily; 1hr); Þingvellir (July–Aug, daily; 30min).

Reykholt to: Geysir (daily; 5min); Gullfoss (daily; 15min); Hveragerði (2 daily; 1hr 35min); Reykjavík (2 daily; 2hr 15min); Selfoss (2 daily; 1hr 15min).

Selfoss to: Eyrarbakki (3 daily; 25min); Geysir (3 daily; 1hr 30min); Gullfoss (3 daily; 1hr 40min); Hella (daily; 35min); Höfn (3 weekly; 5hr 50min); Hveragerði (daily; 30min); Hvolsvöllur (daily; 1hr); Kirkjubæjarklaustur (3 weekly; 3hr 20min); Laugarvatn (2 daily; 1hr); Reykjavík (daily; 1hr); Skógar (7 weekly; 1hr 40min); Stokkseyri (3 daily; 15min); Þingvellir (July–Aug, daily; 1hr 15min); Þórlakshöfn (4 daily; 1hr); Vík (7 weekly; 2hr 10min).

Skógar to: Hella (7 weekly; 1hr 5min); Höfn (3 weekly; 4hr 10min); Hveragerði (7 weekly; 2hr 10min); Hvolsvöllur (7 weekly; 45min); Kirkjubæjarklaustur (3 weekly; 1hr 40min); Reykjavík (7 weekly; 2hr 40min); Selfoss (7 weekly; 1hr 40min); Vík (7 weekly; 30min).

Stokkseyri to: Eyrarbakki (6 daily; 10min); Hveragerði (1 daily; 1hr); Reykjavík (1 daily; 1hr 40min); Selfoss (3 daily; 15min); Þórlakshöfn (4 daily; 25min).

Vík to: Hella (7 weekly; 1hr 35min); Höfn (3 weekly; 3hr 40min); Hveragerði (7 weekly; 2hr 40min); Hvolsvöllur (7 weekly; 1hr 15min); Kirkjubæjarklaustur (3 weekly; 1hr 10min); Reykjavík (7 weekly; 3hr 15min); Selfoss (7 weekly; 2hr 10min); Skógar (7 weekly; 30min).

Þingvellir to: Laugarvatn (July–Aug, daily; 30min); Reykjavík (May 20–October 9, daily; 50min); Selfoss (July–Aug, daily; 1hr 15min).

Planes

Heimaey to Reykjavík: 2 daily; 30min.

Ferries

Heimaey to Þórlakshöfn: daily; 2hr 45min.

Þórlakshöfn to Heimaey: daily; 2hr 45min.

CHAPTER THREE

WEST COAST

The panorama of the bay of Faxa Fiord is magnificent – with a width of fifty miles from horn to horn, the one running down into a rocky ridge of pumice, the other towering to the height of five thousand feet in a pyramid of eternal snow, while round the intervening semicircle crowd the peaks of a hundred noble mountains.

Letters from High Latitudes, Lord Dufferin, who sailed his yacht *Foam* to Iceland in 1856

Reykjavík and the Reykjanes peninsula together form the southern edge of Faxaflói, the sweeping bay which dominates Iceland's west coast and any journey north of the capital – the Ringroad clings to its shores as far as the small commercial centre of Borgarnes before striking off inland on its way towards Brú and the north coast. Although the scenery is not Iceland's most dramatic, it provides visitors travelling around the country in a clockwise direction with their first taste of small-town Iceland and as such makes a satisfying introduction to the rest of the country. If you can it's a good idea to break your journey at one of the small towns hereabouts to get a feel for what rural Iceland really is all about – in summer the views of flower meadows dotted with isolated farms sheltering at the foot of cloud-topped mountains are picture-postcard pretty. Travelling north, the first town you come to, the disappointing, ugly Akranes, with its concrete factory and fish-processing plants, is best passed over in favour of nearby Borgarnes, a small commercial centre that also makes a good jumping off point for the historical riches of Reykholt and the excellent hiking around Húsafell.

The "pyramid of eternal snow" to which Dufferin, who sailed his yacht *Foam* to Iceland in 1856, was referring is the glacier, **Snæfellsjökull**, which sits majestically on top of a dormant volcano at the tip of Snæfellsnes, a long arm of volcanic and mountainous land jutting out into the sea and the highlight of any trip up the west coast. Divided by a jagged mountain ridge, the peninsula not only marks the northern edge of Faxaflói bay but also the southern reaches of the more sheltered

---

ACCOMMODATION PRICE CODES

Throughout this guide, prices given for **youth hostels, sleeping-bag accommodation** and **campsites** are per person unless otherwise specified. **Hotel** and **guesthouse** accommodation is graded on a scale from ① to ⑧; all are high-season rates and indicate the cost of the cheapest double room. The price bands to which these codes refer are as follows:

① Up to 4000kr	③ 6000–8000kr	⑤ 10,000–12,000kr	⑦ 15,000–20,000kr
② 4000–6000kr	④ 8000–10,000kr	⑥ 12,000–15,000kr	⑧ Over 20,000kr

(See p.26 for a full explanation.)

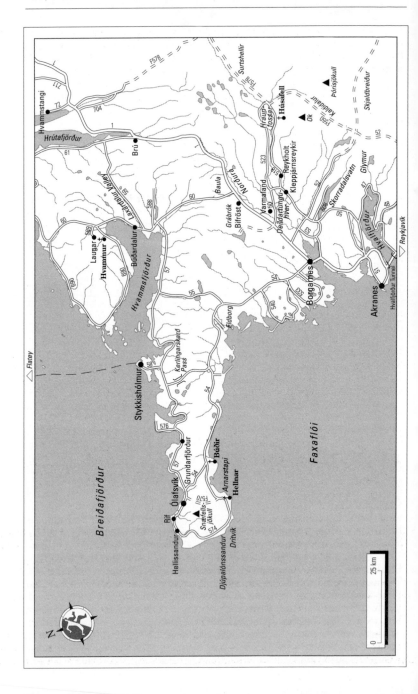

Breiðafjörður with its hundreds of islands and skerries, over which lie the table mountains of the west fjords. On a clear day the snowcap is clearly visible across the water from both Reykjavík and the west fjords. The best **whale watching** in Iceland can be experienced off the western point of Snæfellsnes aboard catamarans sailing from the fishing village of **Ólafsvík** – this is undoubtedly the best place to come to see the biggest mammal on Earth, the blue whale, regularly spotted off shore as well as the more common humpback whale. From **Arnarstapi** on the peninsula's southern coast it's possible to take a **snowmobile** up onto the glacier for some of the most exhilarating driving – and vistas – you'll ever experience. Of all the west coast's towns and villages, only **Stykkishólmur** on the northern coast of Snæfellsnes with its wooden houses and its vibrant harbour busy with chugging fishing vessels is immediately appealing and it is the only town on the peninsula worth an overnight stay. Occupying a sheltered spot in the neck of land which links the west fjords with the rest of the country, **Laugar** in Sælingsdalur with its hot springs is a good place to break the long journey from Reykjavík to the west fjords as well as offering a few cultural diversions. For splendid isolation there can be few better places than **Búðir** on the southern coast of Snæfellsnes – a wide sandy bay, home only to a charming hotel complete with creaking floorboards and ocean views.

What the west coast may lack in scenic splendour, it makes up for in historical and cultural significance – landscapes here are steeped in the drama and tragedy of the Sagas. Close to **Búðardalur**, to the north of Snæfellsnes, Haukadalur valley was the starting point for **Viking** expansion westwards which took explorers first to Greenland and later to the shores of North America as heroically recounted in the **Saga of Eirik the Red**. The farm at **Eiríksstaðir** was once home to the eponymous hero and his wife, who together pioneered the settlement of Greenland having been outlawed from Iceland. It's also thought that **Leifur Eiríksson**, the first European to set foot in North America, was born on a farm that has now been reconstructed on the original site. Although the farm is remote and difficult to reach without your own transport, it's worth making the effort to get here since there are few places in Iceland where historical events are more tangible – standing beside the turf-rooved farmstead overlooking the barren expanses of the valley westwards out to sea it's easy to see what inspired the early Icelanders to take to the ocean to search for lands anew. Equally rich in history is the tiny village of **Reykholt**, just forty-five minutes outside Borgarnes, and home to arguably the most famous and influential man who lived during the age of the Sagas, **Snorri Sturluson** (see p.142). Here you can still see the outdoor warm pool where the great man bathed and received visitors. More Saga history can be found in Laxárdalur valley, northeast of Búðardalur, where characters from the **Laxdæla Saga** (see Contexts, p.303) lived out their feud-torn lives.

Getting around the west coast

The west coast is one of easiest areas in Iceland to explore by **public transport**. From the ESSO station forecourt in **Borgarnes**, the transport hub for the entire west coast, five different **bus routes** depart several times south to Akranes and Reykjavík, east to Reykholt, west to Snæfellsnes, and north to Búðardalur and the southern west fjords, as well as continuing along the Ringroad to Brú and all points north. In fact, three stick to Route 1 on their way to their final destinations (Akureyri, Siglufjörður and Hólmavík), with several daily departures between

Borganes and Brú. The tiny settlement of **Brú** is also a strategic interchange point for passengers travelling between the west fjords and destinations along the north coast such as Akureyri.

Two services operate between Reykjavík and **Snæfellsnes**; one travels along the south coast of the peninsula along Route 54 via Búðir to Ólafsvík and Hellisandur, whereas the other bears right onto Route 56 (shortly after the farm Gröf) to head for the north coast and Stykkishólmur and Grundarfjörður. Unfortunately there is no public transport around the tip of the peninsula, but it is possible to connect at Búðir crossroads with an **excursion bus** round the glacier in summer. This service operates twice daily (June–Aug Mon–Fri) from Ólafsvík and travels first in a clockwise direction via Búðir, Arnastapi and Hellisandur before performing an anti-clockwise circuit via the same villages back to Ólafsvík. Connections exist in both directions at Búðir crossroads for passengers travelling to and from Reykjavík on the scheduled bus.

Travel up the west coast also offers three alternative ways of reaching the west fjords. One option is to take the bus the entire way from Reykjavík to Ísafjörður via Brú and Hólmavík. The other is to take the bus to Stykkishólmur, connect there to the ferry, *Baldur*, across Breiðafjörður to Brjánslækur from where another bus leaves for Ísafjörður (see Travel Details for details). A third but more limiting option is the bus from Reykjavík to Reykhólar via Búðardalur and Laugar. This service may be regular but there are no onward connections at all from Reykhólar.

Akranes and around

Once beyond Reykjavík and its adjacent overspill town, Mosfellsbær, the Ringroad makes its way round the towering form of Mount Esja (see p.71) towards industrial Akranes, one of the most economically vibrant towns in Iceland. Until recently, to reach the town, the national artery was forced to weave its way around **Hvalfjörður**, or Whale Fjord, the biggest in southwest Iceland, named after the large number of whales seen here ever since the time of the Settlement. More recently, during World War II, the fjord's deep anchorages made it one of the most important bases in the North Atlantic, when British and American naval vessels were stationed here, providing a port and safe haven for supply ships travelling between Europe and North America. Today though, the fjord is no longer the obstacle to travel it once was, and an impressive **tunnel**, opened in 1998, has dramatically improved communications. Nearly 6km in length, of which around 4km lie below the seabed, it slices through the mouth of the fjord, a massive engineering project by Icelandic standards that took just over two years to complete. Blasting through the basalt bedrock began simultaneously on both shores of the fjord in 1996 amid commercial concerns from the people of Akranes that the shorter distance to the capital (48km through the tunnel compared with a massive 108km round the fjord) would kill off their local shops and services – fortunately their fears have proved unfounded. Twenty-four hour **toll booths** are in place at both ends currently charging a hefty 1000kr per car, which, although expensive, is well worth it to save a tedious detour.

Just beyond the exit from the tunnel, Route 51 strikes off west from the Ringroad for **AKRANES**, the west coast's biggest town and home to 5200 people and one of the few places outside Reykjavík experiencing population growth. Although you'd never guess by wandering around the modern streets today,

HVALFJÖRÐUR AND WHALING

At the head of Hvalfjörður, the disused open-air **whaling station** is a poignant reminder of Iceland's days as a whaling nation and of the key role Hvalfjörður played. In fact, until the late 1980s, tourist buses from Reykjavík would even wiggle their way round the fjord to allow visitors to watch the grisly spectacle of a whale being sliced up alfresco.

Iceland began **commercial whaling** in 1948 and was still doing so right up until the summer of 1989, at the end of a four year period that the Icelandic government termed "scientific research whaling". During this period, specially equipped ships (four of which now stand idle in Reykjavík harbour) harpooned fin, sei and sperm whales in the deep waters off the west coast of Iceland and towed them back to the Hvalfjörður whaling station. Minke whales were also caught from ordinary fishing boats. In latter years, however, there was immense international opposition to the slaughter from various quarters, not least a boycott of Icelandic seafood instigated by Greenpeace, and direct action, when a Canadian craft sank two Icelandic whaling vessels and destroyed the whaling station here in November 1986.

With its economy declining as a result of the boycott, Iceland withdrew from the International Whaling Commission in 1992, claiming the organisation set up to manage whaling had become one devoted solely to preventing all hunts. As an island nation, the Icelanders passionately believe in the right to harvest all living marine resources, and opinion polls consistently show a vast majority of the population, generally around eighty percent, in favour of resumption. Indeed, every year the contentious issue resurfaces, with the owner of the remaining four whaling ships claiming he could have the vessels ready for service within a matter of weeks. Matters came to a head in March 1999 when, after much debate, the Icelandic parliament voted by a huge majority to **resume whaling** and called on the government to begin preparations. However, since Iceland's most important markets for fish are in Britain, France, Germany and the United States, where opposition to whaling is strongest, ministers are treading carefully – and slowly – painfully aware that a country where three-quarters of all exports are fish related simply cannot risk another boycott.

Akranes traces its history all the way back to 880 AD when, according to the Book of Settlement, Landnámabók, the area was first settled by two Irish brothers, Pormódur and Ketill Bresason, most probably monks. Over the following centuries the tiny village grew into a successful agricultural settlement as the town's name, literally "field promontory", indicates – corn was grown on the fertile land around Mount Akrafjall. However, around the middle of the seventeeth century, one of Iceland's leading bishops, **Brynjólfur Sveinsson**, from the Skálholt bishopric stationed a number of his fishing boats in Akranes and unwittingly gave birth to the country's first fishing village. The town never looked back and today fishing and fish processing account for roughly half of the town's economy.

Although fish processing, ship maintenance, cement making and the production of ferro-silicon for export are the four mainstays of the local economy, smaller firms, including banks and insurance companies, are also based here, lending the town a busy, commercial air. However, Akranes is best known for its sporting prowess – the local **football** team, Íþróttabandalag Akranes, have been national champions seventeen times – and its two sports halls, swimming pools and soccer stadium are of a correspondingly high standard. Despite this, gritty Akranes is hard to like, entirely without architectural charm and a terribly cold spot even in summer, as the icy winds straight off the sea howl round street corners, sending the hardiest locals scurrying for cover. However, it's a good base from which to explore the heights of **Mount Akrafjall**, which dominates the easterly skyline and where there's some decent hiking to be had, or, when the sun is shining, the long sandy beach, **Langisandur**, a fifteen-minute walk from the town centre. Before leaving town, however, there's a chance to get to grips with the history of the cod wars and to see the actual cutters used to slice through British trawler nets in the 1972 and 1975 disputes, housed in the Gardar **folk museum**, the town's one cultural grace.

Arrival, information and accommodation

All **buses** arrive at Skútan petrol station on Pjódbraut, from where it's a right turn and a 15min walk to the **tourist information office**, at Skólabraut 31 (Mon–Fri 9am–noon & 1–5pm; ☎431 3327) on the first floor of the building which also houses Landsbankinn. Here you can get practical information from the friendly staff about Akranes as well as leaflets containing suggested hiking routes up Mount Akrafjall.

One of the town's two **hotels** is just a stone's throw from the tourist office; *Hótel Barbró* (☎431 4240 or 431 4067, fax ☎431 4241), at Kirkjubraut 11, is plain and simple. The décor is outdated and overly flowery but it does have perfectly decent en-suite doubles (②–③) and sleeping-bag accommodation (1700kr); breakfast is included in the price. *Hótel Ósk* (☎431 3314; ③) at Vogabraut 4, is located in a boarding school and is only open mid-May to August; note that breakfast is extra

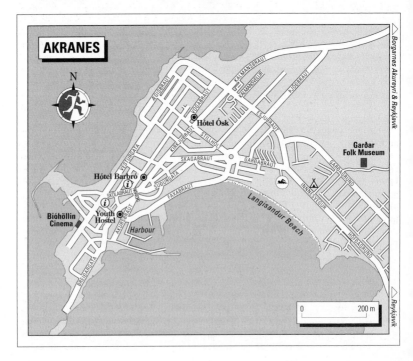

here. Its rooms are spartan but spacious, complete with simple cooking facilities and a shower. The **youth hostel**, *Bermúda* (☎431 3478, fax ☎431 5030; 1450kr), is close to the harbour at Akursbraut 9. To get to the **campsite,** it's a fifteen-minute walk along Innesvegur, past the sports centre and swimming pool, to Víkurbraut.

The Town

Although there are no sights as such in Akranes, sooner or later you'll come across the concrete buildings of the Haraldur Bödvarsson **fish-processing factory**, one of Iceland's largest, which completely dominate the **harbour** area, emblazoned with the name of their founder in bold red letters. Close by, the **shipyard** of Porgeir Og Ellert is at the cutting edge of not only Icelandic but also world technology in fishing-trawler production. However, it's the founding of the **Icelandic National Cement Works** (Sementverksmidja Ríkisins) in 1958 that really gets locals excited, an environmentally friendly plant, close to the harbour at Mánabraut, which uses crushed shells from the sea bed rather than lime as raw material; mercifully, the cement works are closed to visitors.

Once you've exhaused the handful of streets in the centre of town, take a stroll up to the **Gardar folk museum** (May–Aug daily 10.30am–midday & 1.30–4.30pm; Sept–April Mon–Fri 1.30–4.30pm; 250kr) close to the campsite and off Gardagrund. The granite stone in front of the museum inscribed in Gaelic and Icelandic commemorates the Irish role in Akranes's history and was given to the town by Ireland in 1974 to mark 1100 years on settlement in Iceland. Close by, also in front of the museum, the twin-masted cutter, **Sigurfari**, built on the River Humber in Britain in 1885, carries the honour of working as the last sailing ship in the Icelandic fleet before being sold to the Faroe Islands where, remarkably, it fished until 1970. Although it's possible to board the ship via a wooden walkway, it's easier to gain an impression of how agile and speedy it was by walking around the hull in its dry grassy moorings. However, the museum's most interesting exhibits are the hook-shaped cutters which were used to sever the nets of British trawlers during the cod wars of 1972 and 1975. Though quite ordinary to look at, they proved devastatingly effective when dragged across British trawler wires by the Icelandic coastguard.

The best **swimming pool** and sports centre in town are found off Gardabraut at Jadarsbakkar; the modern changing rooms at the swimming pool contain a steam room, whereas outdoors there's a pool and four hot pots. Behind the sports centre complex lies the one kilometre long stretch of sandy **beach** known as **Langisandur** – a must in Akranes when the sun is shining, since the southern aspect of the shore will do wonders for your tan. Bear in mind, though, that although the water can look tempting on a sunny day it fails the big-toe test by a long way; it's barely 5°C warm at the height of summer.

Eating and drinking

The best bet for **eating** is the popular *Hrói Höttur* at Skólabraut 14, essentially a glorified pizzeria serving good-value burgers and fish and chips for around 500kr as well as decent pizzas; a takeaway service is also available. Alternatively, further down the road at number 30, *Pizza 67* has a good range of better, takeaway-only pizzas. For finer fare, head for the restaurant inside *Hótel Barbró* at Kirkjubraut 11, – the décor may be dark and uninspiring but the food is fresh. The best bet here is the fish of the day, but be prepared to shell out at least 2000kr. At lunch time *Café 15*, at Kirkjubraut 15, is a good choice for sandwiches, soups and filling snacks. Otherwise, there's the Hardarbakarí **bakery** at Kirkjubraut 54, with the usual range of white loaves, Icelandic flatbread and cakes. Come Friday and Saturday evening, the town's youth can be found **drinking** at either *H-Barinn*, at Kirkjubraut 8, a pleasant bar in the town centre, or the dingy-looking *Báran* bar, close to the cinema, at Bárugata 15, which also doubles up as a low-key disco.

Mount Akrafjall and Glymur

On approaching Akranes from the Ringroad you'll have driven by **Mount Akrafjall**, which, at 643m, is not only 200m higher than Reykjavík's Mount Esja, but also dominates the skyline east of town. The mountain offers one of the best panoramas in the west of Iceland, with spectacular views not only of Akranes but also, on a clear day, of Reykjavík. On a sunny day you'll find most of the town out here either climbing the flat-topped mountain or picnicking in the lush meadows at its foot – during summer you'll also find copious numbers of **seabirds**, especially kittiwakes, nesting on the mountain's craggy sides. Of the mountains two peaks, the eastern one, **Háihnúkur** (555m) is easiest to climb thanks to a well-defined **path** leading to the summit from the car park below. The left peak, Gerimundartiundur, measures in at 643m, split from the other by a river valley through which most of the town's water supply flows. For details of the various ascents ask at Akranes's tourist office (see p.136) for their free **map**, *Uppgönguleidir á Akrafjall*.

From the mountain, Route 47 winds its way east around the northern shore of Hvalfjörður towards Iceland's highest waterfall, **Glymur**. The falls drop nearly 200m from the boggy ground to the west of **Hvalvatn**, but it can be difficult to find a vantage point from where to see the spectacle at its best. A rough **track** leads up through the valley at the head of Hvalfjörður towards the falls – allow about an hour from the road. Incidentally, according to Icelandic folklore, a mythical creature, half-man half-whale, which once terrified locals from its home in the dark waters of Hvalfjörður, was tricked into swimming out of the fjord, up the river and the Glymur falls, before dying in the waters of Hvalvatn – where, oddly, whale bones have been found.

Borgarnes and around

On leaving Akranes the Ringroad covers a lonely and exposed 38km before reaching **Borgarnes**, the principal town of the Breiðafjörður region, which not only enjoys a spectacular setting on a narrow neck of land which reaches out into the eponymous fjord but also has excellent views inland to the glaciers of Eiríksjökull and Langjökull. The stretch of road from Akranes, particularly around Hafnarfjall, on the southern approach to Borgarnes, is one of the most hazardous in the entire country – facing westwards, it takes the full brunt of violent storms which drive in from the Atlantic and not surprisingly closes frequently during the winter months, as cars have been overturned here by the brute force of the wind. In summer things are not quite so severe but it is still an extremely windy spot.

Unlike most other coastal settlements, Borgarnes isn't dependent on fishing – powerful tidal currents in the fjord have put paid to that – but is primarily a service centre for the surrounding dairy farmers who rely on the town's slaughterhouse and good roads for their livelihoods. However, the town's main claim to fame and your attention is its historical association with Skallagrímur Kveldúlfsson, father of **Egill Skallagrímsson**. A ninth-century pirate, thug and poet, Egill was the hero of *Egill's Saga* and is commemorated here by a statue of himself carrying his drowned son, Bödvar, who's buried alongside his grandfather in the town.

The Town

If Borgarnes has a town centre it's the area around **Brúartorg** square and the ESSO station that merits the title, though like so many other provincial Icelandic towns, the place is so small and compact that its handful of suburban streets can easily be seen in an hour. From the bus station at the filling station, it's a short walk down the main drag, Borgarbraut, containing the town's main shops and services, to Borgarnes's main attraction, **Skallagrímsgardur**, a small but pleasant park at the junction with Skallagrímsgata. By the entrance on the left is the **burial mound** of one of Iceland's earliest settlers, **Skallagrímur Kveldúlfsson**, complete with horse, weapons and various other Viking accoutrements. Originally just plain Grímur, he obtained the first part of his name, Skalla ("bald"), because he lost all his hair at an early age. Skallagrímur's son, **Egill**, is portrayed on the accompanying monument carrying home the body of his own son, Bödvar. According to the Saga, Egill's son fell to his death in the Hvitá river during a severe storm and was laid to rest, here, next to his grandfather. Distraught, Egill fell into a deep depression and vowed to neither eat nor drink until the day he died. However, his daughter-in-law tricked him into sipping a cup of milk and persuaded him to write a poem in memory of his beloved son. Egill soon became so involved in his composition that he forgot his vow to die; his work, *Sonatorrek*, is remembered by a statue by Ásmundur Sveinsson in nearby Borg á Myrum (see p.140).

Continue down Borgarbraut and you'll soon come to **Safnahús Borgarfjardar** (Mon–Fri 1–6pm, plus Thurs 8–10pm; free), the regional **museum** with its pedestrian and somewhat tedious displays of local art, natural history and folk exhibits. Spare yourself and head instead for the excellent open-air **swimming pool** and sports centre on Porsteinsgata, a continuation of Skallagrímsgata, situated right by the water's edge with great views of the fjord and the surrounding hills; there are also a couple of hot pots here, a waterslide, a steam room and a sauna.

Practicalities

All **buses** from Akranes and Reykjavík cross the long and exposed bridge over Breiðafjörður before pulling into the forecourt of the Esso **filling station** on Brúartorg square, which doubles as the town's **bus station**. The transport hub for all bus services along the west coast, direct **buses** run to and from Reykjavík, the Snæfellsnes peninsula, Búðardalur (for Eiríksstaðir), the west fjords, Akureyri and Reykholt; for timetables, ask at the tourist office, *Hótel Borgarnes* or at the *Hyrnan* restaurant (see below). Buy tickets on board the buses.

In the service building here there's a branch of Búnadarbanki Íslands **bank** (Mon–Fri 9.15am–4pm), complete with ATM, and a small **supermarket**; there's another ATM at the western end of town in the doorway of the KB department store on Brákarbraut – follow the main Borgarbraut through the town centre to get here. The travel agency, Ferdaskrifstofa Vesturlands, across the road on Borgarbraut, also serves as the **tourist information office** (June–Aug Mon–Fri

9am–5pm, Sat & Sun 11am–4pm; Sept–May Mon–Fri 9am–5pm; ☎437 2323) and has a good supply of brochures and maps.

There's just one **hotel** actually in town, the plain *Hótel Borgarnes* (☎437 1119, fax ☎437 1443; ④) at Egilsgata 14–16; although the en-suite doubles here are comfortable, tastefully decorated and quiet, they are terribly overpriced. Alternatively, across the fjord and a twenty-five walk over the bridge back towards Akranes in a stunning setting at the foot of Hafnarfjall, the *Mótel Venus* (☎437 2345, fax 437 2344; sleeping-bag accommodation 1400kr, ②–③), on Hafnarskógur, has simple but cell-like doubles with wobbly tables and venetian blinds; all buses pass the motel. For cheaper **farmhouse** accommodation, it's hard to beat the working farm, *Bjarg* (☎437 1925, fax ☎437 1443; sleeping-bag accomodation 1400kr, ①), a twenty-minute walk north of town following Borgarbraut all the way; here, the smells and sights will give you a real taste of Icelandic country life, as well as a healthy appetite for their traditional cooking. Although the **youth hostel**, *Hamar* (June to mid-Sept; ☎437 1663 or 437 1040; 2200kr), is inconveniently situated a good hour's walk north of Borgarnes, it sits right on the Ringroad and is therefore reachable by bus, and the gabled farmhouse that houses the hostel is charming. The **campsite** (☎437 1529) is back in town on Borgarbraut, just behind the ESSO station.

The best-value **place to eat** is the *Hyrnan*, inside the service building attached to the filling station. Popular with truckers and holidaying Icelanders, it serves up main dishes such as fresh fish as well as smaller snacks such as burgers and sandwiches – reckon on around 1000kr for something filling. Alternatively, try the plain and simple *Matstofan* café on Brákarbraut, beyond the museum, but bear in mind that drinks-wise it only serves light beer. For a more upmaket dining experience, head for the expensive and fussy restaurant inside *Hótel Borgarnes* (see above). For evening **drinking**, if you don't fancy the quiet and prohibitively expensive hotel bar, make sure you stock up during the day at the ÁTVR **state alcohol shop** inside the miniscule Vöruhus KB department store on Brákarbraut.

Borg á Myrum

Another site mentioned in the Sagas, the farm of **Borg á Myrum**, just a couple of kilometres north of Borgarnes off Route 54, is easily reached by buses to the Snæfellsnes peninsula. First settled by **Skallagrímur Kveldúlfsson**, this spot is, to Icelanders at least, of double historical significance because of its association with one of Iceland's greatest writers, Snorri Sturluson (see p.142). The fact that all that remains today is the *borg*, or large rock, after which Skallagrímur's original farm was named, seems to matter little to the misty-eyed home-grown tourists who make the visit here. That said, you're unlikely to find crowds of visitors as most stay no more than ten minutes or so before moving on, because the original farmhouse is long gone and there's precious little to see here today other than a small white church, the *borg* itself and a sculpture by Ásmundur Sveinsson entitled *Sonatorrek* (*The Great Loss of my Sons*) in memory of the moving poem written by Egill mourning the death of his sons, Bödvar and Gunnar.

Like so many of Iceland's historical sites, archeological remains are thin on the ground, so you'll have to arm yourself with the facts and let your imagination do the rest. Skallagrímur ended up here very much by chance after falling foul of his king, Harald Fairhair of Norway. Together with his father, Kveldúlfur (literally

---

EGILL'S SAGA

Although there's no concrete evidence, historians generally believe that **Egill's Saga** was most likely written by Iceland's greatest thirteenth-century writer and politician, **Snorri Sturluson**. It tells of the Viking age adventures of **Egill Skallagrímsson** (*c*910–990) on his many seaborne forays, first to Norway and then later to England. Key to the story is Egill's conflict with King **Eric Bloodaxe** of Norway (*c*895–954), son of Harald Fairhair. Following in his father's footsteps, Egill decides to challenge the growing central power of the Norwegian crown and manages to humiliate King Eric publicly, kill his son and survive an attempt by Queen Gunnhildur to poison him – all in one night. Having lost the respect of his subjects and accordingly shamed out of Norway, King Eric takes up residence across the North Sea in Viking Jórvík (York) only to receive an unexpected visitor – Egill had been shipwrecked on the Yorkshire coast and soon stood face to face with Eric and Gunnhildur again. Although condemned to death, he composes a poem in praise of King Eric and is spared. According to the Saga, Egill returned to Borg in Iceland in 957 and lived out his final years in Mosfell just outside Reykjavík.

"evening wolf", so named because he grew tired and irritable in the evenings), he fled the wrath of King Harald and set sail westwards for Iceland. However, during the lengthy and stormy voyage, Kveldúlfur fell ill and ordered that, on his death, his coffin be tossed overboard and his grieving family settle wherever it washed up. Following his father's instruction, Skallagrímur first set foot in Iceland in an area rich in bogs, forests and salmon rivers, at Borg á Myrum (Rock in the Bogs), where he raised his family, naming the surrounding area, accordingly, Borgarfjörður (rocky fjord). The family struggle against the Norwegian king continued when Skallagrímur's son, **Egill**, who also lived at Borg, returned to Norway to do battle with his arch enemy, Eric Bloodaxe (see box above).

The third great man to live at Borg was **Snorri Sturluson** (see p.142). At the age of nineteen Snorri married the only daughter of Father Bersi the Wealthy, of Borg, and moved to the farm following his father-in-law's death in 1202 to run the estate as his heir. However, his marriage was not a happy one and just four or five years later, around 1206, he decided to move inland to Reykholt leaving his wife behind.

Reykholt and around

The cultural highlight of any trip up the west coast, **REYKHOLT** is immediately appealing. Not only does this little hamlet set in the wide open spaces of the fertile Reykholtsdalur valley enjoy a stunning setting amid dusky mountains and the sleepy meanders of the Reykjadalsá river, but it also contains much more tangible memorials to **Snorri Sturluson**. The excellent museum here is is by far and away the best place to get to grips with Iceland's rich and, at times, downright confusing history of Saga events, characters and writing. However, don't view a trip here as simply a way of mugging up on Icelandic history. Reykholt is also a fantastic place to fetch up for a couple of days to enjoy the pastoral delights, solitude and fairly reliable weather of the west coast at its best.

The hamlet itself now consists of little more than a few geothermally heated greenhouses and a church. At the foot of the hillock on which the former school

SNORRI STURLUSON

Born at the farm of Hvammur (see p.148) near Búðardalur in 1179, **Snorri Sturluson** was descended from some of the greatest figures in early Icelandic history; on his father's side were influential chieftains, on his mother's, amongst others, the warrior poet Egill Skallagrímsson. At the age of two he was fostered and taken to one of Iceland's leading cultural centres, Oddi (see p.110), where, over the years, he became acquainted not only with historical writing but also the court of Norway – a relationship that would eventually lead to his death. In 1206, following his marriage to a wealthy heiress, he moved to Reykholt and consolidated his grip on power by becoming a chieftain, legislator and respected historian and writer; he also developed a distinct taste for promiscuity, fathering three children to women other than his long-suffering first wife, Herdís.

Snorri Sturluson is the most celebrated figure in Icelandic literature, producing first his *Edda* then *Egill's Saga* and *Heimskringla*, which from its geographical detail shows that Snorri spent several years living in Norway. During this period he developed a close bond of allegiance to the Norwegian earl who reigned alongside the teenage king, Hákon. However, following a civil war in Norway, which resulted in the earl's death, the Norwegian king declared Snorri a traitor to him and ordered one of his followers, Gissur Þorvaldsson, to bring the writer back to Norway – dead or alive. On the dark night of September 23, 1241, seventy armed men led by Gissur burst into Snorri's farmhouse in Reykholt sending him fleeing from his bed down into the cellar. Five of the thugs pursued Snorri, where, unarmed and defenceless, they hacked Iceland's most distinguished man of letters to death.

(due to be developed into a library and museum) stands, Snorri's pool, the **Snorralaug**, provides a rare visual example of a piece of medieval Iceland and is even mentioned in the *Landnámabók* (Book of Settlements) and the *Sturlunga Saga*. A four-metre-wide geothermally heated pool ringed with stones, it's believed this is where Snorri would bathe and receive visitors, and next to it are the restored remains of the **tunnel** thought to have led to the cellar of Snorri's farmhouse, where he was assassinated in 1241 (see box). The pool is fed by an ancient stone aquaduct from the nearby hot spring, Skrifla. Back up the steps from the pool, the Snorri **statue** which graces the front of the former school was presented to Iceland by Norway's King Olaf shortly after independence in 1947. It's a clear reminder of the continuing wrangle between the two Nordic nations over Snorri's origins; the Norwegians strongly maintain that Snorri is theirs and claim he was born in Norway. Although the Icelanders have gratefully accepted over three million Norwegian kroner to help set up the Snorri exhibition hall, the new library and Snorri research centre attached to the village church (see below), suspicions remain that the Norwegians haven't yet renounced their claims on Snorri.

Although Reykholt grew up around the old church, which today stands marooned between the village hotel and the former school, it's the new, snow-white **church,** with its steep V-shaped roof, which is the centrepoint today. Underneath the church, the **Heimskringla exhibition hall** (June–Aug daily 10am–6pm; Sept–May open on request, ☎435 1490; 300kr) is a good place to get to grips with Snorri and his writings. Here you'll find more information on Snorri than you can shake a stick at and much on Reykholt's role as a centre of culture and learning over the centuries in the history of Iceland. The large prints of the Sagas hung on the walls will give you an idea of what the documents actually looked like if you failed to see examples in the Árni Magnússon manuscript institute in Reykjavík. The church itself, with its specially designed acoustic walls, is used to host the **Reykholt Music Festival** during the last weekend in July when visiting singers and musicians from across the Nordic region gather here for a series of classical music concerts open to the public – look out for details posted around the village.

Practicalities
Getting here from Borgarnes is a straightforward affair – a daily **bus** (except Sat) covers the 18km along Route 527 in about an hour; on Fri & Sun there's also a direct service from Reykjavík. Arriving from the north of Iceland, connections can be made at Borgarnes but generally require an overnight stay, since the Reykholt bus currently leaves at 9.15am. Services arrive at and depart from the filling station at the eastern end of the village, where there's also a small **shop** (daily 10am–10pm) which sells most basics, including food.

Originally built as a boarding school in 1931, friendly *Hótel Reykholt* (☎435 1260, fax ☎435 1206; sleeping-bag accommodation 1450kr, ②) with fantastic views of the Okjökull and Eiríksjökull glaciers is a wonderfully peaceful **place to stay** right at the centre of the tiny village; Snorri had his farmhouse next to where the hotel now stands. The plain rooms are comfortable; breakfast is an extra 750kr, though there are self-catering facilities available. The adjoining **restaurant** serves the dish of the day for 1090kr, but beer here is expensive. The only other place to stay is the independent *Runnar* **hostel** (☎435 1185), 7km west of Reykholt on Route 516 beyond Kleppjárnsreykir, which offers sleeping-bag accommodation for 1200kr. There's also a swimming pool, hot pots, sauna and sports centre here.

Deildatunguhver

Whilst in the Reykholt area, it's well worth checking out Iceland's biggest **hot spring** of **Deildatunguhver**. Drawing on the geothermal reserves that lie all around Reykjadalir, and pumping out a staggering 180 litres of boiling water a second, the billowing clouds of steam created by this mighty fissure are truly impressive, reaching up high into the cool air – in fact it's water from here that runs via a specially constructed 60km-long pipeline to heat the nearby towns of Borgarnes and Akranes. As in so many other geothermal areas around Iceland, water from the spring is also used to speed up the growth of plants and vegetables by heating up the surrounding greenhouses and during the summer local farmers often set up stalls here to sell their produce to passing visitors. The spring is located by the side of Route 516, 1km north of Kleppjárnsreykir, south of the Hvítá river. From the road, a walkway leads to the spring; although, the spring is safe to visit, it's wise not to get too close to the steam to avoid the risk of burns.

Húsafell and around

The main draw of **HÚSAFELL**, a favourite activity centre for holidaying Icelanders, 25km east of Reykholt, amid birchwoods and a geothermal area where many Reykjavíkers own summer cottages, is the vast lavafield,

THE KALDIDALUR INTERIOR ROUTE

From Húsafell, Route F550 winds its way through the haunting beauty of the **Kaldidalur** valley on its way to the Hallbjarnavörður pass and the junction with Route 52, a distance of 40km. If you're short of time but want a taste of the barren expanses of the Icelandic Interior, this is a good option. Not only will you come face to face with the four **glaciers**, Eiríksjökull (see opposite), Okjökull (see opposite), Langjökull (see opposite) and Þórisjökull, a small oval-shaped ice cap rising to a height of 1350m at the southwestern edge of Langjökull, but you'll pass through a vast grey **desert** where ferocious sandstorms can appear in seconds transforming what was once a clear vista of majestic ice caps and volcanic sands into an impenetrable cloud of grit and dirt. As the neck of land carrying the road narrows to pass between the Ok and Þórisjökull glaciers, the route climbs and rides along the straight Langihyrggur ridge affording spectacular views of the glacier opposite.

In July and August a daily **bus** leaves Reykjavík at 8am for Kaldidalur and Húsafell, continuing from Húsafell at 3.15pm towards Hraunfossar, Reykholt and Borgarnes before returning to Reykjavík. Note this bus only runs in an anti-clockwise direction, meaning there is public transport from Húsafell to Reykholt but not vice versa. It's possible to break your journey at any point en route and to pick up the same bus either the next day or a couple of days later. However, because the bus only operates north through Kaldidalur (in an anti-clockwise circle from Reykjavík), it's not possible to travel from Húsafell into the valley. The only way to do this would be to try to **hitch** a lift – your chances, however, are not likely to be high because of the low amount of tourist traffic which uses this road.

Hallmundarhraun (named after a local cave-dwelling giant who features in *Grettis Saga*). However, the area also offers some excellent **hiking** with trails leading off into the **Húsafellsskógur** forest and, more adventurously, up to the **Eiríksjökull** and **Okjökull** glaciers. The village itself consists of little more than a church, originally built in 1170 but today dating only from 1905, and a hundred or so private summer cottages, mostly owned by the trade unions (whose employees use these cottages in rotation) and individual families. There's also a number of **campsites** (all contactable on ☎435 1550), a **service centre** with a food **store** and **filling station**, and a fantastic geothermally heated outdoor **swimming pool** offering great views of the surrounding hills and glaciers. For information on **cottages** to rent (5-berth for 32,500–37,500kr) ask at the store or call ☎435 1550. There are six **rooms** for rent in an old farmhouse, the *Gamli bærinn* (2,200–3,500kr; ☎435 1325); sleeping bag accommodation is also available here for 1,500kr.

Annoyingly, there is no **public transport** from Reykholt to Húsafell – the only way to get here by public bus is to take the once daily Kaldidalur service (see box above) and alight in the village.

Hallmundarhraun

From the centre of the Húsafell, a rough fourteen-kilometre track leads via **Kalmanstunga** farm (turn right) along Route F578 to the edge of **Hallmundarhraun**, formed when magma poured out from underneath the northwestern edge of the Langjökull and entered the Hvitá. You can walk on the lava, but it is hard going and requires tough-soled soles; take care not to twist an ankle. **Surtshellir** here is a 1500-metre-long cave thought to have been a hideout of the eighteenth-century outlaw, Eyvindur á Fjöllum, and his friends. Exercise extreme caution if you decide to go inside as the uneven floor and darkness can prove disorientating, so you'll need to bring a torch with you. Nearby **Stefánshellir**, part of the same cave network, is also worth a quick look but is essentially more of the same.

Back at Kalmanstunga farm, follow the road left for Fljótstunga, from where another rough track heads for a short distance to the world's largest lava tube, **Víðgelmir**, which may only be entered with a guide (contactable on ☎435 1198). **Accommodation** is available here in farmhouse rooms (①), as sleeping-bag accommodation (1500kr) and in three small cabins (2300–3850kr). All are bookable on ☎435 1198.

Hraunfossar and Barnafoss

Six kilometres west of Húsafell and reached on the Kaldidalur bus from Reykjavík (see box opposite), the waterfalls of **Hraunfossar** and **Barnafoss** are two of the most well-known natural features in Iceland. Although both are on the Hvítá, it's Hraunfossar that make for the best photographs: however, don't expect thundering torrents of white water – the falls here are gentle cascades of bright, turquoise water, emerging from under the moss-covered lava to tumble down a series of rock steps into the river. From here, a track leads upstream to **Barnafoss** (Children's Falls), so called because it was here that two children fell to their deaths when crossing the narrow stone arch that once spanned the river linking the districts of Hálsasveit and Hvítársída.

Okjökull and Eiríksjökull

One of Iceland's smaller glaciers, **Okjökull** is perfect for a **day hike** from Húsafell. At a height of 1141m, the glacier sits in a dolerite shield volcano and is easily reached from Húsafell by first following the western edge of the Bæjargil ravine up to the Drangsteinabrún ridge. Cross to the eastern side of the small ponds which lie south of the ridge and continue straight up to Ok. On a clear day the **views** from here are truly spectacular – west you can see to the coastline and the town of Borgarnes, inland there are sweeping vistas of the Interior. Allow five or six hours and take enough food and drink to last for a day.

Eiríksjökull (1675m) is the highest mountain in western Iceland and the long **hike** here should only be undertaken by seasoned walkers. Before setting out, get detailed information and a map from the service centre in Húsafel, where you can also get helpful **maps**; the following description, however, should help you trace your route along them. Head along the hard, dry grass of the northern slope of the Strútur, east of Kalmanstunga farm, from where there are difficult trails across Hallmundarhraun to Hvítárdrög at the foot of the glacier. Begin the climb itself by hiking up the prominent ravine on the western edge of the glacier, remembering your route to help your descent – it can be very disorientating up here. Beyond the ravine, the going gets considerably easier but watch out for crevasses. Allow a full day and bear in mind that sun-melt can make the hike a lot harder.

Langjökull

Just 20km east of Húsafell, but not readily accessible on foot to the indepedendent traveller due to its isolated location on the western edges of the Interior, **Langjökull** is nevertheless a popular destination for people who want to experience riding across a glacier. At 950 square kilometres, Langjökull (The Long

Glacier) is Iceland's second-largest ice cap, resembling a narrow protruding finger wedged between the Hallmundarhraun and the Kjölur Interior route (see box on p.144). From late May to mid-September there are daily **snowmobile** tours onto the glacier operated from Reykjavík by Langjökull, at Storhöfdi 15, Reykjavík (☎567 1205; 11,900kr) who also provide all necessary protective clothing, including helmets and boots, plus transfer to and from the capital. Skis are also available for rent for anyone who fancies being towed up onto the glacier before making their own way back down. On a clear day, the views out over the ice cap are simply breathtaking, but if it's foggy or raining don't be tempted to make the trip, despite what the party guides may tell you – you'll see absolutely nothing. The snowmobiles can also be booked at the service centre building in Húsafell (☎435 1550).

Varmaland and Bifröst

Regular **buses** from Reykholt to Borgarnes (but not vice versa) pass through **VARMALAND**, a small and uneventful village popular with holidaying Icelanders. To get here from Borgarnes, take a Ringroad bus to Haugar, from where it's a five-kilometre walk along Route 527. Other than its geothermally heated **swimming pool** and the market-gardening centre, Laugaland, where mushroom production began in Iceland, there's little to the place. If you do chose to stay here, *Gistiheimilið Varmaland* (☎435 1303, fax ☎435 1307) has unadorned **rooms** (①) and sleeping bag accommodation (1500kr). The **campsite** (☎435 1280) is a five-minute walk from the guesthouse and pool. Ask at either place for details of the hike (6km) to Laxfoss, from where you could continue on to Bifröst.

A much better option though is to head straight for miniscule **BIFRÖST**, nothing more than a filling station and a hotel, conveniently situated on the Ringroad and a 25-minute bus ride from Borgarnes. Although a mere dot on the map and of little interest in itself, Bifröst's attractions are all close at hand: a couple of kilometres south of the village, spread either side of the Ringroad, the **Grábrókarhraun** lavafield was formed 2–3,000 years ago when lava spewed from the Grábrókargígar cones on the north side of the main road. Over the centuries, various mosses, heathers and shrubs have quite remarkably managed to get a foothold on many parts of the lava. Otherwise, the forested shores of **Hredavatn**, 1km southwest of Bifröst, make for a pleasant stroll and a picnic if the weather's playing along; there's also trout fishing here. Look out for plant fossils in the rocks around the lake. Northeast of the village, the **Grábrók crater** can be ascended by means of a marked trail, as can the **Baula cone**, 11km from Bifröst and reached along Route 60 or by **buses** heading for Búðardalur if you don't fancy walking from the Ringroad. **Accommodation** is restricted to *Fosshótel Bifröst* (June–Aug; ☎435 0005; ⑤) which also offers sleeping-bag accommodation (2500kr) and serves **meals**. There's also a **filling station** here. From the forecourt, **buses** continue north to Bru from where they head for Hólmavík (change here for Ísafjörður) in the west fjords or east towards Akureyri. Limited services also leave for Búðardalur and Reykhólar via Route 60.

Búðardalur and around

North of the Snæfellsnes peninsula lies the wide and sheltered **Hvammsfjörður**, protected from the open sea at its mouth by dozens of small islands. The uninspiring village of **Búðardalur**, at the head of the fjord, although the main service centre for the surrounding hamlets, is best passed over in favour of the rich historical sites close by. From Búðardalur Route 59 runs coast to coast to Hrútafjörður passing through **Laxárdalur**: this is saga country and it was in this valley that one of the best known Viking romances, the **Laxdæla Saga**, was played out. South of here, **Eiríksstaðir**, in Haukadalur, was home to **Eirík the Red**, discoverer of Greenland, and the birthplace of his son, Leifur, who went on to discover North America. Although there's plenty of historical significance in this corner of the country, the towns and settlements listed below can be difficult to reach on public transport – although **buses** do run to Búðardalur, there's no service through Laxárdalur or to Eiríksstaðir.

Búðardalur

Reached by bus from Reykjavík and Borgarnes, **BÚÐARDALUR**, home to just 260 people, provides banking, postal and retail services to the surrounding rural districts. It's an unkempt place, consisting of little more than a collection of a dozen or so suburban streets. In fact, the only reason to break your journey here is to visit nearby Eiríksstaðir. The **tourist information office** (mid-June to Aug Mon–Sat 10am–6pm, Sun midday–6pm; ☎434 1410), located in the same building as the **filling station** at Vesturbraut 12C, can also help out with information about the local sights. Should you wish to **stay** in the village, in order to visit Eiríksstaðir or Laxárdalur, there's **guesthouse** accommodation available at *Bjarg*, Dalbraut 2 (☎434 1644; ②) and a **campsite** (☎434 1126) on Midbraut. For food, head for the **restaurant** in the *Bjarg* or the basic *Dalakjör* restaurant next to the filling station at Vesturbraut 10.

Eiríksstaðir

Twenty kilometres southeast of Búðardalur and reached by Route 586 into Haukadalur valley, the farm of **Eiríksstaðir** is one of the most historically significant locations in Iceland. This was the starting point for all westward expansion by the Vikings first to Greenland and later to the shores of North America. It was on the now abandoned farm, across the waters of the Haukadalsá from the church at Stóra-Vatnshorn, that Eiríkur Þorvaldsson, better known as **Eirík the Red**, lived, father of **Leifur**, who became the first European to set foot in North America (see box on p.148). In 1997, archeologists excavated the ruins at Eiríkstadir and found the remnants of a fifty-square-metre hall dated to 890–980. An evocative **reconstruction** of the original farm now stands close to the ruins and is a must for anyone interested in the Viking period.

The only option for **accommodation** is the comfortable farmhouse at Stóra-Vatnshorn which has single and double rooms (②) as well as sleeping-bag accommodation; traditional home cooking is also available. There are fantastic views out over the Haukadalsá to Náhlíd (557m) from here.

Laxárdalur

The tragedy renowned as one of the great masterpieces of medieval literature, the **Laxdæla Saga**, unfolded in **Laxárdalur**, the valley northeast of Búðardalur and traversed by Route 59. Although there are few remains of the homes of the characters of the tale, the rolling green landscapes are reminiscent of the most romantic scenes in the epic, and the mere mention to an Icelander of virtually any local place name will conjur up images of forsaken love. The story centres on the lives

THE VIKINGS, GREENLAND AND NORTH AMERICA

Although Icelanders don't like to admit it, **Eirík the Red** and his father were actually Norwegian. According to the Book of Settlements, *Landnámabók*, they left Norway to settle in the Hornstrandir region of the west fjords where they lived until Eirík's father died. Eirík then moved south to Breiðafjörður where he met his wife and set up home with her at Eiríkstadir, in Haukadalur, and fathered his first child, **Leifur**. From here the couple moved to the island of Öxney at the mouth of Hvammsfjörður, but Eirík committed several murders and was declared an outlaw. Forced out of the country, he sailed far and wide to the west, eventually discovering land in 985 and, according to the Sagas, promptly named it **Greenland**, "because it would encourage people to go there if the land had a good name".

He settled at Brattahlíd in a fjord he named after himself, Eiríksfjörður, near present day Narsarsuaq. No doubt inspired by his father, Leifur set out to the west from his new home, Greenland, first reaching barren, rocky land that he named Helluland (Baffin Island), from where he continued south to an area of flat wooded land he named Markland (Labrador), in 1000 AD. After another two days at sea he reached more land, where, the Sagas have us believe, grapes grew in abundance. Leifur named this land **Vínland**, which experts believe could mean "Wineland". However, since two days' sailing from Labrador would only take him as far south as current day New England, not exactly known for its wines, speculation remains as to where Viking Vínland is.

of three main characters: the tragic heroine, Guðrún Ósvífursdóttir, Kjartan, the son of **Ólafur the Peacock** (named after his love of finery) and Bolli Þorleiksson, Kjartan's foster brother. Kjartan and the proud and passionate Guðrún fall in love only to be separated when Kjartan leaves for Norway. Bolli persuades Guðrún not to wait for Kjartan to return and to marry him instead. However, on his return to Iceland and hearing of Guðrún's marriage, Kjartan takes another wife instead, Hrefna. Meanwhile, Guðrún falls into despair and begs Bolli to kill Kjartan out of revenge, which he does and immediately regrets. Bolli, in his turn, is killed by Kjartan's brothers in nearby Sælingsdalur. Guðrún married a total of four times and died a hermit at Helgafell (see p.153).

Five kilometres out of Búðardalur just to the north of Route 59 lies the farm of **Hjardarholt**, established by Ólafur the Peacock and later taken over by his son, Kjartan. In the Saga, Ólafur moves his livestock from Goddastadir, now a couple of kilometres to the northeast off Route 587, to Hjardarholt and asks a local chieftain, Höskuldur, to watch the procession from his own farm. The first of Ólafur's animals were arriving at Hjardarholt while the last were still leaving Goddastadir – a visual demonstration of wealth which can still be appreciated today by standing at Hjardarholt and looking at the distant hillside to the northeast. Incidentally, Höskuldur lived next door to Ólafur at **Höskuldsstaðir**, directly located on Route 59 and still inhabited today. Route 59 continues east to Hrútafjörður from where Route 68 heads north into the west fjords and south to the tiny settlement of Brú (see p.141).

Hvammur and Laugar
The other branch of Ólafur the Peacock's feud-torn family lived a little further north in the valleys which run down to **HVAMMUR**. Located 2km off Route 60, beside Route 590, this is one of Iceland's oldest settlements and was first occupied

by Audur Djúpúdga (Audur the Deepminded) around the year 895, the only woman recorded in the Book of Settlements – though confusingly, the Laxdæla Saga refers to her as as Unnuras – as taking land on her own account. There's a small memorial to her here, erected by the University Women of Iceland. She was the first in a long line to prominent Icelanders to live here, the most famous being **Snorri Sturluson** (see p.142), who was born here in 1179. **Árni Magnússon**, whose greatest achievement was to persuade Denmark to return many of the Sagas to Iceland (see p.56), was also born and raised here.

Nearby **LAUGUR**, in Sælingsdalur valley on Route 589, just 2km off the main Route 60, was the birthplace of Guðrún Ósvífursdóttir and remains of the old baths where she had frequent meetings with Kjartan can still be seen at Laugar farm; follow the signs to it along Route 589. This valley is also where her husband, Bolli, was ambushed and murdered by Kjartan's brothers. In Guðrún's day, the geothermal springs here were an important landmark on the long journey to and from the west fjords. Inside the school is a small **folk museum** (June–Aug Mon–Thu 3–7pm; free) with the usual displays on local history.

Today the springs feed a wonderful outdoor **swimming pool** and small steam room (10am–10pm; 200kr) which forms part of the *Edda* **hotel** (☎434 1265, fax ☎434 1469; ②), itself housed in the school; as a result the rooms are somewhat spartan. The **campsite** is adjacent to the hotel. The hotel **restaurant** serves good fish and lamb dishes from 1500kr and provides breakfast. **Buses** to Reykhólar, in the west fjords (see p.184), call at Laugar (1 daily Tues & Thurs, 2 daily Fri & Sun). From here Route 60 continues north to the bridge over Gilsfjörður, marking the start of the west fjords. Just before the fjord, the road runs through Svínadalur, which contains the gorge where Kjartan was ambushed and murdered.

The Snæfellsnes Peninsula

From Borgarnes, Route 54 branches off west past Borg á Myrum (see p.140) through the sparsely populated **Myrar** district, a region of low-lying plains and bogs with a few small lakes, heading for the southern coast of the **Snæfellsnes Peninsula**, a rugged yet beautiful arm of the Icelandic west coast that juts out into the Atlantic between Faxaflói bay and Breiðafjörður. The north and south coasts are divided one from the other by a string of majestic mountains which run down the spine of the peninsula and culminate in the magnificient **Snæfellsjökull**, a glacier at the land's westernmost point. Towns here are mostly confined to the north coast, where harbours are good and plentiful, and it's from picturesque, **Stykkishólmur**, far and away the best place to base yourself on the peninsula, that boat trips can be made across to the peaceful island haven of **Flatey**. From here a road runs west round the tip of the peninsula via **Ólafsvík** where regular **whale-watching tours** leave daily during the short summer months. If you're keen to head straight for the glacier, it's possible to head west along the less rugged and more sandy south coast to **Arnarstapi** where **snow-mobile tours of Snæfellsjökull** can be arranged. Remember though that it's the south coast which more often than not bears the brunt of the moisture-laden low pressure systems that sweep in from the Atlantic, emptying their load here rather than over the mountains on the north coast.

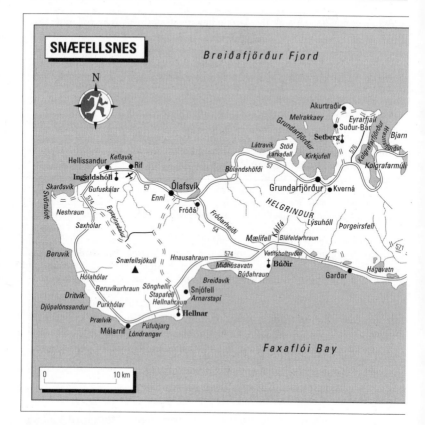

Stykkishólmur

The first town of note on the north coast, be it whether you're approaching on Route 57 from Búðardalur or on Route 56 through the Kerlingarskarð mountain pass from the south, is picturesque **STYKKISHÓLMUR**, with its brightly coloured harbourside buildings. The largest and most enjoyable town on Snæfellsnes, today the place is renowned for its halibut and scallops landed from the waters of Breiðafjörður, which borders the northern coast of the peninsula and is technically more a sea bay than a fjord, full of skerries and rocky islets; incidentally the difference between high and low tide here is one of the greatest in the world at 5–6m. However, during the days of the Sagas, the ancient parliament site, **Þingvöllur**, just to the south of the town was regularly attended and the mountain which marks the entrance to the town, **Helgafell**, became the final resting place for Saga heroine, Guðrún Ósvífursdóttir – both are easily accessible.

Little more than one long straight main street, **Adalgata**, which leads to the **harbour,** is where the first settler in the region, Þórólfur Mostraskegg, found his high-seat pillars; in true Viking seafaring fashion he'd thrown them overboard vowing to settle wherever they washed up. He named the *nes*, or promontory,

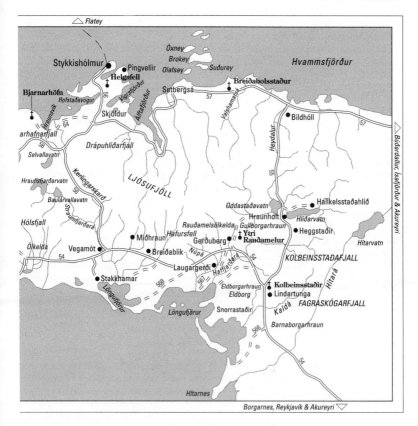

after the god of thunder, Þór, hence the name Þór's promontory. It wasn't until the beginning of the nineteenth century that things really got moving in Stykkishólmur, though, when a man by the name of Árni Thorlacius inherited the town's trading rights from his father. In 1832, he set about building **Norska Húsið**, the Norwegian House (June–Aug daily 11am–5pm; 200kr) at Hafnargata 5, with imported, coarsely hewn timber from Norway as was the tradition in the nineteenth century – Iceland then, as now, had little timber of its own with which to build. Today the building is still the most impressive in the town. It houses a museum that attempts a potted history of Stykkishólmur; look out for the old black-and-white photographs of Árni and his wife, on the second floor. Also up here, the *skautbúningur*, the Icelandic national costume, is worth a fleeting glance. Rather curiously, Icelanders remember Árni not so much for his commerical success in drawing the town into the modern age but for his weather reports from 1845 which are the oldest daily such articles in Iceland and most of northern Europe. If you want more of Árni, you'll find a monument to him and his wife near the tiny harbour opposite.

The only other sight is the space-age looking **church** (Mon–Fri 10am–5pm; free), a ten-mimute walk from the harbour up on a rocky hill off Borgarbraut overlooking the town and with good views on a clear day out towards the waters of Breiðafjörður. Although construction began in 1975, the church wasn't consecrated until fifteen years later; its design includes a vast white ladder-like bell tower rearing up over the doorway and its semicircular domed rear roof. The interior is equally unusual, with hundreds of light bulbs suspended from the ceiling providing the lighting. **Music recitals** (generally classical) are held here every Sunday (mid-June to end Aug; 500kr), generally at 5pm.

What Stykkishólmur lacks in terms of sights, it more than makes up for with its excellent two hour long **bird-watching** and **scallop-tasting tours** (3250kr) operated from the harbour by Eyjaferdir (☎438 1450, fax ☎438 1050) out to the dozens of tiny islands northeast of Stykkishólmur, where you'll see plenty of species including puffins and cormorants; the boat passes the small now uninhabited **Öxney**, east of Stykkishólmur in the Breidasund sound, that Eirík the Red, discoverer of Greenland, and his son, Leifur Eiríksson, who went on to discover North America, lived for several years. They also run **whale-watching tours** from nearby Ólafsvík (see p.156).

Practicalities

Arriving by bus, you'll be deposited at the Gissur Tryggvason **filling station** at Adalgata 25, which also functions as the town's **bus station**, from where it's a ten-minute walk along Adalgata to the **harbour**, where the ferry to and from Brjánslækur and Flatey docks docks (see box on below). On the way you'll pass the **tourist information office** (June–Aug daily 10am–6pm; ☎438 1150; Sept–May call ☎438 1750) on Borgarbraut, which dishes out limited information about the town and surrounding area from its location inside the excellent **swimming pool** and **sports complex**.

For **hotel** rooms with a view, you can't do better than modern and functional *Fosshótel Stykkishólmur* (☎438 2100; ⑥) beyond the tourist office at the top of Borgarbraut. From its hill-top location, the hotel has unsurpassed views of the islands and skerries of Breiðafjörður. The **youth hostel** (May to mid-Sept; ☎438

MOVING ON FROM STYKKISHÓLMUR

Taking the *Baldur* **ferry** from Stykkishólmur harbour across Breiðafjörður to **Brjánslækur** (3hr; 1500kr) in the west fjords, via the island of **Flatey** (1hr 45min; 1100kr) can save a lengthy and time-consuming drive. Sailings are twice daily from June to August (9am & 4pm) and once daily for the rest of the year on Tuesday, Wednesday, Friday and Saturday at 10am, and at 1pm on Sunday, Monday and Thursday from Stykkishólmur harbour across Breiðafjörður to Brjánslækur (3hr; 1500kr) in the west fjords via the island of Flatey (1hr45min; 1,100kr; for more information call ☎438 1120 or check out *www.qknet.is/ferjan*.

By taking the 9am June–August ferry, it's possible to continue by **bus** (Mon, Wed & Sat only) from Brjánslækur to Patreksfjörður (see p.181) and the Látrabjarg bird cliffs (see p.182); the return journey is possible on the same days, using the 4pm sailing from Brjánslækur to Stykkishólmur.

From Stykkishólmur, daily **buses** also run south all year to Reykjavík via Gröf and Borgarnes; on certain days, by changing at Gröf, it's possible to continue along the south coast to Búðir then back over to the north coast to Ólafsvík (see p.155) and Hellissandur (see p.157). From June to August, however, a daily service also runs west to Grundarfjörður (see p.155), Ólafsvík and Hellissandur.

1095; 1500kr) is at Höfdagata 1 whereas **guesthouse** accommodation can be had down the road at Höfdagata 11 at *Heimagisting Maríu* (☎438 1258; ③). The **campsite** (☎438 150) is next to the sports field, off Adalgata.

For **eating** your choices are limited to enjoyable and good-value *Knudsen* at Adalgata 4, which serves up pizzas, burgers, sandwiches as well as more substantial fish and meat dishes at reasonable prices, or the up-market restaurant inside *Fosshótel Stykkishólmur*, which is expense-account stuff although the fish dishes are delicious. Sandwiches can also be found at the Gissur Tryggvason filling station. The **state alcohol shop**, ÁTVR, is at Hafnargata 7.

Þingvöllur and Helgafell

A couple of kilometres south of Stykkishólmur, a small track leads off Route 58 to the east and running parallel with the Nesvogur inlet leads to the old parliament site of **Þingvöllur**, at the mouth of the Nesvogur inlet and right on the water's edge. This became a meeting place for the surrounding area following the death of Þórólfur Mostraskegg (during his lifetime the parliament was on Þórsnes). A few ruins can still be seen, including a sacrificial site that served as the altar to the god Þor. The site is located at the end of the track from Route 58.

From Þingvöllur, the mountain you can see to the southwest (though reached via different route) is **Helgafell**, or Holy Mountain, regarded in pagan times as sacred, when early settlers here believed it was an entrance to Valhalla, into which they would go after their deaths. Even today, local myth has it that Odin will grant three wishes to anyone climbing Helgafell for the first time, on the condition that they climb in silence and come down on the east side without looking back or speaking. This is not as simple as it sounds. The **path** up the west side is easy enough, but the eastern descent is steep and rocky and you have to pick your way carefully. The ascent, as is worth making though: at the top there are ruins of a tiny thirteenth-century **chapel** and striking **views** over the islands of Breiðafjörður and to the mountains of the west fjords. **Guðrún Ósvífursdóttir**, heroine of *Laxdæla Saga*, spent the last years of her life at the farm here and, over 900 years on, people still decorate her grave – outside the nearby churchyard and marked by a headstone – with wild flowers. The monastery which also once occupied this spot was moved here from the island of Flatey and survived until the Reformation. **To get here** it's a four-kilometre walk out of town on Route 58, past the airstrip and beyond the Nesvogur inlet, to the second turn on the left. All **buses** in and out of Stykkishólmur pass this junction.

Services to and from Reykjavík also pass through the narrow **Kerlingarskarð** mountain pass on Route 56, south of Stykkishólmur, named after an old female troll who, local legend has it, was caught by the sun and turned to stone whilst on her way home from a good night's fishing. Locals say she can still be seen with her line of trout over her shoulder on a ridge of the Kerlingarfjall mountain, opposite Hafrafell, at the northern end of the pass. Stories are also rife of drivers experiencing the eerie presence of an extra passenger in their cars as they drive through the pass.

Flatey

The largest of the Breiðafjörður islands, **FLATEY** is a tranquil haven of two dozen or so restored wooden cottages set amid fields of bright yellow buttercups. If you like the idea of having nothing to do all day but stroll through undisturbed meadows whilst taking in magnificient vistas of the west fjord mountains and Snæfellsjökull, then dining by evening on succulent cod caught the same afternoon, this is the place to come. The weather is most dependable in August, but remember if you're coming here out of season the island will be virtually deserted, since most of the houses are only occupied in summer by Reykjavík cityslickers; just four people spend the winter on Flatey.

Although today low key in the extreme, Flatey was once one of Iceland's leading cultural centres, and in 1172 a **monastery** was founded on the island's highest point, a little behind where the present-day church stands, though there's nothing left of it today. The island was also once home to the **Flateyjarbók**, a collection of illuminated medieval manuscripts written on 113 calfskins. Although the book was written at Víðidalstunga, in northern Iceland around 1387, it turned up here and remained in the possession of a local farmer's family until they gave it to the Bishop of Skálholt, who in turn sent it by royal request to King Frederik III of Denmark in 1659. The *Flateyjarbók* finally returned to Iceland in 1971 and is today housed in the Árni Magnússon instutute in Reykjavík (see p.57).

The island
From the ferry jetty it's a ten-minute walk down the rough track that passes as the island's one and only road to the **old village**, a restored collection of painted houses nestling around a tiny **harbour**. It's from here that the island's sheep are painstakingly bundled into boats and taken to the mainland for slaughter – quite a sight if you're around to witness it.

Past the harbour the track bears right, turns into a well-trodden path and climbs a little to the diminutive **Lundaberg** cliffs where you'll find plenty of black **guillemot**, **kittiwakes**, **fulmars** and **puffins** from April onwards, when the birds first start to arrive; half of all the 37 different species of bird that breed in Iceland are found on the islands of Breiðafjörður. Beyond the hill, the path continues towards the eastern part of the island, which has been declared a **nature reserve**, marked by the odd sign or two and closed to the public during the breeding season (May 15–July 20); the birds migrate south in late August or early September. It's possible, though, to pass round the edge of the reserve, following the marked wooden posts, to the island's south coast where you'll be bombarded by arctic tern who show no mercy for man nor beast – even the island's sheep are subject to regular divebombing raids. If you don't mind this (keeping still seems to deter the birds a little), there are some secluded pebbly coves here, home to the odd wrecked fishing boat, with excellent views on a clear day across to Snæfellsjökull. From the shoreline, the path continues up past the campsite (see below) up to the **church** with its dramatic roof and wall paintings of island life – and puffins — by the Catalan painter, **Baltasar**. Quite the entrepreneur, whilst visiting the island in the 1960s he suggested painting the church in return for free accommodation. After much hard work, the yellow building behind the church has been restored to its former glory and proudly claims the title of the oldest and smallest **library** in Iceland, established in 1864.

Practicalities
For details of the **ferry** from Stykkishólmur, see the box on p.152. Right by the harbour's edge is the island's only **guesthouse**, *Vogur* (☎438 1413), a rickety old wooden house dating from 1885 that was once used to accommodate priests sent to serve on Flatey. There are only ten beds here, so it's wise to book in advance.

A steep staircase leads to the two top rooms, right under the eaves, one of which has superb views out over Breiðafjörður. Be sparing with water here since the guesthouse has access to the only clean well on the island; you'll often see people dropping in to fill up their buckets. The **restaurant** here also functions as a small café during the day, serving up good home-made cakes and lunches. By evening, you can sample fresh fish landed just a matter of hours earlier; dinner costs from 1000kr, lunch from 700kr, breakfast from 600kr. The **campsite** is in a field behind Krákuvör farm, on the main track to the main harbour, and looks out over the sea. The island **post office** (Mon–Fri midday–1.30pm) is close to the farm.

Berserkjahraun and Grundarfjörður

From Stykkishólmur, one daily **bus** (June–Aug) heads west along Route 57 to Hellissandur calling at Grundarfjörður and Ólafsvík. Just after the junction with Route 56, the Kerlingarskarð pass, the road veers round the 4000-year-old **Berserkjahraun** lavafield named after the two **Berserkers** who cleared a route through it in 982 AD. Berserkers, periodically mentioned in the Sagas, were formidable warriors, able to go into a trance that made them impervious to wounds. Much valued as fighters but given a wide berth socially, since they were considered to be very dangerous, local man Víga-Styr persuaded the two to undertake this odd task because he had to take a circuitous route round the lava every time he wanted to visit his brother's farm. However, he later killed them after one fell in love with his daughter. Look carefully and you'll see the path, which is still visible in the lava; beside it is the men's burial mound.

Once across the small bridge over Hraunsfjörður, the road soon comes to **GRUNDARFJÖRÐUR**, dominated by the neighbouring Kirkjufell. Established in 1786 by the Danish king as one of six commercial centres in Iceland, the place exerted a strong influence on the west coast; in the early 1800s, for example, traders could only operate in the region if they had a branch in Grundarfjörður. From 1800–60, French fishermen also profited from the excellent harbour here and used the town as a base, owning the church, hospital and shipping operations. When they left, they dismantled their buildings and even exhumed their dead, shipping the bodies back to France. Today the village and its 850 inhabitants depend on their position as the commercial centre of western Iceland, and the local freezing plant, for prosperity, not exactly something that will make you want to linger.

Accommodation can be found at the functional *Hótel Framnes* (☎438 6893, fax ☎438 6930), Nesvegur 6–8, or at *Ásgeirshús* (☎438 6983) at Borgarbraut 2. The **campsite** (☎438 6813) is 1km east of the village at the farm located by the Kverná river. For **eating and drinking** you're better off in Stykkishólmur, but in the village you'll find the basic *Ásakaffi* at Grundargata 59 serving up sandwiches, cakes and light meals. For more substantial dishes, the *Krákan* restaurant, at Sæból 13, has good fish dishes. For pizzas, head for *Kristján IX* at Grundargata 59. The local **swimming pool**, virtually the only place to find life in Grundarfjörður, is on Borgarbraut.

Ólafsvík

ÓLAFSVÍK is not only the most productive fishing town on Snæfellsnes, it is Iceland's oldest established trading town, granted its charter in 1687. Squeezed

WHALE WATCHING OFF SNÆFELLSNES PENINSULA

Whale-watching tours from Ólafsvík on the *Brimrún*, a catamaran operated by Eyjaferdir (☎438 1450, fax ☎438 1050; 4500k) depart one to two times daily from June to August and last from four to seven hours, depending on weather and the number of whales there are to spot. The boat leaves from the western side of the harbour, near the tourist office, and follows the shoreline towards the open ocean, where there's a chance of seeing **killer whales** and **bottlenose dolphins**; once the boat is out on the open sea blue whales and **humpback whales** are common. Humpbacks are spotted very close to the boat, breaching the surface of the water, or "spy-hopping", the technical term for poking their head out of the water and having a look around. Much, much larger than the humpback, the **blue whale** is the largest mammal on earth weighing 120,000kg (the equivalent of 2000 people standing on one spot) and is as long as two coaches. Less frequently, **minke whales, long-finned pilot whales** and **fin whales** are also spotted.

Bring waterproof clothing, a thick woollen hat and gloves – and plenty of camera film. Light snacks and hot drinks are available from the café on board. To be sure of a seat it's wise to book in advance with Eyjaferdir or at the tourist office (see below); alternatively, you can simply pay as you board.

between the sea and the towering Enni (415m), it's a quiet working fishing village whose population goes about its daily business seemingly unmoved by the groups of travellers who turn up here in search of Ólafvík's main attraction, the chance of spotting **whales**, including the biggest mammal on earth, the mighty blue whale (see box). The town is also one of several places to use as a base for climbing **Snæfellsjökull**, the nearby glacier (see box opposite).

Other than whales, Ólafvík's only other sight is the **Gamla Pakkhúsið** on Nordurtangi, a solid-looking timber warehouse built in 1841 by the town's leading trading firm who, naturally, dealt in fish. Today it houses a **folk museum** (late May to end Aug daily 11am–5pm; free), which has a few good black-and-white photographs of the town and the obligatory exhibitors about fishing. The **church** on Kirkjutún is worth a quick look for its three-legged detached bell tower and its sharply pointed spire.

Practicalities

A once-daily **bus** runs all year round from Reykjavík and Stykkishólmur to Grundarfjörður. The **tourist office** (late May to Aug daily 11am–5pm; ☎436 1543) is in the Gamla Pakkhúsið, on Nordurtangi. There are two **guesthouses** in town, both opposite each other on the main road: *Gistiheimilið Höfdi* (☎436 1650, fax ☎436 1651; ⑤) with small but passable rooms with shared bath at Ólafsbraut 20, and the not disimilar but much cheaper *Gistiheimilið Ólafsvíkur* (☎436 1300; ②) at Ólafsbraut 19. The **campsite** (☎436 1543) with showers and hot and cold running water is on Dalbraut, about 1km east of the town centre. The best place for meals is the **restaurant** inside the *Höfdi*, where the dish of the day (usually fish) goes for around 1200kr but there are also burgers and sandwiches. Across the road, in the restaurant attached to the *Ólafsvíkur*, there are meat and seafood dishes for around 1200kr, plus pizzas from 800kr, as well as more sandwiches and burgers. Cheap and cheerful fry-ups and burgers can also be had at *Grillskálinn*, on the main road next to Landsbankinn, at Ólafsbraut 21. The **state alcohol shop**, ÁTVR, is at Myrarholt 12. The indoor **swimming pool** is at Ennisbraut 9.

Rif and Hellissandur

From Ólafsvík, Route 574 continues west past a dramatic beach of black volcanic sand, Hardikambur, on its way towards the miniscule fishing hamlet of **Rif**, which, with a population of just 150 souls, is really nothing more than a well-protected harbour and a few fish-processing plants, and its marginally bigger neighbour, **HELLISSANDUR**, 2km further on. Known locally as just Sandur, the latter of these two places is the westernmost settlement on Snæfellsnes and home to most

---

SNÆFELLSJÖKULL

Enter the Snæfellsjökull crater, which is kissed by Scatari's shadow before the first of July, adventurous traveller, and thou wilt descend to the centre of the Earth.
Journey to the Centre of the Earth, Jules Verne

Made world famous in the nineteenth century by Jules Verne's *Journey to the Centre of the Earth*, **Snæfellsjökull** stands guard at the very tip of the peninsula to which it gave its name, Snow Mountain (Snæfell means "snow mountain", Snæfellsnes means "snow mountain peninsula"). It is from here that Verne's hero, the German geologist Professor Lidenbrock of Hamburg, descends into a crater in the extinct volcano under the glacier and embarks upon a fantastic subterranean journey accompanied by his nephew and Icelandic guide with the very un-Icelandic name of Hans. The Professor has managed to decipher a document written in runic script that leads him to believe that this is the way to the centre of the earth; rather inexplicably he finally emerges on the volcanic Mediterranean island of Stromboli. This remote part of Iceland has long been associated with supernatural forces and mystery, and stories like this only strengthen this belief. In recent years the glacier has even become a point of pilgrimage for New Age travellers who, to the bemusement of locals, consider the area one of the world's great power centres, though they're not much in evidence.

Experienced hikers have a choice of three **ascents** of the 1446-metre-high, three-peaked glacier, which incidentally sits on a dormant volcano; three eruptions have occurred under the glacier in the past 10,000 years, the last around 300 AD. **Maps** and **information** about the routes can be found at the tourist offices in Ólafsvík and Arnarstapi.

The easiest is via Route F570 **from Ólafsvík**, which begins just 1km east of the town's campsite and runs up to the glacier's eastern edge then via the narrow Jökulháls pass down to Arnarstapi on the south coast. Although this road is passable by four-wheel-drive vehicles, it's often blocked by snow, even in the height of summer. Take extreme care once on the ice for hidden crevasses; picks and crampons may be needed; allow three to four hours to reach the glacier and another two to descend to Arnarstapi. This approach is also possible **from Arnarstapi** (see p.160), also via the F570, leading first past the eastern flank of Stapafell (526m) and winding its way up to the glacier; allow at least five hours to reach the ice. This is the route taken by the **snowmobile tours** from Arnarstapi (see p.160).

The third and longest ascent of the glacier begins **from the Hellissandur** (see above); take Route 575 west out town to its junction with the unnumbered road that follows the course of the Módulækur river up through Eysteinsdalur valley to the glacier – note that on some maps this road is not marked. From the road's end a walking path continues up to the glacier's highest point, Jökulpufur (1446m) from where another track leads down the ice cap's eastern flank to join up with mountain road F570.

of the fishermen from nearby Rif. There's very little to do in Hellissandur other than to pay a quick visit to the two old **fishermen's cottages**, complete with turf rooves, which make up the Maritime Museum, **Sjómannagardur** (June–Aug daily except Wed, 9am–midday & 1–6pm; 200kr) beside the main road, Útnesvegur. In the larger of the two buildings is the oldest rowing boat in Iceland, dating from 1826. Otherwise, Hellissandur makes a good base from which to explore the various **hikes** around western Snæfellsnes (see box).

For **accommodation** there's the pleasant and simple *Gistihúsið Gimli* near the ocean at Keflavíkurgata 4 (☎436 6825, fax ☎436 6770; ②) which has some en-suite

---

HIKING AROUND THE WESTERN SNÆFELLSNES

Hellissandur makes a good base for exploring the foot of the Snæfellsjökull and the surrounding **lavafields**. A recommended day hike of around 20km leads from the village to Eysteinsdalur valley; take the unmarked secondary road between the campsite and the maritime museum that leads towards the glacier. After around 1km the road becomes a hiking path which strikes out across the **Prestahraun** lavafield, joining up after 4km with the un-numbered road that runs up through the valley. Here, on the south side of the road, a signed path leads up to the hill, **Raudhóll**, to a red scoria crater. An impressive rift in the lava can also been seen to the east of the hill. Continue another 1km along the road towards the glacier and you'll come to a signposted path to the south of the road, which leads to the prominent basalt spur, **Klukka**, and a beautiful waterfall, **Klukkufoss**, where the Módulækur flows through a narrow canyon lined with basalt columns. Back on the main road and another 1km towards the glacier, a path to the north of the road leads to the **Blágil** ravine, where the Ljósulækir glacial river thunders through the narrow rugged gorge. To return to Hellissandur, retrace your steps along the main road, beyond the turn for the waterfall, to the hiking path that heads out to the north across the **Væjuhraun** lavafield for Rif. From here, simply head west along the coastal road to Hellissandur. **Maps** of these routes are available from the tourist office in Ólafsvík (see p.156) and at the guesthouse in Hellissandur (see above).

Another recommended day hike (18km) leads first to the sandy bay, **Skarðsvík**, walled in by cliffs and crags on its northern and western edges. The lava above the cliffs is overgrown with moss and can be a good place to see rare plants. Excellent **fishing** can be had in the bay's protected waters and it's therefore a favourite spot for local boats. To get here, follow Route 574 west out of Hellissandur to its junction with the unnumbered road signed for Skarðsvík; it's at this point that the main road swings inland, heading for the glacier and the turn for Eysteinsdalur valley. Just 2km west of Skarðsvík the road terminates at the peninsula's westernmost point, Öndverdarnes, a dramatic and weatherbeaten spot marked only by a lonely lighthouse and a stone well which legend has it is linked to three springs: one of fresh water, one of sea water and one of wine. The promontory is a favourite destination for basking **seals**, who favour the pebbly beach here. South of the cape the **Svörtuloft** cliffs are worth a visit; swarming with **seabirds** in summer, the cliffs provided a major source of eggs and birds for the tables of local villagers until the 1950s, when living standards began to rise. The free-standing crag in the sea here, **Skálasnagi**, was once connected to the mainland by a natural stone bridge until it fell victim to the pounding of Atlantic breakers in 1973. From the cliffs, a path heads east, inland through the **Neshraun** lavafield to an area of small hillocks known as **Neshólar** before emerging at Skardsvík.

rooms as well as sleeping-bag accommodation; alternatively, the **campsite** is on the eastern edge of the village by the main road, Útnesvegur, beautifully set by an open meadow. The ESSO **filling station** on Útnesvegur is the best bet for **food** where there's a small grill restaurant. The town's only other facilities are a branch of *Landsbankinn* at Klettsbúd 4 and a **swimming pool**, also on Klettsbúd. A daily **bus** runs from Reykjavík via the south coast of Snæfellsnes and Ólafsvík to Rif and Hellisandur. For details of travelling by bus from Hellisandur to Arnarstapi, see p.160.

Dritvík, Djúpalón and Lóndrangar

On leaving Hellissandur, the horizon is dominated by the huge mast that transmits the long-wave signal for Icelandic national radio, anchored down by wire cables against the brute force of Atlantic storms. Beyond this last sign of civilisation the landscape becomes increasingly desolate and the road surface more and more potholed – there's nothing but wilderness between here and **Dritvík** bay, 24km southwest of Hellissandur along Route 574. Once home to sixty fishing boats and accordingly one of the most prolific fishing villages on the peninsula, today the bay is uninhabited, and centuries of fishing tradition would have been completely lost if it were not for the continuing presence today of four mighty **stones** at nearby **Djúpalón**, a short stroll south from the bay, and each with individual names: the largest, *fullsterkur* (full strength) weighs in at 155kg, next comes *hálfsterkur* (half strength) at 140kg, then *hálfdrættingur* (weakling) 49kg and finally *amlódi* (useless) weighing just 23kg. Any fisherman worth his salt had to be able to lift at least the latter two onto a ledge of rock at hip height to prove his strength. The smallest stone is now broken – perhaps after one too many attempts by weakling tourists.

The lofty rock pillars, **Lóndrangar**, are just 5km southeast of the Djúpalón lagoon and easily reached on foot from Route 574. The taller of the two is 75m high and known locally as the "Christian pillar", with its smaller neighbour called the "heathen pillar" although nobody seems to know why; both are remnants of a basalt cinder cone. There's no public transport here, it's possible to get here on the Snæfellsnes **excursion tour** to and from Ólafsvík (see p.134).

Hellnar

Just like its western neighbour of Dritvík, the tiny settlement of **HELLNAR** was once one of the peninsula's most prosperous fishing communities. Today though the place consists of nothing more than a couple of farm buildings and the odd holiday cottage either side of a steep, dead-end road that winds its way down to a picturesque hoof-shaped **harbour** and a tiny sandy **beach** where the occasional fishing boat is moored. To the left of the harbour, the sea cave, **Badstofa**, is known for its rich birdlife as well as its unusual light shades and hues caused by the swell of the sea.

The old salting house, dating from 1937, still stands on the harbourside, its white stone walls and bright yellow roof now housing a charming **café**, the *Fjöruhúsið* (late May to early Oct daily from 11am; no fixed evening closing time), which serves up home-made cakes and great espresso, as well as some excellent fish soup of an evening when the arty interior lighting is provided by a dozen light bulbs suspended on long wire flexes. If the weather's poor, sit inside and savour the uninterrupted views of the Atlantic through the café's small square windows; in fine weather you can sit on the wooden terrace at the rear, which overlooks the harbour.

Arnarstapi

From the cave at Hellnar, an easy path (2.5km) leads east along the cliff tops to nearby **ARNARSTAPI**, at the foot of Stapafell (526m). The village itself comprises a few holiday cottages and a **harbour**, reached by following the road through the village down to the sea – but beware of the large number of arctic tern that gather here during summer and take pleasure in divebombing unsuspecting intruders. From the harbour, **whale-watching tours** depart at 10am Monday to Friday (3hr; minimum 5 people, 3900kr per person) on board the *Nökkvi*, offering the chance to see **killer whales** and the peculiar rock arches and sea caves that the coastline hereabouts is renowned for. You'll also see the large stone **monument** to the pagan-age figure Barður Snæfellsás, who, according to local legend still lives in Snæfellsjökull and protects the area from evil.

The village is also the starting point for hikes and jeep drives up to **Snæfellsjökull** via Route F570 (see p.157), but its better known for its **snowmobiling** excursions across the glacier. Trips lasting 1–3 hours depart from here and go up onto Stapafell (3900kr per person for two sharing one snowmobile, 4500kr for your own machine). Speeding along the ice top is an exhilarating experience, and the views of the glacier and the coastline are quite simply breathtaking when the weather is good – but don't be tempted to head onto the ice if it's raining because you'll see nothing. If speed isn't your thing, a slower snowcat, a sort of open-top truck on caterpillar tracks, also carries groups of twenty or so across the ice (2500kr). Buses leave from the tourist information office (see below) every two hours between 9am and 7pm (daily May to Sept; other times on request) for the glacier where, once on its snout, you transfer to snowmobile. With your own transport it's possible to begin the tour there; from Arnarstapi, head east on Route 574 to the junction with mountain road F570, from where the snowmobile tours are signed. Although this road can be extremely bumpy, even small cars can use it.

Practicalities

Although there's no public transport to and from Arnarstapi it is possible to get here by excursion **bus** (June–Aug) from Ólafsvík and Hellissandur. From Arnarstapi, the bus leaves at 1.30pm for Hellissandur and Ólafsvík and at 4.40pm for Búðir and Ólafsvík; take the later bus and change at Búðir for Reykjavík. What little life there is in the village is centered on the red-walled, turf-rooved cottage, Snjófell (☎ 435 6783, fax ☎435 6795), by the car park off the main road, which acts as the **tourist information office** and a booking centre for the one and only **hotel**, the yellow-walled *Arnarfell* (☎435 6783 or ☎854 5150; ②), next door. There are just nine doubles here offering cosy farmhouse-style accommodation; alternatively there's sleeping-bag accommodation (1500kr); cooking facilities are also available. Bikes are also available for rent here at 1000kr per day. The **campsite** (☎435 6783 or ☎854 5150) is close by. Although the **restaurant** inside the Snjófell complex is the only place to eat, it does offer a decent menu, with some good fish dishes.

Búðir and Lysuhóll

Nineteen kilometres east of Arnarstapi, and served by all **buses** from Reykjavík, **BÚÐIR** is a romantic, windswept location, a former fishing village at the head of the sweeping expanse of white sand that backs the bay here, Búdavík. The settlement, like so many others in this part of the country, was abandoned in the early nineteenth century and today consists of nothing more than a hotel and a church, both situated just a stone's throw from the ocean. Surrounded by the **Búdahraun lavafield**, rumoured to be home to countless leprechauns, and enjoying unsurpassed views out over the foam-capped waves of the Atlantic, the tiny **church**, which dates from 1703, pitch-black and with three white-framed windows, cuts an evocative image when viewed from the adjoining graveyard with the majestic Snæfellsnes mountain range as a backdrop.

The enchanting *Hótel Búðir* (☎435 6700, fax ☎435 6701; ⑦), located in a timber building dating from 1836, is unfortunately closed until Spring 2002. **Rooms** here, although a little small, have been individually decorated in nineteenth-century style and either enjoy a view of the lavafield or of the sandy bay. Once the hotel reopens it will also be able to arrange **horse rental** around the uninhabited expanses of the Löngufjörur coast east of Búðir as well as over the Arnardalsskard pass to the peninsula's north coast and the shores of Breiðafjörður.

Five kilometres east of Búðir and reached on Route 572, the dot on the map that is **LYSUHÓLL** is one of the few places on the peninsula with its own source of geothermal mineral water. The spring provides natural hot bubbly water for the outdoor **swimming pool** and hot pots which are open daily from mid-June to late August (10am–10pm) and offers fantastic views of the surrounding mountains. For a place to stay here there's a basic but pleasant **guesthouse** (☎435 6730; ②) and a campsite, both on the same site as the swimming pool. The guesthouse **restaurant** is good for small snacks such as soup and home-made bread. All **buses** to and from Reykjavík call here.

East along Route 54 to Borgarnes

From Lýsuhóll, **Route 54** continues east crossing the powerful Straumfjardará flowing down from Seljafell before reaching the lonely Löngufjörur and the **Eldborgarhraun** lavafield. As the road swings east for Borgarnes you get a view of the oval-shaped crater, **Eldborg**, sitting conspicuously amid the flat expanse of the lava. To the east of Eldborg, **Fagraskógarfjall** mountain was the haunt of Grettir of *Grettir's Saga*: "a savage and dreadful place" according to William Morris, who was here in 1871 – though these days it seems much more green and peaceful. North of here, along Route 55, the caves of **Gullborgarhraun** lavafield are a maze of intricate passageways containing coloured stalagmites and stalactites. It's advisable though to seek local advice before exploring them. Once again, **buses** to and from Reykjavík on Route 54 pass these attractions.

travel details

Buses

The bus details given below are relevant for May to September; for winter times, visit *www.bsi.is*.

Akranes to: Bifröst (daily; 1hr); Borgarnes (4 daily; 1hr); Búðardalur (4 weekly; 2hr 15min); Búðir (daily; 2hr); Grundarfjörður (daily; 2hr 45min); Hellisandur (daily; 3hr); Ólafsvík (daily; 2hr 45min); Reykjavík (9 daily; 1hr); Stykkishólmur (daily; 2hr)

Bifröst to: Akranes (daily; 1hr); Borgarnes (daily; 30min); Reykjavík (daily; 1hr 40min)

Borgarnes to: Akranes (4 daily, 1hr); Bifröst (daily; 30min); Búðardalur (4 weekly; 1hr 30min); Búðir (daily; 1hr 15min); Grundarfjörður (daily; 2hr); Hellisandur (daily; 1hr 45min); Ólafsvík (daily; 1hr 30min); Reykjavík (8 daily; 1hr); Stykkishólmur (daily; 1hr 15min)

Búðardalur to: Akranes (4 weekly; 2hr 15min); Borgarnes (4 weekly; 1hr 30min); Reykjavík (4 weekly; 2hr 45min)

Búðir to: Akranes (daily; 2hr); Borgarnes (daily; 1hr 15min); Hellisandur (daily; 30min); Ólafsvík (daily, 15min); Reykjavík (daily; 2hr 30min)

Grundarfjörður to: Akranes (daily; 2hr 45min); Borgarnes (daily; 2hr); Reykjavík (daily; 2hr 15min); Stykkishólmur (daily; 45min)

Hellisandur to: Akranes (daily; 2hr 30min); Borgarnes (daily; 1hr 45min); Búðir (daily; 30min); Ólafsvík (daily; 15min); Reykjavík (daily; 3hr)

Ólafsvík to: Akranes (daily; 2hr 45min); Borgarnes (daily; 1hr 30min); Búðir (daily; 15min); Reykjavík (daily; 2hr 45min)

Reykholt to: Borgarnes (daily; 45min); Reykjavík (2 weekly; 1hr 45min)

Stykkishólmur to: Akranes Stykkishólmur (daily; 2hr); Borgarnes (daily; 1hr 15min); Grundarfjörður (daily; 45min); Reykjavík (daily; 2hr 30min)

Ferries

The ferry details given below are relevant for May to September; for winter times, check the relevant entries in the guide.

Flatey to: Stykkishólmur (2 daily; 1hr 45min)

Stykkishólmur to: Flatey (2 daily; 1hr 45min)

CHAPTER FOUR

THE WEST FJORDS

ttached to the mainland by a narrow isthmus of land barely 10km wide, the West Fjords are one of the most breathtakingly beautiful and least-visited corners of Iceland. This peninsula of 8600 square kilometres, stretching out into the icy waters of the Denmark Strait, with its dramatic fjords cutting deep into its heart, is the result of intense glaciation. Everything here is extreme – from the table mountains that dominate the landscape, plunging precipitously into the Atlantic, to the ferocious storms that have gnawed the coastline into countless craggy inlets. Life up here, on the edge of the Arctic Circle, is tough – even in summer, temperatures seldom rise above 10°C, and drifting pack ice is never far from the north coast.

Since flat land is at a premium in this rugged part of the country, towns and villages have grown up on the narrow strip of lowland that separates the mountains from the fjords. Geologically all but cut off from the outside world, the people of the West Fjords have historically turned to the sea for their livelihood, and today the majority of the 9600 people who still live here are still financially dependent on **fishing** and its related industries. However, the traditional way of life is changing, and the effects of rural depopulation are being felt in every village as outlying farms are abandoned and dozens of young people choose the bright lights of Reykjavík over a precarious and uncertain future on the very edge of Europe.

The unforgiving geography of the West Fjords makes travel here difficult and convoluted. Roads are mainly surfaced with gravel, and they're always potholed and often circuitous. **Route 61**, for example, wiggles its way exasperatingly round no fewer than seven deeply indented fjords en route to the regional capital, **Ísafjörður**. Benefiting from a spectacular setting on a narrow spit of land jutting out into **Ísafjarðardjúp**, the town makes an excellent base from which to explore this 75-kilometre-long fjord network at the heart of the West Fjords, plus **Drangajökull**, the only glacier in the region, as well as the outstanding natural beauty of the uninhabited **Hornstrandir** peninsula, which offers some of the

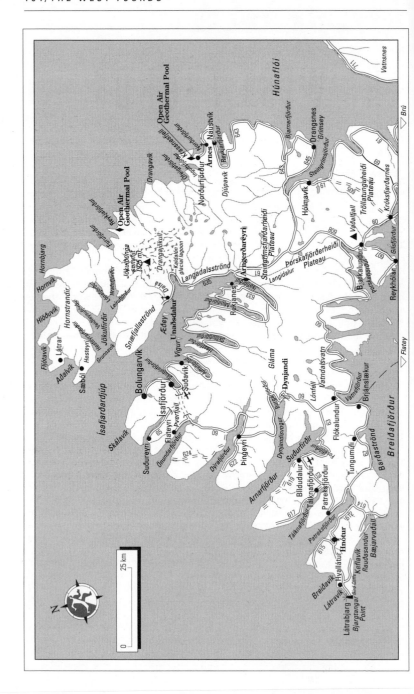

wildest and most rewarding hiking in Iceland. From Ísafjörður, Route 60 weaves its way over mountain tops, round several fjords and past a handful of tiny fishing villages on its way to the ferry port of **Brjánslækur**, from where a daily boat leaves the West Fjords for Snæfellsnes. A brooding, lonely peninsula reaches out into the Atlantic from this point terminating at **Látrabjarg**, Europe's most westerly point, and one of the world's greatest bird cliffs, with large numbers of puffins, razorbills and other seabirds. Nearby **Patreksfjörður**, the second town of the West Fjords, is the only place in the region with a population big enough for life to go on independently of Ísafjörður. Meanwhile, on the other side of the West Fjords, the eastern **Strandir** coast, which stretches north from the busy fishing village of **Hólmavík**, is hard to beat for splendid isolation, its few villages hardly visited by tourists, and with some of the most dramatic, forbidding landscapes this corner of the country has to offer.

As for **getting around the West Fjords**, from June to August it's possible to travel across the region by **long-distance bus**. From Ísafjörður, services run on Tuesday, Friday and Sunday morning via Súðavík (30min), Ísafjarðardjúp (3hr) and the Steingrímsfjarðarheiði plateau to Hólmavík (5hr), from where onward connections can be made to Reykjavík and, on Friday only, to Akureyri. An afternoon service runs back to Ísafjörður from Hólmavík on the same days. On Monday, Wednesday and Saturday, a bus leaves Ísafjörður for Þingeyri, Hrafnseyri, Brjánslækur, Patreksfjörður, Breiðavík and Látrabjarg, a total journey of six hours. The bus waits at the cliffs for 90 minutes before returning via the same route; ferry connections for Snæfellsnes exist at Brjánslækur.

Local buses operate several times daily all year round between Ísafjörður and Bolungarvík and Flateyri. From September to May, two buses daily follow the route between from Tálknafjörður to Patreksfjörður, then back to Tálknafjörður before continuing to Bíldudalur and its airport. On Friday only, a service runs in both directions from Reykjavík to Hólmavík and Drangsnes via Borgarnes and Brú. A connection can be made at Brú for Akureyri.

Ísafjörður

With a population of just over 2900, **ÍSAFJÖRÐUR** is by far and away the largest settlement in the West Fjords and is where most travellers choose to base themselves when exploring the region. All administration for the area is centred here too, and there's also a significant **fishing industry**. It's hard to imagine a much more dramatic location; built on the L-shaped sandspit, **Eyri**, which stretches out into the narrow waters of **Skutulsfjörður** and provides exceptionally good shelter for the ocean-going fishing vessels, the town is surrounded by towering mountains on three sides and by the open waters of **Ísafjarðardjúp** on the fourth. During the long winter months, locals are forced to battle against the elements to keep the tiny **airport** open, which very often provides the only point of contact between the entire region and the rest of the country. Should you be able to arrive in Ísafjörður by plane, however, you'll be treated to an unforgettable experience as you bank steeply around the fjord, then skim past the sheer mountainside of Kirkjubólshlíð before dropping onto the landing strip. In fact, during the darkest months of the year (Dec & Jan), the sheer height of the mountains either side of the fjord prevents the low winter sun from shining directly onto the town for a number of weeks, and the sun's reappearance over the mountain tops at the end of January is celebrated with **sólarkaffi**, "sun coffee" (in fact just normal coffee) and pancakes on January 25.

Although the Eyri sandspit was settled during the ninth century, it wasn't until the late sixteenth century that Ísafjörður gradually became one of the country's main trading centres. This was when the town's most notorious resident, **Jón Magnússon**, a fundamentalist priest, ordered two men on a neighbouring farm to be burned at the stake for sorcery. Today though, Ísafjörður is a quiet and likeable place where you'd be wise to make the most of the shops, restaurants and bars on offer before venturing out into the wilds beyond such as the Hornstrandir peninsula or one of the much smaller West Fjords villages. There's very little of note, though, in the town – Ísafjörður's pleasures are more to be found in strolling through its streets or watching the fishermen busy at work in the harbour rather than taking in tourist sights. The **West Fjords Maritime Museum**, though, one of the very few museums in the region, is worth visiting for an insight into the extreme conditions that past generations have lived under here. That it's located in one of the country's oldest timber buildings is unusual in itself, when you consider that the climate here is so severe that anything made out of wood doesn't normally last long at all.

The Town

Although there are no specific sights in Ísafjörður, it's a pleasant enough place to stroll round for a couple of hours. Shops, banks and the post office can all be found on Hafnarstræti, for camera accessories head for the bookshop opposite the hotel. The brightly painted timber houses on **Silfurgata**, which leads from the hotel to the sea, and on **Tangagata**, which crosses Silfurgata at its eastern end, are particularly beautiful with their mountain backdrop.

At the southern edge of town, beyond the tourist office and on Sudurtangi, are four of Iceland's oldest buildings, all timber structures dating from the late eighteenth century. One, the carefully restored **Turnhús**, with its unusual roof tower, was originally constructed in Denmark before being moved to Iceland in 1744, where it was used a salting house. As the tallest structure in Ísafjörður, it also served as a lookout from where returning fishing boats were spotted – livelihoods depended on being first to the dockside when the boats came in, it being paramount that the fish were processed as quickly as possible. The **Turnhús** now houses the **West Fjords Maritime Museum** (May, June & mid-Aug to Sept daily 1–5pm, July daily 10am–5pm; 200kr). Inside, fishing paraphernalia and old black-and-white photographs give a good idea of what life used to be like during the early twentieth century; look out for those depicting the thousands of fish that would be laid out to dry and salted in the open air; in later years, ice cut from the fjord was used to preserve instead. One photo, from the winter of 1918, was taken when plummeting temperatures and ferocious storms ushered in one of the severest winters for decades, when sheets of ice crept up the fjord, choking up the harbour and freezing the entire fishing fleet – bar one boat – into the ice. Of the remaining buildings on the museum site, the **Tjöruhús** dates from the 1730s, attached to which is the **Krambud**, originally a shop dating to 1761. The fourth building, the **Faktorshús**, from 1765, was once home to the shop manager. None of the three is open to the public.

Practicalities

Buses, which are operated by Allrahanda (☎540 1313), stop outside the central Edinborgarhús at Aðalstræti 7, from where it's a one-minute walk to the Vesturferðir travel agent, which also functions as the local **tourist information office** (Mon–Fri 8am–6pm, Sat & Sun 10am–3pm; ☎456 5121, fax ☎456 5185); head south on Aðalstræti until you come to the office at the end of the block at the junction with Pollgata. Buses also stop in the western part of town outside the summer hotel, *Torfnes*, on Skutulsfjarðarbraut. Passenger **boats** to and from the Hornstrandir peninsula arrive at Sundahöfn harbour, at the eastern end of Mjósund, which leads down to the harbour from the tourist office. The **airport**, 7km out of town, is on a narrow stretch of land on the eastern edge of the fjord;. there are no buses into town, but taxis (800kr) are available.

The only **hotel** in town that's open year-round is *Hótel Ísafjörður* (☎456 4111, fax 456 4767; ⑤), centrally located on Silfurtorg, just off the main street, Hafnarstræti. Don't be put off by the grey concrete exterior, inside the doubles are comfortable, if somewhat plain, are well insulated against the biting wind, and breakfast is included. A considerably cheaper alternative is the **summer hotel**, *Torfnes* (June–Aug; ☎456 4485, fax 456 4767; sleeping-bag accommodation 950–1700kr, ③), set in a boarding school in the western part of town on

Skutulsfjarðarbraut, where rooms comprise nothing more than a bed and a wash-basin; breakfast costs 800kr extra. Ísafjörður also has a **guesthouse**: *Gistiheimili Áslaugar* (☎456 3868, fax 456 4075; sleeping-bag accommodation 800–1500kr, ②) at Austurvegur 7, though the doubles here are rather small and dingy; breakfast is 850kr extra. The **campsite** (☎456 4485; 200kr per tent) is behind the *Torfnes* summer hotel.

The best and liveliest **restaurant** in town is *Pizza 67*, at Hafnarstræti 12, which serves up pizzas from 1200kr, chicken and lamb dishes from 1500kr until 10pm (until 3am Fri & Sat). Similar dishes are served up at *Hrói Höttur*, Mánagata 1, which is handy for the *Torfnes* summer hotel if you don't want to head all the way into town from there. Next door, the elegant *Á Eyrinni* serves delicious but pricey fish dishes from 1500kr. The finest food in town, however, is to be had at the restaurant inside the *Hótel Ísafjörður* although the chances are you'll be dining alone if you come here, as the high prices seem to deter most locals; reckon on 2300kr per person for fresh cod or turbot with with hollandaise sauce and fresh veg.

For **snacks** and microwaved hamburgers head for *Hamraborg*, at Hafnarstræti 7, which is open until 11.30pm, or the **bakery**, Gamla Bakaríid, at Aðalstræti 24, if you fancy a coffee and a sandwich. The one and only **pub** in town is the aptly named *Krúsin* (Thurs–Sat), attached to *Pizza 67*, where young Ísafjörðers gather to quench their thirst or, on Friday evenings, have a dance. Alternatively, the **state alcohol shop**, ÁTVR, is at Aðalstræti 20. The **cinema**, at Norðurvegur 1, generally has several showings a week. The indoor **swimming pool**, at Austurvegur 9, also has a sauna for men on Monday, Wednesday, Friday and Saturday and for women on Tuesday, Thursday and Sunday.

Around Ísafjörður: Bolungarvík and Skálavík

Fifteen kilometres northwest of Ísafjörður along Route 61, the fishing village of **BOLUNGARVÍK**, at the mouth of Ísafjarðardjúp, suffers from one of the most exposed locations in the country. Not only does it receive some of the foulest weather in Iceland, but its position at the foot of three mountains, two of which are close to 700m high, means it's also susceptible to avalanches and landslides, and a large section of Route 61 is protected from rock and snowfalls by sturdy metal nets suspended between posts at the roadside.

Although Bolungarvík is one of the larger settlements in the West Fjords, with a population of around a thousand, it's a workday place with little to entertain visitors. However, it is worth making the twenty-minute trip from Ísafjörður to visit the open-air **Ósvör Maritime Museum** (200kr) at the entrance to town, just before the bridge. The tiny, turf-rooved huts here, with their thick stone lower walls, are reconstructions of structures that were once used to house fishing-boat crews, a salting house and a rack for drying fish, and give a good idea of how cramped conditions were in the early twentieth century. The museum also has a six-oared rowing boat from the 1940s, built to a traditional local design on display. The landing stage, beyond the huts, was used when the weather conditions were too severe for boats to land in more exposed Bolungarvík itself.

The town's only other attraction, the **Natural History Museum** (Mon–Fri 9am–noon & 1–5pm, Sat & Sun 1–5pm; 250kr), is a ten-minute walk from the maritime museum following the main road into town, Þuríðarbraut, across the Hólsá river, and straight on into the main street, Aðalstræti. From here, turn right into

Vitastígur and you'll see the museum down by the harbour. Inside there's a curious collection of various stuffed animals including a polar bear, a seal and, oddly, a cockerel, though nothing that will hold your attention for more than a couple of minutes. The museum, however, is a good place to stock up on decent postcards, which you can send from the nearby post office on Aðalstræti.

Bolungarvík practicalities

A local **bus** arrives and departs from the **post office** at Aðalstræti 19 three times daily Monday to Friday (200kr) for Ísafjörður. The town's only **guesthouse**, in the same building as the Natural History Museum, is *Finnabær* (☎456 7254, fax 456 7534 sleeping-bag accommodation 950kr, ①), Vitastígur 1, a simple affair inside what looks like a small office complex. Rooms are small and plain but cheap, while breakfast is 700kr extra. The **campsite** is at Höfdastígur 1, next to a swimming pool and the Hólsá river, where Route 61 from Ísafjörður enters town. **Eating** is restricted to *Veitingahúsið Finnabær*, on Vitastígur, where fresh fish and other simple dishes can be had from 1000kr.

Skálavík

From the western edge of Bolungarvík, Þjóðólfsvegur continues 12km northwest through the uninhabited Hlídardalur valley until it reaches the exposed **Skálavík** bay, which takes regular batterings from Atlantic storms as they sweep in mercilessly from the northwest. Although Skálavík is today uninhabited bar a couple of summer houses owned by brave souls who don't seem to mind the weather, at the end of the nineteenth century around one hundred people were living here, ekeing out an existence from the surrounding barren land. Given the village's vulnerable location between the Deilir and Öskubakur mountains, **avalances** were always a particular hazard and claimed several lives; perhaps not surprisingly therefore, the last farmer gave up his struggle to keep the village alive in 1964 and left.

There's no public transport to Skálavík but it is possible to **walk from Bolungarvík** in around two hours – simply follow Þjóðólfsvegur all the way. The bay offers a real chance to commune with nature and a night spent **camping** here, battling against the weather, is certainly a memorable experience; bring all the supplies you'll need. There's also some good **hiking** around here; one good route (7km) begins at the western edge of the bay and leads west along the shore round Öskubakar to to the lonely lighthouse on the headland at Galtarvíti. From here, another track (5km) heads inland through the valleys of Norddalur and Bakkadalur back to Skálavík and the beginning of the track back to Bolungarvík. A detailed **map** of these routes is included in the hiking leaflet *Gönguleiðir í Nágrenni Bolungarvíkur*, available free from the tourist office in Ísafjörður (see p.167) and from the guesthouse in Bolungarvík (see above).

Around Ísafjarðardjúp

The largest and most breathtaking of all the West Fjords, the seventy-five kilometre-long **Ísafjarðardjúp** stretches all the way from the mountains around Bolungarvík at its mouth to the shores of Ísafjörður, the most easterly of the nine smaller fjords that make up the western coastline of this great bay. Approaching from the southeast, descending from the Steingrímfjarðarheiði plateau on Road

61, the views of Ísafjarðardjúp are spectacular – remote, uninhabited forbidding fjordlands as far as the eye can see, which form this northwestern corner of Iceland. In fact, from the head of Ísafjörður to the regional capital there's just one village along a very lonely road stretching around two hundred kilometres. Look across the waters of the bay and, on the eastern shoreline, you'll see the sheer, snow-capped mountains of **Langadalsströnd** and **Snæfjallaströnd**, themselves divided by the glacial lagoon, **Kaldalón**, which is fed by meltwater from the only **glacier** in the West Fjords, **Drangajökull**. Until just a couple of decades ago these coasts were dotted with isolated farms making an uncertain living from sheep farming and growing the odd crop, today though most have been deserted, reminders of how difficult life was up here. In addition to working the land, many farmers also eked out an existence as fishermen on Ísafjarðardjúp, where white-fish was once so abundant. Today though, the bay is better known for its rich shrimping grounds, found at its mouth as the whitefish have moved further out to sea.

Súðavík and Reykjanes

Twenty kilometres southeast of Ísafjörður, Route 61 passes through sleepy **SÚÐAVÍK**, the one and only settlement between there and Arngerðareyri. This tiny fishing village, with a population of barely two hundred, is your last chance to stock up with essentials before the start of the circuitous negotiation of fjords involved in leaving Ísafjörður. There's very little of note in the village, consisting solely of the main road lined on each side by a few brightly coloured suburban homes, other than the simple wooden **church**, now next to the main road at the Ísafjörður end of the village but once located in the deserted settlement of Hesteyri (see p.172) across the water on Hornstrandir – when Hesteyri was abandoned in 1952 it was decided that the old church should be dismantled and brought to Súðavík, where several families chose to begin their new lives. The church became a centre for prayer in January 1995, when fourteen people were killed and many homes destroyed by an avalanche that crashed onto the village from the precipitous slopes of Súðavík urhlíd, the steep mountain which bears down over the village. If you need to stay overnight, there's a **campsite** (no tel) next to a swimming pool, at Nesvegur 3, or there are **rooms** available at *Sumarbyggd* guesthouse (☎456 4986, fax 456 4987; sleeping-bag accommodation 1450kr, ①). For a snacks and burgers, head for the Shell filling station on the main road.

As Route 61 leaves Súðavík and begins its course around the Álftafjörður fjord it passes the remains of the Norwegian **whaling station** that provided employment for the village in the early 1900s. The next 150km, as you twist around the fjords, are remarkable only for their dullness – this section is one of the most infuriating in the entirety of the West Fjords, as you'll often drive up to 50km around one of the five fjords that punctuate the road to Arngerðareyri, only to make two or three kilometres of actual headway. With your own transport – and the will to navigate yet another fjord – you can detour northwest off Route 61 onto Route 633, about 100km from Súdavik, and go northeast to the tiny settlement of **REYKJANES**, set on a geothermal area located on a spit of land between the diminutive fjord of Reykjafjörður and much bigger Ísafjörður, and looking out onto the open waters of Ísafjarðardjúp. Virtually the only building here is a **hotel**, the functional *Hótel Reykjanes* (☎456 4844, fax 456 4845, sleeping-bag accommodation 1,400kr, ②), where breakfast costs an extra 700kr. Although there's very little to do here, it's an excellent place for a swim in the naturally **heated outdoor pool** (daily 8am–11pm) and sauna in the village, after or ahead of the long drive to Ísafjörður. Back on Route 61, at the mouth of Ísafjörður, the road then swings right to climb up to the Steingrímsfjarðarheiði plateau; a couple of kilometres after this sharp turn up, Road 635 turns left to head for Kaldalón.

Langadalsströnd: Kaldalón, Drangajökull and Unaðsdalur

The southeastern shore of Ísafjarðardjúp, **Langadalsströnd**, is named after Langidalur (Long Valley), which climbs into the hills immediately east of Arngerðareyri. Just 3km east of there, Route 635 branches north off Route 61 at a bridge over Bæjardalsá river, passing lush green fields and a few scattered farms as it heads north along the shore to the **Kaldalón** glacial lagoon, an exceedingly bumpy thirty-minute drive from the junction in your own transport – there's no public transport on this section of road.

Approaching the lagoon, a U-shaped inlet from Ísafjarðardjúp between the cliffs of Snæfjallaströnd to the west and Langadalsströnd to the east, you spot the trail of brown, muddy meltwater that has come down from the **Drangajökull** as it merges into the saltwater of the bay. From the parking area by the low hills at the head of the lagoon it's possible to walk up to the snout of the glacier along a **trail**, marked by cairns, in roughly ninety minutes; from the car park head east, following the low hills, to the track leading along the eastern side of the valley up to the glacier. Keep to the eastern side of the cairns and you'll find the going easier, although there are still boulders, stones and streams to negotiate. Note that you shouldn't underestimate the time it'll take to walk to the glacier – the clear air makes the ice appear much closer than it actually is. If you spot the unmarked path leading up the western edge of the snout, past Drangajökull's highest point, **Jökulbunga** (925m) before descending into Furufjörður on the eastern shore of Hornstrandir, don't be tempted to follow it – it's strictly for experienced mountaineers only.

From Kaldalón, Route 633 crosses the glacial river, Mórillá, before continuing northwest for another fifteen minutes (drive) to the farming settlement of **UNAÐSDALUR** where there's a small **church** right on the shoreline. From here the now uninhabited mountainous coastline of **Snæfjallaströnd** stretches to the northwest – although it's hard to imagine, this entire coast was once inhabited as far as the cliffs at Bjarnarnúpur, which look across to Bolungarvík on the opposite side of the bay. However, in 1995 the last family, perhaps unsurprisingly, upped sticks and left this remote, chilly coast – not even in the warmest summer does the snow melt from the mountains here – abandoning Snæfjallaströnd to the elements alone.

Hornstrandir

Once you've seen the remote snow-covered hills and cliffs of the Snæfjallaströnd coastline, you'll have an idea of what lies immediately north, on Iceland's very last corner of inhospitable terrain. A claw-shaped peninsula of land bordered by Jökulfirdir to the south and the Greenland Sea to the north, and attached to the rest of the West Fjords by a narrow neck of land just 6km wide, the coastline of

Hornstrandir is the most magnificient the country has to offer. The rugged cliffs, precipitous mountainsides and sandy bays backed by meadows of wild-flowers make up this official nature reserve on the very edge of the **Arctic Circle**, and **hiking** here is an exhilarating experience; it's quite common to walk for an entire day without seeing another person. The highlight of any trip to Hornstrandir is a visit to the majestic **Hornbjarg** cliff (534m) at the eastern end of Hornvík bay and the highest point on the peninsula. The cliff is home to one of the country's greatest **bird colonies** and its many ledges are stuffed full with ful-mars, guillemots, kittiwakes, puffins and razorbills. Elsewhere, where farmed sheep once devoured everything edible, there is now wild, lush vegetation of unexpected beauty and the wildlife is free to roam – the Arctic fox makes regular appearances – while offshore, seals and whales can be spotted.

Life for settlers on Hornstrandir has always been extreme. For starters, the summer is appreciably shorter than elsewhere in the West Fjords and, bar a geo-thermal spring in remote **Reykjafjörður**, there's no natural hot-water source, no waterfall to generate electricity, no natural harbour, and no road or airstrip. In fact, the fertile valleys and inlets throughout this uninhabited wilderness are lit-tered with traces of derelict buildings where hardy farmers and fishermen once eked out an existence here battling against the inhospitable climate. However, the peninsula's two main settlements, **Aðalvík** and **Hesteyri**, are now almost com-pletely deserted, their abandonment marking the end of yet another Icelandic community. Founded in around 1894, the village depended entirely on a Norwegian whaling station – remains of which can still be seen today at the head of the fjord – until a drastic decline in stocks led to the station being taken over for the processing of herring. At this time, around eighty people lived perma-nently in Hesteyri, with another hundred temporarily resident at the factory, but a fall in herring stocks led to the closure of the factory in 1940. One by one, farm-ers and fishermen left, and in 1952 the last families abandoned both Hesteyri and neighbouring Aðalvík. Incidentally, the closing shots of the Icelandic film, *Children of Nature*, by Fridrik Þór Fridriksson, were filmed on the mountains of Straumnesfjall, which form the eastern wall of Aðalvík bay.

Today Hesteyri consists of nothing more than a handful of abandoned cottages, disintegrating skeletons of concrete and timber clothed with bits of corrugated iron, broken stone and blocks of turf, with just one or two being renovated by fam-ilies whose roots lie here. The only functioning building is *Læknishúsið* (☎456 3879), the former doctor's house, on the western side of the Hesteyrará river, which offers **sleeping-bag accommodation** (1000kr) from late June to mid-August, with cooking facilities available.

Practicalities

Since there are no roads to or within this area, **approaches to Hornstrandir** are either by passenger ferry or on foot. Of the **ferries**, the small boats *Bliki* and *Guðrún* operated by Sjoferðir (☎456 3879; *www.sjoferdir.is*) sail between mid-June and late August from Ísafjörður to: Hesteyri (1 Tues, Thurs & Fri, twice daily Wed & Sun; 2600kr single); Veiðisleysufjörður (1 Tues & Thurs; 2600kr); Grunnavík (Mon & Thurs; 2400kr); Hrafnsfjörður (1 Mon & Thurs; 2700kr); and Aðalvík (1 Sun; 2500kr). **Bookings** for all services can be made at the tourist office in Ísafjörður. In addition, the catamaran *Ísafold* operates several times weekly between mid-June and mid-August from Ísafjörður to Ingjaldssandur (Sæból);

(see p.176) and Látrar (see box below) in the northern bay of Aðalvík; check with the tourist office in Ísafjörður (see p.167) for timetables and prices, or see *www.ferja.is*. The boat also occasionally continues on to Fljótavík and Hornvík before returning via the same route to Ísafjörður.

On foot, the main approaches are from Unaðsdalur (see p.171), where a good path heads north for Leirufjörður following the Dalsá on its way up out of the vil-

---

HORNSTRANDIR IN THREE DAYS

An excellent way to see the best of Hornstrandir is to do the demanding **three-day hike** from Hornvík to Aðalvík. By taking the catamaran *Ísafold* to Hornvík (see opposite) it's possible to walk west in time to catch a boat back to Ísafjörður from Hesteyri or Aðalvík.

Day one: from Hornvík to Hlöðuvík
Once ashore there's the option of heading east along the beach at Hornvík, wading across the Hafnarós estuary and climbing up to Hornbjarg to see the birds. Alternatively, head west along the beach and look for the path that leads up from the sand to take you round the headland into Hælavík bay. From here, a well-trodden path heads up the western edge of an unnamed stream heading for the narrow pass in the mountains, which gives access down to neighbouring Hlöðuvík via a rockfield (where the cairns marking the path disappear at times). The steep descent into the bay offers spectacular views. Reckon on around four and a half hours for this stretch.

Day two: from Hlöðuvík to Hesteyri
Head west along the beach at Hlöðuvík and wade across the river that cuts the beach in two. Continue along the beach around Álfsfell, before turning south inland following the cairns which mark the indistinct path to the mountain pass of Kjaransvíkurskard (426m); the last part of the ascent is rather rocky. From here the going is considerably easier as the path leads southeast to a mountain plateau, which follows the shoreline of Hesteyrarfjörður. Note that none of the streams that cross the plateau are bridged and even in July there are still large snowfields on the plateau. At the western edge of the plateau, the path descends the valley wall into Hesteyri; this descent can be difficult if the wall is still covered in snow. This stretch will take you about seven hours in total.

Day three: from Hesteyri to Aðalvík
Cross the chilly waters of Hesteyrará river to the former doctor's house. From here, a good path – actually the old road that led west to now abandoned Slettá – leads up the hill following the course of the river. At the top, the trail strikes out across an extensive rockfield, which can be hard going in parts; even in July, there is a lot of snow left up here. Follow the cairns through the rock field until the track descends into sandy Aðalvík; the bottom of this path is rather boggy. Cross the shallow river to reach the beach and the tiny settlement of Látrar, at the eastern edge of the bay, or Sæból at the western edge, both surrounded by snowy mountains on all sides. The *Fagranes* leaves both places for Ísafjörður; once again there's no jetty, so passengers must take a dingy to the ferry out in the middle of the bay. If you're walking in reverse, note that the path to Hesteyri can be found by crossing the river and heading for the single house on the river bank. From here head up the hill to the right of the house to reach the rockfield plateau to Hesteyri. Either way, this leg should take around four hours to complete.

lage. From Leirufjörður it's possible to cross the tidal flats and head towards the mouth of Hrafnsfjörður and on to Hornvík in four or five days. Take extra care when crossing the Leirufjörður at low tide, however, because the flats are composed of glacial waste washed down from Drangajökull and can be particularly soggy. Alternatively a much longer and more demanding route leads from Ófeigsfjörður, northwest of Norðurfjörður, the last main settlement on the Strandir coast (see p.188). The path follows the coast north to Drangavík, Reykjafjörður and Furufjörður, from where it's possible to cut west into Hrafnsfjörður or continue north to Hornvík; for this, you should allow at least a week.

Unfortunately the **weather** in this part of the country, on the edge of the Greenland Sea, is especially unpredictable. Deep snow often lies on the ground until July and snow showers are not uncommon even in July and August. Fog, too, can be a particular problem. It's essential therefore to bring the following **equipment**: a sturdy tent and warm sleeping bag, waterproof clothing and boots, more food than you'll need in case of unforseen delays (there are no facilities anywhere on the peninsula), a compass and the 1:100 000 **hiking map**, *Göngukort yfir Hornstrandir*, produced by Landmælingar Íslands. Although many routes are marked on the map as clearly defined, this is often not the case in reality; in poor weather conditions it can be all too easy to lose the path, so make sure that you can use a compass properly before setting out. Remember, too, that in June and July it doesn't get dark here, which means you can extend your time hiking if needed. Incidentally, mobile phones do not work in Hornstrandir, but there are landline **phones** for use in emergencies in the orange shelters dotted around the coast and marked on the map. Take extra care if you're crossing tidal flats, such as at Leirufjörður (see below), or rounding headlands at low tide, as the going can often be very boggy. There are no footbridges in Hornstrandir, so bring an old pair of running shoes to cross rivers and streams – and be prepared to grit your teeth against the bitingly cold water.

From Ísafjörður to the southwestern peninsula

Passing through some of the most dramatic scenery the West Fjords have to offer, **Route 60** is the access route for the southern and western sections of this region. It's predominantly a mountain road, winding through narrow passes and deep-green valleys as often as it rounds the heads of fjords. Public buses operate from June to August (see p.165 for details of winter services) through the handful of tiny villages which mark the way between Ísafjörður and the tip of the southwestern peninsula, the Látrabjarg bird cliffs (see p.179). Yet despite this being the main road to the south and west, providing the only access to and from Ísafjörður that avoids the Ísafjarðardjúp fjord system, once you're south of the villages of **Flateyri** and **Þingeyri**, small sleepy fishing settlements where you'll be lucky to see anybody in the one main street which runs through each place, it's actually little more than an unsurfaced and badly potholed gravel track, where driving requires slow speeds, much gear changing and even more patience. Things look up, though, after the hair-raising descent into minute **Hrafnseyri,** the birthplace of Jón Sigurðsson, the man who led Iceland towards independence during the late nineteenth century. The small museum dedicated to him here details the man's life and is a great place to be on Independence Day (June 17) when there's much singing, dancing and celebration of this fiercely proud nation's achievements. Beyond here, look out for the most impressive waterfall in the West Fjords, **Dynjandi**, at the head of the eponymously named fjord, a favourite rest break for the bus from Ísafjörður on its long journey to and from Látrabjarg. One of the main entrance points into the West Fjords lies due south of here, the ferry terminal at **Brjánslækur**, from where the *Baldur* sails to the island of Flatey (see p.179) and on to Stykkishólmur (see p.150) on the Snæfellsnes peninsula – an unusual choice for a regional departure and arrival point, since there is no settlement here at all.

Beginning on the southwestern edge of Ísafjörður, the road immediately enters a tunnel to bypass Þverfjall (752m); after 2km, the tunnel divides in two, with the road to **Flateyri** (Route 60) continuing for another 4km inside the tunnel before emerging into Önundarfjörður fjord where there's a junction with Road 64 to Flateyri. From June to August, a **long-distance bus** service goes from Ísafjörður to Brjánslækur (3hr), departing at 9am on Monday, Wednesday and Saturday and stopping along the way at all settlements in between; it then continues on to Látrabjarg, at the end of the southwestern peninsula itself (see p182), returning late afternoon via the same route, connecting with the evening ferry from Brjánslækur to Snæfellsnes.

Flateyri and around

The small fishing village of **FLATEYRI**, just 26km northeast of Ísafjörður, reached from Route 60 via Route 64, which heads northwest to the village as it leaves the tunnel, is known across the country for its **avalanche** problems, and the unusual clusters of knoll-shaped mounds located close to the roadside on the lower slopes of the omnipresent mountains are man-made barriers against the snowfalls which occur here every year. A memorial stone next to the church, at the entrance to the village, bears the names of the twenty people who died in the most recent devastating avalanche in October, 1995. The tragedy was a painful loss for this closely knit community where the total population is barely over three hundred, not least because the frozen ground and heavy snow prevented the bodies from being buried in the village cemetery; instead, they had to be kept in the morgue in Ísafjörður until the ground thawed and they could be buried in Flateyri. Extensive rebuilding was necessary after the accident.

Founded as a trading centre in 1792, the village was once a base for shark and whale hunting. Today, however, it's thanks to the fish-processing factory that the village has finally shaken off its dependence on Ísafjörður, where until recently all financial and shipping services needed in the village were to be found. In fact, Flateyri prides itself on the fact that all major services can be found in the village despite being so small – there's even a theatre company. However, it's not a good idea to get stuck here since there's very little to do other than marvel at the open vistas of Önundarfjörður and the mountains that tower over Flateyri.

Flateyri has two **guesthouses**, both with self-catering facilities but neither with en-suite rooms: *Gistiskáli Húsverks* (☎456 7621, fax 456 7722), at Brimnesvegur 4b, which charges 2000kr per person per room, or 1400kr for sleeping-bag accommodation; and *Brynjukot* (☎456 7762), at Ránargata 6, where an entire house sleeping six costs 4560kr per day (bedding costs 500kr extra per person). The **campsite** (☎456 7838), with toilets and running water, is near the swimming pool in Tjarnargata, close to the mountains, at the entrance to the village. For eating and drinking there's the dark and dingy *Vagninn* **restaurant** at Hafnarstræti 19, which serves up a basic, heavily fish-dominated menu; for sandwiches and snacks head for *Kjartanshús* in the ESSO filling station at the entrance to the village. Local **buses** operate all year (2–3 daily Mon–Fri) from Ísafjörður and the post office in Flateyri on Ránargata. In summer, the long-distance bus from Ísafjörður to Brjánslækur and Látrabjarg also calls in at Flateyri (see p.165).

Ingjaldssandur

One of the most beautiful beaches in the West Fjords, **Ingjaldssandur** (marked as **Sæból** on some maps) is located at the mouth of Önundarfjörður, across the water from Flateyri at the tip of the mountainous finger of land that separates the fjord from its southern neighbour, Dyrafjörður. Bordered to the west and east by tall, craggy mountains and backed by lush green fields, the beach's grassy foreshore is an idyllic place from which to watch the huge Atlantic breakers crash onto the sand and pebbles below. In summer this is a good place to spot **arctic tern** and various species of waders; **oystercatchers** are particularly common here.

Ingjaldssandur is only accessible with your own transport and entails a circuitous drive of 44km from Flateyri, heading south on Route 64, then rejoining Route 60 and heading for Þingeyri before Route 624 forks off to the west and eventually heads north back towards Önundarfjörður; although the road is in poor condition it is accessible to non-four-wheel-drive vehicles. The farm, *Hraun*, located right on the beach and the only building here, offers **sleeping-bag accommodation** and cooking facilities for 1000kr; for splendid isolation, it's hard to beat.

Þingeyri

Although one of the oldest settlements in the West Fjords, **ÞINGEYRI,** 48km southwest of Ísafjörður along Road 60, is also one of the dullest. The village takes its name from the ancient *Þing* (assembly) mentioned in Gísla saga, the singularly unimpressive **ruins** which can still be seen on a grassy area in the centre of the village. Over the centuries Þingeyri developed into a significant fishing centre thanks to its sheltered location near the head of Dyrafjörður, and even attracted the interest of the French who applied, unsuccessfully, to establish a base here to service their fishing vessels operating in the region.

Today life is centred on the one main street, **Aðalstræti**, where what few services the village offers – a bank and a few shops – are located. There's little of interest in Þingeyri itself beyond a stroll down to the **harbour** to see the fishing boats landing their catch; better instead, head up **Sandafell** (367m), which stands guard behind the village. This is a favourite place for locals to watch the sun go down as it offers fantastic **views** out over the fjord and of the mountain ridge, topped by the highest peak in the West Fjords, Kaldbakur (998m), which separates Dyrafjörður from the much larger and multi-fingered Arnarfjörður to the south. Although steep, Sandafell can be climbed from the village – several clear **paths** lead up the mountainside. Alternatively, a four-wheel-drive track there heads southwest off Route 60 just 1km after climbing up out of Þingeyri heading for Hrafnseyri.

If you have to stay here, *Gistiheimilið Vera* (☎456 8232) at Hlídargata 22 has simple **rooms** without shower and toilet for 2500kr per person, or sleeping-bag accommodation for 1400kr. Breakfast is not included but cooking facilities are available. The **campsite** (☎456 8225; 480kr per tent), with washing facilities, is located next to the modern swimming pool at the western end of the village. **Eating** is limited to the snack bar at the ESSO filling station on the main road, which also functions as the terminus for **buses** on the Ísafjörður–Látrabjarg run (see p.165).

Hrafnseyri

The seventeen-kilometre drive south from Þingeyri to miniscule Hrafnseyri is one of the most hair-raising sections of Route 60. Climbing all the while to squeeze through a narrow pass between mountains over 700m high, the road then makes a heart-stopping descent into Hrafnseyri on the shores of **Arnarfjörður**; when viewed from the village, the road appears to cling precariously to a vertical wall of rock. Named after the fjord's first settler, Örn (meaning "eagle", *arnar* being its genitive case), who lasted just one winter here, and 30km long and up to ten kilometres wide, Arnarfjörður forks at its head to form four smaller fjords, Suðurfirðir, to the southwest and Borgarfjörður and Dynjandisvogur inlet to the northeast. It's widely, and quite rightly, regarded by locals as the most picturesque of all the West Fjords enclosed by towering mountains.

HRAFNSEYRI itself, consisting of a tiny church, a museum and a solitary petrol pump – which is where the summer-only Ísafjörður–Látrabjarg **bus** service stops, see p.165 – is one of only two settlements on Arnarfjörður (the other is Bíldudalur, 79km away). It was named after **Hrafn Sveinbjarnarson**, who died here in 1213, one of Iceland's earliest doctors, who trained in Europe before returning home to practise. A **memorial stone** next to the church here commemorates his life and the grass mound nearby is thought to be the site of his boathouse. This tiny settlement, though, is of much greater historical significance to Icelanders since it was here that **Jón Sigurðsson** (see box overleaf) was born, the man who won independence for Iceland in the nineteenth century. The excellent adjoining **museum** (mid-June to August daily 1–8pm; Sept to mid-June by arrangement with the curator, who lives next door, ☎456 8260; 300kr) records his life, mostly with photographs, some of his letters and contemporary drawings. Particularly evocative is the painting of the meeting of 1851, which Jón Sigurðsson and a number of Icelandic MPs held with representatives of the Danish state in the Grammar School, Menntaskólinn, in Reykjavík, and which helped pave the way of Icelandic independence. The friendly curator will gladly translate some of the information inside the museum and will also tickle the ivories on the church piano and crank out a song from your home country if you tell him where you're from. Jón Sigurðsson himself was born in the restored turf farmhouse open on request by the curator, with three gable roofs, next to the church. At the rear of the building, his bedroom, containing the original desk from his office in Copenhagen, has been kept in its original state and offers an insight into the ascetic life of one of Iceland's most revered figures.

The best time to be in Hrafnseyri is **Icelandic National Day** (June 17), when a special mass is held in the church and prominent Icelanders from across the country travel to the village to remember their most distinguished champion of freedom. Although it's a serious occasion there's a mood of optimism and good humour in the air, with plenty of singing and celebration.

JÓN SIGURÐSSON

To Icelanders, **Jón Sigurðsson** (1811–69) is what Winston Churchill is to the British and George Washington to the Americans. This is the man who, through his tremendous skills of diplomacy, achieved independence from the Danes, who had almost bankrupted Iceland during the time of the Trade Monopoly. Born in Hrafnseyri in 1811, Jón spent the first twenty-two years of his life in his native West Fjords, and after completing the entry examination for university study, he left for Copenhagen where he chose history and political science among his subjects. Although a committed student, he never graduated from the university, opting instead to dedicate his life to the Árni Magnússon Institute, then a powerful symbol of the struggle for recognition against the Danes; this institute fought a long battle to have many of Iceland's most treasured medieval manuscripts, kept in Copenhagen by the Danish authorities, returned home. However, it wasn't until 1841 that Jón Sigurðsson began his political activities, publishing a magazine in which he put forward historical arguments for Iceland's right to independence. A prolific writer about Icelandic history, politics and economics, he was later elected to the Icelandic parliament, which regained its powers as a consultative body in 1843 thanks to his agitation. Further reforms followed as a direct consequence of his influence, including the right to free trade in 1854, and eventually, twenty years later, a constitution making Iceland self-governing in home affairs, though Sigurðsson didn't live to see Iceland become a sovereign state under the Danish crown on December 1, 1918. Iceland gained full independence from Denmark on June 17, 1944, the anniversary of his birth.

Dynjandi

Twenty kilometres east of Hrafnseyri, at the point where Route 60 weaves around the northeastern corner of Arnarfjörður, the most impressive waterfall in the West Fjords, **Dynjandi**, plunges over a hundred-metre-high cliff top into the fjord at Dynjandisvogur inlet, forming a triangular cascade roughly 30m wide at its top spreading to over 60m at its bottom. Below the main waterfall a series of five smaller chutes carries the waters of the Dynjandisá to the sea. With your own transport, it's possible to reach the head of the falls – continue south along Route 60 for around 5km, and once the road has climbed up onto the Dynjandisheidi plateau, you'll see the Dynjandisá, which crosses the road; walk west from here, following the course of the river to the falls.

All **buses** between Ísafjörður and Brjánslækur (see p.165) make a ten-minute stop at the falls, where there are also a simple campsite, toilets and running water. If, however, you choose to stay here bear in mind that the waterfall is incredibly noisy – *dynjandi* means "the thundering one".

Flókalundur and Brjánslækur

South of Dynjandisheidi, Route 60 continues through an extensive rocky highland plateau, passing the turn-off onto Route 63 for Bíldudalur (see opposite) beside Lónfell (725m), before it finally descends towards the road junction that is the setting for civilization at **FLÓKALUNDUR**. Consisting of a hotel, restaurant and a petrol pump, there's little to note here other than the fact that the Viking, **Flóki Vilgerdarson**, who named Iceland (see p.287), once spent a winter here. He climbed Lónfell, only to be dismayed by the icebergs floating in the fjord and named the land "Iceland", as the inscription on the monument in front of the functional but expensive **hotel** *Flókalundur* (☎456 2011, fax 456 2050; ④), overlooking Vatnsfjörður, reminds modern day Icelanders. The hotel **restaurant** is nothing special, but it does serve up decent if pricey food and makes for a good break on the long journey in and out of the West Fjords. The free **campsite** on the same site is run by the hotel and has running water and toilet facilities. All buses between Ísafjörður and Látrabjarg pass through here in summer.

Barely 7km west of Flókalundur, Route 62 leads to **BRJÁNSLÆKUR**, essentially just the ferry jetty for crossings on board the *Baldur* to Flatey and Stykkishólmur. Other than the **snack-bar-cum-ticket office** in the small wooden building on the main road by the jetty, and a free **campsite** with washing facilities (☎456 2020 or ☎456 2033), there are no facilities here. The summer-only long-distance **bus** from Ísafjörður and Látrabjarg (see p.165) is timed to connect with the ferry.

The southwestern peninsula

From its mountain-top junction with Route 60 by Lónfell, Route 63 descends towards the small fjord, Trostansfjörður, one of the four baby fjords which make up the **Suðurfirðir**, the southern fjords, forming the southwestern corner of **Arnarfjörður**. This section of the road is in very poor condition and features some alarmingly large potholes and ruts. Unusually for the West Fjords, three fishing villages are found within close proximity to one another here – barely 30km separates the uneventful port of **Bíldudalur** from its neighbours, **Tálknafjörður**, one of the region's more likeable places, and the larger **Patreksfjörður**, a commercial centre for the surrounding farms and smaller villages. However, it's the **Látrabjarg** cliffs, 60km beyond Patreksfjörður to the west, that draw most visitors to this last peninsula of rugged land. Here, in summer, thousands upon thousands of **seabirds** including guillemots, kittiwakes and puffins nest in the cliff's nooks and crannies making for one of the most spectacular sights anywhere in the region – what's more, the cliffs are easily accessible from nearby **Breiðavík**, an idyllic bay of aquamarine water backed by white sand and dusky mountains.

Other than local buses, from June to August, the **long-distance bus** from Ísafjörður (see p.165) continues on from the Brjánslækur ferry jetty to Patreksfjörður (4hr 10min), Breiðavík (5hr 35min) and Látravík (5hr 45min), arriving at Látrabjarg at 2.55pm. It returns to Ísafjörður at 4.25pm via the same route.

Bíldudalur and around

A thriving fishing port processing vast amounts of local shrimp, there's little to see or do in **BÍLDUDALUR**, a workaday village of just three hundred people at the foot of Bíldudalsfjall mountain on the southern shores of Arnarfjörður. However, the airport, just 7km south of the village at the mouth of Fossfjörður, has made the village a gateway to the southwestern peninsula of the West Fjords with its regular connections with Reykjavík, cutting out the need for the long and tiring journey up hill and down dale from Ísafjörður. Daily **buses** operate all year round between here and Tálknafjörður (see below) and Patreksfjörður (see opposite) from outside the post office in the main street, as well as to the **airport** (information on ☎456 2151) to connect with the once-daily flight to and from Reykjavík, operated by Íslandsflug. Bíldudalur has just one **guesthouse**, *Gistiheimilið Helena* (☎456 2146 or ☎894 1684; sleeping-bag accommodation 1300kr, ②), a ramshackle building down by the harbour on Hafnarbraut. For the **campsite** (100kr per tent) head for the sports field on the southern edge of the village. The one and only **restaurant**, *Vegamót*, located on the main road at Tjarnarbraut 2, once again close to the harbour, serves up decent fish dishes for around 1200kr. Next door, the Shell filling station has **snacks** and sandwiches.

What Bíldudalur lacks in attractions, however, it more than makes up for with stunning scenery; an excellent fifteen-kilometre **hike** (4–5hr) up the Fossdalur valley to the tiny settlement of **Tungumuli** on the Bardaströnd coast (Route 62) begins at Foss farm, 6km south of the airport at the head of Fossfjörður, following the route taken by local postmen in the late 1800s. From the western side of the farm, the track leads up through Fossdalur towards the small lake, Mjósund, beyond which the route forks. Keep right and take the path over the Fossheidi plateau, which has fantastic views over the surrounding rocky countryside, until it descends through Arnbylisdalur valley on the western edge of Tungumúlafjall mountain, to Tungumuli. A couple of kilometres east of here along Route 62 brings you to the equally small settlement of **Kross**, where there's **accommodation** at *Gistiheimilið Bjarkarholt* (☎456 2025; sleeping-bag accommodation 1250kr, ①). It's actually possible to hike directly to Kross by following the left fork just beyond Mjósund, then climbing through the Geilingadalur and Mórudalur valleys. Both routes are shown in the **hiking leaflet**, *Gönguleiðir á Bardaströnd*, available from tourist offices and accommodation establishments. From Kross and Tungumuli, the **bus** (June–Aug) to Látrabjarg departs at around 12.15pm on Monday, Wednesday and Saturday, plus there's one going in the opposite direction to Ísafjörður, via the ferry jetty at Brjánslækur, at about 6.30pm.

Tálknafjörður

Immediately likeable **TÁLKNAFJÖRÐUR**, just 19km west of Bíldudalur on Routes 62 and 617, is a prosperous village located on the eastern shore of the narrow fjord of the same name. Oddly, for a place with a population of just 320, there's a lively feel to the village and it's one of the few places hereabouts with a bar. A walk up and down Strandgata, the main street that hugs the side of the fjord, also bears witness to the fact that the average age here is just 20; those out of pushchairs tend to be pushing them. Most villagers work in one of the four fish-processing factories that are responsible for the growth of the village over the past forty years or so, although tourism now accounts for a significant section of the local economy, with the adventure centre, **Leikjaland** (☎456 2631 or ☎456 2604), located in the centre of the village, offering kayaking, canoeing and windsurfing on the fjord to the Icelanders who turn up here. There's also **bike rental** (700kr per half-day, 1200kr per day), minigolf and go-kart racing. The nearby open-air **swimming pool**, complete with hot spots, has fantastic views over the surrounding mountains. Five kilometres out of the village to the northwest, the **Stóri-Laugardalur** geothermal area has a couple of alfresco hotspots fed by natural water from a nearby spring; get here by following the road west out of the village and taking the first turn on the right once over the cattle grid.

Practicalities

Buses run all year round between here and Patreksfjörður and Bíldudalur, going via to the airport at the latter place. The best **place to stay** in Tálknafjörður is the *Gistiheimilið Skrúdhamrar* (☎456 2631; sleeping-bag accommodation 1700kr, ②), on the main road, run by a friendly and welcoming New Zealander who can provide endless information on the local area, and since the rooms are part of a home, you're encouraged to relax and feel at home. Prices here include breakfast. Alternatively, the *Gistiheimilið Hamraborg* (☎456 2514; sleeping-bag accommodation 1200kr, ①), a little further down the main road, has simple doubles but breakfast costs an extra 600kr. The **campsite** (☎456 2639; 250kr per tent) is in the centre of the villlage next to the swimming pool. Of an evening, locals gravitate towards *Hópið*, the **bar and restaurant** at the western end of the main road, where a dish of freshly caught fish costs around 1200kr; they also do pizzas and burgers. For **snacks**, soft drinks and other provisions, head for the Mettubúd shop and **filling station** on the main street.

Patreksfjörður

Located on the shores of the southernmost of all the West Fjords, **PATREKSFJÖRÐUR**, bears not only the name of the eponymous fjord but also that of **Saint Patrick**, a bishop from the Scottish islands who acted as spiritual adviser to one of the region's first settlers, Örlygur Hrappson. Today with a population of 750, the village is large enough to exist independently of Ísafjörður, 177km away, and is the only place in the West Fjords, outside the regional capital, to boast more than the odd shop and restaurant. Over the years, this tiny village has won a reputation for pioneering excellence; trawler fishing in Iceland began here, a particular style of saltfish now popular in Mediterranean markets was developed here; somewhat less notably, the town also dispatched the only Icelandic vessel ever to hunt seal in the Arctic. Little entrepeneurial spirit is visible in Patreksfjörður today and, although a refreshing change from the other smaller villages to the north, the place is best seen as a stopoff en route to Látrabjarg. Built on two sandspits, Geirseyri and Vatnseyri, the village simply comprises a main road, **Strandgata**, which runs along the shoreside to the **harbour**; here you'll find the tiny Galleri Ísafold, which displays work from local artists, heavily influenced by the sea and the nature of the West Fjords. Several side streets branch off Strandgata's western end – one of which, Eyrargata, has an excellent open-air **swimming pool** on it – while the main shopping street, **Aðalstræti**, runs parallel to it.

Practicalities

Buses run all year round between here, Tálknafjörður, and Bíldudalur and its airport. From June to August, services also go every Monday, Wednesday and Saturday to Látrabjarg (1pm) and Ísafjörður via the Brjánslækur ferry (6pm); they depart from outside the bakery (see p.182). There's an informal **tourist information office** at Strandgata 11 (Tues–Sun 2–7pm; ☎895 7175) inside the Galleri Ísafold.

The **youth hostel**, *Stekkaból* (June–Aug; ☎456 1675, fax 456 1547), at Stekkar 21, charges 1900kr per person for a bed, or 1350kr for sleeping-bag accommodation; breakfast is an extra 700kr. The best place to stay is close to the shore at Aðalstræti 65, *Afahús* (☎456 1280), which has cosy **rooms** for 1750kr per person, excluding breakfast. For **eating**, head for *Pizza 67* up on Aðalstræti, where the restaurant has excellent views out over the fjord and an outdoor wooden terrace, which is a pleasant place on a sunny afternoon to consume snacks from the next door **bakery**, *Nyja Bakaríið*, which does decent fresh bread and pastries. If you fancy striking up a conversation with local fishermen, you'll find them in the cheap and cheerful *Matborg Veitingahús* café and low-key restaurant down by the harbour on Eyrargata, where pizzas are a popular favourite. For a place to drink, head for the *Rabba-barinn* **bar**, at the junction of Aðalstræti and Sigtún inside the blue and white building called Albína, on the eastern edge of the village, where there's occasional live music that stays open until 3am at weekends; it's also possible to get **snacks** and sandwiches here during the day. The ÁTVR **alcohol shop** (Mon–Fri 1–6pm) is on Þórsgata, down by the harbour.

Látrabjarg and around

The cliffs of **Látrabjarg**, 59km southwest of Patreksfjörður along Route 612, rank as the highlight of any trip to the remote southwestern peninsula of the West Fjords. Extending for 14km, from the lighthouse marking the end of Route 612 and also the westernmost point in Europe, **Bjargtangar**, to the small inlet of **Keflavík** to the east, they rise up to 441m above the churning sea below. A **footpath** leads along the cliff tops, with excellent views of some of the one thousand or so seabirds that come here to nest on the countless ledges below. For centuries, locals would abseil down the cliffs to collect their eggs and trap the birds for food – it's estimated that around 35,000 birds were caught here every year until the late 1950s – and, occasionally, they still do.

Although the **guillemot** is the most common bird at Látrabjarg, it's the thousands of **puffins** that most people come here to see. The high ground of the cliff tops is riddled with their burrows, often up to 2m in length, since they nest in locations well away from the pounding surf, ideally surrounded by lush grass and thick soil. They return to the same burrows they occupied the year before, almost always during the third week of April, where they remain until August or September. The cliffs are also home to the largest colony of **razorbills** in the world, as well as to thousands of other screeching breeds of seabird including **cormorants**, **fulmars** and **kittiwakes**; the din from the thousands upon thousands of birds here can be quite overpowering, as can the stench from the piles of guano on the cliff face.

Incidentally, one of Iceland's most daring sea-rescue operations occurred here in December 1947, when farmers from Hvallátur set out to rescue the crew of a British trawler, the *Dhoon*, which had been wrecked off the rocky shoreline during a severe snow storm. After sliding down the ice-covered cliffs by rope, the Icelanders pulled the sailors to safety using a rescue line they fired across to the stricken vessel – although it took two separate attempts to hoist all the men up the treacherous cliff face from where they were taken by horseback to nearby farms to recover. A year later, a film crew arrived in Hvallátur to make a documentary about the accident, in which several locals were to reenact the rescue – however, while they were filming, another British trawler, *Sargon*, became stranded in nearby Patreksfjörður fjord, giving the film makers a chance to catch a drama on film for real.

The best **place to stay** near Látrabjarg is the popular *Gistiheimilið Breiðavík* (☎456 1575, fax 456 1189; 2100kr per person), 12km to the northeast and right on the sandy shores of the remote and idyllic **Breiðavík bay**, enclosed by hills to the west and east but with open views out over white sand to the aquamarine waters of the Atlantic to the west. A former school, the weatherbeaten guesthouse is run by the friendly Birna Mjöll Atladóttir, whose home cooking is legendary (fish suppers cost 1500kr); breakfast is an extra 700kr. Alternatively, an even remoter option involves informal **camping** at **Brunnar** on the white sands of Látravík bay, beyond Hvallátur, where there's a farmhouse that's home to just two people, immediately to the south of Breiðavík and reached on Route 612; other than fresh water from the stream that flows into the bay from the mountains at the western end of the bay, remember that there are no facilities here at all and no habitation other than the farmhouse at the northeastern end of the bay.

From June to August, the long-distance **bus service** from Ísafjörður to Látrabjarg (see p.165) arrives here at 2.55pm. It returns to Ísafjörður at 4.25pm via the same route.

Rauðasandur

The cliff-top path at Látrabjarg continues east, rounding Keflavík bay and finally descending to the serene red-orange sands at **Rauðasandur** bay after around 20km, where a couple of farming families still live. The lush, open fields that slowly give way to the vast expanse of sand that forms this part of the shore of Breiðafjörður have been cultivated for centuries, and today flocks of hardy sheep wander from field to shore in search of patches of grass. East of the lagoon at **Bæjarvaðall**, which marks the eastern end of the sands, simple farmhouse **accommodation** is available at *Melanes* (☎456 1594; 1750kr per person, or for sleeping-bag accommodation 1250kr), a tiny farm at the beginning of Route 614. From here, the road leads down to Rauðasandur from Patreksfjörður, east of the tiny airstrip at **Sandoddi**, which until a couple of years ago, unbelievably for such an isolated location, had regular flights to Reykjavík.

At the mouth of Patreksfjörður, opposite the identically named village of **Patreksfjörður** (see p.181), the **Hnjótur folk museum** (daily 9am–6pm; 300kr), on Route 612 and served by all **buses** to Látrabjarg from Ísafjörður (see p.165), has a simple stone monument dedicated to all the sailors who lost their lives in shipwrecks off the treacherous shores of the southwestern peninsula during the early twentieth century – all bar one were from the British ports of Grimsby and Hull. Inside the museum, a photograph of the *Dhoon* (see opposite) before she became stranded off Látrabjarg in 1947 hangs alongside maritime rescue equipment, old telephones and typewriters bearing Icelandic characters, and other assorted nostalgic paraphernalia. The prize exhibit, though, is a rusting Aeroflot biplane, purchased by the museum in 1994 after an unsuccesful flight from Russia to America, where it was refused permission to land. Swiftly dispatched back to Russia, the plane only managed to make it as far as Reykjavík before its fuel supply ran out. The harsh climate of the West Fjords has taken its toll on the plane's structure to such an extent that it's no longer airworthy. Outside the museum, by the entrance, is a replica of a Viking longship, presented to Iceland by Norway to mark 1100 years of settlement. Close by, the *Mummi*, the country's oldest steam-powered fishing boat, is also worth a cursory glance.

The south coast: Bjarkalundur and Reykhólar

The south coast of the West Fjords is all but uninhabited. As Route 60 rounds the head of Vatnsfjörður east of Flókalundur, 8km northeast of the Brjánslækur ferry jetty, it's well over a hundred kilometres before civilization reappears at **Bjarkalundur**, itself little more than a hotel and a filling station. Although still dramatic, the mountains along this stretch of road are less rugged and angular than those along the northern and western coasts. The coastline is dominated by small bays separated by high bluffs, and wide areas of heavily vegetated flatland that gently slope down to the shores of Breiðafjörður. In fact the only village of any significance along this stretch of road is geothermal **Reykhólar**, one of the few settlements in the West Fjords to have its own source of naturally heated water and, although there's little to do here, it's a good place to break the long journey in or out of the region with an invigorating dip in the outdoor pool. East of here, the dot on the map that is **Króksfjarðarnes** serves as a road junction: from here routes head across Gilsfjörður fjord to Reykjavík and via the Tröllatunguheiði plateau (Road 605) to Hólmavík.

If you have your own transport, another good place to break the long journey towards Gilsfjörður, the southwestern entry and exit point from the West Fjords, is at **Vatnsdalsvatn** nature reserve, a couple of kilometres east of Flókalundur, where an easy **hiking trail** (8km, 2–3hr) begins at the eastern side of the bridge over the lake and leads through along the eastern shore, known for its rich birdlife and a favourite nesting spot for the dramatically coloured harlequin duck, and the red-throated and great northern diver. Don't attempt to cross the Vatnsdalsá at the head of the lake in order to return down the western shore, since the river is very wide and fast flowing; instead, retrace your steps.

More hiking can be found around the small service centre of **BJARKALUNDUR**, now 127km east of Flókalundur, nothing more than a restaurant and a modern and uninspiring **hotel** bearing the same name (☎434 7762, fax 434 7865; sleeping-bag accommodation 1400kr, ②) where they have clean but plain doubles. The **campsite** at the hotel charges 500kr per tent and has toilets and running water but no showers. Roughly 1km east of the hotel a four-wheel-drive track marks the beginning of a **trail** (7km) leading to the twin peaks of **Vaðalfjöll**, an extinct volcano whose outer layers have eroded away, leaving just a bare chimney from where there are fantastic views out over the fjords and islands of Breiðafjörður. To return to Bjarkalundur, head southwest from the mountains to the old road that leads down to Kinnarstaðir farm, from where it's a couple of kilometres east along Route 60 to the hotel. **Buses** run all year on Tuesday and Thursday (1 daily) and Friday and Sunday (2 daily) from Bjarkalundur to Reykhólar (see below) and Reykjavík. There is no public transport, however, between Bjarkalundur and Brjánslækur.

Reykhólar

From Bjarkalundur, buses continue south on Route 607 to **REYKHÓLAR**, a small farming settlement home to just 120 people at the head of the Reykjanes peninsula with attractive views out over Breiðafjörður. Although Reykhólar's history can be traced back to the time of the Sagas, there's little reminder today of the village's wealthy past, when it was considered to have some of the best farmland in all of Iceland; the village once made a handsome profit from selling the wheat grown on the 300 or so offshore islands hereabouts and the surrounding areas on the mainland. One of the few places in the West Fjords to have a ready supply of geothermal energy, today it's been harnessed and provides the village with its main source of activity – the ugly Þörungaverksmiðja plant, located a couple of kilometres south of the village, that produces a form of animal meal from seaweed. There's little to do in the village except enjoy a relaxing dip in the warm waters of the outdoor geothermally heated **swimming pool** (mid-June to mid-August 10am–10pm; rest of the year 6–10pm), which also has two hot spots and a sauna.

Buses to and from Reykjavík operate all year round on Tuesday, Thursday, Friday and Sunday, but remember that there is no connection west or east of Reykhólar; to continue by bus from here you have to backtrack all the way south to Bifröst and then continue north again on a service to Brú – don't get stuck here. **Sleeping-bag accommodation** is available in the village school, *Reykhólaskóli* (☎434 7880; 1200kr) or at the community centre, *Samkomuhúsið Reykhólum* (☎434 7880; 1200kr). The **campsite** can be found next to the swimming pool; it costs 600kr to pitch a tent, and there are toilets, running water and showers. If you have your own transport you can get to *STAÐUR* (☎434 7730), a **farmstay** 10km west of the village, where a bed costs 2000kr per person, sleeping-bag accommodation is 1200kr; alternatively, there's a six-berth cottage with good views out over Breiðafjörður for 5500kr per day. Back in Reykhólar, food is available at the *Arnhóll* **snack-bar** and shop on Hellisbraut.

South to Gilsfjörður and approaches to Hólmavík

From Bjarkalundur, Route 60 heads southeast to **Gilsfjörður**, the narrow fjord that slices into the narrow neck of land connecting the West Fjords to the rest of Iceland, from where it's a drive of 258km south to Reykjavík via Búðardalur (see p.165). A new bridge across the mouth of the fjord thankfully makes this journey a little shorter than it would otherwise be.

From the tiny farming settlement of **KRÓKSFJARÐARNES,** halfway between Bjarkalundur and Gilsfjörður, Route 605 heads northeast over the mountains and the Tröllatunguheidi plateau to Steingrímsfjörður, from where Route 61 continues to Hólmavík. Alternatively, it's also possible to reach Hólmavík from Bjarkalundur by taking the atrociously poor Route 608 from the head of Þorskafjörður, 4km west of Bjarkalundur, over the Þorskafjarðarheiði plateau, to meet Route 61 up on the bleak Steingrímsfjarðarheiði highland plateau marked only by rock ridges and a few small lakes, then following it southeast.

Hólmavík and the Strandir coast

From Brú in the south to Norðurfjörður in the north, the lonely 220km of the **Strandir coast** form one of the least-visited corners of Iceland, and if you're looking to really get off the beaten track, this is the place to come. The coastline is dominated by the vast Steingrímsfjörður, roughly two-thirds of the way up the coast, which provides superb shelter to the main settlement in the region, **Hólmavík**, a busy fishing village and an excellent base from which to explore the surrounding wilderness. South of here, the countryside is characterized by low hills and rolling farmland, set either side of Route 61, which links Hólmavík with Brú (see p.191) – a strategic transport junction for buses to the region at the head of the narrow Hrútafjörður fjord, marking the easternmost reaches of the West Fjords. North of Steingrímsfjörður, the land is much more rugged in nature, with snow-capped mountains and deeply indented fjords, reminiscent of the dramatic scenery around Ísafjörður.

There are very few services along this stretch of coast, and **public transport** expires at Drangsnes on the eastern shores of Steingrímsfjörður. With your own transport it's possible to continue north to some of the country's most isolated communities, dependent on fishing and sheep farming for their existence; remember, though, that **Route 643** north of Bjarnarfjörður is in poor condition – and that it closes during the first snows of the autumn and isn't cleared until late spring. The end of the road, **Norðurfjörður**, marks the jumping-off point for ambitious overland treks north towards the uninhabited wilds of **Hornstrandir** (see p.173 for walking route).

Hólmavík and around

A thriving fishing village on the southern shore of Steingrímsfjörður with a population of around 420, **HÓLMAVÍK** was granted municipal status in 1890 but only really began to grow during the twentieth century. Today life is centred around the natural harbour at the northern edge of the village, home to around a dozen fishing boats and the freezer-trawler, *Hólmadrangur*, that potent symbol of economic independence in rural Iceland, of which locals are justifiably proud. The village economy is dependent on the shrimps that these boats catch – inshore in the fjords in winter, deep-sea shrimping in summer. Hólmavík also functions as a service centre for the surrounding sheep farms and boasts a large supermarket, two banks, a post office and even a car-repair workshop. Although there are no sights to speak of, sooner or later you'll undoubtedly come across the oldest building in the village, **Riishús**, on the main street, **Hafnarbraut**, which runs parallel to the fjord. Built by and named after a local merchant, Richard Peter Riis, the two-storey wooden structure dates from 1897 and now is home to the one and only restaurant in town (see below).

Practicalities

Buses link Hólmavík all year with Reykjavík; from June to early September there's one bus daily at 4pm on Tuesday, Friday and Sunday; during the rest of the year there's just one weekly on Friday. Services call in the ESSO **filling station** at the entrance to the village. The **tourist information office** (June–Aug Mon, Thurs & Fri 8.30am–8pm, Tues & Wed 8.30am–4pm, Sat & Sun 10am–8pm; ☎451 3465) is located at the entrance to the village, opposite the **supermarket** and the filling station. **Accommodation** is available at the wonderfully located *Gistiheimilið* (☎451 3136, fax 451 3413; sleeping-bag accommodation 1250kr, ①), up on a hill at Borgarbraut 4 and overlooking the harbour and the snow-covered mountains on the opposite side of the fjord; from the tourist office, follow the main road into town and you'll find Borgarbraut running parallel with the northern end of Hafnarbraut. Self-catering facilities and TV are available on the upper floor. The **campsite** is located at the entrance to the village next to the tourist office and charges 250kr per person; showers and cooking facilities are available in the building housing the tourist office.

Eating is best enjoyed at the trendy *Café Riis* at Hafnarbraut 39, whose interior has a maritime flavour, with lots of wooden panels and hanging fishing nets; fish dishes cost from 1390kr, lamb is from 2100kr. Otherwise, for cheaper eats such as burgers and sandwiches, there's a small **snack-bar** inside the filling station.

Around Hólmavík: Laugarhóll and Drangsnes

The hamlet of **LAUGARHÓLL**, 30km northeast of Hólmavík and reached by taking Route 61 north to the head of Steingrímsfjörður from where Road 643 heads east to the pool, consists of little more than a couple of farms grouped around a source of geothermal water, which feeds an outdoor **pool** and a **hotel**, the *Laugarhóll* (☎451 3380; sleeping-bag accommodation for 1400kr, ②). Although none of the rooms are en suite, the hotel is a great place to stay to enjoy the slow pace of life in rural Iceland and an early morning swim in the pool, taking in the inspiring views of the gentle Hólsfjall mountains, which form a serene backdrop to the place. In summer, Laugarhóll is only really accessible with your own transport since the timetabling of the once-weekly Friday **bus** from Hólmavík (4pm) to Laugarhóll doesn't allow for a return journey to be made back to Hólmavík the same day. From September to May, however, it is possible to stay for around an hour in Laugarhóll before returning, though again this is Friday only – tell the bus driver of your plans (in English) if you intend to go for a swim, and he'll pick you up again from the pool.

A **hiking trail** leads from the hotel, first going east along Route 643 towards Norðurfjörður before heading up towards the mountains following the eastern bank of the Hallá, beyond the small Goðafoss waterfall, for Þverarvatn lake. The path then descends towards Laugarhóll following the Þverá river; ask at the hotel for the **hiking guide**, *Gönguleiðir í Strandasyslu*, or pick it up from the tourist office in Hólmavík (see opposite).

The bus terminates in **DRANGSNES**, a tiny fishing village home to just one hundred people overlooking the island of Grímsey in the mouth of Steingrímsfjörður, which was formed, according to legend, when three female trolls tried to separate the West Fjords from the rest of the country, but were turned to stone as the sun rose; one of them is said to have turned into the tall rockstack, **Kerling,** just off the shore close to Grímsey. The village itself consists of a **campsite** with full facilities, one petrol pump, one shop and a dozen or so houses. For **accommodation** there's a farm, *Bær III* (☎451 3241, fax 451 3274; ②), 2km to the north of the village and right on the shore, with excellent views out over Húnaflói.

Djúpavík and Norðurfjörður

Very few visitors to Iceland venture north of Drangsnes because of the complete lack of public transport, but for those who do there's a chance to explore a remote corner of Europe, where towering rock buttresses plunge precipitously into the icy sea and where the coastline is strewn with vast expanses of driftwood that originated on the other side of the Arctic Ocean, in Russian Siberia. Tourist facilities in this part of the country are virtually non-existent but if you want to experience the raw side to Iceland – and an area of outstanding beauty – this is the place to head for.

DJÚPAVÍK, a village close to the head of the shadowy Reykjarfjörður, is dominated by the huge carcass of its old herring factory. Opened in 1935, production

HIKING AROUND NORÐURFJÖRÐUR

Between Norðurfjörður and the farm at Árnes, roughly 3km south of Norðurfjörður, a minor road heads west through Melardalur valley to Eyri farm, on Ingolfsfjörður, the last settlement on the Strandir coast. From the farm, a **hike** leads west around the head of the fjord, before hugging the shoreline and rounding the Seljanes promontory, then entering neighbouring Ófeigsfjörður, where there's a **campsite** with toilets and running water. North of here, the trail keeps close to the shore as it heads up to Eyvindarfjörður, Drangavík bay, Bjarnarfjörður and Reykjafjörður, where there's a **campsite** with all facilities plus geothermal swimming pool. From Reykjafjörður, the trail becomes more distinct and heads inland over the Skartaskarð pass before descending for the coast and down into Furufjörður (campsite with toilets and running water). From here another trail heads west through Skoradalur into Hrafnfjörður from where there are boats to Ísafjörður (see p.167). Allow at least a week for this demanding trek. Before setting out ensure you have enough **provisions** with you and make a firm booking for the **boat from Hrafnsfjörður** before setting out; contact the tourist office in Ísafjöður for details. All the above routes are clearly shown on the excellent *Göngukort yfir Hornstrandir* (1:100 000) produced by Landmælingar Íslands.

of salted herring continued until 1950, when the company went bankrupt following a disastrous collapse in fish catches. Today, Djúpavík is a mere ghost of its former self, most of the houses in the village have fallen down and the picture of desolation completed by the rusting hull of a trawler beside the disused jetty. **Accommodation** is available at *Hótel Djúpavík* (☎451 4037, fax 451 4035; sleeping-bag accommodation 1400kr, ②), a former hostel for the women who worked on the dockside and in the herring factory. Breakfast costs an extra 750kr – and the hotel **restaurant** is the only place to eat in the village. There is no bus service to Djúpavík.

Fifteen kilometres northwest of Djúpavík, **NORÐURFJÖRÐUR** is one of Iceland's last places. Occupying a stunning position amid fertile farmland at the head of the fjord of the same name, which opens out into Trékyllisvík bay, the village is dominated by the mountain, Krossnesfjall (646m) to the east and rarely receives any visitors – perhaps not least because the only place to stay here is the **overnight hut** (*sæluhús*) and adjoining tiny **campsite** close to the one and only village **shop**, which is where you'll find toilets, running water and showers. One of the country's most dramatically situated swimming pools, **Krossneslaug**, is just 4km northeast of the village, north of the farm at Krossnes. Here, natural springs provide a continuous source of hot water to feed the open-air pool down on the beach, whose walls are lapped by the icy waters of the Atlantic.

Six kilometres south of Norðurfjörður, a **hiking trail** leads from the farm at Árnes in Trékyllisvík bay via the Göngumannaskard pass across the Reykjanes peninsula to Naustavík bay, on the northern shores of Reykjafjörður. Details of this hike are included in the **hiking guide**, *Gönguleiðir í Strandasyslu*, available from the tourist office in Hólmavík (see p.186) and the hotel in Djúpavík (see above).

travel details

Buses

Bíldudalur to: Patreksfjörður (1 daily; 1hr); Tálknafjörður (1 daily; 30min).

Brjánslækur to: Ísafjörður (3 weekly; 6hr); Látrabjarg (3 weekly; 3hr).

Flateyri to: Brjánslækur (frequency 2hr 40min); Ísafjörður (2–3 daily Mon–Fri; 20min); Patreksfjörður (3 weekly; 3hr 45min).

Hólmavík to: Drangsnes (1 weekly; 1hr); Ísafjörður (3 weekly; 4hr 15min); Reykjavík (3 weekly; 4hr).

Ísafjörður to: Bolungarvík (3 daily Mon–Fri, 20min); Brjánslækur (3 weekly; 3hr); Flateyri (2–3 daily Mon–Fri; 20min); Hólmavík (3 weekly; 6hr); Hrafnseyri (3 weekly; 2hr); Látrabjarg (3 weekly; 6hr); Patreksfjörður (3 weekly; 4hr 10min); Reykjavík (3 weekly; 10hr 15min); Þingeyri (3 weekly; 1hr 30min).

Látrabjarg to: Brjánslækur (3 weekly; 3hr); Ísafjörður (3 weekly; 6hr).

Patreksfjörður to: Brjánslækur (3 weekly; 50min); Ísafjörður (3 weekly; 4hr); Tálknafjörður (1 daily; 30min).

Tálknafjörður to: Bíldudalur (1 daily; 30min); Patreksfjörður (1 daily; 30min).

Þingeyri to: Brjánslækur (3 weekly; 1hr 30min); Ísafjörður (3 weekly; 1hr 30min); Látrabjarg (3 weekly; 4hr 30min).

Ferries

Brjánslækur to: Flatey (2 daily; 1hr 15); Stykkishólmur (2 daily; 3hr).

Flights

Bíldudalur to: Reykjavík (1 daily; 50min).

Ísafjörður to: Akureyri (4 weekly; 1hr); Reykjavík (3 daily; 50min).

CHAPTER FIVE

NORTHWEST ICELAND

C ompared with the neighbouring West Fjords, the scenery of Northwest Iceland is much gentler and less forbidding – undulating meadows dotted with isolated barns and farmhouses are the norm here, rather than twisting fjords and mountains. However, what makes this section of the country stand out is the location of two of Iceland's great historical sites, the first of which, Cingeyrar, is roughly an hour's drive east of Brú, where Route 61 from the Hólmavík meets the Ringroad, past the wildlife rich Vatnsnes peninsula. This site was once the location for an ancient assembly and monastery where monks compiled some of Iceland's most outstanding pieces of medieval literature. As the Ringroad heads northeast of Çingeyrar on its way to Akureyri, it passes through some of Iceland's most sparsely populated areas and Blönduós, a service centre for the surrounding farms and villages. A much better place to break the long journey along the north coast, however, is the likeable, if unpronounceable, Sauxárkrókur, enlivened by stunning sea views out over Skagafjörður and Drangey island, once home to Saga hero Grettir, who bathed here in the nearby hot pool named after him. Close by, just half an hour's drive away, is the north's second great site, Hólar í Hjaltadal, which functioned as the ecumenical and educational centre of the north of the country between the twelfth century and the Reformation. Hard to get to, but worth the sidestep from Route 1 via the Icelandic emigration centre at Hofsós telling the story of the Icelanders who began new lives in North America, is the fishing village of Siglufjörður. Hemmed in on three sides by sheer rock walls, the village more than repays the effort of getting there and is especially worth a visit if you've not managed to make it to the West Fjords since the surrounding scenery is, unusually for the north coast, almost identical.

Slicing deep into the coastline of this part of northern Iceland, **Eyjafjörður**, or Island Fjord, named after the island of **Hrísey** at its mouth, renowned for its rich birdlife, has for centuries been **Akureyri's** window on the world as ships sailed its length to deliver their goods to the largest market in northern Iceland. Today,

---

ACCOMMODATION PRICE CODES

Throughout this guide, prices given for **youth hostels, sleeping-bag accommodation** and **campsites** are per person unless otherwise specified. **Hotel** and **guesthouse** accommodation is graded on a scale from ① to ⑧; all are high-season rates and indicate the cost of the cheapest double room. The price bands to which these codes refer are as follows:

① Up to 4000kr	③ 6000–8000kr	⑤ 10,000–12,000kr	⑦ 15,000–20,000kr
② 4000–6000kr	④ 8000–10,000kr	⑥ 12,000–15,000kr	⑧ Over 20,000kr

(See p.26 for a full explanation.)

though, fisheries have taken over as the town's economic mainstay, profiting from the rich fishing grounds found offshore. With a population of 15,000 the largest town in Iceland outside the Reykjavík area, not only does the town boast a stunning setting at the head of the country's longest fjord, Eyjafjörður, bordered by flat-topped perpetually snow-covered mountains, but it's also blessed with some of the warmest and most stable weather anywhere in the country, a perfect complement to the long white nights of summer. Between June and August temperatures can reach 20°C hereabouts, really quite warm for somewhere just 100km south of the Arctic Circle, much to the joy of the locals who're quick to point out how sunny Akureyri is compared to windswept and rainy Reykjavík. Indeed, there's great rivalry between the two places and although the "Capital of the North", as Akureyri is often known, can't compete with Reykjavík's eclectic bar, restaurant and nightlife scene, the town's pleasant streets are full of shops and services, and the raw beauty of the surrounding countryside is barely a ten-minute drive from the centre.

The fishing villages of **Dalvík**, with ferry connections across to Hrísey, and **Ólafsfjörður**, close to the mouth of Eyjafjörður, both make excellent day trips once you've exhaused Akureyri; Route 82 between the two villages hugs the shore of the fjord and offers spectacular **views** across the chilly water to the rugged peaks of **Látraströnd**, the fjord's northeastern tip, deserted during the middle of the last century, where there's good wilderness **hiking** to be had. Just forty kilometres north of the mainland, the beautiful Arctic island of **Grímsey** is a must for anyone visiting this part of the country; on the ground this rocky island, bisected by the Arctic Circle, is a springy carpet of moor and grassland bursting with flowering plants whilst aloft the skies are alive with around sixty different species of screeching birds, many of which consider you an unwelcome intruder to their territory; if you haven't yet been attacked by an Arctic tern, you will be here – they even divebomb visitors as they board the plane back to the mainland.

From Brú to Akureyri

The stretch of the Ringroad between Brú and Akureyri is, unfortunately, one of its least interesting. A grinding distance of 230km, many travellers see it as an area to be covered quickly in order to reach Akureyri. However, it can be worth breaking the journey at one or two places en route, and indeed, if you're travelling between the West Fjords and Akureyri, sooner or later you'll wind up at the road junction, **BRÚ** (Bridge), 85km from Borgarnes on the west coast and 38km from Hvammstangi, to the northeast, the nearest settlements of any size. Brú, lives down to its name, comprising a bridge over the Hrútafjarðará, which flows into Hrútafjörður, itself part of the much greater Húnaflói bay. The only signs of life here belong to the ESSO filling station, busy with travellers taking a snack break or waiting for an onward bus connection. East of Brú the Ringroad hugs the shores of Hrútafjörður before turning sharply inland towards the next fjord along this stretch of coastline, the miniscule, Miðfjörður. Beyond here, however, things liven up considerably with the possibility of rounding the Vatnsnes peninsula, where there's a good chance of seeing seals, and, further along the Ringroad, of heading for the north's great historical sites, Þingeyrar and Hólar í Hjaltadal, or taking in small town Iceland in Sauðárkrókur or Siglufjörður.

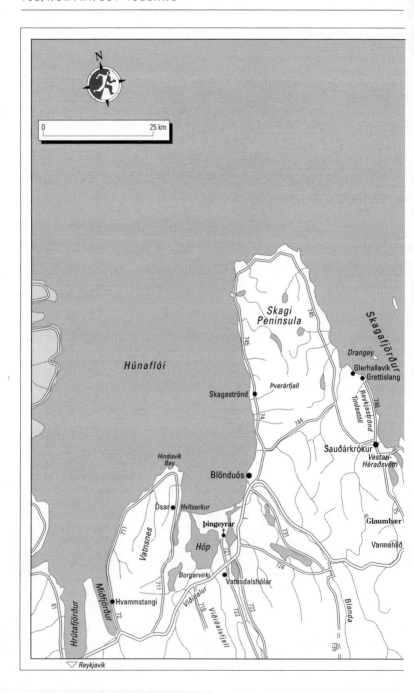

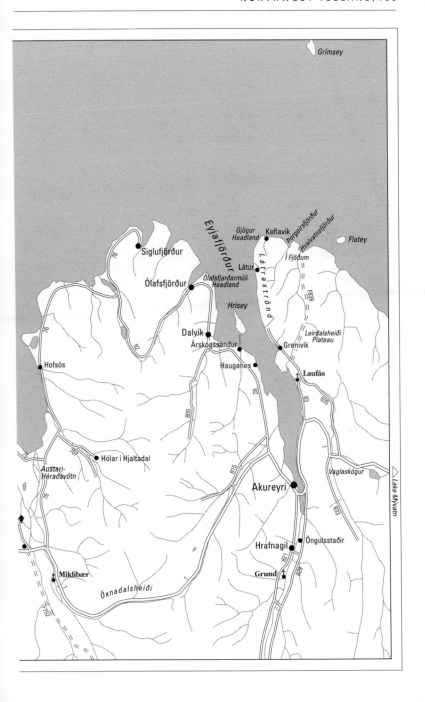

Grímsey

Eyjafjörður

Gjögur
Headland

Keflavík

Þorgeirsfjörður

Hvalvatnsfjörður

Flatey

Siglufjörður

76

Látur

Í Fjöðum

Látraströnd

Ólafsfjörður

Ólafsfjarðarmúli
Headland

82

Hrísey

F839

Dalvík

Leirdalsheiði
Plateau

Árskógssandur

Grenivík

Hofsós

76

Hauganes

Laufás

83

835

82

805

Austari-
Héraðsvötn

767

Hólar í Hjaltadal

815

Vaglaskógur

Akureyri

Lake Mývatn

76

633

Öngulsstaðir

Hrafnagil

821

Miklibær

Öxnadalsheiði

Grund

829

F752

Hvammstangi and the Vatnsnes peninsula

The eastern shore of Midfjörður is the setting for the only town in the area, **HVAMMSTANGI**, although "town" is something of a misnomer since barely 600 people live here. Just 6km north of the Ringroad, and reached by smaller Route 72 (buses will pull in here on request), the place survives on shrimp fishing, and a couple of brightly coloured fishing vessels are often moored in the tiny harbour, right by the one and only main road which cuts through the handful of suburban houses that pass as the town centre. Should you end up needing a **place to stay** here, the *Hanna Siggu* guesthouse, at Garðavegur 26 (☎451 2407; sleeping bag accommodation 1400kr; ①), has plain and uninspiring rooms overlooking the fjord; you might be able to persuade the owner to provide dinner but don't count on it.

From Hvammstangi, you'll need your own transport to follow Route 711 as it heads northeast around the **Vatnsnes** peninsula, a wild and uninhabited finger of land on the eastern side of Húnaflói known for its superb views out over the bay towards the needle-sharp peaks of the Strandir coast in the West Fjords (see p.185). While ascending tiers of craggy, inaccessible hills form the spine of the peninsula, the land closer to the shore is surprisingly green and is given over to grazing land for horses; you'll also spot flocks of **greylag geese**. At **Hindisvík**, close to the head of the promontory, there's a **seal**-breeding ground, where many of the creatures and their young can be seen lolling idly on the low rocks during June and July. Around the headland, on the more sheltered eastern side of Vatnsnes, the friendly **youth hostel** *Ósar* (☎451 2678; 1250kr per person, bed linen 400kr extra), set on a farm, is worth seeking out for its peaceful surroundings and undisturbed views of mountains and ocean across to the rugged Skagaströnd coastline, which marks the eastern edge of Húnaflói bay. If you call ahead, the owners of the youth hostel will pick you up from the Ringroad or from Hvammstangi.

Þingeyrar

As it heads southwards down the eastern shore of Vatnsnes, Route 711 rejoins the Ringroad in Víðidalur, one of the area's most populated valleys and dotted with some beautifully located farms, set against the breathtaking backdrop of the brown and green hues of the Vídidalsfjall mountains (993m).

However, it's not for the scenery that this part of the country is best known, since it's also the location of the ancient site of **Þingeyrar**, which lies just 6km north of the Ringroad along Route 721. If you don't have your own transport, it's a straightforward walk, despite the distance. Originally the site of a **legislative assembly** during the Icelandic Commonwealth (see "Contexts", p.288), the first Bishop of Hólar, Jón Ögmundarson, pledged to build a church and an associated farm here if God were to relieve a severe local famine. When the land began to regain its productivity, the bishop took things one step further and established Iceland's first monastery here in 1133, which remained in existence up until the Reformation in 1550. The monks went on to copy and transcribe some of the country's most outstanding pieces of medieval literature, and it was on this spot that many of the sagas were first written down for posterity.

There's nothing left of the monastery now, but a superb nineteenth-century **church**, Þingeyrarkirkja, now stands adjacent to where the monks once lived and worked. Constructed of large blocks of basalt, brought here on sledges dragged across the nearby frozen lagoon of Hóp, the church was the first building on the site to be made of stone – all previous structures had been of turf – and it brought much admiration from local worthies. Although its grey mass is indeed an impressive sight, clearly visible from miles around, it's the interior that really makes a trip here worthwhile, with its stark white walls setting off the blue ceiling, painted with 1000 golden stars, and simple green pews. The wooden pulpit dates from 1696 and is thought to come from Denmark or Holland, whereas the altarpiece, inset with religious figures made of alabaster, dates from the fifteenth century and was originally made in the English town of Nottingham for the monastery here. The wooden figures of Christ and the twelve apostles lining the balcony were made in 1983 to replace the original figures from Germany that once stood here – the originals are in the National Museum in Reykjavík (see p.56). The building is often locked, so check with the tourist office in Blönduós (see below) about entry or call in to see the church warden, who lives halfway between the Ringroad and the church in the blue and white farm building called Steinnes. You can also ask at the horse farm, next to the church, another place where keys are kept.

Blönduós

From the turn-off to Route 721 for Þingeyrar, it's a further 19km along the Ringroad to **BLÖNDUÓS**, the focal point of Víðidalur, with a huge modern hospital and its modern, multicoloured houses grouped on either side of the Blandaá. Without a good harbour the town is merely a service centre for the locality, pasteurising milk from the surrounding farms, although shrimping does play some part in the local economy. The centre, consisiting of a handful of uneventful suburban streets and the odd shop, is spread over both banks of the river, accessed from the Ringroad by the roads of Blöndubyggd on the southern side and Húnabraut on the northern shore.

Although there's really little reason to break a journey here, if you do, you'll spot the town's astonishingly ugly concrete **church**, right on the edge of the Ringroad opposite the tourist office. Designed to resemble a volcanic crater, the church sits atop a small hill overlooking the town and its charmless grey walls therefore dominate almost any view of Blönduós. The interior is equally austere, with unadorned walls of concrete weaving an austere spell over any visitor – if the church is locked ask at the tourist office for the key. Otherwise, the only other thing to detain you – and frankly it's not going to be the highlight of your trip to Iceland – is the unpronounceable **Heimilisiðnaðarsafnið**, the museum of handicrafts (late June to late Aug daily 2–5pm; ☎452 4067; 300kr) at Árbraut 7, reached by walking along Húnabraut towards the sea, then turning left into Árbraut. The collection here was ssembled by Halldóra Bjarnardóttir, one of the country's leading women's rights campaigners. Part of Halldóra's platform was the elevation of domestic crafts like knitting and weaving to the status of art – an aim, however, that seems hard to justify when looking at the exhibits here. Halldóra also happens to be the longest-lived Icelander ever known – 108 years old when she died in 1981.

All **buses** from Reykjavík via Borgarnes and Brú to Akureyri stop at the ESSO station. The **tourist information office** (late May to Aug daily 8am–10pm; ☎452 4520) is on the northern side of the river on the main street, just over the bridge, by the **campsite** at Brautarhvammur. If you fancy renting out a **cabin** head for the seven wooden ones at *Glaðheimar* (☎452 4123, fax 452 4924; 4100–9300kr) next to the tourist office and overlooking the river; each sleeps up to eight, is complete with kitchen and shower and most also have their own outdoor Jacuzzi on the terrace – you need to have your Icelandic phrasebook at the ready, though, because, unusually, the owners don't speak English. Alternatively, there's the weater-beaten *Hótel Blönduós* (☎452 4126, fax 452 4989; ③), on the southern side of the river at Aðalgata 6, which has very average rooms.

Eating options in Blönduós are poor – the choice is limited to the tasteless and uninspiring fish dishes served up at the *Hótel Blönduós*, the tasty but diminutive snacks and sandwiches available from the *Við Árbakkann* café, at the corner of Húnabraut and Holtabraut, or the greasy burgers, chips and pizzas from both the ESSO filling station, opposite the tourist office, and at *Grillbærinn*, by the main bridge.

Sauðárkrókur and around

Although difficult to get around by public transport, the area around Skagafjörður, over the Skagi peninsula east of Blönduós, is worth exploring for a few days. The best base for this is **SAUÐÁRKRÓKUR**, the second-largest town on the northern Icelandic coast, with a population of 2600 and an immediately likeable place since there are signs of life in the streets on summer evenings, unlike the town's diminutive neighbours. Getting there can be tricky, however, since the town is 23km north of the Ringroad and is only served by buses in summer. As for driving, although it's a tempting shortcut, don't cross the peninsula via the Norðurárdalur valley on Route 744, up over Þverárfjall mountain, unless the weather is excellent and there's no snow; this is a summer-only road and its summit can close with even the lightest snowfall. Instead, take the Ringroad southeast to the tiny village of Varmahlíð, from where Route 75 heads north to Sauðárkrókur, passing, on the way, the historic farmstead of **Glaumbær**, where the first Viking to be born in America lies buried.

The Town

Occupying a triangle of suburban streets stretching inland from the curved shoreline of Skagafjörður, the brightly painted houses and wide streets, with views of the bustling harbour on the edge of its centre, lend a pioneering edge to the town. Although there are few sights to Sauðárkrókur, the wandering around the streets is a pleasant enough way to pass an hour or two – there's no set route to take, but sooner of later you'll wind up on the main street, **Aðalgata**, which is home to shops, restaurants and accommodation. Here, **Sauðárkrókskirkja**, an impressive wooden church from 1892 standing amid an area of residential homes and commercial premises, is worth a look for its fourteen highly unusual stained-glass windows. The futuristic patterns on the centre panes of each portray a variety of scenes from the Crucifixion to the Holy Trinity – although to the untrained eye, they're perhaps not immediately obvious.

North of the church, Aðalgata continues to the **harbour**, from where there are **boat trips** to the steep-sided, flat-topped island of **Drangey**, which resembles an arrow pointing north operated by *Drangeyjarferdir* (May–Sept daily at 10am; 2500kr for a 2hr 30min sail around the island, 4000kr for a 5hr trip onto it; ☎453 6310, bookings necessary). Now a bird sanctuary where kittiwakes and guillemots can be seen in abundance, it was once the hideout of Grettir the Strong, or Grettir Ásmundarson, the courageous but savage outlaw of *Grettir's Saga* (see p.303), who stayed here for three years with his brother, living off the birds and their eggs. The 7.5-kilometre stretch of bitterly cold sea between the island and the mainland is known as **Grettir's Swim**, which the outlaw reputedly swam across to fetch the glowing embers he'd spotted on the mainland after his own fire has gone out; it is still sometimes swum for sport (the latest record is 2hr 10min) despite the water temperature barely rising above 9.5°C. To revive himself after the swim, Grettir jumped into the hot pool at **Reykjaströnd**, which is reached along the very bumpy twenty-kilometre Route 748 from the harbour; take extreme care if you're driving, as it is all but washed away in parts. At its end, walk down to the sea and the black, volcanic sandy beach towards the two turf shacks; the pool, which ever since has borne his name, **Grettislaug**, is to the left, although stone slabs now act as seats and the area around it has been paved with blocks of basalt, As Grettir did, you can cast off your clothes, step into the hot water and steam to your heart's content, admiring the twenty-kilometre-long, snow-splashed moutainface of Tindastóll (989m) on one side, the open ocean and views of Drangey on the other – a quintessentially Icelandic experience.

At low tide only it's possible to reach the enchanting **Glerhallavík** bay from Grettislaug: from the pool, walk along the beach around the foot of Tindastóll to the bay, where the sight of thousands and thousands of shining quartz stones on the beach, buffed by the pounding surf, is quite breathtaking. Note that it's forbidden to remove them from the bay.

Practicalities

Buses from Reykjavík and Siglufjörður arrive and depart from the Haraldar Júlíussonar, at Aðalgata 22. Services run June to September only, leaving at 8.45pm on Friday and at 6.45pm on Monday and Wednesday for Siglufjörður, as well as at 10am on Tuesday and Thursday, plus 4.55pm on Sunday, to Reykjavík. Outside this period there is no service.

Curiously, for such an off-the-beaten-track provincial town, Sauðárkrókur boasts one of the best **hotels** in Iceland, the *Samling Hotel Tindastóll* (☎453 6362, fax 453 5034; ⑥), an odd mix of hi-tech wizardry and old-fashioned charm – one of the rooms was once the temporary residence of Marlene Dietrich, who entertained the British troops stationed in the area during World War II. Each of the ten rooms in this elegant listed timber building dating to 1835 has its own PC, email and DVD facilities, as well as TV, radio and power-showers; out of season, prices fall by around one third. There's even a copy of Grettislaug (see above) at the back of the hotel. Less extravagant is the *Mikligarður* **guesthouse**, opposite the church, at Kirkjutorg 3 (☎453 6880, fax 453 641; ③), a pretty little blue house with a white balcony, with small but perfectly adequate rooms. The *Fosshótel Áning* (☎453 6717; ④), opposite the hospital at Skagfirðingabraut 21, swings into operation during summer in the local boarding school, renting out its numerous box-like rooms. The **campsite** is on Skagfirðingabraut, next to the swimming pool, at the southern end of the town.

Sauðárkrókur's few **places to eat and drink** are all located in the centre of town along Aðalgata. *Kaffi Krókur*, at Aðalgata 16 (summer 11am–midnight, weekends until 3am; evening only in winter), is a good place to meet the locals over a beer and sample good Icelandic and international cuisine, with fish dishes from 1200kr, pizzas from 800kr and burgers from 450kr. Opposite, at Aðalgata 15, the bright blue wooden building houses the *Ólafshús* restaurant, which also serves fish but at much more inflated prices – reckon on 1500kr upwards. For a drink and a dance, most young people gravitate towards the *Royal*, also on Aðalgata, seemingly oblivious to the hideous white and silver décor inside; the dancefloor is upstairs and they have occasional live music.

Glaumbær

Just 8km north of Varmahlíð, on the way into Sauðárkrókur, Route 75 passes the immaculately maintained eighteenth-century farm at **Glaumbær** (June–Sept daily 9am–6pm; 300kr). A private home until 1947, the farm consists of a row of wood-fronted turf-walled dwellings dating from 1750 to 1879, and is a powerful reminder of the impoverished lifestyle many people led in Iceland during the eighteenth and nineteenth centuries. The adjacent timber building houses the Skagafjörður **folk museum** (same hours and ticket) and displays a collection of rustic implements once used on the farm, from spinning-wheels to brightly painted clothes' chests. Not only does the farm demonstrate centuries-old Icelandic building techniques, but it's also where **Snorri Þorfinnsson**, the first American born of European parents (in 1003) is buried; Snorri came to Iceland with his parents and lived out his life on the farm here. **Buses** heading to Sauðárkrókur (see p.196) call here in summer only – or it's a good two-hour walk from the Ringroad.

Around Skagafjörður

The region's greatest historical site lies within easy striking distance of Sauðárkrókur: **Hólar í Hjaltadal**, roughly a thirty-minute drive east along Routes 75 and 76 over the watery expanses of Vesari-Héraðsvötn and Austari-Héraðsvötn at the head of **Skagafjörður** (buses to Siglufjörður pass within 15km), was northern Iceland's ecumenical and educational centre until the Reformation. Today, this tranquil place in the foothills of Hjaltadalur valley consists solely of a redstone cathedral and an agricultural college, a remote and peaceful spot that's worth seeking out – particularly if you fancy **hiking**, since a trail leads from here over to Dalvík (see p.210). Beyond Hólar, Route 76 leads north to **Hofsós**, another diminutive settlement, best known as a study centre for North Americans of Icelandic origin keen to trace their roots, before reaching the end of the line at the fishing village of **Siglufjörður**, the highlight of any trip along this stretch of the trip to Akureyri, and a good base from which to **hike** across the surrounding mountains.

Hólar í Hjaltadal

On the eastern side of Skagafjörður, reached on Route 76 as it heads towards Siglufjörður, then another 15km inland on Route 767, the hamlet of **HÓLAR Í HJALTADAL**, or simply Hólar, was very much the cultural capital of the north from the twelfth until the eighteenth century – monks studied here, manuscripts were transcribed and Catholicism flourished until the Reformation. Now home to just 64 people most of whom work at the agricultural college here – this and the the cathedral are the only buildings remaining – it was the site of the country's first printing press in 1530, set up by Iceland's last Catholic bishop, Jón Arason (who was beheaded twenty years later at Skálholt for his resistance to the spread of the Reformation from the south). A church has stood on this spot since his day, but the present **cathedral** (to enter, ask in the college next door), the successor of earlier religious buildings here, was built in 1759–63 in late Baroque style, using local red sandstone, and is the second-oldest stone building in the country. Inside the fifteenth-century alabaster altarpiece over the cathedral's south door is similar in design to that in the church at Þingeyrar (see p.194), and was likewise made in Nottingham, England. The main altarpiece, with its ornate carvings of Biblical figures originated in Germany around 1500 and was given to the cathedral by its most famous bishop, whose memory is honoured in the adjacent bell tower: a mosaic of tiny tiles by Icelandic artist, Erró, marks a small chapel and headstone, under which the bishop's bones are buried.

There is no public transport to and from Hólar but, with determination, it is possible to walk here from the junction with Route 7. Alternatively, a long-distance hiking path leads here from Dalvík (see p.210). The agricultural college operates as a summer-only **hotel** (June–Aug; ☎453 6303; 2450kr per person). A limited number of rooms is also available at other times of the year but must be booked in advance. There's a swimming pool and hot pot attached. The **campsite** (400kr per person) is located behind the main building. The school's **restaurant** (2–8pm) serves up a changing range of dishes, often including locally reared Arctic char.

Hofsós

Thirty-six kilometres from Sauðárkrókur, **HOFSÓS** is a tiny, non-descript village on the eastern shores of Skagafjörður, consisting of one street and a tiny harbour, with a population of around two hundred. It's primarily a base for the hundreds of Americans and Canadians of Icelandic descent who come here to visit the Vesturfarasetrið, or **Icelandic Emigration Centre** (June–Aug daily 11am–6pm; other times by arrangement; 350kr; ☎453 7935), tracing their roots through the centre's genealogy and information service. Beautifully set on the seafront by the harbour, it makes for an interesting visit whther you have Icelandic blood in you or not, with displays and exhibitions tracing the history of the Icelanders who emigrated west over the sea.

Beside the centre, the wooden **Pakkhúsið** (always open; donation of 200kr) is preserved under the supervision of the National Museum of Iceland as a fine example of a traditional warehouse, built from coarsely hewn timber planks imported from Denmark. Today this hulk of a building, with its sharply pointed roof, is covered in black tar to protect it from the worst of the weather, making the tiny square windows with their white frames all the more striking. Dating from 1777, it was used to store goods for local Danish merchants – it's thought that trading began from Hofsós as early as the sixteenth century. Inside is a cheesy collection of various bird-trapping devices: everything from rafts to snare unsuspecting birds out in Skagafjörður, to nooses made out of stallion's hair – there are also a couple of stuffed puffins, presumably duped by one or other of these techniques.

Opposite the warehouse, the *Brimnes* **guesthouse** (☎453 7434; ②) and, up the hill on the same road, Sudurbraut, the *Sunnuberg* (☎453 7434; ②) both have rooms with sea views, although the *Sunnuberg* specialises in extremely pink walls: doubles at both places cost 5500kr although they're often full in summer with visiting Americans and Canadians. **Eating** is best at the *Sigtún* (daily 11am–midnight, until 3am Fri & Sat), next to the *Sunnuberg*, where haddock or trout will cost you 1200kr, a burger is 400kr and a beer 450kr; there's outdoor seating in summer, with pleasant views out over the fjord. Alternatively there's a small café, *Sólvík*, opposite the warehouse (May–Sept 10am–10pm), serving snacks and sandwiches.

Siglufjörður

Clinging precariously to the foot of steep mountain walls which enclose an isolated narrow fjord on the very edge of Iceland, **SIGLUFJÖRÐUR** is the country's most northerly town, a good a place as any to take stock of just where you've reached: the **Arctic Circle** is barely 40km away and you're as far north as Canada's Baffin Island and central Alaska. Winters here can be particularly severe and the mountain road, Route 82, which links Siglufjörður with its eastern neighbour of Ólafsfjörður, rarely opens before late April. Despite its end-of-the-road location, it's worth making every effort to get here from Hofsós on the winding, switchback road along the shore of the Denmark Strait.

From 1900 to 1970, Siglufjörður was the **herring** capital of the North Atlantic, when hundreds of fishing boats would crowd into the tiny fjord to unload their catches onto the rickety piers that once stretched out from the quayside, where herring girls, as they were known, would gut and salt them – during a good season, casual labour and the number of fishermen (who were, in the early part of the century at any rate, primarily Norwegian) could swell the town's population threefold to over 10,000. Their story is brought to life in film, photographs and exhibits at the **Síldarminjasafnið** herring museum (mid-June to mid-Aug daily 10–6pm, early June & mid-Aug to mid-Sept daily 1–5pm; at other times call ☎467 1604; 300kr), at Snorragata 15, an old salting station that housed around fifty herring girls – you can still see graffiti, daubed in nail varnish, on the walls of the

---

HIKING AROUND SIGLUFJÖRÐUR

Several excellent **day hikes** can easily be undertaken from Siglufjörður. The trails listed below are shown on the hiking **map** of Siglufjörður available at the Síldarminjasafnið herring museum (see above), and you can check out details in advance at *www.siglo.is/en/tourism/hikes/*.

The best of the shorter routes (5–7hr), forming a clockwise circle around the town, begins at the southern edge of Siglufjörður, where the road veers left around the head of the fjord. Follow the walking path up **Eyrafjall**, heading towards the Dalaskarð pass, then over the mountain tops and up **Hafnarfjall**, from where there's an excellent view over the fjord, the surrounding peaks and even Grímsey. From here it's an easy climb up **Hafnarhyrna** (687m), the highest point on Hafnarfjall and the starting point for the easy descent towards the bowl-shaped hollow of **Hvanneyrarskál**, a well-known lovers' haunt during the herring boom. From the hollow, a road leads back down into town.

A second, longer trail (10–14hr) begins beyond the disused airport on the eastern side of the fjord (follow the main road through the village to get there) and leads southeast up the valley of **Kálfsdalur**, which begins just above the lighthouse beyond the airport, past **Kálfsvatn**, over the **Kálfsskarð** pass (450m) before descending into Nesdalur valley on the other side of the ridge. The trail then leads north through the valley to the coast and the deserted farm, **Reydará**. From the farm, the trail leads west along the steep slopes of Nesnúpur (595m) passing a lighthouse and several abandoned huts, built by the American military during World War II as a radar station. Once back on the eastern side of the fjord the path trail continues along the shoreline towards the airport and Siglufjörður.

second-floor room where they once slept, alongside faded black-and-white photographs of heart-throb Cary Grant.

Today, Siglufjörður's heyday is long gone and the place is considerably quieter. It's a pleasant place, consisting of a handful of parallel streets with unkempt multi-coloured homes grouped around the main street, **Túngata**, which turns into **Snorragata** as it approaches the **harbour**, busy with the goings-on of a low-key port, with fishermen mending their nets in the shipyard and fish hanging out to dry – the town still produces kippers (smoked herring) from a factory down by the harbour. Once you've seen the herring museum there's some excellent **hiking** to be had along the trails that lead up out of the fjord (see box opposite).

Practicalities

Accommodation in Siglufjörður throws up precisely three options: the friendly *Hótel Lækur* (☎467 1514, fax 467 1911; ②), where the comfortable rooms (all with shared bath) are decked out in purple and breakfast is included in the price; the much cheaper option *Gistiheimilið Hvanneyri* (☎467 1378; ①), Aðalgata 10, a dreary place with small cramped rooms; and the **campsite** on Snorragata, south of town beyond the harbour. Siglufjörður is one of the few towns on the north coast to boast a *Pizza 67*, in the centre of town on Aðalgata, the only **place to eat** bar the drab restaurant in the hotel, which nonetheless serves up decent fish dishes for around 1100kr. If you're in town take a look into *Allinn Sportbar* (Thurs–Sun on Þormóðsgata, which serves **beer** until 1am (3am on Fri & Sat) and has large screens showing football matches. **Buses** stop at the post office on Aðalgata.

Akureyri

The commercial centre and transport hub of northern Iceland, **AKUREYRI** translates as "the cornfield on the sand spit", the spit of land in question being the point where **Laxdalshús**, the oldest building in town, now stands on Hafnarstræti. However, it was to the sea and its sheltered **harbour**, today located right in the heart of the town between **Drottningarbraut** and **Strandgata**, that Akureyri looked for prosperity. In 1787, when the Danish monopoly on trade with Iceland was finally lifted, Akureyri became one of six places around the country to be granted municipal status, despite the fact that its population then numbered little more than a dozen and most trade remained firmly in the hands of Danish merchants and their families. From then on, however, the town prospered, and in the late nineteenth century one of Iceland's first cooperatives, **KEA**, was established here, going on to play a key role in the economy.

Today, Akureyri is divided into two distinct areas: the town centre, harbour and commercial district north of **Hafnarstræti**, the main street, and the suburban areas to its south, where the distinctive **Akureyrarkirkja**, plus the small university, **museums** and the superb **botanical gardens** can all be found. As far as entertainment goes, the town is a decent enough place to relax in for a day or two, with an excellent open-air swimming pool and enough cafés and restaurants to keep you well fed and watered. That most un-Icelandic thing, the forest, makes a welcome appearance just south of Akureyri in the form of **Kjarnaskógur**, easily accessible on foot from the town centre and a popular destination for locals at weekends who come here to walk the many trails that crisscross the forest and to picnic. If you're doing much touring, you're almost certain to find yourself in town sooner or later, as it makes an excellent base from which to explore nearby Lake Mývatn and the Jökulsárgljúfur National Park (both covered in Chapter Six; see p.222 & p.238). It also serves as a handy jumping-off point for the West Fjords (see p.163) – a flight from Akureyri to Ísafjörður, for example, can save a tiring drive of 567km along the north coast and then up into the West Fjords.

Getting to Akureyri from Siglufjörður involves a long and winding drive along Route 82. However, this route is often closed due to bad weather, and the only other way to reach Akureyri is to backtrack on Route 76 towards Hofsós (see p.199) until you reach the Ringroad again. From this junction, Route 1 makes the steep ascent up to the high moorland of Öxnadalsheiði, where, legend states, many of the victims of the Sturlung Age battles are buried, close to the road at Miklibær. There are countless stories of the ghosts of lost travellers haunting the pass and in winter it's one of the first in the country to become blocked. The government subsidises the highest farm here, ensuring not only that it keeps going but also that help is available for anyone stranded. Bus travellers, though, will have to make do with glancing through the window since services along this stretch of road don't stop.

Arrival, orientation and information

The **airport** is stunningly located on a spit of land in the middle of the fjord, a couple of kilometres south of town, from where it's possible to walk into the centre following the highway, Drottningarbraut, northwards as it runs parallel to the fjord, in around thirty minutes; alternatively, taxis are available outside the terminal building. The airport is served by flights from Reykjavík, Egilsstaðir, Ísafjörður, Grímsey, Vopnafjörður and Þórshöfn; in summer there's also a direct charter flight from Zürich, in Switzerland. **Long-distance buses** terminate in the station at the southern end of **Hafnarstræti**, the main street, which is pedestrianized north of its junction with **Kaupvangsstræti**, from where it leads towards the main square, **Ráðhústorg**. The friendly **tourist information office** (June–Aug Mon–Fri 7.30am–8.30pm, Sat & Sun 8am–5pm; Sept–May Mon–Fri 8am–5pm; ☎462 4442, *tourinfo@est.is*) is in the bus station, and has seemingly endless supplies of maps, brochures and good advice.

Accommodation

There's no shortage of **accommodation** in Akureyri and there's no need to book in advance, even in summer, unless you wish to stay at the cheapest place in town, the excellent and well-appointed **youth hostel** (☎462 3657, fax 461 2549; ②) at Stórholt 1, an easy twenty- to thirty-minute walk north of the main square along Glerágata (Route 1 from Reykjavík), opposite the ESSO filling station and, unusually for Iceland, surrounded by trees. Rooms here sleep up to five people, and there are two kitchens and a TV room; doubles are ②, a room for four costs 1900kr per person, while sleeping-bag accommodation is 1500kr per person (1200kr for HI members). The **campsite** is at Þórunnarstræti next to the university; get here by walking up Kaupvangsstræti, past the swimming pool on Þingvallastræti, and turning left at the crossroads.

Three of Akureyri's four **hotels** are located in the same road, virtually next door to each other and just a five-minute walk from the town centre; as in Reykjavík, **guesthouses** charge pretty much the same prices as each other for rooms of similar standards. **Breakfast** is usually included in the price for both hotels and guesthouses, though we've stated where this is not the case. If you're planning to base yourself in Akureyri and want room to spread out in, it's worth considering renting an **apartment**.

Ás, Hafnarstræti 77 (☎461 2249, fax 461 3810). Conveniently situated opposite the bus station a few of the five rooms in this guesthouse have views out over the fjord, as well as access to kitchen facilities. Sleeping-bag accommodation 1900kr, ②.

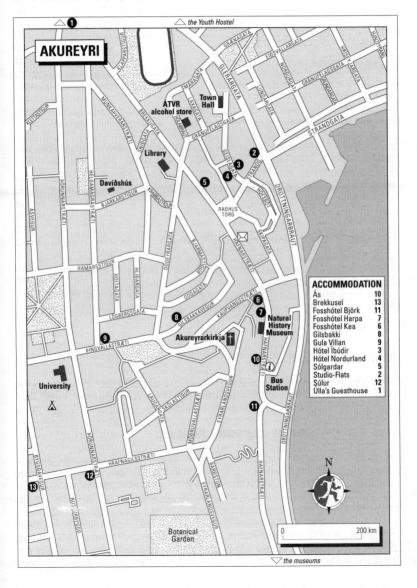

ACCOMMODATION

Ás	10
Brekkusel	13
Fosshótel Björk	11
Fosshótel Harpa	7
Fosshótel Kea	6
Gilsbakki	8
Gula Villan	9
Hótel Íbúdir	3
Hótel Nordurland	4
Sólgardar	5
Studio-Flats	2
Súlur	12
Ulla's Guesthouse	1

Brekkusel, Hrafnagilsstræti 23 (☎ 461 2660 or ☎462 3961, fax 462 3660). A pleasant suburban guesthouse, handy for the town swimming pool, with its own garden and outdoor hot pot. The clean rooms are simple in style, though the omnipresent pink colour scheme is rather intrusive. Breakfast is extra. Sleeping-bag accommodation 1900kr, ②.

Fosshótel Björk, Hafnarstræti 67 (☎461 3030). Located in a house virtually opposite the bus station, in a black- and white-painted house, this is the best of the three Fosshótels in town. All rooms are en suite and have good views out over the fjord, though they are somewhat small for the price. ⑤.

Fosshótel Harpa, Hafnarstræti 85 (☎461 1400, fax 462 7795). Not quite as upmarket at its neighbour, the *Kea*, but a little cheaper, though most of the modern en-suite rooms are functional and unstylish. ⑤.

Fosshótel Kea, Hafnarstræti 87–89 (☎460 2000, fax 460 2080). The largest and most expensive hotel in Akureyri with modern, comfortable en-suite rooms kitted out with satellite TV and a minibar, though the feel is somewhat sterile. Rooms at the front have good views of the town, however. ⑥.

Gilsbakki, Gilsbakkavegur 13 (☎461 2362, fax 461 2723). A good, reliable guesthouse in a quiet suburban street overlooking the town, with three decent rooms sleeping one to three, though breakfast isn't included. ②.

Gula Villan, Þingvallastræti 14 (☎461 2860, fax 461 3040). Five rooms in a guesthouse, with kitchen and TV facilities, opposite the swimming pool on a busy road leading out of town. Sleeping-bag accommodation 1900kr, ②.

Hótel Íbúdir, Geislagata 10 (☎462 3727 or mobile ☎892 9838, fax 462 2300). Pleasant two- to four-room apartments with sitting room and kitchen, usefully located within two minutes' of Ráðhústorg. A two-room affair costs 8000kr per night.

Hótel Norðurland, Geislagata 7 (☎462 2600, fax 462 7962). A good location for this hotel, within easy striking distance of the main square, though the en-suite rooms are rather dreary. Breakfast is included. ⑤.

Sólgarðar, Brekkugata 6 (☎461 1133). Four highly recommended, bright and spacious rooms with TV and access to a kitchen, just one minute from the main square. Breakfast here isn't included. Sleeping-bag accommodation 1300kr, ①.

Studio-Flats, Strandgata 13 (☎461 2035 or mobile ☎894 1335, fax 461 1227). Well-appointed flats right in the heart of the town centre, sleeping up to six, each with own kitchen, shower, TV and telephone. A two-room flat costs 6500kr.

Súlur, Þórunnarstræti 93 (☎461 1160, fax 461 3077). Summer-only (June–Sept) rooms in a guesthouse, with self-catering facilties available, in a guesthouse near the campsite and the botanical garden, a fifteen-minute walk from the centre. Sleeping-bag accommodation 1900kr, ②.

Úlla's Guesthouse, Langahlíð 6 (☎462 3472). Just three simple rooms here, close to the youth hostel north of the centre, on a quiet suburban road that's fifteen minutes' walk from the main square.

The Town: north of Kaupvangsstræti

North of Kaupvangsstræti, the pedestrianized **Hafnarstræti**, the main shopping street, runs to Akureyri's main square, **Ráðhústorg**. This modest street, no more than 150m in length, and its parallel neighbour to the east, Skipargata, together contain virtually all the shops and services that the town has to offer and it's within this rectangle that you'll spend much of your time.

From Ráðhústorg itself, a couple of diversions are within easy striking distance. From the square's northwestern corner, Brekkugata leads up to the **library** (Mon–Fri 10am–7pm; plus Tues & Thurs 10am–8.30pm mid-June to Sept; and Sat 10am–3pm Oct–May), a veritable haven on rainy afternoons with numerous

KEA

Spend any time in and around Akureyri and you can't fail to notice the ubiquitous **KEA** logo, plastered on supermarkets, fishing boats and even Kaffibrensla Akureyrar, the town's coffee-roasting plant. It's said locally that KEA, the Kaupfélag Eyfirðinga Akureyri (Cooperative Society of Eyjafjörður and Akureyri), owns everything except the church and, whilst that's not strictly true, the columns of KEA entries in the phone book gives a good indication of the size of the operation. Established in June 1886 by local farmers keen to win a better price for their wool and meat, ten years later the society opened its first co-op store and never looked back. Today the cooperative is the biggest employer in the region, owning eighty percent of all local retail businesses, concentrating on the food and merchandise sectors. Expansion projects are already well advanced, although quite what the people of Reykjavík will make of plans by their country cousins to rebuild the long-distance bus station in the capital and add a shopping centre to the site, which KEA now owns, remains to be seen.

books in English about Iceland. From here, head south into Oddeyrargata, first right into Krabbastígur and finally left into Bjarkarstígur to reach the austere building at no. 6 known informally as **Davíðshús** (mid-June to Aug 3–5pm; free), the former home of one of Iceland's most famous poets, novelists and playwrights, **Davíð Stefánsson**. Born in 1895 to the north of Akureyri, he published his first anthology of poems at the age of 24 and went on to write verse and novels that were often critical of the state. It was only after his death in 1964 that Davíd was finally taken into Icelanders' hearts and is now regarded as one of the country's greatest writers. Inside, in addition to his many books that adorn the walls, are many of his personal effects, including his piano and writing desk as he left them.

From the top of Bjarkarstígur, the long, straight Helgamagrastræti, named after Helgi Magri (Helgi the Lean), the first settler in the Eyjafjörður region, leads south to Þingvallastræti and the town's excellent outdoor **swimming pool**, which has two large pools, hot spots, a steam room and a **sauna** (1–9.30pm; women only Thurs; men only Fri) and an absolute treat when the sun is shining. Head east down Þingvallastræti and you'll come to the **Art Museum** at Kaupvangsstræti 24 (Tues–Sun 2–6pm; free). Inside is a collection of work from local artists as well as a number of studios where workshops are occasionally held.

It's worth venturing east of the commercial centre of town to explore the harbourside, best reached along the main road, Drottningarbraut, running parallel to Skipagata. Although the small southern harbour, **Akureyrarhöfn**, is close to the junction of Drottningarbraut and Kaupvangstræt, it's really along **Strandgata**, which runs along the harbour's northern edge, where the industrial face of Akureyri becomes more prominent. The shipyard and freighter terminal here make up the largest commercial port outside Reykjavík, a bustling part of town where the clanking of cranes accompanies the seemingly endless unloading and loading of ocean-going vessels at the dockside. In summer it's not uncommon for cruise liners to be moored in the fjord opposite the docks here, awaiting the return of passengers who have been whisked ashore by a flotilla of small boats.

The Town: south of Kaupvangsstræti

Although Akureyri is far from ostentatious, you can't miss the dramatic **Akureyrarkirkja** (daily 10am–noon & 2–4pm), whose twin towers loom over the town, perched on a hill up a flight of steps from the junction of Hafnarstræti and Kaupvangsstræti. Comparisons with Hallgrímskirkja in Reykjavík (see p.59) are unavoidable, especially since both were designed by the same architect, Guðjón Samúelsson, and not only tower over neighbouring buildings but are modelled on basalt columns. Inside, there's are some dazzling stained-glass windows, the central panes of which are originally from the old Coventry cathedral in Britain – removed, with remarkable foresight, at the start of World War II before it was demolished during bombing raids, and sold to an Icelandic dealer who came across them in an antiques shop in London. The church's other stained-glass windows depict scenes from Icelandic history and legends.

A pathway leads round the church to **Sigurhæðir**, at Eyrarlandsvegur 3 (mid-June to Aug daily 2–4pm; free), the former home of **Matthías Jochumsson**, the distinguished poet and author of the Icelandic national anthem. Now a museum containing a small and unexceptional collection of his furnishings and a few portraits, the house was built in 1902 and was his home until his death in 1920. Unless you have a burning desire to immerse yourself in obscure Icelandic poetry, however, it's better to walk right on by, passing close to the university specialising, amongst other things, in degrees in fisheries, and head instead for the glorious **Botanical Gardens** (June–Sept Mon–Fri 8am–10pm, Sat & Sun 9am–10pm; free), known locally as Lystigarður Akureyrar, at the end of Eyrarlandsvegur. Established in 1912 by Margrethe Schiöth, a Danish woman who lived in Akureyri, the gardens are a rich display of plant life enclosed by that Icelandic rarity, fully grown trees. Besides virtually every Icelandic species, there's an astonishing number of sub-tropical plants from South America and Africa – seemingly defying nature by existing at all in these high latitudes, the annual mean temperature for Akureyri being barely 3.4°C. In summer, when the fragance of hundreds of flowers hangs in the air, the gardens, with undisturbed views out over the fjord, are a real haven of peace and tranquility. Incidentally, the dozens of kids you'll see around the gardens, and indeed the rest of Akureyri, are there on behalf of the town council, keeping the place tidy and earning a little pocket money in the process.

Below the gardens is the oldest part of Akureyri, and many of its wooden buildings, including several along Aðalstræti, to the southeast, have been preserved and turned into museums. The first, however, is the least interesting: the **Good Templars Museum**, or Friðbjarnarhús (June–Aug Sat & Sun 1–5pm; free), at no. 46, where the first Icelandic Good Templars Order was founded in 1884 – an occasion recorded inside with uninteresting documents and photos. The museum is named after a local book merchant, Friðbjörn Steinsson, who once lived here.

Further on, at Aðalstræti 54, the black wooden house with white window frames is **Nonnahús** (June to mid-Sept daily 10am–5pm; 200kr), the childhood home of **Jón Sveinsson** – Nonni is the diminutive form of Jón in Icelandic – the Jesuit priest and author of the *Nonni* children's books. Based on his experiences of growing up in northern Iceland, the stories are little known to English-speaking audiences but are are inordinately popular in German-speaking countries – most were written in German – and are translated into around forty other languages. Nonni lived here until he was twelve, when, following his father's death, he moved first to

Denmark, where he became Roman Catholic, then to France and then, in 1914, to Austria, where he wrote his first book, before moving to Germany. Inside the house illustrations from his stories decorate the walls and numerous translations of his dozen books are displayed. Dating from 1850, the house itself is one of the oldest in the town and still has its original furniture, giving a good indication of the living conditions at the time of construction; note the low ceilings and narrow door-ways, which were designed to keep the heat in. Incidentally, when Nonni lived here, the fjord stretched right up to his front door – all the area east of the house, where the main road now runs, is reclaimed land.

A few strides on is the **Akureyri Museum** (mid-June to mid-Sept daily 11am–5pm, rest of the year Sun 2–4pm; 300kr) at Aðalstræti 58, set back a little from the street behind a well-tended garden. The upper floor of the museum has a good assortment of farming and fishing items from Akureyri and Eyjafjörður's past, plus a spectacular wooden pulpit from 1768, which once proudly stood in the church at nearby Kaupangur, hand-painted in subtle greens and blues and bedecked with painted flowers by local Jón Hallgrímsson. Downstairs, an exhibition detailing how the town has developed from the 1700s to the present day contains a glorious jumble of TV sets, typewriters, radiograms and some splendid Art Deco ashtrays.

Heading back towards the town centre, and close to the bus station at the junction of Hafnarstræti and Aðalstræti, Laxdalshús, at Hafnarstræti 11, is the oldest building in Akureyri and is worth a quick glance as you pass. Built in 1795, the grand old wooden structure was home to merchants and their agents virtually without interruption until 1933. Closeby, the **Natural History Museum** (June to mid-Sept daily 10am–5pm, rest of the year Sun 1–4pm; 150kr), a few steps further at Hafnarstræti 81, contains a remarkably wide-ranging collection of both Icelandic and European flora and fauna, including pickled fish, mosses and even a walrus skull. However, it's the display of stuffed animals and birds that really excites the curators, everything from an arctic fox to a wigeon (a species of duck) – you name it, they've got it stuffed.

Kjarnaskógur

Not content with the trees that line most of Akureyri's streets, locals have now planted an entire forest on former farmland roughly an hour's walk south of the town. **Kjarnaskógur**, easily reached by walking south on Drottningarbraut past the airport, is a favourite recreational spot for locals at weekends and on summer evenings, when the air is heavy with the scent of pine. Although birch and larch predominate, there are over fifty species of shrubs and trees here, some of which have grown to over 12m in height, quite a feat for a country where trees rarely reach little more than waist height – witness the long-standing Icelandic joke about what to do when you get lost in an Icelandic forest (answer: you stand up). Within the forest there are easy walking paths complete with picnic sites, a jogging track for the more energetic, which doubles as a skiing trail in winter, plus a children's play area. Camping is not permitted here.

Eating and drinking

Unless you're arrived directly from Reykjavík, you'll feel quite dizzy at the wide choice of eateries in Akureyri. Thanks to the town's small university and its role as a commercial centre for the entire north coast, there's now a fair choice of cafés and restaurants – even the odd bar or two. In short, indulge yourself before moving on.

Cafés and restaurants

Bing Dao, Strandgata 49. Akureyri's only Chinese restaurant close to the harbourside serving up reasonable, if not overly authentic, dishes.

Bláa Kannan, Hafnarstræti 96. No-smoking café in an old wooden building on the main street, good for a cup of coffee or a bite to eat during the day, and popular with local shoppers.

Café Karolína, Kaupvangsstræti 23. Akureyri's most stylish café with works of art hanging from the walls, popular with budding artists and trendy students. Known for its creative fusion cuisine mixing the best of Icelandic and world dishes.

Café Kverið, Hafnarstræti 95. Located in the far corner of the bookstore, Bókval, and good for a coffee whilst browsing.

Fidlarinn, Skipagata 14. Top-notch restaurant overlooking the harbour and the fjord serving expensive but delicious fish from 1500kr and lamb from 2400kr. If you've looking to treat yourself, this is the place to come.

Greifinn, Glerárgata 20. Close to the youth hostel, this pizza and pasta joint makes a welcome change from the ubiquitous *Pizza 67* chain, although the prices aren't too different. Their lunch-time special involves a pizza and salad, or the fish of the day, for 1000kr.

Kaffi Akureyri, Strandgata 7. More bar than café, with a wooden interior touched off by a parquet floor and window blinds. A spacious place popular of an evening for a drink or a coffee, with occasional live music at weekends.

Pizza 67, Geislagata 7. A firm favourite among travellers for its wide choice of pizzas and decent prices. Outdoor seating is available in summer.

Rósagarðurinn, Hafnarstræti 87–89 inside the *Fosshótel Kea*. A good choice for excellent fish or lamb, renowned for its extensive though pricey menu.

Bars and nightlife

Góði Dátinn, Geislagata 14. Dance club where you'll find virtually every young person in Akureyri on Thursday to Sunday evenings grooving to the latest tunes or to live music. Beer in the club is more expensive than in the basement bar, *Ölkjallarinn* (see below).

Græni Hatturinn, Hafnarstræti 96. A popular, evenings-only British-style pub in the basement of the *Bláa Kannan* (see above), and good for a beer (around 550kr).

Ölkjallarinn, Geislagata 14. Great basement bar inside the *Gódi Dátinn* club complex (see above) serving the cheapest beer in Akureyri at 350kr.

Ráðhús Kaffi, Ráðhústorg 7. Red velvet curtains, heavy wooden tables and a floor of green tiles create a trendy atmosphere popular with Akureyri's young things who congregate here from early evening onwards. Occasional DJs, plus a small dance floor.

Við Pollinn, Strandgata 49. An attractive pub located by the harbour in one of the town's oldest buildings, great for a drink before a night out.

Listings

Airlines Flugfélag Íslands, at the airport (☎460 7000).

Bookshops Bókval, Hafnarstræti 91–93, is good for maps and guidebooks. For second-hand books, go to Fornbókabúdin Fródi, Kaupvangsstræti 19.

Cinemas Nyja Bíó, Strandgata 2 (☎461 4666); and Borgarbíó, Holarbraut (☎462 3500).

Emergencies Doctor ☎852 3221; police ☎462 3222.

Hospital The hospital on Eyrarlandsvegur has a 24hr accident-and-emergency ward (☎463 0100).

Laundry Þvottahúsið Höfði, Hafnarstræti 34.
Library Brekkugata 17 (☎462 4141).
Police Þórunnarstræti 138.
Post office Skipagata 10 (☎460 2600).
Supermarket KEA, Byggðavegur 98, close to the campsite.
Travel agent Nonni Travel, Brekkugata 5.

Western Eyjafjörður

Running up **Eyjafjörður**'s western flank from Akureyri, Route 82 affords stunning views over icy waters to the glacier-formed mountains which serve as a protective wall all around the fjord. If you have time, it's well worth making the trip from Akureyri to see not only the mountains but also the rich farmland hereabouts, which is heavily grazed during the summer by cattle and sheep. The long hours of daylight in this part of Iceland, coupled with mild temperatures, make excellent growing conditions for various crops, and the small white dots you'll see in the fields are barrel-shaped bundles of hay, neatly packaged in white plastic, to provide the animals with much needed food during the long months of winter. The highlight of any trip up the fjord is the island of **Hrísey**, noted for its thousands of **wild ptarmigan**, found near the mouth of Eyjafjörður and overlooked by the fishing village of **Dalvík**, itself the starting point for some excellent hiking. Beyond here, a dark tunnel slices through the exposed headland, Ólafsfjardarheidi, to reach the isolated village of **Ólafsfjörður**, although with few attractions itself, it does have an splendid end-of-the-world feeling about it thanks to its location overlooking the Arctic Ocean.

Dalvík

DALVÍK, a nondescript fishing village 42km north of Akureyri with just 1500 inhabitants, enjoys a superbly sheltered location on the western shores of Eyjafjörður overlooking the island of Hrísey (see p.211). Paradoxically though, its poor natural harbour hampered the growth of the fishing industry here until a new harbour was built in 1939 to remedy matters, today used as the departure point for the twice weekly **ferry to Grímsey** (☎461 3600; see p.218 for times). A major shipbuilding and fish-curing centre early in the twentieth century, today Dalvík has lost its buzz, and its quiet **harbour** front, lined by the main road, **Hafnarbraut**, stands guard over the familiar cluster of uniformly shaped modern homes that are so prevalent in the country's smaller communities. Dalvík's lack of older buildings is due to the devastating **earthquake** of 1934, measuring 7.2 on the Richter Scale, which demolished half the structures in the village and caused serious damage to the ones that did survive – two thousand people lost their homes.

The village is really only visited by people en route to neighbouring Hrísey, but should you find yourself with time to kill whilst waiting for the ferry from nearby Árskógssandur take a quick look inside the folklore museum, **Byggðasafnið Hvoll** (June to mid-Sept daily 1–5pm; ☎466 1497; 200kr), one block behind the harbour on Karlsbraut; you'll easily spot the building as it's painted bright red. Divided into four small sections, it's the collection of photographs and personal belongings of Iceland's tallest man, Jóhann Kristinn

HIKES AROUND DALVÍK

Surrounded by magnificient mountain peaks readily accessed through the gentle Svarfaðardalsá valley, which begins at the *Árgerði* guesthouse (see opposite) a short distance south of the town, the scenery around Dalvík makes it one of the best places around Eyjafjörður for hiking. The summer **weather** in this part of the country is often quite stable, making for good walking conditions. Although the valley is popular with locals in summer and autumn for its blueberries and crowberries, which grow in abundance, it's the **whortleberry** that dominates and, after the few short but generally sunny summer months, the bushes turn purple, filling the entire valley with burning colour. Further up the valley, as the land rises, scrub and dwarf birch trees are seen in abundance.

The best **long-distance hike**, lasting two to three or four days, leads over the Heljardalsheiði plateau from Dalvík to the episcopal seat at **Hólar í Hjaltadal** (see p.198). From the *Árgerði*, two roads lead up through Svarfaðardalsá valley as they follow the river: **Route 807** heads up the southern side, whereas **Route 805** hugs the northern bank (no public transport along either). Both meet after roughly 10km at the foot of the wedge-shaped **Stóll**, a mountain dividing the valley in two, though note that the northern road Route 805 is in better condition and is a few kilometres shorter. From here, Route 805 continues another 10km southwest past a couple of farms before petering out, at which point it becomes a track and heads up over the flat-topped mountains of the **Tröllskagi** peninsula, which separates Eyjafjörður from its western neighbour, Skagafjörður, heading for **Hólar**, passing through some of Iceland's best mountain scenery. It should take two or three days to reach this point, but you'll need another half-day to reach the main road, Route 76 (see below), itself reached along Route 767 from here. From Route 76, evening buses head off to Siglufjörður every Monday, Wednesday and Friday from June to September, while during the same months on Tuesday and Thursday mornings, plus Sunday afternoons, there are services to Reykjavík.

North of the Svarfaðardalsá valley, a shorter **day hike** (around 20km in total) leads from Dalvík to nearby Ólafsfjörður via the old road named Drangaleið, once used by locals to reach their northern neighbour. Since the path crosses the Drangar ridge, which is very steep, it's not recommended for anyone who suffers from vertigo. The trail starts a couple of kilometres north of Dalvík, reached by heading north along Route 82 north from town to just south of the now deserted farm, Karlsá, at the foot of the Karlsá, where it flows into Eyjafjörður. Follow the river up through the Karlsádalur valley towards the steep mountain ridge of Drangar (964m), which you'll see in front of you. From here, the track heads east over the ridge to the Burstárbrekkudalur valley, then descends into Ólafsfjörður. A bus (Mon–Fri) returns from Ólafsfjörður at 4.35pm to Dalvík and Akureyri.

Pétursson, born in nearby Svarfaðardalur valley in 1913, that catches the eye. Measuring a whopping 2.34 metres in height (7 feet 7 inches), Jóhann the Giant, as he was known locally, spent most of his life performing in circuses in Europe and America before retiring to Dalvík, where he died in 1984. The museum also contains a collection of birds' eggs, several species of stuffed seabirds and a stuffed polar bear.

The excellent outdoor **swimming pool**, with its mountain backdrop, also has a mixed steam room; it's on Svarfaðarbraut, which runs roughly parallel with Hafnarbraut.

Practicalities

The best place to stay, the friendly *Árgerði* **guesthouse** (☎466 3326; ②) is a fifteen-minute walk south of Dalvík along Route 82 towards Akureyri, in the Svarfaðardalur valley. Beautifully set beside a nature reserve, next to a small river that tumbles down from the mountain tops behind the guesthouse, all eight rooms here are tastefully appointed with plain carpets and light-coloured walls and offer serene views of the surrounding hills. Otherwise, and very much second best for its box-like rooms, *Sæluvist* (☎466 3088 or 466 3188; ③), is in the village at Stórhólsvegur 6, a five-minute walk west along Sunnutún just north of the post office on Hafnarbraut. From June to August, sleeping-bag accommodation (1900kr) is available in the village school, *Grunnskóli*, on Mímisvegur, two blocks south of Stórhóltsvegur. The **campsite** (☎466 3233; free) next door is administered by the swimming pool.

There are two **places to eat** in Dalvík, with little to choose between them. First up is the *Café Menning*, on the main road at Hafnarbraut 14, open for lunch and dinner, which serves pizzas, fish and other light dishes for around 1000kr; a beer here costs 500kr. The *Valensia* seafood restaurant, meanwhile, further west along the main road at Skíðabraut 46, although sounding more upmarket, has essentially the same food on offer at the same prices and opens only in the evening. The décor here is marginally better, with the old black-and-white photographs on the walls of fishermen posing in their best oilskins.

Hrísey

No trip to the north coast of Iceland is complete without seeing the thousands of **ptarmigan** on **HRÍSEY**, a flat teardrop-shaped island at the mouth of Eyjafjörður, reached by ferry from Árskógssandur, about 10km southeast of Dalvík. Although the country's second-largest island (Heimaey in the Westman Islands is the biggest; see p.123), at 6.5km long and 2.5km wide, it's home to barely two hundred people. However, it's also the habitat for more ptarmigan than anywhere else in Iceland, since here they're protected by law and there are no natural predators – such as mink or foxes – on the island. As a result, the birds are very tame and roam the entire island, and you'll spot them in the picturesque village here, laying their eggs in people's gardens or, particularly in August after the breeding season, strolling down the main street with a string of fluffy chicks in tow.

The island's history, however, is more tied to fish than birds and its population peaked at 340 in the mid-twentieth century, when fishing boats from across the country landed their catches in the tiny harbour, making it the second largest herring port on the north coast, after Siglufjörður. Since then things have declined, and in 1999 the main source of employment, the fish-processing factory down at the harbour, which once provided the British supermarkets with fresh North Atlantic fish, closed with the loss of dozens of redundancies, and over thirty people left the island to look for work in Akureyri and Reykjavík. Today, it's the Icelandic National Quarantine Centre, established in 1974 so that stocks of Galloway cattle could be imported from Scotland, that keeps many islanders in employment. Vegetation on the island is particularly lush in summer, since all animals on the island were slaughtered for health reasons when the quarantine centre opened. **Reafforestation** has also begun in a couple of areas, in an attempt to protect the thin layer of soil atop the basalt rock of which Hrísey is formed from further erosion.

Hrísey **village** is tiny, consisting of two or three parallel streets perched on a small hill above the walled **harbour**. Brightly painted houses, unfortunately all of them modern and block-like, look out over the fjord and the handful of small boats that bob up and down in the tiny port. Otherwise, there's a miniscule outdoor **swimming pool** on the main street, Norðurvegur, at the eastern end of the village; at just 12.5m in length, it's heated by geothermal water from Hrísey's very own borehole on the west coast. Even though the village can easily be walked around in 10min there's a map down on the harbourside.

Once you've explored the village, there's some wonderful **walking** to be had along a track that heads north across the island; it begins just ten minutes from the village at the southeastern corner of the island, beyond the couple of colourful private summer cottages that look out over the fjord from the southern coast. Stick to the path, because permission is required to venture into the surrounding heathland where the ptarmigan breed – ask at the guesthouse (see below) for the latest situation regarding the breeding season. It takes roughly an hour to reach the northern top of the island, which is an important breeding ground for the **eider duck**. Unfortunately for visitors, Hrísey also has the largest breeding colony of **arctic tern** in Europe (see box), which means you'll pretty much need hard hats if you get too close to their nesting sites.

Practicalities

A **ferry** shuttles between Árskógssandur on the mainland (where there's a twice daily bus connection Mon–Fri with Akureyri, Dalvík and Ólafsfjörður) and Hrísey every hour 9.30am to 11.30pm from May to August, and every two hours from 9.30am to 9.30pm from September to April (a 15min trip; 250kr single). The island's only **guesthouse**, *Brekka* (☎466 1751 or ☎466 1784; ②), a wooden building painted bright yellow up on the hill behind the harbour at Brekkugata 5, has just three doubles, but if those are full the owners will endeavour to find a room in a private house somewhere in the village. Lunch here, in the **restaurant** overlooking the sea and the jagged mountains of the western shore of Eyjafjörður, is truly excellent; try the fresh halibut with lobster and asparagus (1580kr) or, more adventurously, the pan-fried breast of guillemot in blueberry sauce with red-wine poached figs (1450kr). The **campsite** is located beside the swimming pool on Norðurvegur. The only other facilities are a **grocery** store, Snekkjan, at Sjávargata 2, which also has coffee and light meals, and a bank with a cash machine on Skólavegur.

Ólafsfjörður

From Dalvík, Route 82 winds its way north for 17km to the fishing village of **ÓLAFSFJÖRÐUR**, clinging all the way to the steep slopes of the mountains that plunge into the steely waters of Eyjafjörður, and with superb views of the snowy peaks of the uninhabited Látraströnd coastline on the opposite shore. On a clear day it's easily possible to spot the **Arctic Circle**, which cuts through the island of Grímsey (see p.216), northeast of the fjord's mouth. The village is connected to Akureyri by means of a single lane, claustrophobic, 3.4-kilometre tunnel through the Ólafsfjarðarmúli headland, which divides Eyjafjörður from its smaller cousin, Ólafsfjörður, which gives the settlement its name. On emerging into daylight and turning the corner into Ólafsfjörður, it's not hard to see why the tunnel was necessary – this really is the end of the road, an isolated fishing village walled in by sheer mountains.

Although the drive to Ólafsfjörður and its setting is breathtaking, the village, unfortunately, isn't, an unattractive, workaday place of just a thousand people, set behind the **harbour** on Sjávargata, one block northeast of the main road, **Aðalgata**, where one or two trawlers are moored. There's little here to detain you other than the taxidermist's dream, the well-stocked natural-history museum, **Náttúrgripasafn** at Aðalgata 14 (June–Aug Tues–Sun 1–5pm; Sept–May by arrangement with Sparisjóður bank, in the same building; 200kr), containing the usual suspects – everything from a ringed seal to a stuffed polar bear shot by a local fisherman off Grímsey as he saw it approaching his boat balancing precariously on a piece of pack ice. With over one hundred and forty bird species stuffed for posterity, you'll at least learn the names of some of the living birds you'll see in the wild; pick up the free museum catalogue for the English translations.

Practicalities

Buses to Ólafsfjörður arrive at the only **hotel** in the village, the predictably named and drab *Hótel Ólafsfjörður* (☎466 2400, fax 466 2660; ④), at Bylgjubyggð 2. Doubles here are cramped and so plainly furnished they resemble a school dorm rather than an expensive hotel. Much better are the wooden **cabins** with kitchen and shower, opposite the hotel, where a room costs 8500kr, or, for groups of three or more, 11,000kr buys the entire cabin. The hotel **restaurant** serves simple meals, mostly hamburgers and pizzas though with a little cajoling you may be able to persuade them to rustle up something fishy. The café and restaurant, *Heimaval*, at Ægisgata 10, two blocks west of Aðalgata and right next to the harbour, is popular with local fishermen and the best bet for decent food – fresh fish and light snacks here go for around 1000kr – and a cup of coffee during the day. Alternatively, there's a small **grocery** store, Strax, at the corner of Sjávargata and Aðalgata, next to the harbour. The **swimming pool** and the **campsite** are together, just off Hornbrekkuvegur which heads south from Aðalgata.

If you're thinking of moving on to Siglufjörður from Ólafsfjörður along **Route 82**, which continues southwest from the village up over the flat-topped mountains of Tröllaskagi, be aware that it's essentially a poor, unsurfaced, summer-only track, which closes with even the lightest of snowfalls; out of season, ask at the hotel about its condition, and if in doubt, don't risk it.

Eastern Eyjafjörður

The eastern shore of Eyjafjörður offers something quite rare in Iceland – remote, uninhabited wilderness that is relatively easily accessible from a major town.

North of the small village of **Grenivík**, now the only centre of population on the eastern side of the fjord, the perpetually snow-capped **Látraströnd** coastline is made up of some of the most rugged mountains in the north of Iceland, including the peak of **Kaldbakur** (1167m), which dominates any view of the eastern shore. Excellent and challenging **hiking** routes lead through the wilderness to now abandoned farms which, until World War II, made up some of the country's most remote and desolate communities, where life was a constant struggle against the elements in this area of unforgiving Arctic fjordland, known here as Í Fjördum. The region's other attraction, however, is not nearly so remote: the unusual five-gabled turf farmhouse and church at **Laufás**, 10km south of Grenivík and close to the Ringroad.

Laufás

Although there's no public transport going all the way to **Laufás** (June to mid-Sept daily 10am–6pm; 200kr), a superb example of a nineteenth-century turf farmhouse, 30km northeast of Akureyri, it's worth making the effort to get here. Dating from 1850, the building is timber fronted and has five gabled rooves, all made of turf, giving the impression that it's composed of several separate cottages all joined under one roof. The most remarkable feature, however, is the fabulous herringbone arrangement of turf pieces used to make up part of the front wall. Inside, sadly, is the usual array of mind-numbing how-we-used-to-live parapher-nalia, showing household and farm life from the days when the house was used as a manor farm and a parsonage for the next door **church**, which dates from 1865; the local priest shared the building with his labourers.

From Akureyri, **buses** to Lake Mývatn and Egilsstaðir run along the Ringroad to the junction with Route 83, from where you could either walk or hitch the final 13km to the farm.

Grenivík

Ten kilometres northwest of Laufás, **GRENIVÍK** is a modern fjordside village, which only began life in 1910. Although improvements to the tiny **harbour**, around which the village is situated, brought about a slight increase in trade and thus population, there are still only around 260 people who call the place home. It's principal use is as a starting and finishing point for **hikes** along the fjord to Látraströnd and the Í Fjördum region of the north coast (see box opposite), although there is a **snack bar** in the centre of the village, at Túngata 3, and a **swimming pool** next to the school. For **accommodation**, rooms are available to rent at *Miðgarðar*, at Miðgarður 4 (☎463 3223, fax 463 3260; sleeping-bag accom-modation 1000kr, ②), where breakfast is an extra 700kr. Simple fish meals are also available in the small **restaurant** here. The **campsite** is next to the swim-ming pool beside the village school.

Eyjafjarðardalur

South of Akureyri, beyond the head of Eyjafjörður, **Eyjafjarðardalur** is the wide fertile floodplain surrounding the Eyjafjarðará, which flows down the valley from its source near Nyjarbæjarafrétt, up in the country's Interior. An extensive range of crops are grown here and the animals that graze here produce twenty percent of Iceland's milk. The farms throughout the valley do good business from the rich

HIKING FROM GRENIVÍK TO GJÖGUR

A circular four- to five-day **hike** leads from Grenivík via the Látraströnd coast to the Gjögur headland, guarding the eastern entrance to Eyjafjörður, east through the coastal Í Fjördum region to Hvalvatnsfjörður and the beginning of Route F839, which then returns towards Grenivík.

From Grenivík, follow the unnumbered road northwest from the village to the now deserted farm, **Svínarnes**, where the road ends and a track continues along the Látraströnd shoreline, passing several more abandoned farms, including **Látrar**, which has been empty since 1942. The path continues round the **Gjögur** headland and **Gjögurfjall** (710m), leaving Eyjafjörður behind and following the Arctic shore of the Í Fjördum region. The most notable site here is **Keflavík**, one of Iceland's remotest locations, a now deserted farm that was regularly cut off from the rest of the country for weeks and months in the wintertime. At the beginning of the eighteenth century, people on the farm here were taken ill and died one by one as the harsh winter weather set in – all except for an eleven-year-old girl, who remained alone here for ten weeks until people from the nearest farmstead finally managed to dig their way through the heavy snowdrifts to rescue her. Passing **Þorgeirsfjörður**, the path heads southwest for the next fjord, **Hvalvatnsfjörður**, and the beginning of the mountain road back over the hills up to the **Leirdalsheidi** plateau and finally down into Grenivík; there can often be snow along this route until the middle of July.

On certain dates between late April and mid-August it's possible to do this tour in the opposite direction as part of an **organised tour**; for a cost of 28,000kr, the trip includes transport to Hvalvatnsfjörður and back from Svínarnes, breakfast and dinner – and most importantly horses to carry all your equipment. Contact Jón at the snack bar in Grenivík (see opposite) or call ☎463 3236; for information in Icelandic, visit *www.vip.is/fjordungar*.

soil too, with most of Iceland's potatoes grown here, and in good years the country is virtually self-sufficient in this crop. However, bad weather can – and all too often does – wipe out entire harvests. The further inland the valley stretches, the wider it becomes, before getting lost in the foothills of the vast highland plateau generally known as Hálendið that forms the uninhabited centre of the country. It's here that the F821 mountain road begins, as it heads towards the Sprengisandur area of the Interior (see p.280). If you don't have your own transport, note that highland **tours** arranged through a travel agent in Reykjavík (see p.72) provide the only form of transport to the Eyjafjörður valley from Akureyri.

The drive around the wide Eyjafjörður valley (Routes 821 and 829 run either side of the Eyjafjarðará meeting up 8km south of Grund, see below) offers a chance to escape the mountains that box in so many Icelandic villages and to enjoy wide open vistas of rolling farmland and undisturbed views of the **midnight sun**; the upper reaches of the valley are one of the most enjoyable spots from which to watch the sun dip to the horizon over some of Iceland's greenest countryside, then skim the North Atlantic before rising again towards the east. There are few specific sights – instead, make a trip here to stay on a farm or to enjoy the open countryside around the valley's only real settlement, **HRAFNAGIL**, a mere dot on the map some 12km along Route 821 that runs up the western side of the valley. Home to barely 95 inhabitants, during the time of the Settlement the area around the hamlet was once a chieftain's estate and, later, the residence of Iceland's last Catholic bishop, Jón Arason, although there's nothing today, unfortunately, to attest to the place's historical significance. Five kilometres further south along the same road, the apparantly Byzantine-inspired church in the hamlet of **GRUND**, with its onion-shaped dome and Romanesque mini-spires, is one of the most unusual in Iceland; designed by a local farmer to serve the entire valley, it broke with tradition by being built on a north–south, not east–west, axis. If the church is locked, you'll find the key at the neighbouring farmhouse.

By far and away the best place to stay in the valley is the good *Öngulsstaðir III* **farmstay** (☎463 1380 or ☎463 1227, fax 463 1390; sleeping-bag accommodation 1600kr, ③), whose friendly owners will make you feel at home. The pleasant rooms, simply decorated and en suite, are located in the former cow sheds, whereas the main building, where breakfast (750kr) is served up, is a converted barn. Get here by taking Route 829 (signposted to "Laugaland") up the eastern side of the valley. For **hotel** accommodation there's the **Vin** in Hrafnagil (☎463 1400 or ☎463 1333; sleeping-bag accommodation 1200–1800kr, ③), where breakfast is an extra 750kr.

Grímsey

Forty kilometres north of the mainland, the five-square-kilometre chunk of craggy basalt that defiantly rears up out of the Atlantic is the island of **Grímsey**; straddled by the **Arctic Circle**, where Iceland ends and the Arctic begins. First settled by the Viking **Vestfjarða-Grímur Sigurdsson**, and named after him ("Grímsey" means Grímur's Island), the island supports one tiny settlement, scruffy **Sandvík**, on the southwest coast. Although many come here to cross that magical geographical line (you get a cheesy certificate as proof from the one member of staff who runs the airstrip), it's for the island's amazing birdlife that people come. Sixty or more species, including **puffins**, **razorbills** and **guillemots**, are resident on the island for all or most of the year, found predominantly around the cliffs on the northern and eastern shores, where the din is cacophonous; of these, thirty-six species nest on the island. Take special care when walking around the island since you're likely to be attacked by **arctic tern**, in particular, who will stop at nothing to protect their eggs (see box on p.212).

There's just one road on Grímsey, 3km long, that runs the length of the west coast from the lighthouse at its southernmost point, Flesjar, through the village to the airport at Básar – a total length of 3km. Landing here in one of the light aircraft that link the island with Akureyri can be quite an experience, as planes are often forced to buzz over the runway on the initial approach to clear the hundreds of potentially dangerous birds that gather on it before coming in a second time to land. Taking off is no less hazardous – although one of the island's few cars is sometimes driven up and down the runway to achieve the same result.

Sandvík

SANDVÍK is essentially nothing more than a dozen or so houses grouped around a **harbour**, which is where the ferry from Dalvík docks. Southeast of the harbour, the road leads to the community centre, **Múli**, where every year on November 11, the birthday of the island's benefactor, nineteenth-century American chess champion **Daniel Willard Fiske** is celebrated with coffee and cakes. A prominent journalist during the nineteenth century, and a leading scholar on things

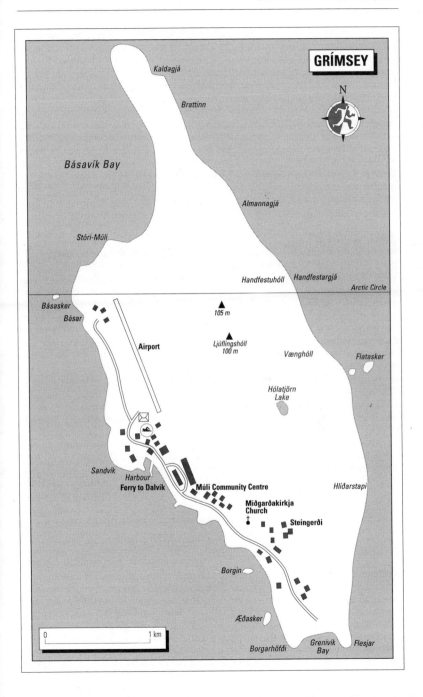

Icelandic, Fiske left the islanders US$12,000 upon his death and gave instruction for a school and library to be built. Oddly, Fiske had never once set foot on Grímsey, but it seems the islanders' reputation as the greatest **chess** players in the whole of Iceland (chess was introduced to Grímsey by the Vikings) furthered his own love of the game; he even donated eleven marble chess sets to the island. The last remaining set can be seen, alongside Fiske's portrait, in the library inside Múli, which stands on the original site of the school he financed. Sadly, hardly anyone plays chess on the island today.

A few steps beyond the community centre, the whitewashed walls of the village **church** cut a sharp image against the heavy skies. It seems to be thanks to one former priest that this isolated community still exists: in 1793, Grímsey came close to being abandoned when a plague swept through the island causing the deaths of many strong and able-bodied men. The six who didn't succumb sailed to the mainland to seek help, but were all drowned when their boat capsized, leaving the priest the only able-bodied man on the island to fulfil his duties.

Practicalities

Arriving on Grímsey by either air or sea will bring you to the west coast; the **airport** and the **harbour** are barely five minutes walk from each other, at the northwestern edge of the tiny village, Sandvík (see above). Most people choose to take one of the **flights** to the island from Akureyri (3 weekly) for the sake of convenience and speed – the trip takes around twenty-five minutes, compared with a total journey time by bus and ferry of four and a quarter hours. However, when the **ferry** runs (6400kr return, 7200kr including bus connection from Akureyri) the little island is often busy – though not overcrowded – with day-trippers. The connecting bus leaves Akureyri on Monday and Thursday at 10am for Dalvík, from where the ferry sails at 11am; it returns on the same days from Grímsey at 5.30pm, arriving in Dalvík at 9pm; a bus then continues to Akureyri, arriving at 9.30pm.

To really appreciate Grímsey's charms you need to stay overnight – simple accommodation is available at the superbly located *Básar* **guesthouse** (☎467 3103; sleeping-bag accommodation 1100kr, ①), whose front door opens out onto the tiny airport runway, whilst the rear of the house has a balcony overlooking the sea. Breakfast is an extra 800kr and, in fact, the guesthouse is the only place to get cooked **food** on the island, too: lunch is 900kr and dinner 1500kr – both consisting of delicious fresh fish. **Camping** is permitted anywhere on the island away from the village. The indoor **swimming pool** is located in the grey building at the eastern end of the runway but it's often closed in summer. Back in the harbour, there's a small cooperative **supermarket** that closes any time between 5pm and 6pm.

Around the island

Setting out from the airport it's possible to **walk round the island** following the path, across the runway. Thereafter, however, it's wise to use the cliff tops as a guide, as the track soon gets lost amid the many springy tussocks, that mark this part of the island as it heads up the hillside to the island's east coast, by far the most dramatic aspect of the island; here sheer cliffs plunge down into the foam and the roaring waves of the Arctic Ocean. The promontory you can see from here, **Eyjarfótur**, stretching out to the north, is a good place to watch the **birds** since it affords good views out over the sea and back over the low fields around the guesthouse and airport where so many species congregate. However, there is no area of the island devoid of birds and simply walking around Grímsey, be it on the cliffs or in the village, will bring you into contact with various varieties of seabirds. Heading south from the headland following the shoreline, the path climbs a little as it goes over **Handfestuhóll** from where you can see the rock fissures, **Almannagjá** and **Handfestargjá**, in the cliff face. Beyond the small islet, **Flatasker**, the coast swings southwest heading for the lighthouse at Grímsey's southeastern point, **Flesjar**. From here the road continues along the west coast into the village and back to the harbour.

travel details

Buses

The bus details given below are relevant for May to September; for winter times, visit *www.bsi.is.*

Akureyri to: Árskógssandur (2 daily; 35min); Blönduós (daily; 2hr); Brú (daily; 4hr); Dalvík (2 daily; 45min); Egilsstaðir (daily; 5hr); Hólmavík (3 weekly; 6hr 30min); Húsavík (4 daily; 1hr 10min); Ísafjörður (3 weekly; 11hr); Mývatn (4 daily; 1hr 45min); Ólafsfjörður (2 daily; 1hr 30min); Reykjavík (daily; 6hr).

Árskógssandur to: Akureyri (2 daily; 35min); Dalvík (2 daily; 10min).

Blönduós to: Akureyri (daily; 2hr); Hofsós (3 weekly; 2hr); Reykjavík (3 weekly; 4hr); Sauðárkrókur (3 weekly; 1hr 15min); Siglufjörður (3 weekly; 3hr).

Brú to: Akureyri (daily; 4hr); Blönduós (daily; 1hr 45min); Hofsós (3 weekly; 3hr 30min); Hólmavík (3 weekly; 2hr 30min); Ísafjörður (3 weekly; 7hr); Reykjavík (2 daily; 2hr); Sauðárkrókur (3 weekly; 2hr 45min); Siglufjörður (3 weekly; 4hr 30min).

Dalvík to: Akureyri (2 daily; 45min); Árskógssandur (2 daily; 10min); Ólafsfjörður (2 daily; 45min).

Hofsós to: Blönduós (3 weekly; 2hr); Brú (3 weekly; 3hr 30min); Reykjavík (3 weekly; 5hr 30min); Sauðárkrókur (3 weekly; 45min); Siglufjörður (3 weekly; 1hr).

Ólafsfjörður to: Akureyri (2 daily; 1hr 30min); Árskógssandur (2 daily; 1hr); Dalvík (2 daily; 45min).

Sauðárkrókur to: Blönduós (3 weekly; 1hr 15min); Brú (3 weekly; 2hr 30min); Hofsós (3 weekly; 45min); Reykjavík (3 weekly; 5hr); Siglufjörður (3 weekly; 1hr 45min).

Siglufjörður to: Blönduós (3 weekly; 3hr); Brú (3 weekly; 4hr 30min); Hofsós (3 weekly; 1hr); Reykjavík (3 weekly; 6hr 30min); Sauðárkrókur (3 weekly; 1hr 45min).

Ferries

Árskógssandur to: Hrísey (hourly May–Aug, every two hours Sept–April; 15min).

Dalvík to: Grímsey (2 weekly; 3hr 15min).

Flights

Akureyri to: Egilsstaðir (3 weekly; 45min); Grímsey (3 weekly; 25min); Ísafjörður (4 weekly; 1hr); Reykjavík (7 daily; 50min); Vopnafjörður (6 weekly; 45min); Þórshöfn (5 weekly; 40min).

CHAPTER SIX

MÝVATN AND THE NORTHEAST

Northeast Iceland – the thinly populated, open expanse between Akureyri and the Eastern Fjords – manages to contain one of Iceland's tourist hotspots while being largely unexplored as a whole. The western part of the region is dominated by the huge, lava-covered Ódáxahraun plateau, which slopes gently from the Interior to the sea, drained by glacial rivers and underground springs; the rest of the land is more varied, with distant peaks rising out of boggy fells and valleys. Tourists, along with most of Iceland's wildfowl population, flock to Mývatn, an attractive lake just over an hour's drive from Akureyri, whose surrounds are thick with hot springs and volcanic formations – many of them still visibly active. A growing number of visitors are also drawn northeast of Mývatn to the impressive canyons and waterfalls at Jökulsárgljúfur National Park, or coastwards to the pleasant town of Húsavík, a prime place to spot whales in summer. Very few, however, bother with the coastal road which runs around from Húsavík to Vopnafjörður; while the rewards here are harder to pin down, it's a great place for purposeless travel, bringing you close to some wild countryside and small, isolated communities – plus the chance to reach the mainland's northernmost tip, which lies fractionally outside the Arctic Circle.

The northeast's **main roads** are the section of Route 1 running east from Akureyri to Mývatn and then across to Egilsstaðir; and Route 85, which mostly follows the coast via Húsavík and Jökulsárgljúfur to Vopnafjörður, before cutting inland and down to the Mývatn–Egilsstaðir stretch of Route 1. Taking them together, you could join them into a circuit from Akureyri, though it's just as easy to continue eastwards out of the region from Vopnafjörður. **Buses**

ACCOMMODATION PRICE CODES

Throughout this guide, prices given for **youth hostels, sleeping-bag accommodation** and **campsites** are per person unless otherwise specified. **Hotel** and **guesthouse** accommodation is graded on a scale from ① to ⑨; all are high-season rates and indicate the cost of the cheapest double room. The price bands to which these codes refer are as follows:

① Up to 4000kr	③ 6000–8000kr	⑤ 10,000–12,000kr	⑦ 15,000–20,000kr
② 4000–6000kr	④ 8000–10,000kr	⑥ 12,000–15,000kr	⑧ Over 20,000kr

(See p.26 for a full explanation.)

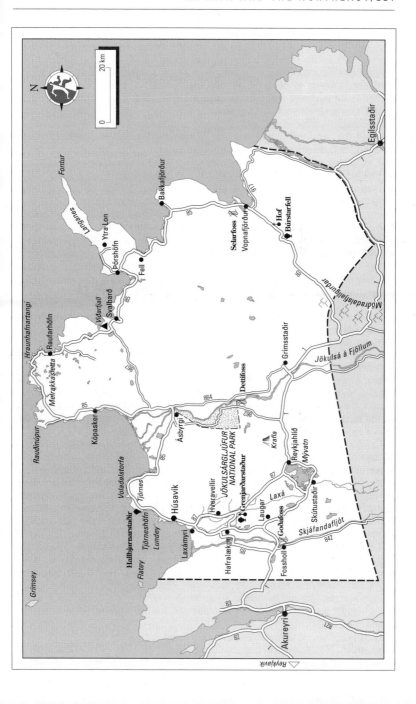

cover both main routes in peak season – roughly June through to September – though at other times services are limited or non-existent; there are also direct **tours** to the area from Reykjavík focusing on Mývatn, and others out of Mývatn and Húsavík. If taking your own transport, note that there are few **fuel stations** between towns, and outside the summer even these may be unattended, with payment made by swiping a credit card on a terminal – it's best to fuel up whenever you can. The main roads are generally sound, though only fragmentarily surfaced and sometimes closed at short notice by snow. Minor roads in the area, while not necessarily needing four-wheel-drives, may only be open for a month or two in summer, so you'll need to find out their condition by asking other visitors or by contacting local information centres before tackling them.

Away from Mývatn and Húsavík, **services** are also thinly spread, though most settlements have at least a bank, a supermarket and somewhere to stay; elsewhere, there are farmstays, a few hostels, and limitless camping opportunities. The northeast's **weather** is much drier and often sunnier than southern Iceland's – and this far north it barely gets dark for three months of the year – though winters are bitterly cold, with heavy snowfalls throughout.

MÝVATN AND AROUND

Around 100km east of Akureyri on Route 1, **Mývatn**, despite the name (it means **Midge Lake**), is one of Iceland's most appealing corners, not only harbouring a veritable treasury of wildlife, but also surrounded by a host of intriguing volcanic formations. Placid and shallow, its unfortunately appropriate name stems from summertime swarms of tiny black **flies**; while visitors seek sanctuary from them behind gauze netting, their larvae provide an abundant food source for both fish and the hundreds of thousands of **wildfowl** which descend on the lake each year to raise their young. All of Iceland's species of duck breed either here or close by on the **Laxá**, Mývatn's fast-flowing, salmon-rich outlet, and one – **Barrow's goldeneye** – nests nowhere else in Europe.

There's plenty more to hold your attention beyond the birds and bugs. Springfed and covering over 36 square kilometres, Mývatn sits on the western side of a major **tectonic fault**, eruptions along which have created an often startling landscape. Mývatn itself reached its current size around 3800 years ago after lava flows dammed and deepened an earlier lake. Long before this, sub-glacial eruptions around 11,000 years ago formed the collection of hulking, flat-topped mountains away to the southeast, while closer to the lakeshore you'll find more recently formed cones, craters and oddly contorted lava. Due east of Mývatn, the land is still smoking and bubbling away at **Bjarnarflag** and **Hverarönd**, though the region's hottest spot lies northeast in the highlands around **Krafla**, where explosively violent fissures were fully active as recently as 1984. All this has made Mývatn a heavily marketed tourist destination – quite a departure from the Middle Ages, when the lake and its steaming surrounds were fearfully dismissed as a pool of the devil's piss – and both the lake and the Laxá are protected as a national reserve.

Most people base themselves at the northern end of the lake at the town of **Reykjahlíð**, Mývatn's small service centre. Here you'll find most of the region's facilities, with a few alternatives dotted elsewhere around the lake – especially at

Skútustaðir on the southern shore. A good **road** circuits Mývatn, with tracks and footpaths elsewhere; without your own transport or the desire to walk, there are numerous **bus tours** offered in season. You could easily spend a week picking over the region, though three days is enough time to take in the main sights – some people even day-trip from Reykjavík by plane.

Mývatn looks its best in summer, but can get very crowded then, with beds in short supply and the **flies** in full force: a few bite, but most just get up your nose or into your eyes – keep them off your face by buying a hat with attached netting. Alternatively, hit a few good days in late spring and, while you'll miss out on some of the bird life, there are no flies, you'll have the place to yourself and could also indulge in **cross-country skiing** to reach some of the sights. If you do this, however, remember that tour operators spend the off-season working elsewhere, and facilities will be limited.

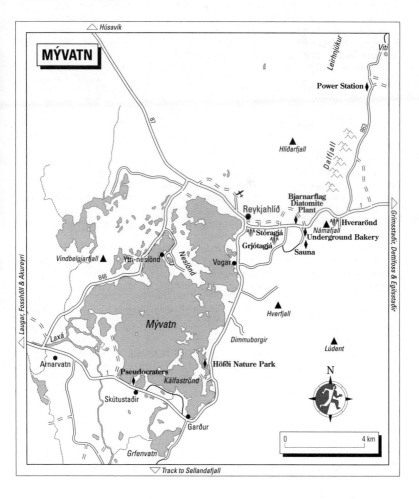

MÝVATN'S DUCKS

In summer, plentiful food and nesting space make Mývatn the best place to see **wild ducks** in northern Europe and, armed with a pair of binoculars and a little patience, you should be able to clock up eighteen species during your stay. Their favourite **nesting area** is in spongy heathland on the northwest side of the lake – not surprisingly, given the country's often treeless environment, all Icelandic ducks are ground-nesting – but as this is closed off during the breeding season you'll have to look elsewhere. Good places to start include Mývatn's southeastern corner; the Laxá outflow on the western side of the lake; and even the shore at Reykjahlíð. **Female** ducks tend to be drably coloured (they need to be camouflaged, as they sit in the open when incubating their eggs): unless otherwise stated, the following descriptions are of breeding **males**.

Two species found here occur only in Iceland and North America. **Barrow's goldeneye** stay at Mývatn all year and are very common: the smart, pied drakes look a little like a scaup or tufted duck, but have a characteristic, comma-shaped white patch between the manic golden eye and bill; females are coloured in a quieter russet and mottled grey plumage. Their courtship displays start in late April: males stretch their necks out towards a potential partner until their beak touches the water, then flick their heads backwards; females respond in a similar manner. Keep an eye open too for their rather cute stripy chicks. The **harlequin duck** has unmistakable chestnut, white and blue plumage, though as indicated by its Icelandic name – *straumönd*, stream duck – is less likely to be seen on the lake than bobbing in and out of rough water on the Laxá. In fact, adult harlequins actually prefer the sea and spend as little time inland as possible, arriving to nest in late April and moving on by mid-July.

Of the other marine ducks spending their summers at Mývatn, most unusual are the **scoter**, a uniquely all-black diving duck, which in Iceland breeds only at Mývatn, and the **long-tailed** or **old squaw**, another strikingly patterned bird with a very long, pointed tail. You'll probably also see **eider**, whose black and white males have subtle pastel pink and green touches on their chests and napes. The eider's bulky build comes into its own at sea, where the birds gather into huge "rafts" and calmly ride out heavy swells, as unsinkable as a fleet of lifeboats. Breeding mostly near the coast through the summer, they pad their nests with special down, and it's this which is commercially collected (after the ducks have moved on) for stuffing cushions, sleeping bags, and the like – a small but profitable business in Iceland.

Otherwise, you'll be fairly familiar with most of Mývatn's ducks, which are primarily freshwater species. Some of the more plentiful include the **mallard**; the long-beaked **merganser** and **goosander**, and the wide-beaked **shoveler**; **wigeon**, with their coppery heads and vertical blond streak between the eyes; the uniformly nondescript **gadwall**; **teals**, who sport a glossy red head and green eyepatch; and the confusingly similar-looking **tufted duck** and **scaup** – both of which have white bodies and black heads, although the tufted duck has a droopy back-swept crest while the scaup has a grey back.

Getting to Mývatn

The quickest way to reach Mývatn is to **fly from Reykjavík or Höfn** into Reykjahlíð. Mýflug Air, based in Reykjahlíð (☎464 4400, fax 464 4401, *www. mmedia.is/myflug*), run a daily service here from Reykjavík from June to August, and from Höfn in July and August. Both flights also link up with an optional bus day tour of the area (see box p.227), allowing you to make a return trip from southern Iceland to Mývatn and pack all its sights in to one very long, exhausting day – though you can, of course, stay longer.

In season, you can also get to Reykjahlíð by **buses** at least daily from Akureyri (mid-May to Sept), Egilsstaðir (June–Aug), and Húsavík (mid-June to Aug); less regular services from Egilsstaðir begin in mid-May, but outside these times there are no buses to Mývatn from anywhere. If you're coming in from Akureyri, it's worth stopping about 40km along at tiny **FOSSHÓLL**, where the ice-blue Skálfandáfljöt (which originates way down south at Vatnajökull) tears through horseshoe-shaped basalt canyons in a pair of **cataracts**. The largest of these, **Goðafoss** (God's Waterfall), is where Þorgeir – the lawspeaker who decided that Christianity should be Iceland's official religion at the historic Alþing in 1000 – destroyed his pagan statues by pushing them over the falls. It's a beautiful spot, and if you decide to stay you'll find that Fosshóll itself comprises little more than a roadhouse, a café-restaurant, and **guesthouse** (☎464 3108, fax 464 3318; sleeping-bag accommodation 1250kr, ①), which also has space for campers. Beyond Fosshóll, the other place to pause before Mývatn is 10km further on at **LAUGAR**, a small town with a **fuel station**, **bank**, and a school where *Fosshótel* run summer **accommodation** (☎464 3340, fax 464 3163; ②). From here, it's another 45km to Reykjahlíð along Route 1, via Mývatn's south and eastern shores.

Reykjahlíð and the lake

Given the number of visitors who invade each summer, **REYKJAHLÍÐ** is a surprisingly small, unassuming place, though there's enough here to keep you busy while getting your bearings. The town sits right at Mývatn's northeastern corner, at the junction of Route 1 and the Húsavík road: coming south down the latter, you first pass the airstrip and **church**, then comes Reykjahlíð's fuel station and small general store. The town's few streets are laid out east of here; there's a clutch of residential homes and then, isolated 250m behind them, the **swimming pool** (200kr). Keep going past the store, however, and you'll meet Route 1, which kinks sharply towards Bjarnafell and Krafla as it heads east or continues south for the **lake circuit**.

The area around the church is worth a look, less for the typically neat structure itself than the **lava flows** either side. These date to August 1729, when erupting fissures 10km northeast at Leirhnjúkur (near Krafla – see p.233) rounded off a prolonged spell of activity. Fast-flowing lava descended from the hills and covered three nearby farms, but was mysteriously deflected around the low-lying church – some say by the cemetery wall, others (in keeping with similar cases elsewhere in Iceland) by prayer. A carving on the pulpit depicts the church of the time under threat, and check out the lava too: there are some good stretches of rope-lava pavements, and plenty of **fissures** caused by escaping gases. Other than this, Reykjahlíð's main attraction is at the school adjacent to the swimming pool (see above), which houses a summer **museum** (June 10–Aug 25 9am–10pm; free), with books, pictures and photos illustrating local folklore, history, and biology, and a sizeable collection of stuffed birds.

On a cold day you'll see steam rising from small cracks in the ground all around Reykjahlíð, and for a closer look walk just southeast of the Húsavík-Route 1 intersection, where you'll find **Stóragjá**, the most accessible of Mývatn's sunken **hot springs**, hidden in amongst the rough scrub and lava. A ladder and rope reach down into the two-metre-wide cleft from ground level, and it was a popular bathing hole until it cooled during the 1990s, allowing a harmful algae to invade. Some people do still swim here, but at the risk of getting any cuts or grazes infected – stick to the town's swimming pool.

The lake shore around Reykjahlíð is flat and gentle and good for **bird-watching**, with a few pairs of **slavonian grebes** – sleek diving birds with yellow tufts behind the ears – now nesting again in the area after lowered water levels kept them away between 1976 and 1992. Ducks aside, there's also a fair chance of spotting **red-necked phalaropes**, small waders with pointy beaks and a distinctive red stripe, which perform "pirouettes" on the water; this creates a whirlpool which sucks up bottom-dwelling bugs on which the birds feed. The northeast bit of Mývatn is also the only place that you don't need a boat to go **fishing** on the lake, though you will require a permit (see "Practicalities" for more on this and gear rental); stocks of trout and arctic char are generally good, though for salmon you're better off on the Laxá (see p.231). Several people in Reykjahlíð have **smoke houses** for curing fish – there's one at the *Eldá* guesthouse (see p.227) – which you can buy direct or through the store; be aware that in the absence of timber they use dried sheep-dung for smoking, and the results are somewhat coarser than wood-smoked fish. Ash from the process is also used to preserve duck eggs by simply burying them in it for several months, turning the yolks green and the albumen a clear, smoky brown – they sound revolting but actually have a pleasantly mild, alkaline flavour.

Practicalities

As you enter town from the south along the Húsavík road, next door to the church is the *Hótel Reynihlíð*, which acts as the **bus stop**, after which is Reykjahlíð's **fuel station**. Reykjahlíð's **tourist information office** (June–Aug; ☎464 4220) is housed in the school, along with the museum (see p.225), and can sort out tours and gear rental, or put you in direct touch with operators. Most accommodation can help with the same things – the travel service operated by *Eldá* (see opposite), which operates many of the tours, is particularly good and also rents out **mountain bikes** (1200kr a day), **horses** (1300kr an hour), and **boats** with fishing tackle and permits (from 800kr an hour). See the box on p.227 for more on tours.

There are **telephones** outside the post office and at the fuel station, with a **bank** and foreign exchange at the *Hótel Reynihlíð*. For **food**, make sure you try some smoked fish, along with *hverabrauð* – bread baked in underground ovens to the east at Bjarnaflag (see p.232) – both of which are available through the small **general store** near the fuel station, which is also stocked with a good range of essentials, including fruit and veg. Good-value meals and not too expensive beer make *Gamli Bærinn*, in a converted farmhouse next to *Hótel Reynihlíð*, the place of choice for a proper sit-down feed: a **café and restaurant** by day, it has more of a bar atmosphere in the evenings. Aside from the reasonable hotel restaurant, the only other option to self-catering is *Hverinn*, next to the store, open from 10am until 11pm in summer for inexpensive roadhouse-style burgers, soft drinks and pasta.

Accommodation

Accommodation opening times are very tourist-season oriented: prices are a little high in summer, falling heavily in winter – if establishments even bother to

Jökulsárlón

Minke whale, off Húsavík

Volcanic desert, the Interior

Geothermal plant

Hot springs, Askja

Icelandic ponies

Landmannalaugar

Valley glacier flowing from Vatnajökull

Laufás

Kverkfjöll

Húsavík

Camping at Landmannalaugar

Basalt columns at Svartifoss

TOURS FROM REYKJAHLÍÐ

Whether or not you have the time to get around the Mývatn area unaided, several of the **tours from Reykjahlíð** offer a trouble-free way of reaching some of the remoter sights, and can also take you right out of the area. Most only operate from around June until September, and need to be booked a day or so in advance.

The *Eldá* guesthouse (see below), and Mývatn Tours (☎464 4196, fax 464 4380, *myvatntours@isholf.is*) are Reykjahlíð's main operators, offering similar tours, though Mývatn Tours tend to be slightly more expensive. Both offer the full-day **Mývatn Tour** (4300kr), a brisk circuit of the lake and most of its attractions before heading up to the Krafla volcano. Both can also tailor **bird-watching** or **fishing** excursions; in addition, Eldá run an unusual trip into the Krafla volcano's **Gjástykki rift** (see p.233) for 3000kr, and are planning regular tours out to **Loftheðir ice caves**, frozen lava caverns discovered only in 1989 and impossible to locate without local knowledge. Mývatn Tours sometimes visit the **Lúdent craters** (see p.229) if there's enough demand.

Further afield, *Eldá*, Mývatn Tours and Sba (☎462 3510, fax 462 7020) run buses up to **Dettifoss** and **Ásbyrgi** for 4600kr (see p.240), which you can catch one day and return the next; Mývatn Tours also specialize in very long **Askja** day trips (see p.282) – contact them for details. Groups of three or more people can set up **four-wheel-drive tours** to the Krafla area and Dettifoss (6–8hr; 7800kr) or Askja (8–10hr; 8500kr) with Super Jeep Tours in advance (☎464 3940 or 897 4846). See p.236 for setting up **whale-watching** day trips to the coast.

---

stay open. **Camping** in the reserve itself is only allowed at designated sites with more around the lake at Vogar, Grænavatn and Skútustaðir (pp.228–231). In town, there are sites at *Eldá* and *Hlíð*.

Birkihraun II, off the swimming pool road (☎464 4196, fax 464 4380). No-frills guesthouse with single and double rooms. ③.

Eldá (☎464 4220, fax 464 4321, *www.elda.is*). Friendly, family-run business utilizing several places around Reykjahlíð; check in at main house near where the lake ringroad leaves Route 1 for either the campsite (including use of showers and kitchen), sleeping-bag accommodation, or singles and doubles. Breakfast costs extra. Camping 500kr, sleeping-bag accommodation 1500kr, ②.

Hlíð, off the airstrip road (☎464 4103, fax 464 4305). There are three options here: a good campsite with a laundry, bathrooms, hot-tubs and kitchen; a roomy, self-catering bunkhouse with a large kitchen and dining area, and favoured by tour groups; and self-catering, four-person cabins. Camping 450kr, sleeping-bag accommodation 1400kr, made-up bed 2400kr, cabin 5000kr.

Reykjahlíð, behind the fuel station (☎464 4142, fax 464 4336, *reykjahlid@islandia.is*). Well-organized, low-key hotel overlooking the lake, whose relaxed furnishings make it feel more like a guesthouse. Breakfast extra. Sleeping-bag accommodation 2000kr, ④.

Reynihlíð, next to the church (☎464 4170, fax 464 4371, *www.mmedia.is/reynihlid*). A modern, motel-like affair with well-furnished rooms, which in summer also offers sleeping-bag accommodation if they've space. Sleeping-bag accommodation 2000kr, ⑥.

The lakeshore

Moving clockwise **around Mývatn** from Rekjahlíð, you follow the Akureyri road down around the lake via **Vogar** and **Skútustaðir** – both with further places to stay – to where the Laxá drains westwards, then cross the river and take a minor road up the west shore and back to town. This circuit is about 35km long in itself, but there are several places to make fairly extensive detours away from the lake, principally **Grótagjá** hot springs; the rough lavafield at **Dimmuborgir** and **Hverfjall** cone, east of the lake; and **Vindbelgjar** peak, on Mývatn's northwestern side. Aside from the highly visible wildfowl, keep your eyes peeled for ptarmigan, arctic foxes and maybe even gyrfalcons. Also note that **erosion** is a serious problem at many popular sites and that you should stick to marked paths where you find them.

How you **get around** the lake depends on resources and time. Realistically, you need some form of transport and a couple of days to take the lake circuit in – you could always hop on Akureyri-bound **buses** or get on and off a Mývatn Tour (see p.227) to spread it over several days, or hire a **bike** or even a **horse** from town (see p.226). Even with your own vehicle, the main sights need a very full day to cover properly, though **lake tours** (see p.227) take in the lot in around four hours. You can, of course, **walk** everywhere – at Easter, many of Mývatn's residents spend Good Friday circuiting the lake on foot in memory of Christ's walk to Golgotha – and you should at least tackle the well-marked **trail** (8km) that links Reykjahlíð with Grótagjá, Hverfell and Dimmuborgir. There's also some longer, harder serious hiking to distant formations south and east of the lake, for which you'll need patience for crossing lava and a copy of the *Landmælingar Íslands* Mývatn 1:50,000 **map** – the tourist information office or *Eldá* might have these, otherwise Akureyri's bookshops are the nearest source.

Vogar and Grótagjá

Heading south from Reykjahlíð, you pass sheep pens built of lava blocks, and the first small stands of **birch**, which appear in patches all down the eastern lakeshore. Big lava blocks by the roadside also mark the edge of a truly vast expanse of volcanic detritus – once out of the woods you'll realize how extensive this is.

Only about 2km along, **VOGAR** is a handful of farms offering comfortable **beds** and **camping** (☎464 4399, fax 464 4341; camping 400kr, sleeping-bag accommodation 1400kr, ②); there's no store but they can furnish breakfast. From here, it's another couple of kilometres northeast along a gravel road to **Grótagjá**, the best-known of Mývatn's flooded fissures. It's impressive, all the more so for being an entirely natural feature; the lava is heaped up in a ridge, and you enter through a crack to find a low-ceilinged, narrow cavern harbouring a couple of clear, long pools (one for men, one for women), all lit by daylight through the entrance. Sadly, however, there's a drawback: unless you're here in winter – when the women's pool is just about bearable for a quick immersion (take care on the rough rocks) – Grótagjá is generally a bit too hot to get into at 48°C, though it is cooling down each year. There are more comfortable hot pools elsewhere at Mývatn, however, and if you're lucky locals may show you their favourites – some are superb in winter, when you have to climb down the ice into them.

Hverfjall and Lúdent

Around 3km southeast of Vogar, **Hverfjall** is Mývatn's most easily identified landmark, looking just how a volcano should: broad, conical and strewn with black rubble and rocks, it's a classic **tephra cone**, made of consolidated ash and pumice. At 2500 years old, Hverfjall is also a bit younger than the lake, and its high rim (400m) presents a very satisfying, straightforward climb from the end of the bumpy access track (1.5km) off the highway. Two hours is ample time for a slow ascent and circuit of the kilometre-wide caldera, which is a great way to orient yourself: immediately west lie the lake's flat blue waters, its scattering of **islands** and convoluted shore; views north take in the town, steaming thermal areas, and the plateau harbouring Krafla (despite the distance, you can usually hear steam vents on the mountain roaring away); southeast lurks Lúdent, beyond which lava stretches out to the distant string of impressively solid rhyolitic table-top formations of **Búrfel**, **Heilagsdalsfjall** and **Bláfjall**. Give yourself an extra hour if you plan to climb down in to Hverfjall's flat-floored crater, where previous visitors have left giant yellow graffiti made by scraping away the dark topsoil – don't add to their destructive mess.

If you enjoyed Hverfjall, it's worth trekking the additional 5km out to see **Lúdent**'s similar formations (if you're driving, you'll need a four-wheel-drive for the soft black sand along the way). The track curls around Hverfjall's south side and then bears southeast, rising to cross a line of rough-edged, overgrown volcanic blisters and miniature outlying craters on the abrupt western edge of the Mývatn fault. A further kilometre across the rift and you're on top of the iron-rich, red gravel slopes of Lúdent's main crater; the rim lacks Hverfjall's symmetry, being partially collapsed and invaded by several secondary cones – the one directly north is almost as wide as Lúdent, and slightly higher at 490m. Look back the way you've come and there's a superb line of sight right along the rift wall. It's possible to carefully circuit Lúdent's crater, but – properly equipped for navigation and a camp-out – you'll get more by following the rift south for 7km from here to **Seljahjallagil**; see "Grænavatn" on p.230 for more on this.

Dimmuborgir

Back on the lake road a kilometre or so south of the Hverfjall junction, another track east – surfaced this time – brings you to **Dimmuborgir** after 1500m, a collection of weird, crumbled and contorted lava towers set amongst the birch scrub. This was once a **lava lake**, whose crust had solidified by the time its containing wall collapsed, allowing what was still liquid to drain out but leaving a broken-up mess behind. Taller formations may have been where steam erupted through the deep pool of molten rock, cooling it enough to form surface-high columns which were left standing on their own once the lava drained away. All this aside, you could easily spend a couple of hours on Dimmuborgir's marked paths, examining the rocks' unexpected and indescribable shapes; none of the forms is very tall but every inch is differently textured, all finished in tiny twists and spires. A moon-shaped hole in a wall at **Gatklettur** beautifully frames Hverfjall to the northeast; otherwise Dimmuborgir's highlight is the lava cave known as **Kirkja**, the Church, about half an hour east from the entrance – what looks like a giant burst bubble of lava, into which around twenty people could comfortably squeeze.

Höfði and Kálfaströnd

A couple of kilometres south past Dimmuborgir on the lake road, the private nature park **Höfði** (daily 9am–7pm; 100kr) marks the first specific lakeside stop. Stack-like formations and tiny islets in the crystal-clear waters here attract birds in some numbers, while relatively dense woodland right along the shore offers good cover for watching them. A local speciality is the **great northern diver** (known as "loon" in the US), which nests here; with luck you'll see the less common red-throated variety too, along with countless **Barrow's goldeneyes**. Across the inlet at Höfði, **Kálfaströnd** is a long peninsula with similar appeal; get here by taking the next turning after Höfði, then walking around the shoreline from the farm area.

Grænavatn and around

Rounding Mývatn's southeastern corner, you pass where the lake's **springs** well up below the waters, though this is invisible except in winter, when their warmth stops the surface from freezing. A kilometre further on, the tiny hamlet of **GARDUR** marks a two-kilometre road south to **GRÆNAVATN**, both a farm and much smaller satellite lake of Mývatn. The lake isn't that interesting, but the **farmhouse** is, roofed in turf and sided in timber and basalt blocks; built in the late nineteenth century and now one of the oldest buildings in the region, it's still lived in.

The farm also runs a basic **campsite** (☎ & fax 464 4194; 400kr), from where you can start some serious cross-lavafield **hikes**. The easiest follows a rough vehicle track for 15km south to **Sellandafjall**'s steep slopes – the northwest corner is the best place to try an ascent. Alternatively, take the track for about a third of the way, then follow the edge of the lava approximately southeast for 4km to the impressive gorge **Gyðuhnjúksgil**. Another option is to head 10km southeast from Grænavatn across the lava to **Bláfjall**'s wild escarpments, north of which are a couple of steep-sided canyons – one, **Seljahjallagil**, is strikingly faced in hexagonal trachyte columns – though there's an easier route here from Lúdent. Don't attempt any of these hikes without at least the *Landmælingar Íslands* Mývatn 1:50,000 **map** and orientation skills; carry all the water you'll need; and give yourself at least two days for a return trip to any one of them – the lava is rough and very slow going. All take you outside the reserve, so you can camp anywhere you're lucky enough to find a suitable spot to pitch a tent.

Skútustaðir

Three kilometres west of Gardur, **SKÚTUSTAÐIR** is an alternative base to Reykjahlíð, a small knot of buildings right by the lake comprising a church, a **store** with basic supplies, a **café** and fuel pump, plus several **places to stay**. Next to the fuel pump, *Hótel Mývatn* (☎464 4164, fax 464 4364, *myvatn@islandia.is*; sleeping-bag accommodation 1800kr, ②) also rents out bikes and runs most of the rest of Skútustaðir's amenities; next door is a guesthouse with very cosy rooms (②), and opposite this is the recently built *Mývatn Lykil Hótel* (☎464 4455, fax 464 4279; ③). In a lower bracket, Skútustaðir's Skjólbrekka community hall offers summertime sleeping-bag accommodation (☎464 4202; 1200kr), while the **campsite** (☎464 4212, fax 464 4322; 500kr) is opposite the *Hótel Mývatn*. If you're after **smoked fish**, the smoke house Reykhusíð Skútustoðum, on the track leading up to the church, sells salmon, char and trout at around 1500kr per kilo.

Whether or not you stay the night, Skútustaðir's **pseudocraters** warrant a close look. Though they look like bonsai volcanoes, pseudocraters are actually created when lava pours over marshland, boiling the water beneath, which bursts through the solidifying crust to form a cone. They tend to occur in clutches around the lake shore, though most of Mývatn's islands are also pseudocraters, including the largest, **Geitey** – a mere 30m high. There are about a dozen closely packed together at Skútustaðir, known as **skútustaðagígar**, and it takes about an hour to walk from the campsite around the collection of grassy hillocks, following paths and boardwalks.

The west shore: Vindbelgjarfjall and Neslönd

Another 4km west from Skútustaðir, *Arnavatn* **farmstay** (☎464 4333, fax 464 4332; sleeping-bag accommodation 1100kr, made-up beds 4800kr; fishing permits) sits right where the Laxá drains quickly out of Mývatn through a collection of low, marshy islands and starts its journey northwest towards the sea at Húsavík. **Harlequin ducks** tumble in and out of the flow, and the calmer stretches and boggy banks attract **greylag geese**, **phalaropes** and **whooper swans** – there's a trail of sorts up along the river's western bank off the Akureyri road.

The lake circuit, however, continues north along Route 848, which runs for 12km along Mývatn's western shore. The first place of note is the unmistakably tall **Vindbelgjarfjall** (529m), halfway along, whose access track leaves the main road at a sharp bend just before Vagnbrekka farm – don't attempt driving this in anything less than high-clearance four-wheel-drive. On foot, it takes about twenty minutes along this track to reach an obscure path up the back of the mountain, marked with white pegs; if you find yourself in a seriously boggy patch, you've gone too far. Once through lowland heather and birch thickets, it's scree all the way around the top – quite slippery and steep – but the scramble to the cairn marking the summit only takes around thirty minutes, from where there are dramatic **views** off the mountain's steep east face and over the lake.

Past the mountain, the main road clips some more pseudocraters – less visited and more tightly packed than Skútustaðir's – before passing a track eastwards into **Neslönd**, a marshy, scrubby bird-breeding area. Access is limited in summer, when the only place you'll be able to get close to birdlife is at **Ytri-Neslönd farm**, whose late owner amassed a truly extraordinary collection of **stuffed birds** covering just about every species that it's possible to see in Iceland. The future of this place is uncertain at present, but you can call in or ask about the latest developments from any of the lake's information offices. From the Neslönd turning, it's another 8km back to Reykjahlíð.

Bjarnarflag, Krafla and around

While Mývatn's immediate surrounds appear fairly stable, the plateau northeast is anything but serene, the barren, pock-marked landscape pouring out lively quantities of steam and – when the mood takes it – lava. Around **Bjarnarflag** and the **Krafla** volcano, you can see not only how destructive such events have been, but also how their energy has been harnessed by the local community. Just 3km east from Reykjahlíð along Route 1, Bjarnaflag is close enough easily to walk to from town, and hikers can follow a 12km track from Reyjahlíð to Krafla via **Hlíðarfjall**'s steep outcrops, though you'd need to use those long hours of daylight to manage the return trip in a single day. Both Bjarnarflag and Krafla – reached along a gravel road off Route 1 around 17km from Reykjahlíð – are also covered by **bus tours**, or you could **cycle** though, unlike the lake circuit, there are some tiring uphill stretches and loose gravel – take a mountain bike. Note too that past all this Route 1 continues east towards Egilsstaðir, with more options for adventurous travel along the way.

Bjarnarflag and around

Only 3km from Reykjahlíð, **Bjarnarflag** is a thermal zone on the lower slopes of **Dalfjall**, a long faulted ridge pushed up by subterranean pressures that runs northeast to Krafla itself. Bjarnarflag has a small geothermal power station – Iceland's first, built in 1969 – but the main focus is the **Kísilidjan diatomite plant**, which processes the silica-rich shells of **diatoms**, single-celled organisms whose massed remains form a thick layer – 5–10m – of sludge on the bottom of Mývatn. Applications are varied: silica is used as a filter in various manufacturing processes, and diatomite itself is used as an insecticide – the fine, sharp-edged particles get into insects' armoured joints and cut them to pieces. **Dredging** the lake for the raw material worries conservationists, though locals point out that the plant is a major employer outside the tourist season, and dredging has relieved siltation and creates deeper, cooler water in which fish flourish in summer. Note the substantial **wall** behind Kísilidjan, designed to deflect potential lava flows from the Krafla area above.

Across from Kísilidjan on the south side of the highway, a brickworks makes a good landmark for locating Bjarnarflag's renowned **underground bakery**. This sounds much more technical that it really is; the "bakery" is simply a few dozen small pits dug into the superheated, steaming soil between the road and brickworks, each covered with weighted dustbin lids or sheets of scrap metal. Rye dough is mixed with yeast and molasses in a cardboard milk carton and left underground for a day, where it transforms into neat, rectangular loaves of heavy **hverabrauð** – "steam bread". This isn't the only such bakery in Iceland, but it is one of the largest; most bread is made for private consumption, though some is sold through Reykjahlíð's store. People sometimes cook other things in here too – such as the Icelandic speciality of boiled sheep's head – so prepare for a shock if you lift lids for a look (though residents would rather you left their ovens alone).

If, on a cold afternoon, you also wish you had a steamy pit to crawl into, follow the track uphill behind the brickworks to where you'll find a wood and fibreglass **sauna**. Though there's a sign outside warning that use is at your own risk, your biggest worry is probably going to be the shock of having to hose the sweat off yourself afterwards with frigid water – but this may well be the point.

Námafjall and Hverarönd

Immediately east of Bjarnaflag, the road twists up and over Dalfjall; on the way, look for a big split in the ridges north, marking the line of the Mývatn rift. The high point south of the road's crest is **Námafjall**, streaked in grey gypsum and yellow **sulphur deposits** – these were once mined and exported for use in gunpowder – and there's an easy twenty-minute track to follow through soft mud to the summit's stony outcrop. The whole Mývatn area is spread below; in particular, look for **Hrossaberg** to the southwest, a large exploded vent with ragged edges simmering quietly away between here and Hverfjall.

The road meanwhile descends Námafjall eastern face and, at the base about 6km from Reykjahlíð, you'll find **Hverarönd**, a large field of **solfataras**, evil-smelling, blue-grey belching mud pools. These are caused by groundwater percolating downwards for over a kilometre to magma levels; heating then forces it back to the surface, where it exits through the sticky red soil at 200°C. It's essential to follow boardwalks and guide ropes here; every year someone leaves them and sinks knee-deep into the scalding pools. These, however, are docile compared with the accompanying **steam vents,** where rocks, gravel and earth have been burst upwards like a bubble to form waist-high, perforated mounds through which vapour screams out ferociously.

Krafla, Viti and Leirhnjúkur

Up in the hills north of Hverarönd, the area around the Krafla volcano has been intermittently erupting for the last three thousand years and shows no signs of cooling down yet. **Krafla** itself (818m) was last active in the 1720s during a period known as the **Mývatn Fires,** which began when the west side of Krafla exploded in 1724, forming a new crater named **Viti** (Hell); earthquakes over the next five years opened up a series of volcanic fissures west of Krafla at **Leirhnjúkur,** producing the lava flows which so nearly destroyed Reykjahlíð's church. More recently, a similar spate of earthquakes caused a new line of activity north at **Gjástykki** between 1977 and 1984 in what came to be called the **Krafla Fires,** and it's this mass of still-steaming lava rubble that is the main draw today.

All this can be explored on foot from the end of the seven-kilometre access road, which runs north off Route 1 just past Hverarönd, passing right under piping from **Leirbotn power station** on the way. By harnessing steam vents in the area it was hoped to achieve a 60 megawatt output, but – aside from construction of the plant unfortunately coinciding with the Krafla Fires – one of the boreholes exploded during drilling to form an **artificial crater** (jokingly known as Sjálfskapar Viti, "Homemade Hell"). For years the station ran at half capacity, though a new 20 megawatt bore opened in 1999 has put things back on track; this is what you can hear (and see) roaring away up on Krafla's flanks.

The road itself ends at **Viti,** a deep, steep-sided, flooded crater, from where you can walk around the rim and then up on to Krafla itself. In the other direction, trails weave across the plain to Leirhnjúkur and Gjástykki, enormously long masses of rough lava, piled into hummocks and stretched into lines, all pitted with smoking craters, cracks and hot spots. As usual, apply common sense to any explorations and, in winter – when you'll have to bring your own gear along and ski out here – avoid shallow depressions in the snow, indicating warm areas beneath.

East towards Egilsstaðir

Past the Krafla junction, Route 1 heads relentlessly eastwards across the seemingly endless, barren flats of the northern **Óðáðahraun lavafield,** the road flanked by neatly made **stone cairns** at 100m intervals. There's actually just enough pasture for sheep here, though their presence is being phased out to reduce erosion – the area gets very bad **sandstorms** in summer. The bus covers the whole 150km to Egilsstaðir in around three hours but, in the right vehicle and at the right time of year, there are several side trips to make along the way – see the "Tours from Reykjahlíð" box on p.227.

The most popular option is to head up to **Jökulsárgljúfur National Park** (p.238). There are two ways to do this, both of which take you north off the Mývatn–Egilsstaðir highway, pass Dettifoss (see p.240) in the south of the park, then continue up to Route 85, around 60km east of Húsavík. The first is Route F862, a four-wheel-drive-only track which heads up through the west side of the park 18km from Reykjahlíð; while the alternative is to cross the Jökulsá á Fjöllum

40km from town and turn off the highway to **accommodation** at Grímstunga I farm (☎464 4294; breakfast by arrangement; campsite 500kr, sleeping-bag accommodation 1450kr, made-up beds 4300kr) at **Grímsstaðir** – note that, despite its prominence on maps, Grímsstaðir is not a town and that there are no stores. From here there's the seasonally open Route 864 north to Dettifoss and beyond. Aside from Jökulsárgljúfur, there's also Route F88 south along the Jökulsá to Askja and Kverkfjöll (pp.282 and 283).

Back on Route 1, it's a further 25km over the Jökulsá, where the road branches, with one route going northeast to Vopnafjörður, the other continuing across to Egilsstaðir – for more on these routes, see pp.220 and 243.

THE NORTHEAST

Only a brief drive north from either Akureyri or Mývatn, **Húsavík** is northeast Iceland's largest town, and the start of the 290-kilometre run eastwards around the coast on Route 85 to **Vopnafjörður**, through Iceland's barren, underpopulated **northeast**. While the regional highlights – **whale watching** out from Húsavík itself, and the gorges, waterfalls and hiking at **Jökulsárgljúfur National Park** – are worth the journey up here in themselves, elsewhere the scattering of small fishing towns and understated landscape of moorland and small beaches have their own quiet appeal. And don't forget that you're almost inside the **arctic circle** here, and summer nights are virtually non-existent, the sun just dipping below the horizon at midnight – conversely, winter days are only a couple of hours long. In summer there's plenty of **public transport** to Húsavík along main roads from either Akureyri or Mývatn, and several services weekly from Húsavík to Vopnafjörður, though at other times you'll have to fly from Akureyri or make your own way through the region.

Essentially, there are two **ways to approach Húsavík**: either directly **from Akureyri** via Route 85; or northwest **from Mývatn** along minor roads that parallel the **Laxá** – the Salmon River – for 50km, to where all routes rejoin near the mouth of the river, just 10km short of Húsavík. The Laxá, incidentally, lives up to its name, and accommodation in the area can provide (expensive) **fishing** licences if you want to try your luck.

The Laugar road

Coming from Akureyri, Route 845 leaves the Akureyri–Mývatn road about 50km from Akureyri at **Laugar** (p.225). Initially you follow the **Reykjadalsá**, one of the Laxá's tributaries, along a well-defined, flat-bottomed valley, but around 10km along the view opens up as you touch the edge of the prehistoric **Aðaldashraun lava flow**, which runs almost all the way on up to the coast. Route 854 turns east here, and about 5km along brings you to **GRENJAÐARSTAÐUR**, where a nineteenth-century **church** and block of turf-roofed farmhouses are well insulated from the icy prevailing winds. Now a **museum** (June–Aug 10am–6pm; 300kr), the estate was founded in medieval times, when it counted as one of the best holdings in all Iceland – a contemporary altar cloth from the original church is now in the Paris Louvre. Just up the road, Staðarhóll farm (☎464 3703, fax 464 3717; sleeping-bag accommodation 1800kr, made-up bed 4050kr) offers year-round **accommodation**, meals and fishing licences. After this, you're at the Laxá itself, just where the road kinks sharply around piping from the small **Laxárstöðar hydro station**. This was due to be expanded in the late 1960s, but fears that a new dam would flood the valley actually drove locals to blow up the construction site in 1970, and further development plans were abandoned.

From here, you can cross the ridge behind the station to the Reykjahlíð road (see below), or follow the river and its marshy surrounds north back on to Route 845, just a couple of kilometres north from you left it. There's further **accommodation** right on the river just east along a side road at *Hraunbær* (☎464 3695, fax 464 3595; self-catering, or meals by arrangement; ②), or 2km up the road at Hafralækur farm (☎464 3561), whose **campsite**, self-catering cabins and dorms sit surrounded by lava rubble, exploded bubbles and pseudocraters – a fine place to spend a day exploring. At this point the road joins up with Route 85, which you follow for the final 22km up to Húsavík.

Along the Laxá from Reykjahlíð

Route 87 follows the west side of the Laxá pretty well directly between Reykjahlíð and Húsavík, though it follows high ground and you don't actually get to see much of the river along the way. Your best chance for a peek is by detouring down to Laxárstöðar hydro station (see opposite); otherwise, the main feature of the route is 40km from Reyjahlíð at **Hveravellir**, a spread of steam-heated **greenhouses** growing house plants and vegetables. Right on the roadside is *Heiðarbær* (☎464 3903, fax 464 3950; 2000kr), where you can **camp** or get dormitory **accommodation** in summer. It also has a good swimming pool.

Húsavík and around

Approaching **HÚSAVÍK** from the south, you come over a crest and see the town sitting below **Húsavíkurfjall** on a rare dip in the otherwise high coastline, the blue-green bay out front patched by cloud shadows and a couple of **islands**. This beautiful setting was the site of one of the earliest recorded settlements in Icelandic history, after the ninth-century Swedish rover **Garðar Svavarsson** wintered here while making the first circumnavigation of the country; the shelters he built gave Húsavík (House Bay) its name. It's also said that two of his slaves decamped during his stay and afterwards established a farm, though later historians – looking for nobler lineages than this – tended to overlook the possibility that they were perhaps the mainland's first permanent residents.

The area's economy focused on sheep-farming until suffering in the nationwide **depression** of the late nineteenth century, when most of those that could switched to commercial fishing, or emigrated to Canada or the US. Continuing hard times forced the remaining farmers, who felt exploited by trade monopolies, to form Kaupfélag Þingeyinga, a cooperative that bypassed middlemen and traded directly with merchants from Newcastle in England, in exchange for whatever the cooperative members needed. In 2000, the cooperative was still functioning, though it was severely debt-ridden.

The town and adjacent coast make a pleasant place to stock up before tackling the northeast's rather less well-supplied stretches, but in recent years, Húsavík's traditional industries have been supplemented by promoting itself as Iceland's **whale-watching** capital (see box on p.236), something it has a fair claim to – with luck, it's possible to see several different species in a single trip, as they move into the rich waters roundabout for summertime feeding.

WHALE WATCHING AT HÚSAVÍK

The whale-watching industry in Húsavík got going in the 1990s, after whalers hit by a 1989 moratorium realized that there was still good money to be made by taking tourists out to find the creatures. Though the Icelandic government allowed hunting to resume "for scientific purposes" in 1999, the decade-long ban means that whale stocks are still high, and if you put to sea in summer off Húsavík the chances of seeing at least one species are good. Dolphins, porpoises and medium-sized **minke** whales are seen more frequently, with much larger **humpback whales** runners-up; these are identified by lengthy flippers and their habit of "breaching" – making spectacular, crashing leaps out of the water. Similar-looking **fin whales** are the next most likely candidates, with rarer sightings of colossal **blue whales**; **orca**, or killer whales; and square-headed **sperm whales**. For some reason, only males of the last species are found in Iceland.

Whale-watching cruises run daily from June through to mid-September, last around three hours, and cost 2500kr. There's a booking office at the harbour, or you can book one through a cruise operator such as Moby Dick (☎ & fax 464 1748, *www.nett.is/whale*); Fjallasyn (☎464 3940, fax 464 3941); and North Sailing (☎464 2350, *www.north-sailing.is*). Evening whale-watching tours can also be arranged, as can day trips out to birdwatch on Lundey. Some operators will also organize transport from Mývatn to Húsavík.

The Town and around

Backed by a newer residential area, Húsavík's small core of early twentieth-century corrugated-iron and weatherboard businesses cluster around the church and harbour, which face each other across the main street, Garðarsbraut. The inevitable **church** is an attractive wooden structure, with complex eaves and a green painted roof, while the **harbour** is a good place to see marine ducks, especially long-tailed (old squaw) and eider – both extremely common all along the coast. Views west across wide **Skjálfandi bay** take in the heights of the peninsula opposite, inhabited until its extraordinarily mountainous terrain prevented roads and power being supplied in the early 1960s, after which its scattered farms were abandoned. Look north up the coast and you may be able to spot **Lundey**, a small, uninhabited flat-topped island famed for its puffins.

The harbour is also the current location of Húsavík's award-winning **whale centre** (June–Sept daily 9am–7pm; call the caretaker on ☎891 9820 at other times; 300kr), though plans are afoot to relocate it to an old fish-freezing plant. Inside, an informative assemblage of models, photos, relics, and even skeletons – all taken from beached or drowned whales – fill you in on cetacean biology, along with a couple of continually playing videos on whales and Icelandic wildlife in general. Pick of the exhibits are pieces of tremendously hairy baleen plates, with which filter-feeding species strain their nourishing plankton diet like slurping soup through a moustache.

Walk up past the church for 150m along Stóragarður, and Húsavík's library is just on your left, housing an excellent **local museum** (Mon–Fri 9am–noon & 1–5pm, Sun 4–6pm; 350kr); turn up when they're quiet and the curator may give you a personal guided tour. Amongst the usual domestic and farmhouse memorabilia, there are bits of medieval weapons found near the town, through to reconstructions of a Viking longboat, and the wooden room in which Húsavík's cooperative was founded. Glass cases house stuffed representatives of Iceland's indigenous fauna, including a hapless polar bear, killed in 1969 after drifting over from Greenland on an ice floe – an event that the staff here are not particularly proud of.

Past the library, the road runs out of town to the lower slopes of **Húsavíkurfjall**, where a belt of trees marks the entrance to winter **ski slopes**. Out of season, it's about an hour's climb to the hill-top transmitter tower, with further views down on the town and gently steaming slopes to the north – locals have private **hot tubs** up there, fed by underground hot springs.

On a bright day, the the coast around Húsavík offers some good, easy **walks** and a chance to rack up your bird-watching tallies. The kilometre-long beach immediately south from the harbour is a fine place to start, or you can head 10km south to **Laxámyri** homestead at the junction of the Akureyri and Reykjahlíð roads. A gravel track here leads out to the mouth of the Laxá at **Ærvík**, a small, flat bay of black volcanic sand. The river itself ends with a steep, turbulent flurry – attractive both to salmon and harlequin ducks – before spilling onto the beach for the final few hundred metres to the sea.

Practicalities

Húsavík is small, with almost all services, including **banks** and the **post office**, near the church either on the highway as it runs north through town – where it forms the 150-metre **Garðarsbraut** – or within a couple of minutes' walk. **Buses** stop outside the church, with summer services daily to and from Akureyri and Mývatn, or several times weekly on via Ásbyrgi in Jökulsárgljúfur National Park and around the coast to Egilsstaðir. The **airstrip** is 10km south on the Akureyri road (for a **taxi** call ☎464 2200), and you can buy tickets for onward travel through the northeast or out of the region at *Flugfélag Ísland*, across from the church at Stóragarði 7 (☎464 1080, fax 464 1084). For **tourist information**, try your accommodation, the whale centre, or the harbourside booking office.

The town is not overburdened with **places to stay** – your options are the friendly *Árból* guesthouse, 100m south of the church at the corner of Garðarsbraut and Ásgarðsvegur (☎464 2220, fax 464 1463; sleeping-bag accommodation 1500kr, ③; breakfast extra); and the slightly gloomy but still welcoming *Hótel Húsavík*, a couple of streets back at Ketilsbraut 22 (☎464 1220, fax 464 2161, *relax@hotel-husavik.is*; ④), where the price includes breakfast and use of a pool. Otherwise, Húsavík's fine **campsite** (500kr), with toilets, a cooking area and sheds for sheltering from inclement weather, is about 300m up the road from the church on the northern edge of town.

Supplies can be bought at the cooperative **supermarket**, 50m north of the church on Garðarsbraut, which has a decent range of meat, fish, fruit and vegetables even in winter; there's also a fishmonger up the road from the *Árból* guesthouse. For **eating**, Húsavík's best restaurant is the harbourfront *Gaumli Baukur*, a wood-panelled, mid-range place with top marks going to their pan-fried haddock and juicy lobster tails. For simpler fare, there's also the *Hloðufell* restaurant and bar across from the supermarket on the main road, which doubles as a branch of *Pizza 67*; while the two fuel stations at either end of town have cheap grills and coffee.

A non-whale-related take on the local coast is offered by Polar Kayaking, at the harbour (☎855 4607 or ☎897 7860), who rent out **kayaks** at 900kr per person for a full day. For mainland explorations, contact Fjallasýn-Mountainview (☎464 3940, fax

464 3938, *www.est.is/fjallasyn*), who, depending on the season, can take you **hiking** or **cross-country skiing, ice fishing**, or on **four-wheel-drive tours** of Mývatn and Jökulsárgljúfur National Park (see below). **Horses** can be hired through Saltvík farm, about 5km south of town on the Akureyri road (☎464 2062); they also offer anything from riding lessons for beginners to a nine-day Sprengisandur traverse.

The Tjörnes peninsula and on to Jökulsárgljúfur

North of Húsavík, the **Tjörnes peninsula** is a rather broad, stubby mass whose roller-coaster roads are cut by numerous small rivers. A few kilometres from town in this direction there's a roadside monument to the locally born patriotic poet **Einar Benediktsson**, one of the key figures of Iceland's early twentieth-century nationalist movement. Past here, now 5km from town, the headlands drop to low **beaches**, reached along vehicle tracks from the road, where you should find the usual melange of **seabirds**, including purple sandpipers, puffins, black guillemots and gannets; in spring, look out for divers (loons) heading to Mývatn. Walking along the beach, it's also not unusual to find yourself being followed offshore by **seals**.

Moving on, the cliffs soon return and 10km from Húsavík there's another track off the main road marked **Tjörneshöfn**, which descends steeply to a tiny boat-shed and harbour looking straight out to Lundey. A shingle beach stretches in both directions below the cliffs, though a small river to the north may stop you heading that way; south there's also seaweed and pleistocene-period **fossil shells** in the headland's layered, vertical faces. These are mostly bivalves, and if you want to see more of them there's a fossil **museum** 2km up the road at **Hallbjarnarstaðir** (☎464 1968; daily in summer 9am–8pm; 300kr).

Tjörnes's northern tip is a further 7km past the museum, where a rough side-road passes a transmitter tower and ends at the short footpath to **Voladalstorfa**, a cliff-top lighthouse from where it's usually possible to pick out a very remote Grímsey to the northwest, and **Mánáreyjar**, comprising a couple of closer vol-canic islets that haven't experienced any stirrings for over a century. From here, the main road rounds the peninsula – at which point you can see northeast over the bay to **Kópasker** – and continues 40km east across the **Bakkahlaup**, a com-plex of shallow lakes at the Jökulsá á Fjöllum delta, to Ásbyrgi and the northern end of Jökulsárgljúfur National Park.

Jökulsárgljúfur National Park

Cutting into the northeast's rocky inland plains, **Jökulsárgljúfur National Park** encloses a 35-kilometre-long stretch of the middle reaches of the **Jökulsá á Fjöllum**, Iceland's second-longest river. Originating almost 200km south at Vatnajökull, for much of its journey through the park the river flows through the massive **Jökulsárgljúfur**, a canyon which is 120m deep and 500m wide in places, forming several exceptional waterfalls and an endless array of rock formations. All this is set against an unusually fertile backdrop – prime grazing land until being made a national park in the 1970s, with over half of the country's **native plants** found here. With three or four days to spare, the park can be thoroughly investigated on foot, though if you're pushed for time, bus tours from Mývatn and Akureyri can still give you the flavour of the place.

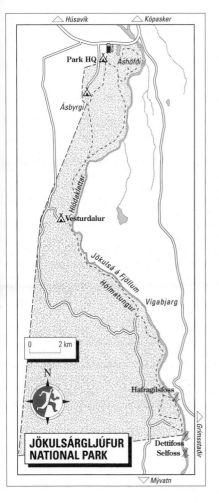

Jökulsárgljúfur has two key sights: the **Ásbyrgi** canyon, located 60km along Route 85 from Húsavík in the north of park; and **Dettifoss**, Europe's most powerful waterfall, at the park's southern boundary and accessed off the Mývatn–Egilsstaðir highway either along the four-wheel-drive-only F862, or Route 864 via Grímsstaðir (see p.233). The F862 then links both ends of the park along the west side of the river, though Route 864 runs up to Route 85 some way to the east. Between June and September, there are daily **buses from Akureyri** via Húsavík and Ásbyrgi to Dettifoss along the F862; coming **from Mývatn**, you'll need to take a tour (see p.227 for practical details of these) or be satisfied with a look at Dettifoss from Route 864.

To really get under the skin of things here, follow the marked **hiking trails** along the west side of the river between Ásbyrgi and Dettifoss. You'll need four days to make the return trek from Ásbyrgi to Dettifoss, but you could also simply spend the time just camped in one spot and exploring in depth. Jökulsárgljúfur's only accommodation is at designated **camping** sites (500kr) at Ásbyrgi – which is where you'll also find the **park headquarters** – and halfway down the park at **Vesturdalur**; it is not permitted elsewhere. Bring all the **supplies** you'll need with you: the nearest shops are wherever you've just come from, though there's a small store just outside the park at Ásbyrgi (see below). For **maps**, hikers should pick up the national park brochure from the park headquarters, or use the similarly scaled *Landmælinger Íslands'* 1:100,000 *Mývatn-Húsavík* sheet, available in Akureyri and Reykjavík. Jökulsárgljúfur's **weather** is quite cool, though rain or sleet are probably the worst you'll experience from July through to September.

The park

The four-kilometre Ásbyrgi road turns south off Route 85 at a small **fuel station** with **store** and **café**, then passes the park headquarters and first campsite, before following the canyon down through unusually tall stands of native birch woodland to a second campsite – extremely crowded at weekends – where **Ásbyrgi** dead-ends in a tight, 90m-tall ampitheatre of dark rock patched in orange lichens. Legend has it that this is the hoofprint of the Norse god Óðinn's eight-legged steed **Sleipnir**, though geologists believe that the canyon was carved out since the last ice age by a series of huge *jökulhlaups* that flooded out from underneath Vatnajökull. With a day to spare there are some fine walks in the area, notably to views of the gorges from the eastern heights of **Áhöfði**.

To hike off into the park proper from Ásbyrgi, **walking trails** head east from the first campsite to cross the gorge before it becomes too extreme, and then bear south; you can either follow Ásbyrgi's rim or the river, though they join up again above the water around 8km later on. A further 4km brings you to the basic **Vesturdalur campsite**, an area of steep cliffs and boggy grassland with craters, caves and some oddly shaped formations to check out. The best of these is **Hlóðaklettar**, where the noise of the river is distorted by hollows in the huge rocks, giving the illusion that the river flows through the rock itself.

Over the next 8km, the trail moves above the river and then down to the marshy **Hólmatungur**, where underground springs pool up to create three short rivers which flow quickly into the Jökulsá through some thick vegetation. The trail crosses the largest of these tributaries, the **Hólmá**, on a bridge just above where it tumbles into the main river. Upstream from here on the Jökulsá's east bank, the prominent face of **Vígabjarg** marks where the formerly mighty **Vígarbjargfoss** ripped through a narrow gorge, before a change in the river's course dried it to a trickle sixty years ago. From here it's another 8km to the 27-metre-high **Hafragilsfoss**, an aesthetically pleasing set of falls whose path through a row of volcanic craters has exposed more springs, which mix their clear waters with the Jökulsá's muddier glacial flood.

A final tricky couple of kilometres of scrambling brings you to the park's southern limits at **Dettifoss**, about 30km from Ásbyrgi. Dettifoss is somehow less attractive than its reputation suggests, though it is colossally powerful, especially during early summer when winter snowdrifts are melting up towards its source. By way of contrast, you might want to make a further 1500-metre foray upstream to **Selfoss**, one of the broadest falls in the area, though only 10m high.

The northeast coast

Route 85 continues north of Ásbyrgi to the northeast coast and a string of small communities – **Kópasker**, **Raufarhöfn**, **Þórshöfn** and **Vopnafjörður** – relying on fish-processing, rather than catches themselves, for their main industry. There are a couple of historical echoes here, but mostly it's the landscapes which are memorable: the flat, marshy **Melrakkaslétta** which lies just outside the Arctic Circle; the fells and dales of the foggy **Langanes Peninsula**; and a score of little black sand beaches with their birdlife and disproportionate numbers of **whale strandings**. These were once something of a windfall for local landowners (the term *hvalreki*, literally "whale wreck", implies "jackpot" and is used nowadays for lottery winnings), providing meat, oil, bone and various tradeable bits, such as sperm-whale teeth. In saga times, people would actually fight for possession of these riches, but today a whale stranding is a bit of a burden, as the law demands that the landowner is responsible for disposing of the carcass – not an easy matter in the case of a thirty-ton sperm whale. Vopnafjörður marks the end of the coastal road, and routes divide here to head inland again, either westwards to Mývatn or southeast to Egilsstaðir and the Eastfjords.

Kópasker

From the Ásbyrgi junction it's another 40km north to the port of **KÓPASKER**, first following the edge of the Jökulsá's broad delta where fish are farmed in large round ponds, then the gravelly Öxafjörður coast. The village looks small on approach, but is actually tiny, with an outlying church marking a short side-road off the highway into the town's simple square of streets beside the harbour. At the **harbour**, look out for locally common, pure white Icelandic gulls, and the church is next to a Settlement-era **assembly site**, giving Kópasker a surprisingly venerable historical anchor, but otherwise the town is best known for suffering a severe force-eight **earthquake** in January 1976, thanks to activity at Krafla (see p.233). Kópasker has just enough room for a school with sculptures made from local rocks decorating its lawn, a **bank**, **post office**, **supermarket**, **fuel station**, and a **youth hostel** (☎465 2121, fax 465 2102, *nyibaer@simnet.is*; sleeping-bag accommodation 1350kr) – they're open all year but you'd be wise to give them advance notice of your arrival, especially in winter.

Melrakkaslétta and towards the Arctic Circle

North of Kópasker, the road passes through the blackened wastes of the low **Leirhafnalfjöll** range, a string of early nineteenth-century cinder cones, and then turns northeast into the empty horizons of the **Melrakkaslétta** tundra, which forms Iceland's northernmost peninsula. It might not look that inspiring, but in its own way the Melrakkaslétta has as much wildlife as Mývatn: a coastline of shingle and sand beaches pulls in plenty of wading birds; while the tundra and an associated mass of small, fragmented lakes attract big nesting colonies of eider ducks and arctic terns, as well as **whimbrel** and the otherwise rare **grey phalarope**, along with both of Iceland's diver (loon) species. To cap all this, Melrakkaslétta is also visited by large numbers of non-resident birds, including barnacle geese, arctic redpoll and knot, migrating between Europe and Greenland or Canada – they pass through in late April and early May, and return with young in September.

For a quick look at the coast, turn north off Route 85 around 16km from Kópasker, and follow an eight-kilometre track to the abandoned farm Grjótnes, from where a footpath follows gannet-infested cliffs for 3km to the flat-topped, sheer-sided headland of **Rauðinúpur**. Meanwhile, the main road brushes the shore between some long lagoons; climb the small rise here and you can look south along the geological fault that runs all the way down to Mývatn. Shortly afterwards, the square-sided **Þórgeirsdys lighthouse** lifts out of the horizon, marking **Hraunhafnartangi**, the mainland's northern extremity – a mere 2.5km outside the **Arctic Circle**. Leave the road when you reach a small bridge, and walk the final kilometre across the moorland, past the lighthouse and cairn, and up onto the loosely piled stone sea wall to see the grey-blue Arctic Ocean pounding the far side.

Raufarhöfn

Iceland's northernmost town, **RAUFARHÖFN** sits on the Melrakkaslétta's eastern coast some 55km from Kópasker and 10km past Hraunhafnartangi. In the 1960s Raufarhöfn was the base for Iceland's **herring** industry, and the town's salting plant processed more herring than anywhere else in the country, providing seasonal work that attracted a floating population of thousands. Times have changed, however, and the town has shrunk to just 400 souls; herring is still landed here, but the new focus is on a plant staffed by Polish workers (Icelanders don't like the work, apparently) which buys cod from Russia, freezes it, and then exports it to the US.

The main road runs straight through town, with the turning to the harbour and church on the northern side. On this road by the harbour you'll find the newly renovated, good-value *Hótel Norðurljós* (☎465 1233, fax 465 1383; ②); the only other place to stay is at the **campsite** on Raufarhöfn's south exit by Raufarhöfn's swimming **pool**. In between are two well-stocked **supermarkets**, with the only **restaurant** in town at the hotel; fuel supplies are uncertain as the main-road **fuel station** may be unattended out of season. The harbour and grassy headland at the end of the church road are good places to admire seascapes from, and the hotel owners give advice on good bird-watching spots and might also rent out **kayaks** to explore Melrakkaslétta's lakes.

Þórshöfn and the Langanes peninsula

Out of Raufarhöfn, it's 65km to Þórshöfn ascending high, rocky heathland as the road heads inland and south. Around halfway there's a glimpse of the coast before rounding the knife-edge scree atop **Viðarfjall**, then it's down to ground level again around Svalbarð, a school offering **summer accommodation** (☎468 1385; ②) and fishing licences for nearby streams; historians reckon the farm here is one of Iceland's oldest, though the modern, nondescript buildings give no visual evidence of this. On a good day, views from the road beyond reach out to **Gunnolfsvíkurfjall**, a ridge of hills at the southeastern end of the goose-necked **Langanes peninsula** – which juts out to the northeast for 35km along the divide between the Arctic Ocean and warmer North Atlantic, and so is frequently **fogbound** – and the higher **Heljardalsfjoll** (931m) to the south, whose summit just brushes the clouds.

ÞÓRSHÖFN is a compact, busy little place with terminally pot-holed roads at the base of the Langanes peninsula. The town is just somewhere to stock up, but Langanes offers some good hiking across grassy fells and moorland out to an uninhabited coast, where – unlike Iceland's more popular outdoor venues – you won't have to share the experience with hordes of drunken campers. The road enters Þórshöfn from the south, and runs for 250m past a church, **campsite** (☎468 1148), **bank**, **post office** and **fuel station** (which has the last fuel and supplies for at least 80km), to an intersection. Turn right here, and the road heads uphill to the supermarket, the green-painted *Lyngholt* **guesthouse** (☎468 1238; ②), an excellent modern pool, and the small *Hótel Jorvík* (☎468 1400, fax 468 1399, *jorvik@netfang.com*; sleeping-bag accommodation 1800kr, ②), which offers meals as well as self-catering accommodation, before running off towards Langanes. Turn left at the intersection for *Hafnarbarinn*, the town's only **bar** and a pizza-oriented **restaurant**, though the fuel station dishes up the usual burgers and coffee.

To bypass town and stay on the coastal road, turn right at the church, but to explore Langanes carry on through town and follow the rough gravel road 15km northeast to Ytra Lon farm, a small, very decent, self-catering **youth hostel** (☎ & fax 468 1242, *ytralon@mmedia.is*; 1500kr). Open year-round, this is also a working sheep farm (they also collect eider down in season); there's the chance to join in or just observe working life, **fish** local streams for trout, or plan a **hike** – staff can give advice on this and might act as guides. There are a couple of good full-day circuits to be made, though to get to the Fontur lighthouse at Langanes' tip you'll need to camp out overnight; keep your eyes peeled for **gyrfalcons** while you walk.

Bakkafjörður and Vopnafjörður

Heading on from Þórshöfn, Route 85 crosses the base of Langanes, then rejoins the coast and meets the Atlantic for the first time, above Finnafjörður, a deep bay with campsite and self-catering **accommodation** at *Fell* farm (☎473 1696, *reimar@simnet.is*; camping 500kr, ②), where you can also pick up fishing licences for the short rivers in the area. From here it's a fairly uninterrupted run to **Bakkafjörður** and **Vopnafjörður** – the smallest and largest of the northeastern communities – and routes out of the region.

The road continues around the coast, dividing 40km from Þórshöfn with a 5km northern spur up to **BAKKAFJÖRÐUR**, an isolated cliff-top community, racked by winds. As the region's smallest settlement the village endures much "butt of the world"-type humour, and in truth there's not much here beyond the store and obligatory salting plant – the **bus** only comes as close as the Route 85 junction, and even buying fuel often means a chase around the place after the attendant. Nor is there anywhere to eat or stay, though in summer you could – with permission – **camp** anywhere in the neighbourhood, and there's a good day walk over the humpy Digranes headland, and around a rocky coastline to the Svatnes lighthouse.

Vopnafjörður

South of the Bakkafjörður junction, the road cuts inland again and suddenly acquires a sealed surface, the first in a long while. About 25km along, a good side road heads for a few kilometres southwest down the **Selá**, to where a small riverside **swimming pool** (free) complete with changing rooms and showers utilizes the northeast coast's only economically viable hot spring. A further kilometre upstream along a jeep track brings you to **Selárfoss**, a five-metre-high tumble of clear, emerald green water – there's a fish ramp beside the falls for the salmon in the river.

It's a final 5km along the main road past Selá, over Nipslón lagoon, to **VOPNAFJÖRÐUR**, a relatively sizeable town arrayed on a steep hillside facing east over a fjord of same name. A pleasant, predictable place with a large harbour and all the usual services, the region around town featured in several interconnected Settlement-era tales of clan feuding known as the **Vopnafjörður sagas**, and Vopnafjörður itself enjoys mild fame for its sunshine and the fact that the 1988 Miss World, Linda Pétursdóttir, grew up here and once toiled in the fish factory. The exposed **campsite** is on the top road across from the school, with a bank and post office one street down near the church, while the **supermarket** and only formal **place to stay**, the very homely *Hótel Tangi* (☎473 1224, fax 473 1146, sleeping-bag accommodation 1500kr, ②), are one street below again on the harbour road. The hotel's **restaurant** has an inexpensive, warming range of lamb, fish, chicken, pasta and pizza dishes, and supplies takeaways for both locals and campers. Otherwise, the two **fuel stations** – one at either end of town – sell snacks.

This slope that Vopnafjörður sits on is actually the eastern side of the **Kolbeinstangi peninsula**, the tip of a narrow, mountainous ridge that runs 35km northeast from the Interior's high plateaus, backing the town in rock. You can follow this right out to the end by taking the road past the hotel and harbour to where it splits; bear left, but leave the track soon after and go cross-country along the stony ridges for 3km to the sea. In the opposite direction, there's a less easy walk to the town's transmitter tower, featuring marshy saddles, rounded stone outcrops and flint-like shards everywhere. The top is extremely barren, with views southwest to Búrstafell (see below) and down off steep cliffs to the broad, black beach south of town – a bit too windswept to justify a trip in its own right – where the remains of a modern shipwreck labour in the shallows.

From Vopnafjörður to Mývatn and Egilsstaðir

If leaving Vopnafjörður in your own vehicle, make sure you **fuel** up before you depart; to the south, there's no fuel available for at least 120km on the main road, while northwards the next reliable source is Þórshöfn.

Buses and the main road follow Route 85 southwest, initially climbing up **Búrstafell**, 18km from town, where there's a turning to an open-air **museum** (mid-June to mid-Sept daily 10am–7pm) featuring well-preserved, turf-gabled farm buildings – worth a look if you haven't seen traditional Icelandic houses before. The heights above are exposed, with sudden snowdrifts possible all through the year, and then the road winds slowly down to join Route 1 some 70km from Vopnafjörður. Buses turn west here for the 65-kilometre run across desolate lava plains and gravel deserts **to Mývatn** via Grimsstaðir (see p.234); or east for the last 100km **to Egilsstaðir**, with the road crossing the **Möðradalsfjallgurðar** range (800m), the highest pass of its entire circuit, before it descends into the long valley of Jökuldalur and passes the turning coastwards to Húsey. In your own transport, there's also a more direct, eighty-kilometre road east from Vopnafjörður to Egilsstaðir, though this is very mountainous and only open in summer; turn off the Búrstafell road just outside town and follow the western side of the fjord up to where the road cuts east across the rugged Hellisheiði, then follow the Jökulsá á Brú south to join Route 1 at the Húsey turning.

travel details

Buses

The details below cover mid-June to early September; contact the Akureyri bus terminal (☎462 4442, fax 462 1817) for exact dates and information on services outside these times.

Ásbyrgi to: Dettifoss (daily; 2hr); Egilsstaðir (3 weekly; 5hr); Húsavík (daily; 1hr); Kópasker (3 weekly; 30min); Raufarhöfn (3 weekly; 1hr 15min); Vopnafjörður (3 weekly; 3hr 30min); Þórshöfn (3 weekly; 2hr 30min).

Dettifoss to: Ásbyrgi (daily; 2hr); Húsavík (daily; 3hr); Reyjahlíð (daily; 1hr 30min).

Goðafoss to: Akureyri (3 daily; 45min); Húsavík (3 daily; 35min); Reykjahlíð (daily; 55min).

Húsavík to: Akureyri (3 daily; 1hr 15min); Ásbyrgi (daily; 1hr); Dettifoss (daily; 3hr); Egilsstaðir (3 weekly; 6hr); Eskifjörður (3 weekly; 6hr 40min); Goðafoss (3 daily; 35min); Kópasker (3 weekly; 1hr 25min); Neskaupstaður (3 weekly; 7hr); Raufarhöfn (3 weekly; 2hr 15min); Reykjahlíð (2 daily; 45min); Reyðafjörður (3 weekly; 6hr 25min); Vopnafjörður (3 weekly; 4hr 30min); Þórshöfn (3 weekly; 3hr 30min).

Kópasker to: Akureyri (3 weekly; 3hr 25min); Ásbyrgi (3 weekly; 30min); Egilsstaðir (3 weekly; 4hr 35min); Húsavík (3 weekly; 1hr 25min); Raufarhöfn (3 weekly; 50min); Þórshöfn (3 weekly; 1hr 55min); Vopnafjörður (3 weekly; 2hr 55min).

Raufarhöfn to: Akureyri (3 weekly; 3hr 50min); Ásbyrgi (3 weekly; 1hr 15min); Egilsstaðir (3 weekly; 3hr 45min); Kópasker (3 weekly; 50min); Vopnafjörður (3 weekly; 2hr 15min); Þórshöfn (3 weekly; 1hr).

Reykjahlíð to: Akureyri (daily; 2hr 45min); Dettifoss (daily; 1hr 30min); Egilsstaðir (daily; 2hr 45min); Goðafoss (daily; 55min); Grímsstaðir (daily; 30min); Húsavík (2 daily; 45min); Krafla (2 daily; 15 min).

Vopnafjörður to: Akureyri (3 weekly; 5hr 10min); Ásbyrgi (3 weekly; 4hr 15min); Egilsstaðir (3 weekly; 1hr 30min); Húsavík (3 weekly; 6hr); Kópasker (3 weekly; 3hr 45min); Raufarhöfn (3 weekly; 3hr); Þórshöfn (3 weekly; 2hr).

Þórshöfn to: Akureyri (3 weekly; 5hr 10min); Ásbyrgi (3 weekly; 2hr 15min); Egilsstaðir (3 weekly; 2hr 30min); Húsavík (3 weekly; 4hr); Kópasker (3 weekly; 1hr 45min); Raufarhöfn (3 weekly; 1hr); Vopnafjörður (3 weekly; 1hr).

Flights

Húsavík to: Akureyri (daily; 25min); Mývatn (daily; 15min).

Mývatn to: Akureyri (daily; 15min); Húsavík (daily; 15min); Reyjavík (daily; 1hr).

Vopnafjörður to: Akureyri (6 weekly; 1hr 15min).

Þórshöfn to: Akureyri (6 weekly; 45min).

CHAPTER SEVEN

THE EASTFJORDS AND THE SOUTHEAST

T he five-hundred-and-fifty-kilometre strip of land and water covering Iceland's Eastfjords and the southeast takes in a quarter of the country's coastal fringe, though for much of this distance the scenery is pretty static, dividing into just two rather different regions. About as far as you can possibly get from the urban comforts of Reykjavík and Akureyri, the Eastfjords are necessarily self-contained but also unexpectedly well settled, with a population evenly distributed between eastern Iceland's main town of Egilsstaxir, and a handful of smaller but relatively substantial coastal communities which are dotted at regular intervals along the fjords' convoluted coastline. The region has been farmed since medieval times, but the coastal villages here – each with its own small harbour and fishing fleet – really took off during the herring boom of the early twentieth century, and a few were even used as Allied naval bases during World War II. While there's a little bit of history to soak up, the big attraction here are the fjords themselves, a mix of brightly coloured cliffs and blue waters, and there are some relatively easy hiking trails along the coast. For something more serious, head southwest of Egilsstaðir, where deer graze the tundra below the solitary heights of Snæfell, the core of an an extinct volcano.

South of the Eastfjords, the landscape becomes more typically bleak and rugged, dominated by the icy vastness of **Vatnajökull**, whose bald cap sprawls inland west of the town of **Höfn**. With a largely infertile terrain of waterlogged moors and black gravel deserts known as **sandurs** to contend with – not to mention a series of catastrophic **volcanic** events over the years – the population cen-

---

ACCOMMODATION PRICE CODES

Throughout this guide, prices given for **youth hostels, sleeping-bag accommodation** and **campsites** are per person unless otherwise specified. **Hotel** and **guesthouse** accommodation is graded on a scale from ① to ⑧; all are high-season rates and indicate the cost of the cheapest double room. The price bands to which these codes refer are as follows:

① Up to 4000kr	③ 6000–8000kr	⑤ 10,000–12,000kr	⑦ 15,000–20,000kr
② 4000–6000kr	④ 8000–10,000kr	⑥ 12,000–15,000kr	⑧ Over 20,000kr

(See p.26 for a full explanation.)

tres are understandably thinly spread, though you'll find a couple of easy places to explore glacial fringes, and even the ice cap itself.

Transport into and around the region during summer is plentiful, with scheduled buses covering all towns along Route 1, while local services or tours take you beyond. You can also fly in from Akureyri or Reykjavík to airports at Egilsstaðir and Höfn, while Seyðisfjörður in the Eastfjords offers an alternative entry or departure point for Iceland, via the weekly ferry from Scandinavia. During the winter, buses from Reykjavík can get you as far as Höfn on Route 1, but you'll have to rent a car, hitch or fly to reach Egilsstaðir from any direction. **Weather**-wise, expect cold winters with heavy snowfalls, though the southeast coast tends towards wet conditions, while everywhere east of Vatnajökull seems to have much sunnier weather than the rest of the country – at least when the westerlies are blowing.

EGILSSTAÐIR, SNÆFELL AND THE EASTFJORDS

Far from the flow of things, Egilsstaðir and the Eastfjords form a nicely compact, underrated region, whose low-key attractions offer a very different view of Iceland from that presented by the country's more famous sights. Set on Route 1 exactly halfway around the country from Reykjavík, **Egilsstaðir** makes a good base for excursions inland around **Lögurinn**, a narrow, lake-like stretch of the **Lagarfljót** river, or even for an assault on the rocky spires of **Snæfell**, eastern Iceland's highest peak. The Lagarfljót itself is worth exploring too, as there's plenty of birdlife and seals around its marshy mouth. Egilsstaðir is also well placed for reaching the **Eastfjords'** settlements, the pick of which are the tiny village of **Borgarfjörður Eystri**, which sits surrounded by the best of the Eastfjord's scenery; and the international port of **Seyðisfjörður**, just 25km to the east. Right at the fjord's southern end near the town of **Djúpivogur**, don't miss the trip across to **Papey**, a small island with plenty of puffins and a surprisingly long history.

This is one part of the country that really has to be seen **in season** (mid-May to Sept), when you can choose between exploring either with your own transport or on public buses, hopping between the small fishing communities along the way. Once out from Egilsstaðir there's generally no need to return, as most of the other Eastfjord towns lie on alternative coastal roads that link up again with Route 1 at the southern end of the fjords. The mountainous coast also provides some good **hiking** between villages on old, mostly unmarked, trails. However, though you can **fly** into Egilsstaðir at any time, there are no buses to the region between October and mid-May, and in winter there's very little point in being here in your own transport, as the landscape will be inaccessible under heavy snow – even main roads can be blocked for days at a time, leaving you stranded. You will, however, find a reasonable amount of accommodation and services open year-round, and tour operators who would love to see the tourist season extended into winter months, if only they had enough visitors.

Egilsstaðir and around

Wherever you've come from, arrival in **EGILSSTAÐIR**, sitting where the roads from Seyðisfjörður, Borgarfjörður Eystri and Reyðarfjörður meet at the highway

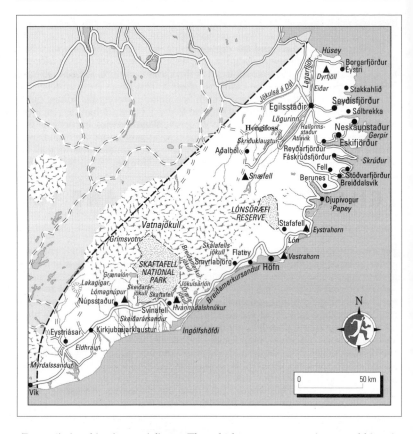

(Route 1), is a bit of an anticlimax. Though the area crops up in several historic texts – most famously in **Hrafnkel's Saga** (see p.252) – the town itself dates only to the late 1940s, when a supermarket, a vet, a hospital and a telephone exchange chose to set up shop where the regional roads converged on a narrow strip of moorland between the glacier-fed **Lagafljöt** river and the back of the Eastfjord fells, bringing the first services into this remote corner of the country. Today Egilsstaðir has grown to fill a couple of dozen streets but remains an unadorned service and supply centre, important to the regional economy but containing little in the way of essential viewing.

Egilsstaðir is, however, a major **transit hub**; the airport has flights to Akureyri and Reykjavík, the port of Seyðisfjörður is nearby, and anyone travelling by bus has to stop here for at least as long as it takes to change services. While the town itself may not slow you down for long, there is, in fact, a reasonable amount to hold you in the area for a day or two. Running southwest from Egilsstaðir, the Lagafljöt forms a long lake known as **Lögurinn**, whose eastern shores are famously forested and whose waters are home to a mythical beast somewhat akin to the Loch Ness monster. Continuing southwest beyond the lake, rough roads and hiking tracks wind up to where **Snæfell**'s isolated peak – clearly visible on a good day from Egilsstaðir – guards the northeastern edge of the Vatnajökull ice cap (see p.253). Meanwhile, heading north from town takes you through moors to the coast around the mouths of the Lagarfljöt and the parallel **Jökulsá á Brú**, a good place to spend a few days fishing, or tracking down wildfowl and reindeer.

The Town

However long you plan to stay in Egilsstaðir, make sure you drop in to the excellent **Minjasafn Austurlands**, the East Iceland Heritage Museum, a ten-minute walk from the bus station on Tjarnabraut (June–Aug Tues–Sun 11am–5pm; 300kr). Amongst the usual examples of local crafts, there are some less ordinary exhibits dedicated to that old Icelandic pastime of **hunting** – mostly guns and ammunition, but a pair of antique wooden snowshoes also feature (rarely seen elsewhere in Iceland), along with a sixteenth-century sword, whose guard and bone handle are decorated with hunting scenes. The museum's two centrepieces are a complete reconstruction of a **turf farmhouse**, which would have been warm but decidedly cramped if ever filled to its fifteen-bunk capacity; and remains from the **Þorisá Barrow**, a local Viking grave dated to 980 AD. Excavated in 1995, this yielded the skeletons of a forty-year-old male and a horse, along with personal effects which included a wooden bowl and two contemporary **English coins**. These were from the reign of Eadwig, the politically inept king of England whose four-year rule saw him lose all authority north of the Thames after nobles ditched him in favour of his brother Edgar, and their presence here throws some light on the extent of trade links and exchanges in the Viking world.

Continue past the museum up Tjarnabraut and you'll pass a modern **church**, whose design vaguely recalls volcanic rock formations, and then reach Egilsstaðir's **swimming pool**, somewhere to unwind on a wet day (Mon–Fri 7am–8.30pm, Sat & Sun 10am–5pm; 300kr). In better weather, there's a brief **walk** to be made uphill from the bus station to a rocky outcrop overlooking the town, with long views down the lake towards a distant Snæfell. If you've got your own transport, it's also worth checking out **Fardagafoss**, a small waterfall in a twisting canyon about 5km northeast of town on the lower slopes of the Seyðisfjörður road.

Practicalities

Egilsstaðir's **airport** is off the highway a kilometre north of town, along with the Flúgfelag Íslands airline office (☎471 1210, fax 471 2208); there are at least four flights a week each way from both Akureyri and Höfn, and daily services to Reykjavík; a bus to town meets flights in summer. These and all long-distance buses wind up at the **bus terminal** just down from the Esso fuel station at the entrance to town. Between mid-May or June and September a number of companies operate regular departures from here north to Borgarfjörður Eystri, Vopnafjörður, Mývatn, Húsavík and Akureyri; east to Seyðisfjörður and through the Eastfjords; and down along Route 1 to Höfn and points west to Reykjavík. Note that between October and mid-May there are no buses either to or from Egilsstaðir.

To enter town, you turn east off this highway onto Fagradalsbraut, immediately passing a knot of services focused around the Esso **fuel station**. About 100m uphill you reach a crossroads, where you'll find a **post office** and **bank**; Tjarnabraut runs north from here to the museum, church, pool and residential areas, while Fagradalsbraut continues east to the Eastfjord roads. The two **car**

rental agents here are based at the airport: Hertz (☎471 1210, fax 471 2208) and Europcar (☎471 1369, fax 471 1621).

The **tourist information office** (June–Aug daily 7am–11pm; ☎471 2320, fax 471 1863, *www.east.is*) is at the bus station, taking all accommodation and bus bookings and helping to sort out **tour** options, such as those operated by Tanni Travel (also contactable through Philip Vogler on ☎471 2190, fax 872 1473, *philip@islingua.is*), the main outfit in town. They offer two separate day trips twice a week in summer: for the whole stretch of mid-May to mid-October, they run north to the coast at Húsey then take in a circuit of Lögurinn (5200kr); and in July and August they head via Hrafnkelsdalur (see p.254) to Snæfell (see p.253) and, weather permitting, the edge of Vatnajökull (5900kr, or 4200kr one-way for those intending to hike on to Stafafell). This latter route is similarly covered by Stefán Sigurðsson of Jeep Tours (☎471 2189, fax 471 1519), whose higher costs reflect the fact that you're in smaller goups (8000kr); he also does cross-Vatnajökull trips to Höfn (see p.266) for 11,700kr.

There are a moderate range of places to stay in town, though it pays to book ahead as accommodation fills up fast in summer. The well-equipped **campsite** with showers, cooking facilities and a laundry is next to the bus station, and also offers dormitory-style beds (book through the tourist information office; camping 500kr, beds 1200kr). For a first-rate **guesthouse**, try *Gistihúsið Egilsstaðum* (☎471 1114, fax 471 1266, *www.isholf.is/egilsstadir/hotel*; sleeping-bag accommodation 1500, ②), 500m west of town on Lögurinn's shore in a converted, solid stone farmhouse with friendly staff and grand views down the lake; they can also rustle up breakfast for guests. As for **hotels**, there's the smart, Icelandair-run *Hérað*, behind the shopping centre (☎471 1500, fax 471 1501, *herad@icehotel.is*; ⑥); the much drabber but comfortable enough *Valaskjálf*, opposite the museum at Skógarlöndum 3 (☎471 1000, fax 471 1001, *valaskjalf@austurland.is*; ④); and an *Edda*, across from the pool off Tjarnabraut (☎471 2775, fax 471 2776; sleeping-bag accommodation 1800kr, ④).

For supplies, Egilsstaðir boasts two very well-stocked **supermarkets**, one behind the fuel station, the other opposite in a new shopping complex. As for eating, the fuel station **café** is well patronized, though only offering the usual grills, pizzas, and sandwiches, with more of the same up at the crossroads at a branch of the ubiquitous *Pizza 67*. Across the road from here next to the bank – though hidden behind trees – the *Café Nielsen* is a folksy coffee shop and gallery. For something more stylish and not too expensive, try the *Ormurrin* **restaurant**'s seafood or pasta dishes, served in a relaxed setting in an isolated house directly behind the fuel station supermarket.

Lögurinn

In common with many Icelandic lakes, **Lögurinn**, stretching directly southwest of Egilsstaðir for 30km, fills a glacier-eroded valley. Unusually, however, the valley is fairly well wooded, at least along its eastern side. Most people don't get much further than these woods' southern reaches around the bay of **Atlavík**, but a decent road runs right around the lake and elsewhere there's saga lore and medieval remains to take in, along with an impressive **waterfall**. Deep and green, the lake itself is home to the **Lagarfljótsormur**, a monster of the Scottish Loch Ness and Swedish Storsjön clans, though so elusive that nobody is too sure what it looks like – a giant snaky form is currently favoured.

You only need one nice day to appreciate Lögurinn, but if you want to stay longer, there's **accommodation** all around the lake, concentrated in the more visited stretch between Egilsstaðir and Atlavík. In your own vehicle, Lögurinn takes an easy few hours to circuit, including time for stops along the way; otherwise you'll have to rely on **tours** from Egilsstaðir (see "Practicalities", opposite) or the twice-weekly **bus**, though this only goes as far as Atlavík. Alternatively, you might pass through en route to Snæfell, as the direct route from Egilsstaðir runs off Lögurinn's southern end. From June to September you can also take a **lake cruise** down to Atlavík with Lagarfljótsormurinn (☎471 2900, fax 471 2901, *www.lagarfljotsormur.is*), whose boats leave twice daily from the wooden-decked roadbridge at **FELLABÆR**, a knot of houses across a long, wooden bridge 2km northwest of Egilsstaðir at the tip of the lake. The cruise to Atlavík takes ninety minutes each way; single/return tickets are 900kr/1400kr, and remain valid for two days, allowing you to spend a night by the lakeshore.

The road to Atlavík

Iceland is not known for its **forests**, which were never very extensive and have fallen to human and grazing pressures since the Settlement. Since the early twentieth century the Icelandic Forestry Commission has put considerable effort into preserving fragmentary pockets of woodland and sponsored **replanting programmes** around the country, and the fifteen-kilometre stretch along Lögurinn's eastern shore at Eyjólfsstaðaskógar and Hallormsstaðurskógar are their showpieces, giving an idea how parts of Iceland might once have looked – and may do so again, given time. Hallormsstaðurskógar in particular is wildly popular with Icelanders, though visitors from more lavishly vegetated climes may feel that the woodland, relatively extensive and pleasant though it is, doesn't warrant so much excitement.

Start by heading south from Egilsstaðir down the highway, where, 11km along, a blue board by the roadside marks a handful of short trails into **Eyjólfsstaðaskógar**, the smaller and least developed of the two wooded areas – the longest takes about three hours return. If you fancy stopping overnight, there's sleeping-bag and cabin **accommodation** at *Eyjólfsstaðir*, a farm across the road (☎471 2147, fax 471 2271; sleeping-bag accommodation 1350kr, cabin 5220kr). Continuing south, Route 1 bends east to Breiðdalsvík and the southern fjord towns; bear right to stay on the lake circuit, which passes a layby with good views over the water before entering **Hallormsstaðurskógar**. Most of the trees here are Icelandic birch – distinguished by its smooth red or silver bark – though there are also plantations of introduced ash, spruce and larch. If you've spent any length of time in Iceland there's real novelty value in being surrounded by close woodland; if not, savour the experience for later. By now you're 24km from town, and close to a range of **summer accommodation**; first is a lakeshore **campsite**, while another kilometre on there's a **fuel station** and small **store** opposite the 200-metre sideroad to **HALLORMSSTAÐUR**, which comprises the modern *Fosshótel* (☎471 1705, fax 471 2197; sleeping-bag accommodation 1500kr, ③), hidden away in the woods with the only **restaurant** around the lake; and *Hússtjórnarskólans* (☎471 1763, fax 471 2761; sleeping-bag accommodation 1350kr, ②), a nice elderly schoolhouse on the forest fringe. There are marked **walking tracks** out of the woods and up onto the fellsides here, the longest of which takes around five hours return; *Hússtjórnarskólans* also hires out **horses** for these trails.

Back on the lake road, it's another couple of kilometres past the fuel station to the **forestry office** and **arboretum**, offering a half-hour stroll around century-old native and imported trees, impressively tall and all labelled – a chance to put names to branches. Past here is another turning lakewards to **Atlavík**, a bay with another popular **campsite** 28km from Egilsstaðir, where lake cruises dock and you can rent rowboats.

Hrafnkelsstaðir and western Lögurinn

Atlavík marks the start of gravel roads around the rest of lake, but they're pretty good and shouldn't give you any problems. Almost immediately, you exit the woods and find yourself well towards Lögurinn's southern end; a few kilometres later and the road squeezes between farm buildings at **Hrafnkelsstaðir**, the holding that features in the latter stages of **Hrafnkel's Saga** (see box, below). Some 40km from Egilsstaðir you cross a long wooden bridge to the lake's western shore; on the far side, turn south to **Valþjófsstaður**, another historic farm founded by the influential twelfth-century chieftain Þorvarður Þórarinsson. The otherwise unremarkable **church** here once sported an ornately carved wooden door of similar vintage, now in Reykjavík's National Museum.

Heading north up the lake from the bridge, it's around 3km to **Skriðuklaustur**, site of a medieval monastery and now graced by a distinctive stone house built in the 1930s by author **Gunnar Gunnarsson**, whose bronze bust adorns the front lawn and who set several of his early psychological novels in the northeast, before switching his attentions to writing about key events in Icelandic history. Next comes the junction with the track up to **Snæfell** (see opposite), which branches west up the valley wall; by this point the lakeside is very open, with scattered home-

---

HRAFNKEL'S SAGA

Lögurinn and the lands to the west form the stage for **Hrafnkel's Saga** (*Hrafnkel's saga Freysgoða* in Icelandic), a short but striking story set in the mid-tenth century, before the country had converted to Christianity. Long debated by scholars as to whether it's a straight history or a complex moral tale, it tells of the landowner **Hrafnkel**, a hard-working but headstrong devotee of the pagan god Freyr, who settled what is now known as **Hrafnkelsdalur**, a side-valley off the Jökulsá á Dál some 35km due west of Lögurinn. Here he built the farm **Aðalból**, and dedicated a shrine and half his livestock to Freyr – including his favourite stallion, the dark-maned **Freyfaxi**, which he forbade anyone but himself to ride on pain of death.

Inevitably, somebody did. Hard times forced **Einar**, the son of a neighbouring farmer, to find work as a shepherd with Hrafnkel, who treated him well but warned him not to touch Freyfaxi. But one day Einar wanted to ride in search of some errant ewes and took Freyfaxi, thinking that Hrafnkel would never know. The sheep were found eventually but, in a seemingly deliberate act, the horse ran back to Aðalból before Einar could clean him. Hrafnkel saw Freyfaxi filthy and exhausted, and, realizing what had happened, felled Einar with his axe.

Though Hrafnkel had never before given compensation in similar circumstances, **Þorbjörn**, Einar's father, demanded redress. Hrafnkel unexpectedly admitted having overreacted and offered a generous settlement that Þorbjörn nevertheless rejected, wanting to set his own terms. Looking for legal help, Þorbjörn enlisted his sharp-witted nephew **Sámur**, who reluctantly took the case to court at the next Alþing at Þingvellir in southwestern Iceland (p.88). But Sámur found that

steads set amongst good grazing land. Seven kilometres from the bridge, look for a small roadside sign marking the walking track to **Hengifoss**, whose 118-metre drop makes it Iceland's third-highest falls. It takes about an hour to walk to them, passing excellent columnar rock formations and the smaller **Litlifoss** along the way; Hengifoss itself forms a dramatic, narrow curtain against the banded red and black cliffs behind. The final 35km back along the lake to Egilsstaðir from Hengifoss is fairly bland, passing a few old turf farmhouses before rejoining Route 1 at Fellabær.

Snæfell

Permanently snow-capped and sharply ridged, **Snæfell** rises to 1833m above the high moorland 80km southwest of Egilsstaðir, right at the very edge of the Vatnajökull ice cap (see p.264). The mountain is one of Iceland's highest, formed from the eroded core of a long-extinct **stratovolcano**, a type that erupts at intervals over long periods, slowly building ejected tephra and lava into tall, bulky cones. While climbing Snæfell needs experience and equipment, reaching the base and exploring the surrounding moors and fringes of Vatnajökull (see p.264) is straightforward enough during midsummer, though unless you've your own four-wheel-drive – and some skill at using it – you'll have to either take a tour or trek in from Egilsstaðir. Hikers can also continue south from Snæfell to Lónsöræfi (see p.265), skirting around Vatnajökull in an increasingly popular **trail** that needs experience with glacier traverses but no mountaineering skills. Aside from beautiful alpine scenery, you'll almost certainly encounter **reindeer** all through the area – they're very common up here – and possibly **gyrfalcon** too, at least up around the peak.

---

nobody wanted to support a dispute against such a dangerous character as Hrafnkel, until a large party of Westfjord men, led by Þorgeir, offered their services. As Sámur presented his case, his allies crowded around the gathering and Hrafnkel, unable to get close enough to mount a defence, was outlawed.

Disgusted, Hrafnkel returned home where he ignored his sentence, but Sámur and the Westfjorders followed him in secret and descended on his homestead early one morning. Dragged out of bed, Hrafnkel was hung up by his Achilles tendons and told to choose between death or giving his property to Sámur. He took the latter option, leaving Aðalból and moving east over the Lagarfljót to **Hrafnkelsstaðir**, a dilapidated farm that he was forced to buy on credit. Back at Aðalból, Sámur destroyed the shrine to Freyr and drowned Freyfaxi as the unlucky cause of the dispute; hearing about this, Hrafnkel renounced his god.

Over the next six years Hrafnkel laboured hard to build up his new property and, his former arrogance deflated, became a wealthy and respected figure. Meanwhile, Sámur's noble brother **Eyvind** returned from a long overseas trip and landed in the Eastfjords at Reyðarfjörður, where he decided to visit Sámur at Aðalból. Riding past Hrafnkelsstaðir, Eyvind was spotted by one of Hrafnkel's servants who, upset by Eyvind's ostentatious finery, goaded her master into taking revenge against his persecutor's brother. Stung by her rebukes, Hrafnkel and his men cut Eyvind down in a bog and then launched a lightning raid on Aðalból, capturing Sámur and giving him the same choices that Sámur had given him: to die or hand over the farm. Like Hrafnkel, Sámur chose to live and – having vainly tried to reinvolve his friends in the Westfjords – retired unhappily to his former estate. For his part, Hrafnkel retained his power and influence and stayed at Aðalból until his death.

Whichever way you plan to get there, **routes to Snæfell** are generally only viable in July and August, and you still need to come prepared for wind, rain or snow. There's nowhere to stock up along the way, so bring everything you'll need with you; **accommodation** involves camping out or staying in shelter huts or proper mountain huts, which need to be booked in advance. From Egilsstaðir, Tanni Travel (see "Practicalities", p.250) run twice-weekly **tours** to Snæfell via Hrafnkelsdalur, and can also organize **guides**, **pickups** and **transport** (from jeeps to horses), and have details about booking **huts** along the route – either contact them, or Karen Erlingsdóttir, Stekkjartröð 12, in Egilsstaðir (☎471 1562, *stekk12@binet.is*). If you're hiking to Snæfell from Egilsstaðir, the track is fairly obvious but you'll need to seek advice from Tanni Travel about your route – some of the rivers along the way may not be fordable on foot – and at the very least carry Landmælingar Íslands' *Austurland* 1:250,000 **map** and a compass. The tougher Snæfell–Lónsöræfi route requires **survey sheets** (from bookshops in Reyjavík and, if you're lucky, Akureyri), and good hiking and navigation skills – otherwise, join in one of the annual group hikes organized by Ferðafélag Íslands and Útivist (see p.35).

Routes to Snæfell and Lónsöræfi

There are two **routes to Snæfell** from Egilsstaðir. The most direct starts at Lögurinn's southwestern corner near Skriðuklaustur (p.252), following the **F910** in a steep, twisting ascent of the valley walls and on to the top of the fells. Once up here, it's around another 10km to the first **shelter hut** near Garðavatn, one of many small lakes to dot the tundra. If you've a sufficiently detailed map and know what you're doing, Hrafnkelsdalur (see p.252) and Aðalból (see below) lie 20km due west via another **hut** in the pass through the Eyvindarfjöll range, though you'll have to negotiate some more lakes and seriously boggy patches along the way. Otherwise, the F910 continues southwest for another 25km to wind up below **Laugarfell's** prominent peak (835m), with a further **hut** a couple of kilometres east along a track near the upper reaches of the Jökulsá í Fljótsdal, one of Lagarfljöt's main feeders. The track takes you past a small waterfall, and there are natural, open-air **hot springs** that you can bathe in right next to the hut too. From here there are several rough routes and as many options to Snæfell, which is only 11km southwest as the raven flies but rather more once you start weaving around the outlying peaks and fording rivers along the way; your ultimate target is the full-blown **mountain hut** (bookings ☎471 1616 or 853 9098) and unadorned **campground** on Snæfell's western side.

A longer route to the mountain follows **Route 1** for 53km west from Egilsstaðir to where the unsurfaced and rough **Route 923** branches down along the Jökulsá á Dal, which becomes the Jökulsá á Brú further up towards the sea. After 30km along there's another bathable **hot spring** at Brú farm, and then a further 10km down the four-wheel-drive-only **F910** lands you in **Hrafnkelsdalur**, where there's self-catering **accommodation** at a farm named *Aðalból* (☎ & fax 471 2788; sleeping-bag accommodation 1300kr, ②), the prize around which Hrafnkel's Saga revolves (p.252). From here, there's a possible twenty-kilometre detour south to the spectacular **Dimmuglúfur**, a steep-sided, layered canyon, though the track there is awful; further west is the similar **Hafrahuammagljúfur**, where there are plans to dam it with a hydroelectric plant. Continuing beyond Aðalból, the final 40km to Snæfell is on very rough tracks and crosses a half-dozen or more rivers, with the only shelter provided by a basic **hut** about a quarter of the way into the journey.

It's another four or five days for the **hike from Snæfell to Stafafell** in Lónsöræfi, the route first traversing the tip of **Eyjabakkajökull**, a glacier at Vatnajökull's northeastern edge, before hopping between three **mountain huts** along the route at Geldingafell, Kollumúvatn and Illikambur, the last well inside the Lónsöræfi reserve but still a day's journey from Stafafell. Before starting, it's essential to make enquiries about the state of rivers along the way, which have to be forded – you may need to arrange a pickup from Stafafell from within the reserve.

North of Egilsstaðir: Eiðar and Héraðflói

North of Egilsstaðir, a broad, waterlogged valley contains the last stages of the silt-laden Lagarfljöt and Jökulsá á Brú as they wind their final 50km to the coast at **Héraðsflói**, an equally wide bay. Moors along the way are a prime place to see **reindeer** in autumn and spring, and birds in summer, while the coast has **seals** all through the year.

There are two separate **roads through the region**, and while there is limited accommodation in the area, arranging transport might be tricky. For the moors, drive or catch the bi-weekly **bus** along the Borgarfjörður road, which starts east out of town and then bends sharply north, paralleling the Lagarfljöt. A radio mast and scattering of houses along the roadside 12km along heralds arrival at the tiny community of **EIÐAR**, which started out as a medieval farm before an agricultural college was founded here in 1883. There's good **trout fishing** in nearby Eiðavatn, **hiking** trails out to fragmented ponds favoured by nesting divers (loons) and, from June until September, you can find **accommodation** at the *Eiðar Guesthouse* (☎471 3846, fax 471 3866; sleeping-bag accommodation 1100kr, ②), where you can also **eat**, and the *Edda* hotel (☎471 3803, fax 3804, *edda@edda.is*; sleeping-bag accommodation 1500kr, ②).

The bus turns around here and heads back to Egilsstaðir but, with your own transport, the moorland **north of town** is well worth checking out in winter for reindeer, which come off the highlands to forage on the tundra, and in summer the whole area is packed with wildfowl and plants. The best place to get a good look at all this is 18km further towards Borgarfjörður where there's a signposted gravel track east to **Hjaltastaður church** – park the car at a spot that takes your fancy, and walk off across the boggy lands towards the distant fells.

Héraðsflói

To head to the coast at **Héraðsflói**, follow Route 1 for 20km northwest of Egilsstaðir to the Jökulsá á Brú, from where Route 925 heads 30km coastwards along the east side of the river to a tongue of land between the Jökulsá and Lagarfljöt. Fringing the sea, these black gravel flats are known as **Héraðssandur**, and there's **accommodation** here at the working farm and self-catering hostel of *Húsey* (☎471 3010, fax 471 3009; sleeping-bag accommodation 1500kr), an excellent place to spend a few days observing an Icelandic farm in action and getting to know the region. The farm breeds horses and offers **riding tours** of up to eight days' duration; there are plenty of nesting ducks, terns, skuas, swans and geese to spy on in the vicinity; and you can join in netting for salmon and trout. Be aware too, however, that the farm is one of the last in Iceland to still **hunt seals**, selling the skins and meat – though they'll point you in the right direction if you want to see them in the wild. Without your own transport, you can reach *Húsey* by calling them in advance to arrange a pickup from Route 925, then catching a westbound bus to the pickup point from Egilsstaðir.

The Eastfjords

The **Eastfjords** cover a 120-kilometre stretch of eastern Iceland's convoluted coastline between Borgarfjörður in the north and southern Berufjörður, with many of the fjords – none of which is particularly large – sporting small villages, mostly given over to fishing. The fjord scenery can be vivid, particularly in summer, with the villages sitting between flat blue sea and steep, steel-grey mountains, their peaks dusted in snow and lower slopes covered in greenery and wildflowers. Each community has its own character; seabirds and seals abound; and there are plenty of relatively easy hiking trails to stretch your legs on. In purely practical terms, you'll also wind up here if you're catching the ferry from Seyðisfjörður to Scotland or Scandinavia.

There are regular summer **buses** from Egilsstaðir to the Eastfjord villages, with the exception of Borgarfjörður Eystri, though not all are interconnected and you'll have to backtrack at some point if you want to check out the coast thoroughly. You can also bypass most of the Eastfjords by taking Route 1 south from Egilsstaðir, which cuts down through the wonderfully stark **Skríðadalur** and **Breiðdalur** valleys to rejoin the coastal road at **Breiðdalsvík** – for more on which, see p.263. Almost all the Eastfjord villages have accommodation, a bank, post office, supermarket and swimming pool, though, as usual, services might be limited outside the main season and it's always worth phoning ahead to check.

Borgarfjörður Eystri

BORGARFJÖRÐUR EYSTRI, also widely known as **Bakkagerði**, is an isolated community of just 120 people, overlooking a small fjord 70km northeast of Egilsstaðir. Backed by mountains, it's a charming location, with heaps of local lore to soak up, along with some of the Eastfjords' most rewarding **hiking trails**.

Past Eiðar (p.255), the road from Egilsstaðir runs towards the sea and then cuts up and over the steep flanks of Geldingafjall, joining the coast on the far side at Borg farm. The bay here, **Njarðvík**, is sided in dangerously loose cliffs, and slips across the road are traditionally attributed to the malevolent spirit of **Naddi**, who was part human, part beast. Naddi was vanquished in the fourteenth century by a farmer who pushed him into the sea and erected a protective **cross** by the roadside, and the one here today still bears the original Latin inscription: *Effigiem Christi qui transis pronus honora* – "You who hurry past, honour Christ's image". By now, you're rounding the tip of **Dyrfjöll**, a long rhyolite mountain which rises behind Borgarfjörður, and reach the village itself within a couple of kilometres.

Borgarfjörður itself sits at the mouth of a ten-kilometre-long valley oriented south, with Dyrfjöll to the west and smaller fells to the east. The village is fairly spread out, with a slowly dwindling population just about getting by on fishing, fish processing and sheep farming, though the latter industry has been hit very hard by disease in recent times. Orientation points include the **jetty**, along with the nearby blocky buildings of **Fjarðarborg school** and attached community centre; the **fish factory** 500m further east and the adjacent Álfasteinn, a **rock shop** which sells polished rhyolite and basalt knick-knacks – there's a mineral display here too if you want to know what you're walking over later on. On the way here, you'll have also passed **Lindarbakki**, a fully restored, century-old turf house, now a holiday home.

Close to the village is the small hill **Álfaborg**, meaning "elf-town", after which Borgarfjörður is named and, according to folklore, where Iceland's fairy queen lives. Below, the **church** is a standard nineteenth-century affair, though the altarpiece, depicting the Sermon on the Mount as delivered atop Álfaborg, was painted in 1914 by the Borgarfjörður-born artist **Jóhannes Kjarval**, who often incorporated local landscapes into his work. Check out returning fishing boats too, for the bizarre-looking **greenland shark** – source of the notorious speciality *hákarl* (see p.30) – which are often landed in Borgarfjörður. For a quick look at the coastal **birdlife**, there are some low cliffs out behind the fish factory from where you'll see eider, puffins, fulmar and gulls; a couple of kilometres around the bay, the islet of **Hafnarholm** is a local nesting reserve, closed in May when birds are setting up house but open for visits during afternoons in June and July, and all day in August.

Practicalities

There are no public buses to Borgarfjörður, so without your own transport you'll have to either join up for the one weekly **tour** from Egilsstaðir – which doesn't allow much time to look around – or contact Borgarfjörður's **mail truck** (☎472 9805 or 854 8305), which makes four runs a week from Egilsstaðir. Once here, Borgarfjörður has the usual service trinity of **bank, fuel station-cum-store** and **post office**, and the Álfasteinn rock shop (see above) doubles as a helpful **tourist information office** (☎472 9977, fax 472 9877, *www.alfasteinn.is*). For accommodation, there's the **campground** next to the church, which is free but has no facilities; or you can sort out **homestay accommodation** at *Borg*, on the main road about 50m past the jetty (contact Skúli Sveinsson on ☎472 9870, fax 472 9880, *www.austurland.is/borg*; sleeping-bag accommodation 1500kr, made-up bed 2200kr); or in Fjarðarborg school (☎472 9920, fax 472 9962, *fjardarborg@centrum.is*; sleeping-bag accommodation 1500kr, made-up bed 2300kr). Another option is the farm *Stapi* (☎472 9983; sleeping-bag accommodation 1500kr, ②), which has **cabins** west along the bay just outside Borgarfjörður. For **food**, the school also has a summer restaurant, serving light meals and home-made bread.

Hikes around Borgarfjörður

There are some excellent **hikes** around Borgarfjörður, though a general lack of trail markers, the very real presence of dense summer fogs, plus the strong possibility of atrocious weather and heavy snow on higher trails, make it essential to ensure you're properly equipped, and to seek local advice on routes before setting out. If you want to tailor four-wheel-drive **tours** – or to go reindeer hunting – contact Skúli Sveinsson at *Borg* (see above).

Extremely prominent behind Borgafjörður, **Dyrfjöll**, the "Door Mountain", gets its name from the huge gap in its sharp-peaked, 1136-metre-high basalt crest. The base is a good seven-hour hike from the village, but if you're heading out this way you should also take in **Stórurð**, a valley strewn with black basalt boulders below a small, semi-permanent glacier west again of Dyrfjöll's spine – there are marked walking tracks here south off the Egilsstaðir road at **Vatnsskarð**, where the road crosses Geldingafjall.

A good general introduction to the area is to hike 4km or so west to the next bay of **Brúnavík**, whose steeply sloping valley was farmed until being abandoned in the 1940s. This is a story typical to the whole northern Eastfjords; as the herring industry fizzled out after World War II, and roads and services began to bypass the region, farms founded in Settlement times were given up as people moved on. There's only a small **hiking shelter** here today, where you could have lunch and head back; if you're keen, however, continue south across the loose-sided fells to **Breiðavík**, where there's an emergency hut – the return hike from Borgarfjörður via Brúnavík takes around fourteen hours.

The truly ambitious can extend the above into a three-day trek all the way south to Seyðisfjörður, though there's also a four-wheel-drive track – frequently snow-bound well into summer – which bypasses Brúnavík and Breiðavík but still takes in some superb scenery. This runs down to the next major bay south of Breiðavík, **Húsavík**, whose lush meadows once supported four farms. The highlight here is **Hvítserkur**, a pink rhyolite mountain, wonderfully streaked with darker bands and stripes and rising above lightly greened slopes. There's another **cabin** here, and the track continues down to **Lóðmundarfjörður**, most of whose population clung on into the 1970s. A partly restored **church** remains, built in 1891, and you can stay overnight at *Stakkahlíð* farm, now up and running as a **guesthouse** (☎472 1510, fax 472 1590; meals available; camping 400kr, sleeping-bag accommodation 1200kr, made-up bed 1900kr). Lóðmundarfjörður marks the end of the four-wheel-drive road, but hikers can follow a rough trail through a pass over **Hjálmárdalsheiði** and then down to Seyðisfjörður.

Seyðisfjörður

Twenty-five kilometres east of Egilsstaðir over a good mountain road, **SEYÐISFJÖRÐUR** is an immediately attractive town set at the base of a long, tight fjord. It has a strong Norwegian heritage: first settled by a tenth-century Norwegian named Bjólf, it was entrepreneurs from Norway who, a thousand years later, established Seyðisfjörður as a booming herring port, also importing the town's attractive wooden architecture. During its herring heyday, Seyðisfjörður looked set to become Iceland's largest port, but geography limited expansion. Used as a US naval base during World War II, the town remains an active fishing and processing centre, with a continuing Scandinavian link embodied by the **ferry** *Norröna*, which calls in every Thursday during summer on its Iceland–Faroes–Norway and Denmark route. The town's summer rhythms follow the ferry schedule and it's generally busy only on Wednesdays, when an afternoon craft **market** is laid on for departing visitors.

Scattered along a kilometre or so of road, Seyðisfjörður gives a good first impression of the country to new arrivals, with its smart, neatly arranged core of older wood and corrugated-iron houses backed by steep fjord walls and greenery. If you're coming from Egilsstaðir, the road follows the shallow river Fjarða down to the coast, where you bear left (north) along Ránargata for the older centre around the church and ferry terminal, or right (east) over a small bridge onto Austurvegur and the newer quarter. There's not much to see here; in the older part of town, **Bláa kirkjan**, the Blue Church, is one of the nicest examples of Seyðisfjörður's chocolate-box architecture, painted in pastel hues and hosting classical **concerts** on Wednesday evenings in summer. East on Austurvegur, you cross the bridge and pass Seyðisfjörður's **swimming pool**; further along, a **can-**

non opposite the post office was salvaged from the 1944 wreck of the *El Grillo*, an oil carrier hit by a German bomb. Another few hundred metres up the fjord takes you past the small-boat **harbour** to the East Iceland Technology Museum, **Tækniminjasafn** (June 15–Aug 31 daily 2–6pm; 300kr), whose orderly collection of historical exhibits are outshone by the imposing museum itself, built in 1894 as east Iceland's first telegraph office. Aside from this, make enquiries with accommodation or the tourist information office as to the **Skaftafell Cultural Centre**, a newly opened art gallery in another restored old building; they may also organize historical tours once they're fully up and running.

Practicalities

Buses connect Egilsstaðir with Seyðisfjörður between June and mid-September only, when there's a twice daily service from Monday to Friday, and an extra Wednesday bus to cope with passengers taking the *Norröna* the following day.

Seyðisfjörður's well-stocked **tourist information office** (Mon–Fri 9am–noon & 1–5pm; ☎472 1551, fax 472 1315, *www.sfk.is*) is at the **ferry terminal**, off Ránargata at the end of Fjarðargata; aside from brochures, you can also buy Icelandic **bus passes** here (see Basics, p.22). There's a **bank** next to the church with slightly restricted hours (Mon–Fri 9.15am–12.30pm & 1.30–4pm), while the **supermarket** and **post office** are across the bridge on Austurvegur. Budget accommodation is found either at the **campsite** (☎472 1551, fax 472 1315; 500kr), just back from where the Egilsstaðir road meets Ránargata; or at the *Hafaldan* **youth hostel**, 700m further on along Ránargata outside town (☎472 1410, fax 472 1610, *www.simnet.is/hafaldan*; 1500kr), a friendly place with a well-equipped kitchen, warm, wood-panelled rooms, and great views over the fjord – make sure you book in advance for Wednesday nights. The alternative is a night in the *Seyðisfjörður* **hotel** (☎472 1460, fax 472 1570; sleeping-bag accommodation 1250kr, made-up bed 1990kr, ③), right by the bridge, which has Seyðisfjörður's only **restaurant**, specializing in fish dishes. For lighter **snacks and coffee**, try either of the town's fuel stations, or the basement café in the Cultural Centre (see above).

Around Seyðisfjörður

As ever, there are several **hikes** to be made around Seyðisfjörður, but for something different, you can also **cruise to Skálanes** at the mouth of the fjord with

---

INTERNATIONAL FERRIES FROM SEYÐISFJÖRÐUR

Operated by Smyril Line, the *Norröna* **vehicle and passenger ferry** calls in at Seyðisfjörður every Thursday between mid-May and early September, arriving at 9am and leaving at noon. First stop is Tórshavn in the **Faroe Islands** (arriving Fri at 6am), followed by Hanstholm in **Denmark** (Sat at 4pm); the vessel then returns to Tórshavn (Mon at 6am), before setting out for Lerwick in the Scottish **Shetland Islands** (Mon at 10pm), and Bergen in **Norway** (Tues at noon). From here it's back to Lerwick, Tórshavn and Seyðisfjörður.

Facilities on board are good, with a range of **berths** available, from a couchette – a mattress with no other bedding supplied – to de luxe cabins. Note that the price of a berth does not include your vehicle or even a bicycle, should you be taking one along; for full details of the journey see "Basics", p.3.

Bátaferðir (☎472 1551 or 854 8230) – a good place to see seals and birds; they also head up to Lodmundarfjorður (p.258), at the head of hiking and jeep trails to Borgarfjördur Eystri, taking about ninety minutes each way.

One popular walk starts by following Ránargata for a couple of kilometres past the *Hafaldan* hostel (see p.259) to the **Vestdalsá**, the first real river you'll encounter on the way. Just before you reach it, a trail heads uphill along **Vestadalur**, a valley heading up into the hills to a small lake, **Vestdalsvatn**, past several pretty waterfalls; allow five hours to make the return hike from town. Alternatively, follow the main road as it continues over the Vestdalsá and runs for 14km to the mouth of the fjord at **Brimnes**, where there's a lighthouse and even more decaying ruins from farming times. On the way, you'll pass the trail north over the mountains to Lodmundarfjorður and Borgarfjördur Eystri.

In the opposite direction, take Austurvegur and then the coastal vehicle track for 8km along the south side of the fjord to the site of **Þórarinsstaðir**, a former farm holding where archeologists have recently unearthed the foundations of a church dating from the eleventh century, believed to be the oldest such remains in the country. Not much further on, **Eyrar** is yet another abandoned farm, though here the buildings are far more substantial; it's hard to believe now, but this was once one of the region's busiest settlements. Experienced hikers can spend an extra half-day walking south across mountains from here to the narrow and virtually uninhabited **Mjóifjörður**, the next fjord south, where there's limited accommodation and the chance to catch a ferry on to Neskaupstaður – see opposite.

Route 92: Reyðarfjörður, Eskifjörður and Neskaupstaður

From Egilsstaðir, Route 92 runs southeast for 60km to the sea at the tiny inlet of **Norðfjörður**, passing the fishing villages of **Reyðarfjörður**, **Eskifjörður** and **Neskaupstaður** on the way. Norðfjörður is the top end of the most "typical" part of the Eastfjords, from where its settlements – plain at a distance but more personable on the ground – are distributed down the coast in what, for Iceland, passes as a relatively dense grouping. Once out of Egilsstaðir in this direction there's no need to head back, as Route 96 branches south just before Reyðarfjörður, cutting down to the southern fjords and then out of the region. Between May 25 and August 30 you can catch at least one **bus** daily in each direction between Egilsstaðir and Neskaupstaður; for the southern fjords, see p.262.

Reyðarfjörður

First stop on the Norðfjörður road, and around 20km from Egilsstaðir, **REYÐARFJÖRÐUR** is a small port surrounded by imposing, flat-topped mountains either side of town, their faces ground flat by now-vanished glaciers. The town itself is fairly functional, however, built up as a naval base in World War II and now set for a decline with the expected closure of its fish factory, with the loss of sixty or more jobs – though locals hope a planned aluminium smelter will compensate. The main point of interest here is Stríðsáasafnið, the **Icelandic Wartime Museum**, located back towards the hills off Austurbegur at the end of Heiðarvegur (June 18–Aug 31 daily 1–5pm; 300kr), which details wartime activities with photos and artefacts. North of Reyðarfjörður, **Grænafell** isn't particularly high at 581m, but it is accessible along a two-hour track that climbs up through a narrow gorge to reveal an excellent fjord panorama from the top. Try also to track down the grave of **Völva**, which according to local tales was a supernatural being who watches over the town – the name is applied throughout Nordic countries to a range of benevolent female spirits.

The Norðfjörður road runs through Reyðarfjörður as the town's 700-metre-long main street; the west half is called Búðareyri, and the eastern end Austurvegur. Most of the town's services are along Búðareyri, including the post office, bank and **bus stop**; there's also a **supermarket** down towards the water here on Búðargata. The **campground** (☎470 9090; 450kr) is right on Reyðarfjörður's western boundary, with a small *Fosshótel* next to the post office on Búðareyri (☎474 1600, fax 474 1601; ⑤), or cosy *Tærgesen* **hostel**, in an old timber and iron house across from the supermarket on Búðargata (☎ & fax 474 1447, *gistirey@mmedia.is*; sleeping-bag accommodation 1250kr, made-up bed 2000kr). The *Tærgesen*'s **restaurant** and bar has good pizzas and grills.

Eskifjörður

Set in its own mini-fjord 17km east of Reyðarfjörður, **ESKIFJÖRÐUR** reeks of fish and revels in fishing, managing to maintain a busy fleet despite the fact that most other Eastfjord towns have fallen on hard times. Road junctions are marked by huge propellers and anchors salvaged from trawlers; the fishing fleet are either clogging up the harbour or out on business between Finland and Ireland; and the town's centre is focused around a huge **fish-freezing plant** whose walls are covered in bright murals and whose director, Elfar Adalsteinsson, is also part of the Icelandic consortium that owns English football club Stoke City. Unsurprisingly, across from the freezing plant you'll also find *Sjóminjasafn*, the **Maritime Museum** (June 15–Aug 31 daily 2–5pm; 300kr), housed in an early nineteenth-century trading house made of dark, creosoted timber, and full of maritime memorabilia – a skiff, models of bigger boats, nets, and bits and pieces from the sea. Just down the road, across from the post office, look too for the bronze statue of kneeling sailor, a general symbol for protection at sea.

Outside of town, 8km up the Norðfjörður road right at the mouth of a tunnel that bores through the mountains and down to Neskaupstaður, there's a small winter **ski slope**, featuring a large wooden hut and chairlift – though there's nowhere to stay and you'll need all your own gear. If you want to stretch your legs, head back a few kilometres towards Reyðarfjörður from Eskifjörður to **Hólmaborgir**, the tall headland that prevents the spring and autumn sun from reaching Eskifjörður. This is actually a nature reserve, and the hour-long walk to the summit is pretty easy, with fine views down on the town from the top.

Though appearing from a distance to be spread out along the fjord shore, Eskifjörður's centre is very compact, with a **post office**, a **bank**, a **bus stop** and **supermarket** within 50m of the freezing plant on Strandgata. Around 200m west along Strandgata is a branch of Egilsstaðir's Tanni Travel (☎476 1399, fax 476 1599), offering **tourist information** and trips to Vatnajökull every Saturday in July and August. For somewhere to stay, the free **campground** is further out again, back towards Reyðarfjörður near the church, while in town your only option is *Hótel Askja*, a characterful old **guesthouse** not far up from the post office on Hólsvegur (☎476 1261, fax 476 1561; ②). **Food and drink** are served up by a branch of *Pizza 67*, just across from the museum.

Neskaupstaður

NESKAUPSTAÐUR curls around the northern side of Norðfjörður at the end of the road, Iceland's easternmost town and the Eastfjords' largest settlement, but again proving a thinly spread one. A two-kilometre road runs, under various names, right along the waterfront, with a core of services and backstreets around halfway along, past which the road eventually runs out. Neskaupstaður may be insubstantial but the setting is splendid, the town backed by tall, unstable fells (**avalanches** have occasionally killed townspeople) and facing a similar view across the fjord; judging by the number of antlers hung over front doors here, there's also a healthy reindeer population up in the hills.

Between June 20 and August 20, you can organize **cruises** with Fjarðaferðir (☎477 1820 or 893 3249), whose office is right next to the bus stop, up to the next fjord north, **Mjóifjörður**, which offer the chance of seeing whales, seals and plenty of birds along the way. The journey takes a couple of hours, costs 2200kr, and there's camping or sleeping-bag **accommodation** in Mjóifjörður at *Sólbrekka* farm (☎476 0005, fax 476 0019, *mjoi@simnet.is*), which also runs a small store and can provide **meals** with advance warning. Alternatively, you could spend two days **hiking** southeast from Neskaupstaður to **Gerpir**, a sheer set of cliffs marking Iceland's easternmost point and famed for their seabird colonies – rocks here are also some of the oldest in the country at 13 million years. The hike is a difficult proposition over rugged country, and you'll need to be completely self-sufficient; contact the *Egilsbúð* hotel (see below) for more information about the routes and the possibility of finding a guide.

Most of Neskaupstaður's facilities are near the harbour on Egilsbraut: the **bus stop**, two **banks** and the **supermarket** are here, with the **post office** two streets back from the bus stop on Þiljuvellir. The free **campground** is a kilometre further on, right at the end of the road; in town, the *Trölli* **guesthouse** is back towards Eskifjörður on Egilsbraut (☎477 1800, fax 477 1370, *www.islandia.is/~island*; ②); there's an *Edda* hotel east off Nesgata (☎477 1331, fax 477 1361, *hotelnes-@eldhorn.is*; sleeping-bag accommodation 1350kr, ②); and the *Egilsbúð* summer **hotel**, near the harbour on Egilsbraut (☎477 1321, fax 1322; ②), whose good **restaurant** and **bar** are open through the year.

The southern fjords

South of Reyðarfjörður the Eastfjords begin to open up, and the mountains – if no lower than before – have room to move into the background, softening the scenery until the fjords themselves fizzle out 160km further on. There are two **routes from Egilsstaðir** to the fjords: either by continuing south around the coastal road from Reyðarfjörður, taking in the successively smaller settlements of **Fáskrúðsfjörður**, **Stöðvarfjörður**, **Breiðdalsvík** and **Djúpivogur**, after which the fjords begin to end; or by following Route 1 south from Egilsstaðir direct to Breiðdalsvík and points south. Between early May and the beginning of October, the Egilsstaðir–Höfn **bus** runs six times a week through the southern fjords, taking either the coastal road or the direct Breiðdalsvík road on alternate days, so you need to make sure you're on the right bus.

Fáskrúðsfjörður and Stöðvarfjörður

The fifty-kilometre coastal road south of Reyðarfjörður offers some nice seascapes as it passes headlands, the orange **Vattarnes lighthouse** and an assortment of sharp peaks and loose scree slopes flanking the road before it reaches **FÁSKRÚÐSFJÖRÐUR**. This typically quiet, spread-out hamlet was, until the early twentieth century, the seasonal base for French fishing fleets from

Brittany, who had "discovered" Iceland's rich herring grounds some fifty years earlier, and you pass a French cemetery on the way into town. Set back from the sea, Búðavegur is the kilometre-long main street, where you'll find the **bank**, **post office** and **supermarket** all within spitting distance of Fáskrúðsfjörður's main **accommodation** prospect, the wooden *Hótel Bjarg* (☎475 1466, fax 475 1476, *hbjarg@centrum.is*; ②) – the other option is the **campsite**, on the far exit of town. The hotel **restaurant** has a reasonable grill menu and a bar, and *Bjarg* can also get together half-day **boat trips** out to the three small islands of Andey (very flat), Æðey, and the high, wind-sharpened Skrúður, famed for its gannet colonies.

Another 25km of fjord scenery as you head southwards lands you at **STÖÐVARFJÖRÐUR**, where you'll find big racks of fish drying in the sun on the slopes above town. A small but nice place with diminutive **harbour**, if you're here in spring, you're likely to find snow-white **ptarmigans** wandering fearlessly down the streets, eating ornamental berries in people's front gardens. Everything of note can be found on the through road, Fjarðabraut: on the west side of town, **Gallerí Snærós** displays graphic work and ceramics by local artists; while **Petra Steinasafn** (200kr) is an extraordinary private collection of thousands of rocks and mineral samples from all over the place, accumulated over a lifetime of fossicking. Aside from the **campsite** just back towards Fáskrúðsfjörður, the only place to stay is on the hill above town at *Kirkjubær*, a church converted into a self-catering **hostel** (☎592 3319, fax 475 8938; 1500kr); they also sell fishing licences. The **bus stop** and all other services are huddled together near the Esso **fuel station** on Fjarðabraut; for a night out, try the *Svarti Folinn* (Black Stallion) **restaurant**, which does some excellent and unusual variations on standard themes – such as cod pizza – and also gets in **live bands** from time to time.

Breiðdalsvík, Djúpivogur and Papey

It's only another 18km south past Stöðvarfjörður to **BREIÐDALSVÍK**, which comprises the standard knot of services and not much else, though the *Hótel Bláfell* (☎475 6770, fax 475 6668; sleeping-bag accommodation 1500kr, ③) is a friendly **place to stay** for the night. It also has a good **restaurant** and sells fishing permits for **Breiðdalsá**, a river valley due west of town, along which a largely unsurfaced Route 1 runs up to Egilsstaðir (see p.247) through a steadily narrowing panorama of impressively sharp-edged mountains, frequently snowbound into early summer. Four kilometres along at the wide valley mouth, *Fell* farmhouse (☎475 6679; sleeping-bag accommodation 1500kr, ②) is a little rundown but has decent enough self-catering **accommodation** and **camping**, and makes a good base to try out your salmon- and trout-fishing skills in the river.

Back on the coastal road, it's another 26km past **Streitishvarf lighthouse** and some spectacular basalt cliffs to *Berunes* farm on Berufjörður (☎ & fax 478 8988, *berunes@simnet.is*; breakfast available; camping 500kr, sleeping-bag accommodation 1500kr, ②, 6-person cottages 6500kr), a **summer hostel** that occupies a beautiful but exposed position looking out to where distant mountains float on the horizon like icebergs. Ask at the hostel about **hiking routes** in the area – some are quite challenging – and trips southeast across the water to **Papey** (see below). Not far up the road, **Gautavík** is where the fiery Norwegian evangelist Þangbrand (see p.289) landed in Iceland in the late tenth century to convert the country to Christianity.

Set slightly off the main road, at the southern tip of Berufjörður, **DJÚPIVOGUR** is the southernmost of the Eastfjord settlements, founded by

German traders in 1589, and now a small, pretty village surrounding a sheltered **harbour** which fishing boats share with rafts of eider and long-tailed ducks. For some good views, take the short walk up **Búlandstindur** (1069m), the pyramidal basalt mountain looming behind town. Much better, however, is the trip over to **Papey**, a two-square-kilometre island about 8km southeast of Djúpivogur. The name means "Monk's Island", and Papey is believed to have been inhabited by Irish monks before Settlement, though they appear to have moved on when the Vikings arrived. Farmed intermittently into the twentieth century, there are remains of homesteads here along with Iceland's smallest **church**, built in 1807 – about three people can squeeze inside – but the main point of a visit is to get close to the thousands of **puffins** that nest here each year. Papeyjarferðir (☎478 8119, fax 478 8183) run four-hour trips here from Djúpivogur through the summer, including a couple of hours on Papey itself, for 2800kr.

Back in town, and overlooking the harbour, the newly renovated and welcoming *Hótel Framtíð* offers **accommodation**, a **bar** and **restaurant**, and even provides **camping** space (☎478 8887, fax 478 8187, *framtid@simnet.is*; camping 500kr, sleeping-bag accommodation 1900kr, ②). Opposite is *Langabúð* (10am–6pm or later), a long wooden building that has variously served as a store, warehouse, slaughterhouse, managers' residence and meeting hall since its construction in 1850, and currently houses a **café**. It's also home to a collection of works by the woodcarver Ríkarður Jónsson, along with a memorial to former Progressive Party leader and fellow local Eysteinn Jónsson.

THE SOUTHEAST: VATNAJÖKULL

About 50km south of Djúpivogur the fjords finally recede into the background and you enter the altogether different world of **southeastern Iceland**, a coastal band between the Eastfjords and Vík, which is totally dominated by Europe's largest ice cap, **Vatnajökull**. Almost 150km broad and up to a kilometre thick, Vatnajökull's vast size gradually sinks in as it floats inland for hour after hour as you drive past, though from the road your view is restricted to the numerous glacier tongues flowing in slow motion from Vatnajökull's heights to sea level, grinding out a black gravelly coastline as they go. To see much more you'll have to leave the highway and visit the fells and valleys that border the ice cap, though flying over is a better way to absorb Vatnajökull's full immensity: glaring ice sheets shadowed in lilac; pale blue tarns; and grey, needle-sharp *nunataks* – mountain peaks – poking through the ice.

Vatnajökull's cooling presence – and the frequently devastating **jökulhlaups** (see p.272) that flood out from beneath its icy skirt from time to time – have limited the southeast's settlement, leaving you with no distractions from investigating the scenery. Following Route 1 through the region, the eastern side of Vatnajökull is accessed at **Lónsöræfi**, a private reserve managed by **Stafafell farm**, close to the southeast's main town of **Höfn**. Continuing southwest, the ice cap's southern glaciers can be explored at **Skaftafell National Park**, after which you cross the **Skeiðarársandur**, a huge glacier-induced wilderness between Vatnajökull and the sea. On the far side and moving away from Vatnajökull, **Kirkjubæjarklaustur** is the only other town in the region, near where lava fields and craters at **Lakagígar** stand testament to perhaps the most violent volcanic event anywhere on earth in recorded history.

Coming **from Reykjavík**, you can reach the southeast year-round on flights and buses to Höfn, from where, in winter, *Stafafell* farm will pick up guests by arrangement. In summer, you can also get into the region by bus **from Egilsstaðir** and the Eastfjords, though there is no bus service in this direction between October and early May. Once here, there are plenty of **tours** on offer, covering everything from short guided hill walks to snowmobile assaults on Vatnajökull itself.

Lón and Höfn

Lón is a glacial river valley whose thirty-kilometre-wide estuary is framed by **Eystrahorn** and **Vestrahorn**, two prominent spikes of granite to the east and west. The central **Jökulsá i Lóni** is a small but typical glacial flow, its gravel bed crisscrossed by intertwined streams that are crystal clear and shallow in winter but flow murky and fast in summer. A sandbar across the mouth of bay has silted the estuary up into **lagoons** – *lón* in Icelandic – with good birdlife, trout fishing (though the Löni is too small and erratic to suit salmon), and reindeer herds descending from the upper fells in winter. Inland, the heights above the valley are **Lónsöræfi**, the Wilderness of Lón, actually a starkly beautiful area of steep rhyolite hills and streams, capped by Vatnajökull's eastern edge – though this is invisible from the main road. It's fantastic **hiking** country, where you could spend a couple of days or more on remote tracks, all incorporated into the private **Lónsöræfi reserve** accessed through *Stafafell* farm (see below). Southwest of Lón, **Höfn** is a transit point and somewhere to dry off and stock up before heading off to attack the score of glaciers further west.

Stafafell and Lónsöræfi

Halfway across Lón and just east of the river, a short road off Route 1 heads inland to **Stafafell farm**, behind which the **Lónsöræfi reserve** stretches back into the mountains. Stafafell has been settled for a long time, and the unassuming **church** here, surrounded by birch trees, was founded a generation after the tenth-century Norwegian missionary **Thangbrand** – armed with a sword, and a crucifix instead of a shield – killed Stafafell's pagan owner in a duel. Thangbrand went on to spread the Christian message across Iceland, narrowly surviving sorcery and attacks by a berserker in the process, dividing the country and forcing the Alþing to restore unity by accepting Christianity as the national religion in 1000.

The estuary itself is worth investigating, not least for the thousands of **whooper swans** which nest on the eastern side of the lagoons between Stafafell and **Eystrahorn**, which is on the main road 15km east of Stafafell. From here you can walk out past the **Hvalnes lighthouse** onto the sandy spit which stretches halfway across the mouth of the bay. The same distance in the opposite direction, triple-pronged **Vestrahorn** is the site of suspected ninth-century ruins off the highway on the shores of Papafjörður, the lagoon below Vestrahorn's eastern face.

The only other buildings back in Stafafell besides the church form the adjacent *Stafafell* farm, which offers hostel-style **accommodation** (☎478 1717, fax 478 1785, *www.eldhorn.is/stafafell*; camping 500kr, sleeping-bag accommodation 1300kr, ②) and commands a fine view of the bay, set just where hills begin to rise off the estuary flats. You stay in the old farmhouse and it's a self-catering affair, unless you make prior arrangements. The manager can advise and provide **guides** for guests wanting to trek in Lónsöræfi reserve, and also runs horse-riding and four-wheel-drive **tours** as alternate modes of transport through the reserve.

Hiking in Lónsöræfi

Access into **Lónsöræfi** reserve from Stafafell is either on very limited jeep tracks, or along the dozen or so **hiking trails**, which cover everything from return walks of a few hours' duration to the week-long trek northeast to Egilsstaðir. However long you're going for, take some warm clothing, food, water, and a tent; weather or navigation errors can see even day-walks accidentally extended. Without a guide, you'll also need the relevant 1:100,000-scale **maps** (from bookshops in Reykjavík) and advice from the farm about conditions on the longer routes – the reserve's waterways are all glacier-fed, making for very unpredictable flow rates in summer.

For a brief introduction, spend five hours following the marker posts up the lower slopes of **Lambafell**, the hills immediately behind Stafafell, and then west through the wildly coloured **Grákinn** valley down to the river, where you join a rough vehicle track leading south past holiday homes and cliffs full of nesting fulmar to rejoin Route 1 only a couple of kilometres west of the farm. More ambitious trails follow the west side of the river to **Illikambur** – though you'll probably need vehicular assistance to ford the rivers along the way – and the start of the hike to Egillstaðir via Snæfell (see p.254 for more of this route); even if you don't fancy the entire trek, it's worth at least reaching the **Egilsell hut** at Kollumúvatn for views of Vatnajökull's easternmost edge and weird rock formations at **Tröllakrókur**.

Höfn

Crossing the saddle in Vestrahorn on Route 1 around 15km west of Stafafell, you're suddenly confronted by the first roadside view of Vatnajökull, a hazy white streak on the horizon with more sharply defined glaciers sliding seawards. The steep descent on Vestrahorn's far side lands you more quickly than expected at **HÖFN**, a small town on the tip of a flat peninsula dividing a bay into two. While Vatnajökull makes a splendid backdrop – at least on days when the pernicious fogs abate – there isn't much to do in Höfn besides making use of its services or arranging a tour up onto the ice cap, though with its bus station and airport, the town makes a useful staging post for the southeast.

The western half of the bay, **Hornafjörður**, offered good landing for vessels in Viking times, and is the main reason that Höfn exists at all. The town actually began life in 1863 as a tiny trading post east at Papafjörður, in Lón, but went into a decline with the advent of modern vessels, whose deep keels prevented them from landing in the shallow bay. Tired of having to ride all the way to Reykjavík for supplies, the traders simply moved shop to deeper anchorage at Hornafjörður, though Höfn – which means "harbour" – only took off with the fishing boom of the 1950s and the establishment of a fish-freezing plant, still the largest local employer. You can come to grips with all this – or just take shelter in wet weather – at Höfn's **museum** (June–Aug daily 1–6pm; 300kr), *Byggðasafn*, housed in the original store just up from the bus station on the main road into town; look for the bright orange snowcat exhibit outside.

Practicalities

Höfn stretches for around 2km along Hafnabraut, which turns off the highway and runs past the **supermarket**, **tourist information office** (☎478 1500), **post office** and **bank**, to terminate at the **harbour**. The **airport** is 6km west, with daily flights to and from Reykjavík throughout the year; you'll have to hire a taxi from the desk here to reach town. Höfn's **bus station** is on Hafnabraut about a kilometre from the harbour; in summer there's at least one bus daily passing through either way along the highway bound east to Egilsstaðir or west to Reykjavík, but between October and May the service shrinks to three buses a week to Reykjavík and none going eastwards.

Höfn's **campsite** (☎478 1000, fax 478 1901; 500kr), with showers, laundry, and plenty of space, is right next to the bus station, with other **places to stay** scattered around town. West of the bus station, on Víkurbraut, *Hótel Höfn* (☎478 1240, fax 478 1996; ⑤, 30 percent discount May & Sept) is a comfortable, characterless modern pile open from May to September. For cheaper and more attractive lodgings, head down to the harbour, where the *Nýibær* youth hostel (☎478 1736, fax 478 1965 *nyibaer@simnet.is*; sleeping-bag accommodation 1500, ③) and *Hvammur* guesthouse (☎478 1503, fax 478 1591, *lulu@eldhorn.is*; ②) both provide cosy rooms with shared facilities. For farmstay accommodation, check out *Arnanes* farm, near the airport (☎478 1550, fax 478 1819, *www.eldhorn.is/arnanes*; sleeping-bag accommodation 1600kr, ③).

For **eating**, *Kaffi Hornið*, a café on the Hafnabraut–Víkurbraut intersection, does fine coffee and hot crepes, burgers, grills, and even vegetable gratin and salad. More grills and pizzas are on offer just down Hafnabraut at *Osinn* (Lighthouse), while east along Víkurbraut at *Vikin* restaurant, where they serve up excellent seafood, there's also a **bar**.

Regional tours focus on spending a couple of hours bouncing across Vatnajökull in snowcats or jeeps, and cost from 5000kr per person; operators include Glacier Jeep Tours (contact Bjarni Bjarnason on ☎478 1567, fax 478 2167) and Glacier Tours (☎478 1000, fax 1901, *www.glaciertours.is*), the latter also taking in Jökulsárlón, at Breiðamerkursandur (see p.268), on quick lagoon cruises. Alternatively, buses from the bus station offer similar day trips to Vatnajökull, and also to Lónsöræfi and Skaftafell; while out near the airport Arnanes farm offer glacier tours and horse riding. For a more intimate view of the area – including **hiking** trips through Skaftafell and Lónsoræfi, **bird-watching**, **skiing** and **climbing** – contact Sigurður Bjarnason or Einar Sigurðsson (☎ & fax 478 1682).

Skálafellsjökull and Skaftafell National Park

It's 125km west along Route 1 from Höfn to **Skaftafell National Park**, with Vatnajökull – or rather, its score of outrunning glaciers – staying with you the whole way, never more than a few kilometres from the roadside. With the clear atmosphere playing tricks with your eyes and making it difficult to judge scale, it's only by the length of time it takes to pass them that you realize that some of these glaciers are real monsters, scored and scarred with crevasses and with a light powder of white snow covering the blue-green ice of the glacier tongue itself.

Not far west of Höfn you can see four of these glaciers at once – from east to west they're Hoffellsjökull, Fláajökull, Heinabergsjökull and **Skálafellsjökull**. Several **farmstays** along the way give you the opportunity to stop off: both *Flatey*, 40km from Höfn (☎478 1036, fax 478 1598, *flatey1@mmedia.is*; sleeping-bag accommodation 1650kr, ②), and *Smyrlabjörg*, another 5km west (☎478 1074, fax 478 2043; ②), offer self-catering facilities and guided tours up onto the snowline at Skálafellsjökull, reached along a nineteen-kilometre gravel track from Smyrlabjörg that ends at a **restaurant** overlooking the glacier. Glacier Tours, based in Höfn (see p.267), run **snowmobile tours** from here from 4800kr and, unless you're a seasoned Arctic explorer, they are an exceptional experience. Being on the glacier on a sunny day is remarkably warm, and the glare from the snow can be intense; half-day tours provide good views, but to get the feeling of having *been* somewhere, opt for the full-day rides that cross the glacier to remote mountain peaks jutting up through the snow. Returning, the sun will have melted the glacier's fringes creating little rivulets between the now highly slippery ridges, and it becomes easy to appreciate the dangers of the ice.

Jökulsárlón, Ingólfshöfði and Svínafell

Southwest of Smyrlabjörg, the road is forced ever closer to the sea by the encroaching glaciers, and after 35km you reach a short bridge spanning the mouth of **Jökulsárlón**, Glacier River Lagoon. This is a perfect description of this large pool between the nose of the huge but slowly diminishing **Breiðamerkurjökull** and the sea, full of great slabs of ice which have split off the glacier and float idly in the lake as if performing some slow ballet, tinted blue or pink by the water and sub-arctic evening light. All transport stops for a few minutes for a view from the bank, though it's also possible to make short **boat trips** (1800kr) around the lake, or even **camp** here – though there are no facilities and it's decidedly cold, even in good weather.

From here the road continues southwest for another 30km, the coastal strip comprising the black rubble and grit of **Breiðamerkursandur**, with the surf breaking on shingle just metres from the road. This provides ideal nesting grounds for **greater skuas**, avian pirates who chase and harass other seabirds until they drop their catches. Skuas resemble brown, bulky gulls, and are best watched from a distance as they take exception to being disturbed while raising their young. At the end of the sandur the road bends sharply northwest at a **fuel station** and small **supermarket**, as you round the base of **Öræfajökull**, a glacier covering the Öræfi volcano, whose devastating eruption in 1362 covered the whole region in tephra and caused its abandonment. Öræfi's protruding peak, **Hvannadalshnúkur**, is the highest point in Iceland at 2199m; if you fancy a crack at the summit, contact Skaftafell-based Icelandic Mountain Guides (see "Skaftafell" below), who offer a fifteen-hour ascent of Hvannadalshnúkur for the fit and fearless (8000kr), though you don't need previous mountaineering experience.

Jutting 10km out to sea at this point is the flat prong of **Ingólfshöfði**, said to be where Iceland's first official settler, **Ingólfur Arnarson** (see p.288), made landfall. Tipped by a lighthouse, Ingólfshöfði's soft soil and low cliffs attracts summer colonies of puffins, razorbills and guillemots; you can arrange trips out here from Höfn or *Hof I*, a **farmstay** 5km up the road (☎478 1669, fax 478 1638, *hof@vortex.is*; sleeping-bag accommodation 1650kr) – the farm's nineteenth-century **turf church** was built on the site of a pagan temple.

The final twenty-kilometre run up to Skaftafell crosses the easternmost fringe of **Skeiðarársandur** (see p.271), a desert of rubble and boulders with the massive spread of **Skeiðarárjökull** – one of Vatnajökull's largest, most active glaciers – filling the distance but seeming to recede the closer you come. Just short of the national park, and sitting within a few hundred metres of the snout of **Svínafellsjökull**, modern farmhouses mark out **Svínafell**, once the residence of the **Njál's Saga** character Flosi, who headed the burning of Njál and his family. It was also where Njal's son-in-law Kári, the only one to have survived the burning, finally forgave Flosi in the closing chapters of the tale; see p.108 for the full story.

Skaftafell National Park and around

Bordered by **Öræfajökull** to the east and **Skeiðarárjökull** to the west, **Skaftafell National Park** covers 1700 square kilometres of southeastern Iceland, encompassing barren lowland sandurs, grassy valleys and morraine slopes brimming with wildflowers, through to lengthy glacial tongues and the Interior fringes of Vatnajökull itself. The most accessible part of the park is **Skaftafellsheiði**, a high, wide vegetated tongue of land dividing the lengthy **Skaftafellsjökull** from westerly **Morsárjökull**. Both glaciers shrank during the twentieth century, but there's plenty left of them, plus associated valleys to check out. Even without ice-climbing skills you can follow fairly straightforward **hiking tracks** right up to the flanks of the glaciers – most are clearly marked – or explore further with the proper equipment.

For a bit of Skaftafell's history, follow the road past the **service centre** at the foot of Skaftafellsheiði for a couple of kilometres to its end on Skaftafellsheiði's southwestern slopes at **Sel**, an old turf-roofed farmhouse built in the 1920s and abandoned a generation later. The Skaftafell region has been farmed since medieval times, though much of the original grazing land has since been covered by sandurs, and Sel was forced to relocate to higher ground in the nineteenth century.

One of the shortest **walks** at Skaftafell takes you east of the service centre to Skaftafellsjökull itself, an easy thirty minutes through low scrub around the base of yellow cliffs where ravens tumble overhead. The woods end at a pool and stream formed from glacial meltwater, beyond which stretches ice-shattered shingle and the four-metre-high front of the glacier, streaked with mud and grit and surprisingly unattractive. Crevasses, and the generally unstable nature of glacier extremities, make it inadvisable to climb onto the tongue unless you've previous experience. Another fairly brief hike – allow two hours for the return journey from the campsite – runs up onto Skaftafellsheiði to **Svartifoss**, the Black Falls. Pretty rather than spectacular, it's not the water that gives the falls their name, but the surrounding dark basalt cliffs, whose underhanging columns inspired the architecture of Reykjavík's National Theatre.

Longer walks cross west over Skaftafellsheiði to **Morsárdalur**, the flat-bottomed glacial valley left by the retreating Morsárjökull. On Morsárdalur's western side, **Bæjarstaðarskógar** is a small but thriving wood of willows and birches, close to a **thermal springs** area – great for soaking feet but a touch too hot for a full immersion. You can carry on up the valley from here to the noisy front of Morsárjökull, and then bear west to **Kjós**, a strikingly beautiful valley of bare, fractured boulders and sharp yellow crests, which peak at 1000m. The trek to Bæjarstaðarskógar takes around four hours return, but you'd need around ten for Kjós. The best hike of all,

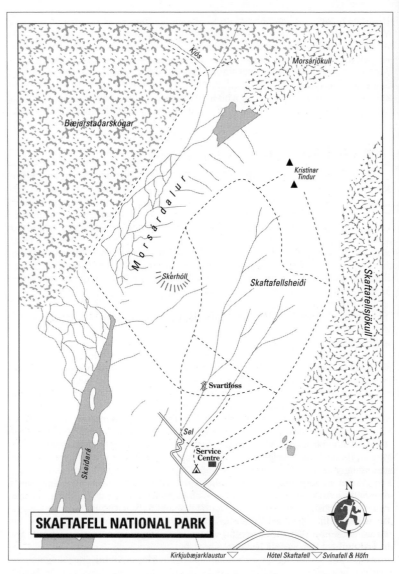

SKAFTAFELL NATIONAL PARK

Morsárjökull

Kjós

Bæjarstaðarskógar

Kristínar
Tindur

Morsárdalur

Skerhóll

Skaftafellsheiði

Skaftafellsjökull

Svartifoss

Sel

Service
Centre

Skeiðará

N

Kirkjubæjarklaustur ▽   Hótel Skaftafell ▽ Svínafell & Höfn

however, is the day-long return trip on a circuit track north around the top of Skaftafellsheiði to the double-peaked **Kristínartindur**; the rewards are a delightful hike across Skaftafellsheiði's upper moors, and awesome views over Morsárdalur and down onto Skaftafellsjökull. You could also climb Kristínartindur's summit (1125m) – it's steep but not technically demanding – but make sure you start early enough to pack all this into even an Icelandic summer's day.

Practicalities

The best place to base yourself is at the Skaftafell **service centre** (May–Sept daily 8am–10pm; ☎478 2288, fax 478 2388, *skaftafell@mmedia.is*), just off the highway at the foot of Skaftafellsheiði, which provides **tourist information**, **fuel**, a **café** and a **supermarket**. There are also extensive **campgrounds** here with showers and laundry, which, despite their size, can get extremely busy in summer; note, however, that camping out in the park itself is not permitted without prior permission. The alternative is to find a bed and board at *Skaftafell* **hotel** at Freysnes, 5km east of the park turn-off on highway near Svínafell (☎478 1945, fax 478 1846; sleeping-bag accommodation 1550kr, ④).

As always, seek advice on routes and what to take with you before setting out on any lengthy walks; the service centre has some park brochures but it's wise to carry Landmælingar Íslands *Skaftafell* **map**, which has 1:100,000 and 1:25,000 sheets covering the Skaftafellsheiði area. There are also plenty of hiking **tours** available if you don't want to go it alone: Icelandic Mountain Guides, based in Reykjavík (☎587 9999, fax 587 9996) and Skaftafell (☎854 2959, *www.solver.is/guide*), take beginners onto Svínafellsjökull for a couple of hours to teach them how to use an ice axe and crampons (2100kr), plus they do glacier traverses and ascents of Hvannadalshnúkur (see p.268) for the more experienced. Hofnes i Öræfum (☎478 1682, fax 478 2382, *www.simnet.is/coast-mountains*) have similar deals, along with cross-country **skiing** and **bird-watching** tours.

Across Skeiðarársandur to Kirkjubæjarklaustur

West of Skaftafell, the highway skirts the massive crescent edge of **Skeiðarárjökull**, the most active glacier in Iceland, whose twenty-kilometre-wide front is so vast that it somehow manages to turn its 1000m drop off the top of Vatnajökull into what appears to be a gentle descent. Over the centuries, the scouring action from Skeiðarárjökull and other glaciers running west off Öræfajökull, combined with titanic outflows from the volcanic glacial lakes **Grænalón** and **Grímsvotn**, have created **Skeiðarársandur**, and much of the 66km of highway between Skaftafell and the tiny hamlet of **Kirkjubæjarklaustur** is spent scudding over this bleak gravel desert, which stretches 15km south from the road to the sea, and where winds can whip up sandstorms strong enough to strip the paint off your car. Surprisingly, then, Skeiðarársandur is the largest European nesting grounds for the **greater skua** – keep an eye open, too, for **arctic foxes**, which feed on the birds. Near Kirkjubæjarklaustur, you can detour inland to take in the stark gorges and glacial rivers of **Núpsstaðurskógur**, and to **Lakagígar**, the site of Iceland's most destructive volcanic event of historic times.

Grænalón and Grímsvotn

Skeiðarársandur is crossed by a complex network of turbulent, ever-shifting glacial rivers, which created such an obstacle to road-building that it was only with the construction of a series of bridges in 1975 that the Ringroad around Iceland was completed – prior to which, anyone living east of here had to travel to Reykjavík via inland roads or Akureyri. These bridges – including **Skeidarárbrú**, Iceland's longest – had to be designed to cope with **jökulhlaups**, massive floods that erupt out from under Vatnajökull regularly and carry untold tonnes of boulders, gravel, ice and water before them. One cause of these is **Grænalón**, a lake formed by a short river whose outlet is blocked by the western side of Skeiðárarjökull, damming a two-hundred-metre-deep valley; every few years the lake fills enough to float the glacier dam wall and empties.

Far more destructive, however, is **Grímsvotn**, a crater lake above a smouldering volcano buried 400m under Vatnajökull's ice cap. Like Grænalón, Grímsvotn fills and empties every few years, but in October 1996 a force-five earthquake signalled abnormal activity under Vatnajökull and over the next few days the ice cap's surface gradually sagged and collapsed inwards to reveal a six-kilometre-long volcanic vent stretching northwest of Grímsvotn. For ten days the new volcano erupted continuously, blowing steam, ash and smoke 6km into the sky and inspiring the fear that a new lake was forming under the ice, but when activity later ceased it was assumed that the waters were somehow being contained. Then, at 8am on November 5, Grímsvotn suddenly drained, sending a wall of water 5m high spewing across Skeiðarársandur, sweeping away 7km of road and – despite design precautions – demolishing or badly damaging several bridges, including Skeidarárbrú. Fourteen hours later the flood rate was peaking at 45,000 cubic metres per second, and when the waters subsided a day later, the sandur was dotted with house-sized boulders and chunks of ice ripped off the front of Skeiðarárjökull. Though the ice has long gone and the boulders have been shifted, you'll still notice the effects of all this, at least in the atrocious condition of the road and the sparkling new bridges, though they're still only single lane and surfaced in wood.

Núpsstaðurskógur and on to Kirkjubæjarklaustur

Nearing Skeiðárarjökull's western end, the huge red and black outcrop of **Lomagnúpur** gradually rises up out of the scenery, marking the glacier's former limit before it began to retreat almost a century ago. In doing so, it allowed access to **Núpsstaðurskógur**, a highly scenic valley with sheer cliffs and twisted glacial streams stretching 15km north along the side of the glacier towards Grænalón. You'll need a high-clearance four-wheel-drive to negotiate the fords on the way in, so it's best to line up transport for camping, or join a **tour** from Kirkjubærklaustur (see opposite). Just past the access track and right at the foot of Lomagnúpur, have a quick look at **Núpsstaður**, a neat line of turf-covered buildings including an eighteenth-century stone farmhouse and an older church – the buildings themselves are fairly unremarkable, but the stark location evokes the hardships of farm life in Iceland a century ago.

Past Núpsstaður, the scenery changes quickly as you leave Vatnajökull behind, hugging a band of low cliffs inland fronted by rounded hummocks rising over grassland and decayed lavafields, though sandurs still persist to the south. Around 15km along at **Foss**, you can see how the cliffs were pressed down under the weight of now vanished ice, with a thin waterfall falling over the lowest edge above the farm. Across the road, a short **walking track** from a parking area circuits a pile of twisted hexagonal trachyte known as **Dverghammrar**, the Dwarf Cliffs, whose form indicates rapid and uneven cooling.

Kirkjubæjarklaustur, Lakigígar and around

If it were anywhere else you'd hardly register passing the tiny township of **KIRKJUBÆJARKLAUSTUR**, but as the only place of any size between Höfn and Vík, what few services it harbours are most welcome. The town sits at the foot of an escarpment on the **Skaftá**, whose rather circuitous path originates on the western side of Vatnajökull and is flanked by lavafields from eruptions by Lakagígar in 1783, centred some 75km to the northwest (see below). Kirkjubæjarklaustur (whose tongue-twisting name indicates a now-vanished convent) has had religious associations since Irish monks set up camp here before the Settlement, but it was during the Lakagígar eruptions that the town's **church** achieved national fame through the pastor, **Jón Steingrímsson**: as lava flows edged into the town, Steingrímsson delivered what became known as the "Fire Sermon", and the lava halted. The modern church, which stands on a granite slab halfway down Kirkjubæjarklaustur's single street, has an unusual facade resembling a ski lodge. It's possible to climb the escarpment behind it by means of a chain, and from the top there's a fine view southwest over Landbrot, a collection of a thousand-odd **pseudocraters** (for more on these, see p.295), formed when lava flowed over a lake during another eruption in 950. For a final geological hit, walk a kilometre or so along the road heading north from town, to where you'll find a field paved in a flat cross-section of hexagonal basalt "tiles" known as **Kirkjugólf**, or "Church Floor".

Practicalities

Kirkjubæjarklaustur is more or less a single street stretching for 100m west off the highway as it kinks over the river, complete with **bus stop**, **bank**, **post office**, **supermarket** and **fuel station**. The town's **tourist information office** (daily June–Sept) is on the main road at the kink; it also sells local crafts such as sweaters. The **central campsite** is opposite the post office, while across from the church you'll find an *Edda* **hotel**, managed by nearby *Hótel Kirkjubæjarklaustur* (both ☎487 4799, fax 487 4614, *klaustur@icehotel.is*; sleeping-bag accommodation 1350kr, ④). Alternatively, a kilometre north of town along the Kirkjugólf road brings you to *Kleifar* **campsite** (☎ & fax 487 4612), an open field but with a kitchen, showers, toilets and laundry; 2km in the same direction is *Geirland* farm, which has self-contained **cabins** sleeping four (sleeping-bag accommodation 1200kr, made-up bed 2500kr, cabin 7950kr). There's a **café** at the fuel station, while *Hótel Kirkjubæjarklaustur* has the town's only **restaurant**.

Tours to Núpsstaðurskógur (see opposite) and Lakagígar can be organized through the tourist information office or by contacting the English-speaking Hannes Jónsson (☎487 4785, fax 487 4890), who runs full day-tours to Núpsstaðurskógur, which include a guided trek (3–4hr).

Lakagígar

Reached off the highway along a 45-kilometre jeep track some 5km west of Kirkjubæjarklaustur, **Lakagígar** – the Laki Craters – stand in testament to the most catastrophic volcanic event in Iceland's recorded history. In June 1783, the earth here split into a 25-kilometre-long **fissure** that, over the next seven months, poured out a continuous thick blanket of poisonous ash and smoke and enough lava to cover 600 square kilometres. So thick were the ash clouds that they reached as far as northern Europe, where they caused poor harvests; in Iceland, however, there were no harvests at all, and livestock dropped dead, poisoned by eating fluorine-tainted grass. Over the next three years Iceland's population plummeted by a quarter – through starvation, earthquakes and an outbreak of smallpox – to just 38,000 people, at which point the Danish government considered evacuating the survivors to Jutland.

A succession of difficult river crossings means that you can only get to Lakagígar on **tours** (see p.273), but it's certainly worth the expense to see the succession of low, black craters surrounded by a still sterile landscape, though the flows themselves are largely covered in a carpet of thick, spongy moss. Pick of the scenery is on the journey in at **Fagrifoss**, the Beautiful Falls, and the view from atop **Laki** itself (818m), which takes in an incomprehensible expanse of lava.

West to Vík

As you head west out of Kirkjubærjarklaustur, a big orange sign warns of sandstorms and within a few kilometres you've cleared the Landbrot pseudocrater fields and the Lakagígar lava legacies – for the final 60km to Vík and the southwest. It's not an exciting journey: around 23km along you pass **Eystriásar farm**, which marks the eastern end of the Fjallabak route through the southern Interior (p.283), after which Vík is a brief drive away across the equally eventless **Mýrdalssandur** – though for some interesting detours along its fringes, see pp.119–120.

travel details

Buses

Note that there are no northbound bus services from Egilsstaðir between September and June, while from October until May there are no southbound services from Egilsstaðir or any transport from the Eastfjord towns between Egilsstaðir and Höfn. Buses run south from Höfn year round.

Breiðdalsvík to: Berunes (7 weekly; 15min); Djúpivogur (7 weekly; 1hr); Egilsstaðir (7 weekly; 2hr); Fáskrúðsfjörður (3 weekly; 45min); Höfn (7 weekly; 2hr 30min); Reyðarfjörður (3 weekly; 1hr 30 min); Stöðvarfjörður (3 weekly; 15min).

Djúpivogur to: Breiðdalsvík (7 weekly; 1hr); Egilsstaðir (7 weekly; 3hr 30min); Fáskrúðsfjörður (3 weekly; 1hr 15min); Höfn (7 weekly; 1hr 30min); Reyðarfjörður (3 weekly; 3hr); Stöðvarfjörður (3 weekly; 1hr 45min).

Egilsstaðir to: Akureyri via Mývatn (daily; 5hr); Akureyri via Vopnafjörður (3 weekly; 8hr 30min); Ásbyrgi (3 weekly; 5hr 45min); Berunes (7 weekly; 3hr); Breiðdalsvík (7 weekly; 2hr); Djúpivogur (7 weekly; 3hr 30min); Eskifjörður (1–3 daily; 40min); Fáskrúðsfjörður (3 weekly; 1hr 20min); Höfn (7 weekly; 4hr 45min); Húsavík (3 weekly; 7hr 30min); Kópasker (3 weekly; 5hr 15min);

Neskaupstaður (10 weekly; 1hr); Raufarhöfn (3 weekly; 4hr 30min); Reyðarfjörður (daily; 25min); Seyðisfjördur (3 daily; 20min); Stöðvarfjörður (3 weekly; 1hr 45min); Vopnafjörður (3 weekly; 1hr 30min); Þórshöfn (3 weekly; 3hr 30min).

Eskifjörður to: Egilsstaðir (1–3 daily; 40min); Neskaupstaður (1–3 daily; 25min) Reyðarfjörður (1–3 daily; 15min).

Fáskrúðsfjörður to: Berunes (3 weekly; 1hr 10min); Breiðdalsvík (3 weekly; 45min); Djúpivogur (3 weekly; 1hr 55min); Egilsstaðir (3 weekly; 1hr 15min); Höfn (3 weekly; 3hr 25min); Reyðarfjörður (3 weekly; 45min); Stöðvarfjörður (3 weekly; 30min).

Höfn to: Berunes (7 weekly; 2hr 15min); Breiðdalsvík (7 weekly; 2hr 30min); Djúpivogur (7 weekly; 1hr 30min); Egilsstaðir (7 weekly; 4hr 45min); Fáskrúðsfjörður (3 weekly; 3hr 25min); Kirkjubæjarklaustur (3–7 weekly; 2hr 30min); Reykjavík (3–7 weekly; 8hr 30min); Reyðarfjörður (3 weekly; 4hr 45min); Selfoss (3–7 weekly; 7hr 30min); Skaftafell (3–7 weekly; 1hr 30min); Skógar (3–7 weekly; 5hr 45min); Stöðvarfjörður (3 weekly; 3hr 30min); Vík (3–7 weekly; 3hr 50min).

Kirkjubæjarklaustur to: Höfn (3–7 weekly; 2hr 30min); Reykjavík (3–7 weekly; 6hr 30min); Selfoss (3–7 weekly; 5hr 30min); Skaftafell (3–7 weekly; 1hr 5min); Skógar (3–7 weekly; 2hr); Vík (3–7 weekly; 1hr 20min).

Neskaupstaður to: Egilsstaðir (1–3 daily; 1hr); Eskifjörður (1–3 daily; 30min); Reyðarfjörður (1–3 daily; 45min).

Reyðarfjörður to: Berunes (3 weekly; 2hr); Breiðdalsvík (3 weekly; 1hr 30 min); Djúpivogur (3 weekly; 3hr 45min); Egilsstaðir (daily; 25 min); Eskifjörður (1–3 daily; 15min); Fáskrúðsfjörður (3 weekly; 45min); Höfn (3 weekly; 4hr 15min); Neskaupstaður (1–3 daily; 45min); Stöðvarfjörður (3 weekly; 1hr 5min).

Seyðisfjördur to: Egilsstaðir (3 daily; 20min).

Skaftafell to: Höfn (3–7 weekly; 1hr 30min); Kirkjubærjarklaustur (3–7 weekly; 1hr 5min); Reykjavík (3–7 weekly; 5hr 30min); Selfoss (3–7 weekly; 4hr 30min); Skógar (3–7 weekly; 3hr 50min); Vík (3–7 weekly; 2hr 20min).

Stöðvarfjörður to: Berunes (3 weekly; 55min); Breiðdalsvík (3 weekly; 15min); Djúpivogur (3 weekly; 1hr 45min); Egilsstaðir (3 weekly; 1hr 45min); Fáskrúðsfjörður (3 weekly; 30min); Höfn (3 weekly; 3hr 15min); Reyðarfjörður (3 weekly; 1hr 5min).

Flights

Egilsstaðir to: Akureyri (4 weekly; 40min); Reykjavík (daily; 1hr).

Höfn to: Reykjavík (daily; 55min).

Ferries

Note that ferries operate May–September only.

Seyðisfjörður to: Bergen, Norway (weekly; 5 days); Hanstholm, Denmark (weekly; 55hr); Lerwick, Shetland Islands (weekly; 4 days); Tórshafn, Faroe Islands (weekly, 21 hr).

CHAPTER EIGHT

THE INTERIOR

S tark, desolate and charged with raw beauty, nothing you might see else-where in Iceland prepares you for the barren upland plateau (500–900m) that is the Interior, Europe's last true wilderness. The strength and unpre-dictability of the elements here means that the country's heart is a deso-late and uninhabited place, with no towns, villages or sights, just cinematic vistas of seemingly infinite plains, glacial rivers and lavafields punctuated only by ice caps, volcanoes and jagged mountains, all reminiscent of lunar landscapes – this is, after all, where the Apollo astronauts came to train for their moon landing. Sheep are virtually the only living things that manage to survive here, but pasture and vegetation, where they do exist, comprise only scattered clumps of ragged grass, and it's a daunting task for the farmers who venture out into this no-man's-land to round up their livestock every autumn.

Historically, the Interior was used as a shortcut between the north coast and the parliament site at Þingvellir, when whole families would set out on horseback to make the hazardous journey to attend the law-making sessions. Today, with the advent of the Ringroad and direct flights to Reykjavík from all corners of the coun-try, the need to traverse this area has long gone, and there are no roads, just tracks (the main ones are listed below) marked by stakes, and hardly any bridges across the rivers, causing some hairy moments when they are forded. The weath-er, too, is Iceland at its most elemental. Not only can fierce **winds** whip up the sur-face layer of loose grit in a matter of seconds, turning a beautiful sunny spell into a blinding haze of sand and dirt, but **snow storms** are common even in July and August – the summer here is very short indeed, barely a matter of weeks, the win-ter long and severe, when the tracks are blocked by deep snowdrifts and closed to traffic. Indeed, every couple of years, the Interior claims more victims through drownings in the icy rivers, while others perish in the snow storms. Occasionally, some simply disappear without trace.

There are two main north–south **routes through the Interior**: the most dra-matic and barren is the **Sprengisandur** route, the **F26**, which leads from the

---

ACCOMMODATION PRICE CODES

Throughout this guide, prices given for **youth hostels, sleeping-bag accommo-dation** and **campsites** are per person unless otherwise specified. **Hotel** and **guesthouse** accommodation is graded on a scale from ① to ⑧; all are high-season rates and indicate the cost of the cheapest double room. The price bands to which these codes refer are as follows:

① Up to 4000kr	③ 6000–8000kr	⑤ 10,000–12,000kr	⑦ 15,000–20,000kr
② 4000–6000kr	④ 8000–10,000kr	⑥ 12,000–15,000kr	⑧ Over 20,000kr

(See p.26 for a full explanation.)

Þjórsá, east of Selfoss, to the Bárðardalur valley between Akureyri and Lake Mývatn. It's also possible to approach Sprengisandur from Skagafjörður on the **F752** and from Akureyri on the **F821** – these two tracks join the F26 close to Nýidalur. The second main route, **Kjölur**, the **F35** and also known as Kjalvegur, runs from Geysir to the Blöndudalur valley south of Blönduós, and is considered an easier route but with less dramatic scenery; it's also the only route on which you can use normal cars. Other routes lead into parts of the Interior from the north and east but don't offer a route across it. Most of these converge on the area to the north and east of Vatnajökull: the F88 follows the course of the mighty Jökulsá á Fjöllum east of Lake Mývatn, to the Askja volcano, from where the F902 continues towards the glacier and to **Kverkfjöll**; heading inland from Egilsstaðir, the F910 and F909 wind their way to **Snæfell** and the northeastern flank of **Vatnajökull**; while to the west of the glacier lies the **Fjallabak** area, reached on tours from Reykjavík along the F208.

It is possible to get a taste of this utter isolation in safety on **bus tours**, essentially normal bus services but (usually) with a guide, though even then it's a bumpy ride. Should you decide instead to cross the Interior under your own steam, it's essential to be properly prepared before departure; note too that the majority of routes are accessible only by **four-wheel-drives**, and that when on them, you should stick to them, as **off-road driving** is not only illegal, but carries substantial fines and does irreparable damage to the land. **Cyclists** and **hikers** are limited to the Kjölur route.

Bus tours

Six **bus tours** penetrate the Interior in summer, all operated by BSÍ, who can be contacted at the long-distance bus station in Reykjavík (see p.46). Most include a **guide**, although large parties on the more popular trips tend to make the guides inaccessible. Remember that neither the Full Circle bus nor the Omnibus passes

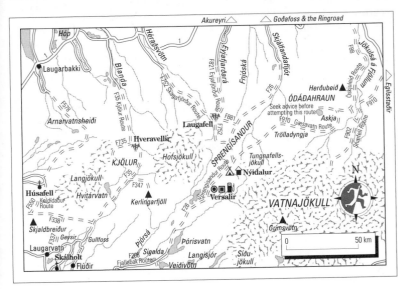

(see p.22) are valid for services across the Interior, although they do entitle the holder to a five-percent **discount** off the fares given below. Note that all the trips listed below last a day unless otherwise stated, though it is possible to hop off the buses at any of their stops – there's at least one hut and campsite on each route – and get back on another service the next day.

The journey over **Kjölur** crosses between Reykjavík and Akureyri daily in July and August (US$81 one-way), while the **Sprengisandur** bus operates between Reykjavík and Mývatn twice weekly from mid-July to late August, departing on Wednesday and Saturday from Reykjavík, and on Thursday and Sunday from Mývatn (US$129 one-way). Trips to **Askja** leave from Mývatn on Monday, Wednesday and Friday from mid-July to mid-August only (US$88 round trip), although a longer three-day version is also available on Monday and Friday (US$205 round trip). The **Fjallabak** tour from Reykjavík operates daily around the Hekla volcano, on to the **Landmannalaugar** geothermal area, the Eldgjá fissure before continuing on to Skaftafell (see p.296), for US$89 one-way. It's also possible to reach the Interior from Egilsstaðir – a twice weekly trip (Wed & Sat July–Aug) runs to **Vatnajökull** and the **Snæfell** mountain (US$86 round trip). Lastly, a three-day excursion to **Kverkfjöll** runs on Monday and Friday from July to mid-Aug only and includes two nights' accommodation and a day's walking on a glacier (US$205 round trip).

Self-driving, cycling and hiking

Any self-driving, cycling or hiking trip through the Interior must be carefully planned and considered. Never underestimate the extreme conditions, climatic and geological, which you may encounter en route. Remember too that in poor weather, low cloud obscures what precious little there is to see, and one part of cold grey desert looks very much like another. Whichever way you choose to see the Interior, always wear warm and brightly coloured protective **clothing**, and choose your time of departure carefully, basing it on the latest **weather forecast** from the national newspapers, television or at *www.vedur.is/ english/*. Also, and most importantly, check the condition of the mountain roads and Interior routes in advance with the Icelandic Highways Department, Vegagerðin (☎1777, *www.vegag.is/indexe.html*); although we've given the official **opening times** for routes in the box below, these can vary according to the weather.

For **cyclists** and **hikers**, the only Interior route is the F35 Kjölur track, since there are no rivers to wade through whilst heavily laden with packs and cycles, and the terrain is less severe. It is essential to carry all **spare cycle parts** with you and to carry more **food** than you anticipate needing should anything go wrong. A **compass** is essential because at times it can be difficult to determine a route where several sets of car tracks meet.

INTERIOR ROUTE OPENING TIMES

Askja/Öskjuleið (F88) June 20; **Eyjafjörður** (F821) July 20; **Fjallabaksleid** (F208) Sigalda–Landmannalaugar section June 25, Landmannalaugar–Eldgjá section July 2, Skaftártunga–Eldgjá section May 28; **Kaldidalur** (F550) June 15; **Kjölur** (F35) June 20; **Kverkfjöll** (F902) June 20; **Skagafjörður** (F752) July 14; **Sprengisandur** (F26) June 29

If you're **driving** across the Interior, check your **car insurance** policy, as four-wheel-drives aren't usually covered for breakdowns when crossing rivers. **Essential equipment** to take includes a tow rope, shovel, basic spare parts – and a rudimentary knowledge of how the engine works. It's best to travel in groups of two or more vehicles, and remember to carry plenty of **fuel**, as consumption across the Interior can be a third more than on well-surfaced roads. Never venture from the marked tracks – the off-road tyre marks you'll see here and there, made by illegal off-roaders, take years to heal and only worsen the country's uphill struggle against soil erosion.

Don't expect to find many bridges in the Interior, as they really only exist on the Kjölur route. Instead, **crossing rivers** involves looking for a safe place to ford one, preferably one that has been used recently (look for tyre tracks). Never follow vehicle tracks into a river without checking the **depth of the water** first though – glacial rivers can fluctuate by anything up to 1m in depth depending on the time of day and prevailing weather conditions. They are at their lowest during the early morning and after a dry spell of weather; conversely, they can be much deeper in the afternoon once the sun has melted the glacial ice that feeds them, or when it's raining. Always wear a **lifejacket** and tie yourself to a lifeline when entering the river to check its depth, and try to **cross in convoy** so that help is available should anything go wrong. Glacial rivers also carry large amounts of mud and sand, making it difficult to see **boulders** and rocks on the river bed when crossing. Be sure to engage a low gear and four-wheel-drive before entering the water – don't stop or change gear once in the river and don't go faster than 18kph. If in doubt, it's much better to wait for the river to subside or for the weather to improve than to take risks.

Overnight huts and camping

The mainstay of accommodation in the Interior is the network of **overnight huts**, or *sæluhús*, open all year and provided by Ferdafélag Íslands, the Touring Club of Iceland, Mörkin 6, 108 Reykjavík (☎568 2533, fax ☎568 2535). Marked on **maps** of the Interior, available in the two main bookshops in Reykjavík (see p.72) and from the capital's tourist office (see p.46), the huts are very busy during summer, and it's essential to book them well in advance. Although they differ – the better ones have self-catering facilities and running water – you'll always need to bring your own sleeping bag and all sleeping space is in dorms. The huts are located in three main areas in the Interior: south and east of Langjökull, on and close to the Kjölur route; between Landmannalaugar and Þórsmörk; and north of Vatnajökull around Askja and Kverkfjöll; we've given **contact numbers** in the guide text; costs are 1200kr per person in each hut.

If you're **camping** make sure to take enough tent pegs with you to anchor down your tent since the wind which howls uninterrupted across the Interior plain can be truly ferocious – among seasoned Iceland-travellers tales of blown-away tents are alarmingly common. **Campsites**, some of which have running water, are at Þórsmörk, Emstrur, Álftavatn, Hrafntinnusker and Landmannalauga, for the Þórsmörk–Landmannalaugar trek (covered in Chapter Two, see p.115); Hveravellir and Hvítárnes, for the Kjölur route; at Nýidalur, for the Sprengisandur route; at Laugafell, for the F752 to Skagafjörður; at Herðubreiðarlindir, Dyngjufjöll (Dreki) and Kverkfjöll, on the Askja and Kverkfjöll routes; and at Snæfell, for the F909 from Egilsstaðir.

Across Sprengisandur: the F26

Featuring the most desolate terrain found in Iceland, the **Sprengisandur** trip runs from Reykjavík to Mývatn, first taking the Ringroad to Hella before turning inland and following the course of the Ytri-Rangá river. The Interior section of this route, from Sigalda to Godafoss, covers 244km. On coach trips, you pass within 10km of the foot of Hekla prior to reaching Þjorsárdalur valley and the reconstructed Saga Age farm at Stöng (see p.105) – easily missed unless the guide points its out. You then pass **Þórisvatn**, a lake whose waters find their outlet in the Þjorsá river and feed a hydroelectric power station. After this, the route climbs into the stony highlands between Hofsjökull and the western edge of the mighty Vatnajökull, which mark the beginning of Sprengisandur proper, an incredible journey through mile after mile of grey sand, stones and rocks that have lain untouched for thousands of years. The enduring image is of nothingness: the glaciers and mountains that fringe the desolation seem a long way off.

Glacial rivers are periodically crossed until you reach the **café**, **guesthouse** and **filling station**, *Versalir* (☎487 5078; ②), deep in the heart of nowhere, where it's possible to break your journey for a day or two. Immediately north of here, the fate of the extensive marshland, **Þjórsárver**, the breeding ground of many of the world's population of **pink-footed geese**, attracted world attention in 2000 when the government's plans to flood the area to provide hydroelectric power for a new aluminium smelter became widely known outside Iceland. Following sustained pressure from environmentalists – and a petition signed by one in four Icelanders – the plans were shelved. Sixty kilometres further east from *Versalir*, the route's only **campsite** and **overnight hut** (☎568 2533) occupies a lonely, cold and windswept spot at 800m; **Nýidalur** valley leads southeast from the track past the small **Tungnafellsjökull** up towards the enormous Vatnajökull.

Three kilometres further on comes the turn for the Gæsvatn route, the F910, which weaves its way over some quite appalling terrain and through an alarming number of rivers, around the north of Vatnajökull, to meet up with the F88 to Askja. Get local advice if you're thinking of taking this route and only travel in convoy.

Past the turn for the F910, the Sprengisandur route continues to the grey waters of Fjórdungsvatn, which marks the turn for the F752 Skagafjörður route, via the **Laugafell** hot springs and overnight hut (☎854 9302), to Varmahlíd and the Ringroad. Then, slowly, the Sprengisandur route gains traces of green, reaching **Aldeyjarfoss** before descending into the Bárðardalur valley, whose scattered farms seem positively lively after hours spent looking at barren waste. The road down from Bárðardalur hits the Ringroad close to Godafoss, where coaches turn right for Mývatn. Allow at least eight hours if you're driving this route yourself.

Across Kjölur: the F35

Kjölur (or Kjalvegur) is the easiest of all the Interior routes to drive, since its surface has been greatly improved and all its rivers bridged over recent years, and if you've got a non-four-wheel-drive, this is the only route you can consider using. If driving a rental car, however, check with the agency to find out whether your insurance covers you for this journey. This account begins on the north coast and ends in Reykjavík, though it's possible to travel from south to north; from

---

THE KJÖLURVEGUR

The **Kjölurvegur trek** is an excellent two- to three-day hike from **Hvervellir** to the glacial lake of **Hvítárvatn**, following the original Kjölur route that ran west of the present F35, hugging the slopes of **Langjökull**, punctuated by overnight huts roughly four to six hours' walk apart. From the springs, follow the F735 west towards the glacier and after roughly 14km, at the *Þjófadalir* **overnight hut**, the jeep track peters out into a walking path as it swings southeast, around the tiny Hrútfell glacier, for another overnight hut at *Þverbrekknamúli*. From here, it's a further straightforward hike of around four to six hours to reach the *Hvítárnes* hut, an idyllic if somewhat lonely place to break the journey – the hut is supposedly haunted by a young woman who lived hereabouts when the area was farmed – though only men who sleep in a certain bed in the hut will see her, apparently. From the hut, it's an easy eight-kilometre walk back to the F35 and the bus to either Reykjavík or Akureyri passing the beautiful **Hvítárvatn** glacial lake, at the foot of Langjökull, on the way. This is where meltwater accumulates before flowing into the Hvítá and on towards Gullfoss – occasionally, icebergs can be seen floating in the serene, pale-blue waters.

Akureyri, buses follow the Ringroad west before turning off along the course of the Blandaá, passing a hydroelectric power station that's built mostly underground. From the power station to Gullfoss it's a distance of 161km; if driving yourself, allow at least five hours.

Once into the Interior, the outlook is similar to Sprengisandur – grey sands and stones. For much of its duration, the route follows the line of a barbed-wire fencing erected to keep the sheep from the west separate from those in the east and restrict the spread of disease (someone is actually employed to ride back and forth along the fence to check that it hasn't been breached). **Kjölur** itself, the highest point on the route, is a broad rocky pass between the massive icesheets of Langjökull and Hofsjökull. Here the F735 leads the short distance west (around 2km) to the **Hveravellir hot springs, campsite** and the well-appointed **overnight huts** (☎568 2533). Of the several springs and pools here, the most intriguing is **Eyvindarhver**, named after an outlaw who's reputed to have boiled up sheep here for his dinner. In summer, the springs can get busy, so try to time your dip to avoid the daily bus trips between Reykjavík and Akureyri (arriving around 2pm from Reykjavík and 1pm from Akureyri) – or stay overnight here and have the springs almost to yourself.

Beyond Hvítárnes, tours pause briefly at Gullfoss (see p.95) and then later at Geysir (see p.94) before a late afternoon stop at Laugarvatn (see p.93). There's another brief stop at Þingvellir (see p.88) on the way to Reykjavík, which makes this tour an excellent – and cost effective — way of also seeing these Golden Circle attractions.

Herðubreið and Askja: the F88

The crownlike formation of **Herðubreið** has earned it the nickname "Queen of the Icelandic Mountains", and at a height of 1682m, it towers over the featureless Ódáðahraun (Desert of Misdeeds) lavafield, to which outlaws were once banished, north of Vatnajökull. Orginally formed by a sub-glacial eruption in the ice cap that once covered this part of the country, you can get within a few kilometres of it on

---

HIKES FROM HERÐUBREIÐARLINDIR

Using Herðubreiðarlindir (see below) as an overnight base, it's possible to undertake a couple of excellent hikes in the immediate area. A good **day hike** leads from the hut to the foot of Herðubreið, covering 5km each way, from where a trail leads around the mountain. Alternatively, it's possible to climb the mountain from its western side: follow the path around the mountain until you reach another track leading up to the summit – the ascent is relatively easy but the final stretch can be difficult depending on the snow conditions on the peak and loose gravel. From Herðubreiðarlindir, this lasts around twelve hours in total.

A third option from Herðubreiðarlindir is the **two-day hike to Askja**: from the hut, follow the path around the mountain until it meets the trail up to the summit (see above). Here you turn left, away from the mountain, heading for the shield volcano of **Kollóttadyngja**, where there's an **overnight hut**, *Brædrafell*, belonging to the Touring Club of Akureyri – allow roughly six hours to cover the 17km here from Herðubreiðarlindir. The route on the second day (20km; 6hr) leads due south from *Brædrafell* across the lava to the foot of the Askja volcano and the **overnight hut**, *Dreki*, at Dyngjufjöll.

---

tours, which leaves the Ringroad not far east of Mývatn, heading along the F88 track and leading eventually to Askja (it's also possible to reach the mountain from Egilsstaðir along the circuitous F910 track, which crosses the Kreppá by bridge before looping back to join up with the F88). Marked initially by wooden posts and tyre tracks, the F88 Askja route (*Öskjuleið* in Icelandic) subsequently hits a mass of jagged lava. Picking a tortuous path, it follows the course of the glacial river, Jökulsá á Fjöllum – in places up to a kilometre wide – until arriving at **Herðubreiðarlindir**, an oasis of poor grass and **hot springs** where there's a **campsite** and an **overnight hut** (☎854 9301).

The track then veers away from the river towards the Dyngjufjöll mountains, and **Askja** itself, the volcano responsible for creating the grim and forbidding surrounds in 1875, when ash and volcanic dust from an eruption carried all the way to Scandinavia. Within the crater are two lakes, the 217m deep **Öskjuvatn** (the form *Öskju-* is the genitive variant of *Askja*) and the smaller **Víti** – whose name means Hell. In 1838, the vent that later formed Víti was described by one local traveller as "a complete Devil's cauldron from which all living things fly; horses quake with mortal fear and can hardly stand when taken to the brink". Although the volcano remains active, with the last eruption in 1961, it has quietened down a lot since then and you can walk around the rim in about an hour. You can also scramble down its steep sides, dotted with sulphur springs, to bathe in the opaque waters of Víti, which can be a little tepid sometimes but perfect for a quick dip. At the foot of the volcano is an **overnight hut** (☎853 2541) and **campsite**.

From Askja, the F910 wiggles around the northern flank of Vatnajökull to join up with the F26 Sprengisandur route north of Nýidalur (see p.280), but this should only be driven in convoy and after seeking expert local advice.

Routes to Kverkfjöll

The main track (F905) to the ice-covered Kverkfjöll begins 4km south of **Möðrudalur** – a tiny settlement 8km south of the Ringroad, halfway between

THE FJALLABAK ROUTE

The **Fjallabak route** runs from Reykjavík through the uninhabited lands north of **Mýrdalsjökull** (covered in Chapter Two, see p.118) to **Kirkjubæjarklaustur** and **Skaftafell** (both covered in Chapter Seven, see p.273 and p.269), a trip that can also be made in the opposite direction. As the route twists between mountains of green or earthy brown, there are two specific halts of 45–60 minutes. First off is **Landmannalaugar**, said to have been the scene of many baptisms during the Conversion and where the series of warm pools provides good bathing. The second is at **Ófærufoss**, a waterfall spanned by a natural lava bridge. You rejoin the Ringroad 28km west of Kirkjubæjarklaustur, where the bus pauses briefly before continuing on to Skaftafell.

Vopnafjörður and Lake Mývatn – crossing undulating gravel and passing the small lake. Twenty kilometres south of Möðrudalur, the route links up with the F910, which leads over the Kreppá, which is bridged, to the junctions with the F902 and F903. The latter leads to the hot springs of **Hvannalindir**, an oasis where eighteenth-century outlaw Eyvindur fashioned a rough shelter using lava blocks around a hollow on the edge of the lavafield. He also built a sheep pen with a covered passageway to the nearby stream, so the animals could drink without being spotted and hence not give away his location. Both can still be found but are well concealed, as Eyvindur intended. Beyond the springs, route F903 joins up with its neighbour to the north, the F902, before reaching **Kverkfjöll** via a maze of ash hills. There's a **campsite** and an **overnight hut** here (☎853 6236) overlooking the braided streams of the Jökulsá á Fjöllum's upper reaches. Low white clouds hover overhead during the long hard slog up the dormant volcano, which erupted to great devastating effect in the fifteenth century, and once at the top these are revealed to be steam issuing from deep fissures in the ice. Nearby sulphur springs, hissing like boiling kettles, prevent ice from forming in their immediate area and the bare yellow earth is in stark contrast to the surroundings. The outstanding views from the glacier take in the entire expanse of Ódáðahraun lavafield, the Dyngjufjöll mountains, Herðubreið mountains, and even the jagged peaks that mark the distant northern coast.

Jökulsá á Fjöllum rises from hot springs under Vatnajökull, and its heat forms an **ice cave**, 5km from the hut. Some daylight penetrates a few metres into the cave, but visibility rapidly diminishes in the thick, damp fog that fills it. The walls and roof are sculpted by constantly dripping water, and the debris embedded in the ice gives a marbled effect. Not far from here the slopes of the glacier are climbable, but they shouldn't be attempted without a guide.

travel details

Buses

Akureyri to: Reykjavík, via Kjölur (1 daily July–Aug; 9hr).

Egilsstaðir to: Snæfell (2 weekly July–Aug; 10hr return).

Mývatn to: Askja (3 weekly July–Aug; 12hr return); Kverkfjöll (2 weekly July–Aug; 3 days return); Reykjavík, via Sprengisandur (2 weekly July–Aug; 12hr).

Reykjavík to: Akureyri, via Kjölur (1 daily July–Aug; 9hr); Landmannalaugar, via Fjallabak (1 daily July–Aug; 7hr); Mývatn, via Sprengisandur (2 weekly July–Aug; 12hr).

SOME HISTORY

Iceland is not only one of the more geologically recent places on earth, it was also amongst the last to be colonized. European seafarers may have known that something lay out beyond Scotland as far back as 300 BC, when the historian Pytheas of Marseille wrote about "Ultima Thule" – possibly Iceland – a northern land on the edge of a frozen ocean, where it never became dark in summer.

It wasn't until considerably later, however, that Iceland was regularly visited by outsiders, let alone settled, and it's still unclear who might have been the first to try. Whoever they were, the first arrivals would have found the country much the same as it appears today, but well forested with willow and birch, and with no large animals.

DISCOVERY

Much of the uncertainty in deciding who discovered Iceland, and when it happened, is down to the lack of archeological and written records. **Roman** coins from around 300 AD, found at several sites along Iceland's south coast, provide the earliest evidence of visitors, and suggest that ships from Britain – which was then a Roman colony and just a week's sail away – made landfall here from time to time. These coins could have been brought in at a later date, however, and no other Roman artefacts or camps have been found. Similarly, the age of a **Norse** homestead on Heimaey in the Westman Islands is disputed; archeologists date it to the

seventh century, but medieval Icelandic historians – accurate enough in other matters – state that it was founded two hundred years later. What is certain, however, is that by the late eighth century **Irish** monks, having already colonized the Faroes, were visiting Iceland regularly, seeking solitude and, according to contemporary accounts, believing that they had rediscovered Pytheas' Ultima Thule. Oral tradition and place names link them to certain spots around the country – such as Papey, "Monks' Island" in the east – but they left no hard evidence behind them and were driven out over the next century by new invaders, the **Vikings**.

Vikings were Scandinavian adventurers, armed with the fastest ships of the time and forced by politics and a land shortage at home to seek their fortune overseas through war and piracy. They had already exploded into Britain and Ireland in the 790s, which is why Irish monks had sought out Iceland as a more peaceful place to live. Though a few Vikings may have been Christian, the majority believed in the **Norse** gods, the Æsir, which included Óðinn, the creator of mankind; his wild and adventurous hammer-wielding son Þór; and Freyr, the god of fertility and farming. The Æsir themselves were children of the first beings, the Giants, who had also created dwarfs and elves; they lived above the world in Ásgarður, where the great hall Valhalla housed the souls of Champions, men killed in warfare. Fearsome in battle, honour was everything to the Vikings, and the faintest slur could start a century-long blood feud between families.

According to tradition, the Vikings came across Iceland by accident when a certain mid-ninth-century freebooter named **Naddoddur** lost his way to the Faroes and landed on the eastern coast of what he called **Snæland**, or Snowland. He didn't stay long, but his reports of this new country were followed up by the Swede **Garðar Svavarsson**, who circumnavigated Iceland in around 860, wintering at modern-day Húsavík in the northeast, where two of his slaves escaped and may have settled. At about the same time, **Flóki Vilgerðarson** left his home in Norway intending to colonize Snæland, which he was led to by following his pet ravens – hence his other name, Hrafna-Flóki, Raven-Flóki. But a hard winter in the northwest killed all his livestock; climbing a mountain he saw a fjord on the other side choked with ice and, frustrated, he renamed the country **Ísland**, Iceland, and returned to Norway.

SETTLEMENT

While Flóki's experiences were unpromising, the idea of so much free space proved tempting to two other Norwegians, **Ingólfur Arnarson** and his brother-in-law **Hjörleifur Hróðmarsson**. Nobles who had lost their own lands in Norway as compensation for killing the son of a local earl, in around 870 they set sail with their households and possessions for Iceland, intending to settle there permanently. When they came within sight of land, Ingólfur dedicated his wooden **seat-posts** – the cherished symbol of his being head of a household – to his gods and threw them overboard, vowing to found his new home at the spot where they washed up. While his slaves searched for them, Ingólfur spent three years exploring Iceland's southern coast, wintering first at Ingólfshöfði (near Skaftafell), Hjörleifshöfði (just east of Vík), and then at Ingólfsfjall (Selfoss). The posts were duly found in a southwestern bay and there Ingólfur built his homestead in 874, naming the place **Reykjavík** ("Smoky Bay") after the steam rising off nearby hot springs, and becoming Iceland's first official resident.

Although Hjörleifur had meanwhile been murdered by his own Irish slaves, things went well for Ingólfur and this attracted other migrants to Iceland, who spent the next sixty years snapping up vacant land in what has become known as the **Settlement**, or Landnám. These first Icelanders, who were mostly Norwegian, were primarily **farmers**, importing their pagan beliefs along with sheep, horses, and crops such as barley, while also clearing forests to create pasture and provide timber for buildings and ships. While it was available, a man could take as much land as he could light fires around in one day, while a woman could have the area she could lead a heifer around in the same time. Landowners became local **chieftains**, whose religious responsibilities earned them the title of *goðar*, or priests, and who sorted out their differences through negotiations at regional **assemblies** (Þing) – or if these failed, by fighting. Conditions must have been very favourable to those in Norway, however, as by 930, when the last areas of the country were claimed, an estimated 60,000 people already lived in Iceland.

THE COMMONWEALTH: 930–1262AD

By the early tenth century, Iceland was firmly occupied and had begun to see itself as an independent nation in need of national government. The chieftains rejected the idea of a paramount leader, and instead decided, in 930, on a **Commonwealth** governed by a national assembly, or **Alþing**, which came to be held for two weeks every summer at **Þingvellir** in southwestern Iceland. Here laws were recited by a **lawspeaker** so that everyone would know them, and disputes settled by four regional courts, with a supreme court formed early in eleventh century. Legal settlement typically involved payment to the injured party or their family; the highest punishment was not death but being declared an **outlaw**, thus being exiled from Iceland. Courts had no power to enforce decisions, however, only make recommendations, and though they held great public authority, in practice their decisions could be ignored – something which was to undermine the Commonwealth in later years.

The first century of the Commonwealth was very much a golden era, however: the country was united, resources were rich, and farming profitable. This was the **Saga Age**, the time when the first generations of Icelanders were carving out great names for themselves in events that passed into oral lore and would only later be written down.

Contact with the outside world continued too, and – in the same way that Iceland itself was discovered – Icelandic seafarers came across their own new worlds. In 980, Eiríkur Þorvaldsson (better known in English as **Eric the Red**) was outlawed for killing his neighbour and sailed from the Westfjords to follow up earlier reports of land to the northwest. He found a barren, treeless coastline, then returned to Iceland to whip up support for colonizing what he called **Greenland** – a misleading name, chosen deliberately to arouse interest. Enough people were hooked to emigrate along with Eiríkur, and two settlements were founded in Western Greenland which lasted until the sixteenth century. And it was from Greenland that Eiríkur's son Leifur – **Leif Eiríksson** – heard that land had been sighted even further west, and set sail around the year 1000 to discover Baffin Island, Labrador, and "**Vínland**", an as-yet unidentified area of the north American coast. A couple of attempts made by others to colonise these distant lands came to nothing, however, and America was then forgotten about until Columbus rediscovered it.

THE COMING OF CHRISTIANITY

Meanwhile, the late tenth century had seen Norway convert to **Catholicism** under the fiery king **Ólafur Tryggvason**. Ólafur then sent the missionary **Thangabrand** to evangelize Iceland, where – despite battling, literally, strong resistance from pagan stalwarts – he baptized several influential chieftains. Back in Norway, Thangabrand's unfavourable reports infuriated Ólafur, who was only prevented from executing all Icelanders in the country by the Icelandic chieftain **Gizur the White**, who promised to champion the new religion at home. Gizur mustered his forces and rode to the Alþing in 1000, where civil war was only averted by the lawspeaker **Þorgeir**, who – having made pagan and Christian alike swear to accept his decision – chose Christianity as Iceland's official religion, though pagans were initially allowed to maintain their beliefs in private. Gizur the White's son **Ísleifur** became Iceland's first **bishop** in 1056, and his homestead at **Skálholt** near Þingvellir was made the bishop's seat, with a second, northern diocese founded in 1106 at **Hólar**.

The new religion brought gradual changes with it, notably the introduction in 1097 of **tithes** – property taxes – to fund churches. As their wealth increased, churches founded **monasteries** and **schools**, bringing education and the beginnings of **literature**: Iceland's **laws** were first written down in 1117; and in 1130 the church commissioned Ari the Learned to compile the **Íslendingabók**, a compendium of the Icelandic people and their lineages. Importantly, Ari wrote not in Latin, the usual language of education and the Church at the time, but in Icelandic, an expression of national identity that was followed by almost all later Icelandic writers.

COLLAPSE OF THE COMMONWEALTH

Despite these benefits, several factors were beginning to undermine the Alþing's authority. During the twelfth century, for instance, life in Iceland became tougher. The country's unstable geology made itself felt for the first time with the **eruption** of the volcano Hekla in southern Iceland in 1104, which buried around twenty farms. The climate cooled too; **tree felling** had become so extensive that there was no longer enough timber for ship building; and **erosion** from logging and overgrazing meant that viable farm land was shrinking, making the country dependent on **imports**.

The tithes had also created a split in Iceland's formerly egalitarian society. With its taxes, the Church became rich and politically powerful, as did chieftains who owned Church lands or had become priests, and so took a share of the tithes. These chieftains formed a new elite group of **aristocrats**, who bought out their poorer neighbours and so concentrated land ownership, wealth, and inherent political power in the hands of just a few clans. At the same time, in 1152 the Icelandic Church came under the jurisdiction of the **Archbishop of Nidaros** in Norway, giving the expansionist Norwegian throne a lever to start pressuring Iceland to accept its authority. Backed by the Archbishop and **Þorlákur Þórhallsson**, bishop at Skálholt from 1179 and later beatified as Iceland's first saint, the Church began to demand freedom from secular laws.

The Alþing's lack of effective power now became clear, as it proved unable to deal with the Church's demands, or the fighting that was breaking out between the six biggest clans as they battled for political supremacy. The period from 1220 is known as the **Sturlung Age** after the most powerful of these clans, led by the historian, lawspeaker and wily politician **Snorri Sturlusson**. Travelling to Norway in 1218, Snorri became a retainer of King Hákon Hákonarson, and returned to Iceland in 1220 to promote Norwegian interests. But his methods were slow, and in 1235 the king sent Snorri's nephew, **Sturla Sighvatsson**, to Iceland to win it over for Norway, by force if necessary. In the ensuing **civil war**, forces led in part by **Gissur Þorvaldsson**, head of the Haukadalur clan, killed Sturla and virtually wiped out the Sturlungs at the battle of **Örlygsstaðir** in 1238. Snorri escaped by being in Norway at the time, but was later killed by Gissur after his return.

Amongst this violence, Iceland was also experiencing a literary flowering: Snorri Sturlusson wrote the **Prose Eddas**, containing much of what is known about Norse mythology; his relative Sturla Þordarson compiled the **Book** of **Settlements Expanded**, accounts of the original landowners and their lives; and it was during this period that the **Sagas** were composed, recalling the nobler events of the early Commonwealth. Meanwhile the war continued, and by 1246 only two chieftains were left standing: Gissur Þorvaldsson, who held the south of the country; and Sturla's brother **Þordur**, who controlled the north. Rather than fight, they let King Hákon decide who should govern the country; the king chose Þordur, who ruled Iceland until 1250, sharing power with the two bishops – also Norwegian appointees. In the end, the bishop at Hólar denounced Þordur for putting his own interests before Norway's, and the king replaced him with Gissur who, after a further decade of skirmishes, finally persuaded Icelanders that the only way to obtain lasting peace was by accepting **Norwegian sovereignty**. In 1262, Iceland's chieftains signed the *Gamli sáttmáli* or **Old Treaty**, which allowed Iceland to keep its laws and promised that the Norwegian king would maintain order, in exchange for taxes and replacing the chieftainships with government officials. While the treaty didn't give Norway absolute control of the country, and demanded a return for Icelandic obedience, it marked the beginnings of seven centuries of foreign rule.

DECLINE, THE ENGLISH CENTURY AND THE REFORMATION

With the Alþing discredited by over forty years of conflict, Iceland turned to Norway to help draft a new constitution. After some wrangling, this resulted in the **Jónsbók**, in 1280, a set of laws that were to remain partly in force until the nineteenth century. The country was to be overseen by a **governor**, with twelve regional **sheriffs** acting as local administrators; all officials would be Icelanders, though appointed by Norway. The Alþing would still meet as a national court, retaining some legislative power, but its decisions would have to be approved by the king.

The new system should have brought a much-needed period of stability to Iceland, but it was not always administered as planned – officials often abused their position, leading to several **revolts**, such as when the brutal governor Smiður Andrésson was killed by farmers in 1361. At the same time, the fourteenth century heralded a succession of **natural disasters**:

severe winters wiped out crops and livestock; Hekla became active again; and the volcano under Öræfajökull in the southeast exploded in 1362, covering a third of the country in ash. But most devastating was the **Plague** or Black Death, which had ravaged Europe in the 1350s and arrived in Iceland in 1402, killing half of the population in the following two years. Compared with this, it seems inconsequential that the Danish "lady king" **Margaret** had meanwhile absorbed the Norwegian throne under the **Kalmar Union** of 1397, thereby placing Iceland in Denmark's hands.

THE ENGLISH CENTURY

While all this was going on, the underlying struggles between landowners, the Church and the king were escalating, typified by events during what is known as the **English Century**. At the time there was growing demand in Europe for dried **cod**, which after 1400 became a major Icelandic export, exchanged for linen, wine and grain. **Fishing** – formerly a secondary income – boomed, providing a new source of funds for coastal landowners. Soon English and German vessels were vying for trade with Iceland and even beginning to fish themselves; the English gained the ascendancy after setting up a base on the Westman Islands (where they also indulged in kidnapping and piracy), and managing to get an English bishop – **John Craxton** – appointed to Hólar in the 1420s. Denmark, alarmed at England's rising influence and the taxes it was losing through uncontrolled trade, appointed its own **Jón Gerreksson** as bishop at Skálholt, although this violent man – who had his own military and spent his time levying illegal taxes and harassing his neighbours – ended up being drowned by locals in 1433.

Trying to restore order, Denmark passed laws stopping the Church from raising illegal taxes and banning the English from Iceland. The English response was to kill the Icelandic governor in 1467, so the Danish king encouraged the German trading organization known as the **Hanseatic League** to establish trading bases in the country – a popular move, as the League had better goods than the English and gave better prices. The English returned with cannons, a forceful stance that after 1490 gained them the right to fish Icelandic waters as long as they paid tolls to Denmark. All went well until 1532, when trouble flared between German and English vessels at the trading post at **Grindavík** on the southwestern Reykjanes Peninsula, culminating in the death of the English leader. English involvement in Iceland dropped off sharply after this, leaving Icelandic trade in the hands of Danish and German interests.

THE REFORMATION AND ITS EFFECTS

The Church, which by now had complete jurisdiction over Iceland's lands, and profitable stakes in farming and fishing, became even more powerful in 1533 when the two bishops – **Jón Arason** and **Ögmundur Pálsson** – were appointed as joint governors of the country. But outside Iceland, a new Christian view first proposed by the German Martin Luther in 1517 had been gaining ground. **Lutherism** revolted against what was seen as the Catholic Church's growing obsession with material rather than spiritual profits, and encouraged a break with the Rome as the head of the Church – a suggestion that European monarchs realized would therefore place the Church's riches and influence in their hands.

During the 1530s, all Scandinavia became Lutheran, and converts were already making headway in Iceland, though threatened with excommunication by the bishops. In 1539, the Danish king **Christian III** ordered the Icelandic governor to appropriate Church lands, which led to the murder of one of his sheriffs and a subsequent military expedition to Iceland to force conversion to Lutherism. This was headed by **Gissur Einarsson**, a former protégé of Ögmundur but covert Lutheran, who replaced Ögmundur as bishop at Skálholt in 1542. A skilful diplomat, he encouraged Lutherism without, by and large, antagonizing Catholics. His appointment left Jón Arason at Hólar as the last Catholic bishop in Scandinavia, and on Gissur's death in 1548, Arason unsuccessfully pushed his own Catholic candidate for Skálholt, an act that got him declared an outlaw. Gathering a band of supporters, Arason marched south and captured Skálholt, but was subsequently defeated and executed along with two of his sons on November 7, 1550, allowing Lutherism to be imposed across the entire country.

The consequences of the Reformation were severe, with the new faith forced on an initially unwilling population, who – in common with many other countries at the time – may have

disagreed with Catholic abuses of power but not with Catholicism itself. The Danish king acquired all Church holdings and their revenues, profits from which had previously stayed in Iceland; monasteries were abolished and, deprived of funds, the Church found it hard to sponsor education – though it did manage to publish a translation of the Bible in 1584, the first book printed in Icelandic.

Politically too, the Church was now an instrument of the king, and the Danish crown gained a far more direct hold on the country. Technically, however, Iceland remained an independent state through its treaty with Norway, but in 1661 King **Frederick III** declared his rule absolute over all Danish lands, and the following year sent an armed ambassador to Iceland to make its people swear allegiance. During an assembly at **Bessastaðir**, near Reykjavík, the Alþing's lawspeaker and Skálholt's bishop were forced to submit, removing their final vestiges of authority and handing complete control of the country to the Danish crown.

In the meantime, Iceland's economy – still based on farming and fishing – suffered a severe blow through the **Trade Monopoly** of 1602. This restricted all trade between Iceland and the outside world to a select few Danish merchants, who charged steeply for their goods, while giving poor prices for Icelandic products. By 1700, the monopoly had ruined the country, creating a mostly poor, dispirited population of tenant farmers and landless labourers. Fishing was also on the wane, partly because a shortage of timber meant that Iceland's vessels were basic and small, and easily out-competed by foreign boats. Aside from a fruitless attempt to introduce **reindeer** as livestock, the only concrete action taken to redress trade imbalances was made by the bailiff **Skúli Magnússon**, who in 1752 founded a company at Reykjavík – still just a small farming settlement at the time – to improve agricultural practices and modernize the wool and fishing industries. Though the company was only moderately successful, its warehouses became the core of Reykjavík town, soon to become Iceland's largest settlement and de facto capital.

Unfortunately, a fresh wave of disasters now swept the country, the worst of which was the catastrophic **Laki Eruptions** of 1783–84 in the southeast. Poisonous fallout from Laki wrecked farming over the entire country, and the ensuing **famine** reduced the population to just 38,000. Denmark briefly considered evacuating the survivors to Jutland, but in the end settled for easing the economy by replacing the trade monopoly with a **Free Trade Charter** in 1787, which allowed Iceland to do business with a greater range of Danish merchants. Another effect of the eruptions were accompanying **earthquakes** which knocked over the church at Skálholt and caused subsidence at the Alþing site; the bishopric was moved to Reykjavík, and the Alþing – which by now only met irregularly to discuss minor matters – was finally dissolved.

NATIONALISM

European political upheavals during the early nineteenth-century Napoleonic Wars had little effect on Iceland, though there was brief excitement in 1809 when opportunistic Danish interpreter **Jörgen Jörgensen** deposed the governor and ran the country for the summer. However, the increasingly liberal political climate that followed the war encouraged **nationalism** throughout Europe and was championed in Iceland by the romantic poet **Jónas Hallgrímsson** and historian **Jón Sigurðsson**, a descendent of Snorri Sturlusson, who pushed for free trade and autonomy from Denmark. Bowing to popular demand, the Danish king reconstituted the Alþing at Reykjavík in 1843, which met every other year and had twenty elected regional members of parliament and six representatives of the king. Jón Sigurðsson was amongst the first members elected.

Even greater changes were on the way, sparked by the French Revolution of 1848, after which Europe's other royal families began to cede real power in order to avoid a similar fate. After uprisings in Denmark, the **monarchy** there became constitutional, allowing Jón Sigurðsson to point out that Iceland's 1662 oath of allegiance to the king as an absolute ruler was therefore no longer valid, and that the Old Treaty was now back in force. This didn't make him popular with the king, a situation exacerbated when he led the defeat of a bill at the Alþing, in 1851, that would have legally incorporated Iceland into Denmark. Sigurðsson also managed to have remaining trade restrictions finally lifted four years later, an act which did more than anything else to improve life in Iceland by bringing in modern farm implements

and wood for boats at affordable prices, while allowing the profitable export of livestock, wool and fish.

In 1871 Denmark politically **annexed** Iceland, an event that, though not accepted by Icelanders, gave them a favourable **new constitution**. Broadly speaking, this returned full legislative powers to the Alþing and was ratified by King Christian IX himself, while attending celebrations at Þingvellir in 1874 to mark a thousand years since Settlement. Home control of lawmaking saw further benefits to living conditions: the tithe system was abolished; infrastructure improved; schooling was made compulsory; improvements in boats and fishing equipment caused the growth of port towns; and farmers formed the first Icelandic co-operatives to deal directly with foreign suppliers. There followed a sizeable population boom, despite heavy **emigration** mostly to Canada and the US during the late nineteenth century following another spate of harsh weather, disease and livestock problems.

HOME RULE, UNION AND INDEPENDENCE

The concept of total political autonomy from Denmark grew from ideas planted by Jón Sigurðsson before his death in 1879. By 1900, differences in the way this could be achieved led to the formation of **political parties**, who in 1904 pressured the king into granting Home Rule under the **Home Rule Party** led by **Hannes Hafstein**. Hafstein's decade in office saw the start of trends that were to continue throughout the century: an emerging middle class led a gradual population shift from the land to towns, communications picked up with the introduction of **telephones** in 1906, and new technologies were adopted for farming and fishing, boosting output. Workers also founded the first unions, and women were granted rights to an equal education and allowed to vote.

Hafstein's biggest defeat came in 1908 when the Alþing rejected the **Draft Constitution**, a proposal to make Iceland an independent state under the Danish king. Yet a decade later, a referendum found ninety percent of voters approved of the idea, and in December 1918, Iceland entered into the **Act of Union** with Denmark, where it received recognition as an independent state while still accepting the Danish king as monarch.

World War I pretty well bypassed Iceland, and after it ended in 1918 the economy consolidated, though stalling along with the rest of the world during the 1930s **Great Depression**. As **World War II** loomed in Europe, Iceland – dependent on trade with both Britain and Germany – decided to stay neutral, but, after the outbreak of hostilities in 1939, the country's strategic North Atlantic location meant that, neutral or not, it was simply a matter of time before either Germany or Britain invaded. The **British** were first, landing unopposed in May 1940, so gaining a vital supply point for the Allies' North Atlantic operations. The following year **US forces** replaced the British with the approval of the Alþing, on condition that they respected Icelandic sovereignty and left once hostilities were over.

Though fighting never came to Iceland itself, World War II was to trigger the end of foreign rule. When Germany invaded Denmark in 1940 the Alþing decided that, as the king could no longer govern, the Act of Union should be dissolved and therefore that Iceland should declare its full **independence**. The formal ratification took some time, however, as the government was in disarray, with none of the four political parties holding a parliamentary majority. In the end, acting regent **Sveinn Björnsson** had to found an apolitical government, which finally proclaimed independence from Denmark on June 17, 1944, with Björnsson elected as the first president of the **Icelandic Republic**.

THE REPUBLIC: FROM 1944 TO THE PRESENT

One of the biggest challenges for the new republic came immediately after the war. The US troops departed in 1946 as requested, but as the **Cold War** between the Soviet and Western powers began to take shape Iceland felt uncertain about its lack of defence. With neither the population nor desire to form its own military, in 1949 the Alþing voted that Iceland should instead join the US, Britain and others as part of **NATO**, the North Atlantic Treaty Organisation, and in 1951 agreed to have US forces operate an airforce base at **Keflavík**, using facilities the US had already built during World War II. Though the need for defence was widely accepted, the idea of having foreign influence back in Iceland after having only just got rid of it for the first time in 700 years was not popular; the decision to join NATO caused a **riot** in Reykjavík, and today, with the Cold War long past, the continuing US presence at Keflavík remains a contentious issue.

The country has also had to deal with a rather different defence matter: that of preserving its **fish stocks**, and hence most of its export earnings, in the face of foreign competition. Following skirmishes dating right back to the English Century (see p.290), in 1896 Iceland's **territorial waters** – the area from which it could exclude foreign vessels – had been set as extending three nautical miles from land. As commercial fishing picked up again after World War II, fish stocks through the Atlantic declined, and most countries increased their territorial limits. In 1958, Iceland declared a twelve-mile limit which Britain protested, sending in naval boats to protect its trawlers fishing in these new Icelandic waters in the first act of the **Cod Wars**. These flared on and off for the next thirty years, with Iceland continuing to expand its claims as fish stocks continued to dwindle, and employing its coastguard to cut the cables of any foreign trawlers that were caught poaching. Things came to a head in 1975, when Iceland declared a two-hundred-mile limit around its shores, at which point Britain broke off diplomatic relations and ordered its Navy to ram Icelandic coastguard boats, which happened on several occasions. The situation was only resolved in 1985, when international laws justified Iceland's position by granting the two-hundred-mile limit to all countries involved in the dispute.

Domestically, Iceland has become predominantly urban since 1944, with over half the population of 270,000 living in the Greater Reykjavík area, and just 24,000 remaining on the land as farmers. Standards of living are now equal to any European country – in fact, with little industry and low pollution levels, Icelanders are in some ways better off. Virtually all Icelanders are literate and well educated, and communications are as good as they can be given the natural conditions – the Ringroad around the country was completed in 1974, and Iceland's per-capita usage of **computers** and the Internet is one of the world's highest. New technologies, such as the harnessing of **hydro** and **geothermal energy** for electricity, heating and growing **hothouse** foods, have also been enthusiastically embraced. On the downside, the fact that **fishing** is the single main source of export earnings has made the economy very sensitive, and a reliance on **imports** means that prices are high, with many people needing more than one job in order to make ends meet. The runaway inflation of the 1970s (in part caused by the 1973 eruption of the volcano on Heimaey, which disrupted the season's fishing) has been capped, though at the cost of rising **unemployment** figures – although many Icelanders will tell you that if people don't have jobs in Iceland, it's because they don't want them.

At the beginning of the twenty-first century, three thorny issues dominate the political scene in Iceland: **European Union membership**; the resumption of whaling, and the environment. Following the decision by fellow Nordic nations Sweden and Finland to join the EU in 1995, the question of whether Iceland should follow suit is rarely out of the headlines. At issue is the EU's Common Fisheries Policy, which opponents of membership claim would open up Iceland's territorial waters to other member states and do serious damage to the country's economy, eighty-percent of which is dependent on fish and fish-related products. Supporters argue that, as a tiny nation, Icelanders need the international stage offered by the meetings in Brussels that are shaping Europe's future. Public opinion on the issue swings back and forth, monitered closely by politicians of all parties, eager to gain political capital from the mood of the people.

The question of whether to resume **whaling**, and to what degree, is linked to that of EU membership. The Icelandic government, having been instructed by parliament in 1999 to research the impact any resumption would have on the economy, is carefully gauging the mood of the international public and that of the European Commission in Brussels, fearful of a repeat of earlier boycotts of Icelandic fish that sent the economy into freefall.

However, the burning issue for most Icelanders is the protection of their unspoilt **environment**. Following a successful public campaign, a recent decision to postpone the building of vast dam in the uninhabited Interior to provide hydroelectric power for a new aluminium smelter planned for the East Fjords was greeted with much jubilation. Herein, however, lies the crux of Iceland's dilemna – how the country's outstanding natural beauty, fierce independence and pride can be protected from the economic and political pressures of a world upon which Iceland is totally dependent for its existence.

LANDSCAPE AND GEOLOGY

Iceland's lunar landscapes are one of the country's prime attractions, but its apparently ancient façade is in fact an illusion. Geologically, Iceland is actually very young, with its oldest rocks dating back a mere 14 million years, to a time in the Earth's history when the dinosaurs had long gone and protohumans were yet to evolve.

The reason that its landscape appears so raw is because Iceland sits on a geological hot spot on the mid-Atlantic ridge, where the **Eurasian** and **American continental plates** are drifting east and west apart from each other. As they do so, Iceland is continually tearing down the middle, allowing **magma** (molten rock from the Earth's core) to well upwards towards the surface. When the surface cracks – in an earthquake, for instance – magma erupts through as a volcano, and when groundwater seeps down to magma levels it boils and returns to the surface as a **thermal spring**, or even a **geyser**.

Almost all such geological activity in Iceland is located over this mid-Atlantic tear, which stretches northeast in a wide band across the country, taking in everything between the Reykjanes Peninsula, the Westman Islands and Mýrdalsjökull in the southwest, and Mývatn and Þórshöfn in the northeast. As this band is where volcanoes are creating all the new land, it's here that you'll find the most recent rocks; conversely, the oldest, most geologically stable parts of the country are around Ísafjörður in the Westfjords and Gerpir cliffs in Iceland's extreme east.

At the same time, Iceland is close enough to the Arctic for its higher mountains and plateaus – most of which are in the south of the country – to have become permanently ice capped, forming extensive **glaciers**. Melt from around their edges contributes to many of Iceland's **rivers**, which are further fed by **underground springs** – also the source of the country's largest **lakes**. Cold, dry **air** formed by sub-zero temperatures over the ice caps is also responsible for some of the weird **atmospheric effects** you'll encounter here, while others have an extraterrestrial origin.

VOLCANOES

Though Iceland's volcanoes share a common origin, they form many different types, based on the chemical composition of their magma, which flows out of the volcano as **lava**. Where the lava is very fluid and the eruption is slow and continuous, the lava builds up to form a wide, flattened cone known as a **shield volcano**, a type that takes its name from the Skjaldbreiður (Shield-broad) volcano at Þingvellir. Where an eruption is violent, the lava is thrown out as a fine spray, cooling in mid-air and forming cones of ash or **tephra**, a cover-all name for volcanic ejecta; typical examples of tephra cones are found at Mývatn's Hverfjall, and Eldfell on Heimaey in the Westman Islands. Common elsewhere but relatively rare in Iceland, **strato volcanoes** are tall, regular cones built from very long-term lava and tephra accumulations; westerly Snæfellsjökull is a good example, though the country's most consistently active volcano, Hekla, has formed in a similar manner but along a line of craters rather than a single vent.

Less familiar forms of volcanic eruptions include **crater rows**, which is where lava erupts at points along a lengthy **fissure**, such as occurred at Leirhnjukur north of Mývatn in the 1970s, and Lakigigar in southeast Iceland during the 1780s. Both eruptions produced a string of low, multiple cones and large quantities of lava – in Lakigigar's case, flows covered 600 square kilometres. **Submarine eruptions** also occur off Iceland and are how the Westman Islands originally formed, as demonstrated by the creation of the new island of Surtsey in the 1960s. Looking like mini-volcanoes but actually nothing of the sort, aptly named **pseudocraters** – like those at Mývatn and Kirkjubæjarklaustur – form when lava flows over damp ground, vapourising the water beneath, which explodes through the soft rock as a giant blister.

Most **rocks** in Iceland were created in volcanic eruptions, and two common forms are easily identifiable. **Basalt** forms fluid lava solidifying into dark rock, weathered expanses of which cover the Reykjanes Peninsula and elsewhere. Where basaltic lavas cool rapidly – by flowing into a river or the sea, for instance – they form characteristic hexagonal pillars, with excellent examples at Svartifoss in Skaftafell National Park and Hjálparfoss at Þórsárdalur. In contrast, **rhyolite** forms a very thick lava, which often builds up into dome-like volcanoes such as Mælifell on the Snæfellsnes Peninsula. Cooled, it normally produces distinctive grey, yellow and pink rocks, typified by the peaks of the central Landmannalaugar region, though in some cases rhyolite solidifies into black, glass-like **obsidian**. Types of tephra to look for include black or red, gravel-like **scoria**; solidified lava foam or **pumice**, which is light enough to float on water; and **bombs**, spherical or elongated twists of rock formed when semi-congealed lava is thrown high into the air and hardens as it spins – they can be as big as a football but are usually fist-sized.

Aside from their cones and lava fields, volcanoes affect the landscape in other ways. Historically, dense clouds of tephra have destroyed farms and farmland on a number of occasions – such as the twelfth-century eruption of Hekla that buried Stöng in Þórsárdalur. Volcanic activity under ice caps can also cause catastrophic flash floods known as **jökulhlaups**, the most recent being at Grímsvotn in 1996. On the other hand, extinct volcano craters often become flooded themselves and form lakes, or **maars**; one of the biggest is Öskjuvatn in the Askja caldera, but there are also smaller examples at Grænvatn on the Reykjanes Peninsula and Kerið crater near Selfoss.

THERMAL SPRINGS AND GEYSERS

Thermal springs are found all over Iceland, sometimes emerging at ground-level literally as a hot-water spring – such as at Hveragerði – or flooding natural depressions or crevasses to form hot pools, which can be found at Mývatn and Landmannalaugur. In some cases the water emerges from the ground as steam through a vent; where this mixes with clay, boiling mud pits or **solfataras** are formed, of which the most extensive are those at Hverarönd, east of Mývatn. Natural steam is harnessed in Iceland to drive turbines and generate **geothermal power**, and also as heating for homes and hothouses.

While **geysers** tap into the same subterranean hot water as thermal springs, nobody is quite sure exactly why they erupt – it's either a gradual buildup of water pressure or a subterranean hiccup. Since the Krísuvík geyser blew itself to pieces in 1999, Iceland's only example of note is at **Geysir**, northeast of Selfoss.

GLACIERS, RIVERS AND LAKES

Glaciers can be thought of as giant, frozen rivers or waterfalls that move downhill under their own colossal weight. Usually movement is slow – maybe a few centimetres a year – though some can shift a metre or more annually. In Iceland, they're all associated with ice caps, the biggest of which, **Vatnajökull** (which more or less means Glacial Sea), spreads over 150km across the country's southeast. These caps sit atop plateaus, with a few isolated rocky peaks or **nunataks** poking through the ice, off which scores of glaciers descend to lower levels.

As glaciers move, they grind down the rocks underneath into fine gravel or sand, which is ultimately deposited at the front of the glacier and carried away by streams or rivers which are also the product of glacial friction. The sediments are deposited as desert-like **sandurs**, such as those that occupy much of Iceland's southeastern coastline.

It's also possible to see the effects that the glaciers themselves leave on the landscape, as both ice caps and glaciers were formerly far more extensive than they appear today. During previous ice ages – the last of which ended around 12,000 years ago – much of the country was beneath the ice, but there has been considerable fluctuation in glacier limits even in recorded times, and at present most are shrinking. The intricate inlets of the Eastfjords and Westfjords were carved by vanished glaciers, as were the characteristically flat-topped mountains known as **móbergs** southeast of Mývatn. Former glacial valleys – typically broad and rounded – can be seen along the Ringroad southwest of Akureyri; and Iceland's most mobile glacier, Skeiðarárjökull in Skaftafell National Park, has been retreating over the last eighty years leaving raised **morraine** gravel ridges in its wake.

The majority of Iceland's **rivers** are fairly short, glacial-fed affairs, though the two largest – the **Hvíta** in the southwest northeastern **Jökulsá á Fjöllum** – each exceed a respectable 200km in length. Both have quite spectacular stretches where they have carved **canyons** and **waterfalls** out of the landscape: at Gullfoss on the Hvíta; and Dettifoss and Ásbyrgi along the Jökulsa. Icelandic **lakes** are not especially large and tend to be caused – as with Mývatn or Þingvallavatn – when lava walls dam a spring-fed outflow, causing it to back-flood.

ATMOSPHERIC PHENOMENA

One of the strangest features of being in Iceland during the summer is the extremely **long days**. The northernmost part of the mainland is actually just outside the Arctic Circle, and so the sun does set (briefly) even on the longest day of the year, though you can cross over to the little island of Grímsey, whose northern tip is inside the Arctic and so enjoys midnight sun for a few days of the year. Conversely, winter days are correspondingly short, with the sun barely getting above the horizon for three months of the year.

One consequence of Iceland's often cold, dry atmosphere is that – on sunny days at least – it can play serious tricks on your sense of scale. Massive objects such as mountains and glaciers seem to stay the same size, or even shrink, the closer you come to them, and sometimes phantom hills or peaks appear on the horizon. Another effect – best viewed on cold, clear nights – are the **northern lights**, or **Aurora Borealis**, which form huge, shifting sheets of green or red in the winter skies. They're caused by the solar wind bringing electrically charged particles into contact with the Earth's atmosphere, and you'll have to be in luck to catch a really good show – they improve the further north you travel.

WILDLIFE AND THE ENVIRONMENT

Iceland's first settlers found a land whose coastal fringe, compared with today, was relatively well wooded; there were virtually no land mammals, but birdlife and fish stocks were abundant and the volcanic soil was reasonably fertile. Over a thousand years of farming has brought great changes: big trees are a rare sight, fish stocks have plummeted, and introduced mammals have contributed to erosion and other problems, but a growing regard for Iceland's natural heritage is beginning to redress the imbalance, and the country's natural history remains very much alive.

FLORA

Though fossils indicate that around 12 million years ago Iceland had stands of maples and other broad-leaved trees, dawn redwood and even giant sequoias, subsequent ice ages had wiped these out long before humans ever landed here. It's likely that the Vikings found woods mostly comprising **dwarf birch** and **willow** that you still see here today. Both can grow up to 10m or so in height, but generally form shrub-like thickets – original forests, however, would have been fairly extensive, reaching from the coast up into highland valleys. Clearances for timber and pasture have reduced Iceland's tree cover to just one percent of the land, though since 1994 over four million trees – including commercial stands of **pine** – have been planted in an attempt to restore levels to pre-settlement estimates.

The most widespread flora – **mosses** and **lichens** – tend to get overlooked, but they cover almost every lava flow and cliff in the country and provide a colourful mosaic of greens, greys and oranges, especially after rain has darkened the surrounding rocks. In mid-summer you'll also see plenty of flowering plants, including **heather**, large areas of fluffy **cottongrass**, and blue **harebells**. In early autumn, **berries** are also plentiful, and many people collect them to eat.

MAMMALS

The **arctic fox**, which feeds almost exclusively on birds, was the only land mammal in Iceland when the first settlers arrived. Common throughout Iceland, they're chubbier than European foxes, with short, rounded ears, bushy tail, and a coat that turns white in winter. **Polar bears** have never flourished here, though every decade one or two float over on ice floes from Greenland, only to be shot as a dangerous pest by the first person who sees them.

Domestic animals arrived with the Vikings. The **Icelandic horse** is a unique breed descended from medieval Norwegian stock, as none have been imported since the tenth century. Cattle numbers are fairly low, but **sheep** outnumber the human population by four to one. **Reindeer** were introduced from Norway and Finland in the late seventeenth century for hunting purposes – today they're restricted to eastern Iceland, where they stick to high altitude pasture in summer, descending to coastal areas in winter. Iceland's cold climate has limited the spread of smaller vermin such as **rats** and **mice**, which were unintentionally brought in on boats and only occur around human habitations; escaped **rabbits** have recently established themselves around Reykjavík and on Heimaey, however. **Minks** have also broken out of fur farms and seem to be surviving in the wild, much to the detriment of native birdlife.

Offshore, Iceland has a number of **whale** species. Traditionally, their valuable meat, bones and teeth were most frequently obtained from washed-up corpses, and battles were even fought over the rights to their carcasses until **commercial whaling** fired up in the nineteenth century. A decade-long moratorium on hunting ended in 1999, though numbers remain high for the time being and you've a good chance to see some if you put to sea. Most common are a couple of species of **dolphin** and the five-metre-long **pilot whale**, but there are also substantial numbers of far larger **fin whales**, **sei whales** and **minke whales**, all of which feed by straining plankton from sea water through moustache-like baleen plates inside their mouths. Far less common are **orca** (also known as killer whales), square-headed **sperm whales**, and **blue whales**, which reach 30m in length and are the largest known animal in history.

Grey and harbour **seals** are found in Iceland, with the biggest numbers seen around the north coast and off the Westman Islands. Both seal species are also hunted, despite being depicted as almost human in Icelandic folktales, appearing as "were-seals" who have human families on land and seal families in the sea. According to these stories, if you walk along a beach and find a seal following you out from shore, it may be looking to see if you're one of its children.

BIRDS

Iceland has some 300 recorded bird species, of which around 80 breed regularly. The **gyrfalcon**, a large bird of prey with variable grey-white plumage, is a national icon, once appearing on the Icelandic coat of arms and exported for hunting purposes until the nineteenth century. They're not common, but occur throughout mountainous country; rather oddly, in folklore the gyrfalcon is said to be brother to the ptarmigan, its main source of food. Another spectacular bird of prey

ICELANDIC BIRDS

Below is a partial list of **Icelandic birds**, with English and Icelandic names (US names are given in brackets where they differ substantially from British usage). You won't have to be an ardent twitcher to clock up most of these, though a couple of less widespread species are also included.

Arctic skua	Kjói	Pink-footed goose	Heiðagæs
Arctic tern	Kría	Pintail	Gröfönd
Barnacle goose	Helsingi	Ptarmigan	Rjúpa
Barrow's goldeneye	Húsönd	Puffin	Lundi
Black guillemot	Teista	Purple sandpiper	Sendlingur
Black-headed gull	Hettumáfur	Raven	Hrafn
Black-tailed godwit	Jaðrakan	Razorbill	Álka
Black-throated diver (Loon)	Himbrimi	Red-necked (Northern)	Óðinshani
Brünnich's guillemot	Stuttnefja	phalarope	
(Thick-billed murre)		Red-throated diver	Lómur
Cormorant	Dílaskarfur	Redpoll	Auðnutittlingur
Dunlin	Lóuþræll	Redshank	Stelkur
Eider	Æðarfugl	Redwing	Skógarþröstur
Fulmar	Fýll	Ringed plover	Sandlóa
Gannet	Súla	Scaup	Duggönd
Golden plover	Heiðlóa	Scoter	Hrafnsönd
Goosander	Gulönd	Shag	Toppskarfur
Great auk*	Geirfugl	Short-eared owl	Brandugla
Great skua	Skúmur	Slavonian grebe	Flórgoði
Greater black-backed gull	Svartbakur	Snipe	Hrossagaukur
Guillemot (Murre)	Langvía	Snow bunting	Snjótittlingur
Gyrfalcon	Fálki	Starling	Stari
Harlequin duck	Straumönd	Storm petrel	Stormsvala
Herring gull	Silfurmáfur	Teal	Urtönd
Iceland gull	Bjartmáfur	Tufted duck	Sítúfönd
Kittiwake	Rita	Turnstone	Tildra
Lesser black-backed gull	Sílamáfur	Wheatear	Steindepill
Little auk (Dovekie)	Haftyrðill	White wagtail	Maríuerla
Longtail duck (Old squaw)	Hávella	White-tailed sea eagle	Haförn
Mallard	Stokkönd	Whooper swan	Álft
Meadow pippit	Þúfutittlingur	Widgeon	Rauðhöfðaönd
Merganser	Toppönd	Wren	Músarrindill
Merlin	Smyrill		
Oystercatcher	Tjaldur	*Extinct	

is the huge **white-tailed sea eagle**, though their numbers were seriously reduced in the 1980s through taking poison baits intended for escaped minks. Around a hundred breed in the Westfjords, though juveniles travel quite widely over the country.

The **ptarmigan** is a plump game bird, plentiful across Iceland wherever there is low scrub or trees. They're well camoflaged, patterned a mottled brown to blend with summer vegetation, and changing – with the exception of black tail feathers and a red wattle around the eye – to snow-white plumage in winter. Aside from being preyed upon year-round by foxes and gyrfalcons, ptarmigan are also a traditional Christmas food, though actually protected in certain areas. Other common heathland birds include the **golden plover**, a migrant whose mournful piping is eagerly awaited in Iceland as the harbinger of summer; and **snipe**, identified by their long beaks, zigzag flight, and strange drumming noise made by two stiffened tail feathers which protrude at right angles to its body. In fields and eastuaries you'll see **pink-footed geese**, the most common of Iceland's wildfowl species, and even in downtown Reykjavík you'll find **whooper swans**; and just about everywhere are **raven**, held by some Icelanders to be highly intelligent, though often associated in tales with portents of doom.

Many of Iceland's **ducks** are coastal, though you can see almost all recorded species either on or around Mývatn, a lake in the northeast. **Eider** are probably the most famous Icelandic duck, known for their warm down, but birders will want to clock up **harlequin** and **barrow's goldeneye**, which occur nowhere else in Europe; for more about these species and others, see the box on p.299.

Of all the country's birdlife, however, it's the huge, noisy, teeming **seabird colonies** which really stick in the mind. There are several types of gull – including the uniformly pale **Iceland gull**, and slight, graceful **kittiwake** – but far more common are narrow winged, stumpy **fulmars**, which look gull-like but are actually related to albatrosses. They nest in half-burrows or overhangs on steep slopes and cliffs, and are relatively fearless, often allowing you to approach fairly close – come too near, however, and they spit a foul-smelling oil from their double-chambered beak.

In summer, flat, open places around the coast are utilised by colossal numbers of ground-nesting **arctic terns**, small, white birds with narrow wings, black caps and bright red beaks. It's interesting to watch the activity in a tern colony, but bear in mind that the birds relentlessly attack anything that threatens their eggs or chicks. **Skuas** are heavily built, brown birds with nasty tempers and a piratic lifestyle – they chase and harass weaker sea birds into dropping their catches. Like terns, they also nest on the ground in vast colonies across the southeastern coastal sandurs, and are equally defensive of their territory.

Iceland's equivalent to penguins (which are only found south of the equator), are the similar-looking **auks**, a family that includes **guillemot** (murre), **razorbill**, and **puffin**. Like penguins, these hunt fish, live in huge seaside colonies, and have black-and-white plumage. Unlike penguins, however, they can also fly. Auks' **beaks** are distinctively specialized: long and pointed in guillemots; mid-length and broad in razorbills; and colourfully striped, sail-shaped in puffins – all aids to their specific fishing techniques. The best place to see puffins is on Heimaey in the Westman Islands – for more on them see p.122 – but you'll find other auks anywhere around Iceland where there are suitable nesting cliffs. One exception is the arctic-dwelling **little auk**, or dovekie, now seen only rarely on Grímsey, Iceland's northernmost outpost.

BOOKS
AND SAGAS

With a population of barely over a quarter of a million, Iceland boasts more writers per capita than any other country in the world. The long dark winter months are said to to be the reason so many folk put pen to paper, and native-language books on all matters Icelandic can be found in shops across the country. Conversely, as the Icelandic-language market is so small, print runs are generally small, prices can be inordinately high – specialist publications cost the equivalent of hundreds of dollars, and even a popular-fiction paperback can come in at around 2000kr.

The availability of books on Iceland in English is, unfortunately, remarkably scant. To many foreign authors, Iceland is still an unknown topic, a reason, perhaps, for the tendency of many writers to lapse into "land of fire and ice"-style clichés. Below, however, is a selection of the better publications, the pick of a very meagre crop.

LITERATURE AND FICTION

W.H. Auden & Louis MacNeice *Letters from Iceland* (Faber & Faber). Amusing and unorthodox travelogue, the result of a summer journey the young poets undertook through Iceland in 1936. Especially enjoyable are the irreverent comments about local people, politicians and literature.

Gúðbergur Bergsson *The Swan* (Mare's Nest). The story of a young girl sent to a country farm to serve her probation for shoplifting – a characteristic Icelandic sentence. Here she becomes torn between ancient tradition and new attitudes, but by submitting to the inevitable restraints of remote rural life she finds a new kind of freedom.

Mark Cawardine *Iceland Nature's Meeting Place* (Iceland Review). Plenty of colour photos and maps in this wildlife guide which provides useful information for the amateur naturalist. Advice, too, on where to go to see individual species of birds.

Eirík the Red and other Iceland Sagas (Oxford University Press). The tale of one of Iceland's most notorious Viking heros, whose

son went on to discover North America. Full of blood and guts and a real page turner.

Robert Kellog & Jane Smiley *The Sagas of Icelanders* (Allen Lane-Penguin). Hefty compendium of a dozen key sagas, including *Laxdæla* and *Egil's* but strangely omitting that of *Njál*. A few less well-known short tales and the introduction also make interesting reading.

Halldór Laxness *Independent People* (Vintage). Excellent novel by Iceland's Nobel Prize winning author about the toils and troubles of sheep-farmer Bjartur to live free and unbeholden to any man – only to see his one and only daughter live unbeholden to him.

Magnus Magnusson (ed) *Njal's Saga* (Penguin). The longest of all the sagas, this is a thoroughly compelling, visceral account of the schemings and characters involved in a fifty-year medieval blood feud.

Tim Moore *Frost on my Moustache* (Abacus Paperback). Highly enjoyable account of the author's attempts to follow in the footsteps of adventurer Lord Dufferin, who sailed to Iceland in 1856. A critical and well-observed account of the Icelandic nation makes this book a must-read.

David Roberts *Iceland Land of the Sagas* (Villard). Beautiful glossy pictures by photographer Jon Krakauer accompany the rich text in this coffee-table book of Iceland.

Snori Sturlusson *Egil's Saga* (Penguin). A powerful and lucid narrative – few of the Icelandic sagas can match this one for the vivid presence of the central figure, Egil (see p.303).

Snorri Sturlusson *King Harald's Saga* (Penguin). Part of the Heimskringla, recording the turbulent life of King Harald of Norway, felled in battle at Stamford Bridge, in Yorkshire, when invading England in 1066, just three weeks before the Battle of Hastings – had he won, English history might have been very different.

Þór Vilhjálmsson *Justice Undone* (Mare's Nest). Ásmundur, a magistrate, travels into the remote Icelandic wilderness to hear his first case, a charge of incest and infanticide. Haunted by an ancient drowning and his own troubled past, he is tested to the limit during his time among desperate people in a desolate landscape.

HISTORY AND WILDLIFE

Sigurður Ægisson *Icelandic Whales* (Forlagið). Slim, pocket-sized guide to the 23 species recorded from Icelandic waters, well illustrated and with entertaining, informative text.

Erroll Fuller *The Great Auk* (Harry N. Abrams). An exhaustive labour of love that breathes some life into the history of this now-extinct species of seabird, the last pair of which were bludgeoned to death off southwestern Iceland by hunters in the mid-nineteenth century.

Mark Kurlansky *Cod* (Vintage). Brilliantly entertaining and offbeat account of the cod in history, and a trade in it which reached from Iceland to the US and Spain. A good number of recipes too, if you want to see what all the fuss was about.

Terry Lacy *Ring of Seasons* (University of Iceland Press). An interwoven, perceptive and lively account of Iceland's history, mythology, culture, and daily life, seen through the eyes of a long-term foreign resident.

Christopher Perrins *Birds of Britain and Europe* (Collins). One of many similarly handy field guides covering all the birds you'll see in Iceland. Text and distribution maps are overly Brit-centric but illustrations are excellent.

Anna Yates *Leifur Eiríksson and Vínland the Good* (Iceland Review). An excellent and readable account of the discovery of North America by Icelandic Vikings. A thorough argument of where exactly Vínland is accompanies debate on why the Norse settlements in North America died out.

SAGAS

Icelanders will tell you that the greatest of the sagas contain everything you need to know about life. And while it is certainly true that no other ancient literature can match them for gripping, laconically told tales of individuals caught in inexorable, often terrible fates, getting acquainted with them will also reveal something of the people, culture and history of Iceland.

The word *saga* itself simply means "thing told", and several types exist. Written between the twelfth and fifteenth centuries, in a language similar to the Icelandic spoken today, that we have the manuscripts today is down, in the main, to just one man, **Arni Magnusson** (1663–1730). As the Icelanders became increasingly poor under Danish rule, when many manuscripts could be found stuffing holes in farmhouse walls, Arni

Magnusson made it his mission to save them and take them to Copenhagen for storage. Once there, however, they were nearly all destroyed in a fire, though Arni saved many himself. Following Iceland's independence in 1944, a strong political movement arose to return the manuscripts from Copenhagen and an institute was established to receive them. Such was the political importance attached to these priceless artifacts that some were brought back by gun boat (for more on this, see p.56)

On reading a saga, the first thing you notice is the hard-boiled style: unemotional and sparing on external description, but with details given early on that become deeply significant as the tales unfold. When we first meet Hallgerd as a child in *Njal's Saga*, for example, we are told of her striking long hair, which goes on to play a key part in the death of one of the saga's heroes.

Whether these tales are actually true or not is a matter of intense scholarly debate, with one school believing them to be the final, written stages of a long oral tradition, and another arguing that they are creative outpourings of individual artists. In the end, this doesn't matter – what does is that, when read today, they feel immediate and believable. There are many good **translations** available, most of the major ones published by Penguin (especially *Egil's Saga*, *Njal's Saga* and the *Laxdæla Saga*). A recent anthology *The Sagas of Icelanders* (see p.301) collects a number of good translations, taken from the complete series of English translations *The Complete Sagas of Icelander's* (Leifur Eiríksson Publishing).

Sagas range in subject from those about Icelandic bishops (**biskupasögur**); saints' lives (**heilagra manna sögur**); the massive saga of the Sturlung age (**Sturlunga saga**); sagas of the Norse Kings, either individual sagas or collected in Snorri Sturlusson's **Heimskringla**; and chivalric stories of knights in armour (**riddarasögur**) and the **fornaldarsögur**, stories of mythical times past, with dragons, dwarves and heroic figures.

The most famous and original of all, however, are the so-called "sagas of Icelanders", or **Íslendinga sögur**. These were written down mainly in the thirteenth century, but tell of events around the Settlement three hundred years earlier, during what became known as the **saga age**. They read like histories, being set in real places (many of which still bear the same name today), and usually begin with a series of genealogies establishing the "historical" origins of the main characters. Some are biographies of individuals – such as poets, such as **Egil's Saga** (see below), or of outlaws, such as **Grettir's Saga** (see below). Many tell of long-running feuds, from origin to conclusion – such as **Njal's Saga** (see p.108). Others are identified by a focus on a particular area – the **Laxdæla Saga** (see below) is a good example of this.

EGIL'S SAGA

Egil Skallgrimsson, poet and hero of *Egil's Saga*, is born an outsider. His grandfather, Kveld-Ulf (Evening Wolf, or Shape Changer), is a man of two distinct personalities – wise and hard-working by day, but brooding and withdrawn at night, and Egil inherits the dark side of his grandfather's personality. Small, dark and ugly, he does, however, have a prodigious poetic talent by the age of three, he has composed his first poem. He is also destined for an eventful life – aged seven, he kills a playmate.

The bulk of the story tells of his often bloody and unforgiving adventures as a Viking and the enmity he earns from Eirík Bloodaxe and his witch-queen Gunnhild, by stabbing the king and erecting a *niðstöng* (insult pole) to them. He subsequently visits King Athelstann in England, but is shipwrecked and ends up in the hands of his enemy Eirík, himself exiled from Norway. However, he saves his own life by reciting a poem called *Höfudlausn*, or *Head Ransom*, and wins the king's favour and pardon. Towards the end of his life his beloved son dies and, like his grandfather did before him, he withdraws from the world. One of his daughters persuades him to put his grief into the composition of a poem, which he does, producing *Sonnatorrek*, one of the greatest poems of early modern times in Europe, with complex allusive imagery, which tells of his sorrow and his disillusion with Odin.

GRETTIR'S SAGA

Egil is an outsider by dint of his personality, but **Grettir Asmundsson** is a more straightforward outlaw hero in *Grettir's Saga*, a "coal biter", a youth who, after a slow beginning, eventually makes something of himself. In Grettir's case, the centre of his saga is his encounter with the

monstrous Glam, the ghost of a slave – a version of the Old English epic *Beowulf*. Eventually, after a long fight, and just before Grettir destroys him, the moon comes out and the monster turns his eyes towards it with a look so terrible "that Grettir said it was the only sight that made him tremble". Later, after one killing too many, he is outlawed and dies a hunted, wounded fugitive.

LAXDÆLA SAGA

The *Laxdæla Saga* has three main characters – the tall, blonde and heroic **Kjartan**; the beautiful **Gudrun Osvífrsdóttir**; and Kjartan's cousin **Bolli**, who lurks in the background to complete a classic love triangle. It takes thirty or so chapters before the three figures are centre stage, but before they have met, a wise man predicts that Gudrun will have four husbands. Later that day, seeing Kjartan and Bolli swimming together he predicts that one day Bolli will stand over the dead Kjartan, and be killed for his deeds; and thus the inescapable template for the characters' lives is set out to the reader.

Gudrun is married to her first husband against her will and divorces him after two years. She then marries Thord, who incurs the enmity of a family of sorcerers and is drowned as a result. Gudrun then meets Kjartan, and they become close, but Kjartan decides to seek his fortune abroad, and asks Gudrun to wait three years for him, but she refuses.

While in Norway, Kjartan is held hostage, but still finds time to have an affair with the beautiful princess Ingibjorg. Bolli, who has been with his cousin during his courtship and on Viking expeditions, now returns to Iceland and tells Gudrun that Kjartan intends to settle in Norway, whereupon Gudrun's family persuade her to marry Bolli. Kjartan subsequently returns and marries another woman, Hrefna, giving her a priceless headdress as a wedding gift, a gift actually bestowed on him by Ingibjorg, who had told him to give it to Gudrun as a wedding present.

There is no love lost between the two neighbouring households, and things only worsen when the headdress is stolen. In revenge, Kjartan lays siege to Gudrun and Bolli and humiliates them by not letting them go to the lavatory for three days. Eventually, Gudrun goads Bolli and his brothers to try to kill Kjartan – Bolli is reluctant but eventually joins the fight, dealing a death blow to a barely injured but exhausted Kjartan, who gives himself to be killed by Bolli and dies in his arms. Gudrun gloats over his death but Bolli is inconsolable. Kjartan's brothers revenge him by eventually killing Bolli – Gudrun is pregnant at the time, and one of the killers wipes his sword on her dress.

Eventually Gudrun gives birth to a son whom she names Bolli, after his father. She decides she won't marry again until her husband is avenged, and makes a promise to Thorgils Holluson that she will marry no other man in the land than him if he kills her husband's murderer. This he does, at which point Gudrun reveals she is betrothed to another, Thorkel Eyjolfsson, who is abroad. She does indeed marry Thorkel, but he drowns, after which Gudrun becomes a nun. Before she dies, her son Bolli asks her which man in her life she loved the most, to which she replies "I was worst to him I loved the most", one of the best-known lines of saga literature.

LANGUAGE

Notwithstanding the odd change in pronunciation, today's Icelandic is essentially the same language the Vikings spoke over 1300 years ago. As a result, it is an oddly archaic language, heavy with declensions, genders and cases, not to mention Norse peculiarities. Whereas the other principal members of the North Germanic group of languages, Danish, Norwegian and Swedish lost much of their grammar over time, **Icelandic has proudly maintained features that make even the most polyglottal language student cough and splutter.**

It is also one of the most linguistically pure languages in Europe in terms of **vocabulary**, and a campaign to rid the language of foreign (mostly English) words has led to the coining of many new, purely Icelandic, words and phrases, devised by a committee of linguistic experts. Modern inventions especially have been given names from existing Icelandic words, such as *sími* for telephone (literally "long thread"), and hence *bréfasími* ("letter telephone") for "fax machine"; *eggjakaka* ("egg cake") for "omelette"; and even *fara á puttanu* ("to travel on the thumb"), for "to hitchhike". Although there's no Icelandic word for "interesting" (the closest is *gaman* – "fun"), there's a plethora of words to do with fish and the sea: *pín porskur!* ("you cod!") is a term of abuse, whilst "to give up" is often rendered as *leggja ára í bát*, "to lay one's oars in the boat". If something isn't up to much, it's *ekki upp á marga fiska* – "not worth many fish". Rural life has also left its mark on the language: on Friday nights in Reykjavík you'll find plenty of people who're

---

PRONUNCIATION

Stress in Icelandic is always on the first syllable. Below is a guide to the pronunciation of Icelandic vowels and consonants – some have no equivalent in English, but the nearest sound has been given to facilitate pronunciation.

Vowels

a	as is f*a*ther	ó	as in s*o*w
á	as in c*ow*	u	like u in c*u*te
e	as in g*e*t or a*i*r, depending on whether long or short	ú	as in f*oo*l
é	like y*ea*h	y	see "i", above
i	as in h*i*t	ý	see "í" above
í	as in l*ea*n	æ	as is *eye*
ö	as in f*u*r	au	as in French f*eui*lle
		ei	as in h*ay*

Consonants

As in English except:

j – as in *y*et

ll and rl – like the Welsh *ll*, or *dl* pronounced together in English

f before l or n – pronounced *b*, eg Keflavík

rn – pronounced as *dn*

Note that Icelandic Þ/þ is the same as English "th" in *th*is
And Icelandic Ð/ð is the same as English "th" in *th*ing

ICELANDIC

BASIC PHRASES

English	Icelandic
Yes	Já
No	Nei
Hello	Halló/hæ
How are you?	Hvernig liður þér/ hvað segirðú?
Fine, thanks	Mér liður vel, takk; ég segi allt ágætt
Goodbye	Bless/bæ
Good morning/ afternoon	Góðan dag
Good night	Góða nótt
Today/tomorrow	Í dag/á morgun
Tonight	Í kvöld
Please	Afsakið
Thankyou	Takk fyrir
I'd like . . .	Ég ætla að fá . . .
Excuse me	Fyrirgefðu
Here you are	Gerið svo vel (plural)/ gerðu svo vel (singular)
Don't mention it	Ekkert að þakka
Sorry? (as in "what did you say?")	Ha?/hvað sagðir þú?
Where/when?	Hvar/hvenær?
What/why?	Hvað/hvers vegna?
Who/how?	Hver/hvernig?
How much?	Hvað mikið?
I don't know	Ég veit ekki
Do you know (a fact)?	Veistu . . . ?
Is there/are there . . . ?	Er/eru . . . ?
With/without	Með/án
And/not	Og/ekki
Something/nothing	Eitthvað/ekkert
Here/there	Hér/þar
Near/far	Nálægt/fjarlægt
This/that	Þetta/þetta/það
Now/later	Núna/seinna
More/less	Meiri/minni
Big/little	Stór/lítill/smár
Open/closed	Opið/lokað
Men/women	Karlmenn/kvenmenn
Toilet	Snyrting
Gentleman/ladies	Herrar/konur
Bank	Banki
Post office	Pósthús
Stamp(s)	Frímerki
Where are you from?	Hvaðan ertu?
I'm from . . .	Ég er frá . . .
. . . America	. . . Bandaríkjunum
. . . Australia	. . . Ástralíu
. . . Britain	. . . Bretlandi
. . . Canada	. . . Kanada
. . . England	. . . Englandi
. . . Ireland	. . . Írlandi
. . . New Zealand	. . . Nyja sjálandi
. . . Scotland	. . . Skotlandi
. . . Wales	. . . Wales
What's your name?	Hvað heitirðu?
My name is	Ég heiti
How do you say . . . ?	Hvernig segir maður . . . ?
. . . in Icelandic?	. . . á íslensku?
Do you speak English?	Talarðu ensku?
I don't understand	Ég skil ekki
Could you speak more slowly?	Gætirðu talað hægar?
How much is it?	Hvað kostar þetta?
Can I pay, please?	Ég ætla að borga?
The bill/check, please	Reikninginn, takk

GETTING AROUND

How do I get to . . . ?	Hvernig kemst ég til . . . ?
Left/right	Vinstri/hægri
Straight ahead/back	Beint áfram/tilbaka
Bus (in towns)	Strætó
Bus (long distance)	Rúta/áætlunarbíll
Where is the bus station?	Hvar er biðstöðin?
Where is the bus stop?	Hvar er strætostöðin?
Does this bus go to . . . ?	Fer þessi rúta (strætó) til . . . ?
What time does it leave?	Hvenær fer hún?
What time does it arrive?	Hvenær kemur hún til?
When is the next bus to . . . ?	Hvenær fer næsta rúta (strætó) til . . . ?
Can you let me know when we get to . . . ?	Gætirðu sagt mér Þegar við komum til . . . ?
Is anyone sitting here?	Er þetta sæti laust?
Is this the road to . . . ?	Er þetta leiðin til . . . ?
Where are you going?	Hvert ertu að fara?
I'm going to . . .	Ég er að fara til . . .
Here's great, thanks	Hérna er ágætt, takk
Stop here, please	Stansaðu hérna, takk
Single ticket to . . .	Einn miða, aðra leiðina til . . .
Return ticket to . . .	Einn miða, báðar leiðir til . . .

ACCOMMODATION

Where's the youth hostel?	Hvar er farfuglaheimilið?	Can I see it?	Má ég sjá það
Is there a hotel/ guesthouse round here?	Er hótel/ gistiheimili hér nálægt?	I'll take it	Ég ætla að taka það
		How much is it a night?	Hvað kostar nóttin?
		It's too expensive	Það er of dýrt
I'd like a single/ double room . . .	Gæti ég fengið einsmanns herbergi/ tveggjamanna herbergi . . .	Do you have anything cheaper?	Áttu eitthvað ódýrara?
		Can I leave the bags here until . . . ?	Má ég geyma farangurinn hérna þangað til . . . ?
. . . with a bath/shower	. . . með baði/sturtu	Can I camp here?	Má ég tjalda hérna?
Bed	Rúm		

DAYS AND MONTHS

Days and months are never capitalized. Days are declinable but months are not.

Monday	mánudagur	March	mars
Tuesday	þriðjudagur	April	apríl
Wednesday	miðvikudagur	May	maí
Thursday	fimmtudagur	June	júní
Friday	föstudagur	July	júlí
Saturday	laugardagur	August	ágúst
Sunday	sunnudagur	September	september
		October	október
January	janúar	November	nóvember
February	febrúar	December	desember

NUMBERS

1	einn	14	fjórtán	60	sextíu
2	tveir	15	fimmtán	70	sjötíu
3	þrír	16	sextán	80	áttatíu
4	fjórir	17	sautján	90	níutíu
5	fimm	18	átján	100	hundrað
6	sex	19	nítján	101	hundrað og einn
7	sjö	20	tuttugu	110	hundrað og tuttugu
8	átta	21	tuttugu og einn	200	tvö hundruð
9	níu	22	tuttugu og tveir	500	fimm hundruð
10	tíu	30	þrjátíu	1000	þúsund
11	ellefu	31	þrjátíu og einn	1,000,000	milljón
12	tólf	40	fjörutíu		
13	þrettán	50	fimmtíu		

NUMERALS

Numerals 1–4 are all inflected as follows:

ONE	Masculine	Feminine	Neuter	THREE	Masculine	Feminine	Neuter
Nominative	einn	ein	eitt	**Nominative**	þrír	þrjár	þrjú
Accusative	einn	eina	eitt	**Accusative**	þrjá	þrjár	þrjú
Genetive	eins	einnar	eins	**Genetive**	þriggja	þriggja	þriggja
Dative	einum	einni	einu	**Dative**	þremur	þremur	þremur

TWO	Masculine	Feminine	Neuter	FOUR	Masculine	Feminine	Neuter
Nominative	tveir	tvær	tvö	**Nominative**	fjórir	fjórar	fjögur
Accusative	tvo	tvær	tvö	**Accusative**	fjóra	fjórar	fjögur
Genetive	tveggja	tveggja	tveggja	**Genetive**	fjögra	fjögra	fjögra
Dative	tveimur	tveimur	tveimur	**Dative**	fjórum	fjórum	fjórum

sauðdrukkinnn – "as drunk as a sheep"; the word for sheep, *fé*, is also the generic term for money. Dogs also speak Icelandic and can quite clearly be heard to say *voff* (small children will refer to a dog as a *voffi*) whilst cows on the other hand say *mö*.

Icelandic has also maintained many old names for European cities that were in use at the time of the Settlement, such as Dyflinni (Dublin), Jórvík (York, in Britain, hence Nya Jórvík for New York) and Lundúnir (London) in London).

Anyone learning Icelandic will also have to grapple with a mind blowing use of grammatical cases for the most straightforward of activities: "to open a door", for instance, requires the accusative case (*opna dyrnar*) whilst "to close a door" takes the dative case (*loka dyrunum*). Not only that, but "door" is plural in Icelandic, as is the word for Christmas, *jólin*, hence *jólin eru í desember*, literally "Christmasses are in December" (as opposed to the English "Christmas is in December"). Thankfully, there are no dialects anywhere in the country.

BASIC GRAMMAR

There are 32 **letters** in the Icelandic alphabet. Accented á, é, í, ó, ú and y count as separate letters. Letters þ, æ and ö come at the end of the alphabet in that order. Hence a dictionary entry for *mögulegur* comes after *morgunn*.

Verbs come in many classes and are either strong and characterized by a vowel change (*tek, tók, tekinn*: "take", "took", "taken") or weak (*tala, talaði*: "speak", "spoke"), without a vowel shift. Verb endings agree with **pronouns**, which are as follows: *ég* ("I"), *þú* ("you", singular), *hann* ("he"), *hún* ("she"), *það* ("it"), *við* ("we"), *þiz* ("you", plural), *þeir* ("you", masculine plural), *þaer* ("you", feminine plural), *þau* ("you", neuter or mixed gender plural).

Icelandic **nouns** can have one of three genders (masculine, feminine or neuter) and can appear in any one of four different grammatical cases (nominative, accusative, genitive and dative). For example, the masculine word *fjörður*, meaning "a fjord", is *fjördur* in the nominative case, *fjörð*, in the accusative case, *fjarðar* in the genitive and *firdi* in the dative case. The case of a noun is determined by many factors, including the use of a preceding preposition, for instance, *í Reykjavík* ("in Reykjavík") but *til Reykjavíkur* ("to Reykjavík"). Watch out

for this particularly at airports on the arrival and departure boards: planes to Egilsstaðir for example will be marked *Egilsstaða* (genitive), but those arriving from Egilsstadir are labelled as *Egilsstöðum* (dative).

Vowels also have an unnerving ability to shift – for example, *hér er amma* ("here is grandma") but *ég sé ömmu* ("I see grandma"). This even happens with proper nouns: *þetta er Lada* ("this is a Lada car") but *ég á Lödu* ("I own a Lada"). There is no **indefinite article** in Icelandic with the result that *fjörður* can mean both "fjord" and "a fjord". The **definite article**, as in the other Scandinavian languages, is suffixed to the noun; for example, *maður* means "a man", but *maðurinn* means "the man". The definite article is declined according to the gender and number of the noun.

Adjectives generally precede the noun they qualify and are inflected according to the gender and case gender of the noun. The strong declension is used with indefinite nouns, as in *góður maður* – "a good man". Definite nouns (those with the definite article or other determinatives) require the weak declension, so *góði maðurinn*, "the good man".

NAMES AND NUMBERS

Icelanders take the forename of their father as the first part of their own **surname**, plus the Icelandic word for son (*son*) or daughter (*dóttir*). For example, the son of a man whose forename is Jón will have Jónsson as a surname; a daughter of the same man will have Jónsdóttir as a surname. A family of four in Iceland will therefore have four different surnames, which can certainly throw things into confusion when they travel abroad. When asking someone's surname Icelanders will enquire "*hvers son er Kristbjörn?*" ("Whose son is Kristbjörn?") for example, to which the reply might be "*hann er Egils son*" ("He's Egil's son"). Formally or informally, Icelanders are always addressed by their forename and are listed accordingly in the telephone directory. Even the Prime Minister can be found under his forename, David, his surname, Oddsson, seems very much an afterthought.

When giving their **addresses**, Icelanders put their street names in the dative case but their town and country in the nominative case. They decline their own names, for instance, *ég tala við Önnu* – "I'm speaking to Anna" (*Önnu* is the accusative, genitive and dative form of "Anna") and *bókin er eftir Ingibjörgu Sigurðardóttur* – "the book is by Ingibjörg Sigurðardóttir".

When **counting**, the nominative masculine form of the numerals is used, i.e. einn, tveir, þrír, fjórir. However, **street numbers** and the **time** are given in the neuter form. It's a good idea to familiarise yourself with the feminine and neuter forms because they are frequently used in shops and restaurants, since *króna* (plural: *krónur)* and *þúsund* (thousand: plural *þúsundir)* are feminine, whilst *hundrad* (hundred: plural *hundruð)* is neuter. Note however *tvær hundruð þrjátíu og þrjár krónur* where *tvær* and *þrjár* are both feminine, to agree with *krónur*.

LEARNING ICELANDIC

In theory, the Germanic roots of English and Icelandic, coupled with over two centuries of Norse influence in England during the Viking era should make Icelandic a fairly easy language for English speakers to learn. It doesn't – and any foreigner who has mastered even a smattering of the language will find Icelandic jaws dropping at his every turn. Conversely, most Icelanders speak excellent English, and young people in particular are only too keen to try out turns of phrase on you.

If you want to teach yourself **Icelandic**, however, your best bet is the widely available Linguaphone's course, which provides a good grounding in the language, though it is old-fashioned. Otherwise, *Teach Yourself Icelandic* (Routledge) by P.J.T. Glendening is handy for reference but is terribly dry. German speakers have access to by far the best Icelandic course on the market, *Lehrbuch des Isländischen* (Langenscheidt), by Ríta Duppler and Astrid van Nahl, which is accompanied by two cassettes. There is only one Icelandic reference work in English on the subject of **grammar**, *Icelandic Grammar, Texts and Glossary*, by Stefán Einarsson. Originally published in 1945 and still printed today by the John Hopkins Press it offers a very thorough, if somewhat stodgy analysis of the language (it is included in the Linguaphone course).

DICTIONARIES AND PHRASEBOOKS

Dictionaries are exceptionally thin on the ground outside Iceland, but the pocket sized *Icelandic–English, English–Icelandic Dictionary*, published by Hippocrene Books, New York, is good for basic reference and is fairly easy to get hold of. German-speakers again have the best option, with *Universal-Wörterbuch Isländisch* (Langenscheidt), being by far the best small dictionary. Larger dictionaries are best bought in Iceland, where they're much less expensive – though reckon on at least 5000kr for an English–Icelandic or an Icelandic–English one, and double that for one referencing in both directions.

Of the **phrasebooks**, most useful is Berlitz's *Scandinavian Phrase Book and Dictionary*, which includes a hundred-page section on Icelandic.

GLOSSARY

Á river
ÁÆTLUN timetable
ÁS small hill
BÆR farm
BÍLL car
BJARG cliff, rock
BRÚ bridge
DALUR valley
DJÚP deep inlet, long fjord
DRANGUR rock column
EY island
EYRI sand spit
FELL/FJALL mountain
FERJA ferry
FJÖRÐUR fjord
FLJÓT large river
FLÓI bay
FLUGVÖLLUR airport
FOSS waterfall

GATA street
GIL ravine, gill
GISTING accommodation
HEIÐI heath
HERBERGI room
HNJÚKUR peak
HÖFÐI headland
HRAUN lava
HVER hot spring
JÖKULL glacier
KIRKJA church
LAUG warm pool
LÓN lagoon
REYKUR smoke
RÚTA long distance coach
STAÐUR place
STRÆTÓ city bus
TJÖRN lake, pond
VATN lake
VEGUR road
VÍK bay
VÖLLUR plain, flatland

INDEX

Stay in touch with us!

ROUGHNEWS is Rough Guides' free newsletter. In three issues a year we give you news, travel issues, music reviews, readers' letters and the latest dispatches from authors on the road.

I would like to receive ROUGHNEWS: please put me on your free mailing list.

NAME ....

ADDRESS ....

Please clip or photocopy and send to: Rough Guides, 62–70 Shorts Gardens, London WC2H 9AH, England or Rough Guides, 375 Hudson Street, New York, NY 10014, USA.

ROUGH GUIDES: Travel

Alaska
Amsterdam
Andalucia
Argentina
Australia
Austria

Bali & Lombok
Barcelona
Belgium &
  Luxembourg
Belize
Berlin
Brazil
Britain
Brittany &
  Normandy
Bulgaria
California
Canada
Central America
Chile
China
Corsica
Costa Rica
Crete
Croatia
Cuba
Cyprus
Czech & Slovak
  Republics

Dodecanese &
  the East Aegean
Devon &
  Cornwall
Dominican
  Republic
Dordogne & the
  Lot
Ecuador
Egypt
England
Europe
Florida
France
French Hotels &
  Restaurants
  1999
Germany
Goa
Greece
Greek Islands
Guatemala
Hawaii
Holland
Hong Kong &
  Macau
Hungary

Iceland
India
Indonesia
Ionian Islands
Ireland

Israel & the
  Palestinian
  Territories
Italy
Jamaica
Japan
Jordan
Kenya
Lake District
Languedoc &
  Roussillon
Laos
London
Los Angeles
Malaysia,
  Singapore &
  Brunei
Mallorca &
  Menorca
Maya World
Mexico
Morocco
Moscow
Nepal
New England
New York
New Zealand
Norway
Pacific
  Northwest
Paris
Peru
Poland
Portugal
Prague
Provence & the
  Côte d'Azur
The Pyrenees
Romania
St Petersburg
San Francisco

Sardinia
Scandinavia
Scotland
Scottish
  highlands and
  Islands
Sicily
Singapore
South Africa
South India
Southeast Asia
Southwest USA
Spain
Sweden
Switzerland
Syria

Thailand
Trinidad &
  Tobago
Tunisia
Turkey
Tuscany &
  Umbria
USA
Venice
Vienna
Vietnam
Wales
Washington DC
West Africa
Zimbabwe &
  Botswana

AVAILABLE AT ALL GOOD BOOKSHOPS

ROUGH GUIDES: Mini Guides, Travel Specials and Phrasebooks

MINI GUIDES

Antigua
Bangkok
Barbados
Beijing
Big Island of Hawaii
Boston
Brussels
Budapest
Cape Town
Copenhagen
Dublin
Edinburgh

Florence
Honolulu
Ibiza & Formentera
Jerusalem
Las Vegas
Lisbon
London Restaurants
Madeira
Madrid
Malta & Gozo
Maui
Melbourne
Menorca

Montreal
New Orleans

Paris
Rome
Seattle
St Lucia
Sydney
Tenerife
Tokyo
Toronto
Vancouver

TRAVEL SPECIALS

First-Time Asia
First-Time Europe
Women Travel

PHRASEBOOKS

Czech
Dutch
Egyptian Arabic
European
French
German
Greek

Hindi & Urdu
Hungarian
Indonesian
Italian
Japanese
Mandarin
  Chinese
Mexican
  Spanish
Polish
Portuguese
Russian
Spanish
Swahili
Thai
Turkish
Vietnamese

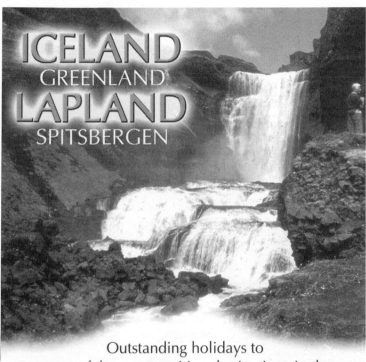

Will you have enough stories to tell your grandchildren?

©2000 Yahoo! Inc.

Yahoo! Travel